D1562295

EUTHANASIA AND LAW IN EUROPE

This book is a successor to J Griffiths, A Bood and H Weyers, *Euthanasia and Law in the Netherlands* (Amsterdam University Press, 1998) which was widely praised for its thoroughness, clarity, and accuracy. The new book emphasises recent legal developments and new research, and has been expanded to include a full treatment of Belgium, where since 2002 euthanasia has also become legal. In addition, short descriptions of the legal situation and what is known about actual practice in a number of other European countries (England and Wales, France, Italy, Scandinavia, Spain, Switzerland), written by local specialists, is included.

The book strives for as complete and dispassionate a description of the situation as possible. It covers in detail:

- the substantive law applicable to euthanasia, physician-assisted suicide, withholding and withdrawing treatment, use of pain relief in potentially lethal doses, terminal sedation, and termination of life without a request (in particular in the case of newborn babies);
- the process of legal development that has led to the current state of the law;
- the system of legal control and its operation in practice;
- the results of empirical research concerning actual medical practice.

A concluding part deals with some general questions that arise out of the material presented: is the legalisation of euthanasia an example of the decline of law or should it on the contrary be seen as part and parcel of the increasing juridification of the doctor-patient relationship? Does the Dutch experience with legalised euthanasia support the idea of a 'slippery slope' toward a situation in which life—especially of the more vulnerable members of society—is less effectively protected? Is it possible to explain and to predict when a society will decide to legalise euthanasia?

Euthanasia and Law in Europe

John Griffiths
and
Heleen Weyers

Maurice Adams

·HART·
PUBLISHING

OXFORD AND PORTLAND, OREGON
2008

Published in North America (US and Canada) by
Hart Publishing
c/o International Specialised Book Services 920 NE 58th Avenue, Suite 300,
Portland, OR 97213–3786
USA
Tel: +1 503 287 3093 or toll-free: (1) 800 944 6190
Fax: +1 503 280 8832
E-mail: orders@isbs.com
Website: http://www.isbs.com

© John Griffiths, Heleen Weyers and Maurice Adams 2008

John Griffiths, Heleen Weyers and Maurice Adams have asserted their right under the Copyright,
Designs and Patents Act 1988, to be identified as the author of this work.

Hart Publishing, 16C Worcester Place, OX1 2JW
Telephone: +44 (0)1865 517530 Fax: +44 (0)1865 510710
E-mail: mail@hartpub.co.uk
Website: http://www.hartpub.co.uk

British Library Cataloguing in Publication Data
Data Available

ISBN: 978–1-84113–700–1

Typeset by Hope Services, Abingdon
Printed and bound in Great Britain by
TJ International Ltd, Padstow, Cornwall

FOREWORD

Although it is inspired by and a successor to Griffiths, Bood and Weyers, *Euthanasia and Law in the Netherlands* (1998, referred to throughout as 'GB&W'), this is not a 'second edition' of the earlier book. Its coverage is different and while two authors (Griffiths and Weyers) are the same, we are joined by Adams (for the situation in Belgium) and by a number of colleagues who treat several other European countries.

A variety of choices underlie the contents of this book. Most important of these is the addition of Belgium, reflecting the fact that in 2002 Belgium became the second country in the world to legalise euthanasia, and also the influence of the Dutch experience on Belgian developments and the close collaboration between Dutch and Belgian scholars in this area. A second major choice was to include, in part III, several other European countries. In short, the approach in this book is far more comparative than it was in the earlier book.

In part I, dealing with the Netherlands, we have chosen to avoid as much as possible repetition of material dealt with in the earlier book (most importantly, the history of legal change and the findings of Dutch research up to 1997). Where appropriate we briefly summarise the Dutch situation as it was in 1997 and devote our attention to developments since then. The reader interested in a detailed treatment of the earlier history and the situation as it was in 1997 is referred to the earlier book, which will remain in print. The different way in which we now treat current Dutch law reflects the somewhat different emphases that the intervening years seem to require.

We have written this book, as we did its predecessor, as a collective project. Nevertheless some of us are more responsible for some chapters than for others. Weyers bears primary responsibility for chapters 2, 3 and 20, Griffiths for chapters 4, 5, 6, 10, 17, 18 and 19, and Adams for chapters 7, 8 and 9 (in collaboration with Herman Nys). In Part III we are joined by scholars from other European countries who have written reports on the specific legal and empirical situations in some eight countries. The three of us bear responsibility for the overall conception and editing of the book.

Griffiths' work on this book is a continuation of a project that began almost 20 years ago and has resulted in a number of publications, particularly on problems of effective regulation of socially problematic medical behaviour such as euthanasia. Weyers completed her dissertation on the Dutch history of legal change concerning euthanasia in 2002 and since then has devoted particular attention to the question how this change, until very recently unique to the Netherlands, can be explained. Adams has written on the political and parliamentary developments leading up to the Belgian legalisation in 2002, and on some problems of interpretation and administration of that law. All of this earlier work is reflected in the pages of this book.

In the years after *Euthanasia and Law in the Netherlands* was published, a substantial research programme on the regulation of socially problematic medical behaviour (RSPMB), under Griffiths' responsibility, came into being at the University of Groningen. Weyers has been a senior member of the programme from the start, and Adams an associated member. The RSPMB programme includes socio-legal research (much of it international and comparative) concerning advance treatment directives, decision-making processes in connection with withholding and withdrawing treatment, judicial decisions in hard cases involving the end of life, knowledge and interpretation by doctors of the legal rules applicable to their behaviour, self-regulation by medical professionals, termination of life in neonatology, the concept of medical futility and its use in practice, the influence of legal and other factors on the implementation of organ-donation programmes, and so forth.[1] These, then, are the sources of the ideas upon which this book rests.

A book such as this could not have been written without the support we have received from a number of institutions. We are in particular grateful for the generous support the RSPMB programme has for many years enjoyed from the Department of Legal Theory and, more generally, the Faculty of Law of the University of Groningen. Some of the research projects that, among other things, have contributed to the work of the programme and thereby to this book have had financial support from the Faculty of Law of the University of Groningen, the University of Antwerp, and the Netherlands Foundation for Scientific Research (NWO). Finally, we acknowledge the continuing stimulating support of the CHAZERAS Fellowship.

Specific thanks are due to a number of colleagues and others who furnished us with data and/or helped us improve the accuracy of our presentation and interpretation of data derived from their research, or who facilitated access to important sources of information: Esther Dekkers (Regional Review Committees), Agnes van der Heide (Erasmus University Rotterdam), a staff member of the Central Bureau of Statistics (whose puristic rules do not allow us to identify him/her), Eduard Verhagen (University Medical Centre Groningen), Bert van den Ende (Albert Schweitzer hospital), Frances Norwood, Wim Distelmans (Free University of Brussels), Esther Pans, Eric Vermeulen and Cristiano Vezzoni.

For reading and commenting on (parts of) the book and saving us from greater and lesser errors of law, fact and interpretation, we would like to acknowledge the contributions of the authors of the country reports in part V, all of whom have also

---

[1] For more information about this programme (formerly known under the acronym MBPSL—Medical Behaviour that Potentially Shortens Life), see its website (where its newsletter is to be found): <http://www.rug.nl/law/research/programmes/rspmb/index> accessed 20 April 2008.

given important assistance on other parts of the book. We would also particularly like to thank Alex Bood, Govert den Hartogh, Albert Klijn, Donald van Tol, Nicolle Zeegers, Herman Nys and Dirk Vanheule for their critical help.

Winnie Schrijvers, documentalist of the RSPMB programme, has been responsible for a number of years for the rapidly expanding documentation collection, without which this book could not have been written; she also did the bibliographical work reflected in the List of References. Marion Beijer rendered research assistance of all sorts.

It goes without saying that while all of those mentioned, and many others, made important contributions to the book, only we are responsible for the flaws that undoubtedly remain.

John Griffiths and Heleen Weyers (Groningen)
Maurice Adams (Tilburg and Antwerp)
1 January 2008

PS On 19 February 2008, too late for inclusion in this book, a Bill to legalise euthanasia (including physician-assisted suicide) along the lines of the Dutch and Belgian laws was provisionally adopted by the Luxembourg parliament (*Proposition de loi sur le droit de mourir en dignité, No 4909*). At the same time, a law on palliative care was adopted. The two laws only become effective after differences between them have been resolved. As far as we are aware, no emperical data on medical end-of-life practice exist for Luxembourg.

CONTENTS

DETAILED CONTENTS

LIST OF TABLES, BOXES AND GRAPHS

Tables

Boxes

Graphs

ABOUT THE AUTHORS

MAURICE ADAMS studied law and philosophy of law at the Universities of Maastricht (the Netherlands), Leuven (Belgium) and Oxford (UK). He did a PhD in law at the University of Leuven. Since 1997 he has been professor of law at the University of Antwerp in Belgium, teaching mainly in the field of jurisprudence and comparative law. As of September 2007 he is professor of law at Tilburg University, and part-time professor of comparative law at the University of Antwerp. In his research he has a particular interest in issues of regulation, and in the relation between law and politics (and political theory) and law and ethics. He has written extensively on the regulation of euthanasia. He functioned twice in an advisory capacity to the Belgian parliament in connection with pending legislation on euthanasia, and also for the House of Lords in the United Kingdom.

GEORG BOSSHARD is a doctor and originally specialised in Family Medicine. He later completed a master's degree in applied ethics at the University of Zurich and began an academic career in medical ethics at the University of Zurich's Institute of Legal Medicine in 2000. In 2006 he was appointed 'Privatdozent' for Clinical Ethics and became a member of the newly created Institute of Biomedical Ethics, where he is responsible for Clinical Ethics at the Zurich University Hospital. Medical end-of-life decisions in general, and the Swiss model of assisted suicide in particular, are amongst the key areas of his research, in which empirical investigations play a central role. He is a member of the Central Ethics Committee of the Swiss Academy of Medical Sciences (SAMS) and participated in the SAMS's expert committee to establish new Medical-Ethical Guidelines for the Care of Patients at the End of Life.

REIDUN FØRDE received her degree in medicine from the University of Oslo in 1978. She practised as a clinician until 1998. From 1995 to 2007 she was employed at the Research Institute of the Norwegian Medical Association, where she was involved in research on doctors' attitudes towards, and experience with, various ethical problems. Parallel to this she worked part-time as professor at the Section for Medical Ethics of the University of Oslo, where she became full-time professor in 2007. Since 2000 she has been in charge of the coordination of the clinical ethics committees established at all Norwegian hospital trusts. She was a member of the Ethical Council of the Norwegian Medical Association from 1994–2005, and in the period 1998–2005 she chaired the Council. She was a member of the Ethics Task Force on Palliative Care and Euthanasia of the European Association for Palliative Care (EAPC).

JOHN GRIFFITHS studied philosophy (Berkeley) and law (Yale) in the United States and taught law there and in Ghana for several years before being appointed in 1967 to the chair in sociology of law at the University of Groningen in the Netherlands. He retired in 2005. His research and writing in recent years have concerned legal effectiveness and the social working of law, and in that context he has been particularly interested in problems of effective regulation of euthanasia and other medical behaviour that potentially shortens life. He is author (with A Bood and H Weyers) of *Euthanasia and Law in the Netherlands* (1998) and of many articles—mostly in Dutch and English—on the regulation of euthanasia.

STÉPHANIE HENNETTE-VAUCHEZ is a graduate of the Institut d'Etudes Politiques de Paris as well as of the Université Paris I Panthéon-Sorbonne Law Department where she received her PhD in 2000. After being a Fulbright postdoctoral scholar at Northwestern University Law School in Chicago (2000), she was appointed professor of public law at Université Paris 12 Créteil. Her research focuses mostly on legal regulation of biomedical issues. She has published several books and many articles on these matters, and recently edited *Bioéthique, Biodroit, Biopolitique. Réflexions à l'occasion de la loi du 6 août 2004.* Paris, LGDJ, Coll Droit & Société (2006).

PENNEY LEWIS studied mathematics, law and philosophy in the United States, Canada and the United Kingdom. She clerked for Mr Justice Iacobucci at the Supreme Court of Canada and is qualified as a barrister and solicitor in Ontario. She is professor of law at King's College London where she teaches medical law and criminal evidence in the Centre of Medical Law and Ethics and the School of Law. In the area of medical law, her research focuses on end-of-life issues. She is the author of a number of articles on assisted dying. Her book *Assisted Dying and Legal Change* was published in 2007 by Oxford University Press. She has also published articles and chapters dealing with a wide range of medical law topics, including wrongful life, advance decision-making, refusal of treatment, medical treatment of children and medical procedures which are against the interests of incompetent adults, such as non-therapeutic research.

LARS JOHAN MATERSTVEDT holds a PhD in philosophy (on Nozick and Kant) and is professor at the Norwegian University of Science and Technology (NTNU) in Trondheim, where he teaches history of philosophy, theory of science, ethical theory and medical ethics. As a postdoctoral research fellow with the Norwegian Cancer Society he carried out research on the relationship between euthanasia and palliative medicine. He chaired the Ethics Task Force on Palliative Care and Euthanasia of the European Association for Palliative Care (EAPC). For three years he was a member of the Norwegian Government's National Committee for Medical Research Ethics. He is former head of the Medical Ethics Unit, NTNU, and is currently Visiting Research Fellow at the International Observatory on End of Life Care of Lancaster University. He is author (with Georg Bosshard) of the chapter 'Euthanasia and physician-assisted suicide' due to appear in the fourth edition of the *Oxford Textbook of Palliative Medicine* (2008). His home page, containing his downloadable publications as well as links to euthanasia laws and bills, is http://www.materstvedt.net.

SOFIA MORATTI received her degree in law from the University of Pavia and is currently a PhD candidate at the University of Groningen. Her research deals with the concept of medical futility and its use in connection with decisions to withhold or withdraw treatment in Dutch neonatal intensive care units.

GRACIELA NOWENSTEIN studied sociology and anthropology in Paris (Université Paris 10-Nanterre, Institut d'Etudes Politiques, Ecole des Hautes Etudes en Sciences Sociales). She has a PhD in sociology from the European University Institute in Florence. Her dissertation is a study of the failure of an attempt by French political authorities to modify organ donation practice by means of a law presuming consent to organ donation. She has been a research fellow at the ESRC Centre for Genomics in Society at the University of Exeter where she did research concerning the ethical regulation of gene therapy in the United Kingdom. She is currently a Marie Curie Fellow in the Department of Legal Theory of the University of Groningen where she is conducting comparative research on the regulation of brain death and organ procurement in Spain, Italy, France and the Netherlands, and its effect on everyday practice in hospitals.

HERMAN NYS studied law at the Catholic University of Leuven, receiving his PhD in 1980. He teaches medical law in the medical and law schools of the Catholic University of Leuven. He has also been professor in international health law at the University of Maastricht in the Netherlands (2000–05). He is consultant to UNESCO for bioethical law. His standard work on Belgian medical law was published in Dutch (1991/ revised 2005) and French (1995), and he is the editor of the *International Encyclopaedia of Medical Law* (a loose leaf review of medical law of many national states). His main research interests are patients' rights, genetics, biomedical research with human beings and end-of-life issues. He is member of the Belgian Advisory Committee on Bioethics and various institutional ethics committees. He was the first president of the Belgian Federal Commission on Patient Rights (2004–05).

ASLAK SYSE studied medicine, history of ideas and criminology at the University of Oslo. From 1972–90 he held various positions as a doctor, among them as District Medical Officer in Mtoko District, Zimbabwe (1982–85) and as Chief Consultant for the Health Services for the Mentally Retarded in Finnmark, the northernmost county of Norway (1981–89). After finishing a law degree he joined the Department of Public and International Law of the University of Oslo in 1990. He holds a PhD in law, and was appointed professor in 1997. His main publications are in health law, welfare law and criminal law, in particular on criminal responsibility, mental health legislation, and euthanasia.

HELEEN WEYERS studied philosophy and history at the University of Groningen and received her PhD in sociology of law in 2002 with a dissertation on the process of legal change with respect to euthanasia in the Netherlands. She teaches sociology of law and political science in the Department of Legal Theory of the University of Groningen. She is co-author (with J Griffiths and A Bood) of *Euthanasia and law in the Netherlands* (1998). Her current research deals with the explanation of legal change.

NOTE TO THE READER

Throughout this book (except in part III where we follow the preferences of the various authors) we use 'he' to include 'she' whenever gender is unknown or irrelevant.

We use abbreviated references to literature that is frequently cited. The abbreviations are explained at the beginning of the List of References. In the List of References we identify items by using the abbreviations, so that all references in the footnotes can be found in exactly the same form in the List of References.

We use acronyms for the names of organisations and of categories of medical behaviour (in particular, MBPSL) that appear frequently in the text. These are explained, where appropriate, in the text, and also at the beginning of the List of References.

Since the Dutch and Belgian governments make English translations of their respective statutes legalising euthanasia available on the Internet, it has seemed to us best to use those translations in this book, even though at some points they seem to us not entirely felicitous. In the Dutch case, we think our own translations in *Euthanasia and Law in the Netherlands* of some of the relevant terms is more accurate (or less likely to give rise to wrong associations by an English reader). Where relevant, we have noted our reservations concerning the official translation. Unless otherwise noted, the translations of legal and other texts in part III has been done by the authors of the respective chapters.

We have tried to make the book useful for a wide variety of readers (among them doctors, lawyers, policy-makers, scholars in the fields of health law, comparative law and sociology of law, ethicists, and interested members of the general public). Not all readers will be equally interested in all of the subjects covered in the various chapters, or in the level of detail at which some subjects are treated. Some readers, for example, will want to know precisely how the Dutch Regional Review Committees are dealing with the large number of very diverse problems that they are confronted with. On the other hand, someone interested in confirming or refuting some version of the 'slippery slope' argument will look for more empirical detail concerning euthanasia practice than may interest some lawyers. We have tried to accomodate divergent interests by providing readers with a detailed Table of Contents and an Index that will take them to exactly where they want to be.

Finally, a note on sources. Wherever possible, we have referred to secondary sources in English and have relied as little as possible on secondary sources in other languages. The local secondary literature, particularly in Dutch, is very extensive, and it would be impossible and pointless to try to do justice to all of it. On the other hand, as far as primary sources are concerned we have tried to be as exhaustive as possible, on the assumption that others may want to use this book as their point of entry into the local situation.

TABLE OF CASES

European Commission of Human Rights

European Court of Human Rights

France

Italy

Switzerland

United States

TABLE OF STATUTES

References such as '325n106' indicate that the provision is only mentioned in footnote 106 on page 396, whilst '296b9.1' indicates box 9.1 on page 296. A reference in the form '224nn' indicates mention in multiple notes on page 224.

Council of Europe

Sweden

Switzerland

1

Introduction

1.1 This Book and its Readers

This book is about euthanasia and other medical behaviour that potentially shortens life (MBPSL), and about their legal regulation. The primary focus will be on the Netherlands and Belgium because presently they are the only countries in the world in which euthanasia, under specific circumstances, is legally permissible.[1] In the Netherlands, considerable attention has been paid over a number of years to the problem of regulating it. Information has been systematically collected concerning actual practice. Legal and open euthanasia practice in Belgium is of very recent date (2002) and legalisation took place without the decades of debate and experimentation that preceded legislation in the Netherlands, so that legal, ethical and practical experience—and systematic data—are less richly available. Nevertheless, taken together, the two national cases are of considerable interest both to the Dutch and Belgians themselves and also to people elsewhere who are considering whether or not to make similar practices legal and, if this is done, how they might most effectively be regulated.

In parts I and II we deal with the legal norms and procedures currently in place in the Netherlands and in Belgium, respectively, and with how these have come to be what they are; we will also critically consider the available evidence bearing on actual practice and on the effectiveness of current law as an instrument of control. Part III consists of contributions on the situation in several other European countries. Part IV consists of some comparative and explanatory reflections stimulated by the material presented earlier in the book.

We have written this book with a reader in mind who is unfamiliar with the Dutch and Belgian situations, and with those in the other countries covered in part III, and has no specific technical knowledge of the law in these countries. We do assume that our reader is interested enough in the problems of public policy surrounding euthanasia to want an account that goes beyond generalisations and

---

[1] There are a handful of partial exceptions to this generalisation, all of them as far as we are aware concerning assistance with suicide. The most important are the State of Oregon in the United States (see Hillyard & Dombrink 2001), where as the result of a referendum and a recent decision of the United States Supreme Court (*Gonzales v Oregon*, 546 US 243, 2006) physician-assisted suicide is legal, and Switzerland, where assistance with suicide by non-doctors is not illegal and is an institutionalised practice (see ch 16).

superficialities and includes as much as possible of the legal and factual information important for an informed assessment of end-of-life medical practice and its regulation. Our intention has been to present such a reader with reliable information and serious, balanced assessments.

1.2 The Definition of 'Euthanasia' and of Other 'Medical Behaviour that Shortens Life'

'Euthanasia' in the strict and, in the Dutch and Belgian context, the only proper sense refers to the situation in which a doctor ends the life of a person who is suffering 'unbearably' and 'hopelessly' (without prospect of improvement) at the latter's explicit request (usually by administering a lethal injection). When a distinction is made between the two, 'euthanasia' is reserved for killing on request, as opposed to 'assistance with suicide', but generally the two are treated together. We will follow this practice and will often loosely use the single term 'euthanasia' to cover both where the distinction is not relevant.

As we will see in the course of the book, euthanasia in this limited sense is only separated by rather problematic boundaries from related phenomena, such as pain relief in doses known to be likely to hasten the death of the patient, and the withholding or withdrawing of life-prolonging treatment. These other practices are generally considered unproblematic in both Belgium and the Netherlands (as in many other countries), even—perhaps especially—by many vigorous opponents of euthanasia. They are widely regarded in medical law as 'normal medical practice' and thought to give rise to a 'natural death' (that is, one due to the patient's underlying condition). On the whole, they are regarded as quite different from euthanasia and are not thought to require specific control.

There is another sort of behaviour which is also closely related to euthanasia but which—while legal in the Netherlands under narrowly-defined conditions, and known to occur with some regularity in many other countries as well—is everywhere far more controversial than euthanasia: the administration of lethal drugs to shorten the life of persons who cannot or do not explicitly request this (severely defective newborn babies, persons in long-term coma, persons in the final stages of dying).

Together with euthanasia proper, all of the behaviour mentioned above, when engaged in by doctors, is part of a complex of 'medical behaviour that potentially shortens life' (MBPSL). Although there are, of course, important distinctions between different sorts of MBPSL, and some may well be morally and legally more problematic than others, for purposes of legal and ethical analysis, empirical description and effective regulation the whole complex must be considered together.

A terminological note: We use the expression 'shortening of life' when referring to behaviour that a doctor knows is likely to cause the patient to die earlier than he otherwise would have done. We use the expression 'termination of life' to refer to behaviour of a doctor that is expected to shorten the patient's life *and for which there is no medical indication* (such as to relieve pain or to avoid 'futile' treatment). 'Termination of life' thus includes not only euthanasia (and assistance with suicide), together with termination of life without an explicit request, but also the administration of drugs that are normally used for pain and symptom control in doses that in the circumstances are not medically indicated, and the withholding or withdrawing of life-prolonging treatment that the patient or his representative have not refused and that is not medically futile. These terminological choices are explained in chapter 4.2.3.

1.3 The Legal Status of Medical Behaviour that Terminates Life in the Netherlands and Belgium

Chapters 4 and 9 treat the legal status of euthanasia, physician-assisted suicide, and the other sorts of MBPSL in the Netherlands and in Belgium in detail. To get the reader started, we present here only the bare bones of the legal situation.

In the Netherlands, euthanasia was until 2002 explicitly and apparently absolutely prohibited by two articles of the Dutch Penal Code. Article 293 prohibits killing a person at his request (the offence is a 'qualified' variety of homicide, in the sense that the homicide would otherwise be murder). Article 294 prohibits assisting suicide (suicide itself is not a crime in Dutch law and, but for article 294, assisting suicide would not be either). Despite these apparently unqualified prohibitions, the Supreme Court held in the *Schoonheim* case in 1984[2] that a doctor can rely on the defence of justification due to necessity if he administers euthanatica to a patient who asks him to do so and whose suffering is 'unbearable and hopeless'. In the period preceding and following the *Schoonheim* case the courts, generally following the lead of the Royal Dutch Medical Association, worked out the 'requirements of due care' that must be followed in such a case. As we will see in chapter 4, legislation became effective in 2002 which in effect ratified the solutions arrived at by the courts. A doctor who carries out euthanasia or assists with suicide must first have consulted an independent colleague, who gives a formal opinion as to whether the legal requirements have been met, and he must report what he has done in the context of a special, non-criminal review procedure. Only if he is found to have acted 'not carefully' is the case forwarded to the prosecutorial and medical disciplinary authorities.

What has been said of euthanasia does not apply to situations in which a doctor administers lethal drugs without the patient having made an explicit request, although here, too, the general contours of the emerging legal norms are becoming

---

[2] Supreme Court, 27 November 1984, *Nederlands Jurisprudentie* 1985, no 106. An English translation can be found in GB&W: 322*ff.*

clear. In the case of severely defective newborn babies (and probably of coma patients), recent legal developments seem, as we will see in chapter 6, to point the way to a generally acceptable outcome, but these matters remain far more controversial than euthanasia proper.

In Belgium, euthanasia (but probably not physician-assisted suicide) was illegal until 2002, when legislation was passed legalising it along lines generally similar to those in the Netherlands. Before that time, it undoubtedly took place in actual medical practice, but there had never been a prosecution or court decision in which the possibility of a legal justification could be tested. The same still applies to termination of life without a request from the patient.

1.4 Reactions from Abroad to the Dutch and Belgian Situation

Dutch society has over the centuries attracted considerable foreign attention. Admiration for Dutch achievements in commerce, social organisation, science, the arts and engineering (especially water control and land reclamation) has been mixed with scepticism, disapproval, and dismay, especially at Dutch 'toleration' (of unorthodox religion, illegal drug use, novel sexual relations and so forth). But foreign characterisations of Dutch society, favourable or unfavourable, often tell us more about the situation in the observer's own country than they do about the Netherlands.[3] Thus what the German traveller in the 17th century who was shocked at the fact that 'servant girls in Holland behaved and dressed so much like their mistresses that it was hard to tell which was which,'[4] principally tells us is that social differences were expected to be highly visible in contemporary Germany.

Of no current subject is this more true than it is of euthanasia. Although the Dutch experience with euthanasia has attracted a great deal of comment, until recently little of this went much beyond expressions of enthusiastic welcome or of moral outrage to consider what is actually happening in the Netherlands. The Dutch experience has mostly been seen by foreign observers as a source of ammunition to be used for domestic purposes. Those who are inclined to react to Dutch and, more recently, Belgian developments in this polemical way are invited in the course of this book to consider the complexities of the legal, moral and empirical questions involved. On close examination, none of these seem to lend themselves to simple, absolute answers.

The criticisms from abroad do raise some fundamental questions, in particular with regard to the problem of adequate legal control. Unfortunately, on the whole, such concerns were in the past often voiced in a way which did not invite serious

[3] Compare Van Ginkel 1997: 15–42.
[4] Israel 1995: 2.

response. Imprecision, exaggeration, suggestion and innuendo, misinterpretation and misrepresentation, ideological *ipse dixitism*, and downright lying and slander, took the place of careful analysis of the problem and consideration of the Dutch evidence. It is perhaps understandable that the Dutch reaction tended to be dismissive, since such critics did not seem to deserve attention and keeping up with their misrepresentations would have been a full-time job.

The previous paragraph is how, almost 10 years ago, we characterised the situation in the international debate.[5] Since then the whole subject seems to have become normalised and the general tone of the professional literature is less hostile and more respectful, if not necessarily less critical. The serious press, too, is prepared to investigate Dutch and Belgian developments carefully and report on them in a reasonably objective way. Thus, when the 'Groningen protocol' dealing with termination of life in neonatology was suddenly and briefly international news—the Vatican newspaper *Osservatore Romano* having compared the doctor most prominently involved to the Nazi doctors—responsible newspapers like the *New York Times* and the *Guardian* had experienced reporters do careful and accurate articles about what was really going on.[6]

The more relaxed atmosphere that now prevails is all to the good. Other countries may, like Belgium, choose to follow the Dutch lead, or they may decide to deal with the enormous problems arising from the medicalisation of death in modern health care systems in some other way. In either case, the relevance of the Dutch and Belgian experience to efforts elsewhere to deal with the problems of achieving adequate control over behaviour of doctors that affects the manner and the timing of death, can only be properly discussed after one appreciates, in detail, what Dutch and Belgian euthanasia practice entails and how the legal norms and enforcement processes that regulate it are working in practice.

1.5 Four Theoretical Themes

Our first objective, as we have noted, is to give as full and as accurate a description as we can of the law on euthanasia and other medical practices that potentially shorten life, of actual medical practice, and of the functioning of the control system, and to analyse the meaning of all this material for various questions in the international public debate. We focus in particular on the Netherlands and Belgium, but we approach the matter in a comparative spirit, and in part III there are country reports on a number of other Western European countries.

But we would not be true academics if we were prepared to leave it at that. In fact, we have a number of more 'theoretical' interests to which we hope this book will also make a contribution. We will return to these at various points in the book

---

[5] GB&W: 20–21.
[6] See ch 6, n 1.

(in particular in part IV) but this is the place to let the reader know what our theoretical agenda is.

1.5.1 The Emergence and Diffusion of Euthanasia Law

The process of legal change in the Netherlands and Belgium has been extensively documented, but the question *why* euthanasia was legalised in these two countries, and not elsewhere, is hard to answer. Two important variables that might offer such an explanation come to mind: public opinion supportive of such change[7] and the political opportunity for change to take place. Whether a population thinks euthanasia should be legal depends on widely held values concerning, on the one hand, the importance of treating human life with respect (the 'sacredness', if one will, of life[8]) and on the other hand, the importance of respecting individual autonomy with regard to fundamental choices in life. Changes in such values, in turn, reflect more global processes of secularisation and individualisation. Whether a change of values leads people to make new demands on the political system depends among other things on the degree of trust they have in their fellow citizens and in their political and social institutions. In the case of euthanasia, this trust concerns in particular those who will be involved in carrying out euthanasia and the institutional (and social control) context within which it will take place.[9] Finally, the mere fact that public opinion supports it can never in itself explain legal change. There must also be a political agent willing to put the issue on the agenda of the relevant institutions, and a political opportunity structure that makes a proposal for change likely to succeed.[10]

All this—value change, its translation into political demands and the political reaction to such demands—does not take place in splendid national isolation. Certainly nowadays in Europe, processes of legal change are heavily influenced by international interaction and cooperation, in particular in the context of the European Union and other European institutions such as the Council of Europe, the European Convention on Human Rights and the European Court of Justice. Thus a second question to be considered in connection with legal change concerns influence and diffusion: does the fact that one country has successfully experimented with a legal change (such as legalisation of euthanasia) increase the likelihood that another will do so? With respect to abortion, legal recognition of same-sex couples and the like, it has been argued that legal change in one country leads to parallel change in other countries.[11] It seems plausible that legalisation of euthanasia in the Netherlands was an important factor supporting legalisation in neighbouring Belgium. Will the Swiss practice of legal physician-assisted suicide, now that it is becoming widely known, have a similar effect on other countries? And what will be the effect of the Dutch and Belgian legalisation of euthanasia on

---

[7] See Dicey 1905.
[8] See Dworkin 1993.
[9] See Weyers, 2006.
[10] See Green Pedersen, 2007; Kriesi *et al* 1995.
[11] See Eser & Koch 2005; Boele-Woelki & Fuchs 2003.

legal developments elsewhere (especially in Europe)? We will return to these questions about legal change in chapter 20.

1.5.2 The Quantity of (Euthanasia) Law

When a taboo is shattered, it is often supposed that what takes place is a radical reduction in what can be called 'regulatory pressure': there are fewer (or less serious) binding rules and less actual enforcement. At first sight, one might even think that this must be true by definition: the very idea of the end of a taboo being that things that were formerly unthinkable become thinkable and also do-able. Pessimists often see all this as a decline in the level of civilisation—a return to barbarism. The case of euthanasia affords a good chance to examine this whole idea critically.

Our thesis, explored further in chapter 18, is that the legalisation of euthanasia, far from representing a decline in the quantity of law, in fact has been the occasion of an astonishing increase in the number of legal rules, their impact on end-of-life medical practice, and the intensity of their enforcement. Legalisation of euthanasia fits neatly, we will argue, into a more general, long-term development that has been noted in many countries: increasing juridification of the doctor–patient relationship.

1.5.3 The Spectre of a 'Slippery Slope'

One of the questions that lies at the heart of public debate on the possible legalisation of euthanasia concerns the safety of doing so. Will such a potentially dangerous practice be susceptible to effective control? Will it victimise the weak and defenceless, the psychologically unstable, the poor and otherwise disadvantaged? Will legalisation lead to a decline of moral restraints, so that what began as fairly innocent legal change gradually erodes fundamental foundations of the sort of society we want to live in? This sort of question lies just beneath the surface throughout the book. We will treat it head-on in chapter 19.

1.5.4 Varieties of (Legal) Comparison

This book can be considered an essay in comparative law. Our methodology is to a large extent that of comparison, in time as well as in place. We will concentrate on Belgium and the Netherlands, comparing them and their respective paths of legal development. But all along the way we are going to be comparing these two countries, which first explicitly legalised euthanasia, with a number of other European countries which have not yet done so. Our reason for doing so is not mere idle curiosity. It is based in the wisdom of the observation that, '*He who knows one society knows no society.*'[12]

---

[12] A Köbben, 'De vergelijkende methode in de volkenkunde,' in *Van primitieven tot medeburgers* (Assen, Van Gorcum, 1974), p 24 (quoting Fahrenfort).

The approach we take to comparison is *functional*, by which we mean that it seems to us to make little sense to study the regulation of euthanasia by focusing just on the rules concerned. In describing the legal regulation of euthanasia in the Netherlands and Belgium (chapters 4 and 9) and in the countries treated more briefly in part III, our point of departure is not the rules themselves but the behaviour (mostly of doctors) that they regulate.[13] We begin with an exploration of the whole range of 'medical behaviour that potentially shortens life' (MBPSL) in order to locate 'euthanasia' in the context of other sorts of medical behaviour with which it shares important features and from which it cannot always easily be distinguished, either analytically or in practice. The questions we address are these: what, if any, rules are applied to medical behaviour that potentially shortens life? and how and why is 'euthanasia' separated out for special treatment?

The approach we take to comparison is also *non-formalistic*. We do not have to take a position on the question whether such an approach would be necessary in every area of law, but in studying the law concerning euthanasia and the other MBPSL, even in one country but certainly when one engages in comparison, it is essential to take the concept of 'law' in a broad sense. As it regulates everyday medical practice, and in particular as it develops and changes, the law consists of much more than formal 'legal' texts such as statutes or judicial decisions. These are preceded by, surrounded by, and followed by a vast amount of 'para-legal' sources of law. It would, in every country we know of, be impossible to state what the law 'is', let alone what it will be tomorrow, without taking account—to name a few of the most obvious and important other sources of law—of parliamentary reports (such as that of the House of Lords Select Committee on the Assisted Dying for the Terminally Ill Bill), of reports of official advisory committees (such as those of the French National Ethics Committee), of reports and guidelines of official organs of the medical profession, and so forth.

It is also important to compare the rules concerning euthanasia and other MBPSL in a *multilayered* way. The rules themselves are the first layer, and we will pay careful and detailed attention to them. But rules are always *embedded* in an historical, institutional, political, cultural and social environment, without which their meaning cannot be understood. The second and third layers of comparison, in our case, concern specifically the (organisation of the) health care system within which the rules are situated, and more generally the political culture and constitutional background of the legal system of which they are a part. In effect, we are thus engaged in comparative institutional and political sociology.

Finally, in making comparisons we do so from the point of view of the *social working* of legal rules.[14] This book is not the place to go into the theoretical difficulties of a simplistic instrumentalist approach to the 'effectiveness' of law, one

---

[13] Compare the approach to comparative law developed by Kagan (Kagan 1990; Kagan & Axelrad 2000; Gunningham, Kagan & Thornton 2003). We use 'rules' in this context as shorthand, referring to the varying mix of rules and principles characteristic of law (*cf* Braithwaite 2002).

[14] See Griffiths 2003.

that treats legal rules as direct (potential) causes of behaviour. But looking at the place that euthanasia law plays in the social practice of euthanasia does afford a wonderful opportunity to consider how complex the relationship between rules and behaviour can be, and we will be engaged in doing so at many points in this book.

From the perspective of the idea of the social working of legal rules, it is obvious that in studying euthanasia law comparatively it is not enough to look at what the rules are and how they came to be that way, it is also essential to take account of what happens to them on the 'shop floor' of everyday life. How and when do people use the rules? Do the rules make a difference in social interaction? What difference? How does this come about? Because the 'social working' approach assumes that the social meaning of a legal rule lies not in legal texts but in the difference the rule ultimately makes in social life, in engaging in comparative law in the way we seek to do, we are also necessarily engaged in comparative sociology of law.[15]

---

[15] Our approach to comparative law owes much to the writings of Twining (eg 2000, forthcoming). We take comparative law to be a *descriptive* discipline, subservient to efforts to explain difference and change in law. Its task is to enable us to describe (some aspect of) law in a way which permits answers to the questions, whether there are differences in time or place and precisely what they are.

Part I

The Netherlands

2

The Netherlands and the Dutch Health Care System

The Netherlands is, together with Belgium, the principal setting in which we will be examining the legal regulation of euthanasia and other medical behaviour that potentially shortens life. In interpreting the information and arguments to be presented in the coming chapters, it is necessary to know something about the local context. In this chapter we give some basic information about the (political) structure and culture of the Netherlands, about the Dutch health care system, and about Dutch public and professional opinion with respect to euthanasia. In chapter 7 we do the same for Belgium. The various chapters in part III give more summary information about the countries covered there.

2.1 Dutch (Political) Structure and Culture

The Netherlands is a small, mostly flat country of some 16 million inhabitants, one of the most densely populated in the world. It emerged as an independent country in the 17th century. In the latter part of the 19th century, the contours of the modern parliamentary system emerged, in which the Government is responsible to the Second Chamber of Parliament (Lower House) and requires the support of the members of that House. After passing the Second Chamber a law requires the approval of the First Chamber (the Senate).

Dutch elections are on the basis of proportional representation, so that a party's share of the national vote determines its share of the seats in Parliament. From the time universal suffrage was achieved (1917), voters have been able to choose from a large number of parties: a catholic party, protestant parties (some now merged with the catholic party as Christian Democrats), and several secular parties of which the most important are liberal and socialist in orientation. None of these parties has ever had a majority of the seats in the Lower House of Parliament. The Dutch Government is therefore always based on a coalition, and from 1917 until 1994 the christian parties were always pivotal members of any coalition.

Dutch political culture at the beginning of the 20th century and until well after the Second World War can best be characterised with the term '*verzuiling*', which literally means 'pillarisation', that is, the systematic organisation of many social institutions such as political parties, trade unions and employers' organisations, sport clubs and schools, along the lines of the 'pillars' of society, defined in largely religious terms. The well-known student of Dutch political culture, Lijphart, distinguishes three 'pillars': catholic, calvinist and secular, the last consisting of a socialist and a liberal bloc.[1]

Another important feature of Dutch political culture was 'corporatism', based on the originally catholic social philosophy that rejects both the socialist idea of class struggle and the bourgeois-capitalist idea of competitive individualism, in favour of an ideology of common responsibility for the common good, subject to general supervision by the state. In its Dutch version, 'corporatism' traditionally emphasised the responsibility of middle-level social organisations, in which, for example, trade union leaders and representatives of employers' organisations are included, for the regulation of the economic life of the various branches of the economy.

Despite its segmented character, the Netherlands has been a stable democracy. The reason for this lies in the specific political style adopted by the Dutch elite. Pacification of the differences between the 'pillars' was accomplished because the elites of the various 'pillars' practised a pragmatic toleration, were businesslike in their dealings with each other, and tended to solve differences concerning the distribution of scarce goods on the basis of proportionality. Once the decision was taken to support a particular activity—radio, schools, hospitals—this was arranged organisationally in pillarised institutions and financed in proportion to the number of radio listeners, students, patients, etc of the various pillars.[2]

When an issue could not be solved by applying the principle of proportionality—for example, in case of ideological yes-or-no questions like decolonisation or abortion—avoidance of a definitive resolution was the solution generally sought. Such avoidance took three forms: postponing consideration of the issue (for example, by referring the issue to a prestigious committee), redefining it in such a way that the state was no longer responsible for dealing with it, or 'depoliticising' it. 'Depoliticising' involved making the issue appear a 'procedural' or a 'technical' one and therefore politically neutral.[3]

The 1960s and 1970s were a crucial watershed for Dutch society. From a conservative, tradition-bound country the Netherlands transformed itself into a hotbed of social and cultural experimentation. The Netherlands took a prominent place in the sexual revolution, the legalisation of abortion, the acceptance of drugs, the democratisation of educational institutions, the questioning of religious authority (in particular that of the Catholic Church), and so forth. Societal relationships changed in this period too, becoming far more egalitarian and far less authoritarian—much more 'democratic', as the Dutch would say. The social distance between ordinary people and those to whom they had formerly been

[1] See Lijphart 1968: 17.
[2] *Ibid* at 127–8.
[3] See Andeweg & Irwin 1993: 38.

deferent declined, and ordinary Dutchmen (workers, students, those affected by public building projects, etc) now generally expect to have their views listened to on issues that affect them. In public discussions of important social questions, among them euthanasia, politicians can no longer speak with the authoritative voice they used to enjoy.

That the Dutch have changed is shown by the findings of the European Values Study.[4] In his well-known writings on value orientations, Inglehart concludes that there is a correlation between prosperity and value orientation. People who grow up without a threat to their livelihood tend to think of values such as freedom, self-expression and improvement of the quality of life as more important than values such as social security and personal safety. Inglehart speaks of a shift from a 'materialistic value orientation' to a 'post-materialistic value orientation'.[5] A correlation between increased prosperity and an increasing number of people who consider 'post-materialist values' important has been found in almost all European countries. In the early 1990s, the Netherlands and Denmark were special because in these two countries for the first time people with a 'post-materialistic value orientation' outnumbered those with a 'materialistic value orientation'.[6]

The consequences for politics of these recent developments are twofold. On the one hand, the electorate is no longer divided in a predictable way and the biggest political parties (Christian Democrats, Social Democrats, and Liberals) have become more or less 'catch-all' parties. On the other hand, a new political division has emerged between those who defend personal freedom with respect to non-material issues and those who defend christian values such as the sanctity of life.

2.2 Health Care in the Netherlands[7]

2.2.1 The Dutch Health Care System

The Dutch are relatively healthy compared with the inhabitants of other countries. Most inhabitants will live to an advanced age. Life expectancy at birth in 2005 was 77.2 years for men and 81.6 years for women. Both men and women can expect to spend about 60 years of their lives in good health and about 70 years of their lives without physical constraints.[8]

The Dutch tend to have a high opinion of their health care system. Doctors enjoy a high level of societal trust (thus, for example, there is little objection to

---

[4] Since the 1970s, extensive data on values in a large number of countries have been collected three times. The findings of the first study were not published separately. The findings of the second study (1990–93) are published in Inglehart, Basañez & Moreno 1998; the findings of the third study (1999/2000) are published in Halman 2001.

[5] See Inglehart 1977: 28.

[6] *Ibid* at 139.

[7] Except where otherwise noted, Van Rooij *et al* 2002 is our source here.

[8] See Mackenbach & Van der Maas 2004: 51.

doctors having access to privacy-sensitive information in medical records[9]). And the results of a health care-consumer panel in 2004 show that 90% of the panel members have great trust in their GP and in specialists.[10] More than three quarters of the population consider the quality of medical care good to excellent.[11]

Health care policy in the Netherlands reflects the country's cultural commitment to social equity and solidarity. In 2006, after 30 years of discussion, a new universal system of health care insurance was introduced, replacing the older combination of a public system for those with lower and a private system for those with higher incomes. Everyone who lives in the country is now legally required to take out 'private' insurance, the terms of which are highly regulated. There is a fixed monthly premium for every adult of about €90 and an additional income-dependent premium. The mandatory coverage includes basic care (GP, prescription drugs, hospital care), and the costs of euthanasia are included. Coverage can be broadened (eg to cover dental expenses, 'alternative' therapies, and so forth) if one opts to pay extra. Although health care insurance is mandatory, the fact is that there have been problems of enforcement, and at present the number of uninsured persons is supposed to be about 1% of the population. Exceptional costs (such as costs for rehabilitation, home care, and a stay in a nursing home or a residential home) are covered by a compulsory national health financing scheme (AWBZ). Every person living in the Netherlands is covered by the scheme.

2.2.2 Institutions for Health Care and Care of the Elderly

Health care institutions in the Netherlands derive historically from the activities of churches, later taken over by private organisations affiliated with the various 'pillars' of Dutch society. There were, and still are, non-denominational, catholic, protestant and humanist institutions. The recent history of Dutch health care is one of a changing relationship between the state and these originally private institutions. The 'pillarisation' of health care continued long after the state assumed responsibility for the financing and regulation of health care and some remains are to be found in the institutional organisation of the health care system.

There are more than 800 health care institutions that provide 24-hour nursing care in the Netherlands. Leaving aside institutions such as nursing homes for children and special institutions for the blind and the deaf, these include, in addition to hospitals and nursing homes, mental hospitals (76 institutions with some 23,000 beds) and institutions for the mentally handicapped (154 institutions with some 36,000 beds).[12]

---

[9] See *Medisch Contact* 61: 943 (2006).
[10] See <http://www.nivel.nl/oc2/page.asp?pageid=5435> accessed 11 January 2007.
[11] See SCP 2002: 293.
[12] See CBS 2003b: 200.

Hospitals

There were 130 hospitals (*ziekenhuizen*) with over 55,000 beds in 2001. These include 8 university hospitals in various parts of the country, 100 general hospitals and 20 specialised hospitals which limit their care to certain illnesses (such as cancer) or sorts of patients (such as burn victims).[13] The costs of hospital care are paid for by health care insurance.

Almost all hospitals are private, and all are run by non-profit organisations. Merger and cooperation between hospitals has been important during the last four decades with the number of general hospitals declining from 212 in 1963 to about 130 in 2001. Since mergers often take place between two or more hospitals originally founded on different denominational principles, the 'pillarisation' of hospitals has been declining.

Because hospitals are private institutions, they have a certain degree of freedom in determining their own policy, among other things with regard to end-of-life care generally and euthanasia in particular. Most hospitals permit euthanasia.[14] Until recently most doctors who practised in hospitals were not employees of the hospital, and the degree of control a hospital had over doctors was limited. Legislation in 1998 changed the relation between hospitals and specialists by introducing the figure of a 'contract of admittance' (*toelatingsovereenkomst*). The contract provides that the specialist is ultimately responsible for the medical treatment of his patients but he must respect the organisational and financial framework of the hospital. The board of the hospital is ultimately responsible for the quality of the medical care given. Nowadays, in many big hospitals (including all university hospitals) doctors are employees of the hospital.

Nursing Homes

Nursing homes (*verpleeghuizen*) are institutions for the care and nursing of persons who do not require hospital care but who cannot be taken care of at home, the costs being born by the public scheme for exceptional medical expenses. Residents pay an income-related share of the costs of stay.

In 2004 there were 335 nursing homes in the Netherlands with 56,000 beds, 46% for somatic patients and 54% for psychogeriatric patients (most of them suffering from dementia). More than 90% of the persons admitted to nursing homes are over 65 years old; the average age is 80 years. For most elderly patients, the nursing home is their last home. The average length of stay is nearly three years.[15]

Like hospitals, nursing homes have some freedom to determine their own policy with regard to euthanasia and related medical behaviour that potentially shortens life. Since the doctors who are responsible for patients in a nursing home are usually employed by the institution, nursing homes can generally exert

---

[13] See Mackenbach & Van der Maas 2004: 202.
[14] See ch 5.4.1.
[15] See Mackenbach & Van der Maas 2004: 205–8.

considerable control over medical decision-making. In most nursing homes, euthanasia is in principle acceptable.[16]

Residential Homes

Admittance to a residential home (*verzorgingstehuis*) (publicly financed old-age homes and the like) is possible for (usually elderly) persons who, because of a disability, lack of social contacts, or anxieties are not capable of living independently. Residents must be able to carry out most daily tasks for themselves. The costs of stay in a residential home are borne by the public scheme for exceptional medical expenses; residents pay an income-related share of the costs of their stay.

There are 1,346 residential homes in the Netherlands with about 110,000 beds.[17] The average age of residents is increasing. The proportion of residents 85 and older rose from one-third in 1980 to almost two-thirds in 2002. This group consists chiefly of women who are single. The average length of stay is at most five years. Such an institution is the last home for most of its inhabitants.[18]

People who live in a residential home have their own GP (which means that a number of different GPs have patients in any given home). This in principle means that euthanasia is a matter between a resident and his GP, although from incidental information it appears that, at least in the past, a residential home with a strong religious orientation might find euthanasia so objectionable that it would be difficult for a GP to carry it out there.

Institutions for Terminal Palliative Care

The development of palliative care in the Netherlands differs from that in for example the UK, because in the early years attention was not focused on founding a new kind of institution. This different history can partly be explained by the important role nursing homes have in terminal care and partly by the terminal care provided by GPs. The first residential 'hospice' was set up in 1988 and by 2006, there were about 200 specialised institutions for terminal palliative care.[19] Some of these institutions are hospices (run by professional staff), some of them are 'almost home houses'—facilities managed predominantly by volunteers—and the rest are wards in nursing homes, residential homes and hospitals. Depending on the institution where it is given, terminal palliative care is paid for by the patient's health insurance or by the public scheme for exceptional medical expenses. In most palliative care institutions euthanasia is an option. The quality and availability of terminal palliative care in the Netherlands is currently considered, relative to other countries, very advanced.[20]

---

[16] See ch 5.4.1.
[17] See CBS 2003b: 203.
[18] See Boot & Knapen 2005: 137.
[19] See Mistiaen & Francke 2007: 9.
[20] See C Ross-van Dorp (Secretary of State for Health), speech 1 November 2006, available at <http://www.minvws.no/toespraken/cz/2006/nederland-koploper-in-palliatieve-zorg.asp> accessed 24 September 2007.

Home Care

People who cannot care for themselves but remain at home qualify for home care. Home-care organisations offer a package of services comprising nursing, domestic care and counselling, in connection with maternity, illness, recuperation, disability, old age and dying. In 2002, 164 home care institutions were officially recognised and they assisted some 370,000 clients, mainly with domestic care.[21] However, many more people need this kind of assistance. Those who do not receive professional home care must look for assistance to family, friends, neighbours, etc. It is governmental policy to encourage this sort of informal care. Most of the financial costs of home care are born by the public scheme for exceptional medical costs, the rest by individuals.

Where People Die

In 2004 about 65% of all deaths took place in an institution, usually a hospital (33%), a nursing-home (22%) or a residential home (11%); about 28% of all deaths took place at home and 7% elsewhere.[22] Five per cent of all deaths take place in a hospice or other specialised institution for palliative terminal care.[23] Most Dutch people (73%) would prefer to die at home or a place that resembles home.[24]

2.2.3 Health Care Professionals[25]

The professionals involved in the care of a dying patient, and the nature of their relationships with one another, vary widely from one place of death to another.

In hospitals, apart from doctors and nurses, social and pastoral workers are usually involved, sometimes also a psychologist or psychiatrist. Other specialists (eg anaesthesiologists) are called in when needed. These various professionals tend to regard themselves as a 'team' and to discuss and coordinate the various aspects of terminal care with each other. Final decision-making responsibility rests, however, with the doctor who is at the relevant moment responsible for the patient's treatment. There is usually little contact with the patient's former GP.

In nursing homes, the professionals principally involved in the care of a dying patient are nursing-home doctors and nurses, pastoral workers and physiotherapists. Here, too, the working relationship is conceived of as 'teamwork'; coordination of care is the responsibility of the nursing staff but ultimate responsibility for decisions concerning care is with the doctors. There is little contact with specialists (hospitals) or a patient's former GP.

---

[21] See Boot & Knapen 2005: 106.
[22] Data received from the Central Bureau of Statistics.
[23] Mistiaen & Francke 2007: 9.
[24] See De Boer 2006: 160.
[25] Except where otherwise noted, Schrijvers 1997 is our source here.

In a residential home the principal professionals as far as terminal care is concerned are the home's nursing and service personnel and an inhabitant's own GP. Coordination of care is the responsibility of the home's staff, medical treatment (including all contacts with specialists) is the responsibility of the GP. Since many GPs may have patients in a given home, coordination can be problematic and the communication of doctors with the home's staff is often considered by the latter inadequate.

In the case of patients who die at home, the primary professionals involved are the patient's GP and the personnel of a home care service, especially a visiting nurse. Although they usually work closely together, visiting nurses sometimes criticise GPs for excluding them from the decision-making on questions such as euthanasia.[26] Physiotherapists, social workers and pastors are sometimes also involved, but often not in coordination with the GP, who 'just happens to come across them' when he visits the patient.

2.2.3.1 Doctors

In 2001 there were about 24,000 doctors engaged in clinical practice (GPs, specialists and nursing-home doctors).[27] About 60% of all practising doctors are members of the Royal Dutch Medical Association (KNMG),[28] which is a purely private association. The KNMG has since the 1980s supported the legalisation of euthanasia, and its guidelines have heavily influenced the substance of Dutch euthanasia law.

General Practitioners

Dutch primary medical care has three major system characteristics: 'listing', 'gatekeeping', and 'family orientation'. 'Listing' means that in principle every Dutch inhabitant is registered with a GP. This guarantees patients continuity of care. Dutch GPs see three-quarters of their patients annually, averaging 4 contacts per patient per year (however, 16% of the population are responsible for two-thirds of the total number of visits).[29] The 'gatekeeping' function refers to the fact that patients generally do not have direct access to specialists or hospital care but must be referred by their GP. The impact of gatekeeping is reflected in the low referral rate: more than 90% of all complaints are treated by GPs. The third characteristic, 'family orientation', refers to the fact that a Dutch GP generally serves as the personal physician for a patient's entire family. Moreover, GPs make home visits: 4% of all contacts are visits to the patient's home, especially in the case of the elderly or very sick.

---

[26] See Van Bruchem-Van der Scheur *et al* 2004: 142.
[27] See Mackenbach & Van der Maas 2004: 217.
[28] See Dillmann 1996: 65.
[29] See Mackenbach & Van der Maas 2004: 180.

Roughly a third of all clinical practitioners are GPs. In 2001 there were about 8,000 GPs, almost all of them working in private practice.[30] About a third of all GPs are in solo-practice, another third in duo-practice, a quarter in group practice or in a multi-disciplinary health centre.[31] The proportion of duo-practices, group practices and health centres is increasing. GPs who are in solo- or duo-practice always have more or less intensive contact with a number of other GPs in their immediate surroundings, with whom they form a 'substitution group', so that access to first-line medical care is guaranteed for their patients 24 hours a day throughout the year regardless of an individual doctor's absence on weekends, vacations, illness, etc.

Since the beginning of the 1990s, the relationships between GPs have become gradually more organised. In the past, apart from duo- or group practices, the only formal contact between them was in 'substitution groups'. Recently, however, both the government and the National Association of GPs (NHG) have been promoting a national organisational structure at the base of which are 'GP-groups' (in which several 'substitution groups' participate). These are responsible for the organisation of substitution, continuing education, contacts with other professionals, etc; they are also supposed to arrange for inter-collegial quality control.[32] Since 2006, another occasion of increased cooperation is the organisation of the new health-insurance system. GPs must make financial arrangements with the insurers of their patients, and they do this not as individuals but as groups (usually GP-groups). Nevertheless, GPs remain highly individualistic and they have considerable freedom in conducting their practice. Formal control is limited, and implementation of what control there is, is weak.[33]

GPs are the responsible doctor in about 44% of all deaths, including both those of people who die at home and those of residents of residential homes. They are responsible for 87% of all euthanasia deaths.[34]

Specialists

In 2002 there were about 13,500 specialists of whom 90% were connected with intramural institutions.[35] Specialists are the responsible doctor in about 33% of all deaths and in 2005 they were responsible for 9% of all euthanasia deaths.[36]

---

[30] See Mackenbach & Van der Maas 2004: 217.

[31] See CBS 2003b: 202.

[32] In J Zaritsky's film, *An Appointment with Death* (Corporation for Public Broadcasting 1993), there is a scene in which a GP discusses a request for assistance with suicide with his colleagues in such a 'GP-group'.

[33] Another form of control takes the form of professional standards. The NHG issues practice standards for a large variety of conditions, and in the absence of good reasons a GP is expected to conform to them. In 2000 the NHG won the prestigious German Carl Bertelsmann prize for the quality of its translation of scientific findings into concrete practice standards for GPs.

[34] Onwuteaka-Phlipsen *et al* 2007: 102.

[35] See Mackenbach & Van der Maas 2004: 217. There are many specialist associates, some of which have developed guidelines that will be discussed for example in chs 4.2.3.4(B) and 6.

[36] Onwuteaka-Phlipsen *et al* 2007: 102.

Nursing-Home Doctors

'Nursing-home doctor' is in the Netherlands a medical specialty. In 2001 there were about 1,100 specialised doctors working in nursing homes.[37] More than most GPs and many other specialists, nursing-home doctors function as members of a treatment team, usually as its head. Most of them are employed by the institution where they work. Nursing-home doctors are the responsible doctor in about 22% of all deaths and in 2005 they were responsible for 4% of all euthanasia deaths.[38]

2.2.3.2 Nurses and Nursing Assistants

In 2001 there were about 72,000 nurses and nursing assistants working in hospitals, more than 118,000 in elderly care (nursing homes and residential homes) and more than 142,000 in home care.[39]

The nursing profession has a long tradition of professional organisation. As in many areas of Dutch society, 'pillarisation' plays an important role, and nurses are still largely organised along religious lines. Nurses' organisations increasingly promote professionalisation, concentrating on the following three areas: autonomy in professional practice, a voice in policy-making processes, and organisation of the professional group. However, in actual practice autonomy and professional responsibility are limited. The content and pace of work are largely determined by third parties. Nurses are often consulted in euthanasia cases but legally their direct involvement must, for reasons we will see in chapter 4.2.3.3(J), be limited.

2.2.3.3 Pharmacists

When a doctor proposes to administer a controlled drug (which includes all drugs used as euthanatica) the drug must be supplied by a pharmacist. Pharmacists are expected not to supply blindly whatever a doctor orders but to exercise some marginal control. Thus, for example, pharmacists are supposed to make sure that the proper instructions for use, warnings about side-effects, etc are given to the patient, and to check on the combinations of drugs prescribed for a patient (sometimes by different doctors) to ensure that taking them together is pharmacologically responsible.

In 2005 there were over 5,000 registered pharmacists. About 1,600 of them are self-employed in pharmacies directly accessible to the public, 300 are responsible for the pharmacies of hospitals, and some 500 GPs, especially those in areas where no pharmacy is available, function as their own pharmacist.[40]

Dutch pharmacists are organised in the Royal Dutch Association for Pharmacy (KNMP) which issues guidelines on appropriate euthanatica and on the involvement of pharmacists in euthanasia (see chapter 4.2.3.3(J)).

[37] See Mackenbach & Van der Maas 2004: 217.
[38] See Onwuteaka-Philipsen *et al* 2007: 102. The specialist association of nursing home doctors has developed guidelines for end-of-life care that are discussed in ch 4.2.2.2.
[39] See Van der Windt *et al* 2003: 45.
[40] See CBS 2003b: 202.

2.2.3.4 Municipal Pathologists

The Law on Burial and Cremation requires, before burial or cremation can take place, that a doctor attest that a person's death was due to a natural cause. If the patient's own doctor cannot do this, he must report this fact to the municipal pathologist,[41] who examines the body and decides himself whether the death was a natural one; if not, he reports the case to the local prosecutor (see further chapter 4.2.4.1).

Every municipality in the Netherlands has at least one municipal pathologist. Persons authorised to practice medicine are eligible for appointment and in small municipalities a local GP in private practice is usually appointed, with several colleagues as his deputies. In larger cities, municipal pathologists are usually doctors in the city health service. There is general consensus among those responsible for medical policy that in the future municipal pathologists should be public employees.

2.2.3.5 The Medical Inspectorate and Medical Disciplinary Law

The Medical Inspectorate is responsible for the enforcement of legal provisions relating to public health, institutions such as hospitals and nursing homes, and health care workers such as doctors and nurses, and for giving advice and information to the Minister of Health. Among other things, the Inspectors are authorised to initiate medical disciplinary proceedings.

All doctors in the Netherlands who are authorised to practice medicine, as well as other professions involved in the health care system (including nurses and pharmacists), are subject to medical disciplinary law.[42] The primary purpose of disciplinary law (since its reform in 1993) is to guarantee the quality of medical care and to protect the general public against incompetence and carelessness. Disciplinary measures can be imposed for actions or omissions that are inconsistent with the care to which patients are entitled, or with the demands of good medical practice. Complaints can be lodged by an Inspector, by the governing body of the institution in which a health care professional works, or by a person directly affected by the behaviour in question. A complaint is handled in the first instance by one of the five regional Medical Disciplinary Tribunals; appeals are to the Central Medical Disciplinary Tribunal. The meetings of the Tribunals are, in principle, open to the public. One of the following measures must be imposed if the person charged is found guilty of a disciplinary offence: a warning, a reprimand, a fine, suspension from practice for at most one year, or revocation in whole or in part of the authority to practise.[43]

---

[41] This translation of the Dutch word *lijkschouwer* (literally: 'examiner of corpses') is used in the official translation of the Euthanasia Law of 2002. It may well be a better translation than the term 'coroner' used in the predecessor of this book since, unlike the British coroner, the legal responsibility of the *lijkschouwer* is very limited (see ch 4.2.4.1).

[42] Law on Professions Concerned with Individual Medical Care *Wet op de Beroepen in de Individuele Gezondheidszorg, Staatsblad*, 1993a, no 655. In addition to medical disciplinary law, both civil law (malpractice and breach of contract) and criminal law bear on the behaviour of medical practitioners. It is possible that for a single incident, a doctor is liable under two or even three of these bodies of law.

[43] See on Dutch medical disciplinary law Hout 2006.

2.3 Public and Professional Opinion concerning Euthanasia

Reservations concerning the way public opinion data is usually collected, and the meaning and (political) significance of the 'opinions' collected, are discussed in chapter 17.1. We present some of the better Dutch data here.

2.3.1 Dutch Public Opinion concerning Euthanasia

For almost half a century polls have specifically investigated the opinion of the Dutch public concerning euthanasia.[44] These polls tend to suffer from one or another of the sorts of defects characteristic of opinion polling. The formulation of the question posed usually leaves much to be desired (in particular, 'euthanasia' is often inadequately defined or poorly distinguished from other MBPSL) and in any case differs from one poll to the next without the poll-takers apparently being aware of the different things they are asking (whether the respondent might consider euthanasia, approves of it, thinks a doctor should accede to a patient's request, thinks the law should allow it, etc). The result of all this is that the results are difficult to interpret or compare. The first poll was conducted in 1950 and the question posed was rather good: 'If a person is suffering from a painful and incurable illness and the patient and the family request it, should a doctor be allowed painlessly to hasten the moment of death?' Fifty-four per cent of all respondents were opposed to allowing this, but 55% of non-religious respondents were already in favour.[45]

Since 1966 the Social and Cultural Planning Bureau (SCP) has polled Dutch opinion using a consistent, rather poorly formulated, question: 'Should a doctor give a lethal injection at the request of a patient to put an end to his suffering?' The results are shown on Table 2.1. As the SCP polls show, the greater part of the change in public opinion from roughly balanced to strongly positive had occurred by about 1975. Since the middle of the 1970s, a majority of the Dutch population has consistently been 'in favour of' euthanasia; the percentage of unqualified opponents has declined from about 25% in 1970 to about 10% in 1991, and the latter group seems to have remained more or less constant since then. Since the end of the 1990s, there may have been a minor shift from unreservedly positive toward the (more sophisticated) answer 'it all depends'.[46]

---

[44] For discussion of some of these polls see Catsburg & De Boer 1986; Van Holsteyn & Trappenburg 1996: 51–3; Blad 1996: 390–401. For a discussion in English of various Dutch opinion polls concerning euthanasia see Hessing, Blad & Pieterman 1996: 161ff.

[45] See Hessing, Blad & Pieterman 1996: 161.

[46] In 1993 the SCP conducted an opinion poll (N=1874) with a different question: 'It should be possible for a patient to have euthanasia carried out if he or she wants it.' The results (ages 16–74, excluding a very small number of 'do not know') were as follows: strongly agree (19%), agree (46%), neither agree nor disagree (14%), disagree (15%), strongly disagree (5%). Source: SCP, *Culturele Veranderingen* [Cultural Changes] survey 1993 (data received from SCP).

Table 2.1. SCP public opinion polls concerning euthanasia, 1966–2004

'Should a doctor give a lethal injection at the request of a patient to put an end to his suffering?'

	yes	depends	no
1966	40	12	49
1975	53	24	24
1980	52	36	12
1985	55	33	12
1991	58	33	9
1995	58	35	8
1998	50	40	9
2004	51	39	9

Source: through 1991: SCP 1992: 475. *Source* after 1991: SCP, *Culturele Veranderingen* surveys (data received from SCP). A very small 'do not know' category has been eliminated for the sake of simplicity. The results of the SCP polls are available in English in more detail for 1966 and 1991 in Van der Maas *et al* (1995). The number polled ranges from about 1,700 to about 2,250.

We take the unconditional 'no' answers on this and other polls we will discuss to be the least ambiguous indicator of (changes in) public opinion. Table 2.1 illustrates why. Since no one could sensibly be 'for' euthanasia under any and all conditions, the 'yes' answers must reflect various positions on a spectrum of 'it depends'. Whether there is any difference between the opinions of those who answer 'yes' and those who answer 'it depends', and if so what leads people to prefer one to the other, is unknown.

The SCP discontinued this series of polls after 2004. The most recent SCP poll uses an entirely different sort of question. From a recent report it appears that 71% of those polled think that euthanasia will be generally accepted in 2020, and 72% think that this is desirable.[47]

The general picture given by the above polls can be observed for all the various segments of the population whose opinion has been separately measured. There are essentially no differences between men and women. Younger people are slightly more positive than older people. Supporters of the non-confessional (social-democratic and liberal) parties have long been strongly positive, whereas a positive majority among Christian Democrats only emerged in the mid-1980s. A majority of persons who report no religious affiliation were already supportive in 1966 (28% 'no'), and they remain the most supportive group (in 1991, 3% 'no'). A majority of

---

[47] See SCP 2004: 425. The 2001 national survey of euthanasia practice (discussed in ch 5.1.2) included a survey of a sample of the Dutch population as a whole, in which among other things some questions were asked about opinions concerning medical behaviour that potentially shortens life. The questions were not very precise but the answers nevertheless seem to confirm that there is very strong public support for the essentials of Dutch euthanasia practice (Van der Wal *et al* 2003: 69).

catholics were opposed in 1966 (55% 'no'), but by 1991 catholics were essentially indistinguishable from the rest of the population. Dutch reformed are now only slightly less supportive than the general population (16% 'no'), and the stricter calvinists (*gereformeerden*) are least supportive of all (34% 'no').[48]

According to the SCP, there is every indication that with regard to euthanasia, as with a variety of other issues, a process of cultural diffusion has taken place. Until the middle of the 1960s, values were rather traditional throughout the country. Beginning in the cities a process of modernisation set in, and traditional attitudes toward a variety of issues (marriage, sexuality, emancipation of women, homosexuality, abortion, euthanasia, political protest) began to change. The process of change began somewhat later in the less urban areas of the country. In the case of euthanasia, convergence set in from about the beginning of the 1990s. At present, there is little remaining difference between the urban and rural population.[49]

Less superficial data comes from Van Holsteyn and Trappenburg's extensive study of Dutch public opinion, not only about euthanasia but also about a number of other MBPSL.[50] Their findings generally confirm those of earlier polls. In 1995, about 10% of the Dutch public were of the opinion that euthanasia should 'always be forbidden', whereas 64% considered that it should 'always be allowed' if requested by the patient. Some 80% of those who answered the question considered that the doctor in a case described in the questionnaire (based on a widely shown television film of an actual case of euthanasia[51]) had done the right thing.

Van Holsteyn and Trappenburg analyse the reasons their respondents gave for their opinions on the various questions. They conclude that these tend to correlate most strongly with a person's attitude toward personal autonomy on such matters. In general, those who believe autonomy is important are much more likely to support the various MBPSL (even in a case where the patient's autonomy must be exercised by a parent or other family member). Attitudes toward the principle of beneficence—in particular, whether a respondent considers it the primary role of a doctor to relieve the patient's suffering or to keep him alive—are of some, but not major importance. Weekly church attendance is associated with opposition to the various MBPSL but it is also very strongly associated with a person's attitude toward autonomy (4% of those who have never had a religious affiliation reject the idea of personal autonomy, as against two-thirds of those who regularly attend church). According to Van Holsteyn and Trappenburg, the autonomy effect remains even when religious affiliation is held constant.[52]

[48] Most of the above data are taken from Van der Maas *et al* 1995: 1413; for data on political party affiliation in 1988, see NVVE 1989.

[49] See SCP 1996: 516–25.

[50] Van Holsteyn & Trappenburg 1996 (see for a summary in English, Van Holsteyn & Trappenburg 1998).

[51] M Nederhorst, *Dood op verzoek* [Death on Request], documentary television film, first broadcast on 20 October 1994.

[52] For further details about Van Holsteyn and Trappenburg's study, in particular relating to other sorts of MBPSL, see GB&W: 199–201. Their research shows that, in general, Dutch public opinion is quite close to Dutch law, except with regard to the legal right of parents to request withholding of life-prolonging treatment from a baby with Downs syndrome (public opinion seems to be against this) and

2.3.2 Dutch Medical Opinion concerning Euthanasia

The Royal Dutch Medical Association (KNMG) has for two decades supported the legalisation of euthanasia (see chapter 3.1). The professional opinion of individual doctors has been studied in the Dutch national surveys of euthanasia practice. The results are shown on Table 2.2.

Table 2.2. Opinions of Dutch doctors concerning euthanasia (percentages in agreement with statement)

Statement	1990 (N = 405)	1995 (N = 405)	2001 (N = 410)
'Everyone has the right to self-determination concerning life and death.'	64	52	56
'In the past five years, my views on euthanasia–			
• have become more permissive.'	25	18	12
• have become more restrictive.'	14	12	20
• have not changed.'	61	70	69

Source: Van der Wal *et al* 2003: 68 (interviews with doctors). No comparable data for 2005.

On its face, Table 2.2 seems puzzling. Are the views of the general population and of doctors changing in opposite directions? The formulation of the first question is unfortunate (it not being at all clear what the contents of such a 'right' might be) and the declining frequency of endorsement of such a statement may simply reflect increasing sophistication among doctors. The answers to the second question, concerning the direction in which doctors' views are changing over time, seem to indicate what one would expect: a stabilisation of professional opinion after a period of change (although there may be some indication of a change in the direction of more 'restrictive' views, whatever that might mean).

A better indication of professional opinion is probably given by doctors' statements about their own (likely) behaviour. The answers of Dutch doctors to the question whether they have performed or would be willing to perform euthanasia or assisted suicide are shown in Table 5.7 in chapter 5. No indication of a change toward more restrictive attitudes can be distilled from these answers. The proportion of Dutch doctors in principle willing to perform euthanasia remained essentially constant after 1990 at between 84% and 89%. The proportion that is unwilling has also remained stable at 11 to 15%, but those unwilling even to refer a patient had declined to 1% by 2001. GPs (who, as we have seen, are responsible for the bulk of all euthanasia) are much more positive than other doctors: in 2005, 64% had 'ever' performed euthanasia (more than double the rate for other

the 'right' of elderly persons who are 'tired of life' to receive pills from their doctor with which they can commit suicide at a time of their own choosing (public opinion would support such a right).

doctors) and over a quarter had carried it out within the preceding year (about five times the frequency for other doctors).[53]

2.4 Concluding Remark

The Netherlands is a prosperous country. Thanks, among other things, to a high level of social solidarity and a health care system that is accessible to almost every inhabitant, the Dutch are among the happiest people in the world.[54] Together with growing prosperity in the decades after the Second World War, a new value orientation developed that emphasises autonomy in choices about how to live one's life, and this came to include some room for the choice to end one's life in a humane way (which in practice has meant, with the help of a doctor). Since the Dutch tend to trust their fellow countrymen and their professionals, entrusting such a sensitive task to doctors has not seemed overly dangerous. All this, together with a history of tolerance and a culture of making formerly taboo subjects discussable and of preferring transparency to secrecy, constitutes the cultural soil in which the public debate on euthanasia could take root and the context within which the legal developments and medical practices described in the following chapters must be understood.

---

[53] Onwuteaka-Philipsen *et al* 2007: 99.
[54] See Veenhoven 1998: 63.

3

Recent Legal Developments
in the Netherlands

The Termination of Life on Request and Assisted Suicide (Review Procedures) Act (the Law of 2002) came into effect in April of 2002. The Netherlands thereby became the first country in the world in which euthanasia is formally legalised by statute. Foreign attention was intense but for the Dutch the Law of 2002 did not change very much: in effect the statute ratified judicial decisions, guidelines of medical professional associations, and prosecutorial practice that had already brought about legal change in the 1980s.[1] As we noted in the Foreword, we have tried as much as possible to avoid repeating in this book what we wrote in its predecessor, *Euthanasia and Law in the Netherlands* (1998). This chapter therefore focuses on legal developments from 1997 to the present, and in particular the events leading up to the Law of 2002. In section 3.1 we summarise developments before that. The reader interested in the details of the prior history is referred to the earlier book.[2]

In the following five sections we discuss the enactment of the Law of 2002 (section 3.2). Then we deal with other important events and developments between 1997 and 2007. These latter sections focus in particular on several important new court cases, covering four different questions. The first is whether a doctor should be allowed to assist a patient with suicide if the patient is 'tired of life' (section 3.3). The second concerns the boundaries of medical behaviour at the end of life in the case of a non-competent patient (section 3.4). The third concerns patients suffering from dementia (section 3.5). And the fourth discusses recent developments concerning the possibility of assisted suicide by non-doctors (section 3.6). We close with some reflections on the changes over the past decade (section 3.7).

3.1 Legal Developments through 1998[3]

The Dutch Penal Code provides in article 293 that a 'person who takes the life of another person at that other person's express and earnest request' is guilty of a

---

[1] The Ministers who defended the bill in Parliament repeatedly stated that it codified existing practice.

[2] For an even more comprehensive history (in Dutch), see Weyers 2004.

[3] Unless otherwise noted, this paragraph is based on GB&W, ch 2.

serious offence (but less serious than if the behaviour were treated as murder). Article 294 provides that 'a person who intentionally incites another to commit suicide, assists in the suicide of another, or procedures for that other person the means to commit suicide' is guilty of a serious offence, although suicide itself is not illegal. Prosecutions under these articles were almost unknown until the 1970s.

The 1970s saw a few criminal prosecutions for euthanasia or physician-assisted suicide. These cases led the highest authority in the prosecutorial system—the Committee of Procurators-General (PGs)—under guidance of the Minister of Justice, to develop a policy on such cases. They decided that in every case of euthanasia that came to the attention of the prosecutorial authorities,[4] the PGs— and not the local prosecutor—would decide whether to prosecute. The criteria to be used in making this decision were taken from the few court cases there had been. These criteria, not yet well worked out, were the presence of a voluntary and well-considered request and of unbearable and hopeless (in the sense of: without hope of improvement) suffering, the involvement of a doctor and the consultation of another professional (not necessarily a doctor).

In the early 1980s some doctors began reporting that they had performed euthanasia and the PGs decided to prosecute some of them to produce clarity both with respect to the grounds on which euthanasia might be justified and the precise content of the requirements of due care a doctor has to comply with. This action of the PGs can be seen as the beginning of the unique course of legal development the Dutch have followed with respect to euthanasia.

Some of the cases resulting from the decision of the PGs led to appeals to the Supreme Court. However, before the Supreme Court for the first time ruled on a case of euthanasia, important societal and political developments had taken place. In 1982, at the request of Parliament, a State Commission on Euthanasia was set up to advise the Government on the desirability of amending the law on euthanasia. The State Commission asked a number of organisations for information about the current views on euthanasia. One of these organisations was the Royal Dutch Medical Association (KNMG).

The Board of the KNMG appointed a committee that in 1984 formulated a position. The committee thought it wise that the Association not take a position for or against euthanasia. Instead, in the committee's view, the Association should make clear that if euthanasia takes place, it should be performed by a doctor, and the Association should clarify the requirements of due care applicable in such a case. With respect to these requirements, the committee took the position that there must be a voluntary and well-considered request and 'unacceptable' suffering (a

---

[4] The prosecutorial authorities usually learn about a case of euthanasia only if a doctor, after ending a life on the patient's request, has 'reported' the case by not filing a certificate of natural death (see ch 4.2.4.1 for a full description of the reporting procedure). Before 1980 there had never been a doctor who, after ending a patient's life, did not file a certificate of natural death. In the early 1980s some local prosecutors set up reporting and investigating procedures designed to encourage doctors to report euthanasia. This policy bore fruit: in districts with such a procedure the reporting rate was higher than in other districts.

phrase intended to summarise 'unbearable and hopeless'). The committee formulated two procedural requirements: a second doctor should be consulted and a certificate of natural death should not be filed.[5] The KNMG adopted the committee's report, thereby making clear and public that the medical profession (highly respected in the Netherlands) was prepared to take responsibility for euthanasia.

When the first case concerning euthanasia (the *Schoonheim* case[6]) was decided by the Supreme Court later the same year, the willingness of the medical profession to take responsibility for euthanasia apparently made it easier for the court to come to the conclusion that a doctor who in a case of euthanasia complies with the requirements of due care can successfully invoke the justification of necessity (conflict of duties). The Supreme Court referred the case back to a Court of Appeals which ruled that the defence of necessity was supported by the facts in the case and acquitted the doctor.

In the same year 1984, a member of the left-liberal party—D66—submitted a bill providing for the legalisation of euthanasia. A majority in Parliament—consisting of the social-democrats (PvdA), left-liberals (D66) and right-liberals (VVD)—supported the bill. This majority, however, could not effectively be mobilised because the christian-democratic party (CDA) was at the time an essential part of any coalition government and used its position to block such legislation.

The next year, in 1985, the State Commission on Euthanasia issued its report. A majority took the position that euthanasia, performed under certain conditions, should be legalised. From that time on, euthanasia has been continuously present on the Dutch political agenda. But the Dutch political culture continued to keep a legislative solution out of reach until the late 1990s.

During the years that followed, a number of legal questions concerning euthanasia were dealt with by the courts. In 1987 the Supreme Court held that a doctor who complies with the requirements of due care can assume that he will not be prosecuted. Thereafter, the Minister of Justice promised the Medical Association that the prosecutorial authorities would not bring charges in such a case. From this time on, euthanasia has been effectively legal in the Netherlands, although the Government (in particular the CDA) and various commentators often found it convenient to describe it as still illegal.

In the 1990s attention shifted from the legality of euthanasia to the problem of effective control. In 1990 the first steps were taken to design a special reporting procedure. The new procedure assured doctors that the police would investigate reported cases in a discrete way. If a doctor, after performing euthanasia, notified the municipal pathologist of this fact and filled in a form which showed that he had met the requirements of due care, the police would not investigate the case.

The first national research into the practice of euthanasia was carried out in 1990. The results showed that most doctors, after performing euthanasia, did not

---

[5] In 1987 the Medical Association added the requirement of appropriate record-keeping.

[6] *Nederlandse Jurisprudentie* 1985, no 106. For an English translation with explanatory notes, see GB&W: 322–8; the case is discussed in its historical context at *ibid*: 62–5.

report what they had done. Only 18% of all euthanasia cases were apparently being reported as such.[7] Because the new reporting procedure was nevertheless considered useful, the Government decided to give it a legal foundation. When the 1990 study was repeated in 1995, the reporting rate had increased to 38% but this was thought to be still far from satisfactory. The Government decided that doctors might be more inclined to report if the 'criminal' character of the reporting procedure were reduced. It was therefore decided to put a 'buffer' between doctors and prosecutors by creating Regional Review Committees to review reported cases. The committees, composed of a lawyer, a doctor and an ethicist, would judge whether a doctor had complied with the requirements of due care. If a committee found that this was the case, it would advise the prosecutorial authorities not to prosecute. In principle, the prosecutorial authorities would follow the advice of the committee.[8] The Regional Review Committees were created by Order in Council and commenced work at the end of 1998.[9]

In 1998 another new facility was created—a service (known under the acronym SCEN) that provides trained consultants for GPs who are considering performing euthanasia. The consultant informs GPs about the requirements of due care and functions as a check on whether in a specific case the requirements of due care have been met.[10] Because of its great success the service has recently been extended to nursing homes and hospitals.[11]

3.2 Statutory Legalisation

In 1998 elections were in the offing. The Government, in which for the first time since 1917 none of the confessional parties was represented, had not seized the opportunity to legalise euthanasia during its first term. D66, the political party that had introduced the first euthanasia bill in 1984, took the coming elections as an opportunity to put euthanasia back onto the legislative agenda. Together with parliamentarians of the PvdA and the VVD, the other parties constituting the coalition government, D66 introduced a bill to legalise euthanasia.[12] The elections resulted in a second coalition government of PvdA, VVD and D66, and the new Government adopted the legislative proposal as a government bill. This bill, which became The Termination of Life on Request and Assisted Suicide (Review Procedures) Act, specifies a number of requirements of due care, amends articles 293 and 294 to provide that a doctor who meets the requirements and reports the death of his patient to the municipal pathologist is not guilty of

---

[7] See ch 5.4.3 concerning the reporting rate.
[8] *Second Chamber of Parliament 1996–1997*, 23 877, no 13.
[9] See RRC 1998/1999: 3.
[10] See Onwuteaka-Philipsen & Van der Wal 1998.
[11] See ch 4.2.4.4.
[12] *Second Chamber of Parliament 1997–1998*, 26 000.

an offence, and gives the Regional Review Committees a statutory foundation, making their determination that a doctor has met the statutory requirements final.[13]

As far as the legality of euthanasia is concerned, the Law of 2002 does little more than ratify what the State Commission, the Medical Association, the courts and the prosecutors had already accomplished. The only genuinely new provisions concern the legality of euthanasia pursuant to a prior written request by a person who has become incompetent, and the position of minors. Formally the law puts more emphasis on the requirements of consultation and reporting by making these prerequisites to legal euthanasia (something the courts had not done). However, during the parliamentary debates the Minister of Justice assured Parliament that prosecution policy with respect to these requirements would not change.[14]

Parliament discussed the bill between February 2000 and April 2001. Recurring themes were the central values underlying the bill, the significance of the advanced written request provided for in the bill, the position of minors who ask for euthanasia, the legality of assisted suicide for patients whose suffering is not due to a medical complaint but is 'existential' in nature ('tired of life')[15] and the role of nursing personnel in cases of euthanasia.[16]

The Preamble to the bill emphasises its central objectives: transparency of euthanasia practice and legal certainty. In their defence of the bill, the Minister of Justice and the Minister of Health pointed to the lack of legal certainty caused by the 15-year postponement of statutory legalisation and argued that the low rate of honest reporting of deaths due to euthanasia as 'not natural' was a result of doctors' feelings of legal insecurity.[17]

Perhaps surprisingly, the value of patient self-determination was not prominent in the Government's arguments for the bill. The word self-determination (*zelf-beschikking*) does not appear in the Preamble. The situation to be codified is taken to be the conflict of duties which forms the basis of the justification of necessity required by the courts. Self-determination is not a part of *this* conflict (although it is a substantive part of the legitimacy of euthanasia) and the ministers emphasised that self-determination is not a right provided for in the bill: the new defence is only available to a doctor who complies with the requirements of due care, and a doctor has no duty to perform euthanasia in an appropriate case.[18]

Nevertheless, opponents of the bill thought that self-determination was the hidden, underlying principle of the bill. They considered the difference between the *value* of self-determination, considered by the minister and other supporters of

---

[13] The Law of 2002 is discussed in detail ch 4.2.3.3.

[14] See ch 4.2.4.2 on the effective status of the two requirements.

[15] A recurring item was the *Brongersma* case in which a GP assisted a well-known political personality to commit suicide. The patient was characterised as suffering only from being 'tired of life'. The *Brongersma* case is discussed in section 3.3.

[16] See eg *Second Chamber of Parliament 1999–2000*, 26 691, no 5: 58–72; *2000–2001*, no 8.

[17] See eg *Second Chamber of Parliament 1999–2000*, 26 691, no 6: 33–4; *2000–2001*, no 9: 13; no 22.

[18] See eg *Second Chamber of Parliament 1999–2000*, 26 691, no 6: 16–17; 24; *2000–2001*, no 9: 17–18.

the bill as underlying many fundamental human rights,[19] on the one hand, and a *right* of self-determination on the other, as artificial.[20]

The ministers argued that a doctor must balance respecting the wish of an unbearably suffering patient to die in a dignified way and the importance of respect for human life (*beschermwaardigheid van het leven*). Invoking public opinion surveys, the ministers argued that the meaning of respect for life had changed: For many people respect for life includes the possibility of avoiding an ultimate loss of personal dignity and giving people the opportunity, according to their own convictions, to say farewell and to die in a dignified way.[21]

A controversial provision in the bill recognised the possibility of an advance written request for euthanasia. A doctor whose patient is suffering unbearably but is no longer competent can honour such a request. The patients referred to most often in this connection in the parliamentary debates are patients in a late stage of dementia.[22]

The original D66 bill had provided that parents of children between 12 and 18 could reject the request of their child for euthanasia. The Council of State advised the Government to change this provision so as to make it correspond to the age requirements for informed consent in the Law on Contracts for Medical Treatment (WGBO):[23] minors between 16 and 18 should have the right to decide for themselves and for those between 12 and 16 only a veto of the two parents together should be a decisive obstacle. The Government accepted this advice and added to the bill a provision that the request of a minor between 12 and 16 for euthanasia could be honoured by a doctor even if one of the parents objected. This provision provoked a storm of criticism both from within the Netherlands and abroad. When it became clear that in the opinion of the doctors concerned the provision was superfluous, it was withdrawn.[24]

The legal position of nursing personnel involved in a case of euthanasia was also a point of debate. No one questioned the principle that a nurse may not himself end the life of a suffering patient. However, the boundary between a case of normal medical practice (pain relief) and euthanasia is not always clear to a nurse. The ministers complicated the matter even more by not keeping the differences clear between preparatory acts (which nurses are allowed to perform) and actually carrying out euthanasia (which is limited to doctors).[25] Because questions regarding nurses kept being raised—for example, should they be included in the composi-

---

[19] *Second Chamber of Parliament 2000–2001*, 26 691, no 24 (PvdA, D66 and GreenLeft).

[20] *Second Chamber of Parliament 2000–2001*, 26 691, no 8: 10 (two smaller christian parties: GPV and RPF).

[21] *Second Chamber of Parliament 2000–2001*, 26 691, no 6: 28 (in an answer to the christian party SGP).

[22] Dementia as such is, according to current medical insight, not an illness that can be said to cause unbearable and hopeless suffering. The advance request of a patient with severe dementia was supposed to be important only for those patients who, besides dementia, also suffer from other illnesses.

[23] See ch 4.2.2.1 on these aspects of the WGBO.

[24] *Second Chamber of Parliament 1999–2000*, 26 691, no 7.

[25] See ch 4.2.3.3(J).

tion of the Regional Review Committees? should a requirement of consulting a nurse be added to the requirements of due care?—the Minister of Health announced in Parliament that she had arranged for research to be carried out into the role of nursing personnel.[26]

Despite the many questions that arose during the debates, the Second Chamber of Parliament accepted the bill in November 2000 without many changes. Forty Members (of the christian parties and the left-socialist party SP) voted against and 104 in favour of the bill. In April 2001 the First Chamber likewise accepted the bill with 46 senators in favour and 28 against. The law became effective on 1 April 2002.

The new law was heavily criticised from abroad. There was not much reaction to this criticism in the Netherlands. The same laconic reaction met the report of the United Nations Human Rights Committee, which criticised the alleged weakness of the system of control.[27]

Apart from discussions on the bill, parliamentary debate on euthanasia in the period 1998–2006 was mostly limited to reactions to the Annual Reports of the Regional Review Committees and the report of the third national survey of euthanasia practice in 2001.[28] The main subject of these discussions was the disappointingly low rate at which doctors were accurately reporting deaths due to euthanasia as 'not natural'.[29]

3.3 The *Brongersma* Case

On April 22 1998 a GP assisted one of his patients to commit suicide. The patient, ex-senator Brongersma, 86 years old at the time of his death, had had a very active, politically and socially engaged life. But in recent years his physical condition had begun to deteriorate and among other things he had problems of incontinence and balance. The consequence was increasing social isolation. Brongersma found his situation unbearable and sought his GP's help to end his life.[30] The GP, Sutorius—who happened to be a SCEN doctor specially trained as a consultant in cases of euthanasia—had a number of discussions with Brongersma about his wish to die. He had two independent consultants examine and talk to Brongersma. When they confirmed his view of the situation, Sutorius agreed to Brongersma's request. After Brongersma's death Sutorius properly reported what he had done.

---

[26] *Second Chamber of Parliament 1997–1998*, 23 877, no 26. See for the results of this research Van Bruchem-Van der Scheur *et al* 2004.

[27] See *Second Chamber of Parliament 2000–2001*, 26 691 and 22 588, no 42: 1–4.

[28] Regulation of termination of life of newborns also attracted attention (see ch 6).

[29] See ch 5.4.3 on the reporting rate.

[30] In 1996 he had tried to end his life himself but the attempt failed (Court of Appeals Amsterdam, LJN-no: AD6753; case no: 23–000667–01 B).

In his report Sutorius characterised the reasons for Brongersma's request as: 'lonely, feelings of senselessness, physical deterioration, and a long-standing wish to die not associated with depression'. To a question concerning Brongersma's suffering Sutorius reported: 'The person in question experienced life as unbearable.' And to a question whether there were treatment alternatives, he answered: 'No, the person in question "weighed the pros and cons", and there was no disease [to treat]'.[31] The prosecutorial authorities decided to prosecute.[32]

The trial took place in the District Court, Haarlem, on 30 October 2000—the same day preparatory deliberations on the Government's bill took place in the Second Chamber of Parliament. The prosecutor took the position that ageing, deterioration and fear of losing control over the end of life do not justify a doctor assisting with suicide. The District Court found no reason to doubt the voluntariness of the request, the unbearable suffering, the consultation and the careful carrying out of the assistance. Relying heavily on one of the expert witnesses, the court accepted the view that Brongersma's suffering was hopeless (in the sense of there being no reasonable prospect of improvement). The court accepted the appeal to necessity and acquitted Sutorius.[33] The prosecution appealed.[34]

The judgment of the District Court generated a great deal of public reaction. Through its Chairman, the Royal Dutch Medical Association publicly distanced itself from the judgment.[35] The KNMG decided to appoint a committee to advise it with respect to the boundaries of the legitimacy of a doctor's assistance in dying and whether the currently existing framework of rules regarding assistance with suicide should be changed.

On 6 December 2001, the Court of Appeals reversed the judgment of the District Court. In reaching its decision, the Court of Appeals asked two professors—a physician and a lawyer—to advise it regarding the legitimacy of life-ending behaviour in cases of unbearable suffering that does not stem from a

---

[31] Sutorius was aware of earlier decisions not to prosecute 'tired of life' cases. He expected the case to be dismissed. Otherwise he apparently would have reported Brongersma's physical problems more explicitly (Crul 2001b).

[32] Since the case antedated the creation of the Regional Review Committees, Sutorius' report went straight to the prosecutorial authorities.

[33] District Court Haarlem, 30 October 2001, no 15/035127–99; *Tijdschrift voor Gezondheidsrecht* 2001/21.

[34] The Committee of Procurators-General took the position that the District Court's decision would lead to an unqualified right of patient self-determination. The PGs also doubted whether the suffering had been hopeless and unbearable. They pointed that the case differed from the earlier *Chabot* case (see ch 4.2.3.4(A)) because Brongersma did not have a psychiatric disorder but was 'a very gifted man who saw no further opportunity to exercise his capacities, and also apparently wanted to exercise control over his suffering' (*Second Chamber of Parliament 2000–2001*, 26 691, no 24).

[35] The Chairman wrote:

> As the criterion of unbearable and hopeless suffering is extended, the request of the patient becomes the central issue and the medical professional judgment disappears to the background. Such a route leads ultimately to self-determination, as the NVVE [Dutch Voluntary Euthanasia Society] calls it . . . This differs greatly from our ideas about how to deal with death . . . and the role doctors play (*Trouw*, 2 November 2000).

somatically or psychiatrically classifiable disorder. They were also asked to give their opinion with respect to a doctor's professional competence in such a situation and whether there was consensus on the matter in the profession. Both experts were of the opinion that such behaviour does not fall within the professional competence of a doctor and that there was no consensus within the medical profession as to its justifiability. The Court of Appeals followed these opinions. Although the court regarded it as desirable that even in cases of purely existential suffering due to a lack of any perspective in life, doctors are concerned about the suffering of their patients and seek to relieve it, it nevertheless ruled that relieving suffering that does not have a medical cause is not a part of the professional duty of a doctor. Therefore, the appeal to the justification of necessity—based on the conflict of duties to which a doctor in his professional capacity can be exposed—was rejected. Sutorius was found guilty but the court used its discretion not to impose punishment. Sutorius appealed.

In December 2002 the Supreme Court ruled on Sutorius' case. The Supreme Court rejected all of Sutorius' defences, its most important conclusion being that the reasons given by the Court of Appeals for rejecting the justification of necessity were legally correct. A doctor who assists in suicide in a case in which the patient's suffering is not predominantly due to a 'medically classified disease or disorder', but stems from the fact that life has become meaningless for him, acts outside the scope of his professional competence.[36]

The *Brongersma* case is unique in the development of Dutch euthanasia law in that judicial decision-making and parliamentary debate were closely interwoven. Many questions about the case were asked during the parliamentary debates on the pending bill and the key question was whether situations comparable to the *Brongersma* case would be covered by the new law. It was obvious that many members of Parliament were opposed to this. The Minister of Justice stated explicitly in Parliament that the bill was not intended to cover such a case.[37] The questions raised and statements made about the coverage of the new law figured prominently in the decision of the Supreme Court as arguments for rejecting Sutorius' appeal.

The Supreme Court's decision in the *Brongersma* case did not put an end to uncertainty. The trials in the District Court and the Court of Appeals had made clear that the concept of 'disease' is open to more than one interpretation. One annotator of the decision predicted that the main effect of the road chosen by the court would be to induce doctors to use the concept of disease in a strategic way: they will stress the patient's disease or disorder as a cause of his suffering.[38] The indistinctness of the criterion will also mean, according to some, that doctors will

---

[36] *Nederlandse Jurisprudentie* 2003, no 167.

[37] See *Second Chamber of Parliament 2000–2001*, 26 691, no 22: 60. The Minister of Health took an opposite stance when she revealed as her personal view that 'situations as these should not be excluded completely' (*Second Chamber of Parliament 2000–2001*, 26 691, no 22: 76).

[38] See *Nederlandse Jurisprudentie* 2003, no 167 (annotation by Schalken).

have to make decisions not knowing exactly where the legal boundary lies,[39] which may have an adverse influence on their willingness to report.[40]

In 2003, the report of the third national survey of medical practice at the end of life gave special attention to the situation in which the patient being 'tired of life' is the reason for assisted suicide.[41] It appeared that although doctors do receive such requests, they hardly ever regard them as a sufficient reason to give the requested assistance.[42] 'It is not part of my job', was the reason most often given.[43] By contrast with doctors, the Dutch population is rather positive concerning assisted suicide in such a case: 45% of the population thinks that if they ask for it elderly people should be able to receive drugs to end their life.[44]

In December 2004 the committee appointed by the KNMG delivered its report on assisted suicide for patients who are 'tired of life'.[45] The committee emphasised the importance of the matter by noting the probability that requests for this kind of assistance with suicide will increase in the near future. In the committee's opinion such assistance should be lawful because of the unbearable and hopeless suffering involved. On the committee's view the source of the suffering is not decisive: people without classifiable diseases can suffer unbearably and hopelessly. The dividing line relied upon by the Supreme Court does not solve the practical problems involved, given 'the possibility of suffering without disease and of diseases without suffering'.[46] Development of the criteria used by doctors to assess the suffering of a patient is a more promising way to deal with the limits of medical authority than trying to distinguish between 'medically based' suffering and other suffering. In the committee's opinion, doctors, especially GPs and nursing home doctors, can be experts with respect to existential suffering at the end of life[47] but the committee also argued that this expertise should be further developed. To date, the Board of the KNMG has neither rejected nor accepted the committee's ideas. The board does agree with the committee that the issue is

---

[39] See the KNMG press release of 24 December 2002 at <http://www.knmg.artsennet.nl/content/dossiers/909791707/715499849/AMGATE_6059_100_TICH_R1146171138319079/?PHPSESSID=2f8143af7d40110b3ff3c495fc2d1207> accessed 24 September 2007. Individual doctors made similar comments (see eg *NRC/Handelsblad*, 30 December 2002).

[40] Gevers 2003: 316; Pans 2003: 876–7; KNMG 2004b: 8.

[41] Van der Wal *et al* 2003: 102–10.The researchers define 'tired of life' as the situation in which the patient asks for assisted suicide in the absence of a serious physical or psychiatric disorder. GPs were asked to describe the situation of one such patient. The researchers found as characteristics of the patients described: high age (average 78) and lack of a partner. Three-quarters of the patients suffered from one or more diagnosed disorders such as a stable situation after cancer or heart problems, visual impairment, hardness of hearing, arthrosis and depression.

[42] Nevertheless, about three-quarters of the doctors questioned stated that complying with a request in such circumstances was conceivable.

[43] See Van der Wal *et al* 2003: 104.

[44] *Ibid* at 107.

[45] KNMG 2004b.

[46] *Ibid* at 21.

[47] The committee characterises such suffering as follows:

Suffering from the prospect of having to go on living in a situation of no or very little quality of life, which results in a persistent desire to die, while the absence of quality of life is not or not preponderantly caused by a physical or mental disorder. (KNMG 2004b: 15)

complex and requires a special and careful approach, and it has promised to stimulate discussion on the subject among doctors.[48]

The subject of the *Brongersma* case—'tired of life'—is closely related to a debate that has been going on since 1991. In that year Drion, a prominent Dutch lawyer and former Supreme Court judge, wrote an influential article in which he argued that very old single persons who are 'finished with life'[49] should have the right to receive lethal drugs from their physician.[50] The NVVE and another smaller right-to-die society (SVL, Foundation for Voluntary Life) have embraced variations on this idea (which came popularly to be referred to as the 'Drion pill'). The *Brongersma* case seems to make clear that doctors will not be able to play a central role in such a non-'medical' case. The NVVE and the SLV have recently sought permission to carry out an experiment to establish whether making a 'last-will-pill' available in such a situation can be done safely. Their proposal is that a person who wants to die would be required to discuss this wish with a staff member of the experiment. If some—as yet not well-defined—conditions are fulfilled, the person would qualify for assistance. D66 was considering taking the lead on this issue[51] but its parliamentary representation was greatly diminished by the elections in November 2006. The new Government has explicitly stated that no permission for such an experiment will be given during its term.[52]

3.4 The Limits of Relief of Suffering in the Terminal Phase

From the first national research in 1990 into the practice of medical behaviour at the end of life it appeared that about 1,000 times a year a doctor administers lethal drugs with the express purpose of ending the life of the patient although the patient has not explicitly requested it.[53] All the patients involved were very sick and dying; they apparently suffered severely and were no longer able to express their wishes. The researchers observed that it is difficult to distinguish termination of life without an explicit request from intensive relief of pain and other symptoms.[54] The

---

[48] <http://www.knmg.artsennet.nl/content/dossiers/303849643/235780274/AMGATE_6059_100_TICH_R144637931820684/> accessed 24 September 2007. The Minister of Justice in turn promised to follow the discussion closely (*Second Chamber of Parliament 2004–2005, Appendix*, no 909).

[49] It has been thought useful to distinguish 'tired of life' from 'finished with life'. A person who is 'tired of life' is supposed to be suffering; and a person who is 'finished with life' is supposed to have come to the decision that on balance the disadvantages of further life outweighs the advantages. 'Finished with life' as a justification for assisted suicide is, on this view, more exclusively based on the principle of self-determination (see Van der Werf & Zaat 2005).

[50] H Drion, 'Het zelfgewilde einde van oude mensen.' *NRC-Handelsblad* (19 October 1991).

[51] *Trouw* (9 February 2002).

[52] *Coalition Agreement*, 7 February 2007: 42. <http://www.overheidsmanagement.nl/regeerakkord/, accessed 24 September 2007.

[53] In about 30% of these cases some discussion with the patient had taken place or the patient had otherwise made clear that he would like to have his death hastened (Van der Maas *et al* 1991: 50).

[54] In most cases typical pain and symptom relieving drugs were used: morphine and/or other sedatives; in only 20% of the cases were muscle relaxants used. The estimated shortening of life was similar to that in cases of death due to the administration of pain relief (Van der Maas *et al* 1991: 53 and 59).

Remmelink Committee, which supervised the research on behalf of the Government, referred in its advice based on the findings of the research to part of this category of medical termination of life, when euthanatica are administered to a patient whose vital functions are successively and irreversibly failing, as 'help in dying' and regarded it as essentially unproblematic. In the view of the Remmelink Committee 'help in dying' is part of 'normal medical practice' and the resulting death a 'natural' one. In response to questions in Parliament, however, the Government made clear that in its opinion such behaviour is not 'normal medical practice' but 'termination of life', and the death of the patient a 'non-natural' one that must be reported as such.[55]

In 1997 a case of termination of life without an explicit request—exhibiting many of the features the Remmelink Committee had had in mind—came to public attention. The doctor involved was the GP Van Oijen.[56] His patient was an 85-year-old severely suffering woman who was being cared for in a nursing home. She had been bedridden for months and by the end had lapsed into coma; administration of morphine was continued to keep her from suffering should she awaken. In anticipation of her imminent death, Van Oijen prescribed palliative drugs which nevertheless were not given by the nursing personnel because they feared that she was so close to death that she might die if given an injection. For the same reason they had stopped washing her or changing her diapers. The next day Van Oijen found her still alive but in a horrible state. After consulting with her daughters, who insisted that an end be made to the degrading situation of their mother, Van Oijen decided to give her a muscle relaxant that he happened to have with him.[57] The woman died and Van Oijen filled in a certificate of a natural death. The director of the institution found the death suspicious and notified the Medical Inspector, who in turn informed the prosecutorial authorities. Both the inspectorate and the prosecutorial authorities initiated legal proceedings.

The Medical Inspector faulted Van Oijen on several grounds. The Medical Disciplinary Tribunal found him guilty of four of these: termination of life without request, filing a false certificate of natural death, administering a drug whose expiration date had expired and insufficient record-keeping. The tribunal imposed the least severe measure available to it—a warning—because Van Oijen's

---

[55] *Second Chamber of Parliament 1991–1992*, 20 383, no 14: 7.

[56] Van Oijen had become a public figure in the euthanasia debate because of his participation in a documentary film broadcast on television in the Netherlands and elsewhere in which the preparation for and carrying out of a real case of euthanasia was shown (*Death on Request*, IKON 1994).

[57] Van Oijen's use of drugs in this case seems not to have been very careful. The drug used was in his bag because he had needed it the day before to perform euthanasia on another patient. The drug had expired 2 years earlier (March 1995). See *Nederlandse Jurisprudentie* 2005, no 217. The Court of Appeals seems to have had little sympathy for Van Oijen, because of the impression of general sloppiness that pervaded his behaviour. It found it particularly reproachful that a SCEN-consultant like Van Oijen, highly familiar with the requirements of due care, should have sought to avoid accountability for what he had done; he was also reproached for not having consulted a colleague. See See Court of Appeals, Amsterdam, AF9392 no 23–000166–02.

motivation had been to serve the interest of his patient.[58] The inspectorate did not appeal because in the meantime Van Oijen was facing criminal charges.[59]

On 7 February 2001, four years after the event,[60] Van Oijen stood trial for murder and filing a false certificate of natural death. The District Court rejected Van Oijen's defence of necessity: at the time the lethal drug was administered the patient was in coma and therefore not suffering. Furthermore, the patient had earlier made clear that she did not want to die. The court also rejected Van Oijen's other defences to the murder charge.[61] Van Oijen's defence to the charge of filing a false certificate of 'natural death' was that he had honestly believed the death was the 'natural' result of 'palliative care'. This defence was also rejected, the court observing that the drugs used are not medically indicated for palliative treatment. The District Court found Van Oijen guilty of both offences and sentenced him to a conditional fine of 5,000 guilders (approximately €2,250).[62] Van Oijen appealed.

The Court of Appeals also found Van Oijen guilty.[63] He appealed to the Supreme Court. On 9 November 2002, the Supreme Court ruled that the justification of necessity in principle can be available in a case of ending the life of a dying patient without the patient's request, but only in extraordinary cases. The court mentioned very urgent circumstances influencing the condition of the patient which place the doctor in a situation of necessity, a situation in which he has to choose between mutually conflicting duties and interests.[64]

In Van Oijen's case there were no such circumstances—his comatose patient was not suffering unbearably and her pitiful situation was not decisive because death was about to occur of its own accord. The Supreme Court therefore left the ruling of the Court of Appeals standing.[65]

Terminal Sedation

During the late 1990s there was growing interest in a 'new' form of end-of-life treatment, 'terminal sedation'. It was recognised that a terminally ill patient can have symptoms that can only be relieved by deep and continuous sedation until

---

[58] Medical Disciplinary Tribunal Amsterdam, 4 May 1998.

[59] See Crul 2001a: 235.

[60] Van Oijen first sought to have the charges dismissed. He described his behaviour as 'palliative care', which in Dutch law means that it would be covered by the 'medical exception' and the death would be a 'natural' one. The District Court ruled that what Van Oijen did was 'termination of life', a ruling that was affirmed by the Supreme Court (see LJN AB 0147, District Court Amsterdam, 21 February 2001, 13/127808–97). After these preliminary proceedings the criminal proceedings themselves began.

[61] Van Oijen argued, among other things, that it had not been proved that the drug caused the patient's death.

[62] District Court Amsterdam, n 59 above. The prosecutorial authorities had asked for a conditional jail sentence of nine months.

[63] The Court of Appeals imposed a conditional jail sentence of one week with two years probation. Court of Appeals, Amsterdam, 3 June 2003, no 23–000116–02.

[64] *Nederlandse Jurisprudentie* 2005, no 217: 9.

[65] See further on the *Van Oijen* case, ch 4.2.2.5.

death occurs. When deep sedation is accompanied by the withholding of artificial feeding and hydration (ANH)—because this is seen as medically futile—the combination of an act (sedation) and an omission (not administering artificial feeding and hydration) can be considered to have hastened the patient's death.

While greeted enthusiastically in several other countries, mostly by opponents of legal euthanasia who regard terminal sedation as a morally and legally unproblematic alternative, more critical observers noted that the practice can be dangerous precisely because of its blurred boundary with euthanasia and termination of life without a request.[66] From a Dutch television programme in February 2003 it appeared that some doctors believe there is no real difference between euthanasia and terminal sedation: they prefer terminal sedation because they thereby escape the reporting and review required in euthanasia cases. This programme provoked questions in Parliament. The Secretary of State for Health avoided answering these questions by arguing that it was wise to await the results of the third national research on medical practice at the end of life, which, among other things, would focus especially on terminal sedation.[67]

In the report of the 2001 research, Van der Wal *et al* concluded that according to the doctors concerned in about 10% of all deaths terminal sedation had been applied. The researchers noted that they themselves had classified some of these cases as euthanasia because the administration of sedatives had been for the express purpose of hastening death, usually at the explicit request of the patient.[68] The head of the prosecutorial service, De Wijkerslooth, reacted publicly to these results arguing that if terminal sedation is so similar to euthanasia then there ought to be some external control. He took the position that it is not the doctor's subjective 'intention' (to relieve suffering versus to hasten death) but the consequences of his behaviour that determines whether what he does is 'termination of life'. The prosecutorial authorities decided to bring a criminal case against a doctor who had apparently shortened the life of a patient with terminal sedation. The case that presented itself for this purpose (although as it happened no withholding of ANH was involved) was that of Peter Vencken, who was temporarily working in a hospital before beginning his specialisation.

On 31 May 2002 Vencken, after consulting the patient's family, gave a dying patient morphine and a sedative, Dormicum.[69] The patient died a quarter of an hour later and Vencken reported this as a natural death. He considered what he had done sedation in the terminal phase, a practice that in his opinion fell under the 'medical exception'. Because another doctor in the hospital had doubts about the death of the patient, the board of the hospital alerted the local prosecutor and the Medical Inspectorate.[70]

---

[66] See Nuy & Hoogerwerf 2000: 124.

[67] *Second Chamber of Parliament 2002–2003, Appendix,* no 1089.

[68] See Van der Wal *et al* 2003: 84. For further data on terminal sedation, see ch 5.2.1.2 and 5.2.2.2.

[69] The patient suffered from a cerebro-vascular accident from which recovery was impossible and was therefore only receiving palliative care.

[70] See Legemaate 2006: 1692.

On 10 November 2004 Vencken stood trial for murder. The District Court ruled that the amount of drugs used was medically indicated in the circumstances and that an intention to kill therefore could not be proved. The court acquitted Vencken.[71] The prosecutor appealed, and in July 2005 the Court of Appeals (which did not address the matter of Vencken's intention) held that it had not been proved that the patient died because of the drugs and likewise acquitted Vencken.[72] The short time it took the Court of Appeals to come to its verdict—two hours—was widely seen as a reprimand of the prosecutorial authorities.[73] They concluded, in turn, that an appeal to the Supreme Court was not called for, and the criminal prosecution of Vencken came to an end.

The Medical Inspectorate doubted the carefulness of Vencken's behaviour and brought the case before a disciplinary tribunal. The tribunal investigated whether the amount and kind of drugs used was indicated or at least justifiable. According to the consulted expert this had been the case. In March 2005 the tribunal ruled that Vencken's behaviour could be considered 'normal medical behaviour'. It emphasised the importance of consulting the family and nursing personnel and of careful record-keeping. The tribunal found Vencken's record-keeping insufficient but did not impose any sanction for this omission because of the lengthy criminal proceedings Vencken had undergone.[74] At first, the Medical Inspector appealed, but in April 2006, after receiving reports from experts on terminal sedation, the inspectorate decided to withdraw the appeal.[75]

The Medical Inspectorate's decision was facilitated by societal developments with respect to terminal sedation. De Wijkerslooth's position, that terminal sedation should be assessed by the prosecutorial authorities, led to questions in Parliament. The Minister and Secretary of State for Health took the position that the medical profession should formulate a guideline regarding terminal sedation.[76] The KNMG appointed a committee to do this and approved the committee's proposed guideline in December 2005.[77]

The KNMG committee's report focuses primarily on what it calls 'palliative sedation', a term the committee prefers to 'terminal sedation' since the committee considers the practice a part of the wider category of 'palliative care'. 'Palliative sedation' refers on the committee's view to inducing a deep and continuous coma in a patient in the last stage of life with the intention of keeping the patient comatose until death occurs. Artificial administration of nutrition and hydration in such a case is 'futile'. The committee proposes to limit palliative sedation to patients with a life expectancy of less than two weeks, so that the death of the

---

[71] *Medisch* Contact 2004: 1876–9; LJN: AR 5394, District Court Breda, 170/03.

[72] LJN: AUO211, Court of Appeals, 's-Hertogenbosch, 20–000303–05.

[73] See eg 'Hof tikt Openbaar Ministerie op vingers in zaak-Vencken [Court of Appeals Slaps Prosecutorial Wrist in Vencken Case].' *Medisch Contact* 2005: 1248.

[74] *Medisch Contact* 2005: 499–502.

[75] 'Inspectie trekt beroep tegen Vencken in [Inspectorate Withdraws Appeal in Vencken Case].' *Medisch Contact* 2006: 640.

[76] *Second Chamber of Parliament 2003–2004*, 29 200 XVI, no 268: 9.

[77] See KNMG 2005.

patient will be from the underlying disease and not from the withholding of ANH. In the committee's view it is the patient's medical condition and not the doctor's subjective intentions that are determinative with respect to the legitimacy of palliative sedation.

The committee formulates some specific requirements of due care in the case of palliative sedation combined with withholding ANH. It is only appropriate in the case of 'refractory symptoms' that cannot be dealt with in a less drastic way. The patient (or, in case of incompetence, his representative) should consent to it. The doctor should use drugs that are appropriate for the purpose. Good record-keeping is important. A doctor who is not expert with regard to the relevant aspects of the case (refractory symptoms, sedation) should consult an expert. In the committee's view palliative sedation as defined is 'normal medical practice' leading to a 'natural death' so that formal consultation with a second doctor is not required and no special reporting and assessment procedure is called for.

The committee's report encountered both praise and criticism. It was praised for defining 'terminal sedation' in objective terms rather than in terms of a doctor's subjective intention but criticised for devoting most of its attention to the relatively unproblematic practice of palliative sedation and for giving so little attention to control.[78] Some authors found the period of two weeks too long: palliative sedation should not exceed a couple of days if one wants to be sure the patient dies from the underlying disease.[79] And some stressed that the decision to apply palliative sedation should always be a team-decision.[80] Fears were expressed that doctors will prefer palliative sedation and therefore press patients, who possibly would prefer euthanasia, in the direction of their own preferences.[81]

At the end of December, in reaction to the KNMG's guideline, the new head of the Committee of Procurators-General stated that if a doctor follows the guideline the prosecutorial authorities see no reason to take action. He agreed with the committee that palliative sedation is 'normal medical practice' and not a form of 'termination of life'.[82] With this reaction, the prosecutorial authorities seemed to abandon the doubts their former head had raised about terminal sedation and to acknowledge that the prosecution of Peter Vencken should not have taken place.[83] However, the legal status of 'terminal sedation', where ANH is withheld for long enough that the death of the patient is probably hastened, remains unsolved (see further chapter 4.2.2.4).

[78] See Den Hartogh 2006a.
[79] Sutorius in *Trouw* (10 October 2005); NAV/JPV 2006: 25.
[80] See Blom *et al* 2006.
[81] That patients may have objections can be concluded from the finding that the general public does not think that palliative sedation—dying while one is unconscious and cannot communicate—can be characterised as a 'good death'. See Rietjens *et al* 2005: 56. See further ch 4.2.3.3(C), 'suffering with no prospect of improvement'.
[82] *NRC-Handelsblad*, 29 December 2005. Not surprisingly, the KNMG was pleased with this new policy <http://www.nieuwsbank.nl/inp/2005/12/30/V053.htm> accessed 10 September 2007.
[83] Vencken was awarded €50,000 by the trial court for having wrongfully been kept in custody. In the opinion of Vencken's lawyer the amount of the compensation reflected the court's view that the prosecution ought never to have taken place. See *Medisch Contact* 2006: 264.

3.5 Assisted Suicide for Patients with Dementia

The number of demented persons in the Netherlands is increasing. Ever more people apparently feel the need to arrange things in advance so as not to die what they consider to be an undignified death. An indication of this can be found in the advance treatment directives developed by the NVVE. In such a directive the author stipulates that in specified circumstances he refuses medical treatment and/or asks for euthanasia. Some 1% of the Dutch population (mostly the elderly) currently has drafted an advance directive[84] and it seems that many of these include dementia among the conditions under which the request is to become effective. A doctor is legally bound to comply with a treatment refusal but not with a request for euthanasia. And although the Law of 2002 explicitly permits this, actively ending the life of a demented patient is generally seen as very problematic. The Dutch Association of Nursing-home Doctors (NVVA) takes the position that actively ending a life merely because of severe dementia is not consistent with the 'good care' required of a nursing-home doctor.[85] The Health Council, however, argues that continuing the debate on actively ending a life in such a case is desirable because a significant part of the population strongly desires the possibility.[86]

In 1999 a GP published an article on the assistance with suicide she had given to a patient with early vascular dementia and the reaction to this of the prosecutorial authorities.[87] The patient was a man who lived in a psychiatric hospital because of his organic-psychiatric disease and who was very unhappy about his situation. After several attempts to kill himself he asked the doctor to assist him with suicide. The doctor found the request understandable and after consulting several experts[88] she decided to give the requested assistance. She reported the death as a non-natural one and the prosecutorial authorities took the position that the doctor had complied with the requirements of due care and decided not to prosecute.

In 2004 it became known that this was not the only case of assisting a demented patient with suicide that the prosecutors had found met the legal requirements. The same doctor made public, at a meeting of the KNMG, that a second case in which she was involved, had also not been prosecuted.[89] The Minister of Justice, when questioned in Parliament, referred to a third such case. According to the minister there had been no doubt that the request was well-considered and the suffering hopeless. Among elements of the unbearable suffering involved was the fact that the patient had witnessed the same kind of deterioration of his

---

[84] See Vezzoni 2008.

[85] See AVVV 2006: 30.

[86] See Gezondheidsraad 2002: 20.

[87] See Van der Meer *et al* 1999. The assistance with suicide took place in 1996.

[88] Among others, a psychiatrist was consulted to establish that the patient was not suffering from a depression.

[89] *De Volkskrant* 4 June 2004.

parents and the feared the 'prospect of loss of decorum'.[90] In answering a follow-ing question the minister said that such suffering is not completely subjective. Referring to the judgment of the Supreme Court in the *Schoonheim* case, he stated that unbearable and hopeless suffering can consist of the fear of further deteriora-tion and the risk of not being able to die with dignity.[91]

As we will see in chapter 4.2.3.3(C) ('unbearable suffering'), the Regional Review Committees have taken the position that suffering due to dementia can be a legitimate ground for euthanasia pursuant to an advance request.

3.6 Assistance with Suicide by Non-Doctors

In the early years of the public discussion about euthanasia it was already clear that it is not only people who suffer from a (terminal) illness who ask for assistance in dying. Others who seek such assistance are old people who are 'tired of life', people with chronic diseases who cannot endure the prospect of many more years to come, and people in psychic distress. Because doctors are reluctant to assist these patients with suicide, even where the legality of doing so is clear, they look elsewhere for help.

Some of those who do not get help from their doctor approach lay organisations. Since the 1980s, the NVVE will give personal advice to a member about effective means to end one's life.[92] Since 1996 members of the NVVE can buy a booklet with information about ways to end their life.[93] Questions have been asked in Parliament about the permissibility of giving information in this way about ways to commit sui-cide. The general opinion seems to be that giving information ought not to be pro-hibited.[94] During the 1990s, another lay organisation began actively offering assistance: *Stichting De Einder* (Foundation the Horizon). *De Einder* not only gives information and the opportunity to talk about one's desire to die but is also willing

---

[90] *Second Chamber of Parliament 2003–2004, Appendix:* 1817. The Minister's opinion was that suf-fering from 'Alzheimers disease' (in fact, this diagnosis was dubious in the case in question—see Hertogh *et al* 2007) is in general without prospect of improvement since no treatment exists. In this case it could be doubted whether the unbearableness of the suffering was objectifiable but this could not be verified because the patient was dead.

[91] *Second Chamber of Parliament, 2003–2004, Appendix:* 2117.

[92] In the early 1990s a doctor closely linked to the NVVE was prosecuted for assistance with suicide. In this case the Supreme Court observed that giving information about how to end one's life does not amount to 'assistance' under art 294 of the Penal Code, but 'steering' the suicide does (see *Nederlandse Jurisprudentie* 1996, no 322).

[93] NVVE 2003. The WOZZ Foundation—a foundation that carries out scientific research into the possibilities of a 'humane self-chosen death'—has also published a book on the subject. The second edition of this book (2008) is available for physicians, pharmacists and professionals, and also for severely ill people and their intimates. For the WOZZ 'humane' stands for dying in the presence of oth-ers without conscious suffering and without physical mutilation; in practice this comes down to the use of drugs or stopping eating and drinking (WOZZ 2006: 7).

[94] *Second Chamber of Parliament 2002–2003, Appendix:* 1143.

to have volunteers be present at the time of the suicide.

Since 1999 four persons working for the NVVE or *Stichting De Einder* have been prosecuted under article 293 of the Penal Code for having assisted in a suicide. Two prosecutions were initiated when family-members of the deceased complained to the prosecutorial authorities; in the other two cases the 'suicide-consultant' either alerted the police or attracted attention by publishing about the case. In the first case, in which a psychologist of the NVVE was involved, the District Court ruled that there is no obligation to prevent the suicide of a competent person. The court held that the psychologist had acted carefully and acquitted her.[95] In the other three cases volunteers of *De Einder* were involved. In one case the suicide-consultant was sentenced to twelve months of which eight were conditional. The Court of Appeals took the position that the consultant had over-stepped many boundaries and that there was reason to fear for repetition.[96] The consultant appealed arguing that preparatory acts are different from assistance with suicide. The Supreme Court, however, affirmed the ruling of the Court of Appeals that the moment at which the assistance takes place is not decisive in answering the question whether article 294 has been violated.[97] In another case the founder of *De Einder* was involved.[98] He had made the suicide possible by exchanging drugs with the woman who wished to die. The District Court gave him an unconditional jail sentence of one year.[99] On appeal, the Court of Appeals reduced the penalty to twelve months, of which eight were conditional, with two years probation, because the defendant showed remorse (he stated to the court that he was ceasing his work as a suicide-consultant).[100] In both cases the courts made very clear that self-determination is not an 'ultimate value' and account-ability is very important. The last case in which a lay person stood trial for assist-ance with suicide ended with an acquittal. The District Court observed that talking, and giving information and moral support, do not amount to assistance with suicide.[101]

---

[95] *Tijdschrift voor Gezondheidsrecht* 2004: 178–9.

[96] The assistance consisted of opening a jam jar and a bottle of alcoholic liquor, putting things such as water, yoghurt, bowls, liquor and a plastic bag near the woman, and helping her to consume the medicines and alcohol and to put a rubber band around her neck. The consultant anonymously called the police about the suicide and one week later he was taken into custody and ultimately held for 40 days (*Tijdschrift voor Gezondheidsrecht* 2004: 173–8).

[97] LJN: AR 8225, Supreme Court, 01853/04. The defendant stopped his work as a suicide-consultant.

[98] The man was well known as suicide-consultant both from the annual reports of the foundation and from his publications.

[99] *Tijdschrift voor Gezondheidsrecht* 2006: 174–83.

[100] LNJ: AY7270, Court of Appeals Amsterdam, 23–006489–05.

[101] In the Spring of 2007 the prosecutor withdrew his appeal (*Relevant* 2007/2: 14). In late November 2007 it became known that yet another member of a right-to-die society—Schellekens, chairman of the *Stichting Vrijwillig Leven* ('Foundation for Voluntary Life')—had been arrested for assistance with suicide. Schellekens and the son of the woman who committed suicide have since been released. The prosecutorial authorities have not yet made a final decision whether to prosecute.

A Second Model?

From Chabot's research[102] it appears that it is not only suicide-consultants but also people in a person's immediate social surroundings who sometimes give support to a person wanting to commit suicide. This varies from direct assistance such as collecting the lethal drugs, to being present so that the person does not have to die alone. According to Chabot, the number of cases of this sort of life-ending exceeds the amount of euthanasia carried out by doctors.[103] Taking all the different forms of assistance of lay persons together—the experiment the NVVE has proposed, the work of suicide-consultants and the support of family and intimates—Chabot believes that a second model of non-medical assistance with suicide may be emerging, and he doubts whether the two models can coexist. The criteria of the non-medical regime will be less strict than those of the current medical regime and both doctors and patients will be inclined to opt for the first.[104]

3.7 Reflections

The process of legal change with respect to euthanasia, like many Dutch political processes concerning sensitive issues, took a long time. The legalisation of euthanasia by the courts in the 1980s has only recently been codified in statutory form. With the benefit of hindsight we can conclude that the time was well spent. As we will see in chapter 4, there has been an enormous production of increasingly well-thought-out substantive and procedural rules governing euthanasia practice, and the control system has been greatly improved. In chapter 5 we will consider the wealth of data on medical behaviour at the end of life that has been produced in the meantime—data that, despite the growing acceptance elsewhere of the Dutch research methodology, is still unequalled. In the course of the process public opinion evolved to the point that, as we have seen in chapter 2.3.1, more than 90% of the population is not opposed to legalisation of euthanasia. Statutory legalisation took place when euthanasia was not really a controversial issue anymore.

The process of legalisation can also be looked at from a different point of view, in which it is not the length of the process that is remarkable but the fact that euthanasia became a political issue at all. Features of Dutch politics and the Dutch political system seem important in explaining why this happened. The first con-

---

[102] Chabot 2001; see for further discussion of this research ch 5.3 ('suicide without the assistance of a doctor'). In the cases Chabot investigated the deceased almost always had earlier asked a doctor for assistance but this had been refused, either because the patient was not in a 'terminal' condition or was not suffering from a 'terminal illness' (neither of which, legally, is a requirement for physician assisted suicide). The doctors concerned did not doubt that the patient's request was well-considered and lasting (nor did the person's relatives).

[103] He conservatively estimates that there are some 4,400 cases per year (Chabot 2007: 261); see further on this research, ch 5.2.2.3.

[104] See Chabot 2003.

cerns the left-right antithesis in politics. In the Netherlands the classical—largely economic—antithesis has been complemented with a new one that opposes materialistic (wealth and security) value orientations with non-materialistic ones (participatory democracy and lifestyle individualism). A related characteristic of modern Dutch political life is the existence of political parties dedicated to promoting non-material issues in the public arena. A third feature of modern Dutch political culture, well-illustrated by the process of legal change with respect to euthanasia, is the involvement of many participants. In the area of end-of-life medical practice, this wide participation has not been limited to euthanasia. With respect to the regulation of palliative sedation, for example, the prosecutorial authorities, the Medical Association, the Medical Inspectorate, patients' organisations, individual doctors and scholars, and politicians all contributed to the public debate.

Legalisation of euthanasia does not rest simply on the value of self-determination. Both the solution initially chosen by the courts—legal acknowledgement of the conflict of duties a doctor can be confronted with—and the ultimate statutory legalisation, address doctors in the first place and not patients: it is the doctor who has the conflict of duties and who must make a justifiable choice. Furthermore, the interpretation of the conflicting duties at stake—to relieve suffering and to respect life—shows that self-determination is not the main principle legalisation is based on. Self-determination is only a precondition for the legitimacy of a doctor's behaviour, in the sense that relief of suffering in such a drastic way is usually only legal if done at the explicit and well-considered request of the patient. In the period, 1997–2007, two opposite movements are visible. On the one hand, we see patients' organisations (but also a committee of the KNMG) seeking to enlarge the room for self-determination by promoting the idea of assisted suicide for patients whose suffering is not 'medical'. On the other hand, we see the courts and Parliament stressing the limits that follow from the involvement of doctors in ending their patients' lives.

The result of 30 years of debate on euthanasia is a well-developed system of control, consisting of expert consultation before euthanasia is carried out and assessment afterwards by the Regional Review Committees, which have been designed to be acceptable to doctors. The road chosen in the 1990s—continuous fine-tuning of the requirements of due care and of the system of control—has not been abandoned. The major example of this in the current decade is the developments with respect to palliative sedation. The debate on palliative sedation reveals some of the progress that has been made: the KNMG Committee, the Medical Disciplinary Tribunals and the Chairman of the Committee of Procurators-General succeeded in keeping subjective intentions out of the debate and thereby opened the road to more objective ways of defining the boundaries of legal end-of-life behaviour by doctors.

The ruling of the Supreme Court in the *Brongersma* case seems to be an anomaly, at least looked at from the perspective of the well-proven approach followed up to then consisting of acceptance, transparency and regulation. By trying to draw a line between suffering that is medically classifiable and other forms of suffering the court seems to choose the route of repression. It seems doubtful whether the demarcation will survive in practice. The reaction of doctors, lawyers and social scientists suggests a Pyrrhic victory for the repressive approach. Similarly, the effort of the prosecutors and the courts to put an end to assistance with suicide by lay organisations that stress self-determination seems unlikely to stop the further growth of an organised practice of lay assistance.

4

Dutch Law on Euthanasia
and Other MBPSL

In chapter 3 we have described the process of public debate and legal change that has led in recent years to the current state of affairs in Dutch law concerning euthanasia and physician-assisted suicide. In this chapter we describe in a systematic and detailed way what that law is. To do so in an adequate way requires that we also describe the surrounding body of law dealing with other forms of medical behaviour that potentially shortens life (MBPSL). We begin in section 4.1 with a brief analytic overview of the way such medical behaviour is regulated. Then, in section 4.2, we deal in detail with current law. Section 4.3 is devoted to some concluding reflections.

The description of current law in this chapter follows a systematic scheme that we have adopted for comparative purposes, both in this chapter and in chapter 5 concerning the law in practice, as well as in part II on Belgium and part III on a number of other European countries. The scheme first covers behaviour by doctors that, although it does potentially shorten the life of the patient, is generally regarded as legally unproblematic ('normal medical practice'), including pain relief with life-shortening effect and abstention (withdrawing and withholding life-prolonging treatment). It then deals with euthanasia and physician-assisted suicide, and thereafter with termination of life without an explicit request. Finally, the system of control is described.

Apart from the importance of the (emerging) legal rules and control system in their own right, we have two additional reasons for the detail into which we will go. The first is that the legal operation involved in 'legalisation' has proved not to be a simple matter. It seems to us useful for people in other countries where legalisation is being contemplated to be aware of the large number of associated problems that will arise, and to be informed about possible ways of dealing with them. The degree of careful attention to detail that has been achieved will probably surprise and interest many of the Dutch as well. In the second place, the sheer volume of regulation—taken together with other indications of the 'quantity of law'—explodes one myth about what happens when euthanasia is legalised: namely that the law withdraws from an area in which it formerly was heavily present—that 'legalisation' amounts to 'less law'. In fact, the behaviour of doctors which leads to the earlier death of patients is more highly regulated in the Netherlands (and more recently, Belgium) than anywhere else, and this is not limited to euthanasia itself. We will return to this point in chapter 19.

Finally, a note about reading this chapter. Especially in the footnotes, it is in places very detailed, because we have wanted to be as complete as possible in referring to primary sources (especially decisions of the Regional Review Committees, which are not generally known even in the Netherlands). We would advise the general reader to ignore the footnotes as much as possible, except possibly on an occasional matter of special interest.

4.1 Law concerning Medical Behaviour that Potetially Shortens Life (MBPSL)

Many things a doctor does or does not do can cause the death of a patient. Like other people, doctors can commit murder[1] or cause someone's death by negligent behaviour such as careless driving. This book is not about such situations, where the fact that the actor is a doctor is irrelevant as far as the legal consequences of his behaviour are concerned. Nor will we be dealing with everything a doctor does as a doctor that causes a patient's death: in particular, medical negligence that leads to so-called *iatrogenic death*—that is, death due to medical mistakes—is not part of our subject.[2]

What we are concerned with is deaths that are not an accident, not the result of negligence, nor the untoward consequences of taking justifiable risks in pursuing legitimate curative or palliative objectives, but the outcome of medical behaviour that the doctor engages in *expecting the behaviour to lead to the earlier death of the patient*. It is possible to define this category in two ways: 'subjectively' (in terms of what the doctor involved actually anticipated) or 'objectively' (in terms of what a reasonable doctor would have anticipated). This opposition runs through the whole of the law in this area, and we will deal with it extensively later on. It is sufficient here to note that our position is that to the extent there is a real difference, it is the 'objective' approach that the law generally takes, and that for good reason.[3] The behaviour we will be concerned with can be described as 'medical behaviour that potentially shortens life' (MBPSL). It consists of a number of legally different sorts of behaviour, as shown on Box 4.1.

---

[1] For a dramatic case in the UK (Dr Shipman) see Esmail 2005; <http://www.the-shipman-inquiry.org.uk> accessed 17 September 2007.

[2] The frequency of iatrogenic death in the Netherlands has been estimated at about 4,000 per year, which the author supposes to be characteristic of modern health care systems (Zelders 1996). A recent publication based on a retrospective study of a sample of hospital patient records comes to an estimated total of 1,735 avoidable deaths in 2004 (Wagner & de Bruijne 2007).

[3] In legal practice, there is rarely any way to know what a doctor 'actually' anticipated other than by taking his word for it or assuming he anticipated what others in his position would have anticipated.

Box 4.1 Varieties of MBPSL

general category		specific category	legitimating principle	legal formulation
'normal medical practice'		honouring patient's refusal of treatment (current or in treatment directive)	autonomy	patient's consent required for treatment
		abstention: with-holding or with-drawing 'futile' life-prolonging treatment	non-malificence	'medical exception'
		pain relief with life-shortening effect	beneficence	
'termination of life'	voluntary	euthanasia	beneficence and autonomy	justification of necessity
		physician-assisted suicide (PAS)		
	non-voluntary	termination of life without an explicit request	beneficence	

Taking the various legal categories of MBPSL in order, from the top of Box 4.1 down, the legal situation in the Netherlands is, very generally speaking, as follows. If a patient refuses life-prolonging treatment, his doctor is obliged to comply, and this also applies to the situation of a currently non-competent patient who, when he was competent, expressed the refusal in the form of a 'treatment directive'.[4] Abstention from life-prolonging treatment on grounds of 'medical futility', and administration of indicated doses of pain relief despite the fact that this may hasten the death of the patient, are considered 'normal medical practice' and fall within the so-called 'medical exception' that permits a doctor to do things that in the case of a non-doctor would be criminal offences (such as surgery or turning off a respirator).[5] 'Termination of life' is in principle homicide (murder or the like). However, if done by a doctor at the explicit request of the patient, 'euthanasia' (including 'physician-assisted suicide', PAS for short) has been made legal.

---

[4] See generally on treatment directives, Vezzoni 2008. Such instruments are often called 'advance directives' but for reasons explained by Vezzoni, the term 'treatment directive' is more precise.

[5] See Leenen 2000: 357–74.

Termination of life in the absence of a request can also be legally justifiable in some narrowly-defined circumstances.

4.2 Current Law in the Netherlands

Dutch law concerning MBPSL is largely to be found in the sources indicated in Box 4.2 opposite.

The most important legal development in the period since 1998 (when the predecessor of this book was published) was the enactment of the Law of 2002, although substantively speaking it does not change much. Its most important effect is to place initial review of reported cases of euthanasia entirely outside the purview of the criminal law authorities. As a result of this, the most important forum for legal development in the ensuing years has been the Regional Review Committees, put on a statutory foundation and given a great deal of autonomy by the Law of 2002. It is largely to the decisions of the committees that one must now look for the fine-tuning of Dutch euthanasia law. Of reports by professional bodies, the most important source of legal development in recent years is that of the Royal Dutch Medical Association (KNMG) on palliative and terminal sedation, to be discussed in section 4.2.2.4.

Over the past decade, the Dutch courts have become less prominently involved than in the past in the development and clarification of euthanasia law. The three most important decisions are those of the Supreme Court in the *Brongersma* case (involving the question whether a 'medical condition' is a prerequisite for assisted suicide) and the *Van Oijen* case (whether 'help in dying' can be considered a form of 'normal medical practice' and hence not subject to the substantive and procedural rules applicable to cases of 'termination of life'), and the decisions of a District Court and a Court of Appeals in the *Vencken* case (whether 'terminal sedation' is 'normal medical practice').

All this has been dealt with in historical perspective in chapter 3, and will be treated at the appropriate places below.

4.2.1 'Normal Medical Practice', the 'Medical Exception' and a 'Natural Death'

Many of the acts and omissions that a doctor engages in in the course of treating a patient violate the literal terms of provisions of the criminal law prohibiting causing bodily harm. From the time of its enactment in 1886 the Penal Code has been generally supposed to include an implicit exception for doctors, the so-called 'medical exception'.[6] In effect, the sections dealing with offences against the per-

---

[6] See Leenen 2000: 325; Enschedé 1985.

Box 4.2 Sources of Dutch Law concerning MBPSL

- the Penal Code, ss 293 (euthanasia), 294 (assistance with suicide), 287 (murder), and 255 (duty to a person in one's care)[7]
- the Termination of Life on Request and Assisted Suicide (Review Procedures) Act of 2002 [referred to in the rest of this chapter as the 'Law of 2002'][8]
- the Law on Burial and Cremation of 1991[9]
- the Law on Contracts for Medical Care of 1995, included in the Civil Code as Title 7, Arts 446–8[10]
- a large number of decisions of the Dutch courts and medical disciplinary tribunals[11]
- the Annual Reports of the Regional Review Committees [RRC] and the reported decisions of the committees in individual cases[12]
- the Report of the State Commission on Euthanasia (1985)
- a number of influential reports of governmental bodies and of the Royal Dutch Medical Association (KNMG) and other medical professional bodies[13]
- prosecutorial policy, publicly announced or implicit in actual practice;
- the policy of the Medical Inspectorate, as reflected in public statements or actual practice (in particular, decisions to initiate medical disciplinary proceedings or not to do so)
- the writings of influential legal scholars[14]

---

[7] See GB&W: app I for the (translated) text of these articles (in the case of arts 293 and 294, as they were before the amendments in the Law of 2002).

[8] *Wet toetsing levensbeëindiging op verzoek en hulp bij zelfdoding, Staatsblad* 194, 2001 (effective 1 April 2002, *Staatsblad* 165, 2002); available online in English under 'euthanasia' at <http://www.minbuza.nl> accessed 3 April 2007 (translations are also available in French, German, and Spanish). Translations in some other languages (eg Italian) are available on the websites of Dutch embassies via <http://www.mfa.nl> accessed 3 April 2007.

[9] *Wet op de lijkbezorging, Staatsblad* 133, 1991; 194, 2001. Amended by the Law of 2002.

[10] *Wet op de geneeskundige behandelingsovereenkomst, Staatsblad* 837, 1994 (effective 1 April 1995, *Staatsblad* 845, 1995). For the historical background and legislative history of this law, see Engberts 1997.

[11] Decisions of the central and regional medical disciplinary tribunals (*centraal en regionale tuchtcolleges*) are incidentally reported in the *Staatscourant, Nederlandse Jurisprudentie, Rechtspraak van de week, Medisch Contact* and *Tijdschrift voor Gezondheidsrecht*, as well as in various collections (eg Rang 1977; De Brauw & Kalkman-Bogerd 1988). They are increasingly available on the website of the tribunals (<http://www.tuchtcollege-gezondheidszorg.nl/home.htm> accessed 3 April 2007).

[12] Some decisions in individual cases are summarised in the Annual Reports (many of these are referred to in the footnotes in this chapter; see the appendix to ch 5 for a complete overview of all judgments that the doctor concerned was 'not careful'). Since early 2006 many decisions are being reported on the committees' website <http://www.toetsingscommissieseuthanasie.nl> accessed 3 April 2007; see further section 4.2.4.3(E).

[13] See for the relevant reports through 1997, GB&W: ch 2 and ch 3; those since 1997 are discussed in this chapter and in ch 6.

[14] In particular, Prof H Leenen who, until his death in 2002, was very influential in this area of health law.

son are to be read as if each of them included at the end the words: 'does not apply to a doctor acting within the scope of his professional authority'. The medical behaviour involved is regarded as 'normal medical practice'; if it should cause the patient to die, the death is considered a 'natural' one.[15] As we will see in section 4.2.4.1 below, this last qualification is of crucial importance for the system of legal control over euthanasia.

The scope of the professional authority of a doctor is largely determined by the so-called 'professional standard', that is, standards of behaviour that are generally accepted within the medical profession itself (these are often written down in the form of guidelines, protocols and the like). There are some sorts of medical behaviour, however, for which there is no professional standard (at least as far as the medical indication for the behaviour is concerned), because they serve no medical purpose. Traditionally, performing a non-therapeutic abortion was the classic example.[16] The legality of this sort of medical behaviour depends upon standards that are not 'medical' in nature. When legal, it does not constitute 'normal medical practice' and does not fall within the 'medical exception'. When, as in the case of euthanasia, the death of the patient is the expected result, the death is considered 'non-natural'.[17]

4.2.2 'Normal Medical Practice'

As we can see from Box 5.1 in chapter 5, 'normal medical practice' that is expected to shorten the patient's life consists almost entirely either of withholding or withdrawing life-prolonging treatment or of the administration of life-shortening doses of pain relief.[18] Taken together they account for almost two-fifths of all deaths in the Netherlands and a comparable number in many other countries. A relatively new sort of MBPSL—'terminal sedation'—is, when it shortens the patient's life, in effect a combination of the two (deep sedation together with withholding of artificial nutrition and hydration). And there is an older idea that continues to lead a sort of subterranean existence in this area, from time to time emerging into public view: 'help in dying', which strictly speaking amounts

---

[15] There is an exception to this, which can sometimes be important: if the patient's medical condition is itself the result of an incident which would be regarded as giving rise to a non-natural death (eg an automobile accident, a criminal offence, or earlier medical malpractice), then the death is considered a 'non-natural' one even though its immediate cause is medical treatment that in itself falls within 'normal medical practice'.

[16] It has been argued from time to time that other treatments such as circumcision, and some sorts of plastic surgery, and other not medically indicated invasions of bodily integrity, should be put in the same category.

[17] See Leenen 2000: 325–6. Powerful arguments in favour of the position that euthanasia should be regarded as falling within the 'medical exception' were made in the past, in particular by Enschedé (1985). This route to legalisation was foreclosed by the Supreme Court in 1987 (see GB&W: 61–5). In section 4.2.5 we broach the question whether something like the 'medical exception' is not nevertheless gradually emerging in law and in practice.

[18] There are some other categories of normal medical practice that may shorten the patient's life, such as radical forms of chemotherapy, radiation and surgery, experimental drugs and so forth. None of these is apparently regarded by anyone as involving problems comparable to those of the MBPSL dealt with here.

to termination of life without a request but has nevertheless been thought by some to constitute 'normal medical practice'.[19]

4.2.2.1 Refusal of Treatment and Advance Directives

Looked at from the perspective of what the doctor actually does, there is no difference between withholding or withdrawing treatment because the patient does not want it and doing so because this is, in the doctor's professional judgment, the right thing to do. The legal underpinnings of the two situations are, however, quite different.

Article 450 (1) of the Law on Contracts for Medical Care recognises in unqualified terms the requirement of informed consent. There seems to be no serious doubt that this entails the right of a competent patient to refuse any treatment for any reason, including wanting to die.[20] There can, of course, be difficulties with regard to the scope of the consent given, the information required as a basis for valid consent, implied consent in emergency situations, and so forth, but these do not affect the binding nature of an explicit refusal.[21] The right of refusal begins at the age of 12, which is the general minimum age of competence for purposes of this law. The right to give consent is more limited, and generally the consent of both the minor and his parents is required in the case of minors 12–16.[22]

A child younger than 12, or a minor between 12 and 18 who is not competent ('cannot be considered capable of a reasonable assessment of his relevant interests'), is represented by his parents or guardian.[23] For persons 18 or over and similarly incapable the law provides for a hierarchy of representatives for purposes of health care decision-making: a court-appointed representative, a representative appointed in a written document by the patient when he was still competent, a spouse or partner who is willing, and finally a parent, child, brother or sister who is willing. The patient's representative is supposed to involve the patient as much as possible in deciding whether to give or withhold consent to treatment. In principle a representative can refuse treatment on any ground which the patient himself might have considered sufficient.[24]

---

[19] See, eg the short, unhappy fate of the suggestion to this effect of the Remmelink Committee in 1991, discussed in GB&W: 132, in ch 3.4, and in section 4.2.2.5 below.

[20] The position of the Catholic Church (*cf* also Keown 2002b), that refusal of non-futile treatment amounts to suicide (see ch 13.2, and the confusion on the subject in the *Welby* and other recent Italian cases—ch 13.3.1), which might entail liability as an accessory for anyone who participated in withdrawing life-sustaining treatment, is not consistent with Dutch law. From the point of view of Dutch law, what was involved in the film *Million Dollar Baby* (Warner Bros 2004) was not 'euthanasia' but respect for a patient's right to refuse unwanted treatment (*cf* Griffiths 2005).

[21] There are a few exceptions to the requirement of consent to medical treatment—eg for blood tests (drivers) and DNA tests (criminal proceedings). These are not relevant for present purposes.

[22] See art 450.2.

[23] Arts 465.1 and 465.2.

[24] A representative cannot take 'highly personal' decisions on behalf of a non-competent person (giving consent to organ donation or requesting euthanasia), and refusal of consent to treatment necessary for continued life is sometimes mentioned in this connection (eg KNMG 2004a: 94, making no distinction between representatives specifically appointed by the person concerned to make just such decisions, and the various other sorts of representatives provided for in the law). There is no support

A third way in which life-prolonging treatment can be refused is through a written treatment directive. Article 450 (3) of the law provides that if a person of 16 or older is not competent (in the sense quoted above), a doctor[25] or a representative of the patient is required to honour a refusal of treatment made in writing when the patient was still competent. The legal status in the Netherlands of such a written refusal of treatment is one of the strongest in the world.[26] There are no limits on the treatments that can be refused nor on the circumstances (eg terminal illness) in which a written refusal is effective. There are also almost no formal requirements (such as witnesses or regular renewal): not even a signature or a date is required. And although the law explicitly requires that the directive be in writing, there can be doubts about even this limitation.[27]

There are few legal limitations on the force of a treatment directive whose meaning, in the concrete circumstances, is clear. There must be no doubt about the authenticity of the document and the identity and competence of the author

for any such restriction in the text of the law itself. In the legislative history, only one example of a 'highly personal' decision was given: euthanasia, as to which there is general agreement in the Netherlands that a representative cannot make a request on behalf of a non-competent patient. Further interpretation of scope of the implicit exception was left to the courts (see *Second Chamber of Parliament 1990–1991*, 21561, no 6, p 54; *1991–1992*, no 11 p 36; *1992–1993*, no 15, p 29).

Especially in the case of an appointed representative, putting refusal of life-prolonging treatment outside the representative's power would be contrary to the whole spirit of the law (compare Leenen 2000: 208*ff.*). Doing so would largely gut the legal right to appoint a representative, a right that for most people who use it is interesting precisely because the representative can prevent the unwonted prolongation of life. The requirement that a representative act as a 'good representative' (art 465 (5)) gives sufficient room for a doctor to override a representative (in an emergency) or to seek judicial appointment of a different representative. This escape-clause does not allow 'subjective value-judgments' and is intended only for exceptional situations in which it is obvious that the behaviour of the patient's representative is plainly inconsistent with the patient's interests. See Sluijters & Biesart 2005: 155.

A pending medical disciplinary case may help to resolve some of the existing confusion surrounding the status of a refusal of further treatment by the representative of a non-competent patient. The doctor concerned initiated tube feeding of the patient over the objections of the court-appointed mentor. The doctor's position, apparently, was that the treatment was not 'medically futile' (which in principle in such a situation is irrelevant); the mentor's position was that the treatment could not return the patient to a life of sufficient quality and that in the circumstances the opportunity to let him die should be taken advantage of. No effort was made by the doctor to have the court replace the mentor on the ground that he was not acting as a 'good representative'. The mentor filed a complaint with the Medical Disciplinary Tribunal. The hearing is expected later in 2008. (Information received from the lawyer for the mentor.)

[25] The law uses the term 'caregiver' [hulpverlener] throughout, so that nurses and others are also covered, which can be important in the case of resuscitation by ambulance personnel, for example.

[26] See Vezzoni 2008. The most recent guideline of the Medical Association describes the patient's right to refuse treatment in a treatment directive in particularly forceful terms (KNMG 2003: 5):

> The requirement of consent plays a key role in the legitimacy of a doctor's behaviour. One consequence of this is that if the patient refuses a treatment (hence does not consent to it) the doctor may not carry that treatment out. This applies also in the situation that the patient's refusal of the treatment will lead to the patient's death. A refusal of treatment must be respected by a doctor, subject to the condition that the patient is competent.

[27] As Vezzoni notes (2008:84 n 147), the legal force of an advance refusal of treatment is based on the fundamental requirement of informed consent. An oral refusal in advance by a competent patient excludes the presumption of consent. Furthermore, doctors and representatives are required to implement the patient's views to the extent these are known. Finally, oral instructions prior, eg, to an operation under narcosis are common in everyday medical practice and, within the context of a contract for medical treatment, are surely binding on the doctor.

nor about the voluntariness of its execution.[28] A doctor can depart from the written instructions 'if he considers that there are well-founded reasons for doing so'. Although the latter formulation is vague, there is general agreement that the doctor's personal views concerning the instructions given in the directive cannot amount to a 'well-founded reason'. The fact that the professional standard indicates that the refused treatment is appropriate, or that following the directive will hasten the death of the patient, is irrelevant. In effect, 'well-founded reasons' refers to doubts about the authenticity of the document, the competence of its author, and the meaning of the instructions.[29]

As we will see in chapter 5, treatment directives are in fact not very effective in actual medical practice. But considered from a legal point of view, taken together with a competent patient's right to refuse treatment and the right to appoint a representative, they afford a patient whose life is dependent on any sort of treatment, including antibiotics and artificial nutrition and hydration, a powerful means to exercise control over continuation of his life beyond a point that he himself determines, one not subject to most of the limitations that apply to euthanasia.[30]

4.2.2.2 Withholding or Withdrawing Treatment Based on 'Medical Futility'

In discussions of the authority of a doctor to make abstention decisions, a crucial distinction is oft-times overlooked: between the situation in which the doctor wishes to initiate or continue treatment but the patient (or his representative) reject it, and the situation in which the doctor wishes to withhold or withdraw treatment but the patient (or his representative) insist on it. In the first situation (dealt with in section 4.2.2.1 above), the patient's word is law. Quite different principles are at stake in the second situation, which is treated here.

The basic principle of Dutch law on a doctor's authority to withhold or withdraw treatment is very simple: it is a violation of the professional standard for a

---

[28] In the early 1990s (prior to the Law on Contracts for Medical Treatment) a doctor was prosecuted for ignoring a written note pinned to the clothing of a woman who, apparently, had attempted suicide. In the note she made clear she did not want to be resuscitated. The note was not signed or dated, and it was not certain that the woman herself had written it. The doctor was acquitted. See Vezzoni 2008:87 n 154. See also the recent medical disciplinary case (Central Medical Disciplinary Tribunal, 19 April 2007, *Medisch Contact* 62: 1227–30, 2007) (complaint by representative of patient; resuscitation after suicide attempt despite written treatment refusal and objections of representative; problems with authenticity of documents and identy of representative; treatment refusal was not available until apparently successful treatment was underway, and stopping it was not considered a responsible option; complaint unfounded).

[29] See Vezzoni 2008: 84–5.

[30] It has been supposed (eg, in Italy—see ch 13) that a doctor, by giving heed to a patient's refusal of treatment, might thereby be guilty of homicide (consent being generally no defence). The short answer to this, as far as Dutch law is concerned, is that the patient's refusal deprives the doctor of any title to give the treatment concerned, so the case is one of an omission not associated with any duty to act. Death due to refusal of treatment is not considered suicide (eg in connection with life insurance). Nor does it break the causal chain between a (criminal) act that gives rise to the patient's medical condition, and the patient's death as a result of refusal of treatment (see the very interesting decision of the Dutch Supreme Court in this regard, in a case in which the victim of a gunshot wound became completely paralysed and refused further medical treatment, leading to her death: *Nederlandse Jurisprudentie* 1997 no 563).

doctor to give medical treatment that is 'medically futile'.[31] This is true even if the treatment will prolong the life of the patient and whether or not the patient or his representative has refused the treatment—in fact, even if they insist upon it. The medical profession itself has argued persuasively that when abstention is being considered, the ethical (and legal) problem is not whether withholding or withdrawing treatment is justifiable, but whether going on with it can be justified when it seems no longer capable of contributing to the welfare of the patient.[32]

But if abstaining from treatment causes the patient's (earlier) death, how is it possible that the doctor who does this on grounds of 'medical futility' is not guilty of homicide? Two approaches have been taken to resolving this dilemma. (1) *The 'omission' approach.* Criminal liability for omission is based on a duty to act and a doctor has a duty to care for his patient;[33] however, there is no duty to administer a futile treatment.[34] (2) *The 'justification' approach.* Although harming a patient by not treating him is potentially criminal, there is an (implicit) justification for the resulting harm if the treatment would have been futile.[35] Neither of these seems entirely satisfactory, however, since they do not account for the fact that there is not only no duty to perform futile treatment, but that doing so is a violation of medical ethics and medical law. The only adequate account of the legality of abstention on a doctor's own authority is one in terms of the professional standard with which every doctor is bound to comply. Whether it involves giving or not giving treatment, only proper medical behaviour—behaviour indicated by the medical standard—falls within the 'medical exception'. Giving futile treatment— like not giving medically indicated treatment—violates the professional standard

---

[31] See KNMG 2003: 5 ('professional duty' to refrain from futile treatment). The violation might have a variety of legal consequences. Such treatment might be considered a criminal offence. It might be a ground for civil damages or penalties. The doctor would expose himself to medical disciplinary sanctions and possibly to sanctions within the context of his employment contract (eg, with a hospital). And the patient's health insurer might refuse to pay the costs of the futile treatment.

[32] See GB&W for an extensive discussion of the reports in which this position is defended. See also KNMG (1997: 11–12, 68–76) for a more recent formulation:

> The added value of medical treatment [which is its justification] can only be determined when one has an impression of the quality of life to which one wishes to add something.

Ignoring that question would entail

> that one always treats the patient, in order to stay on the 'safe side'. There are so many objections to such a course that it cannot be regarded as a realistic alternative. (p. 11)

> [It is not the case] that value judgments can be the *basis* of medical treatment, but it is the case that the wish (mostly from a legal perspective) to limit medicine to a domain of mere facts, is based on a misconception of the structure of clinical behaviour. (p. 70)

[33] This is one reason why the common supposition that because abstention is a 'mere omission' no criminal liability attaches, is wrong. The other reason is that in the circumstances of modern medical practice, at least within institutions, there is hardly such a thing as a 'mere' omission: some active intervention, if only in the form of giving instructions to nursing staff, is always involved.

[34] See Leenen 2000: 357*ff*

[35] See Otlowski (2000: 152–69), who argues that traditional act/omission analysis is insufficient to afford doctors immunity from criminal liability in a case of withdrawing treatment (in her view, withholding treatment, by contrast, is simply an omission, a position that can be questioned). What is really involved, Otlowski argues, is that the behaviour—if appropriate—is *justified*. Compare Kennedy & Grubb 2000: 2117*ff*.

and is therefore an offence under medical disciplinary law and an invasion of bodily integrity in violation of civil and criminal law.

However all this may be—whatever the proper legal characterisation of abstention is thought to be—the fact is that if abstention is medically indicated it is not thought by anyone in the Netherlands to involve potential legal liability for the doctor. As we will see in chapter 5 (Table 5.1), almost a fifth of all deaths in the Netherlands are directly attributable to withdrawing or withholding life-prolonging treatment; such a rate is roughly comparable to rates elsewhere in Europe (see chapter 17, Table 17.2). It has been estimated that 8% of all deaths in the Netherlands are preceded by a decision not to administer artificial nutrition or hydration to a (geriatric) patient who at the end of the course of his disease spontaneously stops eating and drinking,[36] and the Dutch Association of Nursing-home Doctors recommends this as good practice for patients for whom such life-prolonging treatment has become futile.[37]

The idea that 'futility' is purely a matter for a doctor to decide upon in light of the governing medical standard—the case, in other words, for absolute medical authority over decisions not to treat—can easily be overstated. When discussion with other members of the medical staff (including nurses) and with the patient's family is possible, the responsible doctor is obliged to do so, if only to avoid serious mistakes.[38] Similarly, a doctor who comes to the conclusion that (further) treatment would be 'futile' cannot simply turn off life-support. The patient or his representative must if possible be informed and given the opportunity to offer countervailing considerations, and afforded an opportunity to seek a second opinion or even a court order requiring treatment.[39] There is also general agreement that, where possible, there should be some flexibility with regard to the precise timing of the abstention, for example to allow relatives an opportunity to take their leave of the patient.[40]

One way in which determinations of 'medical futility' are made is prospective and conditional: decisions that *if* the patient experiences a particular condition *then* specified treatment would be futile and will not be given.[41] The quantitative importance of such decisions is enormous. It was estimated in 1990 that more than

---

[36] See Van der Heide *et al* 1997a.

[37] See Nederlandse Vereniging van Verpleeghuisartsen 1997; Kruit *et al*, 1998.

[38] See Leenen 2000: 362–3. A 1997 case involving an Alzheimers patient who almost died in a nursing home as a result of uninformed (and erroneous) application of the home's policy of abstaining from further artificial hydration under certain circumstances, but who recuperated when his family had him transferred to a hospital, called attention to the importance of good communication with the family. The man's daughter complained to the prosecutorial authorities who, after consulting the Medical Inspector, decided not to prosecute. See Weyers 2004: 301.

[39] Compare Kleijer 2005. For two cases illustrating these principles, see ch 6.2.2.1 n 28.

[40] See further on the limits of unilateral medical decision-making concerning abstention from treatment based on medical futility, in the specific context of neonatology, ch 6.2.2.1, 'the role of the parents'.

[41] Advance non-treatment decisions sometimes take the form of decisions not to admit a patient to a specialised treatment unit, or to discharge a patient, on the ground that (further) specialised treatment would be futile. Thus, eg, an intensive care unit may, on transferring a stable patient to another ward of the hospital, give the instruction that in the event of further problems he is not to be returned to intensive care (see the case discussed in Kleijer 2005: 40–41). Compare Nederlandse Vereniging voor Intensive Care 2001 (guideline on admission to/discharge from intensive care).

90,000 'do not resuscitate' (DNR) orders are made per year in Dutch hospitals (about 6% of all admissions) and that more than 30,000 deaths are preceded by such an order.[42] It is common for Dutch hospitals and nursing homes to have an institutional policy concerning DNR orders, usually consisting of a protocol for DNR decision-making and a special order form to be kept in the files of individual patients. Development of these policies took place in the early 1990s.[43]

As the foregoing discussion makes clear, in all abstention decisions (except those made at the request of the patient, or on his behalf by a representative) the critical question is whether the treatment withheld or withdrawn would be, or has become 'medically futile'. Treatment is considered 'medically futile' under Dutch law if it has no chance of success in the sense that it cannot 'contribute to solving the medical problem' [*kansloos medisch handelen*], or if it cannot succeed in restoring the patient to a 'minimum level [of functioning]' [*zinloos medisch handelen*].[44] The Dutch health-law authority Leenen regarded these as a matter of medical-professional judgment and therefore entirely up to the doctor.[45]

Leenen rejected the idea that the patient's expected future 'quality of life' could be an 'independent ground for decision' concerning the futility of (further) treatment.[46] In this connection he invoked some general ethical arguments (in particular, that one person can never judge the 'quality' of another person's life) and referred specifically to several judicial decisions which reject decision-making 'grounded in subjective, personal value judgments concerning the future life of a patient'.[47] However, none of the decisions to which he referred appears to reject 'quality of life' considerations as a reason for withholding or withdrawing treatment, so long as the decision is not based on subjective (personal) values.

The idea that 'quality' considerations can be eliminated from decision-making concerning withholding or withdrawing treatment is a fantasy that stands in the way of effective control of medical subjectivity. Even 'chance of success', after all, depends on what one regards as 'success', and there are those who regard the mere continued existence of biological life as having value in itself. Every decision to continue or to discontinue life-prolonging treatment inevitably implies a judgment about the value of the life thereby (not) saved.

In short, the difference between 'no chance of success' and 'too little quality of life' as standards for making a decision to abstain, is not one of kind but of degree: there is a spectrum in which 'quality' considerations gradually increase in relative importance, running from treatment that will not have any life-prolonging effect

---

[42] See GB&W: 215–16.

[43] See Haverkate & Van der Wal 1996.

[44] See Leenen 2000: 357–61. Leenen adds that there must also be a 'reasonable relationship between the means to be used and the objective to be achieved'. While these criteria are not purely medical-technical in nature, the value judgments involved do not concern the value of the patient's life but rather the sense of medical treatment given the patient's condition, and they are 'bounded judgments' [*gebonden oordelen*]: based on the professional expertise of the doctor (*ibid*).

[45] *Ibid* at 362–3.

[46] *Ibid* at 360; Leenen's views were, in the past, less nuanced (see 1994: 310–12).

[47] *Ibid* at 361.

at all, through treatments that may add minutes, hours, days or even years to life but only in an unconscious state, or subject to very severe incapacities or great suffering, all the way to treatments that can restore the patient to a normal life-span but in a somewhat reduced condition. And then we have said nothing about another part of the equation: the proportionality of the treatment (burden to the patient) in relation to the length and the quality of life to be won. Leenen's idea that doctors may and must abstain from life-prolonging treatment only if purely medical considerations indicate that this is the medically appropriate thing to do,[48] cannot work to define the boundaries of legal abstention.[49]

As we will see in chapter 6, in the specific context of neonatology there have been substantial efforts to identify more or less 'objective' elements of a decision on 'quality' grounds in terms of the baby's expected future level of functioning in a number of distinct respects that, *mutatis mutandis*, can also apply in the case of an adult patient.[50] Leenen to the contrary notwithstanding, there is considerable support in the case law for the proposition that when there is such a professional standard for the 'quality of life' aspect of abstention decisions and the doctors concerned have followed it, the courts will accept the outcome.[51]

Decision-making procedures have been designed that go further than such an 'objectification' of futility as a ground for unilateral medical decision-making. The initial medical decision that abstention is appropriate—based on the sort of more or less objective criteria just referred to—can be made 'intersubjective' by ensuring that it is not made by a single doctor but by several doctors, and nurses, together. The medical decision can then be presented to the representative/family of the patient, who can either agree or disagree. If the representative/family remain opposed, a number of further steps follow (second opinion, medical ethical committee), and at each step, if the decision is contrary to the initial medical position, abstention may not take place. Finally, there is room for appeal to a court. Only after the whole procedure has been followed, with the doctor's judgment having prevailed at every stage, may abstention be carried out against the wishes of the representative/family.[52]

Such proposals reject Leenen's rather simplistic idea that since the family (or even the patient himself) cannot insist on 'futile' treatment, they can have no formal role in the decision-making process. 'Medically futile treatment', he said,

---

[48] Leenen 2000: 357–63.

[49] See to the same effect the position of the KNMG, quoted in n 32 above.

[50] See ch 6, Box 6.1.

[51] See GB&W: 126 (discussing the *Prins* and *Kadijk* cases, in which both abstention and active termination of life were carried out according to a professional guideline); *Kort Geding* 1999/834–838F (action against hospital challenging decision of intensive care doctors not to readmit a patient, since further IC treatment would be 'futile'—decision taken according to hospital protocol accepted by court).

[52] See Kleijer 2005 for a proposal to this effect for Dutch intensive care units, based on an earlier proposal of the Council on Ethical and Judicial Affairs of the American Medical Association (see American Medical Association 1999), a proposal for 'shared decision-making' of the International Consensus Conference in Critical Care (Carlet *et al* 2004), and the Texas Advance Directives Act (Fine & Mayo 2003).

'does not become medically indicated just because the patient [or his family] asks for it.'[53] As the Royal Dutch Medical Association observes, whether treatment is futile or not is highly dependent on the patient's own values and hence, if he is incompetent, on what is known about them,[54] something about which the patient's family or representative is likely to be better informed than his doctor.

Kleijer's research into abstention practice in Dutch intensive care units shows that the family of a patient plays a substantially greater role in the decision-making than the notion that a purely 'medical' judgment is involved would lead one to expect.[55] Furthermore, the fact that the patient or his family may want time to seek a second opinion, or to challenge the doctor's decision in court, can require that abstention be postponed, a fact that is often overlooked when authors stress the authority of the doctor to decide when treatment is 'futile' and to withhold or withdraw it when it is.[56] Kleijer's conclusion—combining law, medical practice and the ideas he encountered on the shop floor—is that the family should have 'an important role in assessing the qualitative aspect of "medical futility"' and intensive care units should have a clear procedure for involving the family in the decision-making process (but in fact, very few of them do).[57]

4.2.2.3 Pain Relief with Life-Shortening Effect and the Idea of 'Double Effect'

When medically indicated for the relief of pain or other symptoms, a doctor may administer drugs even though this is expected to shorten the life of the patient. Doing so (absent a situation of necessity) would in the case of someone who is not a doctor amount to intentional killing and therefore be a serious criminal offence. In the case of a doctor, it is generally agreed in the Netherlands and elsewhere that such behaviour is not criminal.[58]

In the medical ethics literature, the legitimacy of such behaviour is generally thought to be based on the so-called 'doctrine of double effect', according to which, if the doctor's primary intention is to relieve suffering, the fact that he knows his action will also cause death does not make it immoral. It is also supposed that the doctrine is the basis for the legal treatment of pain relief that causes death. However, it seems clear that this view is mistaken. Dutch criminal law—like that in many other countries[59]—normally uses an objectified conception of intent that does not permit the fine distinctions between primary and secondary subjective intentions that the doctrine of double effect requires. As far as the law is concerned, it is the fact that pain relief is *medically indicated,* and not the doctor's subjective intention, that protects the doctor from criminal liability. This is the

---

[53] Leenen 2000: 362–3.
[54] KNMG 1997: 11.
[55] Kleijer 2005: 110–29, 192–4.
[56] *Ibid* at 34–42, 185–94.
[57] *Ibid* at 194.
[58] See eg Leenen 2000: 374.
[59] See Otlowski 2000: 170–84.

position taken years ago by the State Commission on Euthanasia,[60] and the obvious implication is what one would expect: such behaviour falls within the medical exception.[61]

Nevertheless, without support in criminal law doctrine,[62] the Dutch discussion on pain relief has proceeded for many years on the assumption that it is the doctor's subjective intention that protects him from criminal liability. The most visible evidence for this is to be found in the reports of the four national surveys of euthanasia and other medical behaviour that shortens life. The researchers in the first survey (1990) seem simply to have assumed that the doctor's 'primary' intention determines the border between pain relief and termination of life (voluntary or otherwise). They even went a step further and distinguished *three* levels of intention: 'knowing' that death would probably be hastened, 'partly intending' to hasten death, and 'explicitly intending' to hasten death. Even under the doctrine of double intent, both the second and third categories would have to be considered immoral. The researchers, however, chose to regard only the third category— explicit intent—as placing the doctor's behaviour outside of the category of 'normal medical practice' and into that of euthanasia (if on request) or termination of life without request. This procedure was repeated in 1995, 2001 and 2005. The fact that 'objective' data concerning the amount of euthanasia taking place have been collected on the basis of behavioural categories so constructed, and that doing so has kept the total apparent amount of euthanasia and other termination of life to very modest proportions, seems to have numbed the critical reaction that might have been expected to such a sleight-of-hand.[63]

Recently, however, there have been signs of a return to doctrinal orthodoxy. In its guideline of 2003, the Medical Association emphasises that it is essential that,

the nature and amount of the doses given be justifiable in terms of necessary pain or symptom relief. . . . If doses are knowingly given that cannot be [so justified] . . . then the

---

[60] Staatscommissie Euthanasie 1985: 43; see further section 4.2.3 below.

[61] Compare Gezondheidsraad 2004: 38. In practice there is much less room for the doctrine of double effect than is often supposed, it having become clear in recent years that the life-shortening properties of opiates are often greatly exaggerated by doctors: pain relief in indicated doses rarely if ever causes the patient's death (see Admiraal & Griffiths 2001; compare Vander Stichele *et al* 2004; Provoost *et al* 2006).

[62] See Van Tol 2005: 89–93. It seems clear from Van Tol's research that it is unlikely that the prosecutorial authorities have ever accepted the doctrine of double intent and the resulting use of a subjective conception of intention. They simply have not been confronted with the issue, since doctors do not report such cases and prosecutors therefore do not see them.

[63] See generally Van Tol 2005: 89–93. Strictly speaking, the in-between category (sometimes called co-intention) would seem to be empty. If pain relief (in the doses given) is medically indicated, then the most the doctor can be said to have done is to accept the likelihood of death as a side-effect of medically-indicated behaviour. If, on the other hand, the pain relief was not indicated, then it would seem that there can have been no reason for giving it other than to cause the death of the patient. It is hard to understand what intention a doctor could possibly have in administering drugs that are likely to cause death, and are not indicated for the relief of pain or other symptoms, other than to bring about the death of the patient. That doctors may be (opportunistically) confused in thinking about their own intentions (see for an example of this ch 6, Box 6.9) is not relevant to the question of their criminal liability for their behaviour.

purpose of the behaviour is apparently . . . to hasten death. A critical line is thereby crossed and the behaviour must be considered euthanasia, with all the resulting consequences.[64]

As we will see in the next section, a recent report for the Medical Association on 'terminal sedation' explicitly rejects a delimitation of acceptable medical behaviour in terms of the doctor's subjective intention. Sedation is permissible *when it is medically indicated to deal with refractory symptoms.*[65] The report was quickly embraced by the prosecutorial service. In short, the position the State Commission took in 1985 with regard to pain relief—that it is covered by the 'medical exception' only if it is 'medically indicated'—seems to be gaining support.[66]

4.2.2.4 Palliative and Terminal Sedation

Over the past few years, a supposedly new sort of MBPSL arrived on the Dutch scene: 'palliative sedation'. This can be defined as 'putting a patient into deep sleep, in the expectation that this will be continued until his death'.[67] If properly administered, the sedation itself will have no life-shortening effect. If the patient's life is shortened, this is because the sedation is accompanied by withholding artificial nutrition and hydration (ANH), either because the patient has refused ANH in advance or because it is deemed 'medically futile' to seek artificially to prolong the life of a patient who will remain unconscious until he dies.

There has been disagreement about what the name of the behaviour should be: *terminal* or *palliative* sedation. On the whole, those in the palliative care movement prefer to call it 'palliative sedation', to reflect their view that it is, or ought to be, part and parcel of good palliative care. Those who prefer the term 'terminal sedation' choose to emphasise the terminal character of the behaviour concerned. Since, from the regulatory perspective of this book, the latter characteristic is particularly important, we distinguish between 'terminal sedation' (which is potentially a cause of death because the sedation is accompanied by withholding of ANH for a period long enough that it can be expected to hasten the patient's death) from 'palliative sedation' (where ANH is given or life-expectancy is short).

The idea of 'terminal sedation' first made its appearance in the 1990s, initially as a supposedly unproblematic alternative for euthanasia. It can be seen as a simple combination of two sorts of normal medical behaviour: pain and symptom relief, and abstention from ANH (based either on medical futility or on the

---

[64] KNMG 2003: 6. *Cf* RRC 2006: 9 ('death as a by-product of *treatment that was necessary to relieve serious suffering*' falls within the medical exception—italics added).

[65] KNMG 2005.

[66] See eg Bood 2007: 2294; Gevers 2007: 284, 286 (proposing legislation explicitly to include 'indicated' pain relief within the 'medical exception'). It is interesting to note in retrospect that during the whole period in which modern Dutch law on the subject was developing, the State Commission was almost the only official or quasi-official body to address the legal status of MBPSL in which criminal lawyers of national standing played a leading role. See Weyers 2004: 156 on the composition of the State Commission (in addition to its chairman, Jeukens, who was a member of the criminal chamber of the Supreme Court, the highly respected prosecutor Meijers was a member, as was Nieboer, a professor of criminal law).

[67] Gezondheidsraad 2004: 31.

patient's refusal). The idea of 'terminal sedation' was seemingly embraced in an offhand way by the United States Supreme Court in the *Quill* case,[68] in which the court held that the US Constitution does not entail a right to physician assistance with suicide. Its holding, the court suggested (encouraged in this by a brief of the American Medical Association), does not reduce anyone's liberty very much, since 'terminal sedation' is an acceptable alternative.[69] This notion, that 'terminal sedation' is a safe, legal and ethically unproblematic alternative for euthanasia, later got picked up elsewhere, in particular by opponents of legalisation of euthanasia (in Norway, for example[70]). And so it arrived in the Netherlands.[71]

The national survey of 2001 sought to measure the extent to which what it called 'terminal sedation' is a cause of death. It seemed that in between 6% and 12% of all deaths 'deep, continuous sedation' until death was given, and that most of these cases involved withholding of ANH.[72] (As far as one can tell from the Annual Reports of the Regional Review Committees,[73] all of the deaths following such 'terminal sedation' were reported as 'natural deaths'.)

In particular the results of the 2001 survey seem to have called the practice to the attention of the prosecutorial authorities, whose highest official reacted by stating publicly that on his view, deaths due to 'terminal sedation' should be reported as non-natural deaths so that they could be properly examined. The Government answered the ensuing questions in Parliament by expressing the hope that the medical profession would clarify the situation. It was in this context that in 2004 the Medical Association appointed a committee to prepare a guideline on the subject.

[68] *Vacco v Quill*, 521 US 793 (1997).

[69] See Burt 1997 for this implication of the court's decision. The message they found in the court's decision was enthusiastically embraced by opponents of legal physician-assisted suicide such as Burt as proof of the proposition that there is no need for it. But Orentlicher, who for years as a lawyer for the American Medical Association had fought legal battles against euthanasia and physician-assisted suicide, commented that if there is one thing even worse than these, it is 'terminal sedation', since it involves all of the dangers without any of the safeguards (Orentlicher 1997).

[70] See Schwitters 2005: 56.

[71] See ch 3.4 for the recent legal history of 'terminal sedation'. See Seymour, Janssens & Broeckaert 2007 for an interesting comparative study of the cultural differences in perspectives on palliative sedation in Belgium, the Netherlands and the UK.

[72] Van der Wal *et al* 2003: 85. The national researchers define 'terminal sedation' as 'bringing the patient into deep sleep while forgoing artificial nutrition or hydration' (Rietjens *et al* 2006: 749).

[73] 'Terminal sedation' is not mentioned until RRC 2003: 15, where it is restricted to the situation in which the sedation is accompanied by withholding of ANH; when this is done with the intention of shortening life and at the request of the patient, the committees state, it should be reported (apparently, as 'euthanasia') (*ibid* at 16; see also RRC 2004: 8). In 2005, apparently under the influence of the report on 'palliative sedation' of the KNMG Committee, the committees' terminology changes to 'palliative sedation' but the substance of its position seems to be unchanged: deep, continuous sedation until death, whereby ANH is withheld as 'futile', is 'normal medical behaviour'; the committees refer to the 2-week restriction but do not address the consequences for the duty to report if this limit is exceeded (RRC 2005: 8; *cf* the much more summary treatment in RRC 2006: 5; for terminological confusion in cases in which the patient refused sedation see n 179). The committees have apparently in fact received no reports of either palliative or terminal sedation. Data from the prosecutorial authorities likewise gives no indication of any cases of terminal sedation having been reported. The prosecution in the *Vencken* case (see ch 3.4) was the result not of reporting by the doctor but of a hospital reporting a doctor to the Medical Inspectorate.

In 2005 the committee's proposed guideline was quickly adopted by the Medical Association without public discussion and shortly thereafter embraced by the prosecutorial authorities.[74] But it quickly elicited withering criticism,[75] and to judge from direct personal experience of the authors of this book (on the occasion of discussion of the report at various symposia and the like) the report has given rise to considerable confusion.

This confusion is at least partly the result of the fact that, without being explicit about it, the guideline addresses a different problem from that which had lead to the committee being set up in the first place. To understand this, one must keep in mind the fundamental legal difference between behaviour (medical or otherwise) that *is a predictable cause of death* and behaviour that perhaps ends with death but is not likely to be its *cause*. Sedation at the end of life can fall into either category. If it is light or intermittent, or deep and continuous but accompanied by the administration of ANH, or deep and continuous without ANH but commenced shortly before death is expected anyway, it will not generally shorten the patient's life. When medically indicated, this sort of sedation—which the guideline appropriately calls 'palliative sedation'—is part and parcel of palliative care. It was not concern about 'palliative sedation' in this sense that had lead to the appointment of the committee.

What had given rise to concern was sedation that, because it is accompanied by withholding or withdrawing ANH over a longer period, can be considered to cause the patient's death. This sort of sedation can appropriately be called 'terminal sedation' and is what the whole debate was really about. But the guideline does not address the question whether or not 'terminal sedation' is relevantly different from euthanasia (or termination of life without a request) and whether or how it should be regulated.

In short, the confusion and criticism to which the guideline gives rise can be attributed to the fact that it is taken to regulate a highly problematic sort of behaviour, whereas it in fact gives some useful requirements of careful practice for the administration of pain and symptom relief (in the form of sedation) at the end of life. Seen in this light, it is to be welcomed for recognising the need to subject 'normal medical behaviour' that causes death to some degree of regulation. Furthermore, it is thanks to the committee that the widespread misconception that sedation accompanied by withholding of ANH is in itself a cause of death was exposed as a fallacy, thereby paving the way for a clear distinction between 'palliative' and 'terminal' sedation.

Read in the way just indicated, the guideline can be summarised as shown in Box 4.3:

[74] See ch 3.4.
[75] See eg Den Hartogh 2006a, 2006b.

Box 4.3 The KNMG Guideline on palliative sedation

1. Palliative sedation—in the sense of deep, continuous sedation until death and withholding of artificial nutrition and hydration—is 'normal medical practice' (and the patient's death can therefore be reported as a 'natural' one, to which no specific control attaches).
2. Palliative sedation is only appropriate if the patient has less than 2 weeks to live (in which case, abstention from artificial nutrition and hydration will usually have no life-shortening effect).[76]
3. Palliative sedation is only appropriate when necessary to deal with 'refractory symptoms' that cannot be satisfactorily dealt with in another way.
4. Opioids should not be used for palliative sedation.
5. The patient or his representative must agree to the proposed course of action.

Considering the serious implications of continuous sedation until death,[77] these special requirements for 'palliative sedation' seem entirely sensible. In particular, item 5 of the guideline, which goes further than existing rules for abstention or for other forms of pain and symptom relief, is important. One can wonder if the guideline should not have required consultation with another, independent doctor, even though this is not generally required in the case of normal medical practice. As Den Hartogh points out, the lack of specific control of 'palliative sedation' is a virtual invitation to doctors not to take the various requirements formulated in the guideline seriously,[78] and also to steer patients who indicate an interest in euthanasia in the direction of 'palliative sedation', thereby depriving those who would have preferred to remain conscious until the time of their death of the option of euthanasia. On the other hand, the nature of the suffering it requires ('refractory symptoms') seems to contemplate only somatically-based suffering, which is more limited than the 'unbearable suffering' required for euthanasia. In short, the guideline may contribute to a reduction in patient choice

---

[76] The two-week rule of thumb cannot, Den Hartogh (2006a) argues, be supported only on this ground, since predictions of when a patient will die are unreliable and while a healthy person can survive for two weeks without hydration, it is not clear that the same applies to a dying patient. Den Hartogh argues that a limit of two weeks can nevertheless be justified in terms of proportionality: the possibly earlier death of the patient from terminal sedation is, within such a brief period, an acceptable consequence of a decision to relieve suffering by means of sedation and to refrain from artificial hydration.

[77] As Chabot (2007: 252) observes, deep, continuous sedation until death excludes the patient from any further participation in the decision-making, making it impossible for him to confirm or to reconsider earlier decisions that this is the way he wants to die. Den Hartogh (2006b) argues that from the patient's point of view, the choice for such sedation is just as drastic as the choice for euthanasia, since it entails the end of his conscious life (from which he concludes, among other things, that consultation with a second doctor should be required).

[78] An indication of the problems of control involved in treating palliative sedation as 'normal medical practice' is revealed in a recent study. It shows that many GPs leave the initiation of sedation entirely to a nurse, do not remain with the patient until the required depth of sedation has been reached, and do not systematically reassess whether the sedation is adequate. See Klinkenberg & Perez 2007.

between the two ways of dying and to reduce the transparency of end-of-life medical practice.[79]

Despite such criticism, an important contribution of the KNMG committee to the Dutch debate on how to characterise the various sorts of MBPSL and subject them to effective control should be emphasised. Following the lead of a report of the Health Council, 'palliative sedation' is defined in terms not of the doctor's 'intention' (to relieve suffering versus to hasten death) but in terms of the medical condition of the patient (refractory symptoms) and what the doctor actually does. As Den Hartogh notes in his critical review of the committee's report, this represents a major step forward in Dutch thinking about how to regulate problematic medical behaviour and how to measure it in empirical research.[80]

In the meantime, the prosecutorial authorities had prosecuted—for murder—a case of what they apparently took to be termination of life without a request: the *Vencken* case, discussed in chapter 3.4. As it transpired, there was no evidence that the sedation administered had hastened the death of the patient, and the doctor was acquitted. In effect, the case turned out to be one of 'palliative sedation'—of exactly the sort shortly thereafter described as 'normal medical behaviour' in the KNMG guideline.[81]

What, then, is the status of 'terminal sedation' in Dutch law—that is, of medical behaviour involving continuous deep sedation together with abstention from artificial nutrition and hydration for a sufficient period that this can be taken to cause the death of the patient? If the sedation is medically indicated (to deal with

---

[79] Den Hartogh 2006a, 2006b. In another report, the KNMG emphasises that palliative care is, for some patients, not an acceptable 'alternative' to euthanasia (KNMG 2003: 6, 14; see also Rietjens 2006: 104: 61% of the Dutch population consider being conscious to the end an important characteristic of a 'good death'). For judgments of the Regional Review Committees in cases in which the patient preferred euthanasia, see n 179.

[80] See Gezondheidsraad 2004: 38, Den Hartogh (2006a). In most other respects, den Hartogh is very critical of the committee's report. He objects to its tendentious way with definitions (problematic cases of 'palliative sedation' being excluded from the scope of the report by defining them as something else—'terminal sedation'), its consequent failure to deal with the question what should be done with such cases, its obfuscatory ideological bent (in particular, the persistent effort to present the practice of 'palliative sedation' as simply an extension of palliative care), and the generally poor quality of its reasoning.

[81] In several ways the courts made plain that in their view Vencken ought never to have been prosecuted (see ch 3.4).

One can have one technical, but not unimportant, reservation about the way the *Vencken* case was decided by the Court of Appeals. Since 'palliative sedation' is 'normal medical practice' it falls under the 'medical exception' (as does, eg, pain relief). It therefore does not matter whether the death was in fact caused by the sedation or not, so long as the sedation was medically indicated under the circumstances. In the *Vencken* case there seems clearly to have been a medical indication of the sort contemplated in the KNMG guideline. The judgment of the Medical Disciplinary Tribunal is in this respect more satisfactory: the fact that the medication given was 'medically indicated' is decisive, not whether or not it hastened the patient's death. The Tribunal notes, further, that the doctor's 'intention—his personal objectives and motives' is irrelevant in assessing his behaviour: the relevant question is whether the medication given was, given the situation of the patient, a professionally accepted way of dealing with the patient's suffering. Vencken's record-keeping was found inadequate, but no sanction was imposed. The Medical Inspector appealed the judgment but later withdrew the appeal, relying on an expert's report by Prof G van der Wal and the guideline of the KNMG, which in the meantime had been adopted.

'refractory symptoms', in the expression of the KNMG) it clearly falls within the 'medical exception' even if it was expected to, and did, hasten the patient's death; the requirements of due care for 'palliative sedation' must be met (and failure to do so will presumably be dealt with by the medical disciplinary authorities). If the withholding of ANH for a period long enough to shorten the patient's life follows upon the medical judgment that giving ANH would be 'futile' in the circumstances, or if the patient has refused it, then even if abstention does cause the patient's death this is no different from any other case of abstention from life-prolonging treatment. In short, it is hard to see how a prosecution for murder, in a case of 'terminal sedation', could succeed, consistently with existing Dutch law.

Perhaps the prosecutor will seek help in the philosophy of action and argue that what the doctor did must be treated as a whole, not reducible to its separate parts (sedation and abstention). He can argue that what the doctor did, taken as a whole, was to cause the (earlier) death of the patient, albeit in a more complicated way than by simply injecting him with a euthanaticum. From the point of view of adequate control over medical behaviour that shortens life, he would be absolutely right. But current Dutch law—as elsewhere in the world—takes account (unwisely) not of the *substance of what the doctor accomplishes* (the earlier death of the patient), but of *the specific way that he does so*, and however you look at it, terminal sedation consists of behaviour that falls within the 'medical exception'. That it is particularly dangerous means that it *ought to be* adequately regulated, not that it actually is (which, of course, applies also to its component parts—relief of pain and symptoms, and abstention, each of which alone is by definition capable of causing the death of a patient).

Terminal sedation calls for adequate regulation, not only in its own right, but also to keep it from becoming an unregulated alternative for euthanasia (and for termination of life without a request from the patient). Otherwise, the regulatory attention paid to the latter will to a considerable degree be rendered toothless: what used to be 'euthanasia' cases being simply dealt with by doctors in a slightly different way and reported as 'natural deaths'. There is some evidence that such a development is in fact taking place (this is a frequently-heard explanation for the apparent decline in the frequency of euthanasia in the course of the last few years). Furthermore, to the extent doctors decline to perform euthanasia where 'terminal sedation' is an available alternative, the range of choice for patients will be reduced.

4.2.2.5 Help in Dying (*stervenshulp*)

The 'Remmelink Committee', which supervised the 1990 national survey, came in its final report to the conclusion that administration of lethal drugs to speed up the dying process in the case of a patient whose bodily functions are successively and irreversibly failing should be regarded as 'normal medical practice' and the patient's death, thus, a 'natural' one.[82] The committee described the practice as

---

[82] Commissie Remmelink 1991: 15, 32, 37. See further GB&W: 131–2, 227, 270.

'help in dying' [*stervenshulp*]. It seems clear that many doctors have long considered such a practice a part of their normal duty to dying patients and their families. However, the suggestion was received in Parliament with expressions of outrage[83] and nothing more was heard of it until the *Van Oijen* case in 2001, which has been discussed in chapter 3.4.

The decision of the Supreme Court in the *Van Oijen* case[84] has been widely read as closing the door on the possibility of legal 'help in dying' as contemplated by the Remmelink Committee. However, it may be premature to read the court's judgment in that way. The case was discussed, from the trial court on up, not in terms of 'help in dying' (no reference was made to this idea nor to the Remmelink report), in which case the legitimacy of the doctor's behaviour would have been a matter of the 'medical exception', but in terms of the justification of necessity, which assumes that the provisions of the Penal Code are *prima facie* applicable. It was in such a context that both the Court of Appeals and the Supreme Court emphasised that Van Oijen's behaviour might, in other circumstances, have been justifiable. The Court of Appeals found as a matter of fact, however, that the patient's suffering could not be considered 'unbearable' since she was in coma, and that she was so close to death that hastening it further was not necessary in order to put an end to an appalling situation of 'inhuman deterioration'. In affirming this holding, the Supreme Court made clear that 'inhuman deterioration' can be assessed objectively by a doctor—that it is not dependent on the patient's awareness of his situation—a point that may become important in connection with the justification of termination of life in other sorts of cases, in particular following upon a legitimate decision to withhold or withdraw treatment that does not lead to a quick and easy death for the patient.[85]

In short, far from closing the door to 'help in dying', a defence that was not considered in the case, the courts' judgments suggest an openness to consider the legality of termination of life in cases not involving a request by the patient, rejecting only the availability of the defence of necessity on the facts of the case at hand. Repeated references were made to medical standards, suggesting that had there been a guideline of the medical profession permitting 'help in dying' in such a case and providing for appropriate requirements of due care, the judicial reaction might well have been quite different.[86]

On the other hand, it can be argued that if a patient is truly at the doors of death, there simply is no justification for 'help in dying', since terminal sedation will eliminate any suffering there might be, and all the observers have to do is to be patient. This argument treats 'unbearable suffering' as limited to consciously-experienced pain, which, of course, can always be dealt with by rendering the

---

[83] See *Second Chamber of Parliament, Proceedings 1991–1992*: 4231–99, 4322–32, 4408–14.

[84] Hoge Raad, 9 November 2004; *Nederlandse Jurisprudentie* 2005 no 217.

[85] This possibility is of particular importance for the status of termination of life in neonatology (see ch 6.2.2.1 on the 'priority principle').

[86] Such professional standards in fact do exist for termination of life in certain specific situations (in particular in neonatology—see ch 6), a matter dealt with in the next section.

patient unconscious. If 'suffering' were interpreted this way, terminal sedation would indeed be the comprehensive alternative for euthanasia and assisted suicide that its proponents believe it to be.

However, 'suffering' has never been so narrowly interpreted in Dutch euthanasia law. From the very beginning the courts have included the *prospect* of inhumane deterioration and an undignified death among the legitimate reasons a person can have for requesting euthanasia, and as we will see in section 4.2.3.3(C), the Regional Review Committees do so too. Deterioration and loss of dignity are things one does not want to think about happening to one even if one is not conscious at the time. Such considerations are taken legal account of in the analogous situation of things one does or does not want to happen to one's corpse after death. But this all concerns interests experienced by the patient himself, even if they are anticipatory rather than current. The ultimate question in connection with 'help in dying' is different: whether *the experience of an inhumane death in the eyes of those in the immediate presence of the dying person*—who himself is and will remain unaware of his situation—can ever justify a doctor in giving 'help in dying'. The common human experience that some forms of dying are simply too awful to accept, *even if the person concerned is not aware of them*, seems too strong to dismiss easily.

The sensitive reader-between-the-lines of some of the judgments of the Regional Review Committees (adopting a broad conception of what can constitute 'suffering'[87]), and the observer of medical practice in neonatology, is inclined toward the conclusion that what is being described as 'suffering' (because that is what the rules seem to require) is sometimes in fact a situation of inhumanity that those who witness it simply cannot bear to allow to continue. If one may venture a prediction, it would be this: the idea of an 'inhumane death' will, in one form or another, come increasingly to be accepted not only as a legitimate (prospective) reason for requesting euthanasia but also as a justification for 'help in dying', subject presumably to some form of legal control.[88] We return to this possible development in section 4.2.5.

4.2.3 'Termination of Life'

So far we have been considering 'normal medical practice': behaviour of doctors that falls (or has been argued to fall) within the 'medical exception' so that a resulting death can be reported as a 'natural' one and the case be subject to no specific

---

[87] See section 4.2.3.3(C).

[88] The proposal of the Remmelink Committee to define *stervenshulp* narrowly and treat it as a normal medical practice would be a possible place to begin. The medical profession could propose some fairly simple procedural requirements. Since there is hardly any doubt that the behaviour involved is fairly common but very easy to conceal, recognising it explicitly in this way and bringing it out into the open would create possibilities for effective, low-intensity control. Otherwise it could be treated as a *sui generis* form of 'termination of life', subject to a simplified control regime (compare the proposal of the Consultative Committee, discussed in ch 6.2.2.4).

control through the criminal law.[89] But there is another sort of MBPSL that the Dutch courts held early on is not 'normal medical practice', so that a resulting death must be reported as not 'natural'.[90] This category is referred to as a whole as '*termination of life*'.[91] Since specific legal control of MBPSL through the criminal law is limited to cases of 'termination of life', the scope of such control is largely determined by the way that idea is defined.

In both the ethical and the legal discussion concerning medical behaviour that shortens life, and in empirical studies that have been made of actual practice, there is much confusion concerning the scope of the concept of 'termination of life'. Definitions—usually more or less implicit—range from extremely broad (all behaviour known to be likely to cause death) to extremely narrow (administration of drugs whose only medical purpose in the circumstances is to cause death: what we refer to in this book as *euthanatica*).

In between the two extremes, most definitions of 'termination of life' leave withholding and withdrawing of life-prolonging treatment out altogether, without limiting the (implicit) exclusion to treatment that is medically futile or that the patient (for example in an advance directive) or his representative have rejected. This entails that a doctor who decides not to give a simple but essential treatment that the patient has not refused would not be regarded as having thereby terminated the patient's life. Such an exclusion is arbitrary: there is neither ethical nor legal ground for it.[92]

A second arbitrary limitation of 'termination of life' is also often made: administration of drugs whose proper use is to relieve pain or symptoms in a manner likely to shorten the patient's life *even if their use (or the dose given) is not medically indicated under the circumstances*. Such cases are often included within the category 'termination of life' only if the doctor administers the drugs with the 'explicit intention' of causing the patient's death; the situation in which pain relief is given in greater than indicated doses and both pain relief and an earlier death are intended (sometimes called 'co-intention') is treated as unproblematic. As we

---

[89] There are, of course, forms of legal control applicable to 'normal medical practice' that are not specific to the end-of-life situation—eg, medical disciplinary law and civil liability for medical malpractice.

[90] See GB&W: para 2.3.1, 3.1.1.

[91] The adjectives 'active' and 'intentional' are often affixed to the concept 'termination of life'. For reasons set forth hereunder, they are unnecessary and misleading.

[92] See for such a limited definition see Gezondheidsraad 2007: 13 ('termination of life is causing or hastening death by administering a drug with the purpose of shortening life'). Compare for criticism of such a narrow approach Otlowski 2000; Bosshard *et al* 2006: 325. Leenen (1977: 80) early on defined 'euthanasia' in terms of an 'action (or omission)'. The point is probably largely theoretical, since in practice in most cases of abstention there will either be a refusal by the patient or his representative, or a legitimate decision by the doctor that further treatment would be 'futile'. Nevertheless, it is not only from the point of view of systematic legal analysis that it is important to insist on the possibility of termination of life by omission. From the standpoint of adequate legal control, it is unnerving to see how casually all forms of withholding or withdrawing treatment are relegated to 'normal medical behaviour' that can be reported as a 'natural death'. In the reports of the national surveys of 1990, 1995, 2001 and 2005, eg, abstention with the explicit purpose of shortening the patient's life is, without any critical reflection, treated as normal medical behaviour (see ch 5.1.2.2).

have already seen in section 4.2.2.3, such a position is inconsistent with existing legal doctrine. The State Commission on Euthanasia stated emphatically in its report of 1985—a report that for the first time officially defined the difference between 'termination of life' and other forms of medical behaviour that shortens life—that if in a concrete case there is no medical indication for pain relief, or the indicated dose is exceeded, or there was an available medical alternative, then what is involved is 'termination of life'.[93]

These considerations lead to the conclusion that the legal definition of 'termination of life' is as given in Box 4.4. 'Termination of life', so defined, falls outside the scope of the 'medical exception', which means that it in principle amounts to homicide. Its legal treatment depends largely, in Dutch law, on whether it is done at the patient's request or not. If so, it will be euthanasia or physician-assisted suicide (legal if done by a doctor who follows the requirements of due care); if pursuant to a refusal of treatment by the patient or his representative termination of life is simply legal. If not requested, it is murder or manslaughter, subject possibly to a defence of justification (see section 4.2.3.5).

Box 4.4 The legal definition of 'termination of life'

'Termination of life' is behaviour:

- that *causes the death* of the patient;
- and that is *intentional* in the legal sense, that is to say, done with knowledge and acceptance[94] of the foreseeable lethal effect—in other words, not accidental;
- and that involves *administration* of a drug[95]

  - that (in the dose given) is *not medically indicated to relieve the patient's suffering*;
  - or for which there is a *medically responsible alternative*;

- or that involves *withholding or withdrawing treatment* that

  - is *not medically futile*;
  - and has *not been rejected* by the patient or his representative.

In the following sections (4.2.3.1 through 4.2.3.5) we discuss the legal status of the various forms of 'termination of life'. We begin with the definition of 'euthanasia' and the treatment of euthanasia and physician-assisted suicide in the Penal Code (4.2.3.1). Then, in section 4.2.3.2 we deal with their legal status before the Law of 2002. Section 4.2.3.3 is the heart of this chapter: it deals at length with the law as it is since 2002. Then, in section 4.2.3.4 we treat the special problems of physician-assisted suicide in the absence of somatically-based suffering. And in section 4.2.3.5 we look at the legal situation of termination of life without a request.

---

[93] Staatscommissie Euthanasie 1985: 77. See more recently, Gezondheidsraad 2007: 8.

[94] See Machielse 2004: 155–60 for the requirement of acceptance of consequences in Dutch law.

[95] Other theoretically possible ways of ending a patient's life (eg the 'plastic bag' method) need not be considered, because they would presumably not be considered 'medical' behaviour at all.

4.2.3.1 Euthanasia and PAS

Article 293 of the Dutch Penal Code provides that a 'person who takes the life of another person at that other person's express and earnest request' is guilty of a serious offence.[96] The effect of the article is to make termination of life on request a lesser offence than murder, which it otherwise would have been. This is what is considered 'euthanasia' in the Netherlands.

In the past—and to this day in many other countries[97]—the term 'euthanasia' covered all of what we in this book refer to 'medical behaviour that potentially shortens life' (MBPSL), as shown in Box 4.5.

Box 4.5 Outdated subdivisions of 'euthanasia'

- 'passive euthanasia' (withdrawing and withholding life-prolonging treatment)
- 'indirect euthanasia' (administering potentially life-shortening pain relief)
- 'non voluntary euthanasia' (termination of life without an explicit request from the patient)
- 'voluntary, active euthanasia'

In the Netherlands, only 'voluntary, active euthanasia' is now considered 'euthanasia' properly speaking. The others have been given distinct names and are considered legally and ethically quite different from 'euthanasia'. The process of terminological clarification began in the Netherlands in the 1970s. In 1977 the prominent medical law scholar Leenen proposed what became the official definition of euthanasia, and this was adopted in the report of the State Commission on Euthanasia in 1985.[98] In more recent years, the Dutch definition of euthanasia has become the standard in the international literature and it can be considered an important Dutch contribution to an ethical, legal and public policy debate free from Babylonian confusion.

Euthanasia, whether or not by a doctor, was on its face illegal in the Netherlands until article 293 was amended by the Law of 2002. However, the Supreme Court had held in the *Schoonheim* case in 1984 that euthanasia by a doctor can, under specific conditions, be legally justifiable.[99]

Killing a person *without* his 'express and earnest request' (non-voluntary termination of life), when done by a doctor, may or may not be justifiable, but it is not 'euthanasia'. It is known in the Dutch discussion as 'termination of life without an explicit request'. Prosecutions in such cases (a number of which will be considered later on in this chapter) are generally for murder.

---

[96] In Dutch: 'Hij die opzettelijk het leven van een ander op diens uitdrukkelijk en ernstig verlangen beëindigt . . .'.

[97] See eg Switzerland, described in ch 16.

[98] For this terminological history, see GB&W ch 2.3.2.

[99] See GB&W: 62–3 for discussion of the Supreme Court's decision in *Schoonheim*; in the appendix of GB&W (322*ff*.) there is a translation of the decision into English.

Assistance with suicide, by contrast with euthanasia, would never have been an offence at all but for article 294 of the Penal Code, since suicide itself is not an offence. Article 294(2) provides that a person who 'intentionally assists in the suicide of another, or procures for that other person the means to commit suicide'[100] is guilty of a serious offence if the suicide takes place. Nevertheless, despite their separate histories and their distinct treatment in the Penal Code, and the fact that euthanasia carries a heavier maximum penalty,[101] Dutch law generally makes no distinction between the two as far as their justifiability is concerned. As noted earlier, in this book we often use the term 'euthanasia' for both except where the difference is relevant.

4.2.3.2 The Legal Status of Euthanasia and PAS before the Law of 2002

The Supreme Court's decision in the *Schoonheim* case—which effectively made euthanasia by a doctor legal, subject to what later came to be called 'requirements of due care'—was based on the defence of justification due to necessity, as provided for in Article 40 of the Penal Code.[102] Article 40 provides that an actor is not guilty of an offence if it was 'the result of a force he could not be expected to resist [*overmacht*]'. Since 1923 this provision had been interpreted to include the defence that the act took place in a situation of necessity in which the actor made a justifiable choice between two conflicting duties. Based on this existing doctrine, the Supreme Court held in *Schoonheim* that a doctor, confronted by the request of a patient who is unbearably and hopelessly suffering, can be regarded as caught in a situation of conflict of duties. On the one hand, there is the duty to respect life, as reflected in articles 293 and 294 of the Penal Code. On the other hand, there is the doctor's duty to relieve suffering.[103] If, in such a situation of conflict of duties, the doctor chooses a course of action that, considering the norms of medical ethics, is 'objectively' justifiable, he is not guilty of an offence, the Supreme Court held.

The requirements of a substantive and of a procedural character[104] that must be

---

[100] In Dutch: 'Hij die opzettelijk een ander bij zelfdoding behulpzaam is of hem de middelen daartoe verschaft . . .'.

[101] Twelve as against three years (see GB&W: 307–08).

[102] Confusingly, both the justification of necessity (conflict of duties) and the excuse of duress are based on article 40, which on its face seems only to deal with duress in the sense of an excuse.

[103] The exact formulation of the conflicting duties on which the justification of necessity rests has taken different forms, of which an important earlier one was the idea that it is a duty to respect the autonomy of the patient that conflicts with the duty to respect life (see GB&W: 171 n 41). Den Hartogh (1996) rejects such an idea because, he argues, a duty to respect the autonomy of the patient can never result in a conflict of duties, since 'the duties that correspond to the principle of autonomy are all negative duties, duties of a non-interfering nature, none of them requires provision of positive help'. See also Bood 1998: 187 n 71 (beneficence qualified by the requirement of a request is more intrinsically consistent than autonomy qualified by the requirement of suffering would be). The Supreme Court in the *Chabot* case (see section 4.2.3.4(A)) specifically referred to the doctor's duty to relieve 'unbearable suffering with no prospect of improvement' (see GB&W: 333) and it is this characterisation that ultimately found its way into the Law of 2002.

[104] In what follows, we distinguish analytically between the conditions that must be fulfilled before the defence of justification can be honoured (substantive requirements), and the legal requirements applicable to carrying out euthanasia that is in principle lawful (procedural requirements). Unfortunately, this

met by a doctor who carries out euthanasia or gives assistance with suicide became fairly clear in the years following the *Schoonheim* decision. Some of these were formulated by the courts in the context of criminal prosecutions, others in a variety of other legal sources, in particular the reports and position-papers of various organs of the medical profession.[105] The following 'requirements of due care' [*zorgvuldigheidseisen*][106] came to be generally accepted.

4.2.3.2(A) Substantive Requirements

The essential substantive conditions of legal euthanasia concerned the patient's request, the patient's suffering, and the doctor–patient relationship (see Box 4.6).[107]
Absent a request, the behaviour concerned does not fall under article 293 of the Penal Code at all and would therefore not be euthanasia but murder. The requirement of a voluntary and well-considered request is also a variant of the general requirement of informed consent required in the case of a competent patient for all medical treatment. If there is a difference in the case of euthanasia, it lies in the oft-heard suggestion that in general the initiative should come from the patient himself, whereas in other cases the doctor could suggest and even recommend a given course of action.[108]

It was not clear to what extent anticipation of a fate one does not want to undergo (eg confinement to a nursing home, or further mental deterioration) could by itself meet the requirement of unbearable suffering, nor whether euthanasia could be carried out on a demented patient who is not currently suffering from the dementia but who in an earlier advance directive requested it in such circumstances.[109]

---

distinction was not clearly made in the period before the Law of 2002, and the drafters of the Law, as we will see, essentially ignored it, at the cost of fundamental confusion about the status of the two sorts of requirements, a situation the Regional Review Committees and the prosecutorial authorities are gradually and delicately seeking to remedy (see further sections 4.2.3.3 and 4.2.4.2 below).

[105] See GB&W: ch 3.1.3 for details.

[106] In the predecessor to this book (GB&W: 8) *zorgvuldigheidseisen* was translated as 'requirements of careful practice' because we thought the association, for an English reader, of 'due care' with the law of tort potentially misleading. We choose now for conformity with the official translation of the Law of 2002.

[107] Before the Law of 2002 there seem to have been no explicit formulations of age limitations, and there are indications that euthanasia may have been practiced in the case of minors (see GB&W: 114 n 81). If the issue had been raised, the general legal rules on decision-making competence would presumably have applied, together with the specific rules in the Law on Contracts for Medical Care of 1995 (which distinguishes between children younger than 12, who are represented by their parents, minors 12–16, whose consent is required for medical treatment but whose parents must in principle also give consent, and minors 16 and older who are treated as independently competent to make medical decisions for themselves).

[108] From time to time, however, one sees suggestions that a conscientious doctor may make a patient aware of the possibility of euthanasia. Thus, eg, Van der Wal and Van der Maas (1996: 174) report the opinion of about half of all doctors that there are 'certain situations in which it is appropriate for the doctor to introduce the possibility of euthanasia'.

[109] This question is explicitly dealt with in the Law of 2002—see section 4.2.3.3(B) below.

Box 4.6 Substantive requirements for legal euthanasia before the Law of 2002

---

1. *The patient's request must, in the terms of article 293, be 'express and earnest'.*

The request requirement was further operationalised as follows:

- the request must be explicitly made by the person concerned;
- the request must be voluntary (competent and not the result of undue external influence);
- the request must be well-considered: informed, made after due deliberation and based on an enduring desire for the end of life (evidenced for instance by its having repeatedly been made over some period of time);
- the request should preferably be in writing or otherwise recorded.

2. *The patient's suffering must be 'unbearable' [ondraaglijk] and 'hopeless' [uitzichtloos]* (in the sense of 'without prospect of improvement').[110]

This requirement was further operationalised as follows:

- the suffering need not be physical (pain etc) nor is a somatic basis required; non-physical suffering can include such things as the prospect of personal deterioration [*ontluistering*] and of not being able to die in a 'dignified' way;[111]
- if the patient's suffering is based on a somatic condition, other possibilities[112] for treating the condition or relieving the suffering must have been exhausted or have been rejected by the patient;[113]
- if the patient's suffering is based on a non-somatic condition, there must be no realistic possibility of treatment.[114]

3. *Only a doctor may legally perform euthanasia.*[115] In principle this should be a doctor who has an established treatment-relationship with the patient [*behandelend arts*].[116]

---

[110] On the whole, these were treated together as a single requirement, and the patient's subjective experience of his suffering was regarded as largely determinative (although it had to be 'understandable'). In 1995 the Committee of Procurators-General proposed to 'objectify' the suffering requirement by separating the two components, but the Minister of Justice refused to allow this (see GB&W: ch 5.3.5). Thanks to the Regional Review Committees it is now clear that there are two distinct requirements (see 4.2.3.3(C)).

[111] See eg the decision of the Supreme Court in the *Schoonheim* case (GB&W: 328); compare the recent formulation in the prosecutorial Guideline for euthanasia cases (n 168).

[112] See GB&W: 150 fn 192 for the suggestion that these are not necessarily limited to *medical* possibilities.

[113] Leenen 2000: 345 (suggesting that if the alternative is a fairly minor treatment that most people would accept, refusing it might stand in the way of euthanasia).

[114] See GB&W: ch 3.5.1 and the decision of the Supreme Court in the *Chabot* case on the question of refusal of treatment in the case of non-somatically based suffering.

[115] GB&W: 103 and n 40.

[116] GB&W: 103 and n 41. The requirement was perhaps even less clear than the words 'in principle' here and in the predecessor of this book suggest. From a series of criminal and disciplinary cases in the first half of the 1990s Weyers (2004: 361) concludes that it had become clear 'that the doctor who performs euthanasia does not necessarily have to be the doctor who has a long-standing treatment relationship with the patient'. In its Guideline of 1995, the KNMG took the position that a patient may change doctor shortly before euthanasia for a variety of reasons (the wish to die at home, lack of confidence in his doctor) and that the 'doctor who takes over the treatment relationship must take the time to get to know the patient well enough to be able to judge whether the requirements of due care have been met'; a few days is in any case too little. (KNMG 1995: 15)

The Medical Association's position from the early 1990s has been that nurses should not be involved in the actual administration of euthanatica.[117] The courts have held in no uncertain terms that a nurse may not administer euthanatica, even under the direct supervision of the responsible doctor.[118] No individual doctor is under an obligation to perform euthanasia, but a doctor who is conscientiously opposed should cooperate in the transfer of the patient to another doctor.[119]

Until the Supreme Court's decision in the *Chabot* case (1994)[120] it was sometimes supposed that the patient must be in the 'terminal phase' of his illness, although the Medical Association had since 1984 rejected such a requirement as medically meaningless, and the lower courts had rejected it from the very beginning.[121] The Supreme Court's decision in the *Chabot* case also made clear that the patient's suffering need not have a somatic origin, so that a psychiatric patient capable of a competent and voluntary request could receive assistance in suicide. More recently the Supreme Court held in the *Brongersma* case that the suffering must be based on a 'medically-classifiable' disease or condition.[122]

A final substantive requirement that was sometimes suggested but appears never to have been accorded any formal recognition was that euthanasia should not be performed if the patient is receiving life-prolonging treatment that has not yet been discontinued. In other words, abstinence should have priority over administration of euthanatica.[123] The idea is essentially the same as the 'priority principle' that has been proposed in the case of termination of life without an explicit request (comatose patients, newborn babies, etc.)[124]

4.2.3.2(B) Procedural Requirements

In addition to the substantive conditions of legal euthanasia, the doctor who performed it had to meet a number of procedural requirements, as shown on Box 4.7.[125] All of these will be treated more fully in connection with the Law of 2002.

---

[117] KNMG 2003: 10. In earlier guidelines, an exception was made for the situation in which the method used (as was frequently the case in the past) takes a considerable amount of time (KNMG 1992).

[118] See GB&W 103 n 40, 108–9.

[119] GB&W: 108.

[120] *Nederlandse Jurisprudentie* 1994, no 656 (see GB&W: 329–38 for an English translation and notes; 80–82, 149–51 for historical and legal context).

[121] See GB&W: 103; Leenen 2000: 345. In 2003 the Medical Association reaffirmed its rejection of the 'terminal phase' as a requirement for euthanasia (KNMG 2003: 14). The prosecutorial Guideline of 2007 (n 353) is explicit that there is no such requirement.

[122] See section 4.2.3.4 below.

[123] Compare KNMG 1975: 11; see the similar suggestion in Zwaveling 1994.

[124] See ch 6.

[125] See for more detail GB&W: 104–7.

Box 4.7 Procedural requirements for legal euthanasia before the Law of 2002

---

1. *Consultation*

The patient's doctor must consult at least one other doctor with respect to the patient's condition and life-expectancy, the available alternatives, and the adequacy of the request (voluntary, well-considered, etc.). The following requirements applied to consultation:

- the consultant should be 'independent' (not a subordinate, a member of a joint practice, a colleague in a group practice of specialists, or a doctor involved in the treatment of the patient);
- the consultation should be timely (not too long before, nor too close upon, the actual carrying out of euthanasia);[126]
- in the case of a patient apparently suffering from a psychiatric disorder the consulted doctor should be a psychiatrist;
- if the patient's suffering is of non-somatic origin, the consultant must himself examine the patient, and in other cases he should do so;
- the consultant should make a written report, that becomes part of the medical dossier of the patient.

(See further, section 4.2.3.3(E).)

2. *Carrying Out Euthanasia or Assisted Suicide*

The termination of life should be carried out in a professionally responsible way (including use of appropriate euthanatica) and the doctor should stay with the patient continuously[127] (except possibly, for good reasons, in the case of assistance with suicide; in such a case, careful arrangements must be made, including the continuous availability of the doctor in case of need) (see further, section 4.2.3.3(F)).

3. *Record-Keeping*

The doctor should keep a full written record of the case (including information covering the above elements) (see further, section 4.2.3.3.(F)).[128]

4. *Reporting*

Death due to euthanasia may not be reported as a 'natural death' (see further, section 4.2.4.1).

---

[126] In 1997 a general practitioner made public his irritation with the Medical Inspectorate, which was investigating a case in which the consultation took place two months before euthanasia was carried out, and hence before the patient's suffering had become unbearable. The doctor vigorously defended the practice of early consultation when the patient is still capable of discussing his situation with the consultant. See 'Open letter to the Medical Inspector, South Holland,' *Medisch Contact* 52: 776–7 (1997). The PGs decided not to bring a prosecution and the Medical Inspector took no further action (information received from the doctor concerned). Recent decisions of the Regional Review Committees have clarified the matter considerably (see section 4.2.3.3(E) below, under *timing*).

[127] See Leenen 2000: 346, referring to a disciplinary case in which the Tribunal had been of the opinion that the doctor must maintain control over the euthanaticum until the moment of administration.

[128] Under the Law on Contracts for Medical Care, doctors are generally required to maintain proper medical records (see Sluijters & Biesaart 2005: 65*ff.*) Before the Law of 2002, maintaining a full and accurate record surrounding euthanasia in the patient's dossier was one of the requirements of due care. (For a criminal conviction in 1997 in which inadequate record-keeping was one of the failures of which the doctor was accused, see GB&W 106 n 56.)

From time to time it was suggested that the doctor should discuss the patient's request with the immediate family and intimate friends [*naasten*] of the patient (unless the patient did not want this or there were other good reasons for not doing so) and also with nurses responsible for the patient's care.[129] The legal status of such requirements was not clear, although both before and after the Law of 2002 questions about both were asked on the model form for reporting.[130]

4.2.3.2(C) Enforcement

If the above requirements for the legally permissible performance of euthanasia had become clear in the almost 20 years following on the *Schoonheim* case, there was less clarity over how, exactly, they were to be enforced. The substantive requirements for justifiable euthanasia were enforced through the criminal law: if the euthanasia was not performed by a doctor, or there was no voluntary and well-considered request, or the patient's suffering was not unbearable and hopeless, the justification of necessity was not available.

A doctor's failure to conform with the 'procedural' requirements, by contrast, did not in itself stand in the way of an appeal to the justification of necessity.[131] This was sensible, since it would be disproportionate to convict a doctor for homicide when the euthanasia itself was otherwise unobjectionable and what he was really accused of was inadequate consultation, record-keeping or the like. However, in a case of multiple violations of these requirements the courts might hold that the defence of justification was not available.[132] The requirement of reporting was enforced with some regularity in prosecutions for filing a false certificate of a 'natural death'.[133] The other procedural requirements could be enforced in medical disciplinary proceedings, although it seems the Medical Inspectorate was not very active in doing so.

4.2.3.3 Euthanasia and PAS under the Law of 2002

Since 2002, the substantive and procedural conditions under which euthanasia can be legally performed are governed by the the Termination of Life on Request and Assisted Suicide (Review Procedures) Act (the 'Law of 2002') which entered into force on 1 April 2002. The law consists of three parts. The first codifies the 'requirements of due care' and makes the Regional Review Committees principally responsible for reviewing reported cases.[134] The second amends articles 293

---

[129] See GB&W 106; for the Medical Association's most recent formulation, see section 4.2.3.3(F).

[130] On this model form, see section 4.2.4.1.

[131] See GB&W: 107. The prosecutorial authorities currently take the same position under the Law of 2002 (see section 4.2.4.2).

[132] See GB&W: 107 n 58.

[133] See Weyers 2004: 282, 362, 379.

[134] The responsibility of the prosecutorial authorities is limited to cases in which the Regional Review Committees have found the doctor 'not careful'. Cases held by the committees to be outside their jurisdiction due to the absence of a valid request or because they consider what the doctor did to be 'normal medical practice', as well as cases that come to their attention in some other way than via the report of a doctor (eg from another doctor, a nurse, the manager of an institution, etc) are dealt with directly by the prosecutorial authorities.

(euthanasia) and 294 (assisted suicide) of the Penal Code to make euthanasia and assisted suicide legal if performed by a doctor who has conformed to the requirements of due care and has reported what he did to the municipal pathologist. And the third part amends the Burial and Cremation Law to provide for the forms and the procedure to be used in reporting a case of euthanasia or assisted suicide.[135]

On the whole, the changes in existing euthanasia law introduced by the Law of 2002 and by case law of the past decade concern only matters of detail (so that unless otherwise indicated the law summarised in the previous section, and more fully in the predecessor of this book, remains valid). The most important changes concern the system of control (which will be dealt with in section 4.2.4).

4.2.3.3(A) The Substantive Grounds and Procedural Requirements

Since the statutory legalisation of euthanasia and physician-assisted suicide takes the form of amendments to articles 293 and 294 of the Penal Code, it is only behaviour prohibited by those articles that, under specified conditions, is made legal. Behaviour that does not amount to 'taking life' or that is not pursuant to an 'express and earnest request', or that does not amount to 'intentionally assisting' or 'procuring the means' (or that does not in fact result in 'suicide') is not affected by the Law of 2002.

The amended sections 293 and 294 provide that the behaviour otherwise prohibited does not constitute an offence 'if it is committed by a physician[136] who fulfils the requirements of due care' set forth in the law *and* the doctor notifies the municipal pathologist in accordance with the procedure set forth in the Burial and Cremation Law as amended. The latter condition is an ill-considered departure from the law previous to the Law of 2002, the courts having consistently held that while filing a false certificate of 'natural death' is in itself a criminal offence, this did not stand in the way of the defence of justification for euthanasia.[137] See section 4.2.4.2 below for the way Dutch prosecutors have dealt with this piece of poor legislative judgment.

For adult patients (18 years or over—minors are dealt with separately below) the statutory 'requirements of due care' (see Box 4.8) are in two respects different from those that applied before the Law of 2002. Both are due to the legislator's failure to distinguish between substantive and procedural requirements.[138] Two

---

[135] In art 22, the Law also makes a technical amendment to art 1.6 of the General Administrative Law, adding 'decisions and actions in the implementation' of the law to a list of matters not covered by the general administrative appeals procedure (the requirement that every public agency have a complaints procedure, however, does apply).

[136] There is no statutory requirement that the doctor be the 'doctor responsible for treatment' [*behandelend arts*]. While acknowledging that there is no (longer) any such formal requirement, the Regional Review Committees have dealt with this apparent oversight in a creative way—see section 4.2.3.3(D) below.

[137] See section 4.2.3.2(C). The effect of the change means that a procedural failure—which in some cases may well be a mistake in classification of the behaviour involved (see Van Tol 2005)—entails liability for a serious criminal offence.

[138] See section 4.2.3.2 above for this distinction.

procedural requirements (consultation and, as just noted, reporting)—which until 2002 were not prerequisites to a successful appeal to the defence of justification—have become a statutory sine qua non for the statutory defence.[139] And a number of other procedural requirements (record-keeping, discussion with nurses and family/intimate friends) seem to have fallen unnoticed by the wayside.[140]

Box 4.8 The conditions of legal euthanasia by a doctor under the Law of 2002

- the patient's request was 'voluntary and carefully considered'[141]
- the 'patient's suffering was unbearable, and . . . there was no prospect of improvement'[142]
- the doctor informed the patient concerning 'his situation and his prospects'
- the doctor and the patient were convinced that there was 'no reasonable alternative in light of the patient's situation'
- the doctor consulted 'at least one other, independent physician who must have seen the patient and given a written opinion on the due care criteria [ie the preceding four items]'
- the doctor 'terminated the patient's life or provided assistance with suicide with due medical care and attention'
- the doctor reported the case to the municipal pathologist[143]

---

[139] It remains, of course, possible that the courts will allow an appeal to the defence of necessity to a charge of euthanasia in a case in which the doctor does not meet the criteria for the statutory defence (because of a failure properly to consult or to report)—the prosecutorial authorities invoke this idea in connection with their policy of not prosecuting in such a case (see section 4.2.4.2). The Regional Review Committees are also interpreting the statutory requirements in a flexible way. Thus, eg, a 'necessity' exception to the statutory requirement of consultation has been allowed (see section 4.2.3.3 (E)). In such indirect ways, the legislative mistake is being corrected in practice.

[140] See, however, section 4.2.3.3(F).

[141] In Dutch: '*vrijwillig en weloverwogen verzoek*'. This and the following requirement is formulated in a peculiar way: the doctor must 'be satisfied that' [*'de overtuiging heeft gekregen dat'*] the request and the suffering meet the required test. Since a person is in any event only responsible for what he can reasonably be expected to know, the expression seems to have no function (similar expressions were sometimes found in formulations of the requirements of due care antedating the law—see GB&W: 104). But see n 240 for a possible function of the expression.

[142] In Dutch: '*uitzichtloos en ondraaglijk lijden van de patiënt*'. In the past, as we saw above (section 4.2.3.2(A)) it was not clear that the expression '*uitzichtloos en ondraaglijk lijden*' implies two distinct tests, as the English translation seems to assume. As we will see below (section 4.2.3.3(C)), the Regional Review Committees have taken the position that two tests are involved.

[143] This requirement, as well as an explicit limitation to doctors, is not included among the requirements of due care in art 2 of the statute, to which the amended arts 293 and 294 of the Penal Code refer, but directly in the Penal Code itself. In earlier legislative proposals the duty to report had been included among the requirements of due care (see Weyers 2004: 390–91). Separating the duty to report from the rest of the conditions of legal euthanasia was a conscious choice made in the private member's bill that later became the Government bill and ultimately the Law of 2002; the choice was motivated by the thought that making reporting a condition of the statutory offence would contribute to improving the disappointing reporting rate (see *Second Chamber of Parliament 1997–1998*, 26 000 no 3: 9).

Interestingly, the oft-supposed (and as often rejected) requirement that the patient be in the 'terminal phase' (or that the illness be a 'terminal' one) is not included in the statute. Nor is there any restriction to suffering of 'somatic' origin.[144]

Since the precursor of this book was published in 1998, almost ten years of practical experience with implementation of the requirements of due care, and in particular the decisions of the Regional Review Committees, have further clarified the criteria for legal euthanasia. The most important developments are discussed on the following pages. It should be emphasised that we deal here only with legal requirements specific to euthanasia. A doctor who performs (or considers performing) euthanasia is also subject to a variety of other legal rules, in particular the civil obligations in the Law on Contracts for Medical Care, of which the most general norm is that he (and other caregivers such as nurses) must act as a 'good caregiver' and in conformity with the 'professional standard'. The Law on Contracts for Medical Care also covers matters such as informed consent, privacy and confidentiality, representation of non-competent patients, record-keeping, and so forth.[145]

4.2.3.3(B) A 'Voluntary and Carefully Considered' Request[146]

Written Request

Although not formally required, a preference for written (or recorded or witnessed) requests can be found throughout the literature, case law, various reports

---

[144] See section 4.2.3.2(A) above for the earlier history of these supposed requirements. The Medical Association recently restated its position, dating back to 1984, that a requirement that the patient's illness be 'terminal' would be impossible to apply in medical practice; it also reiterated its position that no distinction can be made between 'somatic' and 'psychic' suffering (KNMG 2003: 14).

[145] See Legemaate 2005 for an exhaustive survey of the various legal rules that bear on a doctor in connection with euthanasia.

[146] From time to time, an additional requirement—that the request be 'lasting' [*duurzaam*] and 'repeated'—has been suggested (see eg the Order in Council of 17 December 1993 prescribing the form to be used in reporting a case of euthanasia, in GB&W: 311; art 9 and accompanying explanation, Order in Council establishing the Regional Review Committees, 27 May 1998, *Staatscourant* 1998 no 101, included as appendix to the committee's Annual Reports through 2001). In the parliamentary proceedings leading up to the Law of 2002, such a requirement was first included among the requirements of due care (Weyers 2004: 391) but later removed as unnecessary given the requirement that the request be 'well considered' (*ibid* at 395). In the Annual Reports for 1998/99 through 2001, the Regional Review Committees refer to such a requirement. A specific requirement that the request be 'lasting' disappears from 2002 onward in the Annual Reports. In 2002 the committees suggest *en passant* that a request should be 'repeatedly expressed' (RRC 2002: 22). The suggestion is not repeated in later Annual Reports and seems to be unfounded, although repetition in many cases will be good evidence that a request is 'well considered' and not a passing thought (see eg the cases of patients with progressive dementia, RRC 2005: 16, case 4; RRC 2006: 18–19, case 3, in which the fact that the request had been regularly repeated played an important part in the conclusion that it was well considered). The Medical Association notes that repetition is not a 'strict requirement' but that it generally speaking is good practice for a doctor to have the patient repeat his request (KNMG 2003: 13). The prosecutorial Guideline of 2007 (see n 353) refers to a 'consistent (lasting, repeated) request', which is perhaps innocent, but rather confusing considering the prior history noted above.

of the medical profession, legislative instruments and so forth.[147] As a form of self-protection, a doctor is obviously well-advised to insist on requests that can be documented afterwards, and the control system cannot function effectively without them.[148] The Regional Review Committees regularly emphasise the importance of a written or otherwise documented request (and note that in practically all the cases they see, a written request is in fact present).[149] The committees have repeatedly expressed a preference for a request written by the patient in his own words over the use of printed forms.[150]

Timely Request

Although there is no explicit statutory requirement to such an effect, the Regional Review Committees are of the view that a concrete request should generally be made some time before the euthanasia is carried out. A very short period between the first concrete request and carrying out euthanasia—even 'less than a day'—is only acceptable in exceptional circumstances of 'unexpected acute necessity'.[151] The committees observe that in some cases a doctor waits until just before carrying out euthanasia to ask the patient to 'sign the form' and that it is preferable to have the patient prepare his written request at an earlier time when he is not so sick as to be barely capable of writing.[152] On the other hand, the time interval ought not to be as long as 'several weeks'.[153] 'Conditional' requests made sometimes years before (for example, when the form distributed by the Voluntary Euthanasia Association is used) should be reconfirmed shortly before euthanasia is carried out and made concretely applicable to the situation the patient is in, so that it is certain that he wanted euthanasia in this specific situation. In such a case, the request can be considered very well-considered.[154]

Well-Informed Request

The doctor is required to inform the patient fully about his situation, the prognosis, and the possibilities of curative or palliative treatment. This follows both from the general requirement of 'informed consent' to any medical treatment and from

---

[147] See GB&W: 101; KNMG 2003: 13 (not required, but advisable; audio or video recording an alternative). The prosecutorial Guideline (see n 353) observes that the Law of 2002 does not require a written request.

[148] Cases in which a court has had to rely solely on the word of the doctor to the effect that a request was ever made have in fact occurred in the past (see the *Schat* case, District Court, Leeuwarden, 8 April 1997).

[149] See eg RRC 2001: 16; RRC 2006: 17. In the 2004 Annual Report the Regional Review Committees explicitly note that a written request is not legally required (RRC 2004: 14). The case reports for 2006–07 on the committees' internet site as of 26 November 2007 (see n 393) show only 6 of 525 cases in which the request is not explicitly stated to have been in writing.

[150] Eg RRC 2005: 15; RRC 2000: 16–17.

[151] RRC 2001: 17; RRC 2002: 22 (ditto—under heading 'well-considered request').

[152] Eg RRC: 2000: 15.

[153] RRC 2002: 22.

[154] RRC 2000: 16 (see also *ibid* at 14, case 3).

the specific requirement of due care that the patient's request be well informed. The Regional Review Committees regularly emphasise the importance of full and open communication between doctor and patient, carried out where possible over a longer period of time. In their 2006 Annual Report, the committees note that in practice the requirement does not give rise to problems.[155]

Request Not Under Pressure

The Regional Review Committees interpret the requirement that the request be 'voluntary', as it has been in the past, as referring to the absence of external pressure, whether real or imagined by the patient. Concern about being a burden on one's family is often mentioned in this connection.[156] And patients' families are sometimes suspected of putting the patient (or the doctor) under pressure to 'put an end to the situation'.[157]

Request Not the Result of Impaired Capacity

Cognitive or communicative impairment or the existence of a psychiatric disorder does not necessarily preclude a 'voluntary and well-considered request'.[158] In case of doubt, a psychiatric consultation is generally required.[159] Dementia, the

---

[155] RRC 2006: 22.

[156] Eg KNMG 2003: 12. It is not clear why such a normal, perfectly rational and generous concern should be as suspect as it often seems to be (the legal test being whether the request is voluntary, not whether—apart from unbearable suffering—the patient's reasons for making it fit into a modern individualistic ideology).

[157] Eg RRC 2001: 17; 2003: 17 (case 6—doctor believed there was some pressure from the patient's parents but, in the circumstances, did not regard this has having disturbed the decision-making process—'careful'). Compare KNMG 2003: 12–13 (external pressure or fear of being a burden to others); NVP 2004: 18 (ditto; requirement can sometimes be satisfied despite diminished voluntariness).

[158] RRC 2001: 16 (case 4—communicative impairment and degenerative brain disease; two psychiatric consultants consider patient competent—'careful'); RRC 2003: 22 (case 9—elderly patient with metastasised melanoma; suffers from depressivity and fear of increased pain; refuses (further) antidepressives; general euthanasia request antedates the cancer and has been brought up to date; repeated verbal requests before onset of depression; consultant agrees that request is voluntary and well-considered—'careful'); RRC 2003: 16 (case 5—patient suffers unbearably over many years from recurrent serious psychiatric disorders, and in periods of remission repeatedly requests assistance in suicide; psychiatric consultant agrees that patient is competent and his suffering unbearable—'careful'); RRC 2006: 17–18 (case 2—extra psychiatric consultation in case of depressive patient—'careful').

The Netherlands Association for Psychiatry (NVP 2004: 19) suggests a number of tests for the competence of a patient with a psychiatric disorder:

(a) The patient makes a clear choice for death.
(b) He has considered on the one hand a choice for going on living, possibly subject to permanent restrictions as a result of his psychiatric disorder, and on the other hand a choice for suicide, and within the limits of his intellectual abilities can give reasons for his choice for death.
(c) His desire for death is lasting.

[159] The Medical Association's 2003 Guideline provides that if there is reason to suppose that the request may be influenced by the patient's psychiatric condition, a psychiatrist must be consulted (KNMG 2003: 15). The Netherlands Association for Psychiatry notes without comment that in only 3% of all cases of euthanasia is a psychiatrist consulted; it regards such consultation as particularly relevant in the case of non-terminal patients (NVP 2004: 39). See the cases described in n 158, and RRC 2005: 16 (case 4—psychiatric consultation because of doubts concerning the mental capacity of the patient—'careful').

committees observe repeatedly,[160] will generally make fulfilment of the requirements of due care impossible, but it does not entirely preclude euthanasia, since
the patient may have made a written request before becoming incompetent or, if
in the early stages, may still be capable of a well-considered request.[161]

Euthanasia Pursuant to an Advance Written Request[162]

The Law of 2002 makes for the first time explicit that an advance written request
for euthanasia, made by a patient of 16 or older who is currently not competent
but who was competent at the time he made the written request, can satisfy the
requirement of a voluntary request. As with advance treatment directives, there
are no formal requirements such a written request must meet nor are there any
(time) limits on its continued validity.[163] It is widely supposed that this recognition of written requests is largely an empty gesture, especially in the case of patients
with dementia, for whom it was largely intended, since the other requirements of
due care have to be met, one of which is 'unbearable suffering'. Severely demented
persons are believed generally not to suffer from their dreadful condition[164]
and the suffering of other non-competent patients can, it is often supposed, be
adequately dealt with by pain relief and sedation.

   Whatever the case may be as far as patients with dementia is concerned, it would
have been dangerous not to include such a provision for written requests in the

---

   [160] Eg RRC 2005: 9; RRC 2006: 16.
   [161] RRC 2004: 15 (case 3—Alzheimers disease; doctor could come to the conclusion that patient was
competent—'careful'); RRC 2005: 16 (case 4—voluntary, well-considered request can exist in cases of
dementia –'careful'); RRC 2006: 16 (early dementia requires consultation of experts in addition to the
legally required consultant—see for an example pp 18–21, case 3/4, in which two psychiatrists who had
treated the patient supported her request); RRCj 2006, cases 13831, 2421, 13265. See ch 3.5 for further
discussion of the recent public debate and a number of prosecutorial decisions not to prosecute cases
of assistance with suicide for patients with dementia. For some empirical data on such cases, see
ch 5.2.2.1.
   Keizer—nursing-home doctor, philosopher and essayist—recently recanted his earlier position that
early dementia would stand in the way of a competent request and described a case in which (as SCEN
consultant) he had agreed with the patient's doctor that all of the requirements had been met. See
Trouw (22 March 2007), <http://www.trouw.nl/deverdieping/overigeartikelen/article665764.ece/
Dement_en_doodswens_Je_moet_op_tijd_aan_de_bel_trekken> accessed 24 April 2007); he reports
that the Regional Review Committee found the consulting doctor 'careful' (this is presumably the same
case as case 3/4 of 2006, just described).
   [162] The Medical Association's Guideline of 2003 discusses a number of problems to which advance
written requests can give rise in practice, in particular related to the requirements of unbearable suffering and a fully-informed and well-considered request. The more concrete the request, the more it
can form a basis for decision-making by the doctor. It is important that while this is still possible, doctor and patient discuss the written request (KNMG 2003: 20–21).
   [163] Law of 2002, art 2.2. The Medical Association is of the view that setting a general time limit on
the validity of advance written requests would not be desirable, but observes that it is a good idea that
a request be updated from time to time, especially if the health situation of the patient changes, and
that the updating be discussed by doctor and patient (KNMG 2003: 21).
   [164] See for suggestions of the sorts of suffering that might meet the legal requirement, described by
the Ministers of Justice and of Health in their answers to questions raised during the parliamentary
debates on the Law of 2002 (*Second Chamber of Parliament 1999–2000*, 26 691, no 6, p 86): suffering
from disorders other than the dementia and 'extremely unpleasant consequences of the dementia'.

Law of 2002. Before the Law of 2002 explicitly recognised the legality of euthanasia pursuant to a prior written request by a no-longer competent patient, the Review Committees took the position that 'it is generally necessary that communication between doctor and patient continues right to the end'.[165] In practice, however, even in cases for which euthanasia is 'classically' intended (such as cancer), patients often more or less lose consciousness in the period shortly before receiving euthanasia or are no longer capable of communicating, either as a result of the medication they are receiving or from the disease itself. In their 2004 Annual Report, the committees observe that a written request made in advance makes it possible to carry out euthanasia in such a case even though the patient is no longer competent.[166]

4.2.3.3(C) 'Unbearable Suffering with No Prospect of Improvement'

The Regional Review Committees have put an end to an old controversy by emphasising that two different tests of suffering are involved: it must be *both* 'unbearable' *and* 'with no prospect of improvement'.[167]

Unbearable Suffering

Whether suffering is 'unbearable' is 'subjective', that is, it is in principle a matter of 'the patient's perspective, his personality, and his relevant norms and values'. In particular, the extent to which what are often referred to as 'increasing physical deterioration and dependency' and 'loss of dignity', or anticipated suffering (in particular from suffocation), are experienced as unbearable differs from one patient to another. In the particularly problematic case that the medical condition is not acutely fatal (eg MS, ALS, Parkinson, paraplegia, stroke, dementia), such factors can play a key role in the assessment of the unbearability of suffering for a particular patient.[168] The patient's assertion that his suffering is unbearable is subject to

---

[165] RRC 2001: 17.

[166] RRC 2004: 14. The committees note that a written request should be brought up to date regularly while the patient is still competent. See also RRC 2002: 25 (case 10, dealing principally with the requirement of unbearable suffering in a situation of possibly temporary coma, but emphasising also the patient's repeated requests for euthanasia over many years, recently specifically confirmed—'careful').

[167] See eg RRC 2002: 23. See n 108 for earlier doubts about this. The prosecutorial Guideline (n 353) is also explicit that two tests are involved. It emphasises, further, that the requirements 'leave room for the concrete circumstances of an individual case'.

[168] RRC 2002: 23–4; 2003: 19; 2004: 16. In the Annual Reports of 2004 and 2005 (RRC 2004: 16; RRC 2005: 19), the Regional Review Committees add Alzheimers disease to the group of problematic cases. Nevertheless, the patient's suffering has been found to meet the requirements in a number of cases of beginning dementia (see n 161). *Cf* also the prosecutorial Guideline (n 353):

> Suffering comprises not only pain, but also eg invalidity, immobility, (increasing) dependency, fear of suffocation, etc . . . In the *Schoonheim* case the Supreme Court accepted increasing personal deterioration and the prospect of not being able to die in a dignified way as grounds for termination of life on request.

qualification by the more 'objective' requirement that this must be 'understandable' (*invoelbaar*) to a normal doctor (and hence also the Review Committee).[169]

Suffering must be conscious. The Regional Review Committees have taken the position that, since a comatose patient is assumed not to suffer, the requirement of unbearable suffering in general cannot be met in such a case; doctors, they say, should be 'especially restrained'. But they appear to be rather accommodating in accepting things such as groaning, blinking and difficulty in breathing as indications of suffering in such a case.[170] Furthermore, the fact that a patient's coma is possibly reversible and that it would be inhumane to allow the patient to awake, can suffice to meet the requirement of unbearable suffering.[171] In a very recent, as yet unpublished judgment, however, the committees seem to take a slightly more reserved position.[172]

---

[169] See RRC 2004: 16–17, 19 (case 5—in the circumstances of the case, including the personal judgment of the doctor and the consultant that the patient was not suffering unbearably, the requirements had not been met; doctor given warning in medical disciplinary proceeding; decision not to prosecute); 2003: 19 (case 7—requirement of 'unbearable suffering' not met—'not careful'—Medical Inspector speaks to doctor, prosecutors decide not to prosecute); RRC 2000: 20 (case 9—suffering of 97-year-old woman who recently had a stroke, resulting in dependence on others and fear of reoccurrence, held not 'unbearable'; prosecutors disagree and do not prosecute); RRC 2005: 21 (case 6—multiple forms of both somatic and non-somatic suffering as result of automobile accident—Review Committee accepts judgment of doctor that patient's experience of unbearable suffering was understandable). See also the prosecutorial Guideline (n 353), which observes that assessing a doctor's assertion that he found the unbearability of the patient's suffering 'understandable', comes down to the question 'whether the doctor could reasonably have come to [that] conclusion'.

In a number of case reports it appears that at an earlier stage the doctor and/or the consultant had regarded the patient's suffering as 'not yet' unbearable, and euthanasia was only carried out after the patient's situation worsened (eg RRC 2003: 26, case 12); in such a case, the question arises whether there should be a second consultation (see section 4.2.3.3 (E), 'timing').

[170] See RRC 2000: 17 (case 5—'careful'); RRC 2003: 21 (case 8—'careful'). See however RRC 2004: 19–21 (case 5—patient in deep coma 'who gave no signs that could have indicated any suffering . . . and in whose case there was no, or virtually no, chance of partial or full awakening'—SCEN consultant advises negatively—'not careful').

[171] See RRC 2002: 25 (case 10). In RRC 2006: 21–2, case 5, the patient was apparently still suffering despite deep sedation, but the Review Committee's judgment of 'careful' seems also to have been influenced by the fact that the patient had only agreed to the sedation in the first place on condition that euthanasia would be carried out on a specific day if he had not died before then.

[172] See ch 5, appendix, 2007 case A This case involved a 70–80-year-old women in the final stages of cancer, with a long-standing wish for euthanasia and a written euthanasia request, who made a concrete request 4 days before her death. Her suffering was based on her very poor condition (involving total dependence on others), pain, difficulty with breathing and drinking, and the wish to die in a dignified way; she expressly rejected palliative sedation in favour of euthanasia. The consultant was a SCEN doctor who spoke to the woman one day before the euthanasia was carried out and found that all the requirements had been met. The committee held that before she lapsed into unconsciousness on the day the euthanasia was carried out, she had undoubtedly been suffering unbearably and hopelessly. However, once she became comatose, there was no reason to suppose she was still suffering. The committee found the doctor's feeling that she was personally bound by an earlier promise to the patient to carry out euthanasia should the suffering become unbearable 'understandable' but insufficient reason to hasten the patient's natural dying process. The doctor was found 'not careful'.

Suffering with No Prospect of Improvement

Whether the patient's suffering is 'hopeless' [*uitzichtloos*—translated officially as the absence of a 'prospect of improvement'[173]] is, by contrast with the requirement of 'unbearability', a matter of medical expertise.[174] Judging from the Annual Reports of the Regional Review Committees, the requirement (with one exception to be noted in a moment) gives rise to few problems. In the Annual Report of 2005, the committees describe the requirement as follows:

> The suffering of the patient is considered to be lacking any prospect of improvement if there is no realistic treatment possibility. The disease or condition that causes the suffering cannot be cured and there is also no realistic prospect that the symptoms can be relieved. One can only speak of a 'realistic prospect' if there is a reasonable balance between the improvement that can be accomplished with a (palliative) treatment and the burden that such (palliative) treatment entails for the patient.[175]

The main problem to which the requirement can give rise is a fundamental one: it can conflict with the right of the patient to refuse treatment. In the past, it was forcefully argued (and generally supposed) that a patient's refusal of treatment was no obstacle to legal euthanasia, although in the *Chabot* case the Supreme Court did make an exception for the case of non-somatically based suffering.[176] The Regional Review Committees have come to take a more qualified position. Whereas in their first Annual Report the committees seemed to treat the requirement as simply a matter of the existence of a medically indicated (proportionate) treatment,[177] beginning in the Annual Report of 2000, they emphasise that if a patient's refusal of treatment is 'understandable', it does not stand in the way of euthanasia (thus morphine can be refused by a patient who does not want to become less clear-headed, and radiation by a patient for whom the side-effects outweigh the benefits).[178] The Annual Report of 2006 is emphatic: while good

---

[173] 'Improvement' refers to the patient's suffering, not to the underlying medical condition (this is clearer in the Dutch text of the law, where *uitzichtloos* is an adjective modifying *lijden*). In the precursor of this book, we translated the Dutch phrase as 'unbearable and hopeless suffering' (GB&W: 7), which is perhaps slightly more accurate than the current official translation.

[174] See RRC 2006: 19. In the Law of 2002, the requirement is stated twice, in slightly different terms. The patient's suffering must be 'without prospect of improvement' and patient and doctor must have come together to the conclusion that there is 'no reasonable alternative' to euthanasia (see Box 4.8 above). In practice, no attention seems to be paid to the difference in formulation, and it would seem to be the latter that best expresses current law.

[175] RRC 2005: 19; see also RRC 2006: 19. Compare KNMG 2003: 14. The possibility that there might be social or other non-medical alternatives to euthanasia, and that the doctor should explore these (see n 110), rarely receives attention.

[176] See GB&W: 146–7, 150.

[177] RRC 1998/1999: 11. The KNMG had defined a 'real possibility of treatment' in 1997 as: medically speaking there is a prospect of improvement, within a reasonable time, and with a reasonable relationship between the expected results and the burden for the patient (CAL 1997: 164). This definition was frequently referred to during the parliamentary debates on the Law of 2002 (see Legemaate 2005: 41–2).

[178] RRC 2000: 17, 19 (case 8—refusal of further diagnostic treatment in a case of seemingly irreversible paraplegia resulting from cancer in the spinal cord—'careful'); RRC 2001: 18; RRC 2002: 27 (case 11—81 year old cancer patient refuses palliative operation with a low chance of success—

curative and palliative care must be offered the patient before there can be any question of euthanasia, this does not imply that the patient must take advantage of every possible (palliative) treatment. A patient whose suffering is unbearable may refuse (palliative) treatment or care, in which case the refusal will be an important subject for patient and doctor to discuss.[179] The doctor must be satisfied that 'the patient's refusal of a treatment possibility was reasonable in the circumstances'.[180]

In summary: in their interpretation and application of the requirement of unbearable suffering with no prospect of improvement the Review Committees have on the whole been sensitive to the essential subjectivity of suffering and to the fact that people may have reasons they find important for refusing (palliative) treatment. Their judgments—in cases in which both doctor and consultant have come without reservations to the conclusion that the patient's suffering is unbear-

'careful'). In RRC 2004: 21–4 it becomes clear that this approach applies equally to curative and to palliative treatment (cases 6, 8 and 9, in all of which the judgment was 'careful'—the first two involved MS patients with a long history of very serious symptoms: one refused parenteral feeding that would have extended life, the other admittance to a nursing home; in a third case a woman with advanced metastasised breast cancer refused consultation with a palliative care specialist to see if further palliative treatment might be possible—the woman's position was that the existence of further possibilities would not affect her wish for euthanasia).

[179] RRC 2006: 23; see also n 78. Treatment (such as radiation therapy) may have side effects the patient finds hard to bear, and palliative treatment may cause the patient to be groggy or to lose consciousness (eg RRC 2005: 23; RRCj 2006, case 2034—'careful'). The Regional Review Committees' Annual Reports for 2004 and 2005 contain six cases in which sedation was refused by the patient, in all of which the committees apparently (no comment is made on the matter) found this understandable and held the doctor to have met the requirements of due care; in 2004 the committees use the term 'terminal sedation', in 2005 and 2006 'palliative sedation', but in only two cases is withholding of ANH specifically mentioned (see RRC 2004: 13 (case 2); RRC 2005: 12 (case 1), 13 (case 2), 15 (case 3—child of 12—apparently what was refused was terminal sedation), 20 (case 5—terminal sedation refused); RRC 2006: 21 (case 5)). Of 525 judgments of the Review Committees that were available on internet for 2006 and 2007 as of 26 November 2007 (see n 393), the patient had apparently refused 'terminal sedation' in 12 and 'palliative sedation' in 83 (from a check of a number of these judgments it seems that the committees use the two terms more or less interchangeably—that is, whether withholding of ANH was involved is unclear). Where the patient's motive is mentioned, it generally has to do with the wish to die in a dignified, clear-headed way.

The oft-heard suggestion that good palliative care will largely eliminate the demand for euthanasia is not confirmed by the practical experience of at least one oncological specialist. He described to us the phenomenon of terminal cancer patients who, having received good palliative care, request euthanasia, explaining that now that they feel fully in control again, they want euthanasia before there is the inevitable turn for the worse. It seems from a study of one hospice over a period of 12 years (see Zuurmond *et al* 2006) that euthanasia there is far less common than in the general population, but as the authors observe, it is impossible to know whether this is a result of greater attention to palliative care (in particular because, as patients were informed upon admission, euthanasia could not be carried out within the hospice itself).

[180] RRC 2005: 23 (case 7—terminal cancer patient a few days from death refuses the improved palliative treatment suggested by the consultant because in her view it would only prolong her suffering—'careful'). See also RRC 2006: 23–4, case 6 (patient with advanced Huntington's disease requests euthanasia to avoid admittance to a nursing home—reasonable in light of the importance to her of personal independence and of not undergoing further physical deterioration).

able—do not often seem overly paternalistic.[181] On the other hand, no reasonable person could conclude, after reading the Annual Reports, that Dutch euthanasia law is being applied in a way that evidences a 'slippery slope' into unbridled patient autonomy.[182] The committees' decisions thus make quite clear that Dutch euthanasia law not only in its formal legal provisions but also in its practical application, is not based on patient autonomy alone: relief of real suffering that cannot be dealt with in some acceptable other way is also an essential condition.

4.2.3.3(D) The 'Doctor Responsible for Treatment'

As we have seen in section 4.2.3.2, before the Law of 2002 it was generally supposed that euthanasia must (at least, 'in principle') be carried out by the doctor responsible for the patient's treatment [*behandelend arts*]. No such limitation is explicitly included among the requirements of due care in the Law of 2002. The Regional Review Committees seem at first to have been of the view that the law and its legislative history assume the existence of 'a medical treatment relationship between doctor and patient. If the relationship is limited to carrying out euthanasia' the requirement of a treatment relationship has not been met.[183] In 2005, the Review Committees are more guarded.[184] They find in the Law and its legislative history

---

[181] Possible exceptions are, eg, RRC 2000: 20 (case 9—see n 169) and RRC 2003: 20 (case 7—patient with cumulation of somatic and non-somatic complaints arising out of progressive degeneration of the brain due to radiation treatment of an inoperable brain tumour; the patient found his partially paralysed situation, epileptic attacks, inability to read, increasing dependence on care, and lack of any perspective of improvement unbearable, and the doctor and the consultant found the patient's experience of suffering understandable; the Review Committee nevertheless concluded that given the man's considerable life-expectancy (10–20 years) and the fact that he was able to wait for half a year after the positive result of the consultation (which gave him the peace of mind to arrange his funeral, take leave of family and friends, and take part in a special vacation trip for invalids), the doctor could not reasonably conclude that his suffering was unbearable—'not careful'; prosecutors decide not to prosecute).

[182] *Cf* Burt 2005 for a suggestion to that effect.

[183] RRC 2002: 18. For relevant cases see *ibid* at 18 (case 6—substitute doctor knows patient only 1 day and there was also no proper consultation—'not careful'; prosecutors decide prosecution would be disproportionate under the circumstances); and *ibid* at p 19 (case 7—no treatment relationship if 'the relationship between the deceased and the reporting doctor exclusively concerns the wish [of the former] to have [his] life ended'—'not careful'; prosecutors decide not to prosecute). See also RRC 2001: 24 (case 13—relation of friendship, not a treatment relationship—'not careful'—prosecutors decide not to prosecute).

[184] We have been informed by G den Hartogh (a member of the review committee involved) that the change of view of the committees was influenced by Legemaate (2005: 49), who observes that the case law before the Law of 2002 does not support a limitation to the doctor responsible for treatment (compare n 114), and that a single off-hand remark in the parliamentary history of the Law of 2002 is not enough basis for giving it a more limited interpretation than its text requires. Legemaate's position is that,

> The doctor responsible for treatment is to be preferred, because he knows the patient well and is thereby in a better position to assess the requirements of due care, but this does not exclude the possibility that a doctor who is not responsible for treatment [*niet-behandelend arts*] can also acquire sufficient knowledge in that regard. (*Ibid*)

The KNMG's most recent guideline suggests—in connection with the situation in which a patient's doctor has conscientious objections to euthanasia—that it is not necessary that the existing treatment relationship be terminated when the patient seeks help from another doctor, but that the second doctor must be given the opportunity to 'establish a treatment relationship with the patient' (KNMG 2003: 8). Both Legemaate and the Regional Review Committees take an even less limited view, in which a 'treatment relationship' is not required.

'insufficient ground for regarding a treatment relationship as required'. Instead, they take the position that what is decisive is whether 'the doctor had such a relationship with the patient as to permit him to form a judgment concerning the requirements of due care'.[185]

When more than one doctor is involved in treating the patient, it sometimes occurs that both of them consider the patient's request, carry out the euthanasia together, and file a joint report. The committees have occasionally accepted this,[186] but usually they seek to identify the doctor who was principally responsible for what took place.[187] Change or confusion of roles between the patient's doctor and another doctor who is approached for consultation but who later carries out the euthanasia occurs occasionally and gives rise to problems with both the requirement that euthanasia be carried out by a doctor who has a sufficient relationship as well as with the requirement of independent consultation.[188]

4.2.3.3(E) Consultation

The Law of 2002 requires that the doctor consult at least one other, independent doctor, who sees the patient and files a written report.[189] Only in a situation of necessity do the Review Committees occasionally find that the doctor involved used due care even though consultation did not take place.[190] From the reports of the committees it appears that implementation of the requirement gives rise to problems concerning the independence of the consultant, the expertise of the consultant, the timing and quality of consultation, and whether the consultant must agree with the consulting doctor's judgment.

[185] RRC 2005: 27 (case 9—'not careful'; after speaking to doctor, prosecutors decide not to bring charges); RRC 2006: 14–15 (case 1—patient's doctor was satisfied that all requirements were met, but because for emotional reasons he felt incapable of performing the euthanasia himself, he approached a colleague who was willing to do so and who himself fulfilled all the requirements of due care—'careful', but the Review Committee emphasises that such a second doctor cannot limit himself to the actual performance). The cases the committees have considered in this connection have on the whole (but *cf* RRC 2000: 18, case 6) not involved the problem in the mid-1990s of doctors who performed euthanasia when the patient's regular doctor refused to do so (see GB&W: 103 n 41).

[186] See RRC 2003: 14 (case 4); RRC Guideline art 3.3.

[187] For a case in which the Review Committee regarded a doctor as the relevant doctor for purposes of the Law, since he had taken full responsibility for the entire procedure, even though he did not himself administer the euthanaticum (morphine), leaving that to nurses, see RRC 2004: 30 (case 15—it appears more clearly from the description of the facts in a later disciplinary proceeding—see ch 5, appendix—that a SCEN consultant had advised against the use of morphine and that nursing personnel and an intern had therefore refused to set up the intravenous line; in the end this had been done by a colleague of the doctor; the first doctor was found 'not careful'; see further on this case n 213).

[188] See eg RRC 2003: 25 (case 3—consultant carries out euthanasia when patient's condition deteriorates during vacation of patient's doctor—'not careful'—Medical Inspector speaks to doctor but decides not to bring disciplinary charges; prosecutor decides not to prosecute).

[189] 'Failure to fulfill the requirement [that the consultant see the patient and give a written opinion concerning the requirements of due care] entails that the doctor has not met the requirements of due care.' (RRC 2002: 28, case 12—'not careful'—prosecutors decide not to prosecute; Medical Inspector discusses case with doctor).

[190] See RRC 2003: 26 (case 12); RRC 2000: 22 (case 11—sudden, unexpected worsening of patient's condition). For the committees' more usual reaction to a claim of necessity see RRC 2002: 18 (case 6—'not careful'—prosecutors decide prosecution would be disproportionate); 2005: 26 (case 8—'not careful'—prosecutors decide not to prosecute).

Box 4.9 lists a number of different functions of the consultation requirement that one can find in discussions of the requirement and the interpretation given to it.

Box 4.9 Functions of a requirement of consultation

---

1. *Quality control:* the decisions to be made can be medically difficult (diagnosis, prognosis, alternative treatments, possibilities of palliative treatment) and asking the advice of a colleague can contribute to the medical quality of the decision-making (this function is essentially the same as that of consultation in any other medical setting).

2. *Intersubjectivity:* several aspects of the situation require subjective judgments (is the patient's assertion that his suffering is unbearable understandable? is the patient's refusal of treatment reasonable?) and consultation helps to insure that the ultimate decision is not wholly dependent on idiosyncrasies of the doctor involved (this function is essentially the same as that of consultation concerning withholding or withholding treatment on the ground of 'medical futility').

3. *Informational:* for most doctors euthanasia is not an everyday affair and they may not be aware of some of the applicable requirements and considerations.

4. *Preventive and justificatory:* knowing he will have to consult with a colleague, a doctor will try to make sure he has done everything right, and he can use the necessity of consultation in explaining to a patient why, unless the requirements have been met, he cannot accede to the patient's request.

5. *Before-the-fact control:* the consultant ensures that improper euthanasia does not occur (this function is especially relevant in the case of specialised consultants, see chapter 5.4.2). Consistently with this function, it is generally a part of the consultation requirement that in principle the consultant must agree that the requirements have been met.[191]

6. *After-the-fact control:* the requirement of consultation ensures that a second, qualified person knows what the situation was (eg whether the patient really asked for euthanasia) so that control afterwards is not entirely dependent on the word of the doctor concerned.

The first two functions are medical-professional in character and in the early days of euthanasia law it was these that people mainly seemed to have in mind. Functions 2, 3, 4 and 5 all concern ways to strengthen the influence of rules on behaviour. The sixth function concerns the possibility of control after the fact.

---

[191] See KNMG 1995, which in the past regarded it as necessary, if the consultant disagreed, to consult a second doctor (who should be apprised of the negative judgment of the first doctor). If the judgment of the second consultant was also negative, a doctor should not approach still other consultants until one of them agrees with him, but should reconsider his own opinion. The NVP at least until recently took a similar position (NVP 2004: 30). As we will see at the end of section 4.2.3.3(E), the solution ultimately reached by the Regional Review Committees leaves some room in an appropriate case for legal euthanasia despite a negative position of the consultant.

Although as noted earlier it has often been supposed that euthanasia without the approval of the consultant is in principle illegitimate, only the fifth function supports this idea. The first four see the involvement of a consultant as supportive of the judgment of the consulting doctor (who remains responsible for the final decision) and the sixth concerns the transparency of his behaviour. However, as we will see in chapter 5.4.2, the fifth function—before-the-fact control—is increasing in importance.

Independence of the Consultant

The consultant must be independent both of the doctor (no family relationship, partnership, joint practice, or other close or hierarchical working relationship) and of the patient (no personal relationship or (prior) treatment relationship).[192] The Review Committees, who have been confronted with a considerable number of cases in which the consultant's independence is at issue, define independence in a rather flexible way as the situation in which there is an 'independent judgment' of the consultant.[193]

Expertise

According to the Medical Association, 'consultation [with a specially trained SCEN consultant[194]] is to be preferred, because it is clear that in such a case expertise and

---

[192] RRC 2006: 24–25; KNMG 2003: 15. In their Annual Report for 2000 the Review Committees explicitly note a change of policy on their part: before then, members of the same 'substitution group' (GPs who substitute for one another during weekends, sickness, vacations, etc) had not been considered adequately independent (although the judgment 'not careful' did not necessarily follow from a deficiency on only this point). Influenced by the KNMG, the committees changed their view: there is lack of the required independence only if the consultant has actually treated the patient in his capacity as substitute (RRC 2000: 8). In RRC 2006: 24, the committees express their reservations about consultation by a fellow member of a so-called HOED group (GPs who share a building and facilities but have independent practices) and propose in such a situation to examine the degree of (in)dependence on a case-by-case basis.

See, for a clear case of violation of the requirement of independence—the consultant was both a former colleague of the patient and a colleague of the responsible doctor—RRC 2002: 19 (case 7—'not careful'; prosecutors decide not to prosecute). In another case, the consultant had a treatment relationship with the patient and the committee considered that the requirement of independence had not been met, but that in the circumstances a judgment of 'not careful' was not called for (RRC 2000: 21, case 10; the situation was called to the attention of the Medical Inspector, who spoke with both doctors). See also RRC 2004: 26 (case 10—'not careful'—prosecutor decides not to prosecute); RRC 2005: 30 (case 11—'not careful'—prosecutor decides not to prosecute); RRCj 2007 cases B and C (see appendix to ch 5)—'not careful'—outcome not yet known.

[193] RRC Guideline 2003: 4. For an example of a case in which this standard is applied, despite the fact that the consultant was a member of a partnership with the responsible doctor and had also seen the patient earlier when substituting for the latter, and the main reason for the choice of consultant was the patient's preference to talk about her situation with a doctor with whom she had earlier discussed it, see RRC 2001: 21 (case 8); see for a comparable case, RRC 2005: 29, case 10). In their 2005 Annual Report the committees mention the situation in which doctors know each other from other professional contacts such as discussion groups in which difficult cases are presented; whether the independence of the consultant's judgment is affected depends on factors such as the frequency of such contact and whether the case of the patient involved has been discussed (RRC 2005: 25).

[194] See section 4.2.4.4 below on SCEN consultants.

independence are better guaranteed.'[195] The Regional Review Committees share this view, and in several of their Annual Reports are emphatic that the SCEN programme is a very important contribution to the quality and controllability of euthanasia practice.[196]

The importance they attach to the expertise of the consultant manifests itself in the early reports of the committees in the form of comments on the undesirability of psychiatrists as consultants in the case of somatic suffering. In 2004 they appear to modify this view: 'there is in itself no objection to approaching a psychiatrist as consultant, on condition that in his report he express a judgment concerning all of the legal requirements of due care'.[197] On the other hand, the Dutch Association for Psychiatry (NVP) considers it important that non-psychiatrists be alert to the possible psychiatric aspects of requests for euthanasia or assisted suicide and in case of doubt consult with a psychiatrist.[198]

Timing

On the one hand, consultation should not be postponed until it is no longer feasible, either because the patient's physical condition is declining so quickly that waiting for consultation is not possible—eg in the weekend when it is more difficult to arrange—or because he is no longer capable of communicating with the consultant.[199] On the other hand, consultation long in advance has a hypothetical character which makes it unsatisfactory as a double-check that the requirements of due care are met when the euthanasia is actually carried out. The solution to this longstanding[200] dilemma has been found in two-step consultation. In its most recent guideline on euthanasia, the Medical Association recommends, in a case in which the cognitive or communicative ability of the patient is declining, early consultation followed by a short additional consultation when the patient's suffering

---

[195] KNMG 2003: 15 (emphasising the fact that SCEN consultants operate according to a consultation-protocol, follow a comprehensive 'checklist' in preparing their report, and get regular refresher training).

[196] See RRC 2002: 31, 2003: 30, 2004: 25 (quality of reports of SCEN consultants), 2005: 26 (ditto).

[197] RRC 2004: 28 (case 13—the psychiatrist consulted had in the first instance reported only on the competence of the patient). See, for earlier reservations concerning consulting a psychiatrist in such a case, RRC 2001: 21 (case 9—'undesirable'—in the case reported, however, the judgment was 'careful'); 2003: 27 ('not so desirable').

[198] NVP 2004: 39. In the case of a psychiatric patient, a non-psychiatrist should consult two independent psychiatrists. The NVP notes that a psychiatrist is consulted in only 3% of all euthanasia cases. The Annual Report for 2006 reports on two cases in which additional consultation with psychiatrists was sought because of doubts concerning the competence of the patient to make a voluntary and well-informed request and the reporting doctors were found 'careful'. In one (RRC 2006: 17–18, case 2) the patient suffered from depression, but the consulted psychiatrist advised that the request met the requirements. In the other (RRC 2006: 18–21, case 3/4) both a geriatric psychiatrist and a second psychiatrist advised that although the patient was in the early stages of Alzheimer's disease her request was voluntary and well considered.

[199] Often when a Regional Review Committee finds that consultation has not met the requirements (eg insufficient independence of the consultant) failure to arrange for timely consultation is the underlying problem. For a case in which the result was no consultation at all (but the committee found the *arts* 'careful' nevertheless, since he was confronted with a situation of necessity), see RRC 2000: 22 (case 11).

[200] See n 126 above for controversy on this matter in the mid-1990s.

has become unbearable.[201] The Review Committees are of the same view. When consultation takes place well before the euthanasia itself, or if the patient's request is conditional or the consultant's view is that the patient's suffering is not yet unbearable, there should be a second consultation shortly before euthanasia is carried out, when the doctor considers that all the requirements have been met.[202] If the consultant expects that the suffering will soon become unbearable and shortly thereafter this is indeed the case, then depending on the circumstances no further contact with the consultant may be necessary,[203] or telephone contact between the doctor and the consultant may suffice. If the first consultation takes place early on, when there is not yet any question of unbearable suffering and the patient's request has a hypothetical character, then the consultant must visit the patient a second time.[204]

Quality of Consultation and Consultant's Report

Since consultation is a condition of the legality of his own behaviour, it is the doctor who performs euthanasia who is responsible for ensuring that the consultation meets the required standards.[205] Nevertheless, the Regional Review Committees regularly seek additional information from a consultant whose report is too summary.

The so-called SCEN programme, which makes specially trained consultants available, is discussed in section 4.2.4.4. The Regional Review Committees have repeatedly expressed the view that, largely thanks to SCEN, the quality of consultation has greatly improved and it is said to be 'generally excellent' in the case of

---

[201] KNMG 2003: 16.

[202] See RRC 1998/1999: 14 (second consultation desirable in such cases); RRC 2001: 22 (case 10—timely consultation made it necessary that the consultant see the patient a second time when it would have been possible to form a judgment on all of the requirements of due care—'careful'); RRC 2001: 22 (case 11—two-step consultation carried out in an exemplary fashion); RRC 2002: 29 (case 14—second consultation by telephone—'careful'); RRC 2003: 20 (case 7—consultation a half year earlier—in the circumstances, 'a second consultation in which the consultant visited the patient was necessary [to judge whether the patient's suffering was really unbearable and without treatment possibilities]—'not careful'—Medical Inspector speaks with doctor, prosecutors decide not to prosecute); RRC 2003: 26 (case 12—consultant found patient's suffering not yet unbearable because the palliative medicines were effective, but 2 weeks later that was no longer the case and doctor performed euthanasia without a second consultation—'careful' although second consultation would have been better); RRC 2004: 18 (case 4) and 27 (case 12), both cases in which second telephone consultation was sufficient; RRC 2005: 20 (case 5—ditto).

[203] See RRC 2006: 25; RRC 2004: 27 (case 12—no second consultation necessary because consultant had anticipated rapid deterioration and found further consultation only necessary if suffering had not become unbearable within 4 weeks); RRC 2006: 26–7 (case 7—consultation 3 months in advance, when patient's suffering was still bearable; both doctors anticipated its becoming unbearable very shortly, but patient had a longish good period until his condition took a sudden and dramatic turn for the worse; doctor does not consider renewed contact with the consultant necessary—although he did seek advice from a specialist concerning palliative possibilities—'careful'); RRC 2006: 27–8 (case 8—request by patient conditional on the return of unbearable pain despite medication that at the time was effective; consultant's conclusion that the requirements of due care were met was similarly conditional; a week later the pain returns; no further contact with consultant—'careful').

[204] RRC 2005: 25.

[205] *Ibid*; RRC 2006: 25.

SCEN consultants.[206] The frequency of reports on standard forms on which questions are answered 'yes' or 'no'—which the committees regard as quite unhelpful—had declined strongly by 2002,[207] although in the Annual Report of 2003 it is noted that 'some consultation reports are still very summary, especially those from hospitals [ie specialists]'. In such cases the consultant is 'often asked (in the future) to submit a more extensive report'.[208]

Agreement between Consulted and Consulting Doctor

An old point of disagreement about consultation, deriving from differing ideas about what the essential function of the requirement is, concerns the situation in which the consultant disagrees with the judgment of the consulting doctor that the requirements of due care have not been met: is the consulting doctor bound by the disagreement, or is he free to exercise his own judgment? As we have seen above, before the Law of 2002 the rule seemed to be that after one negative consultation, a doctor could approach a second consultant, but that if the second consultation was also negative he should not proceed with euthanasia. The Medical Association recently reconfirmed this position.[209]

The Regional Review Committees recently settled the matter. They expect a doctor who proceeds despite the contrary judgment of a consultant (even if he later consulted a second doctor who did agree with him) to explain his decision.[210] But '[i]n case of a difference of opinion between the doctor and the consultant it is ultimately up to the doctor to make a decision.'[211]

4.2.3.3(F) *Other Requirements of Due Care*

Carrying Out the Decision with 'Due Medical Care and Attention'

The requirement of 'due medical care and attention' gives rise, the Review Committees say, to few problems in practice.[212] (The special problems in connection

---

[206] RRC 2003: 30; RRC 2005: 26; RRC 2006: 15.

[207] See RRC 2002: 31. The committees provide a 'checklist' for consultants (available at <http://www.toetsingscommissieseuthanasie.nl> accessed 4 April 2007), but the explanation at the beginning of the checklist states explicitly that it is only intended as indicative and a consultant is expected to produce an 'open report' which gives as complete and explanatory a picture of the consultation as possible.

[208] RRC 2003: 29.

[209] If the second consultant's advice is also negative, the doctor 'should reconsider his decision to perform euthanasia' (KNMG 2003: 14).

[210] See RRC 2000: 23.

[211] RRC 2005: 25; RRC 2006: 25. For examples of this see RRC 2005: 23 (case 7—responsible doctor proceeds with euthanasia, despite consultant's view that there were additional palliative possibilities, because the patient rejected such treatment, thinking it would only prolong her suffering—'careful'); RRC 2004: 15 (case 3—consulted doctor questions patient's competence; three experts—whom the committee apparently did not regard as formal consultants—disagree; 'the doctor, confronted by the conflicting opinions of the consultant and the experts whose advice he sought afterwards, using his own judgment, properly gave more weight to the latter'). Compare also the prosecutorial Guideline (n 353): 'The opinion of the consulted doctor has the status of an advice. The doctor need not follow it.'

[212] See RRC 2003: 27.

with the involvement of nurses in carrying out euthanasia are dealt with in section 4.2.3.3(J).)

The Review Committees take the position, that it is in principle a violation of the requirements of due care to use a euthanaticum not approved by the Royal Dutch Pharmacological Association (KNMP).[213] In practice, what is usually at issue is morphine, which for many years has been considered unsuitable for euthanasia. As the committees' cases make clear, the use of morphine is generally accompanied by other departures from the requirements of due care: the doctor is not present throughout, and nurses are involved in the administration of increasing doses.[214] Nevertheless, the committees do occasionally find that under particular circumstances no breach of the requirements is entailed when a doctor deliberately departs from the normal requirements.[215]

Before the Law of 2002 the doctor was generally required to be continuously present from the administration of euthanatica to the death of the patient.[216] This requirement—now regarded as an element of the required 'due medical care and attention'—has been reaffirmed in guidelines of the medical profession[217] and in decisions of the Regional Review Committees.[218]

The requirement of continuous presence by the responsible doctor gives rise to a special problem in the case of assistance with suicide. There are some obvious considerations in support of insisting on continuous presence in such a case: maintaining control over the availability of euthanatica, ensuring that the suicide is humane and effective and intervening with euthanasia if it is not,[219] and timely reporting of the death to the municipal pathologist. On the other hand, there are also some important reasons for not (always) insisting on the presence of the

---

[213] See RRC 2006: 28. For the approved euthanatica, see KNMP 2007. See for an example of use of a disapproved drug, RRC 2004: 30 (case 15—'not careful'—Review Committee calls attention of Medical Inspector to procedures and use of morphine in hospital, prosecutors decide not to prosecute, Medical Disciplinary Tribunal 'reprimands' doctor, see appendix; see further on this case nn 187, 214, 218, 231, 280, 392).

[214] See eg RRC 2004: 30 (case 15—administration of morphine by nurses per instructions of doctor; doctor not continuously present—'not careful'—see further on this case n 213).

[215] RRC 2001: 24 (case 12—wish of the patient, who was already receiving morphine intravenously, not to die abruptly; and circumstances in the hospital concerned—'careful'); *Cf* also RRC 2005: 31 (case 11—in circumstances 'careful').

[216] See section 4.2.3.2(B).

[217] AVVV 2006: 41; KNMG 2003: 17; NVP 2004: 30.

[218] See eg RRC 2004: 30 (case 15—' not careful'—see further on this case n 213); RRC 2002: 28 (case 13—doctor delegates administration of euthanatica to anaesthetist and is not present—'not careful'— prosecutors decide not to prosecute). However, in case 12 of 2001, dealt with in n 215, where the use of morphine was deemed acceptable, the committee apparently regarded the 'continuous care' available in the hospital concerned sufficient.

[219] An important concern is that the patient may vomit up the drugs taken, or that the suicide may otherwise be unsuccessful. Horikx & Admiraal (2000) found that in the case of oral administration of approved euthanatica death usually occurs in less than 1 hour but can take as long as 7 hours (and in the past is known sometimes to take as long as 24 hours); in their research death did not take place within the time agreed on with the patient in advance (a practice they strongly advise) in roughly 2 out of 5 cases, and the doctor administered a muscle-relaxant (compare n 223). The absence of this possibility is the basis for the reservations many Dutch observers have with regard to the practice of assisted suicide in Oregon.

doctor, so long as he is immediately available.[220] The Dutch Association for Psychiatry, for example, argues that in the case of psychiatric patients, insisting on the doctor's presence requires that an appointment be made for the suicide, and a patient who is experiencing doubts at the last minute may not want to have made the doctor 'come for nothing'.[221] And some patients have good, personal reasons for preferring to die in private or among intimates.

Up to and including the Annual Report of 2004 the Regional Review Committees insisted that the doctor retain possession of the drugs to be used until the time the patient swallows them and remain with the patient until death occurs.[222] In 2005, however, they took a more qualified position:

> In an exceptional case and for good reasons an agreement can be made in advance to proceed in another way. The doctor must be continuously available to intervene if the drugs are not (sufficiently) effective.[223]

Record-Keeping

As we have seen in section 4.2.3.2(B), before the Law of 2002 adequate record-keeping was one of the requirements of due care. Record-keeping is not specifically included in the Law of 2002 and is seldom mentioned as a distinct requirement, although common sense suggests that it is an essential prerequisite to effective control. The Regional Review Committees occasionally ask a doctor whose report is not complete to provide them with additional information, but they seem never to have criticised a doctor's medical record-keeping.[224]

One of the few places where the special role of record-keeping in connection with euthanasia is dealt with is in the recent joint 'guideline for cooperation' of the Medical Association, the professional organisation of nurses (NU'91) and the Association of Nurses and Caregivers (AVVV).[225] The 'guideline' begins with the observation that,

> [b]ecause a doctor must explicitly justify what he did in the case of euthanasia, record-keeping puts more demands on him than usual. He must be able to demonstrate what decisions were taken and why.[226]

---

[220] See Legemaate 2005: 44.

[221] See NVP 2004: 30.

[222] For three cases in which doctors not present at the time of the assisted suicide were found 'not careful' see RRC 2000: 24 (case 14) and 2003: 27 (cases 13, 14) (in all three cases, the prosecutors decided not to bring charges and the Medical Inspectorate spoke to the doctor).

[223] RRC 2005: 32; RRC 2006: 28. The committees add that in such a case, 'The termination of life must be carried out by the doctor himself.' The position of the Psychiatric Association (NVP) is similar but rather more carefully and flexibly formulated (see section 4.2.3.4(B)).

[224] No such case is to be found in the Annual Reports through 2006 nor in the on-line cases of 2006 (accessed 26 November 2007). Inadequate record-keeping is a medical disciplinary offence and the Medical Disciplinary Tribunal in the *Vencken* case (see n 81 above) found the doctor's record-keeping inadequate but imposed no sanction.

[225] AVVV 2006.

[226] AVVV 2006: 16–17.

This requires special attention in connection with the care of a patient who has requested euthanasia because, apart from its normal functions (such as supporting the continuity and quality of care) proper record-keeping forms the basis for review afterwards of whether the requirements of due care have been met. Good record-keeping makes a good report by the doctor possible, one that gives the Regional Review Committee clear insight into the situation of the patient and the reasons for the doctor's decisions.

> Nurses can contribute to such record-keeping by carefully and continuously observing and measuring the situation of the patient and recording their findings [concerning the patient's health, sense of wellbeing, wishes and needs, and possibilities of everyday activities].[227]

Box 4.10 gives the points to which, according to the 'guideline', particular attention should be paid:[228]

Box 4.10 Relevant items in record-keeping

---

* the euthanasia request and the patient's consistency therein, as well as the standpoint and views of the patient's family and intimate friends (in connection with the voluntariness of the patient's request)
* the hopeless and unbearable character of the suffering:
* the physical symptoms
* the emotional/psychic situation of the patient and his outlook
* social and spiritual aspects
* possibilities of everyday activity
* interventions and their effects, and changes in the patient's situation

---

Reporting (and Supplying the Review Committees with Information)

Before the Law of 2002, for a doctor to file an inaccurate report of a 'natural death' was a distinct criminal offence, and as far as that is concerned, nothing has changed.[229] However, the Law of 2002 amends article 293 of the Penal Code to legalise euthanasia by a doctor who conforms to the requirements of due care *and reports the euthanasia to the municipal pathologist as required by the Law on Burial and Cremation.*[230] When the doctor who reports a case of euthanasia is not the doctor who actually carried it out, the Regional Review Committees treat the latter as the 'reporting doctor' (who must meet the requirements of due care) and

---

[227] AVVV 2006: 28.

[228] AVVV 2006: 28–9.

[229] See GB&W: 114–18 for the legal organisation of the so-called reporting requirement prior to the new law.

[230] See article 20 (A) and (B) of the Law of 2002. A false report of a 'natural death' remains a separate offence.

dispose of the case accordingly.[231] Since the Review Committees do not see non-reported cases, their implementation of the reporting requirement is limited to comments on the quality of the reports they receive and to requesting additional information in the case of an inadequate report.

Both before and after the Law of 2002, a model has been available for doctors to use in reporting.[232] The doctor's duty, the committees note on the current version of the model, is to submit to the municipal pathologist a 'reasoned report' that covers the points in the model and where appropriate explains the answers given. Use of the model itself is not required if the doctor covers all of the requirements of due care. But in practice the model is almost always used.[233]

In general, the committees observe, the quality of reporting by doctors has been improving. They attribute this to the dissemination of information to doctors and feedback from the work of the committees.[234] The committees repeatedly note that when the doctor's and the consultant's reports fully cover all of the information required, it is usually not necessary for the committees to request further information.[235]

In a recent case, a Review Committee found a doctor 'not careful' because he failed to supply it with the information necessary to determine whether the patient, who had been suffering unbearably at the time she requested euthanasia, was still suffering when it was carried out (apparently she had become unconscious in the meantime). The doctor answered the committee's written questions in a perfunctory way and twice did not appear to explain the situation orally to the committee. The committee decided that in the circumstances it could not determine that the requirements of due care had been met and therefore concluded that they had not.[236]

Discussion with Family and/or Intimate Friends (naasten) and with Nurses

Although as we have seen in section 4.2.3.3(A) the Law of 2002 does not explicitly include discussion with the family and intimate friends of the patient among the requirements of due care, the model form for use in reporting a case of euthanasia

---

[231] See RRC Guideline, art 3.1. For cases see RRC 2001: 14 (case 2—patient's doctor regards himself as responsible for the euthanasia, which was in fact carried out by a colleague; although the first doctor reported the case, it was the behaviour of the second that the committee reviewed—'careful'); RRC 2005: 33 (case 14—ditto—Medical Inspector discusses internal procedures with hospital, which decides to make a detailed protocol for such cases—'not careful' for other reasons but prosecutors decide against prosecution). See also RRC 2004: 30 (case 15—see further on this case n 213).

[232] See GB&W: 310–13 for the model as it was before the new Law (in English). The current model is available at <http://www.toetsingscommissieseuthanasie.nl> accessed 20 April 2007.

[233] See RRC 2003: 29. Apparently some doctors were still using the old model, dating from before the Law of 2002, and the committees observed that that model does not cover all of the required points.

[234] See RRC 2001: 25; RRC 2002: 31.

[235] In the online case reports for 2006–07 (accessed 26 November 2007), there are a handful of cases in which inadequate reporting by the doctor concerned lead the committee to request additional written information (14 cases), oral explanation (2 cases), or both (3 cases).

[236] RRC 2006: 29 (case 9); after further inspection by the Medical Inspectorate lead to the conclusion that all of the requirements of due care had been met, the prosecutorial authorities decided not to prosecute (see ch 5, appendix).

does include three questions that deal with this: Were there such discussions? If so, what were their views? If not, why not?[237]

In its most recent guideline (2003), the Medical Association assumes that in normal circumstances a doctor should discuss the patient's request with his family:

[O]bviously there will have to be attention to the views of the patient's family and—in particular if the patient is in an institution—of . . . nurses . . . concerning the request for euthanasia. Neglecting this can disrupt the decision-making process of doctor and patient or give rise to problems after euthanasia has been carried out. In most cases the patient's family will be closely involved in the euthanasia request and be able to respect the wishes of the person concerned. But it is not always the case that the patient and his family, or the family members among themselves, are in agreement. Although what euthanasia is always about is honouring the request of a competent patient, and the opinions of family members are therefore not determinative, it is advisable for a doctor to investigate the objections of family members and try as much as possible to resolve them. That will not always be possible, in particular when family members have objections in principle to euthanasia. It may also be the case that the patient does not want [the doctor to speak] with family members about the euthanasia request. In light of his duty of confidentiality the doctor will have to respect this wish. In such situations the doctor will have to assess whether—despite such disturbing factors—careful communication and decision-making with the patient remains possible.[238]

The family does not play a prominent role in the reports of the Regional Review Committees. When mentioned in a case report, the family is almost always said to be supportive of the patient's request[239]—from which one might infer that when the family is opposed doctors do not perform euthanasia, or that doctors do not mention the family's opposition, or that the committees do not regard the fact as important.[240]

The Law of 2002 is equally silent with regard to a duty to discuss the patient's request with nurses. Here, too, the model provided to doctors for reporting a case

---

[237] See section 4.2.4.1 on this model form.

[238] KNMG 2003: 10. There are also some other incidental references to the family/intimate friends as a source of pressure on the doctor (pp 9, 15), and on the importance of documenting 'possible' discussions (p 13). See Legemaate 2005: 37 for the idea that the doctor's duty of care covers the family and intimate friends as well as the patient.

[239] See RRC 2006: 18–21 (case 3/4—in connection with its judgment of 'careful' the committee explicitly mentions that close friends of a patient with early Alzheimers confirmed to the doctor that for a woman who had always been intellectually and physically active, the gradual loss of her capacities and the prospect of worse to come entailed unbearable suffering). See also RRC 2004: 28 (case 13) for an incidental reference in a case report to the fact that 'the family and the nurses knew of the request and supported it'. It seems from the judgments of the Review Committees that there is usually discussion with the family, which usually supports the patient's request. See ch 5.2.2.1, n 66.

[240] The requirement that the doctor 'satisfy' himself with respect to the voluntariness and well-consideredness of the patient's request and the unbearability and hopelessness of his suffering (see n 141), taken together with the position of the KNMG and of Legemaate (see n 238), would make it possible in an appropriate case for a Review Committee to find a doctor 'not careful' for failure to discuss the patient's request with the family/intimate friends or with a nurse. It should also be kept in mind that the Law of 2002—and therefore the decisions of the Regional Review Committees, the prosecutorial authorities, and the courts—deals only with requirements that are part of the defence to a criminal charge of illegal euthanasia. Other requirements could be enforced in other ways, in particular medical disciplinary law and civil law.

of euthanasia includes three questions dealing with this: Were there such discussions? If so, what were their views? If not, why not?

Especially in hospitals and nursing homes, euthanasia wishes are frequently first made known to nurses. Often this takes the form of diffuse signals and, when appropriate in light of the worsening medical situation, a nurse can ask the patient about his wishes concerning the end of life. If he expresses a desire to die, a nurse should explore with the patient whether this is a request for euthanasia and how urgent it is, and offer to help the patient raise the question with the doctor.[241]

The Medical Association's recent guideline, cited at length above concerning the patient's family, treats it as obvious that the doctor will discuss the patient's request for euthanasia with nurses and others responsible for the care of the patient. Furthermore,

> If the doctor asks for any form of assistance from a nurse or other caregiver, or if a nurse played a role in the request for euthanasia, he should involve them in the decision-making. In practice, a request for euthanasia does not always reach the doctor directly, but sometimes via a nurse or caregiver. Furthermore, they may have important information about, or be able to communicate more easily with, the patient.[242]

Nurses hardly appear at all in the Annual Reports of the Regional Review Committees and there is no indication that the committees consider it an element of 'due care' (eg in relation to the quality of the patient's request or the unbearability of his suffering) that a doctor discuss the case with nurses involved in the care of the patient.[243] As a matter of actual practice, discussion with nurses seems from cases reported to the committees to be fairly common.[244]

4.2.3.3(G) Minors 12–18

In the case of minors (patients under 18 years), the Law of 2002 for the first time[245] contains specific provisions which parallel the age distinctions made in the Law on Contracts for Medical Treatment. A doctor can honour the euthanasia request of a minor over 12 who 'can be considered capable of a reasonable understanding of his interests'. For minors between 12 and 16 both parents, or a guardian, must agree to the euthanasia.[246] For minors of 16 and 17, the parents or guardian must

---

[241] AVVV 2006: 30.

[242] KNMG 2003: 9; see also AVVV 2006: 35 ('very much to be desired' that nurse involved in care of patient who requests euthanasia participate in the decision-making), 39.

[243] *Cf* n 240 for a possible statutory ground for such a duty.

[244] See ch 5.2.2.1, n 63. *Cf* also Van Bruchem-van de Scheur *et al* 2004: 54*ff.*

[245] See section 4.3.3.2(A), n 106, for the legal situation before the Law of 2002.

[246] In the original Government bill, if one or both parents of a minor between 12 and 16 did not agree to the euthanasia, the doctor could perform it anyway if he considered this necessary to prevent 'serious injury' to the minor. 'Serious injury' would have meant 'unbearable suffering with no chance of improvement' (which, ironically, is required for euthanasia anyway) (*Second Chamber of Parliament 1998–1999*, 26 691 no 3: 12). Under pressure from criticism in Parliament and in the Dutch and foreign press, and assured by the medical profession that there was no need for such a provision because in practice parents and their child grow together toward the decision that euthanasia is the only available course of action, the Government withdrew the provision. See ch 3.2 and Weyers 2004: 391–5 for this storm in a teacup.

be included in the decision-making but it is not necessary that they agree with the decision to carry out euthanasia.[247] The reporting and review procedure for cases involving minors is, since the Law of 2002, the same as in the case of adults.[248] The first case of a minor under 16 was reported in 2005; the Regional Review Committee found that the doctor had met the requirements of due care.[249]

4.2.3.3(H) Euthanasia versus Physician-Assisted Suicide[250]

Unlike the situation elsewhere in the world, one of the most characteristic features of euthanasia practice in the Netherlands is that the involvement of doctors is not limited to assistance with suicide. The justification defence worked out by the courts hardly distinguished between killing on request and assistance with suicide, nor does the Law of 2002. While there are of course many other ways in which a doctor can either terminate the life of a patient or assist him to do so himself, in Dutch practice the difference between the two comes down to injection of euthanatica by the doctor versus swallowing them by the patient.[251]

From time to time there have been suggestions in the literature that there ought to be a preference for assistance with suicide.[252] A decade ago the Medical Association adopted Guidelines in which a careful preference was expressed for assistance with suicide whenever this is possible, and this preference is repeated in more emphatic terms in the newest Guidelines of 2003.[253] However, there are no signs of any such preference in actual medical practice, where the preponderance of euthanasia is overwhelming and increased steadily from 1990 through 2006.[254] Nor do the Annual Reports of the Regional Review Committees give any indication that 'due care' involves such a preference, or that a doctor should explain when reporting a case of euthanasia, why assisted suicide was rejected. On the contrary, doctors have been found to have acted with 'due care' in cases in which a preference for assisted suicide—if such a preference had any legal status—would seem to have been appropriate.[255] The only suggestion one can find in the reports of the committees is that the choice for assisted suicide is up to the patient.[256]

---

[247] Article 2 ss 3 and 4 of the Law of 2002.

[248] See section 4.2.4.2 below.

[249] RRC 2005: 9, 15 (case 3—minor of 12—the parents agreed with the request).

[250] See GB&W: 111–14 for a more extensive treatment of this question through 1997.

[251] See RRC 2005: 5 ('In the case of euthanasia the doctor administers the so-called euthanatica; in the case of assistance with suicide the doctor supplies the drugs which the patient thereupon ingests.').

[252] See, for the considerations that support such a preference, Griffiths 2007a.

[253] KNMG 1995: 9; 2003: 9 ('When this is possible, the KNMG is of the view that assistance with suicide should be given instead of euthanasia. Assisted suicide makes the patient's determination and willingness to take responsibility clearer. The nature and weight of the objections of the patient or the doctor to assisted suicide should be made explicit. If the patient has insurmountable objections to taking the drugs himself, this need not always be a reason to reconsider whether the patient's request is well considered.').

[254] See ch 5.2.2.2.

[255] See eg RRC 2003: 17 (case 5—suffering due to psychiatric disorder—'careful').

[256] See RRC 2002: 30 (in the case of assisted suicide the patient himself 'chooses' to ingest the drugs; the word 'chooses' disappears from this definition of assisted suicide in the Annual Report for 2005, RRC 2005: 31). Assisted suicide is said to be preferred by patients for whom their personal autonomy

Despite the general legal indifference to the choice between the two, in the case of non-somatic suffering (psychiatric patients and non-'terminal' patients more generally) it seems to be generally assumed, as we will see in section 4.2.3.4, that if a doctor may be involved at all, this will of course take the form of assistance with suicide.

4.2.3.3(I) The Patient's 'Right' to Euthanasia

As we have seen, legal regulation of euthanasia in the Netherlands has taken the form of a justification, available only to doctors, for what otherwise would be a violation of explicit provisions of the Penal Code. A consequence of this is that the patient, even when his case meets all of the legal requirements, has no 'right' to euthanasia: if he finds a doctor willing to perform it, the doctor can legally do so, but no doctor has any obligation to accede to a request, however well founded. All participants in the public debate have been insistent from the beginning that no doctor can ever be required to carry out euthanasia, and a considerable number of Dutch doctors—not only those with objections of principle—are for various reasons unwilling to do so, either in general or in a particular case.[257]

In these circumstances the availability of euthanasia to a patient is largely a function of who the doctor responsible for his treatment happens to be.[258] It is presumably rare that this doctor was specifically selected at some earlier time for his willingness to perform euthanasia.[259] However, a doctor does have a duty to give his patient accurate and full information and, if he himself is unwilling to accede to a legitimate request, to make this clear to the patient in a timely fashion and to cooperate in the transfer of the patient to another doctor.[260] Nevertheless, it is clear that a patient whose request meets all the legal criteria sometimes experiences great difficulty in finding a doctor willing to carry it out.[261] The whole complex of problems surrounding the access of patients to euthanasia has yet to receive adequate legal attention.

is particularly important. For an example of a case in which the patient chose to 'retain his autonomy to the end', see RRC 2001: 22 (case 11).

[257] See ch 5, Table 5.7. *Cf* Chabot 2007 for some qualitative evidence of this; see also RRC 2006: 14–15 (case 1) for an example of unwillingness in an individual case, which the doctor concerned dealt with by finding a colleague who was willing to carry out the euthanasia.

[258] For the dependence of patients on the willingness of their doctors to perform euthanasia (and on their doctors' willingness to speak to them straightforwardly on the matter) see the qualitative research of Overbeek (1996) and Chabot (2001). Recent research by Van Tol shows that, whereas doctors assess cases of somatic suffering in a reasonably uniform way, in the case of non-somatic suffering there are major differences between them, with as a consequence that whether euthanasia/PAS is available for such a patient is quite arbitrary (see Van Tol 2007).

[259] Furthermore, as Overbeek and Chabot (n 258) observe, a patient may have very good reasons for not changing his doctor in spite of the fact that the doctor makes clear that he is not willing to perform euthanasia.

[260] See KNMG 2003: 8 (no question of a duty actively to approach another doctor, but some help should be given to the patient—such as names and telephone numbers—and the other doctor must be given relevant information about the patient). The NVP (2004: § 2.2) takes the position that a psychiatrist who has conscientious objections does not have to refer a patient himself, but he must explain his position to the patient and inform him of the possibility of approaching another psychiatrist.

[261] See Chabot and Overbeek (n 258) for anecdotal evidence.

Given the monopoly of the medical profession over euthanasia—a position the Medical Association has insisted on from the outset—it has been argued that even though no individual doctor is obliged to perform it, the profession as a whole is bound to ensure the availability of euthanasia to eligible patients.[262] In the past, the existence of institutional policies prohibiting euthanasia was particularly problematic in this connection. The KNMG takes the position that euthanasia is a matter of the 'professional responsibility of a doctor' and that an institutional policy prohibiting euthanasia cannot preclude euthanasia in an individual case by a doctor who meets all of the requirements of due care. Institutional policies that go no further than to exclude the possibility of euthanasia are, the KNMG says, 'irresponsible'.[263]

On the other hand, an institution that takes the position that the personal views of its doctors cannot stand in the way of the availability of euthanasia to its patients can enforce such a policy despite the right of each doctor individually to refuse involvement on grounds of conscientious objections. We know for example of a case in which a doctor with conscientious objections to euthanasia was fired for refusing to cooperate in referring a patient to another doctor in the same hospital.[264]

4.2.3.3(J) The Legal Position of Third Parties

Nurses

The legal position of nurses, as has been noted from time to time over the past two decades, remains in a highly unsatisfactory state.[265] Straightforward application of the criminal law rules relating to accessories would seem in some cases to make the criminal liability of a nurse who participates in carrying out euthanasia dependent on the legality of the doctor's behaviour.[266] Proposals over the years for legislative legalisation tended to treat the liability of the nurse in the same way. The Law of 2002 does not deal with their position at all.

It has from the beginning of legal euthanasia in the Netherlands been quite clear that only doctors may perform it, and it was well established before the Law of 2002 that nurses may not be involved in the actual administration of euthanatica.[267] In

---

[262] See eg Griffiths 1987: 691.

[263] KNMG 2003: 11. By the mid-1990s, almost all hospitals and about half of all nursing homes already had permissive internal policies (see ch 5.4.1 on institutional policies concerning euthanasia).

[264] Account received from the manager concerned. *Cf* also *Trouw* (24 October 2007) ('Verpleger terecht ontslagen wegens uitdragen geloof [Nurse Properly Fired for Imposing her Religious Beliefs]')—the nurse in question attempted to influence the decision-making of patients (among them, persons considering euthanasia; the court upheld the firing, holding that patients in a hospital are entitled not to be confronted with the religious beliefs of those caring for them).

[265] See GB&W 108–9.

[266] See Leenen 2000: 347 (at least if the nurse is involved in carrying out the euthanasia). See also AVVV 2006: 18–20 for a number of hypothetical cases in which a nurse is believed to run or not to run the risk of criminal liability.

[267] In the past it was considered acceptable that nurses increase the dose of morphine to a patient receiving it intravenously. But in a recent case the Regional Review Committee found a doctor in violation of the requirements of due care, among other things for having left the hourly increase of intravenous morphine to nursing personnel of his hospital (see n 214; but *cf* n 215).

the mid-1990's a nurse was convicted of illegal euthanasia when, at the request of the patient and under the direct supervision of the doctor (who was present at the time) she administered the euthanaticum.[268]

The Medical Association's most recent guideline on euthanasia states that no 'actions to carry out the decision' [*uitvoeringshandelingen*] can be delegated to nurses. It distinguishes between 'preparatory' and 'executory' acts as follows:

> The doctor must carry out the . . . [euthanasia] himself. [This includes] . . . giving an injection in connection with termination of life, preparing, attaching and/or opening an intravenous drip in connection with termination of life. Administering euthanatica . . . can never be delegated to a nurse. A nurse can, however, be asked to perform preparatory tasks (such as inserting an intravenous needle in advance) and to give the patient normal care at the end of life.[269]

In a joint 'guideline' of their respective professional associations on the relationship between doctors and nurses in carrying out euthanasia, an attempt is made to clarify the line between preparatory acts—such as inserting an intravenous needle—which are thought not to involve potential criminal liability for the nurse as an accessory, and executory acts which do. 'Preparatory' acts are those which still require an essential act by the doctor to effectuate the termination of life. 'Executory' acts 'have as a direct result the death of the patient'.[270] The Secretary of State for Health, in a letter to the Lower House of Parliament,[271] seems at first even more precise about 'executory' acts: a nurse may not do anything 'which causes the euthanatica, which end the life of the patient, to enter the patient's body'. A nurse can perform preparatory acts that will contribute, some time later, to the performance of euthanasia, so long as these can be considered 'usual medical behaviour'.[272] Unfortunately, the Secretary of State then illustrates the distinction in a way which seems on its face inconsistent with what has just been said. 'Usual medical behaviour' includes giving the doctor instructions, inserting and checking the needle for the intravenous drip, and attaching a line containing a salt solution. Prohibited 'executory' acts include giving an injection, attaching a line containing euthanatica, opening such a line, preparing the euthanatica for administration by intravenous drip or preparing a syringe with euthanatica. Since only giving a lethal injection or opening an intravenous line seem to qualify as

---

[268] See GB&W 108–9. The doctor (who presumably breached the requirements of due care by delegating the task to the nurse) was not prosecuted. As far as is known there have been no disciplinary proceedings against a nurse for involvement in carrying out euthanasia (nurses are subject to medical disciplinary law).

[269] KNMG 2003: 10, 17.

[270] AVVV 2006: 17–22; 38, 41 (doctor and nurse are jointly responsible for maintaining the distinction); 39, 40 (the doctor's instructions to the nurse in connection with preparatory acts should be explicit and in writing).

[271] Brief van de Staatssecretaris van VWS (4 March 2005), *Second Chamber of Parliament 2004–2005*, 29 800 XVI, no 137, p 2.

[272] In Dutch: *gebruikelijk medisch handelen*—an expression very similar to, but presumably intentionally different from, the existing medical-legal term 'normal medical behaviour', which refers to the behaviour of a doctor that is covered by the 'medical exception'.

'executory' acts according to the definition given, the Secretary of State's attempt to clarify the situation ends by spreading confusion.[273]

All this may all not be very important, since everyone seems agreed that the only act nurses are regularly asked to perform—and for which they are said to have an expertise seldom shared by doctors—namely, inserting the needle for an intravenous drip, is 'preparatory'. If they avoid the behaviour that seems 'preparatory' in character but whose status is dubious, thereby keeping well to the preparatory side of the line, nurses can act on the assumption that the doctor's behaviour is in conformity with the requirements of due care and they will not be criminally liable as an accessory should it later be determined that a doctor does not qualify for the legal justification. But the joint 'guideline' does suggest that if a nurse has serious reason to suppose that the proposed euthanasia does not conform to the legal requirements, he could perhaps be subject to criminal prosecution, and if he participates in carrying out euthanasia knowing it to be illegal, he may run a serious risk of prosecution.[274]

This is highly theoretical. So far as is known there has been so only the one prosecution mentioned above of a nurse for involvement in euthanasia carried out under the responsibility of a doctor, and it involved the actual administration of the euthanatica.[275] In light of recent decisions of the Regional Review Committees, finding doctors who delegate the administration of euthanatica to a nurse or to another doctor, responsible for the euthanasia and therefore 'not careful', one could argue that in retrospect even this case was incorrectly decided: it was the doctor who was legally responsible for what took place.[276] However all this may be, both the Minister of Justice and the highest prosecutorial officials are said to have stated more than once that since the primary responsibility for the legality of euthanasia lies with the doctor, criminal or medical disciplinary proceedings against other caregivers who assist a doctor would not be opportune.[277]

Nurses, like doctors, are bound to respect the privacy of patients, and information concerning a patient's request for euthanasia should only be shared with other caregivers to the extent necessary and the wishes of the patient in this regard should be respected.[278] The obligation to maintain confidentiality also applies to contacts with the municipal pathologist, the prosecutor and the Regional Review Committee, after a case of euthanasia has been reported by the doctor: all ques-

---

[273] A reason is given for not allowing nurses to prepare the euthanatica and the syringe: in this way, a nurse cannot be held responsible for any lack of care in connection with the dose of euthanatica administered. However, a similar risk is attached to the other preparatory acts, and in any event, to the extent the examples given rest on such extraneous considerations, they do not illustrate the definition given. See also Legemaate 2005: 48–9 for an attempt to clarify the distinction.

[274] See AVVV 2006: 19–20 to this effect. It is not clear what the legal or other ground might be for these assertions.

[275] See n 268.

[276] See nn 214, 218. If the nurse or the other doctor had been seen as having carried out the euthanasia, then the reporting doctor would not have fallen within the scope of the Law of 2002, the reporting procedure, and the jurisdiction of the Review Committee.

[277] See AVVV 2006: 18; see also Legemaate 2005: 48 for a similar statement during the parliamentary debates on the Law of 2002.

[278] AVVV 2006: 24–5 (including the observation that a patient's insistence on secrecy may stand in the way of honouring his request for euthanasia).

tions should be referred to the responsible doctor. If a doctor fails to report a case, nurses must be able to raise the issue with the doctor or with their superiors and, if this does not suffice, with the Medical Inspectorate or the local prosecutor.[279]

The Medical Association and the professional organisation of nurses agree that a nurse is entitled to decline any involvement in euthanasia if she has conscientious objections.[280]

Pharmacists

Pharmacists (*apothekers*) are involved in euthanasia in the sense that they are the source of the lethal drugs used by doctors. They have, however, been assured by the prosecutorial authorities that if a doctor is prosecuted for illegal euthanasia the pharmacist who supplied the means will under normal circumstances not be regarded as an accessory.[281] The Pharmaceutical Inspectorate has taken the position that the pharmacist must discuss the matter with the doctor concerned, but he does not have to investigate whether the doctor is acting in conformity with the legal requirements.[282] The Royal Dutch Association for Pharmacy (KNMP) has for some years had a number of 'requirements of due care' that a pharmacist who is asked by a doctor to supply euthanatica should follow. Box 4.11 shows what is included in the most recent version (2007) of these requirements.[283]

Box 4.11 Requirements of due care for pharmacists

- there must be timely discussion between doctor and pharmacist, and if the pharmacist is of the opinion that there are possibilities for palliative care he can inform the doctor about these
- there must be a written request from the doctor and this must meet the requirements of and be maintained in the pharmacist's records in the same way as a request that falls under the legislation concerning narcotic drugs
- the doctor must supply the pharmacist with information on those aspects of the case that are relevant for the pharmacist (this can be done orally)
- the pharmacist should orally inform the doctor about the practical and technical aspects of carrying out euthanasia and if necessary give him, together with the euthanatica, written instructions on their use
- the pharmacist may consult another pharmacist about the pharmacological aspects of the case without breaching the confidentiality owed to doctor and patient
- the pharmacist must himself deliver the euthanatica directly to the doctor without involving his staff, but staff can be involved in the preparation
- the euthanatica must be properly labeled
- a pharmacist may refuse to supply euthanatica, but if he does this as a matter of principle he should inform the doctors in his vicinity of this

---

[279] AVVV 2006: 44.
[280] AVVV 2006: 22. *Cf* for an indication that such refusal occasionally takes place, RRC 2004: 30 (case 15—nurses refuse to insert needle for administration of morphine—see further on this case n 213).
[281] See NVP 2004: 34.
[282] See KNMP 1994: 18.
[283] KNMP 2007: 28–9. These criteria were first formulated in 1984 and revised in 1987, 1994, 1998 and 2007.

Apart from criminal liability, pharmacists are subject to medical disciplinary law and to the disciplinary rules of their Association. So far as is known, there has never been any sort of proceeding against a pharmacist in connection with euthanasia.[284]

Lay Persons

Non-doctors cannot legally perform euthanasia. The possibility of their involvement in assisted suicide under the responsibility of a doctor (something similar to the situation in Switzerland, see chapter 16) has received little attention in the Netherlands.[285]

Since 1999 lay assistance with suicide in the absence of any involvement of a doctor has been the subject of several prosecutions. The prosecutorial authorities apparently decided actively to prosecute what are called 'suicide consultants' for the offence of giving assistance with suicide. These 'consultants' are persons working (usually as volunteers) for organisations that give information, advice and support to persons wanting to commit suicide. Interestingly, there have been few prosecutions of persons involved in suicide assistance in a purely 'private' capacity (eg family members or close friends), and all of these of which we are aware took place many years ago.[286] That there in fact are a substantial number of such cases is made clear by Chabot's research on the subject (see chapter 5.2.2.3).

The recent prosecutions of 'suicide consultants' are discussed in chapter 3.6. The key issue in these cases is what constitutes 'assistance'. In an earlier case involving the 'plastic bag' method, the defendant had advised the deceased as to the method, was present at the time, and told him when to pull the bag over his head.[287] The courts held that the 'assistance' prohibited by article 294 requires actual presence at the time of the suicide,[288] and that giving 'moral support' or 'information' are in themselves not enough. The defendant, however, was considered to have gone further than this: what she did amounted to giving the deceased an 'instruction'.[289]

It would be foolhardy to wager a prediction on the direction or the speed of legal development on this matter. So far, while the scope of justifiable euthanasia has

[284] Information received from the KNMP.

[285] An early NVVE bill to legalise euthanasia did provide that it could be done 'by or in close consultation and cooperation with a doctor' (see NVVE 1996).

[286] The *Postma* case (1973)—the earliest case in the development of Dutch euthanasia law—was in effect one of 'private' assistance, the doctor who carried out euthanasia being the patient's daughter; she was given a suspended sentence (see GB&W: 51–2). In another early case—*Pols* (1982)—a psychiatrist carried out euthanasia on a friend and was convicted (for failure to consult another doctor) and given a suspended sentence (see GB&W: 63–4). Early cases in which non-medical family members or others gave assistance, some of whom received significant prison sentences, are discussed in GB&W: 53–4, 58–9, and Weyers 2004: 141*ff.*

[287] See ch 3.6 n 92. Defendant was a doctor but maintained that she had not acted as such.

[288] Note that 'procuring the means' is a distinct ground of criminal liability under art 294.

[289] The decision to this effect by the Court of Appeals, The Hague, was upheld by the Supreme Court (*Tijdschrift voor Gezondheidsrecht* 1993 no 24; 1994 no 65; *Nederlandse Jurisprudentie* 1996 no 322).

been gradually widened, the courts, the prosecutorial authorities, the medical profession and the legislature remain insistent that it must be a purely 'medical' practice. Although the 'medical exception' has been repeatedly rejected, the fact is that
Dutch euthanasia law is exceptional law, for doctors only. As we will see in section
4.2.3.5, this has implications not only for the question who may perform it, but
also for the circumstances in which it is legal at all.

4.2.3.4 Assistance with Suicide in the Absence of 'Somatic' Suffering

It is often assumed that for purposes of the regulatory regime applicable to
euthanasia and assistance with suicide a distinction can be made between somatically based and not-somatically based suffering. Connected with this is the fact
that, although in general Dutch law makes no distinction between the legal
requirements applicable to euthanasia and to physician-assisted suicide, it seems
to be uniformly (if implicitly) assumed that when the patient's suffering does not
have a somatic basis, only assisted suicide is available.[290]

So far as assisted suicide is concerned, any further relevance of the distinction
between somatic and non-somatic suffering was significantly reduced by the holding of the Supreme Court in 1994 in the *Chabot* case (see section 4.2.3.4(A)), to the
effect that not somatically-based suffering can support a valid request for assistance with suicide—that, for purposes of the justification of necessity, the source of
a patient's suffering is irrelevant.[291] The Regional Review Committees have taken
the same position in assessing cases of euthanasia under the Law of 2002.[292]
However, as the *Chabot* case also makes clear, the distinction can be relevant for
the degree of care expected of a doctor, the substance of the consultation requirement, and the consequences of a possible refusal of treatment by the patient.

What ultimately is the intrinsic significance of the somatic/non-somatic distinction? Psychiatric conditions that used to be considered entirely non-somatic in
origin are increasingly being found to include biological factors in their aetiology.
The shortening of life involved in a case of non-somatic suffering will usually be
far greater, but this is not necessarily the case, for example in somatic conditions
such as MS, AIDS, and paraplegia. Precisely where life expectancy is considerable
and the patient's condition has proved untreatable, the prospect of an indefinite
future of the severe suffering that accompanies some non-somatic conditions
can be particularly unbearable.[293] In short, the distinction somatic/non-somatic is
not necessarily congruent with a requirement of proportionality. On the other
hand, when the shortening of life involved is considerable (whether the case
involves somatically based or not-somatically based suffering), the amount of life

---

[290] It has been suggested that a patient whose suffering is non-somatic but who is not capable of carrying out suicide (eg a psychiatric patient who is paraplegic after a failed suicide attempt) should qualify for euthanasia (see GB&W: 151).

[291] This position goes back to the report of the State Commission on Euthanasia (1985).

[292] See RRC 2003: 17 (case 5).

[293] Compare NVP 2004: 22.

lost might itself be thought to support the 'exceptional care' the Supreme Court insisted upon in *Chabot* in cases of not-somatically based suffering.[294]

Finally, as the Supreme Court held in *Chabot*, the idea that in some cases of non-somatic suffering there may be reason to doubt whether the patient's request is voluntary and well considered does not support a general ban on assistance with suicide in all such cases. After all, patients suffering from somatic causes may also suffer from diminished competence, whereas the competence of some patients whose suffering is non-somatic may not be in question at all.

4.2.3.4(A) The Chabot Case

During the 1990s and up to the enactment of the Law of 2002, disagreement and uncertainty reigned with regard to the question, whether and subject to what limitations persons whose suffering is of non-somatic origin meet the conditions for legal assistance with suicide. The subject is covered—through 1997—in some detail in the predecessor of this book[295] so we recapitulate only a few essentials and concentrate on the law as it is under the Law of 2002. Most of the basic questions were settled in 1994 by the decision of the Supreme Court in the *Chabot* case (see Box 4.12).

Box 4.12 Essential holdings of the Supreme Court in the Chabot *case*

- Can assistance with suicide be legally justifiable in the case of a patient whose suffering does not have a somatic basis and who is not in the 'terminal phase'? The court held that it can be.[296]
- Can the wish to die of a person suffering from a psychiatric sickness or disorder legally be considered the result of an autonomous (competent and voluntary) judgment? The court held that it can be.
- Can the suffering of such a person legally be considered 'lacking any prospect for improvement' if he has refused a realistic (therapeutic) alternative? The court held that in principle it cannot be.[297]
- Are there special procedural requirements of due care in such a case? The court held that in the case of non-somatically based suffering, the requirement of consultation (specifically, that the consultant examine the patient) is a condition of the justification of necessity.

---

[294] Legemaate (2005: 41) observes that although no such special requirement is explicitly included in the Law of 2002, since the Law was intended to codify the case law up to 2002 it can be assumed that 'exceptionally great care' is still required in cases of non-somatic suffering. In his view, this is not a separate requirement: it refers to the 'deeper and more extensive attention' that must be paid to the existing requirements (suffering, he argues, should be less easily and less quickly assumed in such a case).

[295] GB&W: 139–51.

[296] Unbearable suffering can, eg, be based on the prospect of becoming demented, in the case of a patient in the early stages of dementia. See Legemaate 2005: 52 (discussing a decision by the prosecutorial authorities in 2003 not to prosecute in such a case).

[297] As we have seen in section 4.2.3.3(C), the Regional Review Committees are currently more willing to accept refusal of treatment in such cases than might have been expected shortly after the *Chabot* case (see GB&W 150 n 193). At the time of the predecessor of this book, there were suggestions in the literature that the interventions that must be tried included 'social interventions that could make the suffering more bearable' (NVP 1998: §3.3.3). The implications of this idea were not entirely clear, and in the intervening years little or no attention has been paid to the matter.

The different treatment of the consultation requirement in the situation of non-somatic suffering followed, in the view of the Supreme Court, from the 'extra-ordinary care' required in such cases. This part of the court's holding is no longer relevant, since such consultation is, under the Law of 2002, a condition of the statutory legalisation in all cases.

4.2.3.4(B) *Suffering Due to a Psychiatric Disorder*

Assistance with suicide to persons suffering from a psychiatric disorder has received attention quite out of proportion to its frequency. As of 1995, Dutch psychiatrists were receiving some 320 serious requests for assistance with suicide per year. Some 2 to 5 of these were granted, in more than half of which the patient was also suffering from a terminal somatic disorder.[298] The Netherlands Association for Psychiatry (NVP), on whose particularly thoughtful and careful guideline much of the following is based, assumes that virtually all cases in which a psychiatrist gives assistance with suicide to a person suffering from a psychiatric disorder with suicide, are reported; in 2001 there were three reported cases in which the suffering was 'primarily of psychic origin'.[299] According to the NVP, 'the view that in very specific circumstances assistance with suicide in psychiatric practice can be justifiable' is widely accepted among psychiatrists.[300] Since 2003, the Regional Review Committees have taken the position that the request of a person whose suffering is primarily of psychiatric origin in principle falls under the Law of 2002 and hence within the committees' jurisdiction.[301]

In general, assistance with suicide in the case of a psychiatric patient will be given by his psychiatrist, and it is that situation that we will be dealing with in what follows.[302] But it should be noted that the NVP does not consider it in principle impossible that a non-psychiatrist—for example, the patient's GP—give assistance with suicide in the case of a former psychiatric patient who is no longer under treatment by a psychiatrist.[303] If the doctor who receives the request is not himself a psychiatrist, he should discuss the case intensively with the patient's psychiatrist(s) (in particular to establish that further treatment is regarded by them as futile) and consult two independent psychiatrists.[304]

[298] Van der Wal & Van der Maas 1996: 204 (no specific study of psychiatric patients was carried out in the 2001 and 2007 studies).

[299] NVP 2004: 4; for a detailed discussion of the NVP's earlier guideline, see GB&W: § 3.5.1. For some (sparse) data on patients suffering from psychiatric disorders, see ch 5.2.2.1 under 'psychiatric patients'.

[300] NVP 2004: 12.

[301] See section 4.2.4.3(B) below.

[302] In the case of psychiatric and somatic co-morbidity, a psychiatrist can give assistance with suicide if he has an existing treatment relationship with the patient, but in such a case a 'second opinion' must be sought from the patient's GP and specialist. If such a person who is not his patient approaches a psychiatrist for assisted suicide, he must either refer the patient to a somatic doctor with whom the patient has a treatment relationship, or himself establish such a relationship with the patient before considering the request (NVP 2004: 39–40).

[303] See RRC 2006: 18–21 (case 3/4) for an example of such a case (it is not clear that the patient was no longer being treated by the psychiatrist).

[304] NVP 2004: 38–9. The Review Committees do not appear to regard such an extreme consultation requirement as necessary (see the case referred to in the previous note).

Voluntary, Well-Considered Request

The NVP defines a 'voluntary request' as one 'free from coercive influence by others'.[305] Psychiatric patients can be particularly susceptible to real or perceived pressure from their social surroundings and a psychiatrist must be alert to the possibility that a patient's request is a response to such pressure. A request is 'well considered' when it meets the tests set out in Box 4.13.

Box 4.13 A 'well-considered' request in the case of a psychiatric patient

---

The request:

- involves a 'clear choice' for death (although a certain ambivalence is inherent in the balancing of reasons for and against, and neither this nor a fear of death that persists up to the last moment are inconsistent with a competent decision);
- is the result of a decision-making process in which the patient has been adequately informed about his situation and its prospects, and possesses enough insight into his disorder and his own personality to be able to weigh the choice for continued life (with the limitations inherent in his psychiatric disorder) against the choice for suicide, and within the limits of his intellectual ability to explain his choice for death;[306]
- reflects a lasting desire for death: the patient must 'over a period of at least several months, in a well-considered way, repeatedly, and also in the presence of others have unmistakably made the request'.[307]

Unbearable Suffering

As in the case of somatically based suffering, how unbearable the suffering of a psychiatric patient is, is largely a matter of his subjective experience, subject only to the requirement that it be 'understandable' [*invoelbaar*] for the psychiatrist. As we have seen, the NVP notes that the often considerable life-expectancy of psychiatric patients entails the prospect, for a patient whose psychiatric disorder has proven untreatable, of lifelong suffering.

The NVP argues that while, in general, every case must conform to all of the legal criteria, the suffering of the patient is the most imperative consideration. In cases in which the patient's suffering is obviously unbearable, some flexibility should be possible with regard to some of the other criteria. There are cases, for example, in which the patient's competence cannot meet a strict standard because of the presence of psychotic elements, but in which the only alternative to assisted suicide is long-term isolation and forced feeding. In such extreme cases there

---

[305] NVP 2004: 18.

[306] The NVP observes that a psychiatrist must be alert to the danger that 'primitive inclinations and drives' that the patient is not consciously aware of may play a role in his choice, but like the Supreme Court in the *Chabot* case, it rejects the categorical assumption that all psychiatric patients lack the capacity for a well-considered choice for death (NVP 2004: 21).

[307] NVP 2004: 21 (italics in original). The NVP rejects a requirement of a written request, out of concern that such a requirement might tend to commit the patient to the request (*ibid*).

should be some room for assisted suicide even if a minor departure from one of the other criteria is involved.[308]

Treatment Perspective

The NVP's position is that a patient's suffering is 'without prospect of improvement' only when 'all treatments that according to scientific medical opinion are appropriate for the patient concerned have been tried and have proven ineffective'.[309] Before reaching the conclusion that there is no treatment that offers hope of improvement, within a reasonable time and with a reasonable balance between the expected results and the burden for the patient, a 'complete psychopharmacological protocol and a complaint-oriented psychotherapeutic treatment' must have been carried out, as well as 'social interventions' that could make the patient's suffering easier to bear. The treatment must be in conformity with guidelines and consensus documents of the profession, and *state of the art*. There is still a 'realistic treatment perspective' so long as it is reasonable to assume that the situation of the patient can improve, that there are possibilities of intervention that have a serious chance of success.[310]

In short, a psychiatric patient's refusal of treatment, unlike that of a patient whose suffering is based on a somatic condition, precludes assistance with suicide if the treatment proposed offers a reasonable chance of success within a reasonable time. However, the NVP notes that an improvement in psychiatric terms will not necessarily always be experienced by the patient as reducing his suffering, and in such a case refusal may be acceptable.[311]

Consultation

Because of the special susceptibility of psychiatric patients to suggestion and influence, and the danger that the psychiatrist, too, may be influenced in his judgment by unconscious motives, the NVP agrees with the Supreme Court's judgment in the *Chabot* case that an especially high degree of care is required in these cases.[312] The NVP distinguishes in this connection between (1) seeking advice from colleagues before deciding what to do (highly recommended), (2) a 'second opinion' for the benefit of the patient, when the psychiatrist considers that the criteria for assistance have not been met, and (3) the requirement of formal consultation before carrying out assistance with suicide.[313] In the case of a psychiatric patient there should be formal consultation with one, and in difficult cases more than one,

---

[308] NVP 2004: 35, 36.
[309] NVP 2004: 24.
[310] NVP 2004: 24–6.
[311] NVP 2004: 26.The NVP does insist, however, that 'indicated biological psychiatric treatments, because of their relatively quick effects and the fact that side-effects are seldom serious' can in no case be refused.
[312] NVP 2004: 27–30.
[313] NVP 2004: 16–17, 28.

independent psychiatrist.[314] In addition to considering the requirements of due care set forth in the Law of 2002, the consulted psychiatrist should give his opinion concerning the psychiatric diagnosis and possible transference and counter-transference aspects of the treatment relationship. It is not in general necessary that two independent consultants be asked to assess the case, but this may be desirable in case of co-morbidity, and in such a case the second consultant might be a non-psychiatrist.

The consulted doctor must have discussed the case with the doctor responsible for treatment, have read the medical files, and have seen and examined the patient (unless it is clear to him from the information the consulting doctor gives him that assistance with suicide is not justifiable). The patient's doctor should himself have decided that assistance with suicide is justifiable before approaching a colleague for consultation (he should not use consultation to resolve his own doubts) but he must not commit himself to carry out assistance with suicide until after consultation has taken place.

If the consulted psychiatrist is of the view that the criteria for assistance with suicide have not been met, but the patient's psychiatrist decides to give the assistance anyway, he 'must have very good arguments that a completely unacceptable situation without any prospects' will otherwise be left unchanged. If the difference of opinion is fundamental, assistance with suicide is not justifiable, and he should approach a second consultant, who must be informed of the judgment of the first consultant. If the second consultant shares the fundamental objections of the first one, then assistance with suicide is out of the question.[315]

Carrying Out Assisted Suicide

In general, the psychiatrist must be present at the suicide. Just before it takes place, he must ask the patient whether he really wants to go through with it. Furthermore, since the drugs used for PAS do not always lead quickly to death, the psychiatrist must be prepared to give an injection of a muscle relaxant if the patient does not die within a reasonable time (at most five hours).

---

[314] Since one of the most important questions the consultant must answer is whether there is a remaining treatment possibility, it is advisable to seek consultation from a psychiatrist with special expertise concerning the patient's specific disorder; in some cases it may be desirable to have the consultation take place in a specialised clinic where there are additional possibilities for examining the patient and for intensive treatment (NVP 2004: 28).

The prosecution Guideline (n 353) asserts that the 'legislator' has determined, in the model form for reporting euthanasia or PAS, that in the case of non-somatic suffering, consultation is required with two independent doctors, one of whom must be a psychiatrist. The guideline refers in this connection to a letter from the Minister of Justice to the Second Chamber of Parliament of 16 September 1994 (*Second Chamber of Parliament 1993–1994*, 23 877, no 1), following the judgment in the *Chabot* case (see section 4.2.3.4(A)). In this letter, such a requirement is indeed formulated (acknowledging that no such requirement is contained in the *Chabot* decision but referring to a revised version of the model form as it then was). However, the current model form contains no such provision, and the model form is in any case merely an appendix to a Ministerial Decree. In short, legal support for such a requirement seems very weak.

[315] NVP 2004: 30.

However, if the patient expressly wants to die in the presence of others but not of the psychiatrist, this is acceptable if there are good reasons for it. In that case it must at the appointed time be possible to reach the psychiatrist immediately and he must be able to be at the scene at short notice. The third persons present may not give any assistance. It is also an option to give the patient the euthanatica for an agreed-upon period such as a week. However, this is only acceptable as a way of making sure the patient does not feel 'obliged' to go through with the suicide. In such cases specific agreements must be made concerning the third persons to be present,[316] the continued availability of the psychiatrist during the agreed-upon period, the place the suicide is to be carried out, and so forth. The patient's GP and close relatives or friends must be notified. The reasons for the decision not to be present, and the agreements made, must be in writing.[317]

Other 'Requirements of Due Care'

The NVP position is that other health professionals who have treated the patient (GPs, other psychiatrists or psychologists) should be included in the decision-making.[318] If the patient is in an institution, the various members of the team responsible for treatment, as well as the superiors of the psychiatrist concerned, should also be involved.[319] The psychiatrist should speak with the family and intimate friends of the patient, both in order to prepare them for the suicide and because they may be a source of important information relevant to the decision-making. If the patient refuses permission for this, the psychiatrist may decide not to go ahead with the assisted suicide, unless the patient has substantial reasons for his refusal (such as very disturbed family relationships, a prior history of abuse, etc), in which case the patient's wishes should usually be respected.[320]

Record-Keeping

The NVP devotes extensive attention to the importance of careful and complete record-keeping. It also adds to the model form for reporting a case of euthanasia or assistance with suicide, a number of questions going deeper into the patient's disorder, the treatments given, the further possibilities of treatment, the reasons for not being present at the suicide and the agreements made in this connection.[321]

---

[316] The NVP is not entirely clear as to whether the presence of others is required, if the psychiatrist himself is not present. The tenor of the rest of the discussion concerning the requirement of actual presence would seem to suggest that some responsible person ought always to be present.

[317] NVP 2004: 30–31. The prosecutorial Guideline (n 353) observes: 'In the case of assistance with suicide the doctor must be present, or available in the near surroundings . . .'.

[318] While the patient must give permission for this, his psychiatrist must make clear to him that if he refuses, assistance with suicide will not be possible (NVP 2004: 31).

[319] NVP 2004: 33. Although they are not responsible in the sense of the criminal law or medical disciplinary law, their responsibility for the institution and its policy requires this. The ultimate decision is, however, the individual responsibility of the doctor and cannot be delegated to a committee or a superior in the institution.

[320] NVP 2004: 31–2; compare CAL 1997: 168–9.

[321] NVP 2004: 41–4.

Institutionalised Patients

An involuntarily committed patient should in principle be discharged before assistance with suicide is given.[322] Consideration should always be given to the possibility of letting the patient live outside the institution for a while in order to establish whether institutionalisation itself was responsible for the patient's unbearable suffering.[323]

The NVP considers particularly difficult the problem of institutionalised suicidal patients for whom there is no treatment perspective but only one of continued physical restraint and who are suffering unbearably from a psychiatric disorder that precludes a well-considered request. 'One is confronted by the limits of what psychiatry has to offer.' The choice, in the view of the NVP, is between giving assistance with suicide even though not all the requirements have been met (and thus running the risk of a criminal prosecution), or following the 'less official route' and letting the patient leave the institution, knowing that he will probably commit suicide. The NVP regards the former course as 'preferable', referring to its position, described above, that assistance with suicide should be possible in exceptional cases in which not all of the criteria have been met.[324]

Conscientious Objections

A psychiatrist is entitled to refuse participation for reasons of principle. He should make his position clear to the patient in a timely fashion and inform the patient about the possibility of approaching another psychiatrist. He need not formally refer the patient to a colleague who is known to be willing to give assistance with suicide, but he should at least give the patient some help in looking for one. He must give the other psychiatrist all necessary information about the patient. It is not necessary that the treatment relationship with the first psychiatrist be ended, but if the patient does not want to continue it he should cooperate in accomplishing a careful ending of the relationship and transfer the patient's medical file to his colleague.[325]

---

[322] NVP 2004: 36. This cannot, however, be done if the involuntary commitment was due to a risk of suicide. The NVP also considers the case of persons involuntarily confined in connection with a pending criminal prosecution or who are serving a sentence: assistance with suicide can only be contemplated after their involuntary confinement is at an end. Some attention is also paid to the special case of persons subject to the special measures for persons found to have committed crimes while of diminished responsibility (NVP 2004: 37).

[323] In general, the NVP regards release in order to enable a patient to commit suicide on his own as subject to the same medical-ethical considerations as assisted suicide: doing so simply because one has personal objections to active assistance, or in order to avoid the risk of prosecution, without informing the patient that assisted suicide is an option and possibly referring him to his GP or to another psychiatrist, is unacceptable (NVP 2004: 11).

[324] NVP 2004: 36.

[325] NVP 2004: 15–16.

Why a Psychiatrist?

According to the NVP, a psychiatrist has only a limited title to give assistance in suicide: the existence of suffering due to a 'psychiatric disorder':

> This [restriction] is intended to establish a border between the context within which [the question of assisted suicide] can be relevant for a psychiatrist, and personal or social suffering that is not directly related to a psychiatric disorder. It is not that such suffering, measured according to humanitarian criteria, necessarily weighs less heavily; but it is not the task of a psychiatrist to alleviate it.[326]

It is thus only within the context of his 'responsibility for giving treatment to a person with a psychiatric disorder', that a psychiatrist can decide to give assistance with suicide.[327] A psychiatrist can only invoke the justification of necessity, based on a conflict of duties, on the basis of his treatment relationship to a person with such a disorder.[328] As we will see in the following section, this idea that a doctor requires a 'medical' title as a basis for giving assistance in suicide—that without such a title, the justification for doctors being involved at all does not exist—is of more general importance in Dutch euthanasia law.

Reporting

Reporting by psychiatrists of cases of assistance with suicide is said to be rare (although the handful of cases known to have been reported to the Review Committees is not so very different from the tiny number that Table 5.11 in chapter 5 shows actually to take place). This may be attributable to the position of the prosecutorial authorities and the Regional Review Committees, until the Euthanasia Law of 2002, that such cases fell outside the jurisdiction of the committees (see section 4.2.4.3(B)). What a psychiatrist who did get reported could expect is illustrated by the following case, which is almost a caricature of the reasons doctors have for not trusting review by the criminal law authorities.

At the end of 2000 a psychiatrist assisted with the suicide of a patient and duly reported what he had done. The prosecutorial authorities apparently took the position that the competence of a psychiatric patient is necessarily questionable and initiated criminal proceedings. In the course of the preliminary investigation two psychiatrists were asked by the prosecutor to give 'second opinions' based on the psychiatric dossier. They concluded (contrary to the two psychiatrists who had actually seen the patient) that the patient had not been competent. The two 'second opinions' also stated that the situation had not been 'hopeless' because there was an available treatment with drugs (this suggestion was later shown to be wrong by an expert specialised in the treatment concerned). In the end, the prosecutorial

---

[326] NVP 2004: 2.
[327] NVP 2004: 13 (*cf* also 14).
[328] NVP 2004: 45.

authorities decided not to prosecute. The case finally ended more than 6 years after the psychiatrist concerned had reported it.[329]

Under the Law of 2002, a Review Committee would have disposed of the case in 3 months, at the most, and in the light of other decisions would presumably have found the psychiatrist 'careful'.

4.2.3.4(C) Assistance with Suicide in the Absence of a 'Medical' Condition

Assistance with suicide in a case of non-somatic suffering, such as that of Ms B in the *Chabot* case, is only in a residual sense 'medical'. Although Chabot himself did not think Ms B was suffering from any psychiatric disorder,[330] the Supreme Court regarded Ms B as in some sense 'sick' and apparently considered this essential. Nevertheless, the decision in the *Chabot* case seemed to some people to represent a shift in the principled basis on which Dutch euthanasia law rests. They believed that the court had taken a hesitant step away from the doctor-centred approach that had dominated legal development from the beginning, in the direction of an approach that would give greater weight to the *principle of autonomy* than to the *principle of beneficence.*

Looked at in this way, the decision in *Chabot* could be seen as having opened the way to a legal development that would accept assistance with suicide to persons whose suffering has no 'medically' recognised character at all, somatic or otherwise. A number of situations in which no 'medical' condition underlies a person's request for assistance with suicide can be distinguished:

- A person who is not psychiatrically 'sick' may suffer unbearably as the result of a traumatic experience, and there may be no treatment acceptable to the person concerned, or none with so favourable a prognosis that its benefits can be considered to outweigh the burden to the patient. (This was the situation in the *Chabot* case, on Chabot's view.)
- As a result of old age, with its accompanying physical deterioration, dependency, loneliness etc, a person may be 'tired of living': life as such has become unbearable. Examples of such cases—in which the prosecuting authorities decided not to prosecute doctors who had rendered assistance—have been described in the literature.[331]
- Although they are not currently suffering, the prospect of dementia, physical deterioration, dependency, confinement to a nursing home, etc is considered unacceptable by some people, who wish to choose their own moment of death in order not to have to undergo these experiences. Years ago, the respected former Supreme Court judge Drion argued that, under very limited circumstances, elderly persons should have the right to be supplied with a 'pill' with which they

---

[329] Information received from the consulted psychiatrist, AJ Tholen. On 27 March 2007 the psychiatrist concerned was formally notified that he would not be prosecuted.

[330] See GB&W: appendix II-2, part 2; Chabot 1996: 153.

[331] See Chabot 1992 and Weisz 1994.

could commit suicide at a time of their choosing.[332] To date, the suggestion has not received serious attention either from the Medical Association or from the Dutch Government or Parliament, although the Voluntary Euthanasia Association continues to promote it.[333]

In effect, two issues are at stake: (1) May a *doctor* be involved if the patient's condition is not a 'medical' one? (2) Should *non-doctors* be permitted to render assistance in such cases?

As we have seen in chapter 3.3, the first question was recently answered by the Supreme Court in the *Brongersma* case (2002). As reported by the doctor concerned, debated in the press and Parliament, and decided by the Supreme Court, the case involved an elderly gentleman who, confronted with increasing immobility and the social isolation consequent both on his advanced age and his disabilities, had come to regard his continuing life as a burden rather than a benefit. He was, as the case was popularly discussed, 'tired of life'. His GP considered that he met the requirements (in particular, of a voluntary request and unbearable and untreatable suffering) and gave him the requested assistance. The Supreme Court held that since his patient's suffering was predominantly based on things other than a 'medically classifiable' disorder,[334] the doctor exceeded the scope of his professional competence in assisting Brongersma to commit suicide. More precisely: the court held that the situation of conflict of duties a doctor can find himself in—relief of suffering versus respect for life—can only arise if, because of the patient's 'medical' condition, the doctor has any special duty at all in the case.

The Supreme Court's emphasis on the 'medical' character of legally justifiable euthanasia and assisted suicide was explicitly embraced by the Government and many members of Parliament in the proceedings leading to the Law of 2002, and thereby became at least a latent part of the new law (although the text of the law contains nothing on the matter).[335]

The possibility of lay assistance in such cases has been discussed in section 4.2.3.3(J) above and in chapter 3.6; the little that is known empirically is dealt with in chapter 5.2.2.3 and 5.3.

---

[332] Drion 1992. For a variety of practical reasons, Drion proposed to limit this to single persons over 75.

[333] See ch 3.3.

[334] In fact, Brongersma suffered from a number of medical conditions, not significantly different from those accepted as sufficient in other cases.

[335] There has been some controversy concerning the question, whether the limitation to 'medically classifiable conditions' is desirable or usable in practice. The chairman of the KNMG announced the Association's disapproval of what the doctor in the *Brongersma* case had done, and two expert witnesses appointed by the Court of Appeals (and who are closely affiliated with the KNMG) argued for a limitation on the involvement of doctors in assistance with suicide, similar to that later imposed by the Supreme Court. Nevertheless, an advisory committee of the KNMG produced a report after the decision in *Brongersma* arguing that there might be some room for participation by doctors in such cases. See ch 3.3.

4.2.3.5 Termination of Life Without an Explicit Request

The final sub-sort of 'termination of life' is termination of life without an explicit request from the person concerned. This does not fall within the 'medical exception' nor is it covered by article 293 of the Penal Code (euthanasia). It is therefore in principle murder. As we will see in chapter 5, Dutch research (Table 5.1) shows that such behaviour by doctors occurs at a small but not negligible rate. International research (see chapter 17) shows that in some other European countries the rate is about as high or higher than in the Netherlands. Were it not for the legally dubious way that the doctor's 'intent' and the act/omission distinction are used in classifying medical behaviour that potentially shortens life (see section 4.2.3 and chapter 5.1.2.2), measurements of such behaviour would probably produce considerably higher rates.

The category of 'termination of life without an explicit request' is in effect a garbage-can category consisting of a number of very different sorts of behaviour. It includes cases of medical corner-cutting or loss of control (eg when under pressure from the patient's family). There are also cases in which the patient made a request but it did not meet the legal criteria. All of this is and will remain illegal, although one can wonder whether it is always appropriate to classify and to prosecute it as 'murder'.

However, the category of termination of life without a request also includes cases in which what the doctor did was consistent with the applicable professional standards. Dutch courts have in several cases involving severely defective newborn babies held such behaviour to be legally justifiable. This situation is dealt with at length in chapter 6.

Finally, despite the suggestion of the Remmelink Committee that 'help in dying' be considered 'normal medical practice' and hence within the 'medical exception', the recent decision of the Supreme Court in the *Van Oijen* case appears to treat such behaviour as termination of life without an explicit request. The doctor involved was convicted of murder.[336]

4.2.4 The System of Control

In this book we are primarily concerned with those areas of the law where specific regulation of medical behaviour that potentially shortens life has developed or is in the process of developing. First, and historically foremost at least as far as legal control is concerned, is the criminal law (medical exception; justification of necessity; amendments to articles 293 and 294 of the Penal Code). Where professional standards have emerged to deal with this sort of behaviour, medical disciplinary law has also become active: both before and after the Law of 2002, the scope of disciplinary law has been rather broader than that of the criminal law, and in addition to the 'requirements of due care' also other rules can and have been enforced

---

[336] See section 4.2.2.5 above.

in disciplinary proceedings.[337] And both before, and on a firmer legal footing after the Law of 2002, the 'requirements of due care' have been enforced in the first instance in a special administrative procedure before the Regional Review Committees (see section 4.2.4.3 below).

Since 2002 the role of the prosecutorial authorities in exercising legal control over euthanasia practice has become much less important both quantitatively and substantively than it was in the early days of legal euthanasia. Nevertheless, the criminal law remains the sanction of last resort in the whole system, and we therefore devote specific attention to the role of the prosecutors in section 4.2.4.2. The involvement of the Medical Inspectorate and the Medical Disciplinary Tribunals in the exercise of legal control has always been sporadic and marginal, and has become even more so since 2002. We will devote no specific attention to this form of legal control, although whenever it has occurred, we have taken note of this in both this chapter and in chapter 5.

While concentrating as we will on sorts of legal control specific to medical behaviour that potentially shortens life, it would be wrong to overlook more general sorts of legal control. A rather important role in the development of Dutch law in this area has been played by the civil courts, largely in cases involving a rough Dutch equivalent of an injunction action (*kort geding*), in which a judicial order is sought to require or to prevent particular behaviour by a doctor. There have been several such cases, mostly involving attempts to require a doctor to withhold or withdraw treatment, or to forbid him from doing so;[338] threats by the representatives of a noncompetent patient to bring such an action seem considerably to increase their bargaining power with doctors.[339] The doctor–patient relationship is conceived of legally as being contractual in nature, so that remedies in contract are in principle available for things like failure to secure informed consent, failure to follow an advance directive or the instructions of a representative, and so forth. Medical behaviour that is negligent or that departs from the professional standard gives rise to potential liability in tort. Employment law can be an important source of control over the behaviour of doctors in general and MBPSL in particular: many doctors are employees of institutions (in particular hospitals and nursing homes) that have policies both with regard to practices they do not permit and with regard to the procedures to be followed, and deviation from these policies can be grounds for ending the employment contract.[340] The law related to health insurance might also be relevant, if for example an insurer were to decline to pay for treatment that is not medically indicated or to which the patient has not consented (eg if there is an advance directive refusing such treatment). Even the law of wills can be relevant, as evidenced by a case in which the family of a woman who died at age 95 by refraining

---

[337] In the *Chabot* case, eg, criminal conviction was followed by a disciplinary judgment, partly for the same behaviour, partly for the additional offence of not having maintained sufficient professional distance from the patient. See GB&W: 338–40. See also the *Van Oijen* and *Vencken* cases (ch 3.4).

[338] The *Stinessen* case (see GB&W: 77–8) and the case mentioned in n 51 are examples of this.

[339] See Kleijer 2005: 130–34.

[340] See the case briefly described in section 4.2.3.3(I). *Cf* Blad 1990: 46, 99.

from eating or drinking in the care of a doctor who was a longstanding friend and to whom she had left a great deal of money in her will, challenged his inheritance.[341]

Still less specific, and in some sense less 'legal' forms of potential control are the national or local Ombudsman (when behaviour by a public agency is involved),[342] and the complaint procedures that health care institutions and general practitioners are required to maintain.[343]

In short, medical behaviour that shortens life is in the Netherlands (potentially) subject to a large number of different forms of legal control, most of which have been actively used and have thereby contributed to the process of legal development. In what follows, we concentrate on the most important of these: the criminal law, and the special administrative control procedure that is grafted onto the criminal law: the Regional Review Committees.

4.2.4.1 The Reporting Procedure in Case of 'Natural' or 'Non-Natural' Death

The system of legal control over euthanasia and termination of life without a request is based on reporting by doctors.[344] Elsewhere in this book we speak rather loosely of the doctor's 'duty' to report a death from euthanasia or termination of life without a request as a 'non-natural' one, which is what the legal situation amounts to in substance. This is the place to describe the applicable legal rules more precisely.

The Law on Burial and Cremation requires the city clerk's permission for burial or cremation. Such permission is granted if the doctor responsible for the patient (or the municipal pathologist) files a death certificate on which he certifies that the patient died from a 'natural cause'.[345] No further legal control takes place

---

[341] See *de Volkskrant* (18 March 2004) p 2. The appeals tribunal for medical disciplinary cases had earlier on sanctioned the doctor for giving the woman medical care in connection with her refraining from eating and drinking, knowing that he had been included in her will (see *Medisch Contact* 59: 427–30 (2004) for the judgment of the appeals tribunal).

[342] See *Algemene Wet Bestuursrecht* [General Administrative Law Act], title 9.2. For the only relevant case known to us, see *Medisch Contact* 57: 1930–32 (2002). The case involved a complaint by a GP—called to the scene of an attempted suicide—against a policeman who overruled his decision to respect a written refusal of treatment and summoned an ambulance. The Ombudsman held that decision-making authority resides with the doctor in such a case. This decision is severely criticised—on the ground that a doctor cannot be expected to have the necessary competence with respect to possible criminal aspects of such a situation—in a reaction in the professional journal for the police (*Algemene Politieblad* (19 October 2002) p 16).

[343] *Wet klachtrecht cliënten zorgsector* (29 May 1995, *Staatsblad* 308, amended 26 September 1996, *Staatsblad* 478). See for a description of the working of this law in practice Friele *et al* 1999. As of 2005, practically all hospitals participated in a national complaints procedure which was processing between 35 and 70 complaints per year (as far as is known, none of these concerned MBPSL). See Stichting Geschillencommissies voor Consumentenzaken 2006: 130*ff.*

[344] The historical development of the reporting procedure through 1997 is dealt with in detail in GB&W: ch 2.3.3 and ch 3.2.

[345] What exactly amounts to a 'natural cause', is a matter of some confusion and disagreement. In the legislative history of the relevant provisions of the Law on Burial and Cremation, acknowledgement that the term 'natural cause of death' cannot be precisely defined is followed by the reassurance that in practice it will be sufficiently clear.

Not only death due to intentional or negligent acts of others is not-natural, but also death due to suicide, even if this is the natural result of mental illness, as well as death due to an accident or external

unless the prosecutorial authorities (or one of the other legal control agencies mentioned a the beginning of section 4.2.4) happens to hear about the case.

If a doctor is not sure that the death was a natural one (believing, for example, that it might have been the result of an accident or a criminal offence), he must notify the municipal pathologist to this effect. If the municipal pathologist is convinced that the death was natural, he files a death certificate to that effect and burial or cremation can take place. Otherwise, he reports the case to the local prosecutor, who must decide whether to notify the city clerk that he has no objection to burial or cremation.

If the doctor considers the death 'not natural' because he himself has terminated the patient's life, there is a special model form (first promulgated in 1993) that he can use in reporting the case to the municipal pathologist. Use of this form is, however, not required.[346] If the doctor reports the case as one of euthanasia, the municipal pathologist sends the file to the appropriate Regional Review Committee.

For a doctor to file a certificate of 'natural' death in a case of euthanasia is a distinct criminal offence (under article 228 (1) of the Penal Code), for which there have been a number of prosecutions.[347]

This reporting procedure has always been applicable not only to euthanasia but also to termination of life without a request, in the sense that it is a criminal offence for a doctor to report such a death as a 'natural' one. In fact, however, while there are known to be a considerable number of such cases, hardly any of them have been reported.[348]

4.2.4.2 Prosecution Policy

As we will see in chapter 5.4.4, quantitatively considered the role of the prosecutorial and medical disciplinary authorities in the day-to-day control of euthanasia

---

violence, even if this is not attributable to human fault.(*Second Chamber of Parliament 1951–1952*, 2410 no 3: 7)

The operational definition in prosecution practice is said to be that a 'natural' death is 'one that comes from within', so that as far as doctors are concerned not only euthanasia but also all deaths due to medical negligence must be considered 'non-natural'. See Van Tol (2005: 61–70) on the tortured history of the idea of a 'natural' death.

[346] See <http://www.toetsingscommissieseuthanasie.nl/verslaglegging/> accessed 23 November 2007, where the text of the form is also available. In fact, over 95% of all doctors do use the form (see Onwuteaka-Philipsen *et al* 2007: 184).

See GB&W: 115–16 for the historical background of the form and pp 310*ff* for the original text (in English). The first version of the form (Order in Council, 17 December 1993, *Staatsblad* 688) was revised when the Regional Review Committees were established in 1998 (Order in Council, 19 November 1997, *Staatsblad* 550, effective 1 November 1998), the 1993 form being retained for termination of life without a request. The form was revised very slightly in 2002 in connection with the Law of 2002 (Order in Council, 6 March 2002, *Staatsblad* 140, effective on the effective date of the Law, 1 April 2002. See for a problem due to the misleading content of the form section 4.2.4.3(B).

[347] In 1987 the Supreme Court rejected the idea that the justification for euthanasia also applies to violation of this article (see GB&W: 72). See Van der Wal & Van der Maas 1996: 146–8 for some incidental prosecution data from which one can infer that prosecutions for falsely reporting a 'natural death' are rare, accidental events.

[348] The tension between the reporting procedure and the privilege against self-incrimination is dealt with at length in GB&W: 116–18; see also Onwuteaka-Philipsen *et al* 2007: 68–9 and Pans 2006: 125–6.

practice has become marginal. Of the 1,800 or more cases reported to the Regional Review Committees each year, the committees hold in almost none that they do not have jurisdiction and in only a tiny handful that the doctor has not been 'careful' (ie met the requirements of due care). In short, as far as reported cases are concerned, the prosecutorial and medical disciplinary authorities have very little to do. To date no case received from the committees with the judgment 'not careful' has been prosecuted (see chapter 5, appendix). The last case of a prosecution based on a case reported as euthanasia/PAS by the doctor concerned was *Brongersma*, dating from before the installation of the Regional Review Committees.[349]

Apart from reported cases, the prosecutorial authorities might be actively looking for non-reported cases. There is, however, no indication of this. Former (and now current) Minister of Justice Hirsch Ballin once suggested that one might compare the number of reported cases of euthanasia in an institution with the number normally to be expected, and investigate the matter further if there seemed to be ground to suspect that underreporting was taking place. Nothing ever came of the idea.[350] The same applies to the idea of one experienced prosecutor, that a national corps of forensically-trained pathologists could investigate *every* death, not just those reported by the doctor concerned as 'not natural'.[351] In effect, the handful of prosecutions in recent years are of non-reported cases that happen accidentally to come to the attention of the prosecutors.

The situation is, in short, very different now from what it was in 1995 when prosecutorial decision-making was the keystone of legal control over euthanasia practice and an important subject of the third national survey of euthanasia practice, whose findings were discussed at length in the predecessor of this book. Over the period 1981–95, over 7,000 cases were disposed of by the prosecutorial authorities, and criminal charges were brought in about 30 of these cases. In the period 1991–95, when euthanasia practice had become fairly well normalised, the prosecutors dealt with over 6,000 cases, 120 of which were given full consideration by the highest prosecutorial authority—the Committee of Procurators-General—resulting in 11 indictments (involving 13 doctors).[352]

In 2003 the Committee of Procurators-General (PGs) issued a guideline for prosecutorial decision-making in light of the new Law of 2002, and in 2007 a revised guideline was issued.[353] Most of the guideline is devoted to a detailed description of the decision-making procedure in reported and not-reported cases, replete with an elaborate flow-diagram of the bureaucratic route to be followed. The prosecutorial authorities will in general, the guideline observes, only have to do with cases in which the Review Committees decide they do not have jurisdic-

---

[349] See ch 3.3.

[350] See GB&W: 293 n 57.

[351] See GB&W: 276 n 28.

[352] GB&W: 241–5.

[353] Aanwijzing vervolgingsbeslissing inzake actieve levensbeëindiging op verzoek (euthanasie en hulp bij zelfdoding). *Staatscourant* 2003, no 248, p 19 (23 December 2003); *Staatscourant* 2007, no 46, p 14 (6 March 2007). Here and elsewhere, references to the guideline are to the most recent version (the differences are marginal).

tion or that the doctor was 'not careful', or cases in which the doctor concerned did not report the case as he should have. In all of these cases, as in the past, the final prosecutorial decision is to be made by the PGs, with the agreement of the Minister of Justice.

The requirement of suffering is of 'such essential importance' that prosecution is in principle indicated if the Review Committee found the doctor 'not careful' because the suffering was not unbearable and without possibility of improvement, or if it was not able to determine this because of the doctor's failure to consult another doctor or to maintain adequate records.

If the Review Committee found the doctor 'not careful' because the patient's request was not voluntary and well-considered (which implies also that the patient was adequately informed) then prosecution is in principle indicated.

If the Review Committee found the doctor 'not careful' because of a failure to consult another independent doctor, but the euthanasia was otherwise properly carried out, prosecution would be unwarranted: a talk with the doctor in which his attention is called to the requirement will suffice.[354]

If the Review Committee found the doctor 'not careful' in the way he carried out euthanasia (presence until the death of the patient, proper euthanaticum), this does not call, in general, for criminal prosecution, and the Medical Inspector should deal with the matter.

Although the Law of 2002 in principle does not apply to a doctor who fails to report, if the doctor can show that he met the legal requirements[355] then prosecution can be considered, not for euthanasia but for the failure to report itself (as we have seen in section 4.2.4.1, this is a distinct offence under the Penal Code) or for an even more minor offence under the Law on Burial and Cremation.

In effect, the PGs distinguish between the substantive requirements for euthanasia (suffering and request) and the procedural requirements, observing that the justification of necessity is in principle still available in cases in which only the latter are at issue. This goes a long way toward repairing the mistakes in this regard that, as we have seen in section 4.2.3.3(A), the legislator made in the Law of 2002.[356]

4.2.4.3 The Regional Review Committees

Regional Review Committees to assess doctors' reports of euthanasia were first established in 1998, with among other things the objective of making the process

---

[354] The guideline notes that the Supreme Court had held, before the Law of 2002, that failure to consult is not an obstacle to invoking the justification of necessity.

[355] The guideline notes that the doctor concerned might invoke either the statutory justification or one based directly on the old defence of necessity. The failure to report gives rise to a 'presumption of guilt' and it will be up to the doctor to show that he met the statutory requirements or was in a situation of necessity.

[356] The report of the national research of 2005 includes recommendations for legislative change which would have the same effect as the prosecutorial guideline of the PGs (see Onwuteaka-Philipsen *et al* 2007: 239–41) and the Government's reaction to that report, while rejecting the idea of legislative change, makes clear that it does approve of what the PGs have done (see Letter of 14 November 2007, n 363).

of review more acceptable to doctors, in the hope that they would be more inclined to report.[357] Between 1998 and the Law of 2002 the task of the committees was to advise the prosecutorial authorities on whether the doctor concerned had conformed to the requirements of due care. They reported their findings to the Committee of Procurators-General, which (subject to the approval of the Minister of Justice) made the final prosecutorial decision. It was prosecutorial policy only to deviate from the conclusion of a committee that the doctor had conformed to the legal requirements under exceptional circumstances. In fact, no prosecution was brought contrary to a committee's advice, and as we can see from the appendix to chapter 5, in most cases where the committee found a doctor's behaviour not in conformity with the legal requirements, the prosecutorial authorities nevertheless decided not to prosecute.

The Law of 2002, in addition to codifying the legalisation of euthanasia, put the Review Committees on a firm statutory footing. A committee's judgment that a reported case of euthanasia meets the statutory requirements now ends the matter and the prosecutorial authorities never see the case. All cases in which a committee finds the doctor 'not careful' are sent both to the prosecutorial authorities and to the Medical Inspectorate.[358]

Neither in 1998 nor in 2002 was provision made for termination of life without a request, and when reported as a 'non-natural death' such cases continued to be reviewed by the prosecutorial authorities pursuant to the procedure that was first established in 1993. Until the Regional Review Committees were created in 1998, the same reporting procedure applied to cases of termination of life with or without a request, much to the dismay of supporters of legal euthanasia.[359] When the Review Committees were set up, the Government announced its intention to create a national review committee for cases in which there was no request, but it was only in 2007 that this was finally in fact accomplished, and then only for the special situation of newborn babies (and third trimester abortion).[360] For a while the Government's position was that cases in which the patient's competence to make a valid request could be in doubt (in particular, psychiatric patients) also fell under the old procedure, and as we will see the model form for reporting cases of euthanasia still contains a misleading note to that effect (see section 4.2.4.3(B)).

---

[357] See Regeling regionale toetsingscommissies euthanasie, 27 May 1998, *Staatscourant* 1998, no 101 (included as an appendix to the Annual Reports of the Regional Review Committees through 2002). For the origins of the idea of non-criminal review committees see GB&W: 278–82.

[358] Law of 2002 art 9.2.

[359] See GB&W: ch 3.2 on the reporting procedure until 1998. The so-called 'points requiring attention' [*aandachtspunten*] to be followed by a doctor who reports a case of termination of life, as these were as of 1993, are to be found in GB&W: 310*ff.*

[360] See ch 6.2.6.6 for the long gestation period of what became the national 'Committee of Experts'.

4.2.4.3(A) The Committees and their Procedures[361]

The Law of 2002 and an Order in Council pursuant to the law provide for five Regional Review Committees with competence over reported deaths due to euthanasia or physician-assisted suicide within a region corresponding to between three and five judicial districts. The basic responsibility of the committees is to make a final judgment whether the doctor who reports a case of euthanasia or physician-assisted suicide has met the requirements of due care specified in the law.[362]

Each committee consists of three members: a lawyer (who is chairman), a doctor and an ethicist; there are three substitute members, of the same three disciplines. All are appointed by the Ministers of Justice and of Health for a period of six years, with the possibility of one renewal.[363] Each committee also has a secretary and one or more substitute secretaries; both are lawyers appointed by the two ministers and exclusively responsible to the committee for which they work. They are responsible, among other things, for preparing draft decisions in cases to be handled by their committee.[364]

The ministers appoint one of the chairmen as coordinating chairman, responsible for initiating and coordinating meetings of the chairmen with representatives of the prosecutorial authorities and of the Medical Inspectorate, at which the procedures and functioning of the Review Committees are discussed. These meetings take place at least twice a year, and one of the main purposes is to strive for uniformity in decision-making.[365] The ministers also appoint a general secretary, who is responsible for coordinating the work of the secretaries, coordinating the preparation of the Annual Reports, initiating consultation among the secretaries and, on request, providing the ministers with information.[366]

In 2003 the chairmen of the Regional Review Committees used their authority[367] to promulgate a guideline for the procedure to be used in assessing whether in a particular case a doctor has met the requirements of due care.[368] The guideline covers the matters in Box 4.14.

---

[361] The competence and procedures of the committees are to be found in bits and pieces in three documents: the Law of 2002, the Order in Council pursuant to the Law (Order in Council of 6 March 2002, *Staatsblad* 2002 nr 141 [hereafter: Order in Council], and the guideline promulgated on 18 June 2003 by the chairmen of the Review Committees pursuant to art 5 of the Order in Council [hereafter: Guideline]. These three documents are included in an appendix to the Annual Reports. Much of what is in the guideline is also to be found in the Law of 2002 and/or the Order in Council.

[362] Law of 2002 art 8.

[363] The composition of the committees is provided for in arts 3–6 of the Law of 2002. The Government has recently indicated that the term should be reduced to 4 years (renewable once) (Letter of the Secretary of State for Health and the Minister of Justice to the Second Chamber of Parliament, 14 November 2007).

[364] RRC Guideline, art 5.

[365] See eg RRC 2000: 8 (coordination of the approach to the 'independence' of a consultant who is a member of the reporting doctor's substitution group; see also RRC Guideline art 9.5); RRC 2003: 8, 16 (competence of committees in case of patients with a psychiatric disturbance; see further section 4.2.4.3(B)).

[366] Order in Council, art 6.

[367] This authority derives from the Order in Council (art. 19).

[368] See RRC 2003: 8, 23.

Box 4.14 Topics covered in the procedural Guideline of the Regional Review Committees

---

- the procedure in case a member of the committee must, on his own motion or on request of the doctor concerned, recuse himself because his impartiality might be questioned
- the procedure in case the reporting doctor is not the doctor who carried out the euthanasia or two doctors report that they did so jointly (see section 4.2.3.3(D) above)
- the procedure to be followed in assessing individual cases (including the requirement in article 9 of the Law of 2002 to notify the reporting doctor of the committee's decision within six weeks—a period that can be extended once for six weeks; and a provision that the committee decide by a majority vote of all members)
- the procedure to be followed if the report filed by the doctor is an insufficient basis for deciding whether he met the requirements of due care (the doctor can be asked to supply additional information in person or in writing; the municipal pathologist, the consultant, or other caregivers can be asked to supply information by telephone or in writing; the doctor or the consultant can be invited to discuss the case with the committee)
- the procedure in case the requirement of independent consultation appears not to have been met (the doctor must show that the criterion of an 'independent judgment' was met—see section 4.2.3.3(E) above)
- the procedure to be followed if a committee is considering a judgment that the doctor in question did not meet the requirements of due care (the doctor is invited to discuss the case with the committee; all members of the committee including the substitute members are asked for advice on the draft judgment; the chairmen and substitute chairmen of the other committees are asked for advice on the draft judgment)
- the procedure in case the judgment is 'not careful' (a copy of the judgment and the dossier are sent to the College of Procurators-General and to the Medical Inspectorate)

The members and secretaries of the Review Committees are specifically forbidden to express a judgment in advance concerning a doctor's inclination to perform euthanasia.[369] They are bound to secrecy concerning information about individual cases that they come to know while carrying out their responsibilities;[370] copies of the dossier made for purposes of a committee's decision-making are to be destroyed after a case is disposed of.[371] The Law of 2002 requires the committees, on request, to provide the prosecutorial authorities with all information they require for assessing a case in which the committees have found the doctor 'not careful', or in connection with a criminal investigation.[372]

---

[369] Law of 2002 art 16.
[370] Law of 2002 art 14.
[371] RRC 2003: art 7.3.
[372] Law of 2002 art 10.

The Review Committees are responsible for the registration of basic data concerning the cases reported to them and for an Annual Report of their work, due before April 1 of each year. The report must at least deal with the number of cases handled, the nature of these cases, and the committees' judgments and the reasons leading to them.[373]

The guideline provides (following the Order in Council) for various forms of training and informational activities of the committees, including their Annual Reports, participation by members in congresses and symposia, publication of articles in professional journals, and participation in the training of SCEN consultants. Public representation of the committees, or contact with the media on matters that concern all of the committees, is in principle limited to the coordinating chairman. Individual members who make public statements should discuss this in advance with their chairman and, in case of doubt, all chairmen should be consulted; in any case, a member should avoid making statements that can be interpreted as reflecting the views of the committees.

4.2.4.3(B) The Jurisdiction of the Committees

Two sorts of cases fall outside the jurisdiction of the Regional Review Committees. A report in such a case is returned by the committee concerned to the municipal pathologist with the request to forward it to the prosecutorial authorities, and the doctor concerned is notified of this.[374]

(1) Cases of 'normal medical practice' and a 'natural' death fall outside the Law of 2002 and therefore outside the jurisdiction of the committees. Thus cases of withholding or withdrawing treatment that is 'futile' or has been refused by the patient, cases of pain relief in indicated doses, and cases of palliative or terminal sedation, do not fall within the committees' jurisdiction.[375]

(2) If there is no (competent) request from the patient, whether what the doctor did is legal or not, it does not amount to euthanasia or assisted suicide and falls outside the statutory legalisation of the latter. These cases involve termination of life of newborn babies, children under 12, and comatose or demented patients who did not make an advance written request while still competent.[376] When the Regional Review Committees for euthanasia were first proposed in 1997, there was to be a single national committee for cases in

---

[373] Law of 2002 art 17. On the basis of the Annual Report, the two responsible ministers report annually to Parliament concerning the functioning of the committees (art 18).

[374] RRC 2003: art 1.3.

[375] See RRC 2003: art I.2.B; for pain relief, see RRC 2002: 17 (case 5—committee not competent); for terminal sedation, see RRC 2005: 8 (referring to a case of sedation and withholding of artificial nutrition and hydration in which a committee found itself not competent—the ground on which ANH was withheld is not specified). Interestingly, the committees suggest (RRC 2003: 16) that if a patient chooses terminal sedation over euthanasia as a more 'natural' form of shortening life, and the doctor performs it with such an intention, then the case should be reported as one of termination of life on request. While sensible, it is not clear that there is support in current Dutch law for this position (see section 4.2.2.4).

[376] See RRC Guideline art I.2.C.

which there was no request or the 'voluntariness' of the request was supposedly subject to doubt (psychiatric patients).[377] However, the Government apparently later got second thoughts and until very recently such a national committee had not been set up. Recently, a non-statutory Expert Committee for cases of termination of life of newborn babies (and third-trimester abortion) has been established. Like the Regional Review Committees before the Law of 2002, its authority is limited to advising the prosecutorial authorities. The extraordinarily long gestational process of this committee is discussed in chapter 6.2.2.6. All other cases of termination of life without a request will continue to be assessed by the prosecutorial authorities according to the procedure first set up in 1993.

Before the Law of 2002 there was doubt about the jurisdiction of the Regional Review Committees in the case of psychiatric patients. The Order in Council that originally established the committees provided in an accompanying explanatory note that cases in which the patient's suffering was 'primarily of psychic origin', and cases in which the suffering was due to a somatic condition but the patient's 'capacity to make a well-considered request might have been disturbed, for example as a result of depression or early dementia', were to be reported pursuant to the procedure for reporting no-request cases.[378] The committees therefore declared themselves without jurisdiction in these cases,[379] so that review remained the responsibility of the prosecutorial authorities.

Under the Law of 2002, both the legality of physician-assisted suicide in the case of a psychiatric patient who makes a voluntary request, and the jurisdiction of the Review Committees, have a statutory basis. Nothing in the statute, nor in the Order in Council which regulates the committees and their procedure, suggests that psychiatric patients fall outside the jurisdiction of the committees. In fact, the voluntariness of the patient's request is explicitly one of the criteria which the Regional Review Committees are statutorily required to assess.[380] In their Annual Report of 2003, the Regional Review Committees observe that they now have jurisdiction in such cases and if, after investigation, they conclude that the patient concerned was not able to make a voluntary and well-informed request, they will find that the doctor has not met the requirements of due care.[381] The committees urged the Government to remove a misleading note to one of the questions in the model form for reporting euthanasia which, despite the new statute and Order in Council, continues to suggest that such cases should be reported according to the

---

[377] See Order in Council, 9 November 1997, *Staatsblad* 550, p 12–13.

[378] See Ministerial Decree of 27 May 1998, *Staatscourant* 1998 no 101, p 10, explanatory note to article 9.

[379] See RRC 2000: 4, 13 (case 2—assistance with suicide of competent psychiatric patient—not within jurisdiction of committee); RRC 2001: 15 (case 3—ditto).

[380] See Tholen 2003 for sharp criticism of the contrary position of the responsible ministers (even after the Law of 2002).

[381] See RRC 2003: 16 (in effect adopting Tholen's position—see n 380); RRC 2003: 17 (case 5—psychiatric disorders, GP gives assistance with suicide after psychiatric consultation—'careful'). See also the prosecutorial Guideline (n 353), *passim*.

procedure for no-request cases.[382] A number of professional organisations, among them the Medical Association, also asked the Government to revise the misleading note on the model,[383] and the Ministry of Justice set up a working group to revise the form which recommended in favour of doing so, but the Government has yet to follow through.[384]

By contrast with psychiatric patients and persons suffering from depression or dementia (who may nevertheless be competent to make a voluntary request), the very same note to the model makes indirectly clear that in the case of minors over 12 (who under the Law of 2002 can make a valid request for euthanasia), the Regional Review committees have jurisdiction to assess the doctor's behaviour.

4.2.4.3(C) *The Committee's Judgments and the Follow-Up*

Formally speaking, the only judgments the Regional Review Committees can render are 'careful' and 'not careful' and the only criteria they can use are the requirements of due care as formulated in the Law of 2002. The fact of the matter is that from the beginning they have not allowed themselves to be straitjacketed in this way. Before the Law of 2002, their judgments were only advisory, so if the prosecutorial authorities did not like judgments of 'careful despite failure to follow the rules strictly', nothing bound them to follow the advice received.[385] Since 2002, the committees' decisions are effectively final, and the committees greeted this change with the supposition that in the future they would have to judge such cases 'not careful'.[386] Nevertheless, it seems quite clear from their Annual Reports[387] that the committees have not abandoned their previous flexible practice of finding a doctor on balance 'careful' even when there are aspects of what took place that were not entirely in conformity with the legal requirements. Furthermore, their decision-making procedure is designed to ensure that the judgment 'not careful' will only be given in cases where it is indubitably deserved (see Box 4.14 above).

---

[382] RRC 2003: 16. The Medical Association, relying apparently only on the note to question 11a on the model, asserted as recently as 2003 that the reporting procedure for euthanasia 'cannot be used for cases of termination of life of patients whose expression of their will *may have been disturbed by a psychic or psychiatric disorder (possibly in the past)*. The judgment of the responsible doctor that in relation to the request the patient is, at the relevant moment, competent, is irrelevant' (KNMG 2003: 21, italics added). The KNMG found this situation undesirable. Nevertheless, the unqualified statement for which, by the time it was made, there was no remaining ground, seems extraordinary.

[383] See *Medisch Contact* 58: 152 (2003): joint letter of six organisations (including the KNMG, the NVP, the NVK and the NVVE).

[384] Information from L Stoop-Bod, secretary of the RRCs, who was a member of the working group. The chairman of the College of PGs apparently has 'has no objection' if the cases to which the note refers are in fact reviewed by a Review Committee (see Onwuteaka-Philipsen *et al* 2007: 210). The Government recently announced its intention to publish a new form, without the objectionable note in early 2008 (see Letter of 14 November 2007, n 363 above). See n 346 for the history of the current form.

[385] See for the committees' practice before the Law of 2002, RRC 2000: 8.

[386] See RRC 2002: 9.

[387] These are discussed extensively in section 4.2.2.3, especially in the notes.

Most cases that reach the committees are quite unproblematic.[388] And in most cases to which the committees give special attention, they ultimately come to the conclusion that the doctor was 'careful'. As Table 5.19 in chapter 5 shows, only a handful of cases is adjudged 'not careful' and referred to the prosecutorial authorities for further consideration. Over the 8 years of their existence, there were 25 such cases, and the rate of 'not careful' judgments was about 2 per 1,000 reported cases.

Even a judgment of 'not careful' is not as black and white as it might seem. In a number of cases the committees note that although a doctor failed to meet one or another of the requirements and therefore must be found 'not careful', his behaviour was 'in good conscience', which looks like a subtle hint to the prosecutorial authorities and the Medical Inspector that prosecution or disciplinary proceedings are not in order.[389]

4.2.4.3(D) The Range of Sanctions

In practice, the range of sanctions available to the Regional Review Committees is far greater than one might imagine from reading the text of the Law of 2002. A doctor whose report is not complete or raises questions can be asked for further information or he can be invited to discuss the case with the committee. In the course of such a discussion it can be made clear to him that the way he carried out euthanasia was not entirely spotless.[390] A committee can go a bit further and make clear in its judgment that although it ultimately finds the doctor 'careful' this is not to say there is no room for improvement; some of these cases the committees call to the attention of the Medical Inspector.[391] Heavier still is the judgment that the doctor was 'not careful' because of a technical violation, but that his behaviour was 'in good conscience'. And finally there is the flat-out judgment 'not careful'.

In addition to the range of sanctions that can be applied to doctors, the committees can on their own, or by encouraging the prosecutorial authorities or the Medical Inspectorate to do so, put pressure on an institution where problems in carrying out euthanasia have arisen in a particular case to adopt or revise its protocol so that such things do not recur in the future. In a number of cases such structural intervention is undoubtedly the most important outcome.[392]

---

[388] See eg RRC 2004: 12 ('most reports hardly afford anything to discuss'). Some recent Annual Reports do give the impression that doctors may be increasingly willing to report cases in which quite a bit went wrong.

[389] See for these cases ch 5, appendix, column g. In one such case, eg, the committee notes that in its discussion of the case with the two doctors concerned they had indicated that the experience gave them reason to change a number of things in their practice, in particular to use SCEN consultants in the future (RRC 2005: 30, case 11/14—consulted doctor not independent—'not careful'—prosecutors decide not to prosecute—see further n 392).

[390] See n 235 on the frequency of requests for additional information. That such 'discussion' can be experienced by a doctor as a serious sanction is revealed in some early protests, and doctors continue to find the experience unpleasant. See ch 5.4.3, n 166.

[391] See eg RRC 2000: 21 (case 21—consultant not entirely independent—on balance 'careful'. but at request of committee, Inspector discusses the matter with both doctor and consultant).

[392] See RRC 2004: 30 (case 15—confusion among doctors involved about their respective roles— 'not careful'; RRC calls attention of medical inspectorate to procedures in hospital and the apparently

4.2.4.3(E) The Case Law of the Committees

From 1998 through 2006, the Regional Review Committees produced published judgments (in their Annual Reports) in some 92 cases. In 2006 they began publishing judgments on their internet site.[393] The contents of these judgments are described at various places in this chapter, depending on the subject. A general appraisal can be short: the judgments are a gold-mine of information. In the first place this concerns the developing law of euthanasia and the problems of medical practice encountered by the system of control and how they are dealt with; less directly it concerns how the system of control is functioning; and still less directly it concerns euthanasia practice itself. Their quality as case law is roughly comparable in these three different respects to that of the decisions of courts and other adjudicatory tribunals.

4.2.4.3(F) An Assessment of the Functioning of the Committees

In the predecessor to this book, when the Review Committees had been proposed but not yet established, we expressed rather low expectations for them.[394] Although we may have been right to doubt they would have a dramatic effect on the willingness of doctors to report,[395] our judgment has otherwise turned out to be quite wrong and in many respects the committees have proved to be a considerable improvement over the previous procedure.

One of the most important advantages of the Review Committees is the transparency of what they do. Prior to 1998, when decision-making on reported cases was entirely in the hands of the prosecutorial authorities, practically nothing was publicly known about what they did, or how, or why. In the report of the 1995 national survey, a separate chapter was devoted to decision-making within the prosecutorial service, which for the first time shed some light on the matter.[396]

---

frequent use of morphine; see further on this case n 213); RRC 2005: 30 (case 11/14—see also n 389—prosecutors decide not to prosecute but call attention of medical inspectorate to inadequate euthanasia protocol; inspector requests hospital to change its protocol; hospital produces extensive protocol and organises symposium for staff); RRC 2005: 32 (case 12—'careful' despite use of inappropriate drugs; committee requests hospital to revise internal guideline advising use of morphine). The Government recently emphasised the importance it attaches to institutional guidelines, and the Medical Inspectorate will make these a part of its regular inspections (see Letter of 14 November 2007, n 363 above).

[393] See <http://www.toetsingscommissieseuthanasie.nl> accessed 26 November 2007. It is the committees' intention to publish all judgments. However, the year 2006 was an experimental, start-up phase, beginning only at the end of April, and nowhere near all judgments of 2006 have been published on the website (as of 26 November 2007: 326); for 2007, 199 judgments had been published by 26 November 2007. Since publication entails the removal of all identifying information, judgments which by their very nature cannot be made anonymous (eg because of the disease) will not be published (information obtained from the national secretariat of the committees).

[394] GB&W: 279–81.

[395] See further on the reporting rate, ch 5.4.3.

[396] Van der Wal & Van der Maas 1996: part III. This part of the report offers not only the first real insight into prosecutorial decision-making in reported cases of euthanasia, it is in fact a too little-known document of more general importance: one of the few systematic descriptions in the literature of any sort of prosecutorial decision-making.

Apart from some interesting insight into the relationship between the Minister of Justice and the prosecutorial authorities,[397] the chapter is primarily interesting for what it reveals about the extreme restraint of Dutch prosecutors in euthanasia cases (13 indictments in 15 years, in which some 7,000 cases had been reported) and about the problems that most occupied prosecutorial attention: apart from doubts about the 'terminal phase' (about which the Minister of Justice was much interested at the time) their concern in about a quarter of all cases was with consultation.[398]

But however interesting as a glimpse into the inner workings of a rather closed institution, the report of the 1995 research cannot remotely compare, in quantity or quality, with the information about legal control of reported cases of euthanasia that the Annual Reports of the Regional Review Committees have made available.

The transparency produced by the Review Committees is not only a matter of their Annual Reports. Each committee consists of three members and three alternates. These people mostly do their committee work on the side, being primarily active professionals in universities, hospitals, the judiciary etc. Several of them are also prominent scholars and authors in related fields. Through their contacts with colleagues who are interested in the workings of the committees, as well as more formal presentations, a great deal of information concerning the functioning of the committees becomes known to scholars, policy makers and others concerned with the way control over euthanasia is working in practice. It would thus be a serious mistake to equate the transparency created by the committees with their published judgments and their Annual Reports alone.

4.2.4.4 The Development of Before-the-Fact Assessment: SCEN[399]

The availability of independent, qualified doctors to function as consultants prior to carrying out a patient's request for euthanasia, and the quality of consultation, have been matters of concern since the beginning of an institutionalised system of legal control.[400] In 1997, the Royal Dutch Medical Association, with financial support from the Ministry of Health, set up an experimental programme in Amsterdam to provide a corps of trained advisors and consultants to be available

---

[397] In particular: the minister did not agree with a proposal of the Committee of Procurators-General that, in connection with the patient's suffering, 'hopeless' and 'unbearable' should be seen as involving different considerations: 'hopeless' referring to the possibility of treatment and being a matter for objective, medical judgment, 'unbearable' referring to the patient's experience and being a matter on which the patient's own view is largely determinative. See Van der Wal & Van der Maas 1996: 141. Thanks to the Review Committees, precisely that distinction is now made (see section 4.2.3.3.(C)).

[398] See Van der Wal & Van der Maas 1996: 139. Other important categories of concern were the request (15%), the way the euthanasia was carried out (13%), and the suffering (in particular, refusal of alternatives: 9%).

[399] See generally on SCEN Jansen-van der Weide 2005.

[400] There were a number of proposals over the years to formalise the consultation procedure, eg by appointing specially qualified doctors to perform the function (see eg the State Commission's proposal for doctors appointed by the Minister of Health, GB&W: app I-C-1).

to family doctors in Amsterdam. This so-called SCEA[401] programme trained a corps of doctors in all aspects of euthanasia consulting (medical, ethical and legal). SCEA consultants were available to family doctors, both for advice about the requirements for euthanasia and for formal consultation.

The project was generally considered to be very successful, and in 1999 it was made permanent and extended to the entire country (now being known as SCEN). In 2002 the Regional Review Committees informed the Ministry of Health that continuation of the programme and expansion to cover medical specialists was in their view very important 'because it makes an important contribution to the quality of due care in connection with euthanasia'.[402] Nevertheless, in 2003 the Government expressed its intention to cease financing the programme. After vigorous protests from the KNMG and the Regional Review Committees, and a parliamentary motion to continue the programme, the Government backed down and agreed to continue the financial support.[403]

In the view of the Regional Review Committees, thanks to SCEN the quality of consultation and of the reports of consultants has improved greatly in cases in which euthanasia is carried out by a family doctor, and they describe the quality of SCEN consultants' reports as 'generally excellent'.[404] Consultation remains a problem when the doctor is not a family doctor.[405] SCEN is currently being expanded to include hospitals and nursing homes, and this expansion was expected to be complete in 2007.[406] In their 2006 Annual Report, the Review Committees are able to note two positive developments concerning consultation by specialists: the increasing number of specialists who have been trained as SCEN consultants, and the increasing use of SCEN consultants (often GPs) by specialists.[407]

SCEN seems to be developing in the direction of before-the-fact control of euthanasia: reviewing the doctor's proposed course of conduct before he carries it out. There are some obvious things to be said for this, after-the-fact control always coming, if euthanasia turns out to have been inappropriate in the circumstances, 'too late'. From the beginning of the Dutch euthanasia debate, the idea of before-the-fact control (special committees, a special division of the courts, etc) has been more or less continuously present as a subterranean theme which, whenever it comes to the surface, has been just as regularly rejected by doctors and by the Government.[408] A

---

[401] SCEA stands for Steun en Consultatie Euthanasie Amsterdam [Support and Consultation Euthanasia Amsterdam]. When the programme was made nationwide, the 'N' for Netherlands took the place of the 'A' for Amsterdam.

[402] RRC 2002: 31. An evaluation of the SCEN programme came to the same conclusion (see Jansen-van der Weide 2005: 68*ff.*).

[403] See letter of 1 April 2004 from the Secretary of State for Health to the Second Chamber of Parliament (*Proceedings 2003–2004*, 29 200 XVI, no 220).

[404] See eg RRC 1998/1999: 14; RRC 2000: 7, 22; RRC 2003: 29–30; RRC 2005: 26.

[405] The committees have voiced their concern about the relatively poor quality of consultation reports by specialists—see, eg RRC 2003: 31. This is a concern that one often hears informally expressed by members of the committees.

[406] See <http://www.knmg.artsennet.nl/content/resources//AMGATE_6059_100_TICH_R113815 11490 70587//>accessed 24 April 2007.

[407] RRC 2006: 25.

[408] See Weyers 2004: 86, 128, 202–4, 236, 326.

variety of reasons have been given for exclusive reliance on after-the-fact control: the traditional resistance of the medical profession to any sort of shared decision-making or dilution of the final responsibility of the individual doctor, practical problems of organising a system of before-the-fact control, the impossibility of anyone giving approval to behaviour that was (until 2002) 'illegal', the undesirability of bureau-cratising the process, ethical objections to involving the state in decisions to admin-ister euthanasia, and so forth.

However all this may be, the fact is—one senses between the lines in the Annual Reports of the Review Committees[409]—that the committees are increasingly inclined to regard a report of euthanasia that is accompanied by the consultant's report of a SCEN consultant, as requiring less attention than other cases. If this is true and becomes known among doctors, one can expect them to be increasingly inclined to make use of SCEN consultants since this will more or less guarantee them against unpleasantness later on. In short, the logical momentum of the way that the committees interact with the SCEN programme seems to be leading to a situation in which the latter gradually take over much of the role of the former. And when that is accomplished, we will have a de facto system of before-the-fact control, with the Review committees principally active as a backup to SCEN in particularly difficult cases.

4.2.5 Concluding Reflections on Dutch Euthanasia Law and the System of Control

As we have seen in section 4.2.3.3, while there has been an enormous growth in the *amount* of Dutch law concerning euthanasia since the predecessor of this book went to press in 1997, and even more so since the Law of 2002, there has not been much change in *substance*. Euthanasia law and euthanasia practice have been nor-malised: largely left to the routine daily practice of those directly involved in med-ical practice and its control. On the whole, politicians and the media have gone on to other things. There is no audible voice in Dutch society or politics calling for turning back the clock. The only real exception to this generalisation is the arrival on the Dutch scene of 'terminal sedation', bringing with it a return to the concep-tual confusion and disagreement concerning the requirements of control that used to characterise the euthanasia discussion.

The Role of 'Intentions'

The most important *fundamental* change going on in Dutch euthanasia law is the gradual displacement of the doctor's subjective 'intention' as the foundation of the classificatory differences between different sorts of MBPSL. Classification of a case as 'termination of life', with as a consequence the duty to report the death as 'not natural', is increasingly being seen as dependent on whether or not there was a

---

[409] Personal communication with several members of the committees supports this idea.

'medical indication' for what the doctor did (eg pain relief). The legal and ethical requirements applicable to a given case of end-of-life medical behaviour are hence determined by 'objective' factors and the medical standard and not by a doctor's self-reported 'intentions'.

As we have seen, until the national survey of 1990, to the extent the doctor's intentions played a role in the legal assessment of his behaviour, this would have been according to the traditional conception of intent in criminal law: foresight and acceptance of consequences. Since these are always present in a case of MBPSL, 'intent' in the criminal law meaning of the term affords no ground for distinguishing between (in particular) pain relief on the one side and euthanasia and termination of life without a request on the other. As the State Commission recognised, the difference between pain relief that is legitimate and pain relief that is homicide lies not in differences in the doctor's subjective intention but in whether the pain relief (including the amount and the way it is given) conformed to the standards of proper medical behaviour which define the limits of the 'medical exception'.

In the national study of 1990 and the three that have followed, the researchers do not classify medical behaviour according to the medical standard, but seek to do so on the basis of self-reported intentions (apparently basing this on a misinterpreted version of the doctrine of 'double effect'). This is a procedure which, whatever its convenience may have been in the collection of data, corresponds neither to what the law is nor to the requirements of sound methodology or effective control (there being few things in life more unreliable than a person's report of his intentions, especially when the choice between competing ones has serious practical consequences[410]).

Other empirical researchers (including those of the pan-European EURELD studies whose results are presented in chapter 17), participants in public and policy discussions, medical law scholars, the authors of position papers of the medical profession—in short, practically everyone involved with euthanasia—began to repeat the mantra of intentions. With one exception: criminal lawyers and, in particular, public prosecutors. As Van Tol has shown, a decade after 'intentions' had become the foundation of research and public policy, Dutch public prosecutors—apparently blissfully unaware of how everyone else was thinking—continued to distinguish between pain relief and abstention, on the one hand, and euthanasia and murder on the other with the help of old-fashioned criminal law doctrine.[411]

The return to doctrinal orthodoxy set in in the early years of the new millennium. In 2003 a new euthanasia guideline of the KNMG stated that if life-shortening pain relief is not justified in terms of the patient's pain or symptoms, it crosses the line between pain relief and termination of life.[412] In 2004 the Health

---

[410] *Cf* Nisbett & Wilson 1977; White 1988 (there is a very interesting discussion of the relevance of this and other research in psychology for the regulation of euthanasia in Wijsbek 2001). See ch 6, Box 6.9, for an illustrative example.
[411] Van Tol 2005: 194–5, 206–7, 213.
[412] KNMG 2003: 6.

Council's report on terminal sedation argued that it is not the doctor's intention but the medical standard that defines 'terminal sedation',[413] and this lead was followed in 2005 by the KNMG's committee on terminal sedation when it defined this 'new' sort of MBPSL in terms of what is medically indicated.[414]

From 'Suffering' to 'Inhumane Death'?

Another, potentially very interesting and important change that may be taking place concerns the interpretation of the idea of 'unbearable suffering' (maybe even its replacement by the more encompassing concept of *menswaardig sterven*—a death consistent with human dignity). It is important to be cautious about this but a number of indications do appear to suggest a trend in legal development.

From the very beginning, the 'unbearable suffering' that is key to the justification of euthanasia in Dutch law has not been limited to pain (and in fact, as we will see in chapter 5.2.2.1—Table 5.9—pain is by no means the most common reason for a euthanasia request). In the 1984 *Schoonheim* case, which effectively legalised euthanasia in the Netherlands, the patient's suffering mostly had to do with the prospect of further physical decline. The Supreme Court specifically referred to an 'increasing loss of personal dignity [*ontluistering*]' and the anticipation of not being in a position 'to die in a dignified manner' as grounds for legally justifiable euthanasia.[415] As we have seen in sections 4.2.3.3(C) and 4.2.3.4(B), so long as it is due to a recognised medical disorder, the conception of 'unbearable suffering' in Dutch law is generous and largely a matter of a patient's subjective experience.

The Regional Review Committees do insist, however, that suffering be subjectively experienced—that is, that a patient who is in coma (whether or not pharmacologically induced) generally cannot be said to suffer. But they also seem (at least until very recently) to accept almost any sort of indication—groaning, restlessness, and so forth—that a patient is in fact experiencing suffering, and they have even accepted the *doctor's* anticipation that the patient would suffer terribly if he awoke from the coma (see 4.2.3.3(C)).

The situations mentioned so far all involve a patient who has requested euthanasia. But the recent decision of the Supreme Court in the *Van Oijen* case (see section 4.2.2.5) seems to open the possibility that in such a case the justification of necessity might be based not only on subjective suffering but also on the prospect—'objectively' ascertainable by a doctor—of an 'undignified death'. In short, there seems to be a subtle addition to the existing grounds for the justification of termination of life going on: not only the patient's subjective experience of suffering, but also the idea in the eyes of intimate beholders that such a death is something one should not let happen to a human being, can suffice. It seems, however, on general principles and on the facts of the *Van Oijen* case, that the family

---

[413] Gezondheidsraad 2004: 38.

[414] KNMG 2005.

[415] A translation of the Court's decision is to be found in GB&W, appendix II; the quoted expressions are at p 328.

or representatives of the patient would have to request, or at least agree to, the termination of life on such grounds.

This line of thought has become very concrete in neonatology, as we will see in chapter 6. The cases in which it has become fairly well settled in Dutch law that termination of the life of a newborn baby can be justified—assuming the parents agree—are those in which further life-prolonging treatment has been withdrawn as futile because of the very poor prospects for the baby, but in which the baby does not die quickly and peacefully; or in which the baby is not (any longer) dependent on life support but its prospects are so poor that it is agreed that when the need arises further treatment will not be given. But the fact is that there is one sort of life-prolonging treatment that could always be withdrawn in such cases, so that the use of euthanatica would be 'unnecessary': namely, artificial administration of nutrition and hydration. The responsible doctors, however, consider doing so utterly impossible, because neither they, nor nursing staff, nor the parents of the baby could bear to witness its slow death from starvation and dehydration, a process that in the case of a newborn baby can take up to two weeks.[416] Since the baby itself would presumably not suffer—being totally sedated—it is the unbearable sight of a drawn-out and inhumane dying process, and the fact that the baby will probably not be able to die in its parents' arms, that in fact steers the decision-making. Both the courts and the prosecutorial authorities seem to have accepted the justifiability of termination of life in such circumstances.[417]

Putting all the above indications together, it does not seem irresponsibly speculative to suggest that Dutch law is slowly but steadily moving in the direction of explicit recognition of a doctor's duty to ensure that his patient dies a 'humane' or 'dignified' [*menswaardig*] death as a distinct ground for the conflict of duties that lies at the basis of the justification of necessity.[418]

The 'Medical' Character of Euthanasia/PAS

Despite efforts by the Euthanasia Association (NVVE) and some other groups, and of writers like Chabot, to create some room for assistance with suicide by non-doctors (more or less along the lines of the situation in Switzerland, see chapter 16)

---

[416] See ch 6, n 34.

[417] See ch 6.2.2.3 and 6.2.2.7. As we will see in ch 6 (6.2.1 n. 8; 6.2.2.1, 'the priority principle') the State Commission on Euthanasia (Staatscommissie Euthanasie 1985) had accepted active termination of life in the case of a patient in irreversible coma when necessary to prevent 'inhumane deterioration' [*ontluistering*] and permit the patient to die a 'dignified death'. The Health Council (*Gezondheidsraad* 1975) took a similar position with regard to newborn babies: where abstention from life-prolonging treatment is indicated, 'active euthanasia' might be considered. The position taken in these early reports seems to exclude the possibility that the only ground for active intervention is subjectively experienced suffering.

[418] G den Hartogh argues (personal correspondence) that allowing 'help in dying' in such cases poses a real risk of a 'slippery slope' (an argument about which he is generally sceptical) because the criteria are rather vague, and there is no request from the patient (which would indicate what he himself regards as a 'loss of personal dignity' and a 'dignified death'. He seems thereby to overlook the possibility of drawing clear lines (other than a complete taboo) that lend themselves to reasonably consistent and reviewable ap-plication, as well as of a degree of 'intersubjective' decision-making to reduce the risk of arbitrariness. See further on the 'slippery slope' idea, ch 19.

the tendency of the last few years has been rather in the opposite direction: increasing insistence on the 'medical' character of euthanasia and assisted suicide. The prosecutors, supported in this by the courts, have done their best to bring as much as possible of the activities of 'euthanasia consultants' within the ban of assistance with suicide in article 294 of the Penal Code (see section 4.2.3.3(J)). At the same time, the Supreme Court in the *Brongersma* case, supported in this by the Medical Association, has sought to limit the involvement of doctors to the situation in which the patient's request is based on a 'medically classifiable' disorder (see section 4.2.3.4(C)). In short, the commitment of the Dutch to the 'medical model' of assisted dying has if anything hardened.[419]

Tightening the Legal Rules

Across the board the procedural rules to which euthanasia is subject have become tighter (on the whole, medical practice has followed suit, as we will see in chapter 5). In this chapter we have seen that the drugs that may be used, the standards to which consultation is held, the way euthanasia is carried out, record-keeping and reporting, are all regulated in a stricter and more detailed way than ten years ago.

As far as the substantive rules are concerned, apart from the developments discussed above concerning the requirement of 'unbearable suffering', and the new possibility of euthanasia pursuant to an advance written request, the last ten years have not seen much change. Indirectly, however, the gradual abandonment of the 'subjective intention' of the doctor as the factor that determines which legal regime is applicable to his behaviour (that for 'normal' or for 'not normal' medical practice) should sooner or later have as a consequence that the hitherto uncontrolled use of heavy doses of pain relief will be subjected to some serious legal control.

The report of the KNMG committee on 'palliative sedation' (see section 4.2.2.4) is the first important step in subjecting pain relief (in this case, in the extreme form of continuous, deep sedation) to some specific regulation. The significance of this development, in the long view, is not diminished by the fact that, as we have seen, the proposed rules are not likely to be very effective (in particular because the committee rejects a requirement of consultation).

The System of Legal Control: Return of the 'Medical Exception'?

While, with the exceptions noted above, changes in the substantive law of euthanasia since the predecessor of this book was published in 1998 have mostly been fairly modest, developments in the system of legal control have been very important. The creation of the Regional Review Committees in 1998 and the statutory status given their judgments by the Law of 2002, together with the institutionalisation and extension of the SCEN programme for consultation, have gone a long way in the direction of a fully satisfactory control arrangement. It is also the case, that the published case law produced by the committees is currently

---

[419] This has, to be sure, been accompanied by some relaxation of the requirement that the doctor who performs it have an existing treatment relationship with the patient. See section 4.2.3.3(D).

the most important source of ongoing legal development, and that through their Annual Reports and in other ways the committees' contribution to the transparency of euthanasia practice and of societal control has been of enormous importance in the 'normalisation' of euthanasia.

At the risk of being accused, as the Dutch would express it, of 'dragging old cows out of the ditch' (which amounts to the same thing as 'beating a dead horse'), we would like to suggest that these changes in the system of legal control can best be described as one in the direction of the 'medical exception'.[420] Euthanasia and assisted suicide, when performed by doctors, have been largely removed from the jurisdiction of the criminal law. This has been accomplished (1) by removing initial review of what a doctor does from the purview of the criminal law authorities and entrusting it to the Regional Review Committees; (2) by the practice of the Review Committees, which dispose over a number of less drastic sanctions but very rarely invoke the ultimate one—finding the doctor 'not careful'—which would entail turning the case over to the prosecutorial authorities; (3) by the policy and practice of the prosecutorial authorities, who hardly ever bring criminal charges in the tiny fraction of all cases that do come to their attention, and in particular not in cases where only 'procedural' faults are at issue.

Two sorts of cases still, in principle, can lead to a criminal prosecution, and both of these can be interpreted as reflecting, not falsifying, the idea of the 'medical exception'. The first involves cases in which the requirement of 'unbearable and hopeless suffering' or of a voluntary request have not been met. In such cases, the committee of Procurators-General has made clear, criminal prosecution is appropriate. But in these cases one can argue that the basic criterion of the 'medical exception' has not been met: that the doctor have acted *as a doctor*. Without suffering (however broadly conceived) based on a medical condition, there is no medical indication for such drastic treatment; without the consent of the patient there is no authority for any sort of treatment. In short, in such a case the doctor does not act as a doctor and he therefore has only the defences possibly available to a lay person who did the same thing.

The second sort of case that might lead to prosecution is the situation in the *Brongersma* case: physician-assisted suicide in the case of suffering not based on any 'medical condition'. Here, again, the problem, as seen by the courts and many commentators, was that the doctor had no medical title to do what he did, since there was no medical indication for it.

In short, the sort of cases still likely to attract criminal prosecution can be seen as falling outside the 'medical exception'. Euthanasia or assisted suicide by a doctor *acting as a doctor* are no longer—to a large extent de jure and for the rest de facto—subject to criminal law control.

To this conclusion we can add the comment that, as consultation by SCEN doctors increasingly becomes characteristic of Dutch euthanasia practice, and as

---

[420] See GB&W: 284*ff.* for a defence of the 'medical exception' as the best approach to effective regulation of euthanasia. As we have seen in 4.2.1 the 'medical exception' was early on rejected as a defence to a charge under arts 293 (euthanasia) or 294 (assisted suicide) of the Penal Code.

the burden of control thereby shifts from after-the-fact control by legal institutions (prosecutors or review committees) to before-the-fact control by medical institutions (SCEN consultants), it is going to seem ever more plausible to describe what has happened, albeit via a roundabout route, as adoption of the 'medical exception' as the solution to the problem of regulation of euthanasia and assisted suicide.

5

Dutch Euthanasia Law in Context and in Practice

The two preceding chapters have dealt with current Dutch law concerning euthanasia and other medical behaviour that shortens life (MBPSL) (chapter 4), and with the process of legal change that led to this set of legal arrangements (chapter 3). The bulk of this chapter considers what is known about actual MBPSL practice and about the operation of the regulatory system. In section 5.1, we present the results of recent quantitative research on the frequencies of the different sorts of MBPSL, in particular the wealth of information collected in large-scale studies in the Netherlands since 1990. Section 5.2 goes into more detail with respect to each of the different sorts of MBPSL. Section 5.3 presents the results of some qualitative research. Section 5.4 deals with data concerning the operation of the special control system for euthanasia and physician-assisted suicide, the chapter ending with the question whether such control can be considered adequate.

The entire subject of MBPSL in neonatology is postponed to chapter 6.

A note to the reader: Even though the data discussed in this chapter are by no means exhaustive and even though they are presented in a simplified and non-technical way, there is undeniably a lot to plough through. This reflects the fact that much of the material presented is not readily available, and certainly not to non-readers of Dutch. We have gone quite far—especially in section 5.2—in presenting data that, while perhaps not always essential for the particular argument we ourselves want to make, may be put to use by some readers for their own purposes. Readers who are less interested in matters of detail may want to skim through the chapter looking for things that particularly interest them.

5.1 Overview of Data on End-of-Life Practice

In this section we deal in detail with quantitative information concerning MBPSL practice, in particular information that became available after the predecessor of this book was published in 1998 (the reader is referred to *Euthanasia and Law in the Netherlands* for an exhaustive discussion of what was known in 1997). The studies on which it is based share some important shortcomings of which it is important that the reader be aware: the reliability of the answers and of their inter-pretation can be problematic (eg, what amounts to a 'request' in practice?); the data derive from doctors so that nothing is directly known from the perspective of the patient or others involved; and the organisational context in which the behav-iour described took place is only known in very general terms (the patient's home, a hospital, a nursing home). Nevertheless, the results of Dutch research afford a wealth of information—food for thought, indications of problems in medical and regulatory practice, highly probable answers to some important policy questions, insights into how legal regulation and social practice are mutually influencing one another—that is unique in the world.

For a proper understanding of the results of most of the studies discussed below, it is important to recall where people die (and, associated with that, what sort of doctor is responsible for their care at the time they die). We dealt with this already in chapter 2.2.2, but just to remind the reader: in the Netherlands, 33% of all deaths in 2004 took place in hospitals (the doctor is a specialist), 28% at home and 11% in old age homes (the doctor is a GP), and 22 % in nursing homes (the doc-tor is a nursing-home doctor).

5.1.1 Frequencies and Characteristics of MBPSL in Four National Studies, 1990–2005

Until 1990, the available information on euthanasia in the Netherlands was frag-mentary, often impressionistic and anecdotal, and of unclear general validity. The first serious effort to establish national frequencies, and to study euthanasia in the context of other MBPSL, was carried out by Van der Wal and covered the period 1986–90.[1] In 1990 the Dutch Government commissioned the first major national study of euthanasia practice, the results of which were published in 1991.[2] In 1995, 2001 and 2005 follow-up studies were carried out.[3]

One of the most important contributions the Dutch national researchers have made to the study of euthanasia has been to place it in the context of other kinds of medical behaviour that potentially shortens life. Beginning in the 1990 research not only euthanasia and assistance with suicide but also other medical behaviour that the doctor expects to lead to the patient's death has been included (pain relief with life-shortening effect, withholding or withdrawing treatment, termination of

---

[1] See Van der Wal 1992; see also Muller 1996. See GB&W: 202–7 for a discussion of this research.

[2] The historical context in which this research was commissioned and the research itself are dis-cussed at length in GB&W: chs 2.4 and 5.1.

[3] The four reports are: Van der Maas *et al* 1991 (an English version was published in 1992); Van der Wal & Van der Maas 1996 (some of the most important findings are published in English in Van der Maas *et al* 1996, and Van der Wal *et al* 1996); Van der Wal *et al* 2003 (some of the more important find-ings are published in English in Onwuteaka-Philipsen *et al* 2003); Onwuteaka-Philipsen *et al* 2007 (some of the most important findings are published in English in Van der Heide *et al* 2007). In the reports of these four studies, the data are allocated to 1990/1991, 1995/1996, 2001/2002 and 2005/2006 respectively, since the data collection spanned the end of the calendar year. For the sake of simplicity, we use throughout only the first of the two years.

life without an explicit request). Precisely because, as we will see, the classification of behaviour in medical practice can be so problematic, it is essential—both from the point of view of empirical research and from that of the design of effective regulation—not to reify 'euthanasia' or any of the rest of MBPSL as distinct sorts of behaviour and study them in isolation. In this regard, the approach first used by Van der Maas in 1990 has been enormously influential; since then, all good survey research into the frequency of euthanasia has followed his example.[4]

In the 1995 and 2001 Dutch studies, in addition to basic frequencies and characteristics of MBPSL, particular attention was paid to consultation, reporting, and prosecutorial policy. In 1995 special attention was paid to newborn babies and psychiatric patients, in 2001 to 'terminal sedation', to persons not suffering from any 'medical' condition, to demented patients, and to newborn babies and children, and in 2005 to 'continuous deep sedation until death' and its relation to euthanasia.

5.1.1.1 Methodology

In 1990 three different sources of information were used: interviews with a sample of doctors ('interview study'); a written questionnaire sent to the responsible doctors in a sample of registered deaths ('death-certificate study'); and a study of the most recent death in the practice of a national sample of doctors. Since 1995 the national studies have repeated the interview and the death-certificate studies, using essentially the same instruments. The 2001 study added interviews with doctors and others involved in a sample of reported cases. In the 2005 study, a questionnaire sent to a sample of over 1,000 doctors was used instead of the earlier interviews ('questionnaire study').

The death-certificate studies produce basic data on the frequencies of various MBPSL (essentially: what did the doctor do? what was his intention? was there a request from the patient?). The interview/questionnaire studies cover matters that go further than the few basic questions concerning an individual case covered in the death-certificate studies. The interview/questionnaire and death-certificate approaches produce slightly different estimates of the frequencies of the various MBPSL, and it is the death-certificate study whose methodology is considered most reliable for these purposes. It has become the international standard. The comparative pan-European EURELD studies covering six Western European countries whose results are presented in chapter 17, are all death-certificate studies using the Dutch methodology.

In interpreting and in particular in comparing the data produced by death-certificate studies, the reader should be aware of two potential sources of confusion. In the Dutch studies and studies elsewhere using the same methodology, in particular those of EURELD, the frequency of euthanasia and other MBPSL is

---

[4] This includes the Belgian research presented in ch 7, the comparative EURELD-studies discussed in ch 17, as well as studies in Australia (Kuhse et al 1997), New Zealand (Mitchell & Owens 2003) and the UK (Seale 2006a, 2006b).

expressed as a percentage of *all deaths*; but in some studies, such as those of Seale for the United Kingdom, the frequencies given are expressed as percentages of *all non-sudden deaths* (ie of those deaths in which a doctor would be in a position to make an end-of-life decision). Rates of MBPSL computed in this way are of course considerably higher than when total deaths are used.[5]

The second source of possible confusion is that most studies, like the Dutch ones, focus on the frequency of various MBPSL as causes of death and therefore count only the *most important end-of-life decision* in a particular case,[6] whereas in some other studies *all end-of-life decisions* are included.[7] The latter approach leads to a considerably higher estimate of the frequency of MBPSL, many of which will not have been the immediate cause of the patient's death. This is because administration of a lethal drug may be preceded, for example, by withdrawal of life support, and the latter will not have been considered the 'most important' of the two.[8]

In this book, unless otherwise noted, we stick to the '*most important decision*' approach and give frequencies on the basis of *all deaths*.

Finally, a note on the reliability of the data. Statistical significance is generally quite high, especially for the more frequent sorts of MBPSL (although the bad habit—which we will not emulate—of reporting frequencies as if they were accurate to a tenth or even to a hundredth of a percent produces an illusion of precision not justified by the nature of this sort of research). We do not indicate statistical significance unless there is special occasion to do so.[9] The main problem with research in this area, as far as reliability is concerned, lies in the response rate. This is usually high in the Netherlands.[10]

5.1.1.2 How to Define Varieties of MBPSL

In the Dutch national studies (and in studies in other countries using the same methodology), 'euthanasia' (and, more generally, all forms of 'termination of life')

---

[5] Thus Seale finds a total frequency of MBPSL in the UK of 70% of non-sudden deaths. As Table 17.2 shows, the rate for all deaths is 64%. The reason for Seale's approach lies in the fact that his data derive from a sample of doctors (who often are not involved in sudden deaths) rather than from a sample of death certificates (see Seale 2006a: 6).

[6] See Van der Heide *et al* 2003: 364 (EURELD study):

> For cases in which more than one . . . [end of life decision was reported] the decision with the most explicit intention prevailed over other decisions, whereas in case of similar intentions . . . [termination of life] prevailed over . . . [intensification of pain relief] and . . . [intensification of pain relief] over . . . [abstention].

[7] See eg Bosshard *et al* 2005 (EURELD study). No explanation is given for the fact that all abstention decisions, not just those that were the 'most important' end-of-life decision in a particular case, are involved, but this is obviously a sensible procedure if one is interested in abstention decision-making as such.

[8] See Van der Wal *et al* 2003: 261–4 for the design of the questionnaire used in the Dutch death-certificate studies.

[9] The researchers of the Dutch national studies seem somewhat more restrained in this regard than their international colleagues (ie the authors whose data are discussed in chs 10 and 17.2).

[10] See n 15.

is distinguished from other MBPSL in an idiosyncratic way. Crucial for the classification of a death is not what the doctor actually *did* nor whether it was *medically indicated* but what his *subjective intention* was. In chapter 4.2.2.3 and 4.2.3 we have discussed the problem of classification of different sorts of MBPSL, concluding that reliance on subjective intentions has no basis in (criminal) law. Here we are concerned with the way legal categories have been operationalised in empirical research.

The researchers have from the 1990 research on distinguished three levels of intentionality in the case of administration of potentially life-shortening drugs to deal with pain or symptoms ('pain relief' for short hereafter). The doctor may act:

1. with the 'explicit intention' of shortening life;
2. 'partly with the intention' of shortening life, that is to say, this is a subsidiary intention associated with a primary intention of relieving pain (hereafter referred to as 'subsidiary intention'; sometimes called 'co-intention');
3. not with the intention of shortening the patient's life but 'taking into account the probability' that what he does to relieve pain will have such an effect (hereafter referred to as 'accepting risk').

In the experience of the researchers, the first and third categories (explicit intention and accepting risk) were, in the case of pain relief with life-shortening effect, not sufficient to describe the range of intentionality they encountered in research: 'there were occasions when, in the opinion of the physician, neither description did justice to his intention'.[11] It was to deal with this problem that they introduced the intermediate level of intentionality: 'partly with the intention' of shortening life.

When the potentially life-shortening pain relief is administered with the 'explicit intention' to cause the death of the patient, this leads to a classification of what the doctor did as 'termination of life' (which, if on request, is 'euthanasia'). The other two levels of intention lead to a classification as 'pain relief with life-shortening effect'. Although such an approach to classification would seem just as applicable to withholding or withdrawing life-prolonging treatment (which we often refer to for short as 'abstention') as to pain relief with life-shortening effect, the Dutch researchers distinguish in practice between the two. In the case of withholding or withdrawing life-prolonging treatment, the doctor's intent is divided into only two categories—'accepting risk' and 'explicit intention'—and, contrary to what one might have supposed, in both cases the death is classified as due to abstention.

In the predecessor of this book, we criticised this reliance by the researchers on the subjective intentions of doctors, on both legal and empirical grounds.[12] At the time, our main concern was that many cases that in substance amount to euthanasia (or termination of life without a request), and that using traditional ethical and

---

[11] Van der Maas *et al* 1992: 21; see also Van der Wal & Van der Maas 1996: 41.
[12] See GB&W: 162–6, 254–7, 271–3.

legal analysis would be classified as such, were being wrongly classified as 'pain relief', thereby artificially reducing the frequency of euthanasia and termination of life without a request. In recent years it has become clear that operationalising 'euthanasia' in the way this has been done to date may also, paradoxically, be responsible for a radical underestimation of the rate of reporting by doctors. We return to this problem in section 5.4.3.

In the later Dutch studies (and those elsewhere using the Dutch methodology), the same approach to classification has been repeated without responding to the suggestion from a number of quarters that it would be better, both legally and empirically, to use the more objective criterion of 'medical indication' to distinguish the various MBPSL.[13] Pain relief with life-shortening effect and withholding or withdrawing life-prolonging treatment would then only be classified as such when there is a *medical indication* for what is done (suffering for which the pain relief given is appropriate; 'futility' of treatment[14]).

The reason for emphasising the problem of classification here is that awareness of the methodology underlying the findings of the death-certificate studies is crucial to understanding the meaning of the results and of the conclusions that can be drawn from them, as well as to a proper interpretation of the 'reporting rates' based on the findings of these studies.

5.1.1.3 Frequencies and Characteristics of MBPSL

Putting aside problems of classification of behaviour as 'euthanasia' or one of the other forms of MBPSL, the Netherlands now has national data on the frequencies of MBPSL spanning a period of 15 years. The results are based on large, carefully composed samples and generally high rates of response,[15] and at least until 2005 have been stable over time. The only other European countries for which in any sense comparable data are available are the United Kingdom and the countries covered in the comparative EURELD project, with which we deal in chapter 17.

---

[13] In the report of the 2005 study, the researchers do raise the question of the relevance of subjective intentions and seem to acknowledge that these are legally irrelevant, but invoke the (supposed but not further identified) 'definition of euthanasia' as justification for continuing to classify medical behaviour in such terms (see Onwuteaka-Philipsen *et al* 2007: 107–8). From time to time the Law of 2002 and the report of the State Commission on Euthanasia of 1985 are invoked as the basis for an operational definition of 'euthanasia' in terms of intentions (see eg Rurup *et al* 2006b; Onwuteaka-Philipsen *et al* 2007: 107). In fact, however, the Law of 2002 is irrelevant (since it contains no definition of 'euthanasia') and, as we have seen in ch 4.2.2.3 and 4.2.3, the State Commission's view was quite different.

[14] Abstention following refusal of treatment by the patient could better be classified separately, since in such a case the doctor is not responsible for the patient's death (in effect, no MBPSL is involved at all).

[15] The samples for the interview studies in 1990, 1995 and 2001 were over 400 and in 2005 that for the questionnaire study was over 1,000; for the death certificate studies the samples were more than 5,000 in all four studies. The response rate for the interview studies was between 85% and 91%; in 2005 the questionnaire study produced a response rate of only 56% (for this and other reasons the questionnaire data are thought by the researchers to be not entirely comparable with the interview data from earlier studies). Response for the death certificate studies was about 75% in all four studies. See Onwuteaka-Philipsen *et al* 2003: 395, 396; Onwuteaka-Philipsen *et al* 2007: 97.

Table 5.1 shows the frequency with which the various sorts of MBPSL were a cause of death, as estimated in the four national studies. Roughly 40% of all deaths are due to something the doctor does or does not do (MBPSL), and this proportion seems to be rather stable and similar to the rate in other Western European countries.[16]

Of MBPSL deaths, almost all were until recently accounted for in about equal proportions by pain relief with life-shortening effect and withholding or withdrawing life-prolonging treatment. However, since 2001 pain relief with life-shortening effect has become a much more important cause of death, being by itself responsible for a quarter of all deaths in the Netherlands. In 1990, pain relief with the 'subsidiary intention' of causing the death of the patient was at 4% twice as frequent as euthanasia, but its frequency declined steadily to only 1% by 2005. Abstaining with the 'explicit intention' of hastening death accounted for almost 10% of all deaths in 1990, its frequency increased somewhat in 1995 and 2001, but by 2005 was back to just under the 1990 rate. Adding termination of life with or without a request, pain relief with a 'subsidiary intention', and abstention with an 'express intention' together, the frequency of death intentionally caused by the patient's doctor was in 2005 about 11%, compared with 16% in 1990, 19% in 1995, and 17% in 2001.

The frequency of euthanasia has always been fairly low. It increased somewhat between 1990 and 2001; but in 2005, according to the death-certificate study, the rate fell suddenly back down to its 1990 level. With the exception of this one finding for 2005, the death-certificate and the interview/questionnaire studies give roughly the same results for all years and the slow upward trend is regular. The frequency of euthanasia/PAS in 2005 according to the questionnaire study (2.5%) is much more in line with the trend in earlier years than is the sudden decline found in the death-certificate study.[17] Thus it may be that the frequency of euthanasia is more stable than appears from the 2005 death-certificate study.

The rate of physician-assisted suicide has always been very low and has declined over the years.[18] Termination of life without a request seems to have declined somewhat since 1990, but the apparent further decline in 2005 is, according to the researchers, not statistically significant.

On Table 5.2 we see some basic characteristics of patients who died from the various MBPSL in 1990, 1995, 2001 and 2005.

People who die from euthanasia are somewhat younger than decedents generally, in particular those who die from pain relief or abstention. Men die slightly more frequently than women from euthanasia, slightly less frequently from pain relief or abstention. Cancer is much more frequent among those who die from euthanasia than it is among decedents generally, but it is also overrepresented among those dying from pain relief (since 1995 it has been underrepresented

---

[16] See ch 17, Table 17.2. If we exclude sudden deaths, in which no behaviour of a doctor is involved, the relative importance of MBPSL is even more striking: 65% in the Netherlands in 2001.

[17] Euthanasia and PAS together accounted, in the interview/questionnaire studies of 1990, 1995, 2001 and 2005, for 2.2%, 2.7%, 2.4% and 2.5% of all deaths. See Onwuteaka-Philipsen *et al* 2007: 102.

[18] The declining relative frequency of PAS is confirmed by the 2005 questionnaire study (*ibid*).

Table 5.1. Estimated frequencies of MBPSL in the Netherlands in national studies: 1990, 1995, 2001, 2005 (percentages of all deaths)

	1990	1995	2001	2005
termination of life on request	*1.9*	*2.6*	*2.8*	*1.8*
euthanasia	1.7	2.4	2.6	1.7
PAS	0.2	0.2	0.2	0.1
termination of life without request	*0.8*	*0.7*	*0.7*	*0.4*
pain relief with life-shortening effect	*19*	*19*	*21*	*25*
accepting risk	15	16	19	24
subsidiary intention	4	3	2	1
withholding or withdrawing life-prolonging treatment	*18*	*20*	*20*	*16*
accepting risk	9	7	7	8
express intention	9	13	13	8
total MBPSL	*39*	*43*	*44*	*43*
total deaths	128,824	135,675	140,377	136,402
estimated deaths from euthanasia/PAS*	2,700	3,600	3,800	2,425

Source: Onweatuka-Philipsen *et al* 2007: 102, 112, 116, 119, 174 (death certificate studies, data rounded off in source). For a summary presentation of the data for 1990, 1995 and 2001 in English see Onwuteaka-Philipsen *et al* 2003; for 2005 see Van der Heide *et al* 2007. Estimates derive from stratified samples; the 95% confidence interval is considerable in the case of the smaller categories of MBPSL—in 2001, for example, this was 2.3–2.8% for euthanasia and 0.1–0.3% for physician-assisted suicide. See also CBS 2007 (including absolute numbers, without, however, indicating that these are estimates based on a stratified sample).

* These estimates do not correspond to the frequencies given: if one multiplies the total number of deaths by the percentage of total deaths due to euthanasia/PAS one gets a different number and the differences are not negligible. No explanation for the difference is given in the reports of the national studies. Contact with the researchers reveals that these estimates are based both on the results of the death-certificate studies and also (to a lesser extent) on those of the interview/questionnaire studies. It is the estimates given here that are used elsewhere in the reports—as in this chapter—to calculate the rate at which requests are carried out (see table 5.7) as well as the reporting rate (see section 5.4.3).

among those dying from abstention). The ethnicity of those dying from the various MBPSL is essentially the same as that of decedents generally. The estimated shortening of life due to euthanasia is about equally divided between less than a week and 1–4 weeks (the former has declined to 46% from 58% in 1990, the latter has increased from 25% to 46%); over the years the estimated shortening of life is more than 4 weeks in about a tenth of all euthanasia deaths. The estimated shortening of life due to the other MBPSL is in the vast majority of cases less than a week, and the trend seems to be toward less shortening of life. The average shortening of life due to all MBPSL taken together is estimated to be four days.[19]

[19] See *CBS Webmagazine* (2 July 2007) available at <http://www.cbs.nl> accessed 3 July 2007. For data for earlier years see Onwuteaka-Philipsen *et al* 2007: 103, 117, 120.

Table 5.2. Characteristics of deaths due to MBPSL in the Netherlands, 2005 (column percentages of each characteristic)

	all deaths	E&PAS N = 311	term. w/o request N = 24	pain relief N = 1,478	abstention N = 767
age					
0–64	19	38	47	17	16
65–79	32	39	28	33	30
80 or older	48	23	25	50	54
sex					
male	49	56	49	47	44
female	51	44	51	53	56
*ethnicity**					
non-western, non-native	3	2	4	2	3
native, or western non-native	97	98	96	98	97
medical condition					
cancer	29	84	23	43	22
cardiovascular	32	6	16	18	31
other/ unknown	39	10	61	38	47
est. shortening of life					
less then 1 week	—	46	88	81	73
1 week to 1 month	—	46	7	2	8
more than 1 month	—	8	6	1	6
unknown	—	0	0	16	13

Source: Onwuteaka-Philipsen *et al* 2007: 103, 113, 117, 120. For further data (covering requests and refused etc. requests, as well as granted requests) see Jansen-Van der Weide *et al* 2005: 1700.

* Non-native, non-western = born in most non-western countries or born in the Netherlands with at least one parent born in one of the same countries.

The very small number of cases of termination of life without a request in the sample makes the reliability of the distribution of characteristics dubious. Cancer seems to be less frequent as underlying medical condition than in the case of euthanasia (the frequency has declined by more than a half to 23% since 1990), and the estimated shortening of life involved is almost always less than a week (as it was in 1990).[20]

The 2001 study examined whether the socio-economic status of patients is correlated with the frequency of euthanasia or other MBPSL. The rate of euthanasia, and the total of all MBPSL, was slightly higher among higher-status patients. According to the researchers, the differences were not statistically significant. Institutionalised patients apparently have a much lower rate of euthanasia, but

---

[20] For the data for earlier years see Onwuteaka-Philipsen *et al* 2007: 113.

rather higher rates of death due to pain relief or abstention, than the population of decedents as a whole.[21]

5.1.2 Data on Reported Cases, 1998–2006

A second source of data are the Annual Reports of the Regional Review Committees. The weakness of these data, compared with those of the national studies discussed in section 5.1.2, is that only *reported* cases are included. To the extent that cases are not reported (see section 5.4.3) the frequency of euthanasia will be understated and the characteristics may be different from those of all cases of euthanasia that actually take place.[22] On the other hand, the data of the Regional Review Committees are available for every year and not subject to sampling errors or non-response.[23]

Table 5.3 shows these data, which on the whole are rather similar to those of the national studies. The dominant role of GPs and the predominance of cancer among those dying from euthanasia or assisted suicide are very similar. Four-fifths of all euthanasia takes place at home.

The part that assisted suicide plays in the total of euthanasia plus assisted suicide is very small in both sources. It accounted for about 5% in 2005, according to the findings of the national studies, having declined from 11% in 1990 (see Table 5.1). And it made up a little under 9% of reported cases in 2006, having declined somewhat since 2000.[24]

---

[21] Van der Wal *et al* 2003: 70.

[22] It is known that this was the case in the past (but the extent of non-reporting was at the time far greater than it is now). See GB&W: 238.

[23] Since 2003 a potential third source of data are the annual mortality statistics produced by the Central Bureau of Statistics (CBS). A so-called 'B-form' must be filled in by a doctor in connection with every death in the Netherlands and sent to the CBS for statistical purposes. It is different from the 'A-form' used to report a death to the municipal pathologist, which forms the basis of the control system for euthanasia. Since 2003 the 'B-form' asks not only about the 'underlying' cause of death but also whether the death was due to 'termination of life' ('this does not include withdrawing or withholding life-prolonging treatment nor pain relief with hastening of death as a side-effect'). Three categories can be checked: 'euthanasia' ('administering a drug with the explicit intention of ending the patient's life at the request of the patient'), 'assistance with suicide' ('providing or prescribing a drug with the explicit intention of ending the patient's life at the patient's request'), or 'other' (no further definition given). Unfortunately, however, it seems that when a doctor reports a case of euthanasia to the municipal pathologist, he almost always leaves the filling-in of the B-form to the latter, and no other cases of euthanasia are reported as such on the B-form. In short, data from the B-form add essentially nothing to what is available in the Annual Reports of the Regional Review Committees (see Griffiths 2007c). (Form, data, and further information received from CBS.)

[24] We have taken the two categories 'PAS' and 'combination' together here, on the assumption that in cases where there was a combination of the two the first choice was for PAS. It may be that the fact the category 'combination' is not used in the national studies (and these cases are presumably classified as euthanasia, that being what leads directly to the patient's death) accounts at least in part for the fact that the frequency of PAS is lower in the national studies.

Table 5.3. Characteristics of reported cases of euthanasia/PAS, 1998–2006 (percentages of all reported cases)

		1998[1]	1999	2000	2001	2002	2003	2004	2005	2006
Total reports		349	2,216	2,123	2,054	1,882	1,815	1,886	1,933	1,923
	euthanasia	90.5	90.3	87.9	88.6	88.8	89.6	90.9	91.3	91.8
	PAS	8.3	8.8	10.0	9.3	9.8	8.2	7.5	7.4	6.9
euthanasia/PAS	combination	1.1	0.9	2.1	2.1	1.4	2.3	1.6	1.3	1.3
	GP	86.2	84.6	84.8	85.7	86.8	85.8	87.3	87.8	88.0
	specialist	11.7	13.4	13.1	12.3	11.0	11.8	10.0	8.8	7.9
reporting doctor	NH doctor	2.0	2.0	2.1	2.0	2.2	2.4	2.8	3.4	4.2
	cancer	84.2	90.3	89.2	88.5	88.1	88.4	87.3	88.6	86.1
	cardiovascular system	3.2	1.6	1.3	1.1	1.5	1.0	1.3	1.2	2.9
	nervous system	4.6	3.1	2.4	2.9	3.2	4.1	3.3	4.4	5.5
	respiratory system	1.7	2.3	2.1	2.0	2.1	1.9	1.8	3.1	3.3
	AIDS	0.6	0.3	0.5	0	0.2	0.2	0.2	0.1	—[2]
medical condition	other/combination	5.7	2.3	4.5	5.5	4.9	4.4	6.0	4.2	2.2
	home	86.5	83.1	83.5	82.7	82.0	81.4	81.1	82.0	79.5
	hospital	10.3	12.4	13.1	12.0	11.1	11.4	9.4	8.2	7.5
	nursing home[3]	3.2	3.7	3.1	3.8	2.2	2.6	3.4	3.8	4.1
	old age home[3]					2.7	2.3	3.3	2.3	4.1
location	other	0	0.8	0.3	1.5	2.0	2.4	2.8	3.7	3.6

Source: Annual Reports, Regional Review Committees.

[1] November and December 1998.
[2] AIDS discontinued as separate category.
[3] Old age homes included under nursing homes through 2001.

5.2 Quantitative Information: Various MBPSL

Having presented some basic overall data on the frequency and characteristics of the various sorts of MBPSL, we proceed now to discuss in more specific detail what is known about medical behaviour of the various sorts. We begin with those MBPSL that are considered to constitute 'normal medical practice'.

5.2.1 'Normal Medical Practice'

One important item of information concerning these MBPSL was systematically studied in the national studies of 1990 and 1995[25] but not thereafter: discussion of the proposed life-shortening behaviour with the patient, his family and nursing staff. Such data are available for 2001, but only aggregated for all MBPSL. If the patient was competent, there was discussion with the patient in 92% of all MBPSL, and with his family in 81%. If the patient was not competent, the decision was nevertheless discussed with him in 19% and with his family in 85% of all cases. Since most MBPSL are either pain relief or abstention, these data must fairly closely reflect what happens in such cases. (These rates were the highest of the six countries covered in the EURELD study, with Belgium and Switzerland consistently relatively high as well.) Discussion was less frequent with other doctors (43%) and with nursing staff (36%).[26]

5.2.1.1 Withholding and Withdrawing Treatment (Abstention)

As we have seen in Table 5.1, 16% of all deaths in 2005 were preceded by a decision to withdraw or withhold life-prolonging treatment, expecting that this would shorten the patient's life. In half of these cases, the shortening of life was the doctor's 'explicit intention'. From Table 5.2 we can see that the age distribution of abstention cases closely resembles that of pain relief, while the role of cancer in such cases is the lowest of all MBPSL. In about three-quarters of abstention cases the doctor estimates the shortening of life at less than a week.[27] As we will see in chapter 17.2, the Netherlands are similar to other European countries with respect to the frequency of abstention, the treatments withheld or withdrawn (mostly medication, and artificial nutrition and hydration), the shortening of life involved, and the presence of an explicit intention to shorten life.

---

[25] See GB&W: 218 for these data.

[26] See Van der Heide *et al* 2003: 348. Interestingly, Belgium scored as high as the Netherlands as far as discussion with other doctors is concerned, and several countries scored higher with regard to nurses (Belgium 57%, Switzerland 50%, Denmark 38%).

[27] The rate has been fairly stable since 1990 (see Onwuteaka-Philipsen *et al* 2007: 120). For more detailed information concerning abstention, based on the 1995 study, see also Groenwoud *et al* 2000a.

Intensive Care Units

Apart from withholding of artificial nutrition and hydration (see below), there is little information available concerning abstention decisions in concrete medical settings. Kleijer's study of withholding and withdrawing treatment in adult Intensive Care Units is a rare exception.[28] Abstention is responsible for about half of all ICU deaths. Extrapolating from Kleijer's data, it appears that Dutch ICUs are responsible annually for about 6,500 deaths following an abstention decision, which is about a quarter of the total yearly mortality due to abstention.

Kleijer focuses in particular on the importance attached to 'intersubjectivity' in the decision-making that leads to the conclusion that (further) treatment would be futile because of the very poor quality of life the patient can be expected to enjoy, and the ways in which 'intersubjectivity' is achieved. In non-emergency situations (patients who remain on the ICU for more than 24 hours), decisions to withhold or withdraw treatment are seldom taken by one doctor alone. In four-fifths of the ICUs, the participation of other staff members takes place in a structured way, in the remaining ICUs the process is informal. But the intensive care doctor is the central figure: he usually initiates the decision-making procedure, his opinion carries the most weight, and if consensus is not achieved he generally makes the final decision. The decision is regarded as a 'medical' one and about two-thirds of the doctors think the consent of the patient's family is not generally required. Nevertheless, two-thirds of them do attribute some or great influence to the views of the family, and in practice most doctors try to achieve 'acceptance' by the family.[29]

Conflict with the patient's family is rare and most ICUs will delay carrying out an abstention decision to give the family time to 'get used to' it. If the patient's family or representative suggest that the proposed decision may have 'legal implications' almost all of the doctors interviewed think that the decision-making process will be influenced, in the sense that there will be 'more documentation', 'more discussion' and 'more time for the procedure'. Although over four-fifths of the respondents think an ICU should have a clear procedure for cases of conflict, in fact none of them does.[30]

The vast majority of the respondents think that every ICU should have a protocol for cases of abstention; they would also favour a national guideline to serve as a model. In fact, however, most ICUs do not have a protocol and those that exist differ considerably in form and content. Furthermore, most of them are not in conformity with existing law on the status of Advance Directives and the role of the legal representative (appointed or otherwise) of the patient.[31]

---

[28] Kleijer 2005. Kleijer's data are from 36 of the 118 Dutch hospitals, selected for size and geographic distribution and including all of the university hospitals. The data derive from structured interviews with both the medical and the nursing head of each ICU.

[29] Kleijer 2005: 69–18, 218–22 (summary in English).

[30] Kleijer 2005: 118–36, 222–3 (summary in English).

[31] Kleijer 2005: 157–81, 224 (summary in English). See Rurup *et al* 2005a for a comparable level of support among nursing-home doctors for guidelines concerning withholding/withdrawing treatment.

DNR Orders

One possible prelude to withholding treatment is a so-called DNR or NTBR order (from the inscriptions 'Do Not Resuscitate' or 'Not To Be Resuscitated' on the patient's chart or in his medical file).[32] Such an order is an instruction (generally in writing), addressed to the nursing personnel or to other doctors, not to intervene in the case of a specified sort of life-threatening situation (such as cardiac arrest). A DNR order does not necessarily result in the death of the patient since the life-threatening situation may not materialise, the patient may not die from it, or intervention may take place despite the instruction. But the sheer size of DNR practice makes it important to include it in any discussion of medical decisions that affect the time of death. DNR practice was covered in the 1990 national study, from which it appears that a few (15%) GPs, a third of all nursing-home doctors, and essentially all medical specialists had made a DNR order within the preceding year. More than 90,000 DNR orders were made in hospitals in 1990: about 6% of all admissions. In about 60% of all deaths for which a specialist was the responsible doctor, a DNR order had been made. Forty percent of all nursing-home doctors said, when asked about their DNR practice, that the question is not applicable to them because in their institution resuscitation *never* takes place (presumably this means: in the case of otherwise dying patients).[33]

It is common for hospitals and nursing homes to have an institutional policy concerning DNR orders, usually consisting of a protocol for DNR decision-making and a special order form to be kept in the files of individual patients. Development of these policies took place in the early 1990s.[34] The standard forms used often specify the treatments to be withheld (cardio-pulmonary resuscitation, antibiotics, hemodialysis, occasionally artificial nutrition and hydration) and provide for regular updating and formal (re)confirmation. Some forms include spaces for information about consultation and about participants in the decision-making (patient, family, nurses, patient's GP).

As we will see in chapter 17.2, recent comparative research indicates that in the Netherlands 60% of all non-sudden deaths are preceded by a DNR order (with an additional 9% of 'institutional DNR decisions'—that is, general institutional policy not to resuscitate). Such a rate is close to that for other countries.

Artificial Nutrition and Hydration (ANH)

In the past few years, withholding artificial nutrition and hydration (ANH) has become a matter of public discussion in connection with 'terminal sedation'. Less well known is the fact that this form of abstention is common practice at the very

---

[32] Strictly speaking, resuscitation covers only cardiopulmonary treatment if the patient's heart or breathing stops. But prospective decisions not to administer antibiotics in the case of pneumonia, or not to return a patient to Intensive Care, for example, are also possible. It is not entirely clear if all anticipatory decisions to abstain or only the two sorts mentioned were covered in the 1990 research .

[33] Van der Wal 1992: 91, 187; see GB&W: 215–16 for further details.

[34] See Haverkate & Van der Wal 1996.

end of life and is the subject of institutional policy in Dutch nursing homes.[35] The 1995 national research addressed specific attention to decisions to abstain from ANH. About 8% of all deaths in the Netherlands were preceded by such a decision (nursing homes: 23%; GPs and specialists: 4%). About two-thirds of the patients concerned were 80 or older and three-quarters were partly or wholly incompetent. The decision to abstain was discussed with the family in 82% of the cases (nursing-home doctors: 89%).[36] Since 1995, decisions to abstain from ANH have been the most common sort of abstention decision, accounting for about a quarter of the total.[37]

Three recent studies deal specifically with abstention from ANH in Dutch nursing homes.[38] The first is a quantitative study of 178 cases (in 32 nursing homes) in which ANH was not administered to patients with dementia who were no longer (or scarcely) eating and drinking. The average age was 85, 4 out of 5 patients were women, and almost 9 out of 10 were entirely incompetent. The primary diagnosis at the time the abstention decision was made was dementia in about four-fifths of the cases and an acute illness in the other cases (stroke, respiratory or urinary tract infection). In two-thirds of the cases there was some advanced care planning, most often in agreement with the patient's children, concerning care to be withheld (admission to hospital, ANH, resuscitation) or to be given (in particular, antibiotics). Only 4% of the patients had an advance treatment directive. The doctor's primary intention was most often to avoid unnecessarily prolonging life, but optimising comfort was also frequently mentioned. In almost a fifth of the cases, an additional intention was to hasten the death of the patient (only incidentally was this the primary intention). The patient's family and nurses were almost always involved in the decision-making; the participants ascribed considerable influence to the doctor and the family. In almost all cases except the few in which the patient was partly or wholly competent, he had no influence on the decision-making. Almost all the other participants were highly satisfied with the decision-making process.

A second, observational study in the psycho-geriatric units of two Dutch nursing homes, generally confirms the quantitative findings just summarised. An interesting additional insight is that in a small number of cases, a nursing-home doctor decides 'in favour of' the family, who want the patient to be given ANH, against his own judgment.

The third study, based on questionnaires sent to doctors, nurses and family members of nursing home patients, reveals a general consensus (over 60% in all three groups) that when a patient with advanced dementia ceases eating or drinking, this should be respected; almost no one considered withholding ANH in such circumstances wrong. There was a similar majority who consider administration of pain medication in such a case legitimate, even though this may hasten death.

---

[35] See ch 4.2.2.2 and 4.2.2.4.
[36] Van der Heide *et al* 1997a (interviews with responsible doctor in a sample of deaths).
[37] Onwuteaka-Philipsen *et al* 2007: 121.
[38] Pasman *et al* 2004a, 2004b; Rurup *et al* 2005a.

Almost all doctors thought such practice usually leads to a 'peaceful death', and most nurses and about half of all family members agreed (most of the rest were ambivalent).

Refusal of Treatment: 'Treatment Directives'

Table 5.1 gave the total frequency of death due to withholding or withdrawing treatment. Table 5.4 shows how much of the total of death due to abstention results from a patient having exercised his right to refuse (further) treatment, either orally or in a written treatment directive.

The part played by the patient in abstention decisions is limited. The proportion of abstention decisions 'accepting the risk' that the patient will die, in which a request by the patient plays a role, is small but slowly growing. When the 'explicit intention' of abstention is to shorten the patient's life, the proportion taken after a request by the patient is a higher (almost a quarter) but stable. Taking Tables 5.1 and 5.4 together, we can estimate that in 2001, of some 28,000 deaths due to abstention, 6000 were at the request of the patient (1800 'accepting the risk' of death and 4200 cases with the 'express intention' of causing death).[39] The total of 6000 amounts to some 4% of all deaths.

In the case of a non-competent patient, refusal can take the form of an advance written refusal of treatment. Kleijer's research on abstention in Intensive Care Units (discussed above), where most patients, of course, are not competent, leads him to estimate that in fewer than 2% of the deaths of patients in ICUs does a written refusal of treatment have a 'steering influence'.[40] Refusal on a patient's behalf by a representative is also rare. Kleijer estimates for Intensive Care Units that in

Table 5.4. Frequency of abstention following a request by the patient (percentages of all abstention decisions with a given intention)

	1990	1995	2001
'accepting risk'	14	17	18
'explicit intention'	23	22	23

Source: CBS 1996: 46–7; CBS 2003a: 23 (death certificate studies). No comparable data from 2005 study.

[39] Total deaths *x* percent with a given intention *x* percent of those at request of patient. It is not clear how many of these cases involve respecting the legal requirement of 'informed consent', since the doctor might have been inclined to abstain anyway. See Vezzoni 2008: 119–20 on the problem of measuring the influence of patient refusal of treatment on the abstention decisions of doctors.

It is somewhat strange to apply categories of 'intent' that refer to the *doctor's* intention, to the situation in which the *patient* refuses treatment. In such a case, the only relevant intention of the doctor is to honour the request, which he is legally obliged to do. It is only the patient who has a relevant intention regarding the withholding or withdrawing.

[40] Kleijer 2005: 97.

less than 1% of all Intensive Care admissions (400 times a year/120,000 admissions) the family/representative definitely want the doctors to withhold or withdraw treatment.[41] Some doctors indicate that they are willing to let their own judgment be influenced, or the moment of abstention advanced, if the position of the family seems reasonable. The situation apparently seldom leads to conflict.[42]

A study by Vezzoni of the social practice of treatment directives in the Netherlands estimates, largely on the basis of information from nursing-home doctors and GPs, that treatment directives are very rare in the population as a whole (less than 1%), somewhat higher for patients in nursing homes (about 5%), and higher again among patients of GPs who died during the preceding year (almost 1 in 10).[43] Although according to Vezzoni the Dutch rate is probably the highest in Europe, the frequency of treatment directives in the Netherlands seems disappointing, at least compared with what has been found in North America.[44] The stated willingness of doctors to allow their medical judgment to be overruled by the written instructions of a patient is also limited. A quarter of the nursing-home doctors and almost half of the GPs in Vezzoni's research would not follow a treatment directive somewhat different from their medical judgment, and if it is directly opposed to their judgment the rate of not following rises to almost 60% (nursing-home doctors) and almost 90% (GPs).[45] These answers are to a hypothetical question in which the instructions in the directive are clear, but in fact, as the international literature on treatment directives (confirmed in Vezzoni's research) shows, treatment directives are rarely concrete and unambiguous, so that their influence in practice is necessarily even more limited.[46]

Dutch doctors rarely take the initiative to suggest to a patient the possibility of a treatment directive and are rarely involved in helping to draft them. The only legal professionals who are involved at all in the social practice—notaries—draft very few of them, and the documents they produce are of low legal and medical quality and therefore unlikely to play much of a role in medical decision-making. The Dutch Government has—beyond enacting a law—done nothing to promote the use of treatment directives, to increase their quality, or to increase the willingness of doctors to abide by the instructions they contain. Neither the Royal Dutch Medical Association or other professional bodies, nor hospitals and nursing homes, have taken steps to promote their use by patients, the involvement of doctors in their drafting, or their implementation in medical decision-making. In

---

[41] Kleijer 2005: 120. Hardly any ICU patients have an appointed representative, and most doctors have confused or erroneous ideas about the legal status of such a figure. In practice they hardly distinguish between a formal legal representative of the patient and 'the family' (one or another of whom will in most cases in fact be the legal representative).See *ibid* at ch 4.5.

[42] Kleijer 2005: 118 (estimated average frequency of conflict: 5 times per year per ICU).

[43] Vezzoni 2008: 201–2. *Cf* also Rurup *et al* 2006a.

[44] Vezzoni 2008: 204–5.

[45] *Ibid* at 208. Kleijer's research in Intensive Care Units shows that fewer than 10% of the doctors considers a written treatment directive 'binding' (Kleijer 2005: 109). *Cf* also Rurup *et al* 2005a (nursing-home doctors).

[46] Vezzoni 2008: 209.

effect, the only significant support for persons interested in drafting one is the Euthanasia Association (NVVE), which for obvious reasons is not a source of help that everyone will feel comfortable turning to. Vezzoni concludes that it is not any defect in the relevant legislation that is responsible for such a low level of use of the facility, such low quality in the few directives actually drafted, and such low willingness of doctors to accept the autonomy of the patient expressed in an advance directive. The responsibility lies in the almost total lack of supportive activity by the government, the medical profession, and health care institutions.[47]

5.2.1.2 Pain Relief with Life-Shortening Effect

As we have seen on Table 5.1, 25% of all deaths in the Netherlands in 2005 were attributed by the doctor concerned to the intensification of pain relief;[48] the Dutch rate in 2001 was similar to rates in other European countries (see chapter 17.2). In 24% of the cases in 2005 the doctor 'accepted the risk' of hastening death and in 1% this was a 'subsidiary intention'. The total frequency of pain relief as a cause of death has steadily increased from 1990 (19%) while the frequency of 'subsidiary intention' has steadily declined (from 4% in 1990). For the characteristics of pain relief cases see Table 5.2. The most important differences between pain relief and euthanasia are that in the case of death due to pain relief the frequency of cancer and the estimated shortening of life is much less and the patients tend to be older than in cases of euthanasia; in all but the last respect, pain relief resembles termination of life without a request much more than it does euthanasia.

There has been little research attention addressed to clinical practice. A rare exception is Kleijer's research, discussed above. In connection with withdrawal of treatment it is common practice in Dutch intensive cares to increase the dosage of opiates/sedatives. Kleijer found that in 6 of 36 ICUs the dosage is increased either not at all or only slightly. In 24 of the 36 it is increased by a factor of 2 to 4 times the existing dosage. And in 6 of the 36 it is increased up to 10 to 25 times and often given in the form of a 'bolus' (single large dose). Kleijer concludes that in many Dutch ICUs, pain relief is administered in connection with withdrawal of treatment in doses that are not medically indicated and that the procedure surrounding this practice often does not meet legal or professional requirements.[49] The same could almost certainly be said of many cases of death due to pain relief in other settings.

Palliative Sedation

For reasons explained in chapter 4.2.2.4, we distinguish between 'palliative sedation'—deep and continuous sedation until death (whereby if ANH is withheld this

---

[47] Vezzoni 2008: 210–12.

[48] 'Attributed' because doctors' knowledge of and ability to predict the life-shortening effect of opiates, in particular, is notoriously poor. See Admiraal & Griffiths 2001.

[49] See Kleijer 2005: 139–43, 223 (English summary). On at least one ICU, muscle relaxants were used. For an illustration of how problematic the distinction between pain relief and termination of life can be in clinical practice, see ch 6, Box 6.8.

is only for a limited period)—which can be assumed not to be a cause of death, and 'terminal sedation' which, because it involves withholding of artificial nutrition and hydration for more than several days, must be considered potentially life-shortening and therefore a form of 'termination of life'. Data for palliative and terminal sedation come from the national research of 2001 and 2005 where they are treated as a single phenomenon, but for our purposes the two need to be treated separately. We deal with the data for both together and more specifically with 'palliative sedation' in this section (using both studies where the 2005 study does not cover points dealt with in 2001); to the extent it can be separated out, 'terminal sedation' is dealt with in section 5.2.2.2 below.

It seems[50] that continuous, deep sedation until death is practised in about a tenth of all deaths in the Netherlands and that there was a slight increase between 2001 and 2005.[51] In 2001, just over half of all interviewed doctors (48% of GPs, 55% of specialists and 75% of nursing-home doctors) said they had ever performed it; respectively 33%, 44% and 65% had done so in the preceding year.[52] In 2005 almost half of it was practised by specialists, about a third by GPs and about a fifth by nursing-home doctors.[53] In 2001, three-quarters of all Dutch doctors (respectively 77%, 64% and 96%) thought that such sedation leads to a 'humane death', but only two-fifths of them considered it a 'good alternative for euthanasia' (respectively 43%, 32% and 38%).[54] The reasons doctors gave for deep, continuous sedation had most of the time to do with pain, restlessness, difficulty of breathing, or fear.[55]

In 2001 there was discussion with the patient in more than half of all cases, and a request from the patient in about a third. If there was no discussion, this was usually because it was not feasible. Over 90% of the time, there was discussion with the family or close friends, and almost half the time with a colleague and with nurses (but rarely with experts in palliative care). The decision for deep and continuous sedation was taken about half the time without the intention to shorten life, the other half with a subsidiary intention to do so. It was rarely the doctor's express intention to shorten life (5% of all cases of continuous, deep sedation).[56]

---

[50] The data in both studies are subject to difficulties of interpretation, and data from different sources (death-certificate and interview studies) give quite different impressions. See Onwuteaka-Philipsen *et al* 2007: 128*ff*.

[51] *Ibid* at 141. A similar indication of the increasing frequency of palliative sedation can be deduced from data on prescriptions for midazolam and other appropriate sedatives. There were almost 20,000 cases of palliative sedation (6% of all deaths) in 2006, an increase of more than a third over 2005 (these data do not include prescriptions by hospital pharmacies or GPs with their own pharmacy). The increase seems to have begun in about 2003. See *Pharmaceutisch Weekblad* 142 no 8 (22 February 2007).

[52] Van der Wal *et al* 2003: 77.

[53] Onwuteaka-Philipsen *et al* 2007: 129.

[54] Van der Wal *et al* 2003: 85.

[55] *Ibid* at 77–8. In about half of all cases, euthanasia had also been considered. The most important reasons for choosing terminal sedation were that the patient preferred it (14%) or had not made an explicit request for euthanasia (10%), or that the requirements for euthanasia could not be met (11%) (*ibid* at 84).

[56] Data in this para from Van der Wal *et al* 2003: 80–84.

These 2001 data are probably not very meaningful, however, because 'terminal sedation' (as it was then called) is—as the research in 2005 shows—a heterogeneous category. Continuous, deep sedation rarely (13% of all cases) occurs in isolation from another medical decision that is itself a potential cause of death. The most commonly associated MBPSL is pain relief (35% of all cases in 2001 and 63% in 2005), whereby in a small number of cases the 'subsidiary intent' is to shorten life (4% and 7% respectively). Association with abstention is also common (53% in 2001 and 33% in 2005); most of this (44% and 22% respectively) is with the explicit intention of shortening life. Continuous deep sedation was associated with euthanasia in 9% of all cases in 2001 and 3% in 2005, and with termination of life without a request in 3% and 2% respectively. In short, the association of continuous deep sedation with other medical behaviour that probably shortened the life of the patient is very strong.[57]

In a large number of cases of continuous, deep sedation (probably rather more than half) it is accompanied by abstention from artificial nutrition and hydration. But in almost half of all cases the patient dies within a day, and in almost another half within a week; in all of these cases no shortening of life was probably involved. The sedation lasted more than a week in only 6% of all cases (and for these we do not know whether or not there was ANH). Whatever the exact proportion is, it is clear that in almost all cases of continuous, deep sedation (including those in which no ANH was given), it probably did not lead to the earlier death of the patient.[58]

The researchers do not discuss the classification of these cases for statistical and legal purposes. Reading between the lines, it seems that most of it will have been classified under the associated MBPSL. In the small number of cases that no (other) MBPSL was involved we can probably assume (see the discussion of 'terminal sedation' in section 5.2.2.2) that the researchers will have classified it as pain relief with life-shortening effect, unless there was an 'explicit intention' to shorten life. How the doctor concerned regarded the matter, in the latter case, is unknown, as is the question whether he reported the patient's death as a 'natural' or a 'not natural' one. No such case has ever been prosecuted,[59] or dealt with by the Regional Review Committees.

5.2.2 'Termination of Life'

The concept 'termination of life' has been discussed extensively in chapter 4.2.3. We came there to the conclusion that the concept should be defined not, as it commonly is (in survey research that uses the Dutch death-certificate methodology), in terms of the doctor's subjective intention, but rather in terms of whether what he does is 'medically indicated'. Such a definition is legally more appropriate

---

[57] Data in this para from Van der Wal *et al* 2003: at 132.
[58] Onwuteaka-Philipsen *et al* 2007: 129, 131.
[59] The *Vencken* case, discussed in ch 3.4 is no exception since it did not involve withholding of ANH.

and empirically more reliable. As we will see, the use by empirical researchers of definitions of termination of life in which the 'intention' of the doctor is critical, is responsible for considerable confusion.[60]

We begin our treatment of the empirical data on termination of life in section 5.2.2.1 with data concerning euthanasia and physician-assisted suicide. Several distinct subjects will then be dealt with in sections 5.2.2.2 and 5.2.2.3.

5.2.2.1 Euthanasia and Physician-Assisted Suicide

The Euthanasia Experience and Willingness of Dutch Doctors

As we have seen in chapter 2.2.3, a third of Dutch doctors are general practition-ers and they are responsible for two out of five deaths in the Netherlands (44%). A bit more than half are specialists, responsible for a third of all deaths (33%). And slightly under 5% are nursing-home doctors, responsible for 22% of all deaths. General practitioners perform the lion's share (87%) of all euthanasia, specialists account for 9%, and nursing-home doctors for 4%.

Dutch doctors have considerable experience with euthanasia. As Table 5.5 shows, about 90% of all doctors (and almost all GPs) report having at least once received a general request. Three-quarters of all GPs have received a concrete request. Almost two-thirds of them have carried it out at least once. These fre-quencies are much lower for specialists and nursing-home doctors. But as Table 5.6 shows, despite these differences in experience, most Dutch doctors of all three types are in principle willing to perform euthanasia.[61]

Table 5.5. Euthanasia/PAS experience of different sorts of doctors (percentages of doctors)

	all doctors				per type of doctor, 2005*		
	Total 1990 N=405	Total 1995 N=405	Total 2001 N=410	Total 2005 N=1032	GP N=264	S N=527	NH N=212
ever had a general request	84	88	90	84	95	65	74
ever had a concrete request	76	77	77	67	78	48	63
ever carried out	54	53	57	51	64	30	25
carried out in preceding year	24	29	30	19	27	5	7

Source: Onwuteaka-Philipsen *et al* 2007: 99 (interview/questionnaire study). See Groenwoud *et al* 2000b for the clinical experience of doctors with carrying out euthanasia and assisted suicide.

* GP = general practitioner; S = specialist; NH = nursing home doctor.

[60] In ch 6.3.4 we will see that another deviation based on a doctor's subjective intention from the legal definition of 'termination of life'—excluding from 'termination of life' the situation in which lethal 'pain relief' is administered in connection with withholding or withdrawing of life-prolonging treatment—similarly has highly unfortunate consequences for the interpretation of the data collected.

[61] Given the consistently higher frequencies in the past, the data for 2005 on requests and perfor-mance are hard to interpret. It is hard, for example, to understand how it is possible that 10% fewer doctors in 2005 than in 2001 had ever received a concrete request. Such peculiarities support the judg-ment of the researchers that something went wrong with the questionnaire that in 2005 for the first time was used instead of interviews. See n 15.

Table 5.6. Willingness of Dutch doctors to perform euthanasia/PAS (percentages of doctors)

	all doctors				per type of doctor, 2005*		
	1990 (N=405)	1995 (N=405)	2001 (N=410)	2005 (N=1,032)	GP (N=274)	S (N=527)	NH (N=212)
ever performed	54	53	57	51	64	30	25
never performed; willing	34	35	32	33	27	42	49
unwilling; would refer	8	9	10	14	7	24	24
unwilling; would not refer	4	3	1	1	1	3	2

* GP = general practitioner; S = specialist; NH = nursing home doctor.
Source: Onweatuka-Philipsen *et al* 2007: 99 (interview/questionnaire studies).

Requests for and Communication about Euthanasia/PAS

A distinction can be made between on the one hand general—often conditional—requests, in which the patient in effect seeks reassurance that if and when the time comes, the doctor will be willing, and on the other hand concrete, unconditional requests. Fewer than a third of all general requests ever reach the stage of a concrete request (see Table 5.7).

Table 5.7. Requests for euthanasia and PAS

	1990	*1995*	*2001*	*2005*
requests in general terms	25,100	34,500	34,700	28,600
concrete requests	8,900	9,700	9,700	8,400
requests carried out (estimates from Table 5.1)	2,700	3,600	3,800	2,425
(% of concrete requests)	(30%)	(37%)	(39%)	(29%)

Source: Onweatuka-Philipsen et al 2007: 100, 108 (interview/questionnaire studies). Extrapolation from the NIVEL panel study (see n 64), shows an increase in the number of concrete requests to GPs from 1,600 in 1979 to 4,000 in 1985, later stabilising at about 5,000 per year (Marquet *et al* 2003: 201); since 2000, however, there seems to be some decline (NIVEL 2007: 134).

It is interesting to note, that not only did the frequency of euthanasia decline in 2005 (at least, according to the death certificate study—see section 5.1.2.3), the number of general and concrete requests seems also to have declined somewhat and the frequency with which requests are honoured dropped dramatically. It is possible to interpret these changes as an artefact of research methodology,[62] or as reflecting both a decline in patient interest and the results of efforts of doctors to 'steer' their dying patients in the direction of a new option: palliative sedation rather than euthanasia. It should also be noted that this way of calculating the rate at which requests are honoured suffers from some serious methodological flaws

---

[62] See n 15 for the researchers' reservations concerning the 2005 questionnaire results.

that make it necessary to take the results with a considerable grain of salt: requests by *patients* are measured by interviewing *doctors*, and cases of euthanasia are produced by the *researchers* (see section 5.4.3 on the problems this last procedure entails). If doctors perceive fewer concrete requests than patients think they make,[63] the rate of honouring requests will be inflated (at least from the patients' point of view). If doctors regard fewer deaths as being due to euthanasia than the researchers do, the rate will also be too high (from the doctors' point of view). In short, these rates of honouring requests should be read as maximal rates.

In the past, concrete requests were frequently oral, but this is a thing of the past (there was a written request in 43% of the doctors' most recent cases in 1990, 70% in 1995, and 93% in 2001). In 2006–07 the request was in writing in virtually all of the cases reported to the Review Committees.[64]

Since 1990 the doctor has usually discussed the patient's request with his family and intimate friends; in 2001 such discussion took place in 96% of all cases, but this declined according to the national study of 2005 to 75%.[65] However, from recent reports of the Review Committees it seems that in 99% of all reported cases there is contact between the doctor and the patient's family, which is generally portrayed as supportive of the request.[66] Discussion with nursing staff seems to be less frequent.[67]

The most important reasons for the patient's concrete request, in cases in which it is honoured, as reported by the doctor for the year 2001, are given on Table 5.8.

Data for 2005 are not readily comparable because they derive from the death-certificate study and relate to the doctor's reasons for carrying out euthanasia in a particular case. More than one answer could be given, and on the average four were mentioned. More than 80% of the doctors mentioned the absence of any

[63] It is well known that a patient sometimes thinks he has made a concrete request but his doctor thinks he was only talking about a possible future situation, or the doctor thinks the patient has withdrawn a request but the patient thinks the doctor has rejected it. See eg Pasman & Onwuteaka-Philipsen forthcoming.

[64] Van der Wal *et al* 2003: 51 (euthanasia, not PAS; in 2001 only GPs and specialists). The question was apparently not asked in the 2005 research. From the judgments for 2006 and 2007 published on the internet site of the Committees (see ch 4, n 393) it appeared as of 26 November 2007, that in 99% the request was in writing.

From a continuous study of a number of aspects of GP practice, based on a representative panel of 56 GPs in 44 practices who report on a weekly basis, it appears that in 88% of the reported euthanasia requests in 2006 (32 requests) the request was accompanied by a written 'euthanasia directive'; in 1984 this had been 15% (NIVEL 2007: 133, 140; *cf* Marquet *et al* 2003: 201).

[65] Van der Wal *et al* 2003: 52; Onwuteaka-Philipsen *et al* 2007: 105.

[66] From the judgments of 2006 and 2007 (see ch 4, n 393) it appears as of 26 November 2007, that in at least 518 of 525 cases the doctor had discussed the request with the patient's family.

A study of the effect of euthanasia on the bereaved family and friends of cancer patients shows that they had less traumatic grief symptoms, less current feelings of grief and less post-traumatic stress reactions than the family and friends of cancer patients who die a 'natural' death. The researchers suggest three possible explanations: euthanasia affords an opportunity to say good bye while the patient is still fully aware; family and friends are more prepared for the time and nature of the patient's death; a patient's request for euthanasia makes it easier for family and friends to talk to him about his impending death (compare Norwood on 'euthanasia talk' in section 5.3 below). Swarte *et al* 2003.

[67] From the judgments of 2006 and 2007 (see ch 4, n 393) it appears as of 26 November 2007, that in at least 148 of 525 cases the doctor had discussed the request with one or more nurses.

Table 5.8. Reasons for patient's request (percent of patients receiving euthanasia), 2001

meaningless suffering	65
deterioration/loss of dignity	44
general weakness/exhaustion	43
avoiding worse or further suffering	36
avoiding deterioration	35
dependence on others	33
pain	29
fear of/avoiding suffocation	23
invalidity/immobility	17
not wanting to be a burden on the family	17
avoiding pain	15
nausea	12
tired of life	5

Source: Van der Wal *et al* 2003: 51 (interviews with family doctors and specialists about most recent case; data concern only euthanasia; more than one answer possible). Data from earlier years give the same general picture. Data for GPs in the period April 2000–December 2002 in Jansen-van der Weide *et al* 2005: 1700, give a generally similar picture.

prospect of improvement, and the patient's wishes; loss of dignity, symptoms (other than pain), pain and expected suffering were all mentioned in roughly half the cases. The wishes of the patient's family were mentioned in roughly a tenth of the cases.[68]

Requests Not Carried Out

About a third of concrete requests are carried out (see Table 5.8). Data on why patients' requests are not carried out is available in the 2001 study.[69] The results are shown on Table 5.9. In short, in 2001 when a concrete request was not carried out, this was (according to doctors) most often—especially among GPs, who account for most euthanasia and PAS—because the patient died of his underlying condition first, and less often because the doctor refused. When the doctor

---

[68] Onwuteaka-Philipsen *et al* 2007: 104. The NIVEL panel study of GP practices (see n 64) reports a trend in the reasons for requests to GPs over the period 1977–2001, with pain becoming 'significantly less important', whereas deterioration became more important' (Marquet *et al* 2003: 201).

[69] In 1995, the 'doctor's judgment' accounted for almost half of all requests that were not carried out and most of the remainder was because the patient died 'before it was necessary to carry out the request'. The most frequently given reasons for the doctor's adverse judgment were that the patient's suffering was not unbearable, that there were still treatment possibilities, or that the request was not voluntary and well considered. Van der Wal & Van der Maas 1996: 61–2.

Table 5.9. **Reasons for not carrying out a request for euthanasia/PAS (2001, percentages of doctors' most recent cases in which a request was not carried out)**

	GP	S	NH	Total
doctor's judgment:	13	35	37	18
suffering was not unbearable	7	14	10	9
treatment alternatives still existed	1	12	17	4
personal objections in this case	4	6	7	5
request was not well considered	1	5	17	3
suffering was not hopeless	1	11	7	4
patient died:	78	44	57	70
before decision-making was complete	29	15	20	26
before decision was carried out	24	20	10	22
before request was operative/				
patient did not (yet) want it	25	9	27	22
carried out by another doctor	3	10	—	4
other reasons	14	16	17	14

Source: Van der Wal *et al* 2003: 53 (interviews). Apparently more than one answer could be given.

refused, this was most often because he did not consider the patient's suffering unbearable.[70]

In 2005, comparable but less detailed data were collected in the death-certificate study. The reasons given by the doctor for not carrying out the patient's request were as follows (more than one answer could be given): 10% patient withdrew request, 18% request not well considered, 6% request not voluntary, 16% suffering not unbearable, 8% suffering not hopeless, 5% principled objections, 2% institutional policy, 39% patient died before euthanasia could be carried out, and 29% other. The

---

[70] These results are confirmed in a more detailed study of requests made to GPs in a 12-month period between 2000 and 2002. It appears that 44% of all concrete requests were carried out, 13% were granted but the patient died before the request was carried out, in 13% the patient died before the decision-making was complete, in 12% the GP refused, in 13% the patient withdrew the request, and in 3% the patient was still alive and decision-making ongoing (Jansen-Van der Weide *et al* 2005). Relative to granted requests, in the case of refused requests there were far more often palliative alternatives (88% vs 32%), the request was sometimes not completely explicit (12% vs 0%), the patient's competence was diminished (39% vs 0%), the suffering was less often to a (very) high degree unbearable (30% vs 93%) and less often completely hopeless (32% vs 84%). Another publication of the same study (Jansen-van der Weide 2005: ch 3) shows that at the time of the concrete request to a GP, palliative options were still available in 11% of granted requests, against 61% in cases in which euthanasia or PAS were refused. The most commonly mentioned palliative options in refused and granted cases, respectively, were medication (71% vs 47%), artificial nutrition and hydration (7% vs 29%), admission to hospital (15% vs 14%), and radiotherapy (12% vs 10%).

It has been estimated on the basis of the findings of the 2001 national study that about 400 elderly persons per year request euthanasia/PAS although they have no serious physical symptoms ('tired of living'). About a third of nursing-home doctors and GPs report having at least once received such a request. These requests are almost never granted (none in the two years preceding the research). See Rurup *et al* 2005b.

researchers observe that problems of timing seem to play a lesser role in 2005 than in 2001, while the requirements of due care seem to play a larger one.[71]

Children

As Table 5.10 shows, very few children between 1 and 16 die each year. In the recent past (2001) MBPSL were somewhat less common as a cause of death of children than of adults (see Table 5.1), largely because the frequency of abstention in the case of children was then quite a bit lower than for adults. In 2005, the differences have largely disappeared (except that euthanasia is less common for children). Euthanasia does occur, but in the order of three times a year (as we saw in chapter 4.2.3.3(G), the Regional Review Committees received the first report of such a case in 2005[72]).

Table 5.10. MBPSL in the case of children 1–16 years, the Netherlands, 2001 and 2005 (percentages of all deaths of children)

	2001*	2005
total deaths of children 1–16	196	564
sample	129	192
no end of life medical decision	65	59
sudden, unexpected death	42	
no MBPSL	23	
end of life medical decision	36	41
euthanasia	0.7	0.6
withdrawing/withholding treatment	12	16
accepting risk	2.8	
express intention	8.8	
pain relief with life-shortening effect	21	23
accepting risk	20	
subsidiary intention	1.1	
termination of life without a request	2.0	1

* August–November 2001
Source: Van der Wal *et al* 2003: 124; Onwuteaka-Philipsen *et al* 2007: 105, 121 (less detail given than in the 2001 research). Reliability of some frequency estimates low due to small numbers.

[71] Onwuteaka-Philipsen *et al* 2007: 108–9.
[72] RRC 2005: 9, 15 (case 3).

The death certificate study of 2005 included 172 paediatricians. Twelve percent had at least once had a general request for euthanasia from a child and 9% a concrete request. Three percent had carried out euthanasia; 62% had never done so but would in principle be willing; 25% would be unwilling but would refer a child to another doctor; 8% would not be willing to refer. Seventy-one percent agreed with the statement that euthanasia is acceptable in the case of a 'minor patient who is capable of a reasonable assessment of his interests' (about half of the GPs and specialists in the study agreed with the statement).[73] A quarter of the paediatricians had at least once terminated a child's life without a request (but most of these cases involved children younger than 1 year) and an additional 15% would in principle be willing to do so; 60% would not.[74]

Psychiatric Patients

In the mid-1990s the question whether a psychiatrist can give assistance with suicide to a psychiatric patient attracted a great deal of attention and a small polemic took place among psychiatrists. The Supreme Court held in the *Chabot* case that the fact that the patient's suffering is caused by a non-somatic disorder is not in principle relevant and that the existence of a psychiatric disorder does not automatically entail that a request cannot be voluntary. And both the Medical Association and the Dutch Association for Psychiatry issued reports taking the position that assistance with suicide should in principle be possible and formulating specific rules of due care applicable in such cases.[75]

The national study of 1995 devoted special attention to the subject and as Table 5.11 shows, the whole affair was, quantitatively speaking, rather a tempest in a teapot, since assistance with suicide by psychiatrists is extremely rare. Furthermore, in most cases the patient is also suffering from a serious, usually fatal, somatic disorder.[76]

Although only a very small number of Dutch psychiatrists have ever given assistance with suicide (6% of those who have ever received a request to do so), most of them consider it in principle acceptable and almost half would be prepared to do so (see Table 5.12).

Psychiatric disorders play a more considerable role in euthanasia practice than the above data on psychiatric patients might suggest. In the 1990 study doctors

---

[73] Onwuteaka-Philipsen *et al* 2007: 105.

[74] *Ibid* at 121. An earlier (2002) interview study (Vrakking *et al* 2005) gave similar results. Responding to a hypothetical question about a 15 year old child with metastasised cancer and pain that cannot be controlled with morphine and who requests euthanasia, 60% of the paediatricians interviewed (and only slightly fewer of the GPs and specialists) would be willing to perform it if the parents agreed (about half as many if the parents did not agree). Only 15% of the doctors considered euthanasia never acceptable for a child below 12. If the child were unconscious, a quarter would be willing to terminate life at the request of the parents. With or without a request from the child, over 80% were willing to increase the level of morphine 'taking into account' that this might hasten death.

[75] All of this is covered in some detail in ch 4.2.3.4.

[76] See Van der Wal & Van der Maas 1996: 210 (this was the case in two-thirds of the most recent cases in which the interviewed psychiatrists had given assistance with suicide); see also Groenewoud *et al* 1997.

Table 5.11. Estimated frequency of requests for physician-assisted suicide in the case of psychiatric patients, and of what happens to the patient, 1995

number of requests	*320*
request seriously considered	21%
PAS given by requested psychiatrist	(2–5 cases/year) 2%
PAS given by another doctor	3%
suicide without assistance by a doctor	16%
natural death	5%
still alive at time of interview	63%
unknown	11%

Source: Van der Wal & Van der Maas 1996: 204–8 (interviews with sample of psychiatrists); see also Groenwoud *et al* 1997.

Table 5.12. Willingness of Dutch psychiatrists to give assistance with suicide, 1995 (percentages)

ever performed	2
never performed, in principle willing	44
acceptable, but not personally willing	19
unacceptable	31
no opinion	5

Source: Van der Wal & Van der Maas 1996: 205; see also Groenwoud *et al* 1997.

reported psychiatric disorders as the most important illness of the patient in about 1% of all cases in which euthanasia/PAS was carried out (and in 14% of the cases in which it was refused).[77] In the 2001 study, a psychiatric disorder was the reason for a patient's request in 3% of all concrete requests (family doctors 4%; specialists 1%; nursing-home doctors 11%); but it was never the reason for the patient's request in cases in which euthanasia was actually carried out.[78] In both 2001 and 2005 doctors attributed the patient's suffering to a psychiatric disorder in about 1% of all concrete requests for euthanasia (for nursing-home doctors in 2005, this was 7%).[79]

As of 1995 psychiatrists were consulted about 300 times a year by non-psychiatrists in connection with requests for euthanasia; such consultation took place in about 3% of all cases of euthanasia. Apparently most or all of these cases involved a somatic disorder.[80]

---

[77] Van der Wal & Van der Maas 1996: 202.

[78] Van der Wal *et al* 2003: 47 (interview study).

[79] Onwuteaka-Philipsen *et al* 2007: 100.

[80] NVP 2004: 39. From the 1995 national study, it appears that almost a third of the interviewed psychiatrists had been approached at least once for consultation by a doctor who was not a psychiatrist, in connection with euthanasia (Van der Wal & Van der Maas 1996: 213); see also Groenewoud *et al* 1997.

Patients Suffering from Dementia

A tempest similar to that of the mid-1990s with respect to psychiatric patients took place later with respect to euthanasia for demented patients—but this one may well prove in the long run not to have been in a teapot. In the 2002 law, as we have seen in chapter 4.2.3.3(B), provision was made for euthanasia pursuant to the prior written request of a person who subsequently has become incapable of making a valid request. The subject was given special attention in the national studies of 2001 and 2005.

As Table 5.13 shows, experience with written advance requests of patients suffering from dementia is not rare among Dutch doctors (the data for 2001 are fuller, those for 2005 are given in italics). Between 2001 and 2005, euthanasia in such a cases had become in principle legal. In 2005 the percentage of doctors who had ever had a demented patient with a written request had increased slightly, but judging from interviews with doctors the frequency of euthanasia in such a case had declined to zero.

Table 5.13. Experience of Dutch doctors with written euthanasia requests of patients suffering from dementia, 2001 and 2005 (percentages of doctors)

	GP	Specialist	NH doctor	Total
ever had such a patient (2005)	*32*	*19*	*80*	*32*
ever had such a patient (2001)	28	23	66	29
• within last 2 years	10	11	50	13
ever discussed honouring such a request (2001)	6	8	48	9
ever carried out euthanasia in such a case (2005)	*0*	*0*	*0*	*0*
ever carried out euthanasia in such a case (2001)	3	1	4	3
• never did so, but thinkable	50	38	22	44
• never did so, unthinkable	47	61	74	54

Source: Van der Wal *et al* 2003: 111–13 (2001 data); Onwuteaka-Philipsen *et al* 2007: 100–01 (2005 data).

From the death-certificate study of 2001 it appears that Dutch doctors treated an estimated 2,200 demented patients who had a prior written euthanasia request, and in 1,600 of these cases there was discussion about whether to honour the request (almost always this was with family, close friends or a representative of the patient). Reliably estimating the number of cases in which the written request for euthanasia of a demented patient was carried out proved to be impossible because of the small numbers involved.[81] Since the Law of 2002 came into effect, the number of cases of euthanasia reported to the Regional Review Committees involving patients with dementia has apparently been very low, but steadily rising: 0 in 2003, 1 in 2004, 3 in 2005 and 6 in 2006.[82]

[81] Van der Wal *et al* 2003: 112–13.
[82] See *Trouw* (22 March 2007), *de Verdieping* p 2. A search of the cases disposed of by the committees in 2006 and 2007 and posted as of 28 November 2007 on the committees' website (see ch 4, n 393) produced only 3 in which the words 'dementia' or 'Alzheimer' appear (it should be emphasised that not nearly all cases have been posted). In the Annual Reports of the committees through 2006, there

In 2001, doctors were about evenly split as to whether they might consider hon-ouring such a request (least willing were nursing-home doctors, who in practice experience the situation most frequently). Two-thirds of all doctors did not con-sider dementia in itself a valid reason for euthanasia, and among nursing-home doctors this was 87%. Most of them considered it impossible to determine the time at which euthanasia in such a case should be carried out.[83] In the 2005 research, about 40% of all doctors agreed with the statement that euthanasia in the case of a patient who has become incompetent is unacceptable, 30% disagreed and 30% were neutral. Over half of all nursing-home doctors agreed, over half of all specialists disagreed, and GPs were roughly equally split.[84] Once again, it seems that nursing-home doctors are much more conservative than doctors who have less experience with demented patients and their advance written requests for euthanasia.

In 2001 nursing-home doctors were asked some questions about their most recent case of a demented patient with a written euthanasia request. Of a total of 44 cases, in two-thirds the doctor was of the opinion that the patient had been in the situation described in the written request and almost all doctors discussed whether to honour the request with the patient's family or close friends. In most cases (almost three-quarters) the family or close friends were not in favour of this, but did favour limiting treatment. The patient in fact almost always died as a result of withholding/withdrawing treatment (39 of 44 cases). The treatments most often not given were artificial nutrition and hydration, antibiotics, or admission to hos-pital and/or an operation. Only 3 of the 44 patients died from euthanasia.[85]

5.2.2.2 Special Topics

Terminal Sedation

In chapter 4.2.2.4 we discussed why, from the point of view of the control system, the difference between 'terminal sedation' (in which continuous, deep sedation is accompanied by withholding or withdrawing artificial nutrition and hydration for more than 2 weeks) and 'palliative sedation' (in which ANH is given, or withheld for less than 2 weeks) is important. 'Terminal sedation' is a form of 'termination of life', whereas 'palliative sedation' is 'normal medical practice'. Unfortunately, as we have seen in section 5.2.1.2, the data from the 2001 and 2005 studies are con-fusing on precisely this point. In neither study are terminal and palliative sedation adequately distinguished, the two studies approach the whole subject in rather dif-ferent ways, and there are in both studies large differences between the results from the interview and the death-certificate studies. In short, in order to estimate

---

are an additional 3 cases in which dementia played a role, and in 2003 there was a case in which the prosecutors decided not to prosecute (see ch 4, nn 146, 161, 296).

[83] Van der Wal *et al* 2003: 115.

[84] Onwuteaka-Philipsen *et al* 2007: 101. See Rurup *et al* 2005a for a similar finding from a 2000 study.

[85] Van der Wal *et al* 2003: 115.

the frequency of terminal sedation in the narrow sense, it will be necessary to cobble an argument together using data from both.

We can make the following rough estimate. As we have seen in section 5.2.1.2, continuous, deep sedation precedes roughly 10% of all deaths; the sedation lasts more than a week in only 6% of these deaths.[86] Six-tenths of a percent of all deaths looks to be the upper limit for 'terminal sedation'. But not all of these deaths involved withholding of ANH. Even if we ignore the close association of continuous, deep sedation with other MBPSL (see section 5.2.1.2), it seems that terminal sedation in the strict sense must account for rather less than 1% of all deaths.

Terminal sedation can be analytically divided into a decision for deep, continuous sedation and a decision to withhold ANH—each with its own distinct and unproblematic justification (see chapter 4.2.2.4), but in practice the decision to administer deep sedation and the decision to withhold ANH are usually (85% of the time) taken together.[87]

It is interesting to note that some commonly supposed reasons why death following continuous, deep sedation might be preferred to euthanasia are apparently of minor importance. The policy of the institution where the patient dies is essentially irrelevant: in only 2% of the deaths in such cases where the doctor is a specialist, and in none in the case of GPs or nursing-home doctors, was there any such influence. Religious considerations, and the wishes of the family or partner, are also rarely important (3% and 2% respectively). Apart from factors that eliminate euthanasia as an option (in particular, the absence of a request from the patient), the most important reason for the choice for sedation, when the choice is discussed at all, is that this is what the patient wants.[88]

From the national study it is not possible to know whether the doctors involved regard their patients' death as 'natural' or not, nor whether, in the latter case, they report it. The number of cases of terminal sedation (in the narrow sense) that are reported and reach the Regional Review Committees seems to be miniscule.[89] We do know, however, how cases of death following deep, continuous sedation were classified by the national researchers in 2001: about half (1.9% of all deaths) were classified as pain relief with life-shortening effect, two-fifths (1.5% of all deaths) as withholding treatment, and one-sixth (0.6% of all deaths) as termination of life (usually at the request of the patient, hence euthanasia).[90]

---

[86] From the 2005 death-certificate study it appears that the patient lived for more than 2 weeks in only 2% of all continuous, deep sedation (with or without ANH) (Onwuteaka-Philipsen *et al* 2007: 131).

[87] Van der Wal *et al* 2003: 78.

[88] *Ibid* at 84 (palliative and terminal sedation are not distinguished here).

[89] See RRC 2005: 8 (committees find a case of terminal sedation—deep sedation plus withholding of ANH—'normal medical behaviour' and therefore outside their jurisdiction); see also RRC 2002: 17 (case 5) for a similar holding in a case in which the patient died while under palliative sedation preparatory to a possible euthanasia.

[90] See Van der Wal *et al* 2003: 86. Classification as termination of life only occurred if a drug was administered with the explicit intention of ending life. According to the researchers, such a classification corresponds to the applicable legislation, which as we have seen in ch 4.2.3 is not the case. In the cases classified as 'termination of life' ANH was presumably withheld, but it does not appear for how long this was (the researchers state, incorrectly, that withholding ANH 'always causes death').

Euthanasia vs Assistance with Suicide[91]

Dutch law treats euthanasia and assistance with suicide by a doctor essentially as equivalents (see chapter 4.2.3.3(H)). But despite the indifference of the law, and everything that can otherwise be said in favour of assisted suicide as the more eligible choice, Dutch doctors perform euthanasia far more often than assisted suicide.

As we have seen on Table 5.1, from the 1990 study to the 2005 study, the part that PAS plays in the total of euthanasia and PAS declined from about 1 in 10 to about 1 in 20.[92] A similar picture emerges from the Annual Reports of the Regional Review Committees covering cases that the responsible doctor reported. For 1998 through 2006 these reports show that the ratio of PAS to euthanasia is roughly 1 in 10.[93]

To be more precise in interpreting these data we would have to limit ourselves to cases in which the patient could have performed the final act himself, for it is only in these cases that there is a real choice. As far as we are aware, such data do not exist. If we make the rather crude assumption that patients with less than a week to live are generally not able to perform the final act, whereas when remaining life is longer than that they generally are, then in the Netherlands in 2005 there were about 1,325 cases of termination of life on request in which assisted suicide was possibly an alternative. There were in fact about 135 cases of assisted suicide: roughly a tenth of the cases where it may have been possible.[94]

We do not know why it is that Dutch doctors so overwhelmingly prefer euthanasia to PAS, the question never having been seriously addressed in research. There are, however, some suggestive hints in the Dutch literature. One possibility is that it is not doctors but their patients who choose euthanasia.[95] However, a doctor who had a preference for PAS could offer only PAS as an option to a

---

[91] This section is largely based on Griffiths 2007a.

[92] A study of ALS patients gives a similar picture (Veldink *et al* 2002). One study suggests that among AIDS patients the frequency of assistance with suicide may be rather greater: about half that of euthanasia (Bindels & Krol 1996).

[93] See Table 5.3. Comparison of the data from the national studies (all cases) with those of the Review Committees (reported cases) shows that the ratio of assisted suicide to euthanasia is apparently not correlated with the frequency with which doctors report.

There may be something wrong with the classification of data in the national studies as far as the distinction between euthanasia and physician-assisted suicide is concerned. Of 227 answers (1998–2000) to a questionnaire distributed to doctors by the Royal Dutch Association of Pharmacists the 'oral method' was reported by the doctor to have been used in 60 (about a quarter) (see Horikx & Admiraal 2000); many or all of these cases may fit the precise definition of assisted suicide used in the death-certificate studies on which table 5.1 is based (furnishing a patient with a drug with the explicit intention of hastening death, which is taken by the patient himself—see <http://www.statline.cbs.nl/StatWeb>accessed 3 July 2007). Cases voluntarily reported to the KNMP are of course not necessarily representative of all cases of euthanasia/PAS, but the difference from the survey data is striking.

[94] Calculations based on Tables 5.1 and 5.2: 136,402 (total deaths) × 1.8% (termination of life) × 54% (estimated shortening of life); 136,402 (total deaths) × 0.01% (PAS).

[95] Curiously, while a patient's choice for euthanasia is never mentioned, there are several cases in the Annual Reports of the Regional Review Committees in which it is said that the patient preferred assisted suicide. See eg RRC 2001: 22 (case 11).

patient, or he could try to convince the patient that it is the better choice, or he could simply refuse to perform euthanasia. In short, a substantial voice in the ultimate choice lies with the doctor.

It has been suggested that at the beginning of the process of legal change in the Netherlands many doctors associated suicide with psychiatric disorder, and proponents of legal euthanasia, such as the Voluntary Euthanasia Association (NVVE), apparently sought in the early years to avoid any such association. Since in the view of the doctors concerned their patients' requests for termination of life had nothing to do with any such disorder, they preferred the form of termination of life that was free from the association. This may be a plausible explanation for the early years but it does not explain why the share of PAS is still so low and actually declining.

In the early years of euthanasia practice Dutch doctors were supported in their preference for euthanasia by influential organisations such as the Medical Association and it was not until 1984 that the Medical Association recognised PAS as a legitimate alternative for euthanasia.[96] But if the position of such organisations was an important influence on doctors, one would suppose that the fact they long since changed their position would be reflected in a change in medical practice. In fact precisely the reverse is true.

Another possible explanation for the preference of Dutch doctors for euthanasia is the fact that from the beginning legalisation in the Netherlands was seen as a matter of the empowerment of doctors and not, as in the United States for example, in terms of the rights of patients. Perhaps doctors find it natural, once they have taken a decision that is conceived of as uniquely theirs, that they should carry it out themselves.

There may also be reasons of a more practical nature for a doctor to prefer euthanasia. Euthanasia can be performed with drugs that act very quickly, so that the dying process is over within a few minutes and the duty of the doctor to be present the whole time is less burdensome than in the case of PAS. The dying process is also in other respects more within the doctor's control. On the other hand, one must not forget that in the formative years of Dutch euthanasia practice, the drug of choice for euthanasia was morphine, whose working is slow and notoriously unpredictable. Any difference between euthanasia and PAS in this respect cannot have been great. Such practical considerations therefore offer no explanation for the emergence of Dutch doctors' preference for euthanasia, at most for its resistance to change.

The risk of failure, that outside the Netherlands is often associated with PAS, might also explain doctors' preference for euthanasia. But when proper drugs are used, these risks are in fact negligible.[97] Furthermore, they are principally relevant in the case of PAS outside the presence of the doctor, something that in the

---

[96] See Weyers 2004: 136–7; GB&W 1998: 57–8.
[97] See Horikx & Admiraal 2000; Oregon Health Division 1999–2006.

Netherlands is permitted, if at all, only in exceptional circumstances.[98] These supposed risks, too, seem not to explain doctors' preference for euthanasia.

In short, the strong preference of Dutch doctors for euthanasia rather than physician-assisted suicide remains something of a mystery. It is, however, perhaps worth mentioning that—considering its rarity in practice—physician-assisted suicide is strongly overrepresented in cases found 'not careful' by the Review Committees: of 15 cases found 'not careful' between 2003 and 2005, 4 concerned assisted suicide.[99] Either PAS is more often problematic than euthanasia, or it is more critically scrutinised.

Termination of Life Without the Patient's Explicit Request

When the results of the first national study were published in 1991, the Dutch public debate on euthanasia was rudely awakened to the fact that a small but significant amount of termination of life was taking place without the request of the patient. From Table 5.1 we have already seen that, according to the operationalisation used in the death-certificate studies (drug, explicit intention, no request) a little less than 1% of all deaths occur in this way. The number of deaths involved was a bit over 1,000 in 1990 and a bit under 1,000 in 1995 and 2001; in 2005 it dropped by almost a half to just under 550.[100] From comparative data, especially from the EURELD study (2001), it appears that this sort of MBPSL occurs in all Western European countries that have been studied (see chapter 17.2, Table 17.2). The Dutch rate was, until 2005, toward the higher end of the range, but at 0.4% now appears to occupy a middle position together with the UK and Switzerland.

Table 5.14 gives some information on the experience of Dutch doctors with termination of life without a request from the patient. It seems that, over the years since 1990, the reservations of Dutch doctors have grown. The number of doctors who say they have ever done so has declined from more than 1 in 4 to less than 1 in 10 (a result that is perhaps not logically impossible but not easy to interpret). A similar decline has taken place in the number who say they have never done so but might be willing. And almost 9 out of 10 now say they would not do so under any circumstances. As we have seen on table 5.1, this considerably decreased willingness corresponds with a decline in the actual frequency of termination of life without a request.

The initial reaction of the Dutch Government when the data were published in 1991 was to regard termination of life without the patient's request as highly troublesome.[101] After the similar finding of the 1995 research the Government reiterated its position that termination of life without a request 'in principle

---

[98] See ch 4.2.3.3(F).

[99] See Onwuteaka-Philipsen *et al* 2007: 198.

[100] Onwuteaka-Philipsen *et al* 2007: 111–12. In 1990, specialists were responsible for more than 70% of these deaths, GPs for less than 30%, and nursing-home doctors for less than 1% (Muller 1996: 97).

[101] See ch 4.2.2.5 (rejection of the Remmelink Committee's suggestion that much of this sort of MBPSL was unproblematic 'help in dying').

Table 5.14. Doctors' experience with termination of life without the patient's explicit request (percentages of doctors interviewed)

	1990	*1995*	*2001*	*2005*
ever performed	27	23	13	6
performed in preceding year	—	8	4	2
never performed/conceivable	32	32	16	7
would never perform	41	45	71	86

Source: Onwuteaka-Philipsen *et al* 2007: 112 (interview/questionnaire studies).

should not take place'[102] and in the ensuing years there have been a number of prosecutions.[103] However, the category is quite heterogeneous, and not all of its component parts are necessarily legally problematic. Included in the category are:[104]

- an estimated 9% (approximately 90 per year) of all deaths of babies under 1 year old (almost always associated with withdrawing treatment)—a category discussed in legal and empirical detail in chapter 6;
- an unknown number of cases in which treatment is withdrawn or withheld and a lethal drug administered to make the final throes of dying pass quickly and in a humane way;[105]
- a presumably very small number of long-term coma/PVS patients;[106]
- a relatively large number of (cancer) patients who are very close to death and no longer able to make their will known, and who appear to be suffering severely.[107]

In many cases, there is some discussion with the patient (who, however, is usually not fully competent—85% in 2005). The frequency of such discussion declined from 46% in 1990 to 26% in 2001 but went back up to 35% in 2005. In 2005, the reasons for not discussing the matter with the patient were largely attributable to incompetence, but other reasons such as the doctor's judgment that this is the best course of action, also played a role.[108] In the past, incidental cases had been found

---

[102] See *Second Chamber of Parliament 1996–1997*, 23 877, no 13: 4.

[103] See chs 3.4, 4.2.2.5, 4.2.2.4 (*Van Oijen* and *Vencken* cases). *Cf* also the *Prins* and *Kadijk* cases discussed in ch 6.2.2.3.

[104] The information given here is mostly a decade or more old; the report of the 2001 research assures us that the situation of 6 years earlier had not significantly changed (Van der Wal *et al* 2003: 58–61).

[105] This situation apparently accounts for only a very small number of cases of termination of life without an explicit request, although the data are not unambiguous on this point. As an important reason for active termination of life, 'treatment was stopped but the patient did not die' was given by the doctor in 2% of all cases of termination of life without an explicit request (see Van der Wal & Van der Maas 1996: 72).

[106] Nothing seems to be known about this category, except that it may in some circumstances be legally acceptable (see ch 5, appendix 2).

[107] See Van der Maas *et al* 1992: 74.

[108] See Van der Wal *et al* 2001: 60; Onwuteaka-Philipsen *et al* 2007: 114. N is small in all years, and in 2005 only 24 cases, which is the reason for presenting the results in global terms here.

in which there had been no discussion with a competent patient, but in 2001 no such cases were found (no data for 2005). There is usually but by no means always discussion with the patient's family and another doctor, and about half the time with nurses.[109]

The shortening of life involved is estimated by the doctors concerned at less than a week in about 80% of the cases, and the drug used is usually morphine. The researchers consider that a large number of these cases resemble death due to administration of pain relief. 'As in previous years . . . what is involved is an ultimate form of relief of pain or symptoms'.[110]

These cases are essentially never reported as 'non-natural' deaths. In the 1995 study the most commonly cited reason for this (mentioned as relevant in their most recent case by 44% of the doctors involved) is that the doctor considers the death a 'natural' one. Saving himself or the relatives the burden of a criminal investigation was mentioned as relevant in roughly a third of such cases, failure to meet all of the 'requirements of careful practice' in 15%, and fear of prosecution in only 9%.[111]

5.2.2.3 'Auto-Euthanasia'

In 2007 Chabot published the results of a quantitative study of the frequency of humane ways (without violence or physical injury) in which people take control over their dying process, in communication with others but without the direct participation of a doctor, a phenomenon he calls 'auto-euthanasia'. In his study, 'auto-euthanasia' is limited to two methods: the use of sleeping pills, or stopping eating and drinking. His data derive from cases described by *rapporteurs*: persons identified in a very large and carefully constructed sample of the Dutch population as having direct knowledge of a relevant case. His key estimate is that in the period 1999–2003, 2.1% of all deaths per year were due to stopping eating and drinking (2,800 cases), and 1.1% (1,600 cases) to the use of sleeping pills, in both cases while in communication with others. The total of 'auto-euthanasia' is 3.2% of all deaths (4,400), which is more than the 2.8% total of euthanasia and physician-assisted suicide in the same period (see Table 5.1).[112]

If we add euthanasia/PAS and 'auto-euthanasia' together, the total is about 6% of all deaths. Adding to this terminal sedation at the request of the patient (some part of the 1% of all deaths due to terminal sedation estimated in section 5.2.2.2), and withdrawing/withholding treatment at the request of the patient (probably about 4% of all deaths[113]), it seems that in roughly 10% of all deaths in the Netherlands the person concerned exercises some degree of control over the timing and manner of his death, without this taking the socially-isolated and often violent form of suicide.

---

[109] Van der Wal *et al* 2001: 59.
[110] *Ibid* at 61.
[111] Van der Wal & Van der Maas 1996: 119.
[112] Chabot 2007: 106.
[113] See section 5.2.1.1.

Chabot's research also produces for the first time some reliable data on the characteristics of cases of 'auto-euthanasia'.[114] It is more frequent among women than among men (3 out of 5 cases). Eighty percent of those who stop eating and drinking are over 60, but only two-fifths of those who use sleeping pills. Deaths due to stopping eating and drinking occur about equally frequently at home or in an institutional setting but deaths due to sleeping pills occur almost always at home. According to the *rapporteurs*, the person concerned was suffering from a fatal illness in about 40% of the cases, from a serious somatic or psychiatric illness in about 30% and from some disability but no serious illness in just under 30%. In a third of all cases the person's life expectancy was more than a month, and in most of these it was more than a half year. According to the *rapporteurs*, the person's suffering was highly unbearable and there were no prospects for improvement in almost all cases. In the few cases in which there was no unbearable suffering, the person concerned was very old, considered his life completed, and did not want to await the inevitable physical decline.

In half of all cases of 'auto-euthanasia' the person concerned had earlier requested euthanasia but the request had been refused. Most often this was because he was not 'terminal' or did not have a fatal illness (as Chabot notes, neither of these is a legal requirement), or because the suffering was not considered unbearable or hopeless. Fear of legal consequences and the personal convictions of the doctor were also mentioned with some frequency.

In half of all cases of stopping eating and drinking, the person concerned did not seek out information in advance, but in a fifth of all cases a doctor was approached for information (printed information and 'someone else' account together for another fifth); right-to-die associations were rarely a source of information. By contrast, in most cases of 'auto-euthanasia' with sleeping pills information was obtained: in a third of all cases, this was printed information, in a quarter a doctor was the source of information, and in another quarter either a right-to-die association or 'someone else'. Doctors were also quite frequently (a fifth of all cases) knowingly helpful in acquiring the necessary pills, but more often (a third of all cases) the pills were acquired under false pretences from a doctor or pharmacy in the Netherlands or abroad. Family and friends were the only other important source of the drugs used.

In about three-quarters of all cases of stopping eating and drinking, death followed within two weeks.[115] When sleeping pills were used, death followed within 12 hours. Looking back on the death, most *rapporteurs* think the person concerned would have considered it a dignified one (this judgment is not much affected by

---

[114] The data that follow are from Chabot 2007: ch 6. Since the data derive from *rapporteurs* Chabot treats it with caution, especially when it may say more about the *rapporteur* than about the person concerned (in particular, assessments afterwards of the 'unbearability' of the suffering).

[115] In the course of constructing his sample, Chabot found a significant number of cases in which the person concerned died within seven days. These were excluded from the sample to ensure that it contained only cases in which the person's persistent and clear-headed wish to die could not be doubted.

whether there had earlier been a request for euthanasia). In about two-thirds of all cases, they think the manner of dying was the first choice of the person concerned. The *rapporteurs* themselves seem on the whole to have more positive memories when the death is the result of stopping eating and drinking.

Chabot does not discuss the matter, but it seems from his results that in many cases of 'auto-euthanasia' with sleeping pills either a doctor who knowingly supplies the pills (22%) or a person present at the scene who prepares the lethal drugs for ingestion (38%), or both, have committed the criminal offence of assistance with suicide.[116] Since the total number of cases in which sleeping pills are used is, as we have seen, in the region of 1,600 per year, a considerable number of serious crimes are involved. Nevertheless, control seems to be essentially non-existent. In two-thirds of the cases the patient's doctor filed a certificate of natural death, but even if the police or the municipal pathologist become involved, the death does not necessarily get registered as a not-natural one. Chabot estimates that at most 200 of the 1,600 cases of auto-euthanasia with sleeping pills (12%) were ultimately registered as non-natural deaths,[117] but it is not clear in how many of these a third person rendered assistance. The bottom line is that there have for many years been no prosecutions of family members or intimate friends for giving assistance in a responsible way (the few prosecutions there have been, have been of volunteers of right-to-die associations—see chapters 3.6 and 4.2.3.3(J)).

5.3 Euthanasia and other MBPSL: the Patient's and the Family's Viewpoint

The fact that euthanasia has been legal in the Netherlands since the mid-1980s, and the continuing public debate and political involvement that this has brought with it, are the direct occasion for the sustained research effort that has lead to the vast amount of empirical information that we have surveyed in the foregoing pages. Inspired by the Dutch research and its methodology, first the Belgians and then researchers in other Western European countries joined in. The result is that we now know a great deal about euthanasia and related practices that shorten the patient's life in quite a few countries.

Most of the information now available, however, shares two characteristics: it is purely quantitative/descriptive and it derives from doctors.[118] That the data

---

[116] Since stopping eating and drinking probably does not constitute suicide, assistance is presumably not a criminal offence, and the death hence a 'natural' one so that the control system for non-natural deaths is not applicable. The responsible doctor certifies a natural death in at least 90% of these cases; the death is almost never registered as a suicide. See Chabot 2007: 164, 227.

[117] *Ibid* at 230.

[118] See GB&W: 246–8 for some minor exceptions prior to 1998. See ch 6 for qualitative research in the specific situation of neonatology.

are almost exclusively descriptive—that they are not addressed to answering any question other than 'how much of something is there?'—means that we still have little insight into any of the 'why' questions one might want to ask, in particular those concerning the social processes that lead to one sort of behaviour or another. That the data—including that concerning patients, their suffering, their motivations and so forth—all derive from doctors means that almost everything we know is filtered through the limited observational capacities of doctors and how they interpret what they observe. What we know is, in effect, limited to what doctors think they know.

The lack of good research into the social processes of decision-making and into the perspective of the patient (and his family) is the biggest and most important gap in existing knowledge concerning the social practice of euthanasia and its regulation. In the period since the precursor of this book, there has been little improvement in this respect. What there is, however, justifies the expectation that much could be learned from a concentrated research effort. Three recent studies stand out in this respect.[119]

'Euthanasia Talk'

Frances Norwood is an American medical anthropologist. Her book deals directly with 25 patients who were dying or had made a request for euthanasia, and their 10 general practitioners, located in Amsterdam and a town in its immediate vicinity.[120] She observed the communication between patient and doctor during house calls, and conducted formal interviews and had informal discussions with the doctors, patients, family members and others. Fourteen of the patients had made a request for euthanasia and during the course of the study (2000–01), 3 of them died from euthanasia, 5 died without euthanasia, and 6 were still alive at the end of the study. One patient who did not request euthanasia died from medical behaviour that hastened death.

The central idea of Norwood's study is that the legality of euthanasia in the Netherlands has made possible a cultural practice in which 'euthanasia is more often a discussion than it is a life-ending act'. This discussion—'euthanasia talk'—includes far more than 'the immediate, the obvious (planning for death) . . . [but also serves] to affirm social bonds and social life at the end of Dutch life'.[121] This is a point that seems to a 'native' both right and important. It corresponds to the Dutch idea that what they have done is to make euthanasia '*bespreekbaar*' [discussable], not only in public discourse[122] but also as a part of the social process of

---

[119] See also Van Dam 2005 for accounts by family and friends of cases in which euthanasia is given, avoided or refused. A more recent book by the same author explores the experience of performing euthanasia from the perspective of the doctor (Van Dam 2007).

[120] See Norwood 2005; some of the results of Norwood's research are also contained in two articles in English (Norwood 2006, 2007).

[121] Norwood 2005: 8–9.

[122] Compare Kennedy 2002.

dying. What Norwood has in mind is wonderfully illustrated in John Zaritsky's TV documentary, 'An Appointment with Death'.[123]

Norwood observes that at each of the several 'stages of euthanasia talk' a family doctor typically waits for the patient to take the initiative of proceeding to the following stage (eg fixing an appointment for a specific time). Requests must be repeated, and a patient must explain his request over and over again. Doctors rarely refuse a euthanasia request outright, they 'pause the process; they slow it down and wait it out'. There are right and wrong ways to request euthanasia. 'I want to die' is wrong, signalling suicidal thoughts or depression—'proper euthanasia requests are not death wishes'—whereas 'I just can't go on' [*ik wil niet meer*] is appropriate.[124]

'Euthanasia is a family matter.' In the context of a GP practice, it takes place at the patient's home and the patient's family plays a very important role in the process: 'the choice for euthanasia is not made in social isolation'. Doctors regard evidence of discord within the family as a danger signal and objections from family members is one of the main reasons euthanasia requests are not carried out.[125]

Slightly fewer than a third of Dutch deaths take place at home—almost two-fifths if one includes old-age facilities (see chapter 2.2.2). This means that a significant amount of 'euthanasia talk'—in particular, that which takes place in hospitals and nursing homes—is not covered in Norwood's study. It would be interesting to know in what respects the characteristics of 'euthanasia talk' in the home are similar to, or different from, that which takes place in an institutional setting.[126] Her research also did not cover settings in which euthanasia may still be somewhat of a taboo (eg some nursing homes and hospices). Finally, it would be very interesting to have some good comparative studies of communication between doctors, patients and their families, and communication within the family itself, in countries where euthanasia is not an option.

Doctor–Patient Communication and Patient Autonomy

Anne-Mei The carried out participant-observation research in a cancer ward of an academic hospital, interviewing both doctors and patients and observing their communication.[127] The patients (middle-aged men) were told that they had an aggressive form of lung cancer for which there was no hope of recovery, and the various possible treatments were described. They were told that 'something can be done' and offered a new experimental palliative therapy that offered some hope of

---

[123] Alexandria VA: KA Productions/TV Ontario, 1992 (on behalf of the Corporation for Public Broadcasting). Compare the quantitative findings of Swarte *et al* 2003 concerning the contribution of euthanasia to open discussion and hence to better coping with grief, see n 66 above.

[124] Norwood 2005: 20–26.

[125] Norwood 2005: 26, 81–92.

[126] One of the cases in Zaritsky's documentary film (see n 123) suggests that 'euthanasia talk' in a Dutch hospital can at least sometimes be very like that described by Norwood for deaths at home.

[127] See The 1999. See also The 1997 (ethnographic study of the role of nurses in cases of euthanasia) and The 2005 (ethnographic study of a psycho-geriatric ward in a nursing home).

postponing the inevitable. Little more was said about the prognosis (which was that the patient would die within 2 years), nor did patients ask about this. In the course of The's research, almost all patients (most of the few exceptions had professional experience with cancer) agreed to the therapy.

Most of the patients were poorly educated men who had always worked hard and were not much given to asking questions about difficult matters. The only exceptions to the general passivity of patients were a small number of people of a higher educational level or with access to family members with a background in medicine: they asked many more questions and received much more information from the doctors. But they, too, ultimately accepted the treatment offered.

The was struck by the optimism she observed among the patients, especially in the early stages of the therapy, despite what they had been told about the inevitable course of the disease. The results of the first chemotherapy were often spectacular and the tumor seemed from the X-ray photographs to have disappeared entirely. In discussing this with the patient, the doctors were enthusiastic, speaking of a 'successful treatment', a 'good reaction to the treatment', and so forth. In fact, as the doctors knew, the apparent disappearance was only because the tumor had become smaller than the resolution of the X-ray: 2.5 million cancerous cells. The perspective of the doctors was short-term and they apparently took this to be true for the patients, too. They assumed that a patient who wants to know more will ask. In fact, however, the patients were giving a long-term interpretation to the doctor's words. Where in the beginning The had assumed that the apparently unwarranted optimism of patients must be because doctors inadequately inform them about the prognosis, she later came to the conclusion that the problem is not that doctors do not tell the truth to patients, but how they tell it, and how patients interpret what they are told.

Later on in the progress of the disease, when the tumor reappears and is treated again, patients become aware that there is little ground for optimism, their physical condition deteriorates, and the pros and cons of further treatment are discussed with their doctor. But they tend to think they have no choice: not doing anything is not an option. When a patient asks concrete questions about the future, the doctors remain vague, in effect adjusting the information they give to the psychological need of the patient to continue believing in recovery. Doctors justify this by pointing out that exact predictions are impossible and that pronouncing a death sentence would only tend to paralyse a patient.

The argues that most terminally ill patients are not much interested in the autonomous decision-making that modern health law presupposes. They prefer to place their lot in the hands of their doctors. When the spread of the cancer cannot be treated any more, a patient is discharged to die at home. He returns to the care of his GP, who knows the patient far better than the specialists in the hospital, and is less oriented toward treatment and more toward the way the patient and his surroundings experience the process of dying. It is this sort of individually tuned care and support, in The's view, that terminal patients need and that helps them to recapture the autonomy they temporarily lose in the hospital setting.

Suicide Without the Assistance of a Doctor

Prior to his quantitative study of 'auto-euthanasia' (see section 5.2.2.3), Chabot had investigated the phenomenon in a qualitative way, reconstructing 20 cases of suicide without the assistance of a doctor from interviews with members of two organisations that give information and support in such cases.[128] At the time, he estimated that there are at least 40 and perhaps as many as 210 such cases per year—a very much lower figure than in his later study. By contrast with the 'anomic suicides' which have dominated the literature since Durkheim's classic study,[129] most of these cases were carefully planned together with a close circle of family or friends (and, if these were not available, with volunteers of right-to-die organisations). It takes a great deal of time and effort for the person concerned to persuade those in his immediate surroundings to accept his wish for death.

The people involved are mostly very old and 'tired of living', people with somatic illnesses that are severely handicapping but not in themselves deadly, and people with seriously handicapping psychiatric disorders for which they have undergone long but unsuccessful treatment. A social practice has grown up around such patients by which they receive counselling, information and help outside the health care system. This practice seems to have its roots in the rejection by doctors (explicit or otherwise) of requests for help.

The patient's doctor, whose refusal of assistance initiates the whole process, usually plays a role later on. Approached by family or friends of the person concerned, or by a volunteer, the doctor can be put under considerable pressure. Often he tries, at least for a while, to prevent the suicide. But some doctors are willing, sooner or later, to cooperate. Some, for example, knowingly prescribe small doses of drugs that, if saved up and taken all at once, can bring about a painless death. Some help conceal what happened by filing a report of a 'natural death'. Some, if the suicide takes place by stopping eating and drinking, are willing to give palliative assistance.

5.4 The Dutch Control System for Euthanasia in Practice

The general outlines of the Dutch control system for euthanasia and physician-assisted suicide, as it has emerged over the course of the past two decades, are as follows. Control at the level of health care institutions (in particular, institutional guidelines) is stimulated by various official and/or professional bodies at the national level, and many institutions in fact have such guidelines (section 5.4.1). Consultation has become institutionalised in the form of specially trained doctors,

---

[128] See Chabot 2001.
[129] Durkheim 1897.

who both advise colleagues confronted by a patient's request and serve as the legally required independent consultants (section 5.4.2). A doctor who carries out euthanasia or assisted suicide must report this to the municipal pathologist and it seems that the rate of accurate reporting is probably higher than until recently was generally supposed (section 5.4.3). Reported cases are reviewed for their conformity to the legal 'requirements of due care' by Regional Review Committees that are independent from the prosecutorial authorities (section 5.4.4). In almost all cases a reporting doctor is found to have acted properly, although the Review Committees do use a variety of informal ways of letting it be known when there is room for improvement. Prosecution is only possible if a committee has found a doctor 'not careful', but prosecution is very rare and since the Regional Review Committees were established in 1998 there has not been a single prosecution based on the adverse judgment of a committee. Nevertheless, precisely because it is focused on stimulation of rule-following by doctors rather than on punishment, the system of control seems to be quite effective (section 5.4.5).

5.4.1 Institutional Policies and Protocols

In the nature of things, euthanasia takes place in a context that has traditionally been surrounded by legal, professional and social guarantees of privacy. Because it is very much wanted by those who receive it (usually with the support of their immediate family), euthanasia is unlikely to produce much in the way of complaints to external authorities. In short, the possibilities for external repressive control are very limited. It is mostly doctors themselves who must apply the rules to their own behaviour.

Transmission of legal information to the 'shop floor' where behaviour to be regulated takes place is always problematic,[130] and the medical shop floor is not different from many others in this respect. Legal texts are often more or less incomprehensible to laymen, and in any case, doctors do not make a habit of reading them. Various intermediaries—the general press, professional journals, and so forth—have reported extensively (if not always accurately) on legal developments, but it is not clear how much of this is read and retained by doctors. It has repeatedly been suggested that medical education should address attention to end-of-life care,[131] but what information medical students in fact are exposed to (and retain) is unclear,[132] and in any event, most doctors now in practice got their medical education before euthanasia became an institutionalised practice.

---

[130] See generally Griffiths 2003.

[131] See, eg, the Report of the Remmelink Commission, responsible on behalf of the Government for having the first national study in 1990 carried out (Commissie Remmelink 1991: 38).

[132] Our attempts to secure such information from seemingly obvious sources such as the KNMG have not produced anything more than vague and partial indications that in some medical faculties, to some extent, some attention is paid to the matter. The report of the national research of 2005 revealed that whereas most doctors consider themselves adequately informed concerning the Law of 2000, substantial numbers of them in fact have mistaken ideas concerning some of its most important provisions (unfortunately, the way the questions were formulated in most cases only sheds light on mistakes that

In such circumstances, it seems fair to assume that the willingness of various institutions close to daily medical practice to engage actively in the transmission of legal information is probably crucial to the success of legal regulation. In fact, for more than 20 years euthanasia policies and protocols have been adopted by general and specialist medical associations, organisations of health care institutions, and local hospitals and nursing homes.[133]

By the mid-1990s most Dutch hospitals and nursing homes had a permissive policy as far as euthanasia was concerned, and in half or more of them the policy was a written one. In many cases, local prosecutors had been more or less actively involved in the development of written protocols.[134] Negative policies were rare in hospitals (about 5%) but much more common in nursing homes (about 33%). The religious affiliation of a hospital appeared to have relatively little influence on its euthanasia policy. In the case of nursing homes the influence was stronger: it was cited as the major reason for a prohibitive policy by half of the institutions with a prohibitive policy. Small hospitals and nursing homes more often had prohibitive policies. Regional location seemed to have no influence. The difference in practice between institutions with a permissive and a prohibitive policy was not great, since many of the latter exhibited in one way or another a certain degree of acceptance of euthanasia.[135] And most non-permissive institutions, in particular nursing homes, indicated they would cooperate in transferring a patient who desires euthanasia to an institution with a permissive policy. They also would cooperate with a patient's GP to have the patient transferred home for euthanasia.[136]

The difference in policy between hospitals and nursing homes seemed largely explainable on practical grounds. Many inhabitants of nursing homes are not considered competent to make a request (a quarter of the nursing homes with a prohibitive policy gave this as a reason). A number of nursing homes were con-

---

make the requirements more strict than they in fact are); the researchers recommend more attention for the Law of 2002 in the medical curriculum (see Onwuteaka-Philipsen *et al* 2007: 148–9, 225–7). In the Letter of 14 November 2007 reacting to the findings of the research (see ch 4, n 363), the Government reemphasised the importance it attaches to adequate legal knowledge and calls on the universities to ensure that medical education include specific attention to the Law of 2002 as well as to palliative care.

[133] See Griffiths 2000 for a discussion of self-regulation by the Dutch medical profession.

[134] See GB&W: 248*ff* and 250 n 131.

[135] In a 1989 study several non-permissive institutions referred explicitly to the fact that the doctor-patient relationship can lead to a conflict of duties, and they accepted the idea that a doctor, in such a situation, might feel 'forced' to accede to a patient's request despite the policy of the institution; the doctor did this, however, entirely on his own authority (Blad 1990: 108, 168–9). One non-permissive hospital acknowledged the fact that it did not know what the euthanasia policy of its specialists was (*ibid* at 107) and several indicated that their policy only applied to their own staff, not to external doctors who had patients there (*ibid* at 167–8). One hospital noted that although its policy was not permissive, euthanasia did in fact occur (*ibid* at 108). Permissive policies generally promised assistance in case of legal difficulties, if a case of euthanasia fell within the institution's policy (Blad 1990: 46, 99). At least some prohibitive institutions would have regarded violation of institutional policy as ground for dismissal (Benjaminsen 1988). Compare ch 4.2.3.3(J), n 264, for an example of use of the employment sanction against a doctor who refused all cooperation with an institution's permissive policy.

[136] Blad 1990: 109–11; 161–7; 186.

cerned about the internal problems that a permissive policy on euthanasia would entail: the policy itself might be unsettling to some patients, and because privacy and secrecy are impossible to guarantee in such institutions, a case of euthanasia would become generally known and lead to fear and insecurity among the other patients.

The 2005 national research included a new study of institutional policy.[137] The difference between hospitals and nursing homes seems largely to have disappeared. Written euthanasia policies are now present in 70% of health care institutions, in particular in 80% of hospitals, 90% of nursing homes, and 88% of hospices. In hospitals, the policy is almost always permissive. In nursing homes policies are now more frequently permissive than in the mid-1990s: only 15% (down from 32%) now prohibit euthanasia entirely. Hospices are quite restrictive: more than half prohibit euthanasia entirely. About four-fifths of all hospitals with a written policy take active steps to make it known to doctors and nurses; nursing homes do the same for doctors, but less frequently for nurses (two-thirds). More than half of all nursing homes but only a few hospitals make their written policy known to patients or their family, and few of either sort of institution make it known to persons outside the institution who refer patients.

Written policies concerning other medical behaviour that potentially shortens life are far less common. Roughly a third to two-fifths of hospitals have such a policy for termination of life without request, palliative sedation, pain relief and abstention. The same is true for nursing homes, except that almost half have a written policy concerning termination of life without a request. Written policies concerning resuscitation are more common in both sorts of institution (three-quarters of all hospitals and four-fifths of all nursing homes).

Most hospitals (83%[138]) and nursing homes (78%) have practice guidelines for euthanasia, and most of these (81% and 60% respectively) date from 2002 or later. Most guidelines refer to most of the statutory requirements of due care, usually explicitly as such, but in many guidelines these are not worked out in much detail. The requirements of a voluntary request, unbearable and hopeless suffering, and consultation are almost always included. Only a third of the guidelines mention the existence of specialised consultants (SCEN) and many guidelines give insufficient information on the requirement that the consultant be independent. Most guidelines make clear that only a doctor may administer euthanatica, but other requirements concerning carrying out euthanasia (continuous presence, the drugs to be used) are less commonly included. It seems that about a quarter of all doctors are unaware of the existence of their institution's guideline.

The guidelines of nursing homes (less so those of hospitals) are often stricter than the Euthanasia Law, categorically excluding patients with dementia, patients in coma or otherwise non-competent, and patients whose suffering is not

---

[137] The information in the following paragraphs is from Onwuteaka-Philipsen *et al* 2007: 151–69.
[138] An additional 6% have guidelines at ward-level.

'physical'. Almost half the guidelines do not mention the possibility that in the case of a non-competent patient an advance written request can satisfy the request requirement.

The Medical Association (KNMG) considers institutional policies that simply exclude the possibility of euthanasia or assisted suicide irresponsible, and it takes the position that such a policy cannot be binding on individual doctors.[139] The Regional Review Committees, the Medical Inspectorate, the prosecutorial authorities and the Government actively promote the formulation of local protocols that accurately reflect the requirements of due care.[140]

The Euthanasia Protocol of the Albert Schweitzer Hospital

The euthanasia policy of the Albert Schweitzer Hospital in Dordrecht (a medium-sised city just upriver from Rotterdam) is an example of the sort of thoughtful euthanasia protocol increasingly characteristic of Dutch health care institutions. The hospital publishes an Annual Report concerning the functioning of its protocol. These reports are interesting documents that nicely illustrate this aspect of Dutch euthanasia policy.[141] The current version of the protocol dates from 2004 and formalises the role of the hospital's 'euthanasia consultant', first established in 1997. The current two consultants—who are spiritual counsellors/pastors in the hospital—are responsible for managing the decision-making process; they advise the responsible doctor and are available to the patient, his family, and the medical staff for counselling.

According to the protocol, the hospital considers euthanasia an integral part of good care for terminal patients, something that the hospital makes available to patients and that people should feel free to talk about. Staff members are not obliged to participate in it, but they should refer a patient who requests it to another caregiver.

The protocol summarises the statutory requirements surrounding euthanasia. To these it adds two hospital guidelines:

- use of morphine-like drugs in increasing doses with the intention of shortening life rather than dealing with pain or other symptoms is not permitted (compare chapter 4.2.3.3(F) for the similar position of the Regional Review Committees);
- assistance with suicide (oral administration) is not advisable, because the dying process in such a case is unpredictable.

---

[139] See ch 4.2.3.3(I).

[140] See ch 4 n 392 for the importance the Government attaches to good institutional protocols. See the appendix to this chapter (nn 10 and 14) for several examples of such action by the Medical Inspectorate in the context of 'not careful' judgments of the Regional Review Committees. In the cases of terminal sedation (see ch 4.2.2.4) and of termination of life in neonatology (see ch 6.2.2.4 and 6.2.2.5), the Government and the prosecutorial authorities have been active at both the local and the national level in promoting self-regulation by the medical profession.

[141] See Albert Schweitzer Ziekenhuis 2004, 2005, 2006.

Requests for euthanasia are to be taken seriously, and the 'euthanasia consultant' is to be brought into the case as soon as a request for euthanasia comes to the attention of a doctor. The 'consultant', a nurse and the responsible doctor form an 'ad hoc team' responsible for a careful procedure. All steps in the procedure should be well documented.

The protocol discusses the whole decision-making procedure in detail, emphasising the need to take sufficient time, to consider alternatives, to make agreements concerning withholding and withdrawing treatment (these are to be recorded in the patient's file), to have the patient sign a written request for euthanasia, and so forth. The responsible doctor (preferably in agreement with the 'team') decides whether to agree to the request; if the request is not agreed to, the reasons for this must be clearly explained to the patient.

If the request is agreed to, concrete decisions concerning the time and place, and who is to be present, are to be made and communicated to the other staff of the ward, the Governing Board of the hospital, the hospital's pharmacist, the patient's GP, and the municipal pathologist (to whom the euthanasia will be reported). Agreements should also be made concerning the nurse who will assist with the euthanasia and with regard to follow-up care for the doctor, the nurse and other staff members, and the family. Two weeks after the euthanasia, all those involved come together to discuss their experiences and to draw conclusions for the future.

According to the Annual Reports, one important result of the protocol is that all cases of euthanasia are known to the hospital and are reported to the municipal pathologist pursuant to the reporting procedure, so that the hospital has a reporting rate of 100%.

Table 5.15 gives a global idea of euthanasia practice in the Albert Schweitzer Hospital in the years 2001–06. Compared with the national study data, over the six years the number of concrete requests (126) that are ultimately carried out (22) seems rather low (17%, as opposed to 33% in the 2001 study data—see Table 5.8). The reasons are also rather different from those in the national study data: among specialists nationally, the most important reason requests are not carried out is the earlier death of the patient (35% in 2001—see Table 5.10), whereas over the 6 years this was only the case 16% of the time in the Albert Schweitzer Hospital. On the other hand, nationally the fact that in the doctor's judgment the patient did not (yet) fulfil the conditions was the reason in fewer than a third of the cases in which a concrete request was not carried out (Table 5.10), whereas in the Albert Schweitzer Hospital this was 46% over the six years.[142] In short, while it is not clear whether this is due to a somewhat more reticent approach or to a more careful procedure, it may be 'more difficult' to receive euthanasia in this hospital than in hospitals in the Netherlands generally.

---

[142] Rough calculation from Table 5.10: 9% where the patient did not yet want euthanasia subtracted from 44% in which the patient died before euthanasia was carried out; 6% in which the doctor had personal objections subtracted from 35% in which doctor's judgment was the reason for not carrying out euthanasia.

Table 5.15. Euthanasia practice in the Albert Schweitzer Hospital, Dordrecht (numbers of cases)

	2001	2002	2003	2004	2005	2006
requests	27	32	29	42	42	35
general	6	10	12	14	21	18
concrete	21	22	17	28	21	17
well-considered, voluntary[1]	21	26	21	32	35	28
prior written euthanasia request	7	8	5	8	11	9
no treatment alternative	21	22	17	28	24	22
unbearable suffering	19	15	17	25	18	16
non-somatic suffering	—	3	3	5	6	1
family opposed	4	1	5	6	2	1
euthanasia carried out	6	2	3	7	2	2
euthanasia not carried out	21	30	26	35	40	33
criteria not (yet) met	12	12	12	23	21	16
request withdrawn	2	6	4	6	5	5
died	2	9	4	5	8	6
released to home[2]	5	3	6	1	6	6

Source: Albert Schweitzer Ziekenhuis 2005, 2006, supplemented with information received from E van den Ende of the AS Hospital. Numbers in italics are included within the preceding general category.

[1] Psychiatric consultation in 2 cases each year, except 1 case in 2003 and 2006.
[2] At least four of these patients, of whom 2 in 2006, died at home from euthanasia.

5.4.2 Consultation

One of the requirements of due care that a doctor who carries out euthanasia must have met is consultation with another, independent doctor (see chapter 4.2.3.3(E)). Consultation currently takes place in virtually all cases reported to the Regional Review Committees. Nevertheless, as can be seen in the appendix to this chapter, defects in consultation (timing, independence) are the most common reason that the committees come to the conclusion that the doctor was 'not careful' (15 of 25 cases from 1998 through 2006).

In the very early days of the euthanasia discussion in the Netherlands proposals had been made, among others by the State Commission on Euthanasia, for various forms of control in advance of carrying out euthanasia or assisted suicide. These were rejected by the Government and the medical profession and none of them ever came to anything.[143] The system of control that was settled upon almost from the beginning was after-the-fact control, attached, as we have seen in chapter 4.2.4.1, to the requirement that a doctor report a death of one of his patients as 'natural' or 'not natural'.

[143] See Weyers 2004: 128, 202–4, 222, 236, 326.

Notwithstanding this prior history, one of the most interesting and important developments in recent years has been the emergence of control before-the-fact. In 1997 the SCEA-project (Support and Consultation Euthanasia Amsterdam) was set up by the Medical Association (KNMG) with financial support from the Ministry of Health to give advice to Amsterdam GPs confronted with a request for euthanasia and to make available to them especially trained consultants (recruited from among practicing GPs). After this pilot programme was favourably evaluated,[144] it was extended to the entire country in 1999 and renamed SCEN (the N standing for Netherlands). The SCEN programme is described more fully in chapter 4.2.4.4. By 2004 there were over 500 registered SCEN consultants.[145] The programme is currently being extended to nursing-home doctors and to specialists in hospitals, and the Regional Review Committees note in their Annual Report for 2006 that an increasing number of specialists have been trained as SCEN consultants, and that SCEN consultants (often GPs) are being used by specialists.[146]

From the 2005 national study, it appears that a SCEN consultant was involved in almost 90% of all cases of euthanasia/PAS (the remaining 10% was about equally divided between cases of no consultation and cases of consultation with a non-SCEN doctor).[147] As we have seen in chapter 4.2.4.4 the KNMG considers the SCEN programme very successful and the Regional Review Committees, who can compare the consultation reports of SCEN consultants with those of other consulted doctors, make no secret of the importance they attach to the programme and its expansion beyond GPs.

Table 5.16 gives an overview of the caseload of the SCEN programme.

As of 2006, 92% of all SCEN consultations were requested by GPs, 4% by specialists and 4% by nursing-home doctors.[148]

The average length of a SCEN consultation in 2004–06 was over three and three-quarters hours.[149] As Table 5.16 shows, in about three-quarters of all cases the SCEN consultant agreed that all requirements had been met, and in almost another fifth that this was not yet the case. In 8% of the cases the SCEN consultant concluded that the requirements had not been met. This was usually because of doubts concerning the unbearability of the suffering (70%), the well-consideredness of the request (30%), or the existence of other treatment possibilities (28%).[150]

Apart from technical questions (legal or medical), most requests for information in 2006 concerned whether in the circumstances euthanasia could be considered

---

[144] See Onwuteaka-Philipsen & Van der Wal 1998.

[145] SCEN 2005. In 2006 there were 532 registered SCEN doctors of whom 508 were active (the rest were not (yet) available to serve as consultants) (SCEN 2007).

[146] RRC 2006: 25.

[147] See Onwuteaka-Philipsen *et al* 2007: 181; the files of the Review Committees for 2005 confirm this frequency (*ibid* at 194).

[148] See SCEN 2007; these frequencies have been fairly stable over the past few years. Relative to their share of all cases of euthanasia (see section 5.2.2.1), GPs are overrepresented in the use of SCEN, specialists very much underrepresented, and nursing-home doctors somewhat underrepresented.

[149] See SCEN 2007.

[150] *Ibid.*

Table 5.16. Role of SCEN consultants in euthanasia/PAS decision-making 2000–2005

	requests for infor- mation by patient's doctor	consul- tations	judgment of consultant concerning conformity with re-quirements of due care (%)			euthanasia or PAS in case of positive consultation (%)		
			no	not yet	yes	yes	no	not known
April 2000–2002[1]	643	3,891	n.d.	n.d.				
2003[2]	n.d.	2,256	n.d.	n.d.				
2004[3]	1,101	2,367	8.3	17.9	73.8	n.d.		
2005[4]	1,202	2,883	5.8	20.0	74.2	73.0	8.8	18.2
2006[5]	1,158	3,019	8.0	18.4	73.5	62.2	25.1	12.5

Sources: [1] Jansen-van der Weide 2005: 55 (complete). [2] SCEN 2004 (appears to be complete). [3] SCEN 2005 (corrected for 90.8% response). [4] SCEN 2006 (corrected for 89.1% response). [5] SCEN 2007 (corrected for 86% response).

(61%), palliative care (26%), and how to deal with pressure from the family or the patient (respectively 18% and 14%).[151]

As argued in chapter 4.2.4.4, given the high quality of SCEN-consultancy according to the Regional Review Committees, we can expect the committees to scrutinise such cases less thoroughly than in cases—becoming increasingly rare—in which no SCEN consultant is used. As this becomes known to doctors, the already high level of use of the programme will increase further until it becomes practically uniform. The committees will become more and more inclined to focus their attention on cases in which there is no written report from a SCEN consultant, or in which the consulting doctor performs euthanasia despite a negative SCEN judgment. As these processes mutually reinforce each other, the weight of control will effectively shift from *after-the-fact* (the Review Committees) to *before-the-fact* (SCEN).

5.4.3 Reporting

The system of legal control over euthanasia in the Netherlands (as in countries where euthanasia is illegal) is crucially dependent on the willingness of those whose behaviour is to be controlled (doctors) to report what they have done. Reporting, and the resulting transparency of euthanasia practice, is important for a number of reasons:

- it helps assuage a legitimate public concern about the dangers of such behaviour;
- anticipation of the necessity of reporting contributes to the 'due care' with which euthanasia is carried out;

[151] See SCEN 2007.

- reporting is essential to adequate control since it is almost exclusively reported cases that are subjected to legal review and if necessary sanction;
- the review process that follows a report is a continuing source of information about the problems that arise in end-of-life treatment and affords a basis in practice for refinement of the applicable ethical and legal rules;
- all of this produces a stream of feedback communication to doctors and others that can be assumed to be a major factor keeping the practice within bounds.

If there are so many good reasons to consider reporting important, why would a doctor fail to do so? A number of 'costs' of reporting should be considered:

- some doctors object to the intrusion of the state into the doctor–patient relationship and therefore refuse to report what they have done (in 1990 about 20% of all doctors had such conscientious objections, but by 1995 this had declined to under 10%);[152]
- reporting violates the relationship of trust with the patient and invades the privacy of his family (percentage negligible);[153]
- reporting exposes the doctor and the patient's family to the hassle and unpleasantness of the reporting procedure itself: filling in of forms, visit by the municipal pathologist immediately after the patient's death, long period of uncertainty (in all of these respects, improvements in the reporting procedure since 1990, and especially after the installation of the Regional Review Committees, have greatly reduced this 'cost');
- reporting brings some attendant risk: especially if one has not met all of the requirements of due care there will at the very least be some unpleasantness and at the worst medical disciplinary or criminal proceedings (this is by far the most important reason doctors give for not reporting[154]).

It is also interesting to turn the question around and ask why any doctor *would* report—what's in it for him? Doctors who report give as most important reasons for doing so that reporting is legally and ethically required, and contributes to the social acceptance of euthanasia practice and the development of the system of control. These are all very idealistic motives. The only practical reasons given are that not reporting can be risky, too, if other people know what happened, and that institutional policy makes reporting mandatory.[155] The number of reported cases of euthanasia per year is shown on Table 5.17. The absolute number of reported cases grew very rapidly in the 1980s and 1990s, from 10 in 1983 to a high point of 2,216 in 1999. It then declined to 1,815 in 2003, and since then climbed back a bit to 1933 in 2005, but in 2006 seems to have levelled off again (see also Graph 5.1).

---

[152] See Van der Wal & Van der Maas 1996: 120–121. It seems that there is a small but in recent years consistent group of under 10% who would not report under any circumstances because they regard euthanasia as a 'matter between doctor and patient' (see Onwuteaka-Philipsen *et al* 2007: 177).

[153] *Cf* Van der Wal *et al* 2003: 144.

[154] *Ibid* at 143–4.

[155] *Ibid* at 142–3.

Table 5.17. Number of cases of euthanasia/PAS reported, 1983–2006

year	1982*	1983*	1984*	1985*	1986	1987	1988	1989	1990	1991	1992	1993	1994
reports	4	10	19	31	84	126	184	338	484	861	1,197	1,303	1,484

year	1995	1996	1997	1998	1999	2000	2001	2002	2003	2004	2005	2006
reports	1,466	1,701	2,096	2,209	2,216	2,123	2,054	1,883	1,815	1,886	1,933	1,923

Sources: 1982–85: *Second Chamber of Parliament, 1986–1987, no 19 700*, ch VI, no 3; 1986–2002: Van der Wal *et al* 2003: 154; 2003–06: Annual Reports Regional Review Committees.

* Data in source differ from total for 1981–85 given in Van der Wal et al 2003: 154 (total = 71).

In 1990, about a quarter of all interviewed doctors said they were prepared to report 'always'.[156] In 1995 75% of doctors who had reported a case said they did so 'always', and in 2001 this was 91%.[157] In the 2005 research doctors who had performed euthanasia since the Law of 2002 were asked whether they had reported it: 97% replied that they had always done so and over 90% of these doctors said they consider not reporting 'unthinkable' (both figures were 100% for nursing-home doctors).[158]

The actual reporting rate, calculated as the ratio of cases in fact reported (see Table 5.17) to the total number of cases of euthanasia as estimated in the national studies (see Table 5.1) has risen from 18% in 1990 and 41% in 1995 to 54% in 2001 and 80% in 2005.[159]

Regarded as the results of an experiment in legal control, such data are little short of spectacular. A new policy concerning behaviour that the state cannot observe directly, that requires expenditure of time and energy and involves some unpleasantness, and that requires the people concerned to run the risk of external criticism or even legal sanctions, started with an effectiveness of about zero, as one would expect. Within a decade and a half, this policy was producing the desired effects in four-fifths of all cases (probably in large measure because the perceived risks of reporting had significantly declined).[160]

The Disappointing Reporting Rate

We must not lose sight of the enormous success of the reporting requirement—nor of the fact that the reporting rate is zero everywhere else in the world except Oregon and Belgium—when we shift our focus from the success of a policy to the unpleasant fact that legal control can hardly be considered adequate when many of the cases to which it is supposed to be applied never come to the attention of the legal authorities, although—to put the matter in perspective—the situation is undoubtedly far better in the case of euthanasia than for most other serious crimes.

Not only are many cases not reported, it is known that at least in the past the problematic behaviour which we would like the authorities to look at more carefully—for example, failure properly to consult a second doctor—is far more common among unreported cases than among reported ones.[161] In other words, we have a control system that, from the point of view of influencing behaviour by legal rules, is an impressive success, one that puts the Netherlands in a class by itself as far as control of euthanasia is concerned, but which nevertheless cannot

---

[156] Van der Maas *et al* 1991: 81.

[157] Van der Wal *et al* 2003: 143.

[158] Onwuteaka-Philipsen *et al* 2007: 176.

[159] *Ibid* at 174. The reporting frequency for specialists is slightly lower (76%) and for nursing-home doctors slightly higher (88%).

[160] Klijn has in a recent lecture (Klijn 2003b) divided the Dutch control regime for reported cases of euthanasia, from before 1985 to the present, into four periods (<1985, 1986–90, 1991–98, >1999), comparing the legal, procedural and institutional conditions prevailing in each period. He argues that the 'costs' of reporting have gone down in each successive period.

[161] See GB&W: 238.

review all cases, and in particular fails to catch some of the legally more problematic ones.

If we look beyond 'euthanasia' to the other sorts of MBPSL, the situation is
worse still, since among the vast number of cases of withholding or withdrawing
treatment, of pain relief with life-shortening effect, and of 'terminal sedation'—
almost all of which get reported as 'natural deaths'—there is an unknown but
plainly substantial number that on further examination would amount to 'termination of life' and therefore require attention. As the head of the Dutch
Prosecution Service observed several years ago, 'terminal sedation' is too similar
to euthanasia to be left outside the arrangements for control.[162] The same argument applies to many cases of death due to pain relief or abstention, especially
when the patient is no longer competent or was not asked what he wanted.

The 'Lying Doctor' Hypothesis

The general assumption has from the beginning been that 'lying' is the problem.
Knowing that what he has done is 'euthanasia' (or 'termination of life without a
request') and must be reported as a 'not natural' death, the doctor chooses for one
or another of the reasons mentioned above not to be honest about the matter and
files a false certificate that the death was a 'natural' one. Dutch policy has been
directed toward reducing the 'costs' of reporting so that 'lying' becomes less attractive an alternative to honesty.

How plausible is the 'lying doctor' hypothesis? Graph 5.1 (which presents the
data given on Table 5.17) shows the development of self-reporting of euthanasia,
from the early 1980s to the present.[163] We must interpret it with care, of course,
since changes in the number of reports per year can reflect either changes in the
amount of euthanasia really going on or changes in the willingness of doctors to
report them. But if we assume that the rate at which doctors perform euthanasia—
whether this rate is going steadily upward or downward or staying the same—will
be less sensitive to temporary external factors than the rate at which they report
what they have done, then some peculiarities in the pattern of steadily increasing
numbers of reports seem to lend support to the 'lying doctor' hypothesis—the
idea that non-reporting is a conscious response to apprehension concerning how
the authorities will react to an honest report. In 1992–93 one sees a temporary
pause and in 1994–95 a temporary decline in the steady upward climb of the number of reports. These are years in which highly publicised prosecutions took place
of doctors who had properly reported what they had done and were prosecuted
due to interventions by the Minister of Justice.[164] At the time, it was predicted that
these prosecutions, by increasing the perceived costs of accurate reporting, would
adversely affect the willingness of doctors to report, and Graph 5.1 appears to

---

[162] See De Wijkerslooth 2003.

[163] Graph 5.1 is inspired by earlier work of Klijn (see Klijn 2003a).

[164] In 1992–93, the *Chabot* case (see ch 4.2.3.4(A); in 1994–95 the *Prins* and *Kadijk* cases (see
ch 6.2.2.3).

confirm these predictions. The same can be said of the period after 1998–99, which saw three new and highly controversial prosecutions,[165] and also the introduction of the Regional Review Committees. While these Committees were intended to increase doctors' sense of security in reporting, the immediate result of a major change in the existing reporting procedure to which doctors had become accustomed may well have been precisely the opposite.[166]

After about 2000, Graph 5.1 becomes more difficult to interpret. One possible explanation for a stagnating number of reports could lie in a real decline in the frequency of euthanasia, a possibility seemingly confirmed by the finding of the fourth national study in 2005 to the effect that between 2001 and 2005 the amount of euthanasia declined for the first time since it was first studied in 1990.[167] After 2003 the number of reports began to rise again. The 2005 national study produced

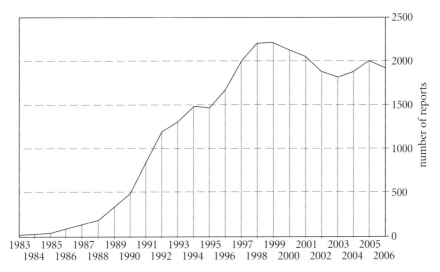

Graph 5.1 Reports per year, 1983–2006

[165] The *Brongersma, Van Oijen* and *Vencken* cases—see ch 3.3 and 3.4; ch 4.2.2.4, 4.2.2.5, 4.2.3.5.

[166] At least in the beginning, the careful scrutiny that the committees gave to reported cases led to negative outbursts from some doctors (see eg Crul 1999). The national research of 2001 found that 70% of the doctors involved in 'difficult' cases (doctor found 'not careful', case sent to Medical Inspectorate, doctor summoned to a meeting of the committee) found the experience unpleasant; 37% of other reporting doctors (in 1995: 53%) found it unpleasant. See Van der Wal *et al* 2003: 164–5. From the 2005 research it appears that most doctors have positive or neutral experiences with the way the Review Committees dispose of a case they report; 20% find the procedure a source of support; 20% find it burdensome and 18% time-consuming. Over 95% considers the committee's judgment good (1% bad). Specialists were the most negative on all questions. In the rare case that a committee requests additional information, the doctors' experiences are less favourable, especially because they find the procedure burdensome (33%) and time-consuming (31%). (Onwuteaka-Philipsen *et al* 2007: 185–6)

[167] See section 5.1.2.3 for the apparent decline, about which we have noted some scepticism at various points in this chapter.

a striking rise in the reporting rate (from 54% in 2001 to 80% in 2005). In the context of the 'lying doctor' hypothesis, these recent developments could be attributed to the growing confidence of doctors in the Regional Review Committees.

In summary, there is at least some indirect evidence that 'lying' has been at least part of the problem of non-reporting, and that actions by the Government or the prosecutorial authorities that increase or decrease the level of uncertainty among doctors about the consequences of honest reporting have an immediate impact on the reporting rate.[168]

An Alternative Hypothesis

In the past few years another possible explanation for the less than perfect rate of reporting has begun to emerge: that doctors do in fact report almost all cases they themselves see as 'euthanasia' and that the major part of the problem lies in the fact that the national studies, which produce the disappointing reporting rates, count many situations as 'euthanasia' that doctors do not consider, and therefore do not report, as such. Not 'lying' but (honest) difference of opinion about whether a case is one of 'euthanasia' or of another sort of MBPSL accounts for a reporting rate considerably less than 100%. This is therefore the place for us to return to the concept of 'euthanasia', the way it has been operationalised in research, and the consequences for the reporting rate.

To understand the argument, one must keep in mind the way the frequency of euthanasia (and the other MBPSL) is constructed in the death-certificate studies. A doctor who, because the death certificate of a former patient is included in the research sample, receives a number of questions about the case from the researchers, is not asked whether the death was due to 'euthanasia'.[169] He is asked whether the death was the result of a drug he administered, what his intention was, and whether the patient requested it. If the doctor answers that he administered a drug with the 'explicit intention' to cause the patient's death, the researchers count the case as one of 'termination of life'. If there was a request from the patient, the case is classified as 'euthanasia', and absent a request it is 'termination of life without a request'. With such a methodology, it is entirely possible that the researchers count a case as one of 'euthanasia' that the doctor himself—despite what he answered to the question about his 'intention'—regarded as one of 'pain relief with life-shortening effect'.

The cases that get reported are classified in a different way, and by the doctor himself. A doctor of course only submits a case to the review procedure for euthanasia if he himself considers it to be one of 'euthanasia'. In effect, a reporting rate calculated as the national researchers do measures cases that doctors consider

---

[168] There is also some informal, anecdotal information to the same effect.

[169] There was at the beginning of the 1990s every reason for this procedure, since given the conceptual confusion surrounding the term 'euthanasia' asking a sample of doctors whether they had performed it would have produced meaningless answers. This is no longer the case in the Netherlands. As Van Tol's (2005) research shows, there is a very strong archetypical case of 'euthanasia' in the heads of most Dutch doctors. But however attractive the approach once may have been for research purposes, no one seems to have taken account of its consequences for the calculation and interpretation of a reporting rate.

and therefore report to the authorities as 'euthanasia' against cases that *the methodology of the researchers* counts as 'euthanasia'. A reporting rate that shows a large number of non-reported cases may not indicate a high level of 'lying' by doctors but simply a different conception of what 'euthanasia' is.

Den Hartogh was the first to recalculate the reporting rate based on the idea that there may be a difference in the way doctors and the national researchers classify cases as 'euthanasia' or as 'pain relief with life-shortening effect'. He did this for 2001 in a rough and ready way, excluding cases of 'terminal sedation' and 'euthanasia with morphine'. He supposed that doctors do not generally consider such cases to be 'euthanasia' regardless of how they describe their intention (he argued that they were legally correct in this).[170] He came to the conclusion that the rate of reporting in 2001 was not 54%, but rather about 90%.[171]

The hypothesis of differences in classification has been confirmed by Van Tol's research into how the actors who are supposed to apply the official legal classifications of MBPSL interpret them in practice.[172] He shows in an ingenious and convincing way that there are major, systematic differences in the way the various participants (doctors, prosecutors, national researchers) classify deaths as 'euthanasia' or as something else. Doctors classify as 'euthanasia' prototypical cases in which a doctor administers by injection an immediately lethal substance (not morphine) to a patient on his request at a moment agreed upon beforehand. Van Tol's interviews with doctors suggest that they report almost all cases they themselves classify as 'euthanasia'.[173]

Although they do not mention his analysis or his conclusions, the researchers in the 2005 national study confirm Van Tol's explanation for the disappointing reporting rate. A question was added to the death-certificate study in which the doctor himself is asked to classify what he did. In about a quarter of all cases in which the researchers classified the doctor's behaviour as termination of life (euthanasia, assisted suicide or termination of life without a request), the doctor classified it differently—usually as palliative or terminal sedation or as pain relief. As Den Hartogh had supposed, not their 'intention' but the drug used is largely determinative of the doctors' classification: in 99% of all cases in which muscle-relaxants are used, the doctor's classification was 'termination of life'; if morphine or benzodiazepines were

---

[170] Den Hartogh's assumption that a doctor's account of his 'intention' does not necessarily determine his classification of what he has done receives qualitative support from Griffiths' experience as a 'participant observer' in a medical ethics discussion group (see ch 6.3.4, Box 6.9): it appears that doctors experience little problem in describing their *intention* as one to shorten life and *what they did* as pain and symptom relief.

[171] Den Hartogh 2003. Without referring to Den Hartogh's hypothesis, the team of national researchers in effect took up his gauntlet and came, on the basis of a more refined analysis of the survey data, to the conclusion that the rate of reporting in 2001 was about 70%. See Rurup *et al* 2006b.

[172] Van Tol 2005.

[173] Van Tol also shows that public prosecutors do not classify cases in the same way as the researchers in the national studies. It follows that there are three possible reporting rates for 2001, depending on whose classification is used: a little over 30% according to the classification of prosecutors, a little over 50% according to the classification used by the researchers, and over 90% according to the classification of doctors. Van Tol concludes that 'The level of the reporting rate is highly dependent on the perspective from which situations . . . are classified.' (2005: 292)

used such a classification was given in only 1% of all cases (in the case of morphine, the classification 'pain relief' was usually chosen; in the case of benzodiazepines 'palliative/terminal sedation').[174]

Earlier suggestions that 'lying' may no longer be the principal reason for not reporting have thus been strikingly confirmed. The reporting rate for 2005 when calculated as in the past was, as we have seen, 80%. The recalculated rate after exclusion of cases involving opioids was 99%. It had been 73% in both 1995 and 2001. The reporting rate when opioids were used was 1–2% in 2005.

The new approach to the reporting rate first suggested by Den Hartogh, given a solid empirical and theoretical foundation by Van Tol, and overwhelmingly confirmed in the 2005 national research, entirely changes the policy problem. It is no longer principally one of inducing doctors to be honest about what they are doing, but rather one of accomplishing a higher degree of what Van Tol calls 'cognitive solidarity' between, on the one hand, doctors whose reporting is the foundation of the entire system of control, and on the other hand those who seek to measure or control what doctors do. It must be decided exactly which cases we want doctors to report, and it must be made clear to doctors what these cases are. At the moment, Dutch euthanasia policy fails rather strikingly in both respects.

The demise of the 'lying doctor' assumption reveals an underlying substantive problem that has been obscured by differences of classification: the extent of largely uncontrolled 'pain relief' that in most respects is hardly distinguishable from euthanasia or termination of life without a request. Those who welcome the apparent decline in the frequency of euthanasia between 2001 and 2005 should feel uneasy about the simultaneous rise in the frequency of pain relief with life-shortening effect. Much of what is currently classified as 'pain relief'—and hence protected from public scrutiny by the mantra 'normal medical behaviour'—is ethically and legally problematic: without a medical indication, without a request from the patient, without consultation with a colleague or other procedural protections.

5.4.4 Review and Sanctions

If a precarious practice such as euthanasia is to be ethically and socially acceptable, it must be under reliable control and also be seen to be so. Non-reporting seems, as we have seen in section 5.4.3, no longer itself to be a major problem. But the question remains what happens to a reported case. In this section we examine how the control systems, whose legal structure has been described in chapter 4.2.2, function in practice. In section 5.4.5 we return to the question whether what has been described can be considered adequate.

---

[174] See Onwuteaka-Philipsen *et al* 2007: 107–8, 122–4. Ninety-one percent of cases classified as termination of life without a request by the researchers were not so classified by the doctors. The effect of the drug used on the doctors' classifications was overwhelming (muscle relaxants being very strongly associated with a classification as 'termination of life'); a life-expectancy of 'several months', the use of a 'disproportional dose' of morphine (doubling the dose every three hours), and an intention to 'hasten the end of life' were also positively associated with such a classification, but to a very much lesser degree.

5.4.4.1 Regional Review Committees

Table 5.18 shows the disposition by the Regional Review Committees of reported cases. They are required by article 9 of the Law of 2002 to inform the doctor in writing of their decision within 6 weeks (with the possibility of extension for another 6 weeks).[175] According to the Annual Reports of the committees the average number of days between the receipt of a report and notification of the doctor has varied from 25 to 30.[176] A formal written decision is given in every case.

Table 5.18. Disposition of cases by the Regional Review Committees, 1999–2006

year	cases reported by doctor	Committee not competent	'careful'	'careful' referred to Medical Inspector	'not careful'
1999	2,216	5	2,206	5	0
2000	2,123	11	2,097	12	3
2001	2,054	8	2,091	4	1
2002	1,882	5	1,872	0	5
2003	1,815	2	1,805	0	8
2004	1,886	0	1,882	0	4
2005	1,933	1	1,929	0	3
2006	1,923	0	1,922	0	1
Total	15,832	32	15,804	21	25

Source: Annual Reports, Regional Review Committees, 1999–2006; further information received from the General Secretary of the Review Committees.

Most cases that reach the Review Committees are quite unproblematic.[177] In 2005 the committees sought further information from the reporting doctor in about 6% of all cases: 1.6% by telephone, 3.8% in writing and in 0.5% by summoning the doctor to a meeting of the committee in question. They requested additional information from the consultant in 2.5% of the cases and, very infrequently (0.3%), from someone else who had been involved. The additional information requested most often (a third of such requests) concerned the consultation or the patient's suffering; a fifth of the requests concerned the carrying out of euthanasia (usually the drugs used) and a tenth the voluntariness of the request. Such requests were much more frequently addressed to specialists than to GPs, and much more frequently to doctors who had not used SCEN consultation than to those who had.[178]

In most cases to which the committees give special attention, they ultimately conclude that the doctor was 'careful'. As Table 5.18 shows, only a handful of cases

---

[175] See ch 4, Box 4.15.

[176] RRC, Annual Reports 1998/99–2006.

[177] See eg RRC 2004: 12 ('most reports hardly afford anything to discuss'). Nevertheless, the recent Annual Reports (2003–06) do give the impression that doctors are increasingly willing to report cases in which quite a bit went wrong.

[178] See Onwuteaka-Philipsen *et al* 2007: 196–7. The data were similar in 2001 except that requests for additional information concerning consultation declined somewhat and those concerning the drugs used increased.

is adjudged 'not careful' and referred to the prosecutorial authorities for further consideration. Over the first eight years of their existence, the rate of 'not careful' judgments was under 2 per 1,000 reported cases (it is a bit over 2 per 1,000 in the years 2002 and thereafter, when the committees' judgments became final).

Of the 15 'not careful' judgments in the period 2003–05, 11 concerned euthanasia and 4 physician-assisted suicide (a substantial overrepresentation of PAS, considering that PAS accounts for less than 10% of all reported cases; in 2 of the 4 cases of PAS, the reason for the judgment 'not careful' was that the doctor had not been present at the time of the suicide). The reporting doctor was a GP in 6 cases and a surgeon in 5 (an underrepresentation of GPs, who account for 88% of all reported cases, and an overrepresentation of surgeons).[179] The principal grounds for a finding of 'not careful' (including 3 cases in 2007) are shown on Table 5.19. This overview confirms the judgment of the committees, often voiced in the Annual Reports, that two aspects of reported cases most often give rise to difficulties on review: whether the consultation was adequate (independence of the consulted doctor; timing of the consultation; etc) and whether the patient's suffering was unbearable (for example, in coma cases).

Table 5.19. Principal grounds for a finding of 'not careful' (1998–2007)

unbearable suffering	8
treatment alternative	1
informing patient	1
treatment relationship	3
consultation	17
performance	6
insufficient information	1

Source: appendix.
N = 28 judgments; more than one ground possible per judgment.

5.4.4.2 Prosecutorial Authorities

Since 1998, prosecution in reported cases is only possible after review of a case by a Regional Review Committee and since 2002 a committee's judgment that the doctor conformed to the requirements of due care has been final. Before examining what the prosecutorial authorities do with cases in which the committee's judgment is unfavourable, it is important to recall what the situation was before the committees were established.[180]

Table 5.20 shows the numbers of cases of euthanasia and termination of life without a request reported to a municipal pathologist and thence to the

---

[179] See Onwuteaka-Philipsen *et al* 2007: at 198–200.
[180] See GB&W: 241–5 for a fuller discussion.

prosecutorial authorities and dealt with by the Committee of Procurators-General (PGs), before and after the introduction of the RRCs. To make short of it: the Committee of Procurators-General paid careful attention to very few reported cases and hardly ever decided to prosecute. The whole procedure was very time-consuming, which was widely supposed to be one of the biggest objections that

Table 5.20. Disposition of cases of euthanasia and termination of life without a request brought to the attention of the Dutch prosecutorial authorities, 1981–2006

	reported by doctor[1]	*discussed by PGs*[2]	*decision not to prosecute after further investigation*[3]	*indictment*
1981–85	71		1	8
1986	84		1	2
1987	126		1	3
1988	184		1	2
1989	338		2	1
1990	484		—	—
1991	861	9	—	1
1992	1,197	13	1	2
1993	1,303	25	11	3
1994	1,484	24	8	3
1995	1,466	36	7	1
1996	1,701	23	1	—
1997	2,096	43	1	—
1998	2,209	15	—	1
1999	2,216	7	1	—
2000	2,123	12	—	1
2001	2,054	4	1	—
2002	1,883	15[4]	2	—
2003	1,815	7	5	—
2004	1,886	2	3	—
2005	1,933	5	1	—
2006	1,923	1	1	—

Source: Van der Wal *et al* 2003: 154; after 2002, see Onwuteaka-Philipsen *et al* 2007: 205–9; RRC 2007. Data from appendix to this chapter used to fill in missing data. The fact that there is a small number of unreported cases such as *Vencken* and *Van Oijen* (see n 165)—correctly or not regarded as 'natural deaths' by the doctors concerned—that in some other way come to the attention of the prosecutorial authorities is one possible explanation for the fact that the number of cases considered by the prosecutorial authorities in the period 1998–2002 is often larger than the number of cases in which a doctor is found 'not careful' by a Regional Review Committee. A further complication is that a case is sometimes not discussed by the PGs in the same year that the doctor reported it.

[1] Before 1990, per date of discussion by PGs; from 1990, per date of death or report.
[2] Number of cases discussed by the PGs for the first time. No data before 1991.
[3] In the rest of the cases discussed by the PGs (except those in which an indictment was sought) a decision not to prosecute was taken without further investigation.
[4] These are all cases reviewed by the RRCs before 2002.

doctors had to reporting. In cases not further discussed by the PGs, the average time elapsed between reporting and a final prosecutorial decision, in 1995, was three and a half months; the longest 10% took six months or more.[181] Prosecutorial decision-making was also completely opaque. Except for the very interesting study of prosecutorial decision-making that was part of the 1995 national research (repeated much more superficially in 2001), nothing was publicly known about these decisions or the grounds on which they were made.

Table 5.21 shows what the prosecutorial and medical disciplinary authorities have done since 1998 with cases in which the Dutch Regional Review Committees find a doctor 'not careful'. Through 2006 there have been no prosecutions in the 25 cases found 'not careful' by the Regional Review Committees. Two disciplinary cases were brought, both of which resulted in the imposition of sanctions.

Despite the enormous increase in the number of reported cases in the course of the 1990s, the significance of prosecutorial control seemed to be declining. Tables 5.21 and 5.22 show that this trend has continued. Since the Regional Review Committees were put on a strong statutory base in 2002, the direct role of the prosecutorial authorities in the control of euthanasia practice has declined to the point of marginality.

There does not seem to be much difference between the questions to which the PGs address particular attention and the reasons the Review Committees have for a finding of 'not careful'.[182] But as we saw in chapter 4.2.4.2, the prosecutorial policy of the PGs is directed in particular to the substantive requirements (in particular, in practice, the requirement of suffering); violation of procedural require-

Table 5.21. Subsequent disposition of cases found 'not careful' by the RRCs, 1998–2006

	number of 'not careful' judgments	*initial decision not to prosecute*	*prosecutor and/or MI discuss case with doctor*	*medical disciplinary case*
1998–99	0	—	—	—
2000	3	1	2	—
2001	1	—	1	—
2002	5	1	4	—
2003	8	1	6	—
2004	4	—	4	2
2005	3	—	3	—
2006	1	—	1	—
Total	25	3	22	2

Source: see appendix to this chapter.

[181] See Van der Wal & Van der Maas 1996: 132–4. There were large differences between the different local prosecutors' offices in the amount of time that elapsed between a doctor's report and the forwarding of the case to the PGs: the average per local office ranged from 8 to 108 days (overall average: 33 days).

ments such as reporting and consultation are not thought generally to call for serious criminal sanctions, and the way euthanasia is carried out is regarded as a medical matter, primarily the responsibility of the Medical Inspectorate.[183]

The role of the Medical Inspectorate is essentially passive. Although all cases found 'not careful' by the Review Committees are sent to the inspectorate as well as to the Committee of PGs, the inspectorate apparently does nothing unless the case is referred to them by the PGs. Occasionally the Review Committees find a doctor 'careful' but bring the circumstances to the attention of the inspectorate, and in these cases an medical inspector discusses the case with the doctor concerned and sometimes with the institution where the euthanasia took place. Usually the problem concerns consultation or the use of an inappropriate drug. When an inspector visits an institution, one of the standard questions asked is whether it has a euthanasia protocol, and if not, the institution is advised to adopt one within three months.[184]

5.4.5 Conclusions concerning the Functioning of the Control System

On first impression, the Dutch control system does not appear to involve much 'sanction pressure' on doctors. Many cases that seem to deserve some specific legal scrutiny are classified (by doctors, but also by the control system itself) as pain relief with life-shortening effect, or abstention, and fall outside the purview of the control system altogether. Of cases that doctors themselves think of as 'euthanasia' some are not reported (although this seems to be much less the case than was generally believed until very recently). Almost all doctors who report are found to have acted carefully. When a doctor is found not to have acted carefully, this rarely results in prosecution or a medical disciplinary case. At the end of the day, out of a somewhat greater number of actual cases of euthanasia, 15,832 cases were reported from 1999 through 2006. Of these, 25 (fewer than 2 per 1,000) of the reporting doctors were found 'not careful'. To date, none of the doctors involved has been prosecuted and only 2 have been sanctioned in medical disciplinary proceedings.

However, before jumping to the conclusion that such a system is all bark and no bite, one should consider the following. In the first place, there have been prosecutions and medical disciplinary proceedings in the Netherlands for doctors who did not report, such as the *Van Oijen* and *Vencken* cases discussed in chapters 3 and 4. There have also been prosecutions of lay persons charged with having rendered assistance with suicide, and these have resulted in several convictions.[185]

In the second place, reporting itself is a form of prospective control: knowing that one will have to report casts a shadow forward upon the behaviour that will have to be reported. The reporting system thus induces doctors not to perform

---

[182] See Onwuteaka-Philipsen *et al* 2007: 206–8.
[183] *Cf* also Onwuteaka-Philipsen *et al* 2007: 210.
[184] *Ibid* at 211.
[185] See chs 3.6 and 4.2.3.3(J).

euthanasia where the rules do not allow it and to carry it out in the right way. Of this there is a great deal of indirect evidence, both incidental but also in the form of the rapidly increasing reporting rate which has not been accompanied by a greater frequency of 'not careful' cases.

The growing use of SCEN consultants in the Netherlands is not only a form of control in advance, but also functions as an institutionalised means of transmitting relevant information to doctors, adding to a variety of other institutionalised (eg hospital protocols) and non-institutional (eg professional journals) ways in which they are kept informed.

Within the control system itself, formal sanctions at the end of the process are not the only stimuli to which doctors are exposed. As we have seen, the Dutch Review Committees ask about 5% of all reporting doctors to provide more information, and in 0.5% (including all cases in which a judgment of 'not careful' is considered) the doctor is asked to explain his behaviour in person to the Committee. In practice, many doctors apparently experience this as a significant sanction.[186]

That few 'not careful' cases are prosecuted does not mean that nothing at all is done. Of the 25 cases of such a judgment in the period 1998–2006, an initial decision not to prosecute was taken in 3 (these doctors will have received a formal notification of the decision, which in itself is an additional reminder that not everything was in order). In 22 cases, a decision not to prosecute was accompanied by a discussion of the case with the doctor, by either the prosecutor or the medical inspector. In 2 cases medical disciplinary proceedings lead to imposition of a sanction. In 2 cases the medical inspector called the attention of the hospital concerned to inadequacies in the local protocol, in 1 case the prosecutors asked the Medical Inspectorate to call the attention of doctors to the problem of consultation (too) long in advance, and in 1 case the medical inspector discussed the case with the consultant.[187]

Such a control system is not focused primarily on repressive control (sanctioning deviation from the rules) but far more on increasing the transparency of medical practice, on transmitting information concerning careful practice to doctors, on keeping doctors aware that by contrast with 'normal medical practice' this sort of medical behaviour is subject to specific scrutiny, and on letting a doctor know in dubious cases that his behaviour was not acceptable. It seems at least highly likely that such a system will be more successful in achieving a high level of conformity with the applicable legal norms (which, after all, on the whole emerged from and enjoy the support of the medical profession itself) than would a system that concentrated on meting out punishment in those few cases of transgression that happened to come to its attention.

Without explicitly saying anything about it, this chapter has been—among other things—an exercise in the application of the 'social working' approach to legal rules,[188] an approach that focuses in the first place on whether and when

---

[186] See n 166.
[187] See the Appendix for these dispositions.
[188] See ch 1.5.4.

people actually use them: apply them to their own behaviour or (by way of expectation or criticism) to that of others. Latent in the phenomena we have described, has been rule-following of various sorts. Patients use the rules when they discuss the subject with their doctor or make general or concrete requests for euthanasia. Doctors do so in their encounters with patients and their families,[189] but also in the decisions they make and in actual euthanasia practice, and in their reporting behaviour. In professional organisations and health care institutions various actors use them in fashioning national or local policy and protocols. Medical professionals (doctors, nurses and others) use them in the exercise of informal social control. In all of these respects, the evidence we have examined in this chapter shows that a great deal of rule-following is going on, and that on the whole Dutch doctors have become very law-abiding. Where there are failures of control, these seem nowadays mostly ascribable to the fact that in a significant number of cases doctors do not classify their behaviour in the way required by Dutch law.

Unlike the situation with regard to many other legal rules, and unlike the situation with regard to euthanasia 15–20 years ago, the participants seem to be reasonably well informed about what the legal requirements are. At least as far as doctors are concerned, very efficient systems for the transmission of legal information are in place (medical journals, the press generally, local protocols, the SCEN programme of trained advisors and consultants).

The Regional Review Committees have proven to be particularly important not only as an institution of legal control, but also from the point of view of legal information. Through the published decisions in their Annual Reports, but also in a large variety of more informal ways, including their participation in training programmes for SCEN doctors, the talks they give from time to time, and last but not least the information about normative developments and persistent problems that spreads from their members to the academic and policy communities to which they belong, they have immeasurably increased the transparency both of euthanasia practice itself and more particularly of the operation of the system of control.

If pressed to explain the apparent success of Dutch euthanasia regulation, the 'social working' approach would point in the first place to the fact that the medical profession itself, from the very beginning and down to the present, has accepted responsibility for euthanasia practice and taken the lead in working out the rules that govern it.[190] For euthanasia itself, most of this took place before the period covered here and is dealt with in detail in the predecessor of this book. Since 1998 the most important contribution of the medical profession to Dutch euthanasia practice is the initiative of the KNMG in setting up what has become a highly-successful system of specially-trained consultants (SCEN). With regard to related sorts of MBPSL, the most important contributions in recent years have

---

[189] See for ethnographic examples the research of Norwood, discussed in section 5.3.
[190] See ch 3.1.

concerned termination of life in neonatology (see chapter 6) and palliative/terminal sedation (see section 4.2.2.4). But also at a local level, doctors and medical institutions have been directly involved in the design of protocols, as the example given in this chapter of the euthanasia protocol of the Albert Schweitzer Hospital illustrates. In short, to put the point in modern management jargon, there is a high degree of 'ownership' by doctors of the regulation of euthanasia, and as the social working approach predicts, this has been associated with a corresponding willingness to follow the rules.[191]

[191] For the much less appealing practices that can take place where euthanasia is taboo, see Magnusson's (2002) study of euthanasia/assisted suicide practice by caregivers (mostly doctors and nurses) specialised in the treatment of HIV/AIDS patients in several cities in Australia and California. Magnusson describes a 'euthanasia underground' that is very effective in making euthanasia available: a hidden 'informal chain of associations between doctors and other care-givers who tacitly approve of, facilitate or directly participate in assisted death' (174–5). The underground euthanasia practice is characterised above all by an 'absence of professionalism'. 'Because euthanasia is an 'under-the-table' procedure, there is no monitoring or accountability, no criteria guiding involvement, and few reliable strategies for achieving death.' In such circumstances 'botched attempts' occur, both doctors and care-givers are put under pressure, doctors get involved in a 'rash or hasty' way in cases about which they know very little, euthanasia is carried out on patients whose situation does not really call for it, and there is an 'all-pervasive culture of deception' (200–02).

Appendix

'Not careful' judgments of Dutch RRCs 2000–2006: principal ground(s) for decision and subsequent history of case

| | | principal ground(s) for decision | | | | | | subsequent history of case | | | | | | | |
| | | substantive | | | procedural | | | mitigation | no charges brought | | | charges brought | | | |
year	case[1]	a) suffering not unbearable	b) existence of treatment alternative	c) patient not adequately informed	d) no or insufficient treatment relationship	e) consultation	f) performance	g) doctor acted 'in good conscience', RRC 'can understand', etc	h) initial decision not to prosecute	i) initial decision not to prosecute; discussion with doctor	j) later decision not to prosecute; discussion with doctor	k) criminal	l) disciplinary	m) outcome	n) outcome not yet known
98–99	—														
2000	9	x						x	x						
	13						x				x[2]				
	14						x			x					
2001	13				x						x				
2002	6			x	x	x		x			x				
	7				x					x[3]					
	12				x				x						
	13				x			x							
	*A	x			x				x						

											warning[8]	repri-mand[12]
2003 7	x				x					x⁴		
10					x		x		x⁵			
11					x		x		x			
13				x	x	x			x			
14	x (coma)			x		x		x				
*A	x (coma)							x				
*B	x (coma)				x		x		x	x¹⁰		
*C	x (coma)				x		x					
2004 5							x		x⁶			
10					x		x		x⁷			
14			x		x	x	x		x⁹			
15				x	x	x	x	x	x¹¹		x	
2005 8					x		x		x	x¹³		
9		x			x		x		x	x¹⁴		
11					x		x					
2006 9	x¹⁵						x		x¹⁶			
2007[17] *A	x (coma)						x				?	? / x
*B					x						?	? / x
*C					x		x				?	? / x
TOTAL (≤ 2006) 25	6	1	1	4	15	6	9	3	8	14		2

Notes over/

Sources: RRC Annual Reports 1998–2006. Further information received from secretariat of RRC; website Medical Disciplinary Tribunals; Public Prosecution

1 Case number in Annual Report of RRCs; cases marked '*' not (yet) in Annual Reports.
2 Medical inspector discusses case with doctor.
3 Also: discussion with consultant; conditional dismissal (*voorwaardelijk sepot*).
4 Prosecutorial authorities request Medical Inspector to call problem of consultation far in advance of euthanasia to attention of the profession as a whole.
5 Conditional dismissal (*voorwaardelijk sepot*).
6 Conditional dismissal (*voorwaardelijk sepot*).
7 Conditional dismissal (*voorwaardelijk sepot*).
8 Reprimand reduced to warning on appeal, Central Disciplinary Tribunal, no 90/2006, 5/12/2006; *Tijdschrift voor Gezondheidsrecht* 31: 165–70 (2007); *Medisch Contact* 62: 436–9 (2007).
9 Conditional dismissal (*voorwaardelijk sepot*) of both doctors involved.
10 Medical Inspector requests attention of hospital concerned to inadequate procedures, hospital makes protocol Conditional dismissal (*voorwaardelijk sepot*).
11 RTC calls attention of Medical Inspector to use of morphine as euthanaticum in hospital concerned.
12 Regional Disciplinary Tribunal Zwolle, no 15/2004, 18/5/2006; *Staatscourant* 17/6/2006, no 136, p 32; *Tijdschrift voor Gezondheidsrecht* 30: 543–6 (2006); *Medisch Contact* 62: 694–6 (2007).
13 Medical Inspector discusses case with consultant.
14 Medical Inspector requests attention of hospital to inadequate euthanasia protocol.
15 Doctor fails to provide Committee with information concerning suffering of patient immediately preceding the euthanasia.
16 Decision not to prosecute after further investigation by the Medical Inspectorate reveals that the requirements of due care had been met (information received from Committee of Procurators-General, 28 November 2007).
17 As of 26 November 2007. Information received from secretariat of Regional Review Committees. Judgments available shortly on website of the RRCs, under 2007 ('*onzorgvuldig*'). Case A involved a woman 70–80; case B involved a man 50–60; case C a woman 50–60. See <http://www.toetsingscommissieeuthanasie.nl/ Toetsingscommissie/oordelen2007/onzorgvuldig/default.asp> accessed 2 October 2007.

6

Termination of Life in Neonatology

6.1 Introduction

It is widely known that the Netherlands was the first country in the world to legalise euthanasia. Less well known, even among the Dutch, is the fact that in the Netherlands termination of life of severely defective newborn babies is also legal under narrowly defined circumstances. Although there has as yet been no legislative change, legal development is far enough along that it is possible to state with reasonable confidence what Dutch law is on the subject.

In this chapter we describe how legal change in the Netherlands came about and what the current legal rules are. We also summarise what is known about actual medical practice and how the system of legal control is functioning. In section 6.3 we discuss some comparative data, in particular concerning Belgium. Some would say the whole state of affairs confirms the prediction of a 'slippery slope' from euthanasia to killing the weak and defenceless—the Vatican has compared Dutch neonatological practice to what was condemned at the Nuremberg trials[1]—so we will end in section 6.3 with some comparative reflections on what is known about differences in actual practice between different countries and over time.

It is useful to begin with a bit of context. The medical behaviour we will be dealing with concerns very sick and often very premature newborn babies. Doctors can keep some of these babies alive with the help of a battery of high-technology treatments, most of which have only existed for a few decades. In the past, the question whether one always does such a baby a favour by keeping it alive hardly arose, since doctors simply lacked the means to do so. And when babies were born with conditions so serious that doctors and nurses thought it kinder to them and their parents to let them die, a number of simple expedients were at hand. As one highly respected Dutch paediatrician was heard to observe, in the early years of his career you would wrap such a baby in non-sterile cloth and put it near a draughty window until nature took its course. He went on to note that in a modern neonatology clinic such simple measures are not at hand: everything is sterile and there are no draughty windows.[2]

---

[1] *Osservatore Romano* [the official Vatican newspaper] (3 September 2004). At about the same time, responsible newspapers like the *New York Times* (19 March 2005) and the *Guardian* (21 December 2004) published thoughtful and accurate articles on the subject.

[2] Personal experience, J Griffiths.

This, in a nutshell, is the root of the problem: While modern medical technology makes it possible to save the lives of many babies who until very recently
would quickly have died, it also keeps some babies alive whose prospects in life
turn out to be so grim that everyone concerned agrees it would have been better if
their lives had not been saved in the first place.

Of the roughly 200,000 babies born each year in the Netherlands, some 1,000
die in their first year (Table 6.1).[3] In over half of these cases, death is preceded by
a decision to withdraw or withhold treatment. There is no reason to suppose that
there is anything unusual about the Netherlands in these respects (see section
6.3.3). However, in the Netherlands in about 100 cases per year, the decision not
to treat is accompanied or followed by termination of the baby's life. It is these latter cases with which this chapter deals.[4]

The vagueness and inconsistency that, as we have seen in chapter 4, surrounds
the concept '(active) termination of life', plays a key and confusing role in discussions concerning medical behaviour that shortens the life of newborn babies. This
makes it important, when discussing the various reports, guidelines and regulations that have been the principal vehicles of legal change, as well as the results of
empirical research into medical practice, to pay special attention to whether the
whole category of 'termination of life', as defined in chapter 4.2.3, or only some
specific part of it, is being covered.

As far as the law is concerned, the main question we will be discussing is,
whether termination of life can ever be regarded as justified, and therefore legal,
and if so, subject to what substantive and procedural conditions.

6.2 The Legal Situation and Medical Practice

6.2.1 The Legal Context

It would be impossible to understand Dutch legal developments concerning termination of life of non-competent patients, in particular newborn babies, without
recalling to mind the most important features of Dutch law on euthanasia and

---

[3] This is among the lowest 'perinatal' death rates in the world (Van der Heide *et al* 1997b: 251).
From a recent report (Achterberg 2005) it appears that the rate in the Netherlands, while low internationally, compares unfavourably with countries such as Finland and Sweden. The two data are not
readily comparable, however, because 'perinatal' death as defined by Achterberg consists of *stillborn
babies* and babies who die in the *first week* of life, while 'neonatal' death as defined for purposes of the
Dutch national studies of medical decisions that shorten life, covers deaths in the *first year* of babies
born alive (of whom roughly 40% die after the first week—Van der Heide *et al* 1997b: 251). To
complete the definitional confusion, the Committee on Perinatal Audit, following the WHO, defines
perinatal death to include stillbirths and 'neonatal' death in the *first 4 weeks* (see Commissie Perinataal
Audit 2005: 8).

[4] We will not deal with an even more controversial—and in practice probably essentially non-
existent—situation: termination of the life of a baby who is not, and will not in the near future, be
dependent on life-prolonging treatment that could be withdrawn or withheld (see Box 6.2, group c).

how it came into being, as those have been described in detail in chapters 3 and 4. In the decade of public debate that preceded the Supreme Court's decision of 1984 in the *Schoonheim* case, holding that euthanasia can be legally justified, it had come to be agreed that 'euthanasia', properly speaking, is strictly limited to the situation of a voluntary request by the patient. The State Commission ratified this consensus in its report of 1985. And since that time, both Parliament and the most active proponents of legal euthanasia have been united in resisting any extension of the term 'euthanasia' or any justification of termination of life beyond those patients for whom it can be regarded as an exercise of personal autonomy.[5]

The emphasis on patient autonomy in Dutch health care law is not limited to the justification of euthanasia. In 1995 the Law on Contracts for Medical Treatment became effective.[6] This law makes self-determination by patients the foundation of the doctor–patient relationship. The law formulates the basic requirement of informed consent in unqualified terms. It creates the possibility of binding advance directives in which a competent patient refuses consent to specified sorts of medical treatment should he later become incompetent. It permits the appointment of a representative to give or withhold informed consent on the patient's behalf, and recognises certain close family members—among them, the parents of the patient—as representatives in the absence of such a written appointment. Such a representative in effect stands in the patient's shoes and can refuse treatment on any ground the patient himself could have done, including the judgment that in the circumstances death is preferable to continued life.[7] Finally, the most recent manifestation of the commitment to patient autonomy in Dutch medical law is the inclusion of the possibility of an advance written request for euthanasia in the Euthanasia Law of 2002.[8]

But despite all this commitment to patient autonomy, the justification of euthanasia in Dutch law has never rested only upon the voluntary request of the patient. From the earliest court decisions on, Dutch judges have referred specifically to the norms of the medical profession as defining the boundaries of legal euthanasia, a position explicitly ratified by the Supreme Court in 1984. And these norms, repeatedly reasserted by the Medical Association and endorsed and adopted by the courts and ultimately, in 2002, by the legislature, require as justificatory conditions *both* respect for the autonomy of the patient and *also* a situation of necessity that the doctor finds himself in because of the patient's 'unbearable and hopeless suffering'.[9]

---

[5] The most prominent representative of this point of view was the late professor of health law, member of the State Commission on Euthanasia and regular advisor of the Government, Leenen (see Leenen 2000: 302*ff*.). Two parliamentary incidents reflect the political commitment to autonomy as setting the absolute outer boundary of the justification of euthanasia: the negative reaction to the suggestion of the Remmelink Committee that some cases of non-voluntary termination of life should be regarded as 'help in dying' (*stervenshulp*) (see ch 4.2.2.5) and the objections raised to the inclusion of termination of life without a request in the reporting procedure for euthanasia (see Weyers 2004: 324).

[6] See ch 3.2.2.1 for the relevant provisions of this law.

[7] See ch 4.2.2.1.

[8] See ch 4.2.3.3(B).

[9] See ch 4.2.3.3.

It is the doctor's duty to alleviate suffering that can be thought in special circumstances to offer a justification for terminating of the life of a patient not capable of making a request for euthanasia. From the beginning this possibility played a role in the background of the euthanasia discussion. A report of the Health Council in 1975, for example, suggested that if in a case involving a new-born baby what was then called 'passive euthanasia'—withholding or withdrawing life-prolonging treatment—is indicated, 'active euthanasia' might also be justifi-able; and the report of the State Commission on Euthanasia in 1985 proposed to make an exception for one specific situation to what the Commission referred to as the 'central principle' that 'intentional termination of life without a request therefor from the person concerned cannot be allowed': the situation in which life support has been withdrawn from a patient in irreversible coma.[10]

Despite the suggestions just noted, by the time—toward the end of the 1980s—that the legalisation of euthanasia had been more or less accomplished, the key role of a voluntary request in the solution ultimately arrived at seemed a formidable barrier to any acceptance of termination of life in the case of non-competent patients, except those who, when still competent, had drafted a written request for euthanasia.

6.2.2 Legal Developments Concerning End-of-Life Treatment

In this section we follow the course of legal development as it took place.[11] With the benefit of hindsight, we can see that the various contributions to the process have not always been entirely unambiguous, especially with regard to the different sorts of situation that can arise, and in particular the situations in which termina-tion of life is thought to be legitimate. In section 6.2.3 we will nevertheless try to summarise the law, as it now seems to be, as clearly and precisely as possible.

6.2.2.1 The CAL and NVK Reports

After the decision in the *Schoonheim* case effectively legalised euthanasia, the Medical Association (KNMG), cognisant of the fact that not all of the problems con-cerning medical practice at the end of life had thereby been solved, appointed a Commission on the Acceptability of Medical Behaviour that Shortens Life (CAL) to report on the legitimacy of termination of life in the case of several categories of not (entirely) competent patients.[12] The CAL issued four interim reports in the period

---

[10] Gezondheidsraad 1975: 27–8; see also Staatscommissie Euthanasie 1985: 44–6 (discussed at n 39 below).

[11] For an exhaustive treatment of the development of Dutch law on this subject, see Dorscheidt 2006.

[12] The earlier history of normative change in neonatology is described in detail by Van der Ploeg (2003). Her historical research reveals that the normative discussion began among, and was to a large extent the work of, a group of doctors trained at the Free University of Amsterdam (a Calvinist insti-tution) and directly influenced by the theologian Kuitert. Central to the perspective of these doctors was the idea that a person is always responsible for the consequences of his acts: in this case, the situa-tion of a patient who, thanks to life-prolonging treatment, has remained alive, but in a state so dread-ful that if one had anticipated it in advance, one ought to have acted differently from the beginning.

1990–93, of which the first (1990) dealt with severely defective newborns.[13] In the same period, the Dutch Association for Paediatrics (NVK) issued a report on the same subject.[14] Both reports were the fruit of intensive discussion with and among neonatologists and were intended to reflect the views of the entire professional group. The positions taken in the two reports are very similar. These reports are among the most thoughtful contributions to legal developments concerning socially controversial medical behaviour at the end of life in the entire Dutch literature.[15] As it turned out, they set the terms for the subsequent course of legal development.

Withholding and Withdrawing Treatment

The CAL and NVK reports deal first and foremost with decisions to withhold or withdraw treatment. If the life of a baby is dependent upon initiating or continuing a life-prolonging treatment, how can a decision to withhold or withdraw[16] such treatment be legitimate? Under Dutch law, a doctor has no obligation to give treatment that according to medical-professional standards is 'futile'; indeed, it is ethically (and legally) improper for him to do so.[17] In this connection, the reports make a distinction that has proved influential, between two basic reasons for withholding or withdrawing life-prolonging treatment: *treatment has no chance of success* and *treatment would be pointless*.[18] In the former case, there is general agreement that the decision to abstain falls squarely within the authority of the responsible doctor, and the wish of the patient or his representative (in the case of a newborn baby, its parents) to have treatment continued is in principle irrelevant.[19]

The idea of 'pointless' treatment is more problematic. As we have seen in chapter 4.2.2.2, it has been forcefully argued that a doctor can only take account of objective 'medical' criteria in deciding to abstain; and since it is based on medical criteria, the decision is up to the doctor just as it is in the case of treatment that cannot succeed. Treatment is thought to be 'pointless' in this narrow sense if it involves a physiological burden to the patient disproportionate to any possible medical benefit, or (because of other medical problems from which the patient suffers) it cannot succeed in restoring the patient to a minimal level of functioning. The idea that 'quality-of-life' considerations could play an independent role in a doctor's decision to withhold or withdraw treatment has been vigorously rejected, it being argued that only the patient himself can refuse treatment on 'quality-of-life' grounds.

---

[13] CAL 1990. A later version of the report (KNMG 1997) is generally more conservative: the 1990 version is discussed here, since it is that version which played a role in legal development.

[14] NVK 1992.

[15] See GB&W: ch 3.3 for a fuller treatment of the CAL and NVK reports.

[16] As we have seen in ch 4.2.2.2, Dutch law does not distinguish between these two forms of abstention from life-prolonging treatment.

[17] See ch 4.2.2.2.

[18] In Dutch: '*kansloos medisch handelen*' and '*zinloos medisch handelen*'. The NVK proposes this pair of concepts as an improvement on the established term 'medically futile' (*medisch zinloos*) that lumps the two situations together (NVK 1992: 23–24, 29–39; see also CAL 1990: 6–7; Spiegel 1997: 12).

[19] Medical authority in this connection is, however, not absolute (see ch 4.2.2.2).

The reports of the CAL and the NVK approach the problem of the justification of withholding or withdrawing treatment from an opposite point of view, one that puts the relevance of 'quality-of-life' considerations in a quite different light. The medical behaviour that requires legitimation, they argue, is not the artificial *shortening* of life, but rather its artificial *prolongation*. Having posed the question in this way, the reports invoke a time-honoured principle of medical ethics: *in dubio abstine* (when in doubt, abstain). Quality-of-life considerations can give rise to sufficient doubt whether the additional life to be won by (further) medical treatment will be of benefit to the patient, that it would be wrong for a doctor to give the treatment.

In the case of severely defective newborn babies the dramatic increases over the past decades in the technical possibilities for keeping a baby alive have led, the CAL and NVK reports argue, to a systematic and troublesome departure from the principle *in dubio abstine*. For a number of reasons—most importantly, to win time in order to make a fully informed diagnosis—doctors have come to apply the contrary principle: *in dubio fac* (when in doubt, act). If there seems to be any chance at all of a favourable outcome, a doctor initially deploys all available means to keep a newborn baby alive. If the baby does not die but the medical intervention leads to a situation that, had it been foreseen from the beginning, would not have justified a decision to intervene, then the doctor is confronted with a choice between continuing treatment that (with the benefit of hindsight) never should have been initiated in the first place, or applying *in dubio abstine* retroactively, as it were:

> Only on the condition that an intervention with which one has begun (without the patient's consent) can later be stopped, is it possible to assure that it is not medical technology, but medical-ethical norms that have proved their value over the years ('in dubio abstine' and 'primum non nocere'), that define the character of medicine and . . . guarantee the well-being of the individual patient.[20]

'Quality of life' refers in this context not to some amorphous and highly personal idea of the worth of an individual human life. As the Health Council much later on emphasised: what is at issue is the 'future quality of life of the child, *as that will be experienced by the child itself*'.[21] The NVK and the CAL give operational substance to the idea of a benefit to the baby in terms of its expected ultimate level of functioning in a number of concrete respects. '[T]he decision should primarily be based on the expected physical and/or mental handicaps of the newborn baby and the limits that these should not exceed.'[22] The situation the NVK and the CAL have in mind they refer to as one in which the prospects for a 'liveable life' [*leefbaar leven*] are too limited to justify life-prolonging treatment.[23] The NVK specifies what it means by a 'liveable life', as shown in Box 6.1, in terms that one can recognise throughout the entire ensuing course of legal development.[24]

[20] CAL 1991: 27.
[21] Gezondheidsraad 2007: 9.
[22] CAL 1990: 17.
[23] NVK 1992: 23; CAL 1990: 7.
[24] NVK 1992: 31–2; see also CAL 1990: 15, KNMG 1997: 72.

Box 6.1 Operationalisation of the idea of a 'liveable life'

- possibilities of communication (verbal and non-verbal) and the establishment of relationships with others
- self-sufficiency for everyday actions like sitting, walking, personal care, household tasks, etc
- non-dependence on continuing (especially intramural) medical care
- capacities for personal development: sight, hearing, reading and writing, work
- absence of suffering (physical and otherwise)
- life expectancy

According to the CAL and NVK reports, Dutch paediatricians are virtually unanimous in the view that refraining from further prolongation of life is legitimate if the baby's prospects are grim in these concrete respects.[25]

The Role of the Parents

Both reports emphasise the importance of the views of the parents. If the judgment is that treatment has no real chance of success, there is, in the words of the CAL, 'no real problem of choice . . . and the views of the parents can therefore play only a marginal role'.[26] If the prognosis is of an 'unliveable life', 'the views of the parents must receive much more weight . . . than seems currently in many cases to be accorded'. In cases in which the 'minimum values' do not unequivocally indicate the proper course of action, it is appropriate for the doctor to adopt a 'modest' position and 'in principle to give the views of the parents a very important role' in the decision-making.[27]

Neither report distinguishes explicitly between two different situations of disagreement between a doctor and the baby's parents: the case where the *doctor thinks withholding or withdrawing treatment is indicated* but the parents insist on further treatment, and the case where the *doctor thinks further treatment is indicated* but the parents insist that enough is enough. In the former case, to which the views just described seem to refer, the question is whether the parents are legally or morally entitled to insist that the doctor give a particular treatment. In principle, not even a competent patient could force a doctor to continue treatment against his professional judgment. Nevertheless, as just noted, the more that judg-

---

[25] A recent documentary film of the practice of withholding or withdrawing treatment in a Dutch neonatal intensive care unit illustrates the use of the CAL/NVP criteria. See P Lataster & P Lataster-Czisch, *If We Knew*, Humanist Broadcast Foundation/Lataster & Films, 2007. (*Cf* <http://www.idfa.nl/en/extra/search/film.aspx?id=30034> accessed 28 November 2007).

[26] CAL 1990: 16. Nevertheless, careful practice requires 'that in all cases the wishes of the parents [with respect to 'help in dying' or the moment of death] . . . be ascertained, and if possible honoured' (*ibid*).

[27] CAL 1990: 16–17.

ment is based on 'quality-of-life' considerations, the more weight should be accorded to the views of the parents.[28]

In the second situation, where the doctor wants to continue treatment but the parents do not, quite different considerations apply. Here the central question concerns the doctor's entitlement to treat over the objections of the parents. Within a couple of years after the CAL and NVK reports appeared, the Law on Contracts for Medical Treatment (WGBO) became effective. Under this law, when a competent patient does not want further treatment, the absolute right to refuse treatment applies, and the professional views of the doctor become irrelevant. If the patient is not competent—leaving aside emergency situations—his rights are exercised on his behalf by his legal representative. The parents represent a young child, and the child's doctor is bound to honour their refusal of treatment on the child's behalf, unless to do so would be incompatible 'with the care expected of a good caregiver'.[29] It would seem, in short, that the parents, deciding on behalf of their child, can in principle refuse treatment for any reason the child itself would be entitled to consider, subject to the outer limits of parental authority. As the NVK observes:

> A doctor who thinks parents are not being sufficiently careful or are not serving the best interests of the child (which after all is primarily entrusted to them), bears the burden of proof.[30]

If the doctor is of the opinion 'that the parents' wish (for example: not to operate) is clearly inconsistent with the child's interests', then, says the NVK, the procedure for temporary removal of parental custody should be used.[31]

Termination of Life

Up to this point, we have been discussing the position the reports take on withholding and withdrawing treatment, a position that has in effect become Dutch law on the subject. The reports describe Dutch neonatologists as being in general agreement with the position set out so far. The only point of real disagreement among Dutch doctors, say the reports, concerns termination of life.

---

[28] See ch 4.2.2.2. The parents must of course be offered the possibility of securing a second opinion, and of transferring the baby to another hospital for further treatment. For application of these principles to cases in which parents seek civil remedies against the decision of a doctor not to resuscitate or ventilate their baby should the need arise, based on the judgment that the medical condition of the baby is so poor that further treatment would be futile, see *Tijdschrift voor Gezondheidsrecht* 1991/28 and 2004/18. In both cases the court held that the doctor's decision that treatment is futile is in principle a medical decision subject only to the marginal test that a reasonable doctor could have come to the conclusion. In both cases there had been extensive consultation and the parents were given full opportunity to challenge the doctor's decision in court.

[29] See ch 4.2.2.1 on these provisions of the WGBO.

[30] NVK 1992: 39.

[31] NVK 1992: 55. As in other legal systems, Dutch law provides for temporary assignment of custody to a guardian if a parent's refusal of medical care is not in the best interests of the child. See Leenen 2000: 170–71.

The NVK report distinguishes three situations in which termination of life might be considered (Box 6.2).[32]

Box 6.2 Situations in which termination of life might be considered

---

(a) as a result of life-prolonging treatment that is no longer necessary, the child has survived, but in a condition that, if it had been foreseen at the beginning, would have led to withholding life-prolonging treatment
(b) withdrawing life-prolonging treatment has not resulted in the quick death of the child and has left it in a situation of unacceptable suffering
(c) independently of any life-prolonging treatment the baby has serious defects that are consistent with life but not with a 'liveable life'

In situations (a) and (b), some neonatologists would consider the use of euthanatica while others would not, but both positions are generally considered legitimate. The CAL considers use of lethal drugs morally acceptable in situation (b) even when this is done preventively to avoid unnecessary suffering.[33] Situation (c) is highly exceptional, among other things because of the possibility of abstaining from fairly routine forms of life-prolonging treatment such as artificial administration of food and hydration.[34] The profession is described by the NVK as divided on the question whether termination of life with euthanatica can ever be legitimate in this situation.[35]

Almost 20 years later, there seems to be no current support for the idea that termination of life could be legal in situations (a) and (c), and we will not discuss them further in this chapter.[36]

[32] NVK 1992: 49–53; the CAL apparently does not consider termination of life acceptable in situation (a).

[33] CAL 1990: 11. The NVK was divided on the acceptability of termination of life in situation (b), but says that almost all paediatricians could respect such a decision; if the parents wish it but the doctor concerned finds it unacceptable, the baby can be referred to another doctor who is willing (NVK 1992: 52).

[34] NVK 1992: 53. As we will see, several later reports similarly suggest that withholding ANH is a real option. In practice, however, condemning a baby to a slow death from starvation and dehydration over a period of up to two weeks—even if the baby itself is kept sedated and in principle not capable of experiencing suffering—is apparently considered so inhumane, so shocking to the sensibilities of doctors, nurses and parents, that it is generally not regarded as a serious option in a neonatal intensive care unit (personal conversation with A Verhagen, NICU, University Medical Centre Groningen).

[35] NVK 1992: 52. Quite apart from possible legal implications, termination of life in such a situation 'it would be medically and morally dangerous, if intentional shortening of life were considered acceptable outside of situations of necessity'.

[36] In a recent report, the Health Council addresses considerable attention to situation (a), noting that there is no support in the case law (the Health Council presumably has *Prins* and *Kadijk*—see section 6.2.2.3—in mind) for the legality of termination of life based only on the idea that the doctor is responsible for the consequences of earlier life-prolonging treatment (Gezondheidsraad 2007: 25–6).

The Priority Principle

Situation (b), in which a legitimate abstention decision gives rise to suffering, seems in practice to be by far the most important of the three. Crucial to the legitimacy of termination of life in this situation is what the CAL refers to as the 'priority principle': termination of life takes place after—and as an extension of—a decision to let the baby die by withholding or withdrawing treatment. As the CAL observed in its later report on long-term coma, since 'the death [of the patient] has already been accepted [when the decision to abstain from further life-prolonging treatment is made] . . . administration of drugs in a fatal dosage can be indicated . . . as a form of help in dying.'[37]

On this view, it is the decision to abstain that is legally and ethically crucial, for it is this decision that necessarily entails the death of the baby.[38] After such a decision has legitimately been made, the only morally relevant consideration left is *how* the baby dies. The priority principle in effect shifts the emphasis of justification from the decision actively to terminate life to the prior decision that the baby is better off dead.

The priority principle has an honourable but little-known prior history in the Dutch literature. When, as we have seen, the State Commission on Euthanasia in its 1985 report made an exception for patients in permanent coma to the requirement of a voluntary request for termination of life, it reasoned in effect on the basis of the priority principle: termination in such a case is only possible after 'treatment that according to current medical knowledge is futile' has been stopped. The legitimacy of termination of life in such a situation lies, in the commission's view, in the 'inhumane deterioration' [*ontluistering*] that the patient would otherwise undergo. Why the State Commission addressed its reasoning only to the case of permanent coma is not clear.[39] In fact, a report of the Health Council had already 10 years earlier suggested that termination of the life of a newborn baby might be justifiable following a decision to withhold or withdraw treatment.[40]

6.2.2.2 The Reporting Procedure

In 1993 legislation was adopted which, as we have seen in chapter 4.2.4.1, authorises the Ministers of Justice and of Health to promulgate a special form on which a case of termination of life (with or without a request) can be reported as a 'non-natural' death. The form they produced includes a list of items on which the

---

[37] CAL 1990: 35. On the idea of 'help in dying' see ch 4.2.2.5.

[38] See NVK 1992: 52.

[39] Staatscommissie Euthanasie 1985: 44–6 (the Commission seems to have assumed that the treatment to be withheld would be artificial feeding). Leenen, leading health law specialist and proponent of the idea that only the request of the patient can ever justify termination of life, and himself a member of the State Commission, later expressed regret that this passage had somehow escaped his attention (interview with H Weyers).

[40] Gezondheidsraad 1975: 27–8.

reporting doctor is required to supply information.[41] In the case of termination of life without a request, the items (insofar as they are relevant to the situation of newborn babies) include the nature and severity of the baby's suffering, the possibilities of relieving it in other ways, discussion of the proposed termination with the parents and with nursing staff, consultation with another doctor, and the manner of administration of lethal drugs. To a large extent, these items track the substantive and procedural requirements formulated by the CAL and NVK.

6.2.2.3 The *Prins* and *Kadijk* Cases

In 1995, murder charges were brought against two doctors who had terminated the lives of babies for whom they were responsible and had properly reported what they had done. In each case, the baby suffered from very serious defects and was not expected to live long; in each case a decision to abstain from further life-prolonging treatment had been made and the baby's death was inevitable; in each case the doctor, in consultation with the parents, decided to administer euthanatica in order to save the baby from dying in an inhumane way.

In *Prins* the termination of life was done in conjunction with the withholding (at the parents' request) of treatment that was considered 'futile' in the circumstances (operations to deal with immediately life-threatening consequences of *spina bifida*). This decision made the death of the baby inevitable, but it was not certain how long the baby would continue to live in a situation of apparently severe suffering that could not be adequately treated in a medically responsible way. At the parent's request, the doctor administered a euthanaticum. He filed a report of a non-natural death.

In *Kadijk* the baby suffered from a fatal and untreatable chromosomal disorder (severe trisomy 13). As a consequence several critical organs were disfunctioning (heart, lungs, kidneys) and the baby was not expected to live long. It was decided in the hospital that in the event of renewed heart or breathing failure, resuscitation would be futile. The parents took the baby home to die, and Kadijk—their GP—was responsible for its care. He knew of and supported the decision not to resuscitate. After a week at home, the baby's condition deteriorated. Its cerebral membrane was protruding through a split in its skull and bled when touched, and the baby was plainly suffering from this. Its kidneys also ceased functioning. Because of doubts about the effectiveness of the pain relief being given (and the judgment that stronger drugs were not a real option) and considering the hopelessness of the baby's situation and the risk that it would die in an inhumane way, Kadijk came to the conclusion that there was no other option than to end its life. After speaking to the paediatrician who had earlier treated the baby and with the

---

[41] See for the original form GB&W: 310–13. In 1998, in connection with the installation of the Regional Review Committees for euthanasia/PAS, the reporting procedures for termination of life with and without a request were separated. A new model form for cases of euthanasia/PAS was provided (see ch 4.2.4.1), but the original form dating from 1993 remains in effect for termination of life without a request (see *Staatsblad* 1998, 280, art 2).

well-considered and explicit agreement of the parents, and having informed the prosecutorial authorities of his intention to do so, Kadijk administered euthanatica. He reported the death as 'not natural'.

The two doctors concerned had followed all of the 'requirements of due care' formulated by CAL and NVK. The prosecutorial authorities recommended against prosecution. In a joint article in *Medisch Contact* (the organ of the Medical Association) the Ministers of Health and of Justice declared that as far as they were concerned what the doctors had done was justifiable.[42] Nevertheless, the Minister of Justice ordered prosecutions for murder, deeming the two cases suitable vehicles for securing legal clarification. In both cases, the doctors were acquitted by the respective District Courts and Courts of Appeals.[43] The responsible prosecutorial officials saw no grounds for an appeal to the Supreme Court,[44] and thereafter have based their decisions whether to prosecute cases of termination of life of newborn babies on the judgments in these two cases.[45]

The upshot of these cases seems to be that the law on the matter is essentially that recommended by CAL and NVK. If the parents agree, termination of life can be justified if necessary to put an end to further suffering in the case of a severely defective newborn baby, where the decision has legitimately been taken to withdraw or not to administer essential life-prolonging treatment in order to let the baby die, but death (while inevitable) does not (or foreseeably will not) take place immediately. The doctor must conform to the applicable requirements of due care and report what he has done to the prosecutorial authorities.

6.2.2.4 The Consultative Committee's Report

A year later, in 1996, a Consultative Committee was appointed by the Ministers of Health and of Justice to formulate requirements of due care applicable to abstention and termination of life in the case of newborn babies and to propose a special reporting and assessment procedure for such cases. The committee consisted of experts in the medical, legal, and ethical aspects of the problem, as well as representatives (*à titre personnel*) of the two ministries and the prosecutorial authorities. According to the committee's report, published in 1997, the creation of the committee was motivated by the fact that doctors were known to consider the existing control system, consisting of a criminal investigation and possible prosecution for murder, unpredictable and offensive, and were therefore not willing to report such cases at all. The prosecutorial authorities were said for their part to have come to the conclusion that the criminal process is not suited for evaluating 'the nuances of medical decision-making'.[46]

---

[42] Sorgdrager & Borst-Eilers 1995.
[43] *Prins: Nederlandse Jurisprudentie* 1995, no 602; 1996, no 113. *Kadijk: Tijdschrift voor Gezondheidsrecht* 1996, no 35. The decision of the Court of Appeals in *Kadijk* is included as appendix II (3) in GB&W.
[44] See *NRC Handelsblad* 22 February 1996.
[45] *Second Chamber of Parliament 2005–2006*, 30300 XVI no 146, p 2.
[46] Spiegel 1997: 6.

In its report, the committee purports to take no position on the acceptability of termination of life of newborn babies. Nevertheless, it explicitly formulates 'requirements of due care' applicable in such a case and proposes that a National Review Committee be created to advise the prosecutorial authorities on how to deal with reported cases, proposals that seem to assume that the behaviour involved can under specific conditions be legal.[47]

Without formulating the 'priority principle' explicitly as a condition of legitimate termination of life, the committee assumes throughout its report that the question of termination of life will almost always be preceded by a decision to withhold or withdraw life-prolonging treatment.[48]

On the role of the parents, the committee follows the lead of CAL and NVK. If treatment has no chance of success, parents cannot require a doctor to give it. But the more the doctor's judgment that treatment is or would be 'pointless' is based on considerations of future quality of life, the greater the weight that must be accorded the views of the parents.[49] Although under the Law on Contracts for Medical Treatment[50] (and the general law on parental authority) it is the parents who decide if a child under 12 is to receive medical treatment, according to the committee the parents cannot refuse treatment that would benefit the child. In the case of disagreement on this between doctors and parents, a judicial order temporarily removing the child from parental custody is the appropriate course of action.[51]

The committee notes that a decision to withhold or withdraw treatment made on 'the wrong grounds' can amount to a culpable omission and give rise to a 'non-natural' death (with disciplinary or criminal consequences). But because 'termination of life' is on its view not involved, the committee does not consider any special procedure necessary for assessing decisions to withhold or withdraw treatment unless this is followed by termination of life. Nor (apparently) does it regard any special procedure necessary in the case of decisions to administer pain relief 'partly with the intention of shortening life'.[52] The influence is clear in this part of the committee's report of the confused thinking introduced into the Dutch discussion of these matters by the report of the 1990 national research (see chapter 5.1.2.2).

As far as termination of life—by which the committee understands the administration of drugs with the 'express purpose'[53] of ending the baby's life—is

---

[47] Spiegel 1997: 25.

[48] See eg Spiegel 1997: 10–11. The committee includes under withholding or withdrawing not only 'advanced or invasive treatment but also basic care such as food, warmth, etc' (*ibid* at p 11).

[49] Spiegel 1997: 23–4. In its formulation of the 'requirements of due care', the committee seems to overstate the role of the parents in the case of withdrawing or withholding treatment on grounds of lack of benefit for the baby: it must be clearly established 'that both parents can agree' (*ibid* at p 28) and 'in principle the wishes of the parents are followed' (*ibid* at p 29). These are rather different formulations from the committee's earlier argument that the role of the parents gradually takes on weight as quality-of-life considerations play a greater part in the decision-making.

[50] See ch 4.2.2.1.

[51] Spiegel 1997: 23–4.

[52] See Spiegel 1997: 8–9, 40–1.

[53] Spiegel 1997: 8; at p 13 the expression 'primarily aimed at' is also used.

concerned, the committee notes that the final decision is up to the doctor, but the agreement of the parents is a necessary condition. The committee follows the lead of NVK and CAL as far as the substance of the 'requirements of due care' in such a case are concerned. It is more explicit and goes into far greater detail, but this need not detain us here.[54]

On the committee's view, decriminalisation of termination of life would encounter fundamental objections on grounds of constitutional and international human rights law. But it argues that the problems currently experienced within the context of criminal prohibition and prosecution could be reduced. The committee proposed three complementary approaches:

1. The further development of criteria and requirements of due care should be stimulated.
2. A multi-disciplinary Review Committee (consisting of doctors, a lawyer and a medical ethicist) should be created to review reported cases of termination of life of newborn babies and advise the prosecutorial officials; in principle, in cases in which the committee finds that the requirements of due care have been met, no prosecution would be brought.
3. A specific prohibition of termination of life by a doctor without the patient's request should be added to the Penal Code; this would afford a better context for the evaluation of such behaviour than that of a prosecution for murder.

According to the committee there is a difference, at least in the experience of doctors, between termination of life and what it calls 'help in dying' (the use of drugs to hasten the final stages of dying). Formally, however, 'help in dying' falls within the definition of termination of life and gives rise to a 'non-natural death' which must be reported. The committee recommended a special, somewhat simplified procedure for assessing these cases.[55]

---

[54] The committee's proposed requirements of due care (Spiegel 1997: 25–31) are confusing on several important points, especially the relationship between the doctor responsible for treatment and the other members of the 'treatment team' (including nurses): there must be 'consensus' over the diagnosis and prognosis (p 27); a decision concerning withholding or withdrawing treatment, palliative care, or termination of life is the responsibility of the doctor but should be 'supported by the team' (p 27); the doctor should 'take their views into account' (p 28); the responsible doctor must ensure that members of the team who do not support a decision to withhold or withdraw treatment or actively to terminate life do not have to be involved in the further care of the patient (p 28).

On consultation, which the committee apparently only considers essential in the case of termination of life, it proposes that the responsible doctor must 'ask the advice' (p 28) of an independent colleague *of another hospital* (which may in practice not always be feasible). Use of the term 'advice' is confusing in light of the fact that in connection with the requirements of due care for euthanasia the more formal term 'consultation' has for many years always been used in this connection. Nor does the committee say anything about what the responsible doctor is to do with the advice he receives.

The committee also proposed a reformulation of the items included in the form for reporting termination of life, to cover the specific case of newborn babies (Spiegel 1997: 30*ff.*).

[55] Spiegel 1997: 41. As we have seen in ch 4.2.2.5 the Remmelink Commission proposed in 1990 that 'help in dying' should be regarded as giving rise to a natural death and therefore fall within the 'medical exception' and outside the criminal law. However, the Government and Parliament had vociferously rejected the proposal.

The report of the Consultative Committee has been quite influential within the medical profession, serving as a source of substantive and procedural standards; it seems also to have been followed by the prosecutorial authorities. But it caused hardly a ripple in the public and political discussion of these matters and until very recently (see section 6.2.2.6), the Government had done nothing with the committee's recommendations.

6.2.2.5 The 'Groningen Protocol'

Until well after the statutory legalisation of euthanasia in 2002, little more was heard publicly about the problem of termination of life in neonatology. Then, in 2004, doctors of the University Medical Centre in Groningen (neonatologists together with neurologists specialised in newborn babies) produced a 'Protocol' to guide the behaviour of doctors in case of termination of life.[56] They did this with the help of a local prosecutor (who could not have participated in the project without at least the acquiescence of his superiors at the national level).

There is some confusion about exactly what category of medical behaviour the Protocol covers.[57] At the outset it proposes to deal with 'active termination of life', defined as the 'administration of drugs to speed up the dying process'. But in the next sentence it limits its coverage to the situation in which the doctor's 'explicit intention' is to end the life of the baby.[58] The rest of the Protocol seems to deal only with an even more limited category, which is revealed when it refers to an annual total of 15–20 cases (according to the national studies, administration of drugs with an 'explicit intention' currently amounts to about 75 deaths per year[59]).

The Groningen Protocol follows the fundamental approach of the CAL and NVK reports and the Consultative Committee: termination of life is legitimate if, after a 'well-founded decision to withhold or withdraw treatment,' the baby remains alive, suffering severely and hopelessly, and there is nothing 'medically responsible' that can be done about the suffering. Most Dutch doctors, the authors of the Protocol assert, find it unacceptable, after having decided that further treatment has become futile, simply to wait until death relieves the baby's suffering.

The priority principle is nowhere mentioned as such and the Protocol is in places somewhat unclear on the question whether actual prior abstention is required. Among those involved in drafting the Protocol an interesting, subtle transformation seems to have taken place, not so much in the way they describe

---

[56] Beatrix Kinderkliniek, Academic Hospital Groningen, 'Protocol actieve levensbeëindiging bij pasgeborenen met een ernstige aandoening [Protocol for Termination of Life in the case of Newborns with a Serious Disorder],' 4th draft, 29 September 2004. See for an account in English, Verhagen & Sauer 2005.

[57] There is similar confusion in the English translation of the Protocol (see Verhagen & Sauer 2005). The same obscurities pervade the empirical studies that have been carried out—see section 6.3.

[58] Implicitly it treats the use of increased doses of pain-relieving drugs 'partly with the intention' of hastening death as unproblematic. It also seems to exclude from its coverage the category of 'help in dying' that the Consultative Committee had distinguished as a special category of termination of life, but nevertheless had insisted involves a 'non-natural death' that must be reported.

[59] See Table 6.1 (9% of 834). In earlier studies, the annual number of cases was roughly 94 (1995) and 98 (2001).

the behaviour with which they are concerned as in the way the descriptive terms are interpreted. In effect, there has been a shift from *behavioural priority* to *decisional priority*. Cases such as *Prins* in which termination of life takes place in the immediate context of the withdrawal of treatment (behavioural priority) are in effect not considered problematic by the authors of the Protocol (see section 6.2.4 for the reflection of this in data on medical practice).

What the Protocol focuses on is the situation of the *Kadijk* case, in which the baby is temporarily not dependent on life-support at the time the termination of life takes place. Apart from palliative care (and, often, artificial feeding and hydration[60]) there is at that time nothing to be withdrawn. However, the baby's ability to survive without life-prolonging treatment is only temporary and a legitimate judgment that further life-prolonging treatment, when necessary, will not be given because it would be 'futile' has been made. It is this *anticipatory decision to abstain* that, taken together with the baby's suffering, legitimates active intervention to end the life of the baby in such a case.[61] It is this narrower focus on an especially problematic group that apparently explains the difference between the 15–20 cases per year referred to in the Protocol and the 75 cases of termination of life per year found in the 2005 national study.

Box 6.3 gives a recent example of the sort of case for which the Protocol is intended.

The Protocol includes requirements of due care derived from those of the Consultative Committee, but covering only the termination of life itself and not the prior decision to abstain from treatment.[62] It assumes that termination will only take place pursuant to a request from the parents,[63] and apparently also—like the Consultative Committee—that the decision will be based on consensus in the medical team.[64] The requirement of consultation is formulated in unusually strict terms: 'The diagnosis, prognosis and unbearable suffering must be confirmed by at least one independent doctor.'[65]

---

[60] See n 34 on the unacceptability in practice of withholding ANH, despite the apparent recommendation of this possibility in the reports of the NVK (n 34) and the Consultative Committee (n 48).

[61] A recent report of the Health Council (Gezondheidsraad 2007: 24) interprets the Groningen Protocol as dealing with the situation of termination of life independently of any life-prolonging treatment. But this is apparently because the Health Council is thinking of life-prolonging treatment *in the past*, whereas what the Protocol contemplates is an *anticipatory* decision to abstain from such treatment when, as expected, it becomes necessary.

[62] Curiously, the Protocol seems to contemplate use both of Leenen's criteria for a judgment of 'futility' and of the 'quality-of-life' criteria of the NVK, which Leenen specifically rejected (see section 6.2.2.1 above). The 'majority of neonatologists in Europe' are said to agree that withdrawing or withholding treatment on 'quality-of-life' grounds is acceptable (see Verhagen & Sauer 2005: 960).

[63] The responsible doctor must satisfy himself that 'the request of the parents . . . is a consistent one'. In the doctor's report, he must specify 'To what extent and at what times [was termination of the baby's life] discussed with the parents?' and 'Did both parents agree to the termination of life?' In the English summary of the Protocol published in the *New England Journal of Medicine* the formulation is slightly different: 'Both parents must give informed consent' (Verhagen & Sauer 2005: 961).

[64] Nothing specifically on this is contained in the Protocol itself. However, the English summary of the Protocol refers twice to 'the final consensus' of 'the participants in the decision-making' (Verhagen & Sauer 2005: 961).

[65] Once again, this is not in the Protocol itself but in the English summary.

Box 6.3 Case of a decision that life-prolonging treatment that shortly will be neces-sary would be futile, followed by termination of life.

Shortly after the baby's birth it was diagnosed with a very serious case of the skin dis-order *dystrophic epidermolysis bullosa*, in which every contact with the skin causes it to come loose. Daily nursing and changing of the dressing was extremely painful for the baby (even when coma was induced, the baby screamed with pain), and the baby's condition was complicated by associated eating and growth disorders and growing auto-amputation of the extremities. The prognosis was for a short life characterised by serious pain and practically no developmental possibilities. It was decided that life-prolonging treatment, which the baby would certainly need, would be 'futile' and would be withheld. At that point, the parents asked the doctors to end the baby's life. There was at the time no treatment being given that could be withdrawn, since stop-ping the daily medical care of the baby's skin was considered irresponsible.[66] The doc-tors considered the baby's suffering unbearable and hopeless; there was no effective way of treating it. It would have been possible to increase the pain relief drastically, thus causing the baby to stop breathing, but in effect this would have amounted to ter-mination of life, and in any case the parents rejected the idea. Following the Protocol, the doctors ended the baby's life when it was about 2 months old. They reported the death as 'not natural'.[67]

Finally, the Protocol requires that termination of life be reported as a non-natural death. In light of the *Prins* and *Kadijk* cases, the authors 'assume that . . . in the circumstances referred to [ie the prior abstention decision and the baby's suffering], and if all relevant requirements of due care have been met,' the prose-cutorial authorities will decide not to prosecute.

The press—in particular, the foreign press—got wind of the Groningen Protocol, and for some weeks in late 2004 and early 2005, media attention was intense.[68] The Protocol was taken by several commentators as a radical new step down the supposed 'slippery slope' from voluntary euthanasia to Nazi practices—despite the fact, which should be quite clear by this point, that the Protocol con-tained little that in the Dutch situation was new.

In July of 2005 the Dutch Association for Paediatrics (NVK) adopted the Groningen Protocol for use throughout the country[69] and later in the year the Government suggested in an answer to questions in Parliament that it regarded the Protocol as a useful step by the medical profession and would take account of

---

[66] Although drinking was extremely painful for the baby, artificial nutrition and hydration was not being given because of the medical risks entailed.

[67] We are grateful to A Verhagen for this example. The baby's death was reported on 12 December 2006, before the new Committee of Experts was accepting cases. The reporting doctor was notified by the prosecutorial authorities on 10 October 2007 of their decision not to prosecute ('the termination of life . . . was carried out in a careful way and was justifiable').

[68] See for example *The Guardian* (21 December 2004); *International Herald Tribune* (11 March 2005); *The Times* (26 April 2005); *New York Times* (10 July 2005). A search for 'Groningen Protocol' on Google (12 January 2006) produced 14,300 hits, of which most appear to be relevant.

[69] Press release NVK, Utrecht, 1 July 2005.

it in formulating a proposal for a special review procedure for cases of termination of life without a request.[70]

6.2.2.6 The Creation of a National 'Committee of Experts'

When in 1998 Regional Review Committees were set up to advise the prosecutor-ial authorities whether a doctor who reports a case of euthanasia has conformed to the requirements of due care (see chapter 4.2.4.3), a parallel national committee to deal with cases of non-competent patients was contemplated. For reasons that were never made public, this committee was not in fact established. The Euthanasia Law of 2002 gave legislative ratification to the Regional Review Committees but, once again, no provision was made for the case of non-competent patients. However, the Government's intention to do so was restated during the parliamentary proceed-ings. Over the years, this intention was reconfirmed on a number of occasions. But despite clear indications of support among doctors, the report of the Government's own Consultative Committee, and requests by the Medical Association and a num-ber of other organisations, until recently nothing was done. There is widespread agreement that the very low reporting rate for such cases, and hence the lack of transparency of medical practice and of effective legal control, has been a direct result of the Government's procrastination.[71]

Finally, on 29 November 2005, the Secretary of State for Health and the Minister of Justice sent a letter to the Second Chamber of Parliament announcing their intention to establish a national 'committee of experts' to advise the prose-cutorial authorities concerning cases of termination of life of newborn babies.[72] It is to assess whether the doctor who reports a case has met the requirements of due care and to forward its conclusions to the prosecutorial authorities. They will make the ultimate decision whether to prosecute, basing their decision on the same requirements, which are taken to define the scope of the justification of necessity in such cases. The procedure is set in motion when the doctor reports the death of a baby as a non-natural one.

---

[70] See *Second Chamber of Parliament, 2004–2005*, no 2145, appendix (15 August 2005).

[71] See eg the report of the Health Council (Gezondheidsraad 2007: 14; *cf* ch 4.2.4.3 for a similar objective of improving the reporting rate in the case of the Regional Review Committees for reported cases of euthanasia). See Dorscheidt & Verhagen (2004) for the history summarised in this section (see also the letter of 29 November 2005, referred to below).

Like the Consultative Committee (see section 6.2.2.4) and the Health Council (Gezondheidsraad 2007: 15), Dorscheidt and Verhagen argue that the European Convention on Human Rights stands in the way of a reporting and assessment procedure for termination of life in the case of non-competent patients entirely outside of the criminal law (as has been accomplished for euthanasia) but that a com-mittee to advise the prosecutorial authorities (as was the case for euthanasia between 1998 and 2002) would pass muster. See Dorscheidt (2006) for an extended argument to the effect that the prohibition of discrimination (in this case, against those with handicaps) in the European Convention on Human Rights makes a non-criminal procedure for reviewing reported cases impossible in the case of termin-ation of life without a request from the patient.

[72] *Second Chamber of Parliament, 2005–2006*, 30300 XVI, no 90. The competence of the committee also includes cases of third-trimester abortion of a viable foetus which suffers from defects that, when it is born, will lead to a decision to abstain from life-prolonging treatment (a so-called 'category 2' case). See appendix 1 on this subject.

The letter of 29 November 2005 assumes that termination of life will be preceded by a decision to withhold or withdraw treatment because the baby is not expected to survive or because the prognosis for its later health is extremely poor. In the latter case the judgment that (further) treatment would be 'futile' is based on the present and future health situation of the baby, in which the items shown in Box 6.4 are considered as a whole in relation to each other. The influence on this list of the criteria for an 'unliveable life' in the NVK's report of 1992 (see Box 6.1 above) is obvious.

Box 6.4 Criteria for the judgment that further treatment would be futile

> • the baby's level of suffering
> • its life-expectancy
> • the burden of future treatment
> • the baby's possibilities for communication
> • its possibilities for living an independent life
> • the degree of its dependency on continuing medical care

If the baby dies as a result of the withholding or withdrawing of treatment, including possible shortening of life due to palliative treatment, 'there is no question of termination of life, but of a natural death. These cases therefore do not have to be reported.' But there are cases in which, while the baby will die shortly, its life is intentionally shortened in light of the 'seriousness of its suffering'. In other cases the baby might remain alive but improvement in its health situation is impossible, with 'constant unbearable and hopeless suffering' as a result and 'no prospect of any form of independent life'. In these cases, termination of life leads to a non-natural death that must be reported to the municipal pathologist. And it is these cases with which the new procedure deals.

The letter of 29 November 2005 observes that 'termination of life of seriously suffering newborn babies . . . must take place with the greatest possible carefulness'. It specifically states: 'If the doctor has acted very carefully, termination of life can be justifiable,' referring in this connection to the Penal Code and to the *Prins* and *Kadijk* cases. The letter formulates 'due care norms' [a novel expression] derived from the case law, the report of the Consultative Committee (which according to the letter had been found by the prosecutorial authorities to 'reflect the case law well'), and the 'Groningen protocol'. The Committee of Experts will use these in judging whether a doctor acted carefully and the prosecutorial authorities will take account of them in deciding whether to prosecute. The 'due care norms' are shown in Box 6.5.

On 14 August 2006 the Secretary of State for Health and the Minister of Justice issued a Ministerial Decree creating the Committee of Experts[73] and on 27 September 2006 the formation and composition of the Committee of Experts

---

[73] Regeling centrale deskundigencommissie late zwangerschapsafbreking in een categorie 2-geval en levensbeëindiging bij pasgeborenen [Establishment of a central committee of experts for late-term abortion in a category 2 case and termination of life of newborn babies], *Staatscourant* 2006, 168 (14 August 2006, effective 1 September 2006).

Box 6.5 'Due care norms' for termination of life in neonatology

---

- the decision to withhold or withdraw treatment must be justifiable (see Box 6.4)
- according to prevailing medical opinion the baby's suffering must be hopeless and unbearable[74]
- in the light of prevailing medical knowledge there must be no doubt with regard to the diagnosis and prognosis
- the parents, being fully informed, must agree to the termination of life, having come with the doctor to the judgment that given the situation of the baby there is no reasonable alternative
- the doctor must consult at least one independent colleague, who sees the baby and gives a written judgment with regard to the requirements of due care; alternatively, the judgment of the treatment team can suffice[75]
- the termination of life must be carried out in a medically appropriate way

---

was announced; it was to begin work on 1 November 2006.[76] However, on 27 February 2007 the decree was withdrawn and a slightly modified decree issued that became effective on 15 March 2007.[77] As of 12 February 2008, the committee had yet to receive its first case.[78]

---

[74] See n 91 on the meaning of 'unbearable suffering' in this context, and note in that connection the specific reference to 'prevailing medical opinion', which seems to indicate an objectified approach.

The letter of 29 November 2005 states at one point that, 'Only actual [*actuele*] suffering supports a decision to terminate life,' which might seem to exclude the possibility of administering lethal drugs immediately before withdrawing treatment (eg breathing support) in order to prevent the baby from experiencing further suffering, a practice that is apparently quite common. But in the context (rejection of the idea that some disorders—the particular reference is to *spina bifida*—always justify termination of life), it seems that what is meant is suffering *in this case* and not suffering *at this moment*. The Ministerial Decree setting up the Committee of Experts (see n 77) does not contain any such restriction, although the explanatory note to the decree does offhandedly (and out of context) repeat the sentence from the letter of 29 November 2005. The recent report of the Health Council criticising what it takes to be an undesirable limitation (Gezondheidsraad 2007: 9, 35; see also Verhagen *et al* 2007a) perhaps attaches more weight than it deserves to the apparently ill-considered and ambiguous word 'actual'. The prosecutorial Guideline (see n 79; *cf* also Verhagen *et al* 2005) gives no indication of any such restriction. Nor (*contra* the Health Council—*ibid* at 35) have the courts or the Regional Review Committees done so in the case of euthanasia (see ch 4.2.3.3(C)).

[75] The prosecutorial Guideline (see n 79) imposes an important qualification: 'This is on condition that the members of the treatment team were in a position to come to an independent judgment.'

[76] Letter of the Secretary of State for Health to the Second Chamber of Parliament, 27 September 2006.

[77] Regeling centrale deskundigencommissie late zwangerschapsafbreking in een categorie 2-geval en levensbeëindiging bij pasgeborenen [Establishment of a Central Committee of Experts for Late-term Abortion in a Category 2 Case and Termination of Life of Newborn Babies], *Staatscourant* 2007, 51 (27 February 2007, effective 15 March 2007) [hereafter: Ministerial Decree]. 15 March 2007 is also the effective date referred to in the prosecutorial Guideline (see n 79).

[78] Information received from the secretariat of the committee. When this fact was recently made public, two of those closely associated with the 'Groningen Protocol' observed that the fact fewer cases than had been expected are being reported is not necessarily due to a failure to report. They suggest that increased use of folic acid during pregnancy and, in particular, the introduction of standard echography at 20 weeks (in time for a legal abortion), have reduced the number of babies born with two of the disorders strongly associated in the past with termination of life (*spina bifida* and the chromosomal disorder *trisomy 13*) (see A. Verhagen & P. Sauer, '*Euthanasie baby's daalt door echo's* [Euthanasia of babies declines due to echo's]' *De Volkskrant* 25 February 2008). This cannot account for the entire short-fall, however, since serious neurological damage due to perinatal asphyxia, for example, would not be affected.

The committee consists of five members: a lawyer (chairman), three doctors from relevant disciplines, and an ethicist (the members whose appointment was announced on 27 September 2006 are a professor of health law, a professor of medical ethics, and three doctors—a neonatologist, a child neurologist, and a gynaecologist). Although the Ministerial Decree contains no such provision, both the letter of 29 November 2005 and the prosecutorial Guideline adopted in connection with the creation of the committee state that the three doctors together have one vote.[79] The committee receives cases from the municipal pathologist to whom the doctor concerned has reported,[80] and makes 'recommendations' to the prosecutorial authorities.[81] Its judgments are based on the 'due care norms' contained in Box 6.5.[82]

Critical Note in Connection with the Committee of Experts

Considering our enthusiastic assessment in chapters 4 and 5 of the functioning of the Regional Review Committees for cases of euthanasia, we are inclined to have high expectations for the Committee of Experts. If this experiment in control succeeds as well as the earlier experiment, the committee will contribute to the further development and clarification of the legal norms concerning abstention and termination of life in the case of newborn babies. The process of external review will become far more transparent and predictable than in the past. All this will encourage doctors to expose their behaviour to external review by reporting cases of termination of life, which in turn will increase the transparency of medical practice and contribute to an open debate about what is going on. These developments will have a feedback effect on the quality of medical practice itself and at the end of the day the protection of the lives and welfare of newborn babies will be improved. This is, in a nutshell, Dutch public policy,[83] and we expect it to be successful.

However, one note of caution may be in order. In giving operational content to what are now fairly general and on some points still unsettled norms, the Committee of Experts will need to be as creative and flexible, and as open to new perspectives, as the Regional Review Committees have been. It is in that connection

---

[79] *Aanwijzing vervolgingsbeslissing levensbeëindiging niet op verzoek en late zwangerschapsafbreking* [Guideline for Prosecutorial Decision-Making concerning Termination of Life Without a Request and Late-term Abortion], valid as of 15 March 2007 [prosecutorial Guideline].

[80] Although article 2 of the Ministerial Decree establishing the committee (see n 77) appears to limit the competence of the committee to 'reported cases', the prosecutorial Guideline for such cases (see n 79) provides that also in unreported cases that come to the attention of the prosecutorial authorities, they can ask the committee for an expert judgment (art. 2.4).

[81] Ministerial Decree, n 77 above, art 2 and 3.

[82] Letter of 29 November 2005 (the Ministerial Decree refers only to the 'due care exercised by the doctor'—art 3). The letter also provides than if the committee finds the doctor not careful, it brings its judgment to the attention of the Medical Inspectorate; an anonymised version is to be published in a 'publicly accessible databank'. The Committee of Experts reports annually to the Secretary of State for Health and the Minister of Justice. These latter provisions are not included in the Ministerial Decree, but will presumably be part of the procedural regulation that the committee is required to adopt; the regulation is also to provide for the way in which the committee carries out its tasks, how and within what period the doctor is informed, cases in which the doctor is requested to appear in person, and the manner in which the committee reports on what it does (Ministerial Decree, n 77 above, art 6).

[83] Compare Gezondheidsraad 2007: 16.

worrisome that there is only one Committee of Experts. Monopolies are not known for creativity, flexibility or openness. The mutual learning and stimulation, and the reciprocal control, built into the structure and procedures of the Review Committees, are not similarly guaranteed in this case. The possibility therefore exists that the Committee of Experts, being subject to no competitive or critical pressure, will behave as an authority unto itself: conservative, formal and restrictive in its approach, or on the contrary idiosyncratic and unpredictable, but in either case without a solid base of support among those regulated and in society as a whole. It may listen above all to the prosecutorial authorities, to the media, to the ministers, or to no one. In short, a single institution presiding alone over a very sensitive and difficult area of normative development and control has its dangers. It would perhaps have been wiser either to set up several such committees—on the model of the Regional Review Committees—or, better still, simply to have added this new responsibility to the task of the Review Committees.

6.2.2.7 Prosecution Policy

How have Dutch prosecutors reacted to the developments described? Reporting, although legally required, is rare: until recently, each year about 3 cases were reported of the 75–90 cases per year of termination of life that the national surveys estimate take place (see Table 6.1, categories C and E).

Verhagen has examined all 22 cases from January 1997 through June 2004 in which the doctor concerned reported the termination of life of a newborn baby (up to 6 months) as a 'non-natural death'. In 14 of these cases, euthanatica were used, in 8 cases pain relief and sedation. The prosecutorial authorities, with approval of the Minister of Justice, decided in all 22 cases not to prosecute, based on conformity with four key requirements of due care: hopeless and unbearable suffering, agreement of the parents, consultation with an independent doctor and use of appropriate means. From Verhagen's discussion of the cases, it seems that the priority principle was followed in all of them: having decided to refrain from further treatment because this was considered futile, the doctor then decided actively to terminate the baby's life because 'it was impossible to reduce the baby's suffering in another, medically responsible way'.[84]

As the letter of 29 November 2005 had announced, a guideline for prosecutorial decision-making was issued by the Committee of Procurators-General (the highest prosecutorial authority) contemporaneously with the Ministerial Decree establishing the Committee of Experts.[85] In general, it tracks the letter of 29 November 2005 and the decree. It explicitly states that the prosecutorial authorities will judge whether the doctor conformed to the 'requirements of due care' (the guideline uses this established term rather than the novel expression 'due care norms' introduced by the letter of 29 November), taking account of the judgment of the Committee of Experts in deciding whether to initiate a prosecution. Prosecution is

---

[84] Verhagen *et al* 2005: 185.
[85] See n 79.

in principle indicated if it is not 'beyond any doubt' that there was unbearable and hopeless suffering or if the parents did not agree. Lack of due care in connection with consultation—if it does not stand in the way of a clear judgment concerning the suffering—is not a sufficient reason for prosecution; in such a case the local prosecutor should discuss the matter with the doctor. Lack of care in connection with carrying out the termination of life does not affect the fact that there was a situation of necessity and should be dealt with by the Medical Inspectorate.[86]

6.2.3 Current Dutch Law on Termination of Life in the case of Newborn Babies

What, in light of the above rather long and at times confusing history, is current Dutch law on the subject of termination of life of severely defective newborn babies? The basic legal facts we have to go on, which on all essential points seem mutually consistent, are as shown in Box 6.6.[87]

In light of these legal facts, it seems safe, despite the absence of a decision by the Supreme Court or any relevant action by the Dutch Parliament, to summarise the

Box 6.6 Sources of knowledge of Dutch law concerning termination of life of severely defective newborn babies

---

- the reports of CAL and NVK (keeping in mind the respect afforded by Dutch courts to the views of the medical profession in cases concerning the justifiability of otherwise criminal behaviour by doctors)
- two prosecutions resulting in very similar judgments by two trial and two appeals courts
- the requirements of due care formulated at the Government's request by the Consultative Committee
- a consistent policy of non-prosecution of reported cases in which the doctors concerned have conformed to such requirements
- the Groningen Protocol, later adopted by the Dutch Association for Paediatrics (NVK) for national use
- the recent establishment of a national 'Committee of Experts', in which connection, as we have seen in section 6.2.2.6, requirements of due care have been formulated which are to form the basis of the committee's judgments and of prosecutorial decision-making
- the prosecution Guideline based on the requirements of due care formulated to guide the decision-making of the Committee of Experts

---

[86] Compare the prosecutorial Guideline for cases of euthanasia, discussed in ch 4.2.4.2.

[87] In May of 2007, the Health Council issued a report on termination of life in neonatology (Gezondheidsraad 2007), specifically intended to contribute to the process of normative development entrusted to the Committee of Experts. Because it appeared after the legal developments dealt with in this chapter, we have not discussed it separately. On the whole, while the interpretation of earlier reports and cases differs slightly from ours—especially concerning the classification of the different sorts of situations in which termination of life may be considered—the general tenor of the Health Council's report and its legal conclusions are similar to those reached here.

relevant law as follows. Termination of life (that is, administering drugs of a sort or in an amount appropriate only for causing the earlier death of the baby, including not only euthanatica but also drugs normally used for pain relief in doses higher than indicated for the relief of pain), is in principle murder, but in the case of a doctor can be justified under the circumstances summarised in Box 6.7.[88]

Box 6.7 Current Dutch law concerning justifiable termination of life of a severely defective newborn baby

- there must be a high level of certainty concerning the diagnosis and prognosis
- a decision to withdraw or withhold treatment on which the baby is or will be dependent for continued life must legitimately have been made[89]
- both parents,[90] being fully informed, must agree
- the baby's suffering must be unbearable[91] and hopeless in the sense that it cannot be alleviated in some other, medically responsible, way
- the requirements of due care must be met, including full discussion within the medical team, consultation with at least one independent doctor (or a sufficiently independent judgment of the members of the treatment team), proper record-keeping, and so forth
- the baby's death must be reported as a non-natural death, that is, subjected to review
- the legal status of termination of life based on current unbearable and hopeless suffering, independently of any concurrent or prospective withholding or withdrawing of life-prolonging treatment, is unclear[92]
- termination of life based only on the prospect of future suffering (an 'unliveable life') is probably not legal
- 'help in dying' constitutes termination of life and the resulting death must be reported as a non-natural one (but it is accepted that appropriate palliative care in connection with withholding or withdrawing treatment may shorten the baby's life, in which case the death is a 'natural' one)

[88] This includes what the Consultative Committee calls 'help in dying'. Despite the position seemingly taken in the 'Groningen Protocol' there is (apart from the early proposal of the Remmelink Committee—see ch 4.2.2.5) no substantial support in Dutch law for the idea that this falls outside the scope of the concept of 'termination of life'. It therefore requires the same sort of justification (perhaps, as the Consultative Committee proposed, with a somewhat relaxed assessment procedure). There seems to be no support in the law or the literature for the suggestion in the report of the national research of 2001 (Van der Wal *et al* 2003: 121) to the effect that administration of euthanatica in connection with withholding or withdrawing treatment does not constitute 'termination of life' (compare Bood 2007: 2295; KNMG 1997: 67, 76).

[89] The occasion on which the decision is to be carried out need not, however, already have occurred (see section 6.2.2.5).

[90] In the Dutch literature predictable situations in which the parents disagree, or one parent is unavailable, or the father of the baby is not the permanent partner of the mother, etc have received no attention.

[91] See n 73 above for the possible additional requirement that the suffering be 'actual'. Verhagen *et al* (2007a), argue that while suffering is a 'personal matter' in the sense that it must be experienced by the individual concerned, this does not mean that it is not objectively measurable even though a newborn baby cannot directly indicate that it is suffering. For pain and discomfort there are external indicia, and it can be clear that 'for every person a given level of pain and discomfort entails unbearable suffering'. Here, as in the case of euthanasia, 'unbearable suffering' seems in practice (eg the *Kadijk* case, section 6.2.2.3; see also section 6.2.4.2 on the use of muscle relaxants to prevent 'gasping') to be used in a broad way to include an inhumane dying process (compare ch 4.2.3.3(C)).

[92] Compare Bood 2007.

Seen from the perspective of the earlier development of euthanasia law and of the Law on Contracts for Medical Treatment (1995), the elements of the law concerning termination of life of severely defective newborn babies seem quite familiar, as summarised in Box 6.8.

Box 6.8 Parallels between euthanasia law and the law concerning termination of life of newborn babies

---

- *the priority principle* reflects the demands of the justification of necessity (if life-prolonging treatment is still being (or shortly will be) given there is no need for active intervention)[93]
- *the baby's (expected) suffering* is what gives rise to the conflict of duties and hence to the justifiability of the doctor's behaviour
- *the requirement that the parents consent* (which would be hard to explain if relief of suffering were the only ground for termination of life in such a case) takes the place of the requirement of a voluntary request for euthanasia
- *the requirements of due care* are in relevant respects very similar to those for euthanasia
- *the system of control* is much the same as that for euthanasia (except that the judgment of the Committee of Experts is not final)

6.2.4 Medical Practice in the Netherlands

6.2.4.1 Data from the Four National Surveys

Let us turn now to what is known about actual Dutch medical practice. The first national survey of MBPSL, held in 1990, had established that Dutch doctors terminate the life of a patient without an explicit request approximately 1,000 times a year. Some small part of this concerned severely defective newborn babies.[94] In light of this finding, and of the CAL and NVK reports, it was decided in the second survey, in 1995, to address special attention to this category of cases, and this was done again, albeit in a more limited way, in the surveys of 2001 and 2005.

According to the 1995 national survey roughly three-quarters of all decisions to withhold or withdraw treatment are based on the judgment that the baby has no real chance of survival, and about a fifth on the judgment that the baby faces an 'unliveable life'. All Dutch neonatologists say they have withdrawn or withheld treatment based on the judgment that the baby has no real chance of survival; almost all have also done so based on the prognosis of an 'unliveable life'. Almost

---

[93] From time to time, an equivalent suggestion has been made in the euthanasia literature (see ch 4.2.3.2(A)).

[94] Van der Maas *et al* 1991: 118, 145. Earlier studies had been limited to a few NICUs (eg De Leeuw *et al* 1996). The NVK (1992: 20) estimated that roughly 10 newborns per year die due to termination of life.

half have administered a drug for the express purpose of ending a baby's life and almost a third more would do so in an appropriate case; a quarter would not do so, but almost all of these would refer the child to another doctor.[95] A more recent study, based on interviews with neonatologists and paediatricians working in Dutch hospitals, confirms that end-of-life decisions are a fairly normal part of Dutch paediatric practice: all neonatologists and almost all general paediatricians have made at least one such decision in their career. Neonatologists, especially, say they almost always include the parents in the decision-making, and that the parents almost always agree with an end-of-life decision. Decisions based on quality-of-life considerations are more frequent in the case of abstention (two-thirds of all cases) than in that of termination of life (about a third).[96]

As we saw at the beginning of this chapter, about 200,000 babies are born each year in the Netherlands and roughly 1,000 die within the first year. Table 6.1 shows the distribution of causes of death of newborn babies in 1995, 2001 and 2005. Comparing the three surveys, it appears that little has changed in the last decade.

In roughly a third to two-fifths of all deaths, no MBPSL is involved. The remaining cases can be divided into five categories (A through E) in terms of the classifications used in the various reports considered earlier in this chapter.[97]

About 85% of all MBPSL deaths of babies under 1 year fall within categories A, B and D. These cases are as a practical matter not currently treated as problematic and are all reported as 'natural' deaths, although as we have seen (chapter 4.2.3) the grounds on which deaths following on administration of doses of pain relieving drugs not indicated for pain relief are properly so classified, are questionable.

The problematic categories are C and E (administration of drugs with the explicit intention to hasten death). These accounted for 9% of all deaths of babies under 1 year in all three surveys, or about 15% of all MBPSL deaths of such babies. Almost all of this falls in category C—termination of life pursuant to the 'priority principle' in connection with withholding or withdrawing life-prolonging treatment—the category with which this chapter has principally been concerned. Category C accounted for about 70 deaths in 2005, and over 80 per year in 1995 and 2001, which would be 5 to 8 times the 15–20 cases per year estimated by the authors of the Groningen Protocol.[98] However, it seems that what the authors of the Protocol had in mind as the group for which it was intended, is category E (if we interpret 'not connected with abstention' to mean: not connected with abstention closely preceding or simultaneous with the termination of life'). In their view, the Protocol applies to the situation in which a *decision* has been made that

---

[95] Van der Heide *et al* 1997b: 252. The answers given in the 2005 study (Onwuteaka-Philipsen *et al* 2007: 121) are not directly comparable because not limited to neonatologists. Twenty-five per cent of all paediatricians have terminated life without a request from the patient (this usually concerns newborn babies), another 15% might do so, and for 60% it is unthinkable.

[96] Van der Heide *et al* 1998: 415. Cases in which the doctor did not follow the request of the parents for an end of life decision slightly more often involve a request for termination of life than for abstention.

[97] See in particular Spiegel 1997: 10.

[98] See section 6.2.2.5.

Table 6.1. Deaths of babies under 1 year, 1995, 2001, and 2005 (percentages of all deaths of such babies)

	1995 N = 299	2001 N = 233	2005 N = 122
sample size			
no end-of-life decision	38	32	[41]**
baby died suddenly	24	20	n.d.
treatment continued until baby died	14	12	n.d.
withholding or withdrawing life-prolonging treatment	57	63	55
not combined with possibly life-shortening drug [A]	26	26	27
combined with possibly life-shortening pain relief [B]	23	29	20
combined with drug* given with the explicit intention to hasten death [C]	8	8	8
intensification of pain relief (not connected with abstention) [D]	4	3	3
drug given with the explicit intention to hasten death* (not connected with abstention) [E]	1	1	1
total deaths under 1 year	1,041	1,088	834

* 'Drug' includes pain relieving drugs.
** Not given in source, calculated from other data on table.

Source: Onwuteaka-Philipsen *et al* 2007: 122; Van der Wal *et al* 2003: 121; Van der Wal & Van der Maas 1996: 181. Estimates based on a sample of all deaths of babies under a year. Because of the small numbers involved, the confidence intervals surrounding these estimates are greater than in the death certificate studies concerning adults.

(further) treatment would be futile and will be withheld (as in the case in Box 6.3 and in the *Kadijk* case, discussed in section 6.2.2.3) but the baby's medical situation is (temporarily) stable and it is not *at the moment* dependent on treatment that can be withheld, so that the use of euthanatica is the only reasonable way of putting an end to its suffering.[99] As we can see from Table 6.1, the number of such deaths in the years 1995–2005 has been roughly 10 per year.

6.2.4.2 End-of-Life Practice in Two Academic Hospitals

Recent research in two academic hospitals sheds new and somewhat different light on the questions we have been discussing.[100] The researchers studied the medical records of all babies who died within the first two months after birth, in the period January–June 2005. They classified each baby into one of three groups: (1) dependent on intensive care, no chance of survival; (2) dependent on intensive care, theoretical chance of survival but with a very poor prognosis; (3) not dependent on intensive care, very poor prognosis and hopeless suffering. 'Deliberate ending of

[99] Personal communication with A Verhagen, one of the authors of the Groningen Protocol.
[100] Verhagen *et al* 2007b; the authors think that their results reasonably reflect Dutch neonatal end-of-life practice.

life' refers in their view to babies in group 3 to whom lethal drugs are administered. No such case was found in either hospital. In addition to data contained in the medical records, all neonatologists who had been involved in the cases in group 2 were interviewed.

Of a total of 30 deaths, 28 (94%) were attributable to a final decision[101] to withdraw (24) or withhold (4) treatment (the other two died despite maximum treatment), a rate higher than in most studies of neonatal end of life care in neonatology.[102] In those 28 cases, the baby had no chance of survival in 18 (group 1). In the other 10 cases (group 2) the final decision was based on quality-of-life considerations, most commonly predicted suffering and predicted incapacity for verbal and non-verbal communication. In most cases, ventilatory support was discontinued, accompanied by alleviation of pain and symptoms. The decision-making in both groups (including the role of the parents) conformed to the requirements we have seen earlier in this chapter. All cases were reported as natural deaths.

Most babies were receiving pain relief before the final decision; in all cases the dosage fell within the normal range.[103] After the decision, additional potentially life-shortening medication was administered in many cases, but it remained within the normal range, and none of the doctors interviewed gave hastening death as the reason for having increased the dosage. The authors note that the role of potentially life-shortening medication as a cause of death may have been exaggerated in earlier studies in the Netherlands, which focused on the intentions of the doctor in defining 'termination of life', rather than on whether the medications used were medically indicated in the circumstances.

In several cases muscle-relaxants were administered shortly before death for symptom management—to prevent gasping—mostly when the parents were insistent that they could not accept (apparent) suffering and agony. The authors note that it has been argued that the welfare of the baby is always more important than comforting the parents, but they argue that the distress of the parents is a legitimate concern (among other things, apparently, because of the importance attached to making it possible for the baby to die in its parents' arms).

---

[101] An important finding is that in 9 cases, two decisions were made: the first, to withhold treatment based on the baby's poor prognosis, was followed by a second decision to withdraw treatment; in 6 of the 9 cases the second decision was because the baby in the meantime was considered to have no chance of survival. The authors note that the phenomenon of successive decisions makes comparison of their results with those of other studies of decision-making based on quality-of-life considerations difficult, since such studies tend to focus only on the final decision. They argue that classification of MBPSL in newborns cannot be based only on the final decision. In their own data, for example, while 10 final decisions were based on quality-of-life considerations, in an additional 6 cases, while the baby was in group 1 (no chance of survival) at the time of the final decision, there had been an earlier decision to withhold treatment based on quality-of-life considerations (see *ibid*, Table 1).

[102] The authors are inclined to attribute the high rate of death due to abstention to the prevailing Dutch approach, that life-prolonging treatment must be justified, and to the 'philosophy of Dutch physicians that when a newborn is clearly dying or going to die despite treatment, all efforts must be made to let the child die in the arms of the parents, disconnected from the ventilator'. *Ibid* at e26.

[103] Two babies were being treated with neuromuscular blockers as part of the hospital's standard treatment for their condition.

In short, from this very detailed study of end-of-life practice in the case of new-born babies, it seems that withdrawing and withholding treatment accounts for almost the whole of neonatal death (the few remaining cases occurring despite maximum treatment), and that medical practice in this regard conforms to the guidelines discussed earlier in this chapter. Death due to life-shortening pain relief seems to be a much smaller category than previously supposed. Termination of life, either after a decision to withhold or withdraw treatment (the situation in the *Prins* case), or in the case of a (temporarily) stable baby who faces the prospect of unbearable suffering (the situation in the *Kadijk* case), is—although legal in the Netherlands—too rare to appear in the practice of two centres in the course of half a year.

What the authors did find, was a small but significant practice of what amounts to 'help in dying', in which the dying process is shortened as a side-effect of the use of muscle-relaxants in order to deal with the distress of the parents at the 'gasping' of their dying baby. The legal status of such 'help in dying' is, as we have seen in chapter 4.2.2.5, an unsettled and controversial topic in Dutch MBPSL law.

6.2.4.3 The Role of the Parents

From a study of the role of the parents in decision-making concerning withhold-ing and withdrawing treatment and termination of life,[104] it appears that, accord-ing to the neonatologists and paediatricians interviewed, in their most recent such case the parents were usually (about 9 cases out of 10) involved in the decision-making and in such cases the decision had always been made with their consent (in about a third of the cases, it was made at their explicit request). A third of the doctors had at least once not carried out such a decision because the parents did not agree (extrapolation gives an incidence for the Netherlands of 20 to 25 cases per year). Most doctors would be prepared to overrule a parental request for an end-of-life decision in an exceptional case; a third of the neonatologists and a fifth of the general paediatricians had had such an experience (the estimated incidence in this case is also 20 to 25 cases per year).[105] All doctors expressed satisfaction with the decision-making in cases of consensus with the parents; most were not entirely happy about cases in which they continued treatment against their own judgment; but only slightly more than half were satisfied in retrospect when they did not accede to the parents' request to discontinue treatment.[106]

Perhaps not surprisingly, when there is consensus between the doctor and the parents the doctor almost always considers the parents able to assess the situation adequately, whereas in about half of the cases of disagreement the doctor consid-ers the parents unable to do so (interestingly, cultural differences do not seem to

---

[104] Van der Heide *et al* 1998; the data do not distinguish between abstention and termination of life.

[105] Unfortunately, the published data do not distinguish here between parental refusals of consent to further treatment and parental requests for termination of life.

[106] A high percentage of cases in which a parental request for an end-of-life decision is not followed involve babies with Down syndrome, where the clinical consensus is that this in itself should not lead to withholding or withdrawing treatment.

the doctors to be a major factor in cases of disagreement: philosophy of life and emotional/relational problems are the most frequently cited factors).

6.3 Comparative Data

6.3.1 Belgium: The Legal Situation and Medical Practice

One can be very brief about the legal situation in Belgium. As far as the law is concerned, termination of the life of a newborn baby is on the face of it murder. However, since there has never been a prosecution of a doctor for the sort of behaviour that would be considered justifiable in the Netherlands, it is not possible to be sure how a Belgian court would react.

A survey using a methodology very similar to that of the Dutch studies (see Table 6.1) has been carried out in Flanders (see Table 6.2). It covers babies who were born alive but died within the first year of life (August 1999–July 2000). Although not directly comparable to the Dutch results because the Dutch data include combinations of 2 MBPSL, the study gives about the same picture as we have seen for the Netherlands.

In half of all cases in which medical behaviour that could potentially shorten life had taken place, the doctor had the explicit intention of hastening the baby's death and in a third, the possibility that this might be the result was taken into account. In two-thirds of all these cases the doctor considered that the baby had no real chance of survival and in one-third that there was no hope of a 'bearable future'.[107] Over 90% of Flemish doctors are prepared to withhold or withdraw life-prolonging treatment and almost 70% would be prepared to terminate the life of a baby.[108] The rate of termination of life is apparently only marginally lower than that in the Netherlands (categories C and E on Table 6.1).

From an interview study with the doctors involved in 136 of the 143 cases in the Flemish study in which an end-of-life decision had been taken,[109] it appears that the parents were consulted in 84% and in a quarter of these cases the parents explicitly requested the course of action. Parents were consulted more frequently (95%) when 'quality-of-life' considerations were involved than when there was no chance of survival (79%). In the 17 cases in which lethal drugs were used, the parents explicitly requested this in 9, were consulted but made no explicit request in 5, and were not consulted in 3.

---

[107] Deliens *et al* 2005: 1317, 1318.

[108] *Ibid* at 1319. It seems, from a study based on the sample discussed in the text, that the religious beliefs of the doctor are not associated with the frequency of medical behaviour that potentially shortens life nor with the place allowed for 'quality-of-life' considerations in the decision-making. It does apparently have some effect on the sort of life-shortening behaviour chosen and on the doctor's characterisation of his intention. See Provoost 2005: ch 6.

[109] See Provoost 2005: ch 4.

Table 6.2. Deaths of babies under 1 year, Flanders,
1999–2000 (percentages of all deaths of babies <1 year)

no end-of-life decision:	
baby died suddenly	23
treatment continued until baby died	20
withholding or withdrawing treatment	34
pain relief with potentially life-shortening effect	16
administration of lethal dose or lethal drug	7

Source: Deliens *et al* 2005: 1316–17. Sample size = 253.

6.3.2 A Qualitative Comparison of Belgium and the Netherlands

Vermeulen, a former intensive care nurse, has studied the way staff members and parents come to decisions about the treatment of extremely premature babies.[110] His research took place for six months each in two neonatal intensive care units, one in the Netherlands, at the Academic Medical Centre of the University of Amsterdam, the other in the Dutch-speaking part of Belgium, at Ghent University Hospital. He observed discussions between staff members and between staff members and parents. A total of 23 cases were closely studied, of which 14 are described at length in the book. On both wards the technological imperative—the tendency to apply every possible treatment—was only partly in evidence. Staff were constantly concerned that they were intervening too much and keeping babies alive with severe handicaps.

The biggest difference between the two wards lay in the different gestational age at which it was considered appropriate to start intensive care treatment. The ward in Amsterdam in principle only provided intensive care for babies born after 26 weeks. At a gestational age of less than 26 weeks the doctor concerned estimated the life chances of the baby and decided whether to commence treatment. In Ghent the doctors started intensive care treatment for all babies over 22 weeks. In both wards treatment was at first provisional and the legitimacy of further treatment was based on the baby's response. In one case, for example, it seemed immediately after birth that a baby's chances of survival were slim so it was not given breathing support but brought to the mother and father to die. After a while the baby started to breathe and the doctor took it to the intensive care ward; after the baby proved its viability with supportive care it was put onto intensive care treatment.

At the time of Vermeulen's research, termination of life with euthanatica (independently of withdrawal of treatment) was not practised in either ward. Nevertheless, Vermeulen observed cases in which life-shortening drugs were given

---

[110] Vermeulen 2001. See also Mesman 2002 for a qualitative study of neonatological practice in a Dutch neonatal intensive care unit (together with a similar study in a NICU in the United States).

to 'accompany' the withdrawal of treatment: in several cases he describes (in both ICUs) morphine/Dormicum and/or muscle-relaxants were used.[111]

On both wards it was the dependency of the child on life-prolonging intensive care treatment that gave rise to decision-making whether or not the child should be allowed to die. If a child was no longer dependent on intensive treatment, terminating life in light of the baby's prognosis was not considered an available option. Thus, in a case in which a child briefly needed intensive care, and it was only afterwards that extensive brain damage appeared, there was no longer thought to be any possibility of 'correcting' the life-prolonging effect of initial treatment. On both wards, the importance of coming to a decision on a child's future before it no longer required intensive treatment played a major role in the medical decision-making and in the communication with parents.

In some situations, parents had only limited possibilities to influence the decision-making. When there was no chance of survival, the decision not to treat or not to continue treatment was seen as a medical decision in which parents have no say. In cases where there was extreme brain damage the decision was also seen as essentially 'medical' and the role of the parents in the decision-making was limited. In Amsterdam, where children under 26 weeks of gestational age were not automatically given intensive treatment, the parents likewise had little or no say in the matter (partly due to a lack of time to discuss it with them).

In other cases, the parents normally had an important role in the decision-making. This was especially the case in situations of doubt about the diagnosis and the prognosis for (the quality) of the later life of the child, which was seen in the perspective of the specific situation of the child and its parents. The staff wanted the decision-making to be a 'joint venture' combining medical and social considerations.

Staff members talked to parents in a way that invited them to contribute to the decision-making and parents who were not able or did not wish to do this were seen as a problem. Parents were informed about the risks and chances in metaphorical language and with euphemisms to keep them from jumping to conclusions prematurely, because staff wanted to involve them in the interpretation of medical facts as they emerged.

Vermeulen's qualitative study confirms the impression from the quantitative studies that medical practice in relation to very ill newborn babies in the two countries is similar. In the two wards he studied, termination of life seems not to have been an acknowledged practice, although in both wards behaviour that falls within the definition did take place in connection with the withdrawal of treatment.

---

[111] Vermeulen 2001: 105, 142, 255, 257–8, 329. See Vermeulen 2003: 294 for a case he observed in the Amsterdam NICU where, after a period of *in dubio fac* in which the baby had become independent of intensive care, it appeared that serious brain damage had taken place. An apparently legitimate decision was taken to refrain from further life-prolonging treatment, and when the baby experienced renewed problems with breathing no breathing support was given. Drugs were then administered to end the baby's life, in order to spare it the suffering of suffocation. Vermeulen regards this as a case in which the 'termination of life' was not really a consequence of a decision to abstain from life-prolonging treatment, since the baby's breathing problems were limited and could easily have been dealt with.

6.3.3 Other European Countries

Is the level of termination of life that the Dutch and Belgian studies reveal what one would expect or is it unusually high or low? One could approach such a question empirically in two ways: by making a temporal comparison (is the level higher than it was in the past?) or by making a geographic comparison (is the level higher than it is elsewhere?).

A carefully done temporal comparison might help answer the question whether legalisation of euthanasia has led to termination of life without a request, although it would obviously be very hard to isolate the legal variable from a host of other contemporaneous social changes. However that may be, temporal comparison is impossible because there are no relevant data available for earlier than 1995.[112]

Geographic comparison with a number of European countries is possible, thanks to a recent comparative study.[113] The study was carried out in 1996–97 and secured data from 1,235 doctors working in 122 neonatal intensive-care units in Italy, Spain, France, Germany, the Netherlands, the UK and Sweden. Most doctors in all countries except Italy reported having at least once 'set limits to intensive interventions', but the number reporting having done so because of a 'poor neurological prognosis' was often rather lower, especially in Italy, Spain and Germany.[114] In all countries except Italy, most doctors accept the risk of earlier death as a side effect of pain relief for a baby with no real chance of survival; in France and the Netherlands, the proportion reporting having given such pain relief is about 90%, and in Sweden about 80%. Of the countries covered, only in the Netherlands and France did substantial numbers of doctors report having administered lethal drugs. The French rate (86%) is almost double that of the Netherlands (45%).

Another report from the same study focuses on attitudes of neonatologists in a number of European countries toward withholding or withdrawing treatment because of a poor neurological prognosis. Dutch, Swedish and UK doctors tend to emphasise future 'quality of life' as particularly important in the decision-making, Italian doctors 'sanctity of life', with Spain, France and Germany in between. Termination of life with pain relieving drugs or euthanatica was not covered in the study.[115]

[112] We do know from anecdotal evidence from persons active in the early days of neonatology, and even earlier—in the Netherlands, Belgium, and elsewhere—that termination of life took place. But we have no way of knowing how frequently it took place.

[113] Cuttini *et al* 2000. A survey of the literature between 1970 and 1995 shows rates (percentages of all deaths) of all 'end-of-life decisions' in NICUs, taken together, ranging from 14% of all deaths (US, 1970–72) to 87% (Netherlands, 1995); after 1990, the rate is well over 50% in all studies. The data derive from the US, the UK, Denmark, the Netherlands and Canada. In all studies except those in the Netherlands, only one NICU was involved (Kollée *et al* 1999).

[114] A more recent Spanish study of 330 deaths in 15 neonatal intensive care units in 1999 shows that 52% of all deaths occurred after an abstention decision. See Grupo de Trabajo 2002.

[115] Rebagliato *et al* 2000. In a related attitude study, doctors in NICUs in the same countries (with Luxembourg added) were asked how they would handle a paradigmatic case of extreme prematurity (24 weeks). Most doctors, except in the Netherlands, would begin intensive care; 63% of the Dutch doctors would not. Should the baby's condition deteriorate substantially, most doctors in France, the

6.3.4 How Meaningful Are Data on 'Termination of Life' in Neonatology?

In chapter 4.2.3 we discussed the definition of 'termination of life', whose justifiability and extent in actual practice in the neonatological context are the central subject of this chapter. All of the data presented in this chapter are based on research that sets more or less arbitrary limits on what is treated as 'termination of life'. The comparative European research does not treat the use of non-indicated doses of pain relieving drugs as termination of life. The Dutch and Belgian data do reveal the frequency with which pain relieving drugs are administered expecting that this will lead to the baby's death. But even in the research done in these two countries, an unknown amount of what amounts to termination of life seems to get classified as 'pain relief'.

This is a point on which qualitative research can shed some light. Vermeulen's comparative study of medical practice in a Belgian and a Dutch neonatal intensive care unit (see section 6.3.2) shows that even where termination of life is not regarded as a possibility, it in fact takes place as an adjunct to—and classified together with—the withdrawal of treatment. Griffiths[116] has described the discussion of a similar case that he participated in as a member of a medical ethics working group (see Box 6.9).

Several recent studies support the judgment that the sort of behaviour involved in this case is quite common, and that the difficulty doctors experience in classifying their behaviour in the legally 'correct' way is characteristic of the operation of the legal control system.[117]

The amount of 'termination of life' would be much higher if 'pain relief' in non-indicated doses were so classified,[118] and to the extent this is the case, all available quantitative research—which, like the reports and protocols discussed above, largely excludes pain relief from consideration—underestimates the amount of such behaviour. What doctors in the Netherlands are generally thought to be required to report to the prosecutorial officials as 'termination of life' is thus an unknown fraction of the behaviour that calls for substantive justification and

---

Netherlands and Luxembourg, and to a lesser extent also Sweden, the UK, Spain and Lithuania would favour withdrawing treatment. There were wide differences between countries in the extent to which doctors would involve parents in the decision-making and allow their decision to be influenced by the views of the parents.

[116] Griffiths 2007b (a few stylistic changes have been made in the description).

[117] See Kleijer's study (2005) of abstention decisions in 36 Dutch adult intensive care units. Compare the findings of the 2005 national survey concerning the way doctors classify their behaviour for purposes of the reporting regime (see ch 5.4.3 for these findings and for further discussion).

[118] Provoost (2005: ch 5) shows that reclassification by an expert panel of the way doctors report their behaviour, based on the probable lethal effectiveness of the drugs used leads to a considerable increase in the frequency of termination of life (at least 7 of 40 cases of pain relief with a possible life-shortening effect were reclassified as use of lethal drugs). Verhagen's recent research (see section 6.2.4.2), however, suggests that this problem may be of more modest proportions—at least in the Netherlands—than previously has been assumed.

Box 6.9 'Intentions' and the classification of MBPSL in neonatology

A baby was born with severe spina bifida. According to the professional norms applicable to this sort of situation, any of the various surgical measures that might have been taken were considered 'medically futile' so the decision was taken to abstain from any life-prolonging treatment. The parents agreed with this decision, but were insistent that the baby must not suffer as a result of it.

The decision to abstain necessarily entailed the death of the baby. However, it might have taken some weeks before this would occur. In the meantime, the baby would experience pain if nothing were done to prevent it. A heavy dose of a drug used for pain relief was administered and the baby died shortly thereafter. The doctors reported the baby's death as a 'natural' one.

In the discussion in the medical ethics working group, the responsible doctors consistently described what they had done as 'pain relief'. There was some discussion about changing medical opinion on the question whether newborn babies experience much pain—apparently in the past it was believed that this was not the case and nothing much was done by way of pain relief. Later on, opinion had changed and *spina bifida* was taken to involve acute pain which was aggressively treated. But, said the doctors, they were having increasing doubts about the actual level of pain experienced by such babies. When someone in the working group asked what sort of pain relief would have been necessary just to deal with the baby's pain, the answer was that Tylenol would probably have sufficed.

This answer was completely unexpected. It lead immediately to the question: 'I thought you said you administered [whatever the drug was] to relieve the baby's pain.' To which the answer was, 'Yes, we did. But we also wanted the baby to die as quickly and humanely as possible.' And to this the reply was, 'How can you call it pain relief when you yourself say Tylenol would have been enough.' Answer: 'But it was pain relief: we used [drug X], which is considered very appropriate for relieving pain, but we just gave rather more than we otherwise would have done.' And so forth.

What were these doctors doing and why were they doing it? Were they lying when they reported the death as a 'natural' one, whereas they 'knew' it was not really due to pain relief? That would be a facile interpretation of what was going on. 'Pain relief' was not just a characterisation they used to avoid having to account for what they had done; it was the characterisation they themselves used in thinking and talking about their behaviour. It seemed, for them, the natural way to look at what had happened. Were they, then, confused about what had happened? There seems to be no evidence for this. They knew exactly what they had done and why and how the baby had died. The point is that the idea of 'intent' is subject to very different interpretations, and that the way doctors think about their 'intentions' (which in their view have in the first place to do with the prevention of suffering) does not afford a stable basis for classifying their behaviour for purposes of legal control or empirical research. It is also quite different from the way a lawyer thinks about intentions.

procedural control. This applies a fortiori to countries in which the whole subject is legally, ethically and empirically taboo.

6.3.5 Concluding Reflection

As far as one can tell from the quantitative and qualitative data surveyed in sections 6.3.1 and 6.3.2, medical practice in the case of very ill newborn babies is largely similar in the Netherlands and in Flanders. The fact that termination of life takes place at about the same rate in both countries, whereas at least some of it is legal in one and all of it is on the face of things illegal in the other, suggests that the legal variable may not be very important as a determinant of the way doctors treat severely defective newborn babies. Quantitative comparisons with other European countries suffer from a variety of methodological and conceptual difficulties but do tend to point in the direction of a generally similar conclusion.

For reasons we have seen, temporal or geographic comparisons using the sort of quantitative data currently available is not adequate to the task of answering the question whether the rate of termination of life of newborn babies in the Netherlands and in Belgium is high, normal, or low relative to the rate in other countries, nor, a fortiori, for answering the question whether legalisation of euthanasia in either country is responsible for whatever differences there may be.

Despite these conservative caveats, let us end with a slightly more daring conclusion. The applicable norms in the Netherlands have assuredly changed in the direction of open acceptance of the legitimacy of termination of life of severely defective newborn babies. As we have shown in this chapter, the influence on these changes of the way euthanasia had earlier been legalised and regulated is obvious. In this sense, one might speak of a normative slippery slope. But where is it sliding to? Some part of all the termination of life that is in fact taking place (as it is in other countries) is now explicitly recognised as calling for formal regulation. Substantive criteria, procedural requirements, and a control system are all in place. Partly because legalisation has not yet been officially recognised by the Government, so that the risk of criminal prosecution remains real, partly because the new system of initial review by a national Committee of Experts has not yet had time to prove itself, and partly because of the unfortunate way that termination of life is still defined in terms of the doctor's subjective intention rather than in terms of actual behaviour and medical standards, it would be fair to say that control over termination of life of severely defective newborn babies cannot yet be regarded as legally adequate. And because of an apparently low reporting rate, it is certainly not effective. What one can be sure of, however, is that it is better than in other countries. In short, as was earlier the case with euthanasia, the Dutch are slipping into ever more transparency of medical practice and ever greater legal control of highly precarious medical behaviour. And along the way, the paediatric profession has taken the lead in developing the sort of regulation of abstention practice that is badly needed not only in neonatology, but also more generally.

Appendices

Appendix 1: Third-Trimester Abortion

A form of termination of life closely related to that in neonatology but that has not played much of a role in the public discussion in the Netherlands concerns third-trimester abortion. Dutch law permits abortion only before the foetus can reasonably be considered capable of surviving outside the womb, and this is generally interpreted to mean 24 weeks. Once the foetus is in that sense viable, abortion is illegal. If serious, non-treatable defects are first diagnosed later in the pregnancy, and the woman urgently requests an abortion, the responsible doctor is confronted with a dilemma similar to that of termination of life in the case of a newborn child.

The Dutch Association for Obstetrics and Gynaecology (NVOG) has adopted a Guideline for such situations that largely derives from the developments in neonatology described in this chapter.[119] If the foetus can only be expected to survive after birth briefly or not at all, the criterion of viability is not met, and abortion is legal.[120]

If the foetus would have a chance of survival after birth, but only if given life-prolonging treatment that would be withheld because it would lead to an 'unliveable life', or if the baby might live without life-prolonging treatment but in circumstances such that termination of life would be considered legitimate, the NVOG considers abortion acceptable.[121] If the foetus survives the abortion, the NVOG observes that recommended practice in the case of severely defective newborns suggest that life-prolonging treatment should not be commenced; the NVOG recommends that gynaecologist and paediatrician should have agreed on this course of action before the abortion. The NVOG proposes a number of procedural rules of careful practice generally similar to those for other MBPSL.

In 1998 a Consultative Committee on Late Abortion appointed by the Minister of Health produced a report which largely follows the position of the NVOG and of the Consultative Committee on Termination of Life in Neonatology (discussed in section 6.2.2.4).[122] The committee proposed a national review committee for these cases.

The competence of the recently created Central Committee of Experts on Late Term Abortion and Termination of Life of Newborn Babies (see section 6.2.2.6

---

[119] NVOG 1994 (discussed in GB&W: 127).

[120] This position is confirmed in the letter of 29 November 2005 (n 72) and the prosecutorial Guideline (n 79). The guideline notes that the requirements of the abortion law must be met and that the death of the foetus must be reported as a non-natural one. The NVOG set up an internal review committee for such cases in 2004, and it reviews approximately 20 reported cases per year, forwarded to it by municipal pathologists (information from G Zeeman, chairman of the NVOG review committee).

[121] The prosecutorial Guideline (n 79) defines the category for which the defence of necessity is available as follows: 'according to medical professional standards it is certain that the disorders of the fetus are of such a nature that medical treatment after birth will be medically futile'.

[122] See Overleggroep late zwangerschapsafbreking 1998.

above) includes, as its name indicates, third-trimester abortion (of a potentially viable foetus) as well as termination of life of newborn babies.[123] In general, in the various documents relating to the committee, the treatment of the two situations, and the applicable requirements of due care, are similar.

Research in one Dutch province (North-Holland) in the early 1990s revealed that more than half of all gynaecologists had performed such a third-trimester abortion and that the practice existed in almost three-quarters of all hospitals.[124] The total number of cases averaged 21 per year (6% of all live or stillbirths involving similar severe defects; about one per ten thousand births). In most of these cases the defect would quickly have been fatal even with extra-uterine life-prolonging treatment (these are thus legal abortions). In a few cases life-prolonging extra-uterine treatment would have been possible but would have led to an 'unliveable life'; in a few cases non-futile life-prolonging treatment might have been possible; and in one case the child might have survived without life-prolonging treatment, but the defect was so serious that it arguably would have been legitimate to have considered termination of the baby's life had no abortion taken place. The requirements of due care proposed by the Association for Obstetrics and Gynaecology (NVOG) were almost always followed, except that in 88% of all cases the death of the foetus was reported as a 'natural death' (more than half of all respondents and two-thirds of those who had performed such an abortion were of the opinion that the death in such a case is a 'natural' one). Although there are said to have been a number of cases reported to the prosecuting authorities (see GB&W: 232), we know of no prosecutions nor of any court decisions clarifying the law on the matter.

Appendix 2: The Case of Coma (and PVS) Patients

The second CAL report (CAL 1991) dealt with patients in long-term coma or 'persistent vegetative state' (PVS), defined as a severe and irreversible form of loss of consciousness in which all communication and normal movement are impossible.[125] It is this report that contains the CAL's most extensive discussion of the legitimacy of withdrawing or withholding treatment in the case of a non-competent patient, with as central argument the idea that it is prolonging treatment, not ending it, that requires legitimation. The legitimacy of termination of life is dependent on the 'priority principle': use of euthanatica to terminate life

---

[123] In connection with this new review procedure the NVOG produced a 'model protocol' covering the requirements of due care and the procedure to be followed in cases both of viable and non-viable foetuses (NVOG 2007).

[124] Van der Wal, Bosma & Hosman-Benjaminse 1996; Bosma, Van der Wal & Hosman-Benjaminse 1996.

[125] CAL 1991: 5–7. In 1994 the Health Council issued a thoughtful and carefully researched report on patients in a 'vegetative state' (Gezondheidsraad 1994); on the whole, the positions taken are very similar to those of the CAL.

should only be considered once it has been decided to discontinue the existing treatment, including artificial feeding.[126]

In early February of 1992 the highest authority of the prosecutorial system (the Committee of Procurators-General) announced its decision, with which the Minister of Justice agreed, not to prosecute a specialist who had ended the life of a 70-year-old, irreversibly comatose patient. The man, who had been found lying unconscious on the street, was brought to hospital and resuscitated (*in dubio fac*). It then appeared that he had had a heart attack that had resulted in severe brain damage from which the chance of recovery was negligible. Since continuation of treatment in these circumstances was considered futile, artificial respiration was stopped in the expectation that the man would quickly die. This did not happen, but his breathing was irregular and in the opinion of the doctor he was suffering severely. After extensive consultation with colleagues, the doctor came to the conclusion that termination of life with a euthanaticum was unavoidable, and he therefore carried it out.

In answering questions in Parliament about the decision not to prosecute, the Minister of Justice said that this was based on 'the combination of concrete, special circumstances, which in this case would have led to a successful defence of [necessity]'. Furthermore, the Procurators-General were of the view that their decision in this case created no 'precedent'.[127] In the predecessor of this book, we wrote that it nevertheless seemed to us likely, in light of the cases discussed in this chapter dealing with termination of life in the case of newborn babies, that the decision not to prosecute accurately reflected emergent Dutch law.[128] There seems to have been no relevant legal development in the years since 1992, but the ongoing legal development concerning newborn babies discussed in this chapter would seem, by analogy, to give more recent support to our earlier conclusion.

---

[126] As early as 1985, the State Commission on Euthanasia had, as we have noted in section 6.2.2.1, proposed that long-term coma should be an exception to its key principle, that termination of life is only justifiable if done at the explicit request of the person concerned.

[127] *Second Chamber of Parliament 1991–1992*, appendix, no 394. From a newspaper account of the case (*De Volkskrant* (14 February 1992)) the following additional facts appear: The decision was preceded by intensive discussions with the patient's family and GP to ascertain what his wishes would have been. Two independent doctors were consulted, and the responsible doctor discussed the case with nursing personnel and with the deceased's 'spiritual advisor'. He informed the coroner of his proposed action beforehand and reported the case afterwards.

[128] GB&W: 131.

Part II

Belgium

7

Belgium and the Belgian
Health Care System

In this chapter we provide the reader with some necessary information about the context in which Belgian euthanasia law is developing. In section 7.1 we describe the political and constitutional background, essential to an understanding of chapters 8 (legal change) and 9 (current law). In section 7.2 we introduce the Belgian health care system. This section deals with the institutional background in which euthanasia (and other MBPSL) takes place, and is particularly relevant in connection with chapter 9 (and to a lesser extent chapter 8). We close the chapter with some information on public and professional opinion with respect to euthanasia (section 7.3).

7.1 Belgian Political Structure and Culture

In order to understand the process of legal change concerning euthanasia in Belgium it is important to keep in mind that as a federal state (and monarchical parliamentary and proportional representative democracy) Belgium has a particularly complex political and constitutional structure.[1] Belgian federalism is organised on the basis of a double subdivision into so-called 'Communities' and 'Regions', each having its own legislative and executive jurisdiction. There are three constitutionally-recognised 'Communities' of which the Dutch and French communities are most important.[2] These communities are mainly competent in relation to specific subject matters of cultural concern to Dutch-speaking and French-speaking and German-speaking people in Belgium. But they also have jurisdiction over so-called personal matters: certain aspects of health care, family policy, education, and the like.

Belgium is further constitutionally divided into three so-called 'Regions': the 'Flemish', the 'Walloon' and the 'Brussels Capital' regions. These regions are

---

[1] For a concise introduction to Belgium's constitutional structure, see Vande Lanotte, Bracke & Goedertier 2006.

[2] There is also a small and constitutionally-recognised 'German Community' in the eastern part of the country.

mainly competent in economic matters in their respective areas. The city of Brussels, the capital, is officially bilingual, but is in fact to an important degree a French-speaking city.

Next to and above this federalised structure, the Federal Government has decision-making powers extending across the whole country. The regulation of euthanasia is a federal competence; hence the Belgian euthanasia legislation has been adopted in Federal Parliament.[3]

Although written law, especially the Constitution, describes the official structure within which the main political institutions function, it only touches marginally on the actual decision-making processes.[4] It is therefore important to address some words to Belgian political culture, since that has had an important effect on the process of legal change concerning euthanasia.

The political scientist Arend Lijphart has famously called Belgium 'the most thorough example of consociational democracy.'[5] 'Consociational democracy' can usually be found in ideologically (albeit not necessarily ethnically) segmented societies. Whereas it was previously thought that a stable democracy could not exist in such countries, Lijphart has shown that this is not true. A stable consociational democracy typically has four characteristics: a grand governing coalition, proportionality (not just in elections, but in everything: cabinets, Parliament, civil service, advisory organs etc), mutual vetoes, and segmental authority (each social segment has its own sphere of authority, either territorial and/or functional). The last condition is also called 'pillarisation' (in Dutch: *verzuiling*). A pillarised society is vertically divided into several segments or 'pillars' according to different religions or ideologies. Each pillar has its own social institutions.

Segmentation makes the stakes of politics at the top level higher than in homogenous societies, since segmentation in consociational societies is always potentially destabilizing. The representatives of the different pillars therefore strive actively for consensus: they seek to find each other and to cherish the common ground as much as possible. Political differences between the ruling groups are therefore not politicised or exaggerated and a substantial portion of the political leaders of significant segments of society cooperate in governing the country. The result is government by grand coalitions and executive power-sharing. Destabilizing tendencies are neutralised by a pragmatic ruling political elite that seeks to solve societal and political problems in such a way that all parties concerned can more or less accept the outcome. This keeps important political groups from becoming estranged from the political system. In other words, although political decision-making in consociational democracies is strongly affected by the interplay of past and present political and ideological and other tensions, it operates in practice so as to defuse these tensions and encourage compromise.[6]

---

[3] See ch 8 on the process of legal change in Belgium.
[4] Mabille 1990: 201.
[5] Lijphart 1981; see also Lijphart 1977.
[6] Mabille 1990: 215.

The political structure of Belgium reflects the various ideological divisions of the country.[7] The three main political segments (liberal, christian democrat and socialist), which date from the middle of the 19th century, are reflected not only in political parties but also in social organisation, and thus not only give form to political party structures, but they also define a social structure from the local to the regional and national level. Religion has long been a major dividing factor in all this: catholicism for the christian democrats, and anti-clericalism among liberals and socialists. Ideological segmentation has long strongly permeated almost all social institutions in the country. Thus outside the political framework, but mostly in close contact with it, there are a whole range of social organisations that reflect the various lines of ideological division in Belgium: there were and still are catholic, socialist and liberal trade unions, catholic and state (non-catholic) schools, hospitals, universities, etc. Until recently these institutions were politically influential, although this influence is waning today. Nevertheless, during the hearings that were organised in the context of the legislative process on the Euthanasia Bill, many of these organisations were invited by various political parties to express their views.[8]

The respective political weight of the three main political groupings had, up till the elections of 1999, been relatively stable. To be sure, the Christian Democrats had been a member of the ruling political coalition for some 40 years. Generally, the Christian Democrats also attracted the largest number of votes throughout the country.[9] The Socialists usually came second as far as voting numbers was concerned, and the Liberals third. Although the Christian Democrats always won the elections, they never had an absolute majority (with one exception from 1950 to 1954). Therefore grand coalition governments have been the norm for decades and are still the norm today.

These coalitions are usually based on a very precise coalition agreement, in which the concessions granted and the advantages obtained for each of the coalition parties (or for the French- or Dutch-speaking parts of the country) are all written down.[10] Thus although the ruling political coalition depends on the support of a majority in Parliament, government by coalition reinforces the position of the Government and weakens the role of the coalition parties in Parliament. The political parties represented in Parliament must exhibit a high degree of discipline so as not to bring the government, which consists of ideologically very different political parties, into danger. Usually it is therefore clear when a new Government is formed what the position of Parliament will be, ie on what issues Parliament will be allowed to legislate and what not. When in 1999 the

---

[7] *Ibid* at 202–3.

[8] See ch 8.4.

[9] It should be noted that in recent decades the Christian Democrats have been much more powerful in the Flemish than in the Walloon part of the country, where up till recently (2007) the Socialists have been very dominant in terms of electoral success and societal influence. See also Mabille 1990: 202–3.

[10] *Ibid* at 210.

Euthanasia and Law in Europe

Christian Democrats were no longer part of the Federal Government,[11] the new coalition agreement clearly stated that the Senate would be allowed to introduce legislation on euthanasia.[12]

So-called 'alternative majorities'[13] (legislation being approved without the consent of one of the governing parties and with the consent of one or more of the opposition parties) are very rare. Where ethical questions were concerned, catholic political parties usually stood opposed to the non-confessional parties. Especially when issues of medical ethics were concerned, this had led to an awkward situation: in 1990 the Belgian abortion law was passed with an alternative majority of Liberals (who were not part of the governing coalition) and Socialists, leaving out the Christian Democrats (who were then part of the Government). As a reaction to this the Christian Democrats had successfully insisted on including in subsequent coalition agreements an explicit ban on such majorities as far as ethical matters were concerned. This in effect gave the Christian Democrats a veto on all such legislation. The veto worked well until 1999, when the Christian Democrats were no longer in the Government.

Having said all this, we should at the same time be aware that a significant part of the societal base that supported ideological segmentation, which was the reason consociational democracy existed in the first place, has in recent years fallen away. Desegmentation in spirit is for a large number of people in Belgium a fact. Institutional segmentation is likewise beginning to wane, with the result that the political influence of segmented social organisations is becoming less and less taken for granted. With secularisation of society, the ideological tensions between the different political parties have at least partly declined.

As far as the organisation of health care is concerned, Caritas Catholica remains very influential because of its sheer power as the overarching coordinating organisation of the majority of Belgian hospitals. In terms of euthanasia policy within the walls of these hospitals, this might be an important fact.[14] But at the same time, because of increasing demands for the managerial professionalisation of hospitals, the influence of Caritas Catholica on hospital policy is decreasing.

Belgian political structure is furthermore characterised by a large number of advisory bodies, formed to help political actors get specialist advice and information from the major interest groups outside the parliamentary framework (and also to give these groups a forum).[15] The task of these advisory bodies is to issue opinions either on their own initiative or at the request of members of the Government. The multilingual character of Belgium has as a consequence that such bodies are usually so organised that Dutch- and French-speaking Belgians are more or less equally represented and the different (and on medical-ethical issues

---

[11] Christian Democrats were excluded from the federal Government until 2007. Having won the elections of 2007, they will almost certainly be part of the new Government currently being formed.

[12] See ch 8.4.

[13] *Majorités de rechange/[Wisselmeerderheid]*.

[14] See ch 9.4.2.3.

[15] Mabille 2000: 213–14.

often opposed) ideological groups are included. One such advisory body is the so-called Advisory Committee for Bioethics which, as we will see in chapter 8.3, played an important role on the issue of euthanasia.

In sum, although today, partly as a result of secularisation, Belgium is probably not as thoroughly ideologically segmented as it was at the time of Lijphart's description, many characteristics of a consociational democracy do still exist. From this point of view, as we will see in chapter 8, the process of legal change concerning euthanasia to a certain extent was in effect a reconfirmation of this type of democracy in Belgium.

The legislative process concerning euthanasia in Belgium was largely conducted in the federal Parliament. The federal Parliament consists of two chambers: the Chamber of Representatives and the Senate. Both Chambers are composed of Dutch- and French-speaking politicians, the Dutch-speaking being in the major-ity (reflecting the fact that the majority of the population of Belgium is Dutch-speaking). For legislation on certain institutional matters, a majority within both the group of Dutch- and of French-speaking members of each Chamber is required. This has resulted in a split within the political families along linguistic lines: each political party represented in Parliament has either a Dutch- or a French-speaking identity. Linguistically unified political parties are not repre-sented in Parliament. As a result there are two independent liberal factions, one for each language group, as well as two christian democratic, two socialist and two green factions.[16]

Although both Chambers have extensive (although somewhat different) legisla-tive powers, the Chamber of Representatives, which has 150 members, is supposed to have political primacy. The Belgian Senate, composed of 71 members[17], is con-ceived of as a so called '*Chambre de réflexion*' in which more reflective discussion is supposed to take place, and fundamental legislative issues are discussed and worked out, for example in the domain of medical ethics. Although both cham-bers of the Belgian Parliament could have initiated legislation on euthanasia, it was in the Senate that the legislative process on euthanasia in fact began.[18]

As in most other countries, the bulk of parliamentary work is done in parlia-mentary committees, which in Belgium are set up as permanent committees. This was also the case with the Belgian Law on Euthanasia.

It is also important to note that when the Senate, by virtue of its right of initia-tive, adopts a draft bill, the bill is forwarded to the Chamber of Representatives.

---

[16] There are also political parties that can be found on just one side of the Belgian language divide, such as the Flemish nationalist extreme right party 'Vlaams Belang'.

[17] Forty-one of its members belong to the Dutch language group, 29 to the French language group, and 1 to the German language group. Additionally the children of the King can be members of the Senate, if they have come of age and have taken the oath (Belgian Constitution Art 72). All three chil-dren of the King are currently member of the Belgian Senate, which makes its official membership 74 persons. The royal members of the Belgian Senate are by constitutional convention not politically active members. They therefore did not play a role in the proceedings leading to the Law on Euthanasia.

[18] To be complete we should add that according to Art 75 of the Belgian Constitution, legislative power in Belgium is also vested in the King: this in effect means that the Federal Government can intro-duce legislative proposals in Parliament.

Within sixty days, the Chamber can give its *final decision* on the bill, by either rejecting or adopting it. If the Chamber amends the bill, it must be returned to the Senate. If the Senate once again amends the bill, it is returned to the Chamber of Representatives, which then makes a *final decision* within fifteen days by either adopting or amending the bill. What is important to note here is that the Chamber of Representatives is clearly the more powerful of the two, in the sense that it can always have the last say on pending legislation. In the adoption of the Law on Euthanasia, the Chamber decided not to change anything in the bill as it came from the Senate. Having done so would have meant sending back the bill to the Senate, which in effect would have entailed a considerable delay.

A final word should be said about the administration of justice in Belgium. A rough division in three institutional lines can be made. In the first place there are the ordinary courts, dealing with civil and criminal matters. As we will see in chapter 9, these courts hardly contributed at all to the development of the law in the area of MBPSL in general and euthanasia in particular. In the second place, the Belgian legal system has a specific Constitutional Court, until recently called the Arbitration Court. In May 2002 the Arbitration Court declared the Belgian Law on Euthanasia in accordance with the Belgian Constitution.[19] In the third place, there is a system of administrative adjudication dealing with political rights and administrative matters, with as a supreme administrative court the so-called Council of State. In addition to its adjudicatory function the Council of State is an advisory body for pending legislation. In May 2001 the Council of State in its advisory capacity issued an important advice on the then Bill on Euthanasia.[20]

7.2 Health Care in Belgium[21]

7.2.1 The Belgian Health Care System

Compared with the inhabitants of other countries the Belgians, like the Dutch, are healthy: life expectancy at birth in 2004 was 76.5 years for men and 82.4 years for women.[22] Both men and women spend about 62 years of their lives in good health,[23] and about 64 years of their lives without physical constraint.[24]

The Belgian health care system is a good example of the complexity of Belgian social organisation. While the federal government plays a crucial role in the financing of health care, responsibility for its organisation is shared between

---

[19] See ch 8.4.
[20] We will refer to this advice regularly in ch 9.
[21] Except where otherwise noted, Corens (2007) is our source here.
[22] Corens 2007: 10.
[23] Bossuyt & Van Oyen 2000: 35.
[24] *Ibid* at 43.

the Federal Government and the Dutch, French, and German speaking 'Communities'.[25] In effect the Federal Government is responsible for health care insurance, for the planning and accreditation criteria for nursing homes, and for pricing policies. The communities are responsible for preventive health care and health promotion, hospital accreditation standards and planning measures, and for coordinating home care and the organisation of elderly care.

Belgium has a system of compulsory national health insurance, which covers almost 99% of the whole population and has a very broad benefits package.[26] The services covered by compulsory health insurance are described in the nationally established fee schedule, which is extremely detailed and lists more than 8,000 services with their reimbursement rate. Services not included in the fee schedule are not reimbursable.[27] Health care policy is further characterised by patients' freedom of choice of providers (GPs as well as specialists) and health care facilities.

Health care insurance covers major risks for the whole population and minor risks for 90% of the population.[28] There are two main schemes: the general scheme, which covers major and minor risks for the whole population (except for the self-employed) and a scheme for the self-employed which covers only major risks.[29] Major risks are hospitalisation, child delivery, elective surgery, dialysis, rehabilitation, implants and specialist care; palliative care is also covered. Minor risks include visits to physicians, dental care, minor surgery, home care and pharmaceuticals for outpatient care.[30] Both schemes cover active and non-active people and their dependants.[31]

The management and administration of health insurance is entrusted to non-government, non-profit organisations: mutual sickness funds (*mutualités*). The mutual sickness funds are organised according to religious and political affiliation. In 2005, christian and socialist mutual sickness funds were predominant, covering 45% and 29% respectively of the Belgian population.[32]

Delivery of health care in Belgium is mainly private. Doctors are self-employed except in university hospitals and large public hospitals. Most doctors are paid on a fee-for-service basis. Patients pay the set fee directly to their physicians and are then reimbursed by their sickness funds. Most services are reimbursed at a rate of 75%, the patient paying 25% of the cost.[33] Inpatient care in hospitals is covered by a third-party payer system. An insured person pays a co-payment, while the bulk of the cost treatment is directly paid by the sickness fund to the hospital concerned.

[25] See above section 7.1; Arneart, van den Heuvel & Windey 2005: 366.
[26] Corens 2007: 59.
[27] *Ibid* at 60.
[28] OECD Economic Surveys: Belgium/Luxembourg, 1999: 75.
[29] As of 1 January 2008, the self-employed will be compulsorily insured against minor risks according to Corens 2007: 59.
[30] Corens 2007: 59.
[31] *Ibid.*
[32] *Ibid* at 40.
[33] *Ibid* at 70.

According to the European Health for All database[34] in 2004 total health expenditure as a percentage of gross domestic product (GDP) was 9.3%. Belgium thereby ranked seventh among the European Union (EU) Member States.[35] In 2005, the three most costly health care services as a proportion of total public health spending were: the hospital budget (27.9%), which covers mainly the costs of accommodation, nursing care and equipment, physicians' fees (27.8%) and pharmaceuticals (17.6%).[36]

In 2003, the largest part of total health expenditure (72.7%) was publicly funded, mostly through reimbursements from the compulsory health insurance system (63.4%). Out-of-pocket payments and voluntary health insurance represented 23.0% and 4.3%, respectively, of the total expenditure.[37]

According to the most recent Eurobarometer (OECD 2002) on the public's satisfaction with the health care system, a clear majority (65.1%) of the Belgian population is satisfied with the present organisation of health care.[38] While according to 23.8% of Belgians the system runs well, 41.3% think that minor changes are needed, 22.7% that fundamental changes are needed, and 5.2% favour reorganising the health care system completely.[39]

7.2.2 Institutions for Health Care and Care of the Elderly

Health care institutions in Belgium derive historically from the activities of churches. This earlier history is still reflected in the importance of the coordinating organisations: Caritas Catholica as the overarching organisation of which the Flemish League of Health Care Institutions (*Verbond der verzorgingsinstellingen*) together with its Walloon counterpart (the *Fédération des institutions hospitalières*) is a part. The influence of Caritas Catholica on both hospital organisations is decreasing as professional management of hospitals requires more flexibility and autonomy. The public hospitals are organised within the Flemish *Verbond van openbare verzorgingsinstellingen* and the Walloon *Association des établissements publics de santé*.

Other health care institutions in Belgium include short-term (hospitals) and long-term residential care (home care, centres for day care, residential homes and 'rest and nursing homes').

Hospitals

In 2005, there were 215 (*Zickenhuizen*) hospitals in Belgium of which 69 psychiatric hospitals and 146 general hospitals. Of the general hospitals 116 are acute care hospitals, 23 are specialised hospitals which limit their care to certain conditions

---

[34] See <http://www.data.euro.who.int/hfadb/> accessed 5 September 2007.
[35] Corens 2007: 53.
[36] *Ibid* at 54.
[37] *Ibid* at 61.
[38] *Ibid* at 38.
[39] *Ibid*.

such as heart and lung diseases or palliative care. Seven of the hospitals are geriatric hospitals and 7 are university hospitals. The university hospitals are all general hospitals.[40]

The majority of hospitals in Belgium are private (70%). Most private hospitals that were originally owned by religious charitable orders are now owned by associations of which most still have a more or less close link with a religious order (more than 80%) while the remainder are owned by universities or sickness funds. Public hospitals are for the most part owned by a municipality, a province, a community or an 'intermunicipal association' (which groups together local authorities, public welfare centres and, in some cases, the provincial government or private shareholders). Both private and public hospitals are non-profit organisations.[41]

Hospitals can have their own policy with respect to withholding and withdrawing treatment and euthanasia. All Belgian hospitals are required to install a medical ethics committee that is responsible for determining this policy.[42] A majority of its members are physicians employed in the hospital so that the policy cannot be imposed unilaterally by the hospital management. (See further chapter 10.3.1 on the MBPSL policies of hospitals.)

'Rest and Nursing Homes'

Elderly persons who need care because of a long-term illness or condition, but who do not have medical problems that require permanent medical supervision in a hospital, can be admitted to a 'rest and nursing home' (*rust-en-verzorging stehuis*) (hereafter: nursing home).[43] The residents must finance the cost of stay themselves, the cost of care falls under the compulsory health insurance system.[44] 40% of nursing homes are public, 40% are private non-profit, and 20% are private for profit.[45]

Each nursing home must have a coordinating and advisory physician who is always a GP. This doctor is responsible for the coordination of pharmaceutical care, medical care and physiotherapy. Each nursing home must have a functional link with a hospital.[46]

Either a physical or a mental dependency is required to be admitted to a nursing home. The majority of the people in nursing homes have somatic conditions (70%).[47]

There were 896 nursing homes in 2000.[48] In 2005 there were 47,243 beds available.[49]

---

[40] *Ibid* at 85.
[41] *Ibid.*
[42] Royal Decree of 12 August 1994. *Belgisch Staatsblad* (27 September 1994).
[43] Corens 2007: 119.
[44] *Ibid.*
[45] Meijer, van Kampen & Kerkstra 2000: 557.
[46] Corens 2007: 119. This obligation can be found in the rules for accreditation of the rest and nursing homes.
[47] Meijer, van Kampen & Kerkstra 2000: 557.
[48] Arneart, van den Heuvel & Windey 2005: 367.
[49] Corens 2007: 119.

The average age of a patient in a nursing home is 83 years old (1.4 % of the population over 65 lives in a nursing home). 75% of the elderly persons in nursing homes are women.[50] The average length of stay is 3.5 years. Psychogeriatric patients stay longer in nursing homes than somatic patients.[51]

Like hospitals, nursing homes can have their own policy with respect to withdrawing and withholding treatment and euthanasia. Unlike hospitals, rest and nursing homes have no obligation to install a medical ethics committee. (See further chapter 10.3.1 on the MBPSL policies of nursing homes.)

Residential Homes

A residential home is a home-replacing environment. The medical responsibility rests with a GP. Historically, residential homes were intended for the elderly who were still in good general medical condition. With well-organised home (*verzorging stehuis*) care it no longer seems necessary to admit elderly people to a residential home when their physical and mental situation makes it possible for them to stay in their own home situation. The distinction between residential homes and nursing homes has therefore largely disappeared in practice. Many residential homes admit elderly in need of care. Many institutions have both traditional residential beds and nursing beds.[52]

In 2001 there were 1,844 residential homes with 79,524 beds available.[53] As with nursing homes the cost of stay is financed by the occupant. The cost of care is covered by compulsory health insurance.

Only 1.4% of the elderly between 60–75 but 83% of the elderly over 95 live in residential homes.[54] The average age of residents is 81 and there are more women than men.[55]

Home Care

If a person is not able to take care of himself at home, he can ask for professional help. Home care (*thuiszorg*) is meant to keep elderly people in their home situation as long as possible. It consists of cleaning and laundry service and assistance with meals.[56] Key disciplines that are generally involved are informal care, general practice, nursing care, home help and social work.

Home care is regulated and organised by the Communities. In 2002, the Federal Government introduced Integrated Services for Home Care to coordinate home care in a defined geographical area. To stimulate multidisciplinary cooper-

---

[50] DeVroey, van Kasteven & Lepeleire 2002: 287.
[51] Meijer, van Kampen & Kerkstra 2000: 557. In 2002 there were 25 psychiatric nursing homes; the total number of beds in 2004 was 2,289 (Pacolet *et al* 2004: 309).
[52] Corens 2007: 119.
[53] Pacolet *et al* 2004: 306.
[54] Arneart, van den Heuvel & Windey 2005: 367.
[55] DeVroey, van Kasteven & Lepeleire 2002: 287.
[56] Arneart, van den Heuvel & Windey 2005: 368.

ation instead of competition, each geographical area can only have one such facility.[57]

Care is provided by home-care nurses or geriatric helpers. 50% of all home care is provided by the White and Yellow Cross (a Catholic organisation).[58]

Palliative Care

In 1985 the first palliative unit was founded. Since the end of the 1990s, many initiatives have been taken at the federal and community levels to support palliative care. Since 2002 Belgium has a Law on Palliative Care.[59] This law defines palliative care as the totality of care for patients whose life-threatening disease no longer responds to curative therapies. The major aim of palliative care is to offer the patient and his next of kin as much quality of life as possible and maximum autonomy.[60]

Palliative care can be offered by the palliative care function of a hospital, in residential homes, in nursing homes and as palliative home care. Since 1997, each hospital must have a so called palliative care function. This function is performed by a multidisciplinary team whose members come from the hospital's medical department, the nursing department and the paramedics department, complemented by a psychologist and a social worker or a social nurse. To develop and to support palliative care in residential homes and nursing homes the coordinating physician and the head nurse of each home are charged with introducing a culture of palliative care and giving advice to the staff.

The aim of palliative home care is to keep terminally ill patients at home as long as possible. Since 1998, multidisciplinary teams have been set up to support the different forms of palliative home care. The team must offer the same quality of care as the palliative care function in a hospital (palliative home care is covered by compulsory health insurance).[61]

Where People Die

Most people over 75 years of age die in hospitals (49%), 30% die in nursing homes, 19% at home and 1.5% somewhere else. Most of those aged between 65 and 75 die in hospitals (60%), 30% at home, 6.4% in nursing homes and 3.1% somewhere else.[62] 70% of the terminally ill would prefer to die at home, but only 28% of them in fact do so.[63]

---

[57] Corens 2007: 119.

[58] See <http://www.witgelekruis.be> accessed 8 January 2008.

[59] The Law on Palliative care of 14 June 2002. Art 2 of the Law expressly recognises a right to palliative care. This right of the patient corresponds to the professional obligation for the treating physician to apply palliative care.

[60] Corens 2007: 120.

[61] *Ibid* at 121.

[62] Data for 2004 received from the Flemish Agency for Care and Health (*Vlaams Agentschap Zorg en Gezondheid*). The data apply only to those living in Flanders who died in Flanders or in Brussels. No data are available for Wallonia. In 2001, over half of all deaths in Flanders took place in a hospital, almost a quarter at home, and almost a fifth in a care home (Cohen *et al* 2006c).

[63] See <http://www.palliatief.be/teksten/evaluatierapport_PZ_JUNI05.pdf> accessed 29 June 2007.

7.2.3. Health Care Professionals

The practice of most health care professionals is regulated by the Law of 1967 on the Practice of Health Care Professions (see chapter 9).

The professionals involved in the care of the dying patient and the nature of their relationships with one another, vary widely from one place of death to another. The situation in Belgium resembles that in the Netherlands with two notable exceptions. First, each Belgian hospital has since 1997 a palliative care function to coordinate palliative care. This does not yet exist in the Netherlands. Second, medical care (including palliative care) in nursing homes in Belgium is coordinated and offered by GPs while in the Netherlands this is the competence of specialised nursing-home doctors.

Doctors

In order to practise medicine in Belgium every physician, must be entered on the register of the Order of Physicians. Apart from a diploma this requires a permit from the Ministry of Health. To be accredited for providing health services within the context of the compulsory health insurance system, health care professionals must notify the National Institute for Sickness and Disability Insurance which administers the programme for most groups of care providers and institutions.[64]

Because, unlike the Netherlands, patients do not have to be referred to a specialist by their GP, GPs do not function as gatekeepers.[65] In 65% of all contacts with a specialist, this is at the patient's initiative, in 34% the patient is referred by a GP, and in 4% another specialist refers the patient.[66]

There were 38,828 doctors in Belgium in 2006, of whom 18,027 were GPs and 20,801 specialists.[67] Belgium has the second largest number of doctors per 1,000 inhabitants in the world (3.9%).[68] In 1997 there were 16 specialists per 10,000 inhabitants and 15 GPs compared with 10 specialists and 5 GPs in the Netherlands.[69] The average number of physician contacts per person in Belgium is relatively high: 7.1 'outpatient contacts' per person in 2004, compared to the average of European Union states, 6.3 contacts per person.[70]

Most physicians (GPs and specialists) operate in solo practice, frequently without staff. However, there are centres, known as integrated health care practices,

---

[64] Corens 2007: 60.
[65] Corens 2007: 107.
[66] Raad voor de Volksgezondheid en Zorg 2003: 160.
[67] Belgian Bureau of Statistics <http://www.statbel.fgov.be/figures/d362_nl.asp> accessed 5 September 2007.
[68] The Netherlands has 3.1% per capita. The rates for nurses, however, are the other way around: 12.8% in the Netherlands and 5.8% in Belgium: see <http://www.rvz.net/cgi-bin/nieuws.pl?niew_srcID=164> accessed 28 June 2007.
[69] SCP 2000: 268.
[70] Corens 2007: 108.

with a multidisciplinary team including (at least) several GPs, nurses, a physiotherapist and a psychotherapist. The number of such practices is growing, although still only a minority of the Belgian population affiliated to them.

The Order of Physicians and Other Doctors' Organisations

The Order of Physicians is established by the law that regulates the Belgian medical profession.[71] Every Belgian physician must be registered on the list of the Council of the Order in the province where he practices medicine. The most important function of the Order is to ensure observance of the rules of professional conduct for physicians and preservation of the reputation, standards of discretion, probity and dignity of the members of the Order. To this end, the councils are responsible for disciplining any misconduct committed by their registered members in, or in connection with, the practice of the profession, as well as serious misconduct committed outside the realm of professional activity, whenever such misconduct is liable to damage the reputation or dignity of the profession. A disciplinary procedure can be started at the initiative of the provincial council, on the complaint of a doctor or a third party (eg a patient), by the Minister of Health, by the National Council of the Order or by the public prosecutor.[72] The sanctions which may be imposed are: warning, censure, reprimand, suspension of the right to practice medicine for a period not exceeding two years, and finally, being struck off the roll of the Order. The National Council of the Order is responsible for establishing the general principles and rules concerning the morality, honour, discretion, honesty, dignity and devotion indispensable to the practice of medicine, which together form the Code of Medical Deontology.[73]

Because of the context of Belgian societal structure (see section 7.1), doctors in Belgium are also organised along different political and ideological lines. This means that next to the official Order of Physicians, there exist a number of private organisations that bring doctors together. Nevertheless, only the Order of Physicians—established by law, given formal rule-making power, and responsible for professional discipline—can be considered as representing all doctors in Belgium. Of course the different ideological positions within the medical profession in Belgium are represented within the Order as the members of its councils are appointed by elections. This makes it very difficult if not impossible for the Order to speak with one voice. The situation in the Netherlands is very different; public functions such as professional discipline being exercised by legally-organised public institutions, and professional policy-making and self-regulation is being left to the formally 'private' Medical Association (KNMG) and a variety of specialist associations.

---

[71] Law no 79 of 10 November 1967.
[72] Corens 2007: 33; Nys 2003: 61–5.
[73] The Code can be found on: <http://195.234.184.64/web-Ned/deonton.htm> accessed 1 October 2007; Dutch, French and German versions.

Nurses

The total number of nurses and nursing attendants in 2006 was 65,952.[74] Nurses are all registered with the RIZIV-INAMI. There is no official code of ethics for nurses but their behaviour is subject to considerable legal regulation.[75]

Pharmacists

Only pharmacists may prepare, sell, distribute and deliver medicine. There are 5,269 pharmacies in Belgium[76] of which 115 are hospital pharmacies. In 2005 the number of pharmacists was 11,882.[77] To be a physician and a pharmacist at the same time is not allowed.[78]

Belgian pharmacists are organised in the Order of Pharmacists. The so-called code of professional deontology, issued by the Order of Pharmacists, provides the ethical rules for the practice of the pharmacist's profession.[79] There is also a federation for all pharmacists: the Belgian Pharmacists Association.

7.3. Public and Medical Opinion

Public opinion concerning euthanasia in Belgium was measured in the international research discussed in chapter 17 (see Table 17.1). In 2000, public opinion was slightly less positive than in the Netherlands (taking the amount of unqualified opposition—'euthanasia never justified'—as the best measure) and at about the same level as in a number of other Western European countries where public support for euthanasia is fairly strong. In 1999–2001, during the parliamentary proceedings on the bill that legalised euthanasia, there was strong public support (roughly three quarters of those polled) for such legislation, and there were no significant differences between the Dutch- and French-speaking parts of the country; support was particularly strong among respondents of a higher educational level.[80]

As Graph 17.1 shows, Belgium is the Western European country in which public support for euthanasia most rapidly increased in the two decades preceding legalisation in 2002, going from one of the lowest levels of support in 1981 to one of the highest in 1999.

---

[74] Belgisch Nationaal Instituut voor de Statistiek <http://statbel.fgov.be/figures/d362_nl.asp> accessed 5 September 2007.

[75] Verpeet, Meulenbergs & Gastmans 2003: 654.

[76] European Observatory on Health Care Systems 2000: 53.

[77] RIZIV Annual Report 2005: <http://www.risiv.fgov.be/presentation/nl/publications/annual-report/2005/index.htm> accessed 5 September 2007.

[78] Philipsen & Faure 2002: 168.

[79] *Ibid* at 166.

[80] <http://www.lalibre.be/article_print.phtml?art_id=15963> accessed 1 October 2007.

The views of doctors were studied in the early 2000s as part of the EURELD comparative European research project (which in Belgium covered only Flanders).[81] As Table 17.1 in chapter 17 shows, 65% of the Belgian doctors who responded agreed with the statement that 'a patient should have the right to decide whether or not to hasten the end of his or her life'. This was the second highest rate in the study (only the Netherlands, at 68%, was higher, and Switzerland, at 61%, was the only other country in which a majority of doctors agreed).

---

[81] Miccinesi *et al* 2005.

8

The Legalisation of Euthanasia in Belgium

In 2002, without much by way of a preparatory societal, medical and legal process comparable to that in the Netherlands, the Belgian Parliament adopted a bill legalising euthanasia. How this came about is the subject of this chapter.

We should note at the outset that public support for euthanasia legislation grew very rapidly in the decade leading up to the beginning of the ultimate legislative process in 1999.[1] Belgian society seems to have become ripe for legislation on euthanasia at the very time the parliamentary process was getting under way.

8.1 The Situation before the Legislative Change of 2002

Although we deal with the law concerning euthanasia and other MBPSL extensively in Chapter 9, it will be helpful to give the reader a brief sketch here of the legal situation before the process of legal change started in Belgium.

Up to 2002 euthanasia was illegal in Belgium. The Deontological Code (Code of Medical Ethics) of the Belgian Order of Physicians also clearly forbade euthanasia. However, although it was clear that euthanasia was in fact taking place, there was no case law on the subject since no doctor had been convicted for performing euthanasia. A certain amount of legal uncertainty surrounded the subject, and it was not known, for example, how a Belgian court would react to a claim of justification based on necessity. The situation was even more complicated when it came to assisted suicide. On the face of it, such assistance was not illegal since suicide itself is not illegal, but here, too, since there was no case law on the matter, it was unclear whether a doctor could safely give such assistance. Finally, it was generally accepted that a doctor is not obliged to continue medical treatment that no longer has any curative or therapeutic effect, and that a possible shortening of life through administration of pain relief is acceptable.[2]

---

[1] See chs 7.3 and 17, Graph 17.1.
[2] See for a full discussion of these matters, ch 9.2 and 9.3.

8.2 The Period Leading up to Legal Change: 1980–1997

The founding in 1980 of two associations—the Dutch-speaking 'Right to Die with Dignity' (*Recht op Waardig Sterven*) and its French-speaking counterpart with essentially the same name (*Association pour le Droit de Mourir dans le Dignité*)—could perhaps be seen as a start—though in a limited way—of organised action to achieve the regulation of euthanasia in Belgium. However, their influence, certainly at that time, was rather small because the subject of euthanasia had not yet become a real public or political issue, and both associations were seen as rather radical in ideology: outspokenly liberal and 'atheist' (ie anti-religious). There was no broad social support for their ideas in Belgium, where social catholicism was still politically dominant. Political support for the agenda of the two associations was miniscule. Even in liberal circles, there was no unqualified support for legislation concerning euthanasia. The most dominant faction in the Government from the 1950s, the Christian Democrats, was strongly opposed. Until the 1990s the Christian Democrats, as a matter of principle, rejected or blocked the regulation of euthanasia.

The First Study Commissions

Political stonewalling did not mean there were no developments on a societal level. From the 1970s on, euthanasia was regularly in the news and was also occasionally the subject of public debate.[3] It seems reasonable to suppose that the Dutch experience with euthanasia had at least some influence in neighbouring Belgium, where more than half the inhabitants speak the same language. However, there is little direct evidence of such influence.

From the middle of the 1980s on, both French- and Dutch-speaking christian democratic parties modified their strict position on the issue. Stimulated mainly by technological developments in medicine and biology, euthanasia and end-of-life decisions generally became at least debatable. This led to the setting up of a commission in 1983 by French-speaking christian democrats to study the ethical issues involved.[4] The premise of their work, according to the commission's report of 1985,[5] was that societal pluralism, increasing democratisation, the growing autonomy of morals from religion, and medical-technological development were all factors that could be expected to bring about social change. Traditional values were therefore also subject to change. The commission looked at a number of issues (mainly of a medical nature), such as the inclination to continue treatment even where there is no longer any benefit for the patient, and the removal and transplantation of organs and tissues, as well as issues involved in medical

---

[3] In 1971, for example, the Belgian state broadcasting network organised a TV debate on the subject.
[4] See Delfosse 1995: 516.
[5] CEPESS 1985: 1–2.

research. Its findings concerning useless medical treatment led the commission to distinguish between 'active' and 'passive' euthanasia. According to the commission the former should be ruled out, whereas the latter was permissible as long as it was accompanied by palliative care and intensive counselling.[6]

In 1986 the Dutch-speaking Christian Democrat Deputy Minister for Health and the Handicapped, Demeester-De Meyer announced a national colloquium entitled 'Bioethics in the 1990s'. Prior to the colloquium, which took place in 1987, there were a number of preparatory meetings held by multidisciplinary and ideo-logically-pluralistic working groups. The working group dealing with 'Ending Life' recommended altering the Penal Code on behalf of doctors who carry out euthanasia.[7] Nothing became of the proposal, among other things because the liberal Minister of Justice was opposed to it.

Nevertheless, the colloquium was from another point of view a significant event: it provided a stimulus for the formation of a pluralistic Committee on Bioethics. The Deputy Minister mentioned above announced the setting up of such a body during the closing session of the colloquium.[8] After years of political wrangling the committee got the final go-ahead in 1993,[9] and was able to commence work in 1996. We return to this development in section 8.3.

The First Draft Bills

In the 1980s, for the first time proposals for a bill concerning euthanasia and related issues were regularly put forward by individual Members of Parliament from virtually the whole political spectrum, with the exception of the Christian Democrats. Since they were all proposed by individuals they did not necessarily have party support. None of these proposals ever reached the stage of being seriously discussed in Parliament.[10] The presence of Christian Democrats in the Government made a government proposal concerning euthanasia and other end-of-life-decisions impossible.

A proposed bill to deal with pointless medical treatment for the terminally ill was introduced in 1984 by French language Liberals[11] (a proposal put forward

---

[6] *Ibid* at 47–50. In 1990 the commission's activities were taken over by another working group, which made a number of recommendations on various medical procedures regarding the end of life. These proposals, however, where largely the same as in the commission report of 1985.

[7] All documents of this colloquium are to be found in Demeester-De Meyer 1987 (two volumes).

[8] See Demeester-De Meyer 1987 (volume II): 139. The idea for such an body had already been put forward in 1984 in the Senate, and in 1986 in the Chamber of Representatives, both times by means of a draft bill. In both cases the impetus came mainly from Christian Democrat representatives. See also Delfosse 1995: 517.

[9] The committee was the result of a cooperation agreement between the State, the Dutch and French and German Communities, and the Joint Commission of the Communities (see *Belgian State Gazette* (3 May 1993)). Such an body was first proposed in 1984 in the Senate, and in 1986 in the Chamber of Representatives, both times by means of a draft bill. In both cases the impetus came mainly from Christian Democrat representatives. See Delfosse 1995: 517.

[10] For an overview of the bills see Coolsaet 1995/96.

[11] Proposal of Law, Senate, 1984–85, no 738/1.

again in 1986[12]). The proposed bill did not deal with euthanasia as such, but would have added to the Penal Code two provisions on the basis of which a doctor would not be obliged to continue 'treatment or reanimation' of a patient, with or without the patient's request. This proposal seemed legally superfluous since it was already generally accepted in Belgium that doctors could stop futile medical treatment. The proposal was mainly intended to provide doctors more legal security.

In 1985, a French-speaking Member of Parliament from the socialist camp proposed a draft bill that laid down rules regarding the doctor/terminally-ill patient relationship.[13] The bill included some provisions concerning patients' rights: (1) the right to full information concerning his health for a patient who asks for such information, and (2) the right of the patient to refuse any treatment. If pain relief was no longer effective, a terminally-ill patient could ask for euthanasia. The request should be made in writing. The doctor could refuse to honour the request, but he should then refer the patient to another doctor. The bill also made provision for ending the lives of patients considered clinically dead. The proposal did not deal with assisted suicide or advance treatment directives.

A proposal for a parliamentary motion in 1988 by a French-speaking Christian Democrat is also worth mentioning. It asked the Federal Government to carry out research into the practice of euthanasia in Belgium, to keep the population informed on the ongoing state of affairs, and to come up with concrete proposals to make sure that human life is absolutely respected. The proposal was rejected, re-introduced in 1992 and rejected again.[14]

In 1993, a member of an eccentric Flemish party submitted a draft bill that reserved euthanasia for patients in the last phase of a 'terminal illness or suffering from a disease leading to death'.[15] It was the only draft bill submitted in all these years that made explicit provision for assisted suicide. It also dealt with the patient's right to information. As with all other draft bills, a doctor would have been allowed to refuse a request for euthanasia, but in that case he was obliged to refer the patient to another doctor.

In the same year a draft bill was submitted by a member of the Dutch-speaking Greens.[16] Ethically, this proposal was the most liberal ever introduced in Belgium, proposing 'medical hopelessness' as the sole medical requirement for euthanasia. It also made provision for a reporting procedure. Euthanasia would only have been possible pursuant to a written request.

In 1995, a French-speaking member of the liberal camp introduced a draft bill. It addressed only euthanasia in the narrow sense, rejecting any form of medical treatment that would result in ending life without an explicit request from the

---

[12] Proposal of Law, Senate, 1985–86, no 19/1.

[13] Proposal of Law, Chamber of Representatives, 1984–85, no 1109/1. A slightly amended version of this proposal was later (in 1986) introduced by a member of the French-speaking Liberal party. A slightly changed version was reintroduced in 1988 and again in 1995.

[14] *Parliamentary Proceedings, Senate,* 1988, no 291/1 and 1991–92, 171/1.

[15] Proposal of Law, Chamber of Representatives, 1993–94, no 1205/1.

[16] Proposal of Law, Senate, 1993–94, no 960/1. Introduced again in 1995, Proposal of Law, Senate, no 1–122/1, and in 1999, Proposal of Law, Senate, no 2–86/1.

patient. It also rejected the idea of written advance euthanasia requests (eg for coma patients) since 'they are only based on abstract considerations and cannot be considered an expression of a concrete desire arising from an actual situation.'[17] Other themes such as palliative care received hardly any attention.

A draft bill submitted by a member of the Dutch-speaking liberal camp in 1996 restricted itself to euthanasia for terminally ill patients. It contained provisions on palliative care and also regulated advance written requests for euthanasia.[18]

Finally, in 1995 a draft bill by the French-speaking Socialist party would have made euthanasia legal, both when the patient can give consent and when the patient cannot personally give consent. In both cases there should be a written request. However, euthanasia could only be considered when the patient's condition (due to illness or accident) is clearly incurable. The proposal stipulated that there must also be persistent and unbearable suffering or distress which a doctor is unable to control sufficiently.[19]

At the time they were proposed, none of the above proposed bills stood a chance of even being dealt with in Parliament. The last three, however, were reintroduced in 1999, virtually unaltered, when the Christian Democrats were no longer in the Government.

8.3 The Second Phase of Legal Change: 1997–1999

The Recommendation of the Advisory Committee on Bioethics

One of the most significant events leading to the legalisation of euthanasia in Belgium is the first Recommendation, on 12 May 1997, of the Advisory Committee on Bioethics, concerning 'The Desirability of a Legal Regulation of Euthanasia.'[20]

This federal committee was set up, according to article 1 of its Founding Statute,[21]

> to inform and advise the Government and the public on problems arising from research and its implementation in the area of biology and health care, and to explore the ethical, social and legal aspects of the issues involved, and in particular the rights of the individual.

The committee consists of 35 members—doctors, lawyers, ethicists, psychologists, and sociologists—and is linguistically and ideologically balanced. In the Belgian context that last means an equal number of catholics on the one hand and

---

[17] Proposal of Law, Senate, 1995, no 1–34/1, p.4. Reintroduced again in the Chamber of Representatives in 1996.

[18] Proposal of Law, Senate, 1995–96, no 1–301/1.

[19] Proposal of Law, Chamber of Representatives, 1995, no 121/1.

[20] Raadgevend Comité voor Bio-ethiek 1997. For an English translation see Nys 1997. On the Recommendation itself, see Vermeersch 2000, Jans 2000.

[21] See Cooperation Agreement between the State, the Dutch and French and German Communities, and the Joint Commission of the Communities, *Belgian State Gazette* (3 May 1993).

of non-religious people on the other. From its inception the committee has been organised into subcommittees consisting of twelve members that again have a balanced composition. The full committee reviews the findings and proposals of the sub-committees, amends them where necessary, and then approves them. The committee can make recommendations on its own initiative, or at the request of the chairpersons of the two chambers of the Federal Parliament, members of the Government, or chairpersons of hospital ethical committees, etc.

The recommendations of the committee do not reflect a 'majority' point of view. No votes are taken and the committee's recommendations include *all* the different and sometimes strongly divergent points of view represented. All views are given equal weight. In this sense the committee is mainly an informative body.

It is notable that the committee's first recommendation was on euthanasia, since this was one of the most sensitive and complex issues it was supposed to deal with when it started working in 1996. The recommendation led to a certain depolarisation of the various differences of opinion, most importantly because it achieved an important precondition of fruitful debate: within its ranks there was broad agreement on a definition of euthanasia. Clearly influenced in this by earlier discussions in the Netherlands[22] the committee defined 'euthanasia' as the 'intentional ending of life by someone other than the person concerned, at the request of the latter'.[23]

The committee's recommendation in effect contained four different proposals for legislation on euthanasia, reflecting the views of four groups within the committee.

Proposal 1 was to change the Penal Code to legalise euthanasia, with a procedure for after-the-fact control. This proposal would have created a legal situation similar to that in the Netherlands after the statutory legalisation of euthanasia in 2002.

Proposal 2 also included a procedure for after-the-fact control. The main difference from the first proposal was that the existing restrictions in the Penal Code were to be retained. However, it would be possible for a doctor to invoke a so-called 'situation of necessity.' This proposal was obviously inspired by the Dutch legal situation between 1994 and 2001.

Proposal 3 provided for a procedure for before-the-fact control not only of euthanasia, but also of other medical behaviour that potentially shortens life. Like proposal 2, this proposal retained the existing provisions of the Penal Code but set out the grounds on which a doctor could invoke a 'state of necessity.'

Proposal 4 was to retain the existing legal situation, which meant that euthanasia would, under no conditions, be allowed.

The committee stressed the need to organise a parliamentary debate on these various proposals and expressed its concern over what in the recommendation was

---

[22] See ch 9.4.2 on this.
[23] Raadgevend Comité voor Bio-ethiek1997: 1.

called 'uncontrolled euthanasia': doctors ending patients' lives without consulting them or their family, often putting pressure on nursing staff to go along with this.[24] This concern was not, however, supported by any empirical data.

The views of the different groups within the committee were, in fact, not as divergent as it might seem. According to one member there was a noticeable degree of support for Proposal 3 (although no unanimity or consensus).[25] This was mainly due to the fact that leading Catholics from both sides of the language divide were prepared under strict conditions to accept euthanasia.

The committee's recommendation and how it was arrived at made mature discussion of the issues possible. It was in this respect notably different from the report of an *ad hoc* committee on abortion in the 1980s. That report consisted simply of a polarised discussion between those for and those against abortion. The painful history leading to the passing of the Belgian abortion law had indirectly been the impulse for setting up the Advisory Committee on Bioethics in 1993. The abortion law had been passed with a so-called 'alternative majority' of liberals and socialists, that is, a majority that did not include the Christian Democrats (who were then part of the Government). As a reaction to this the Christian Democrats had successfully insisted on including in subsequent coalition agreements an explicit ban on alternative majorities on ethical matters, which in effect gave them a veto on all such legislation.

The recommendation of the Advisory Committee formed the basis for a debate in the Belgian Senate on 9 and 10 December 1997 in which both Members of Parliament and outside experts, including members of the committee, participated.[26] It is no coincidence that debate first took place in the Senate, since after constitutional reforms of 1994 the Senate had become the prime vehicle for legislation on ethical issues.[27] That there was consensus in the Senate to proceed with legislation on euthanasia became apparent in the public statements of spokesmen for the most important political parties the week before the debate began.

The French- and Dutch-speaking Christian Democrats felt themselves most in tune with Proposal 3 of the Committee and stated that explicit attention must be given to the development of palliative care to limit the demand for euthanasia. The two Socialist parties were more in favour of Proposal 2. The Dutch-speaking Liberals also opted for Proposal 2, while the French-speaking Liberals had no clear standpoint, except that they believed the existing law offered enough room to provide for any situation that might arise at the end of life. The Dutch-speaking Greens defended the right to life but could support Proposal 3. Finally, the democratic Dutch-speaking nationalists (the then *Volksunie*) wanted more attention to be given

---

[24] Note that by using the phrase 'uncontrolled euthanasia' in this context the committee was using the term 'euthanasia' inconsistently with its own definition, which requires a request by the person concerned.

[25] Schotsmans 1997.

[26] A complete report of this debate can be found in Proceedings of the Belgian Senate 1997–98 and 10 December 1997, 3891–954. To be found via: <http://www.senate.be/www/?MIval=/index_senate&MENUID=12440&LANG=nl> accessed 6 September 2007.

[27] See ch 7.1 on this.

to the development of palliative care, with secondary consideration to the regulation of euthanasia. All these political parties said they wanted to avoid the kind of polarised debate that had taken place on abortion in the 1970s and 1980s. At the end of the day, only the extreme right Flemish Block (*Vlaams Blok)* was against any form of regulation of euthanasia and thought the debate pointless and even dangerous.[28]

During the first day of debate in the Senate the emphasis was on the Recommendation of 12 May 1997 and the opinions of experts. The second day was devoted to debate between the senators themselves. That led, as in the Advisory Committee on Bioethics, to widespread support for Proposal 3, and to political agreement that the Senate Committee for Justice (responsible for criminal issues) and the Committee on Social Affairs (responsible for health care issues) should together frame a bill. The Advisory Committee on Bioethics was asked to formulate a recommendation on non-competent patients and on advance written requests for euthanasia, matters that it had not addressed in its first recommendation, although it had been asked to do so. From the many opinions for and against legislation that appeared in the daily newspapers over the following months, one gathers that the political will to legislate acted as a catalyst for public debate.

The next political step was that three months later, in March 1998, the Dutch-speaking Socialists suddenly declared that legislation that dealt only with euthanasia was too limited. They also wanted legislation to cover comatose patients, handicapped newborns and those suffering from serious dementia. Since the agreement that had been reached to prepare a bill depended on a delicate political balance, this sudden declaration shocked the Christian Democrats. This, together with the attention demanded by other political matters, led to developments coming to a virtual standstill.

However, the decline in political attention to the matter did not mean that nothing further happened. The results of a multidisciplinary pilot study of the actual administration of euthanasia by doctors were published in 1998.[29] The study looked at the situation in only one Flemish city, but it was, nevertheless, the first Belgian scientific study of end-of-life medical decisions. Using the methodology earlier developed in the Dutch national surveys, it showed that euthanasia formed a small but regular part of Belgian end-of-life practice.[30]

The Recommendation of 22 February 1999

On 22 February 1999, the Advisory Committee on Bioethics delivered a recommendation concerning ending the life of incompetent patients.[31] In contrast to its recommendation on euthanasia, all the classic ideological and ethical divisions on the issue were apparent. In the Recommendation regarding euthanasia there had

---

[28] See *Parliamentary Proceedings, Senate,* 1997, no 1–149, p 3940.
[29] Deliens & Bilsen 1998.
[30] See ch 10.1 on the results of this and other studies. *Cf* also Vincent (1999): 6 out of 10 doctors on Belgian intensive care units said they had carried out euthanasia at some time.
[31] Raadgevende Comité voor Bio-ethiek 1999.

been a will to work together, but this time around there was no question of that. The recommendation consisted of three directly opposed positions. The first rejected any form of euthanasia, and thus also any form of ending life without consent. The second would have allowed treatment to end life without current consent but only on condition that there was an advance written request and consent from an impartial representative. Finally, the third position was that treatment to end life should, under certain conditions, be possible in cases where there is no prior or current consent. This recommendation played no significant role in the political debate after December 1999. Nevertheless, the political consensus that had been reached as a result of the first Recommendation and the debate in the Senate, was broken. The way forward turned out to be one of polarisation.

In the run-up to the elections of June 1999, the Socialists emphasised their view that legislation on euthanasia in accordance with Proposal 2 of the committee's recommendation should be adopted, including provision for the incompetent. The Christian Democrats reacted by saying that only a solution in accord with Proposal 3 of the recommendation would be acceptable to them and that they had great reservations in accepting any ending of life without consent. They added that a government with Christian Democrats would only be possible if legislation on this sort of issues could not be approved by an 'alternative majority'.[32]

8.4 The Third Phase of Legal Change: 1999–2002

Autumn 1999: The Majority Bill

National elections took place in Belgium on 13 June 1999. Unexpectedly, for the first time in 40 years it became possible to form a government without one of the key players in Belgian politics: the Christian Democrats. This led to a completely new political situation. The new Federal Government was a coalition of Liberals, Socialists, and Greens, which was quickly dubbed the 'purple-green' or 'rainbow' coalition.

Paragraph 11 of the coalition agreement (July 1999), under the heading 'Ethical Questions', read as follows:

> In recent years biological and bio-medical science has made significant advances. Fundamental interference has become possible in human life. However, our country has not yet succeeded in working out a legislative framework appropriate to this development and suitable for a modern and democratic society. Parliament must be enabled to fulfil its responsibility on such matters, *including euthanasia*, and must do this on the basis of each individual's convictions. (Italics added)[33]

---

[32] See ch 7.1 on the concept of an 'alternative majority'.

[33] The text of the coalition agreement (*Regeerakkoord*) can be found on the website of the Federal Government <http://www.belgium.be/eportal/index.jsp> accessed 7 September 2007.

This call on the Federal Parliament to legislate on euthanasia did not fall on deaf ears. After new Senate hearings in October 1999 with several members of the Advisory Committee for Bioethics, the formal legislative process got underway. Four parliamentary factions of the new governing coalition revived a number of old proposals for a bill and in the media stressed their willingness to come to a definitive proposal in the not too distant future. This was to be done in consultation with the opposition. Both the Dutch- and the French-speaking Christian Democrats also proposed bills, and thus, within a very short period of time, there were six proposals on the parliamentary table.[34]

A common premise underlay all of the proposals except those of the Christian Democrats: the idea of self-determination should be central. They also all proposed legalisation: the Penal Code should be changed so that euthanasia (under specified conditions) would no longer fall within the definition of manslaughter or murder. Otherwise the proposals were very heterogeneous, particularly with regard to the medical preconditions of euthanasia.

In the Dutch-speaking Greens' proposal, 'medical hopelessness' was sufficient ground for euthanasia to be carried out at the patient's request. In the explanatory memorandum this was broadly defined, so that advanced multiple sclerosis, for example, would meet the criterion.

The proposal of the Dutch- and French-speaking Socialist factions required a medical condition due to accident or illness, which was incurable and untreatable. This proposal further required the presence of persistent and unbearable suffering or distress, or irreversible coma (providing there was a prior request).

The proposals of the Liberal factions were the most stringent of the governing parties, reserving euthanasia explicitly for the last stages of life. Thus, the proposal of the French-speaking Liberals required 'approaching and inevitable death' and that of the Dutch-speaking Liberals a 'terminal phase'.

The proposals of the Christian Democratic factions were based not on self-determination but on the concept of mercy, placing strong emphasis on euthanasia as a last resort, only to be considered for those who are terminally ill and beyond palliative care. They rejected any possibility of euthanasia for incompetent patients.

Box 8.1 sums up the contours of the different proposals for legislation that were introduced after the elections of June 1999. It is interesting to note that the differences between the legislative proposals of the political parties of the governing coalition were just as sharp as the differences between the proposals of the governing parties on the one hand and those of the opposition parties on the other hand. To give but one significant example: the criterion of terminality was a necessary condition in the legislative proposals of two parties within the governing coalition (the French- and Dutch-speaking Liberals) but not in those of the

---

[34] An overview and discussion of these proposals can be found in Adams & Geudens 1999–2000: 793–817.

Box 8.1: *Major features of the legislative proposals introduced in 1999*

	Dutch-speaking Greens	Dutch-speaking Christian Democrats	French-speaking Liberals	French-speaking Christian Democrat	Socialist Parties (Dutch and French-speaking)	Dutch-speaking Liberals
Terminal illness/ last phase of life required?	–	+	+	+	–	+
Unbearable suffering required?	–	+	+	+	+	+
Euthanasia conditional on adequate palliative care?	+/–	+	+/–	+	+/–	+
Change of Penal Code?	+	–	+	–	+	+
Written advance request possible for non-conscious patients?	+	–	–	–	+	+

socialist parties (who were also part of the governing coalition). There were further differences of approach between the proposals of the governing parties. Three of them would have permitted euthanasia for non-conscious patients pursuant to a prior written request, for example, but the French-speaking Liberals categorically rejected this possibility. Clear differences were also present with regard to palliative care. Whereas in most proposals this was given little attention, the Dutch-speaking Liberals—like the opposition Christian Democrats—explicitly coupled euthanasia with the provision of a full palliative care package.

On 20 December 1999, a mere six weeks after the issue of euthanasia had been placed on the parliamentary agenda, the coalition parties unexpectedly came up with a bill whose stated aim was 'to embrace the four proposals of the governing parties that had been introduced at the beginning of the Senate hearings'. This would make it easier to have 'an open and comprehensive debate'.[35] In fact, the compromise bill was virtually the same as that proposed by the Socialists. The majority proposal on euthanasia was also linked to proposals for bills concerning

---

[35] See the introduction to Proposal of Law 2–244/1. *Parliamentary Proceedings, Senate,* 1999–2000.

palliative care and establishing a commission to control and evaluate euthanasia practice.

These events amounted to a strong break with the careful political consensus that had been built as a result of the debate in the Senate in 1997. This was not wholly unexpected in the light of what had gone before, because it had been clear since 1998 that the two socialist parties were no longer willing to identify with the consensus but insisted on an independent position.

The most important substantive differences between the governing parties and the Christian Democratic opposition related to five matters:

• The governing parties considered that if a patient suffers from (a) persistent and unbearable pain or distress that cannot be relieved, which (b) is the consequence of a severe and incurable illness, this, in principle, together with the patient's request, is sufficient to justify euthanasia. Whether the situation is unbearable is largely for the patient to decide. The French- and Dutch-language Christian Democrats took the position that the patient must be in a terminal state.

• The governing parties were for legalising euthanasia. Both Christian Democratic parties wanted a construction in which euthanasia remained in principle forbidden but would be justifiable in the case of a legally-defined 'state of necessity'.

• The governing parties proposed to accept, in place of a current request, one made in a prior written request by a patient who (a) is no longer conscious, and for whom (b) there is no means of restoring consciousness, and who (c) suffers from an incurable disease. The Christian Democrats rejected any form of advance request for euthanasia.

• The Christian Democrats proposed to require ethical consultation beforehand, stressing that the purpose was to give support to doctors and patients and not to create an 'ethical tribunal'. The governing parties regarded ethical consultation as unworkable and feared that it would in fact result in an 'ethical tribunal'.

• The Christian Democrats thought palliative care should always be tried before euthanasia was even considered. The majority parties saw palliative care as an option alongside euthanasia.

Notwithstanding the governing parties' stated commitment to an open and comprehensive debate, the presentation of the majority proposal was accompanied by strong statements in the media. The governing parties, so they said, were prepared to have a discussion with the opposition, but the matter had to be rounded off in the Senate by mid-February 2000, just seven weeks later. The Christmas recess came in the middle of that period. In response to the comment of a journalist that real discussion was not possible in so little time the reaction was that the opposition parties were free to introduce amendments in the meantime.[36] The leader of the Dutch-speaking Socialist faction in the Senate did not disguise her resentment of the years when the Christian Democrats had held power: 'The Christian

---

[36] Interview on Flemish Public Broadcasting, 20 December 1999.

Democrats have blocked discussion on this issue for years; now the time has come for legislation.'[37] Her Liberal counterpart let it be known that 'we have been talking about euthanasia for years. Those who do not understand it now, never will.'[38] In fact, the differences between the proposals of the governing parties had been, as we noted already, as wide as those between the majority parties on the one hand and the Christian Democrats on the other. Nevertheless, the governing parties had managed fairly easily to arrive at a common bill.

The Parliamentary Procedure in the Senate

In January and February of 2000 a number of interesting developments took place. Cracks developed in the majority front. Among the Dutch-speaking Liberals this apparently amounted to differences of opinion between the factions in the Senate and in the Chamber of Representatives. There were also differences among the French-speaking Liberals in which the Chairman of the Senate (a French-speaking Liberal himself) played a leading role. On several occasions he let it be known that, in his view, it was not a majority bill that was being discussed but rather a bill proposed by a few individual senators of the governing parties. There were likewise differences of opinion among the Socialists and the Greens. The chairman of the Dutch-speaking Socialists, for example, declared that he was prepared to come to an accommodation with the Christian Democrats, but he was called to order by a number of his colleagues. His efforts at rapprochement were also disparaged by his French-speaking colleague.[39]

Notwithstanding the political desire to proceed as quickly as possible, the Senate Committee handling the bill—a mixed committee consisting of the committees of social affairs and of justice respectively—held hearings with experts between February and May 2000. A wide range of persons from a variety of professional and ideological backgrounds were invited to give their opinions. Many senators of the majority parties initially opposed these hearings ('society has waited long enough for legislation, now it finally has to happen') but it seems that growing societal protest forced the hearings on them.

A very interesting position during the hearings was taken by (the vice-president of) the Belgian Order of Physicians. He observed that

> the National Council [of the Belgian Order of Physicians] does not wish to pass judgment either for or against any legislative initiatives in this matter. Nevertheless, a pressing question in our minds is whether a legislative initiative will bring us greater legal certainty. Of course it will, some say, because everything will be established in a Law. We, the doctors and lawyers of the National Council, are however not so certain that legal certainty will thereby be assured. There is also the question of whether the doctor–patient relationship, to which we attach supreme importance, will not be undermined by the new connotation introduced of the doctor as a bringer of death. As

---

[37] Interview in *De Standaard* (13 January 2000).
[38] Interview in *De Standaard* (13 January 2000).
[39] Personal observation, MA.

doctors, we feel very uncomfortable in such a role, perhaps because we are not yet used to it, but that does nothing to diminish our unease.[40]

The Belgian Order of Physicians thus made it clear that it did not want to play a key role in the legislative process concerning euthanasia. We will come back to this in the concluding remarks of chapter 9.

Despite the many parliamentary hearings the majority parties seemed to have no real intention to hold an open debate on the issue with the opposition. This was evidenced by the fact that none of the hundreds of amendments proposed by the opposition were even considered. However, on 7 July 2000 the Chairman of the Dutch-speaking Socialists reacted positively to an invitation by the Chairman of the Dutch-speaking Christian Democrats to exchange ideas on euthanasia:

> Speaking as a sociologist, society does not change because the law changes. The law follows social evolution. Ideology is thereby not a question of majority or minority. A broad discussion of euthanasia aimed at as wide a majority as possible will influence future approaches to ethical thinking.[41]

A Green senator likewise asked for changes in the bill to accommodate the point of view of the opposition. The chairman of the Dutch-speaking Liberals, however, reacted negatively to the invitation to enter into debate on the issue.[42]

In 1998, shortly before the beginning of the legislative procedure, a second study had been carried out in the Dutch-speaking part of Belgium (Flanders) to investigate medical end-of-life decisions with a possible or certain life-shortening effect. This was a more extensive follow-up of the pilot study mentioned above. The results of the new study were published in late 2000.[43] They were generally similar to those of the pilot study and confirmed that euthanasia had an established place in Belgian end-of-life medical practice. But the most striking finding was that the incidence of death as a consequence of euthanasia was barely the tip of the iceberg of end-of-life decisions: euthanasia and assisted suicide occurred in 1.2% of the total number of deaths examined, but termination of life without a request from the patient was almost three times as common (3.2%). In 39% of the deaths studied, medical decisions had been taken that shortened the life of the patient, including 18% to administer pain relief with life-shortening effect and 16% to withhold or withdraw treatment. But although quantitatively considered, death as a result of pain relief or abstention from life-prolonging treatment was much more common than euthanasia, parliamentary consideration of legislation continued to be focused almost exclusively on euthanasia.

---

[40] *Parliamentary Proceedings, Senate,* 2000–2001, no 2–244/24: 108. Another interesting example of the point of view of medical doctors is the one expressed by one of the chairpersons of a private doctors' organisation (see ch 7.2 on this). When asked during an interview whether or not legislation would provide doctors with more legal protection, he replied:
That is relative, can you cite the most recent conviction of a doctor for carrying out euthanasia? We know of none. Abuse exists but you are not going to alter that through softening the law. (*De Standaard* 24 December 1999).

[41] Interview in *De Standaard* (7 July 2000).

[42] Personal observation, MA.

[43] Deliens *et al* 2000. The results of this study are discussed at length in ch 10.1.

The parliamentary year 2000–01 was quieter than the year before, despite the almost weekly meetings of the Senate Committee dealing with the bill. The respective positions seemed to have become fixed. Societal debate was also on a back burner. The political majority once more set a time limit: they wanted the bill to be completed before the end of the calendar year 2000. This ambition had to be adjusted several times. First there was talk of getting the whole legislative process completed by that time, later of having the bill pass the Senate, and finally of the Senate Committee finishing its work. Nevertheless, discussions on the bill in the Senate Committee lasted until March 2001. There were hundreds of amendments, which led to nightly gatherings of the Senate Committee. Opposition amendments were systematically rejected even when they concerned only simple linguistic changes. The Senate Committee finally approved the bill in March 2001. It was in large measure due to the Chairman of the Senate Committee, a Senator of the French-speaking Greens, that the insistence on speed of a number of members of the political majority had been thwarted.

Since December 2000 the bill of the political majority had undergone a number of changes. One interesting change was that whereas in the original proposal euthanasia was no longer punishable under the Penal Code, in the final version of the Senate bill the Penal Code remained unchanged and it was the Law on Euthanasia that would determine under what conditions euthanasia would no longer be a crime. More importantly, a distinction between terminal and non-terminal patients had been introduced. Whereas in the case of a terminal patient only one consultation was required, in the case of a non-terminal patient an additional consultation was required and a month must elapse between the first request and carrying out the request. The initially separate bill establishing a non-criminal control system was incorporated in the main bill. Finally, a number of adjustments had been made to the provision for advance written requests.

A political development worthy of note came from the Chairman of the Senate, a French-speaking Liberal, who had serious ethical doubts about the bill. In March 2001 he used his authority as Senate Chairman to ask the Belgian Council of State[44] for advice on the bill. The majority faction leaders were initially shocked by this action. The advice of the Council of State appeared at the end of May 2001. Hardly any suggestions were made by the council that could delay the legislative process. The council seemed anxious to avoid interfering with this politically sensitive issue.

Finally, on 25 October 2001, the Belgian Senate approved the bill. In the final plenary debate 136 amendments were introduced, mainly by Christian Democrats. None of them was approved. The final vote on the bill reflected the polarisation between political majority and opposition. Of the 75 members of the Senate, 68 members were present at the time of the vote: 44 voted for the bill,

---

[44] *Conseil d'Etat/Raad van State*. The Belgian Council of State has two functions: it is an administrative court on the one hand and an advisory body for pending legislation on the other.

22 against, and two members abstained (one member of the French-speaking liberal faction and one member of the French-speaking Green party). Of the political majority, three French-speaking Liberals voted against. No opposition senator voted for the bill.

The Procedure in the Chamber of Representatives

Whereas in the Senate preliminary consideration of the bill took place in a so-called mixed committee, in the Chamber of Representatives the choice was made for phased treatment of the bill, with the Committee on Public Health Care providing a report for the Committee on Legal Affairs, which would then formally discuss the bill approved by the Senate.

In January 2002, consideration of the bill began in the Committee on Public Health Care, of which a Dutch-speaking Liberal, who was also a practising doctor, was chairman. Until then, she had been rather critical of the bill, mainly because of its provision for non-terminal patients. The debates in the committee took place in an open atmosphere, with willingness to listen to each others' arguments. As had been the case in the Senate Committee, hearings were organised, this time with (mostly Dutch) experts in palliative care and a few Belgian lawyers and experts.[45]

In its final report[46] the Committee of Public Health Care was unanimously critical of two important aspects of the bill as approved in the Senate. It was of the opinion that psychic suffering should not be a ground for euthanasia. And it wanted a stronger emphasis on the need for palliative care. Two Dutch-speaking Liberal members of the committee supported the protest of the Christian Democrats against the possibility of euthanasia for non-terminal patients.

In the Committee for Legal Affairs, by contrast with the Committee of Public Health, there was no unanimity concerning the bill and the advice of the latter committee was rejected. Although the views expressed were rather critical of the bill, new hearings did not bring any change. The differences of opinion focused on whether or not palliative care should be a precondition for euthanasia[47] and on the possibility of euthanasia for non-terminal patients. The Dutch-speaking extreme right wing party Flemish Bloc (*Vlaams Blok*) was once again the only political party opposed to any form of regulation of euthanasia.[48]

The Final Vote in the Chamber of Representatives

In a plenary session on 16 May the Belgian Chamber of Representatives approved the bill that had been approved in the Senate. As had been the case in the Senate,

---

[45] See the report by the Chamber of Representatives: *Parliamentary Proceedings, Chamber of Representatives*, 2001–02, 50–1488/9.

[46] *Ibid.*

[47] See ch 9.4.3.3. on this so-called 'palliative filter'.

[48] See the report by the Chamber of Representatives: *Parliamentary Proceedings, Chamber of Representatives*, 2001–02, 50–1488/1–12.

some 100 amendments (mainly from the opposition) were introduced, none of which were accepted. The political majority clearly had decided not to allow any amendments, since doing so would have entailed sending the bill back to the Senate. The final vote once again reflected the political and ideological cleavage between political majority and minority: 86 members voted for the bill, 51 against, and 10 members abstained. The last group consisted mainly of Dutch- and French-speaking Liberals. Two French-speaking Liberals voted against the bill, and the Dutch-speaking Christian Democrats announced that they would fight the bill in court (up to the European Court of Human Rights in Strasbourg).[49] On 22 June 2002 the King signed the bill.

In December 2002 the Law on Euthanasia was submitted to the Belgian Constitutional Court[50] on the petition of two pro-life organisations. The court delivered its judgment on 14 January 2004. The court was asked to assess the bill with respect to the principles of non-discrimination (Arts 10–11 of the Belgian Constitution) and the right to life (Art 2 of the European Convention on Human Rights). The complainants were, among other things, of the opinion that people suffering severely cannot make a genuinely free choice. Since the Law on Euthanasia made the principle of self-determination largely determinative, there could be no sufficient protection against abuse by third parties. This constituted discriminatory treatment, since healthy people would be able sufficiently to deter-mine their will. In a mere three paragraphs the court rejected this argument, observing that the complainants overlooked the many guarantees in the law. Moreover, the parliamentary proceedings made it clear that the legislator had paid careful attention to this issue. The court seemed reluctant to interfere with the political decision that had been made concerning euthanasia.

8.5 Reflections on the Process of Legal Change

Despite growing political consensus in the mid-1990s on the desirability of a specific regulation of euthanasia, the parliamentary debate on euthanasia after 1999 was characterised by strong polarisation and antagonistic debate. The new govern-ing parties did not seem willing to enter into a serious debate with the Christian Democratic opposition, and the reverse seems true for the Christian Democrats themselves. One might readily conclude that although the old ideological divisions, based to a large extent on religion (Catholicism versus anti-clericalism), were waning, they nevertheless played a significant role in the parliamentary procedure leading to the Law on Euthanasia. Among other things, this is evidenced by the fact that there was never any chance that any of the hundreds of legislative amendments

---

[49] In fact, they have not carried out this threat.
[50] The so called *Cour d'Arbitrage/Hof van Arbitrage*. The name of this court was changed in 2007 to Constitutional Court.

would be accepted once the bill was approved by the Senate and under consideration by the Chamber of Representatives.[51] And this was true even for sensible technical amendments that had nothing to do with ideology.

The most obvious explanation for the majority's lack of interest in consensus
lies in the fact that after the 1999 elections the Christian Democrats were (unexpectedly) no longer essential to the forming of a governing coalition. A watershed
of resentment had built up in the years that they had dominated government
coalitions and used their strategic position to block political debate and legislation
on euthanasia and other ethical issues. The elections created an opportunity for
political action where it had long been frustrated, and the Law on Euthanasia,
from this point of view, carried an important symbolic meaning: the era in which
Christian Democrats could determine the political process on ethical issues was
finally over. There was an unmistakable inclination on the part of the governing
parties to rub the message in.

Nevertheless, despite the hitherto uncharacteristic polarisation and the way the
Christian Democrats were excluded from the decision-making, the traditional
norms of 'consociational democracy', discussed at the beginning of chapter 7,
were definitely in evidence in the legislative process leading to the Law on
Euthanasia. From the outset of the process of legal change, even before the elections of 1999, the pluralistically composed Advisory Committee on Bioethics
played an important role in preparing the ground for a debate on euthanasia.[52]
The committee introduced a commonly accepted definition of euthanasia and
sketched the broad outlines of possible legislative approaches, thus making sensible discussion about the issue possible. In the committee's approach, the search for
consensus was still apparent.

It should also be noted that in spite of major differences between the various
legislative proposals which the governing parties introduced in parliament
between July and December 1999, they proceeded rapidly in December 1999 to a
coalition proposal. And in spite of differences of opinion during the parliamentary
procedure amongst some members of the parties of the governing coalition, in the
end they voted almost unanimously in favour of the coalition bill. Within the
coalition, techniques for reaching consensus were still functioning very well.

Another characteristic feature of the consociational tradition strongly in evidence in the parliamentary procedure leading up to the Law on Euthanasia is the
time that was devoted to hearings in which a wide range of views were presented
from all relevant sectors of society: universities, medical associations, medics and
paramedics, advisors to government ministers, palliative specialists, people from
abroad, societal organisations, ethicists, practising lawyers, a judge, representa-

---

[51] The fact that so many amendments were introduced reflects the fact that opposition activities
were to a large extent focused on influencing public opinion, the prospects of success for opposition
parties in a parliamentary system being in general very slim. But major objections stemming from
members of the governing parties were also never seriously considered. See for an example of this
section 8.4 on the fate of the report of the Committee on Public Health Care in the Chamber of
Representatives.

[52] See section 8.3 on this.

tives of patient organisations, etc. French- and Dutch-speaking Belgians and representatives of different ideological persuasion were about equally represented.

So much for the actors who played prominent roles in the process of legal change leading to the Law on Euthanasia. With the Dutch experience as a point of comparison, two actors were strikingly absent: doctors and the criminal law authorities. The Order of Physicians clearly preferred there to be no public discussion on the subject at all, and as we have seen were unwilling to play a constructive role in the legislative process. Three reasons may help to explain this. Membership in the Belgian Order of Physicians is, with some exceptions, obligatory for all practising doctors and the association is formally only responsible for medical discipline, the administration of registration and the like. Their role is not really a political one. Moreover, although the Order is not organised along classic denominational lines, it only has access to politics via the denominationally-segregated parties of Belgian consociational politics. It has therefore never been able to speak for all its members with one political voice. In the third place, although doctors were in a situation of legal uncertainty as regards euthanasia, there had in fact never been a prosecution until the legislative process was already underway in 1999. From that point of view, although legislation on euthanasia might theoretically have increased legal certainty, doctors apparently felt comfortable with the situation as it was, and at least their official representatives were definitely leery of formal legal intervention into the doctor–patient relationship.[53]

Unlike the Netherlands, the public prosecutors and the courts had no part in the development of legal norms regarding euthanasia. This is all the more striking since, in the analogous context of abortion, the Public Prosecutor pursued a vigorous policy. Maybe the difference has to do with the fact that thanks to abortion-rights activists abortion became a public issue in the 1960s and 1970s and was therefore not something prosecutors could simply ignore (a suggestion that receives support from the fact that, as we will see in chapter 9.3, prosecutions for euthanasia were initiated once the legislative process did get underway). The fact that abortion, the women who need it and the doctors who perform it were traditionally ascribed a low and disreputable status and thus easily seen as 'criminals', whereas patients asking their doctor for euthanasia and the doctors treating them were probably if anything of rather high status and reputation, may also help to explain prosecutorial reluctance. And finally, as a practical matter euthanasia rarely comes to the attention of the criminal law authorities unless the doctor concerned reports what he has done—something Dutch doctors began doing in the 1980s, but Belgian doctors apparently never did until after the Law on Euthanasia was passed. Belgian prosecutors therefore probably had little or no opportunity to contribute to the process of legal development. But whatever the reasons may be,

---

[53] See more on this in the concluding remarks of ch 9.5. It should be noted that doctors as individuals did make their views known. In 2001 a petition circulated by an anti-confessional association in support of legalisation of euthanasia along the lines of the pending bill was signed by some 12,000 persons, including some 2,400 doctors. See <http://www.rws.be/kwartaalblad/2001/1/10.html> accessed 17 September 2007.

social and political discussion during the political process of legislation on euthanasia was not legally structured. This may help to explain why the debate in Belgium had such a strong parliamentary character.

Having said all this, it might also be important to mention that although there are important differences between the Dutch and Belgian processes of legal change concerning euthanasia, the Belgians clearly did borrow elements of Dutch law. Two striking examples are the definition of 'euthanasia' (although interestingly enough this does not appear in the Dutch statute) and the non-criminal review procedure.[54]

---

[54] See ch 9.4.2 and ch 9.4.4.2 respectively on these two aspects.

9

Belgian Law on Euthanasia and Other MBPSL

This chapter gives an overview of Belgian law on euthanasia (and the other sorts of medical behaviour that potentially shortens life—MBPSL). Because the Belgian process of legal change, and also the social history of discussion and debate on MBPSL (in particular euthanasia) have been much shorter than they were in the Netherlands, the material to draw on is less rich than what we have seen in chapter 4. The classificatory distinctions we used in chapter 4.1 for describing Dutch law on the various MBPSL apply equally in the Belgian case.

We begin in section 9.1 with a brief overview of where the applicable law on euthanasia and other MBPSL is to be found. In section 9.2 we deal with current law on what is considered in Belgium 'normal medical practice'. Section 9.3 will be devoted to the legal status of euthanasia and physician-assisted suicide before 2002, and section 9.4 to euthanasia and physician-assisted suicide under the Law on Euthanasia of 2002. The chapter ends with some concluding remarks in section 9.5.

We make explicit comparisons between Belgian and Dutch law here and there in the course of the chapter. It suffices to note here that while there are striking differences in the formal expression of the applicable legal rules (largely non-statutory in the Netherlands, largely statutory in Belgium), and while the density of regulation is much higher in the Netherlands than in Belgium, substantively the way the two countries regulate euthanasia and the other MBPSL is largely the same.

9.1. Current Law in Belgium

Belgian law relevant to MBPSL is largely to be found in the sources given in Box 9.1.

9.2 'Normal Medical Practice'

In Belgium, as in the Netherlands and elsewhere in the world, many things a doctor does in the course of treating a patient are considered 'normal medical practice'

Box 9.1. The sources of Belgian law on MBPSL

- the Penal Code, articles 393–4 (homicide and murder), 425 (intentionally not providing food or treatment to minors or incompetent persons), 426 (not supporting a minor or incompetent person), 422bis (not helping a person who is in a situation of 'great danger'), and 418 (unintentional homicide)
- the Law on Euthanasia of 28 May 2002[1]
- the Law supplementing the Law on Euthanasia with provisions on the role of the pharmacist and the availability of euthanatica of 10 November 2005[2]
- the Law on Palliative Care of 14 June 2002[3]
- the Law on Patients' Rights of 22 August 2002[4]
- the Parliamentary Proceedings concerning the Law on Euthanasia[5]
- the Advisory Report of the Belgian Council of State on the Euthanasia and Palliative Care Bills[6]
- the Advisory Report, 'The Desirability of a Legal Regulation of Euthanasia,' of the Advisory Committee on Bioethics[7]
- the Deontological Code [Code of Medical Ethics] of the Order of Physicians[8]
- the Royal Decree of 2 April 2003 establishing the way an advance request is drafted, confirmed, changed or revoked[9]
- the Royal Decree of 27 April 2007 regulating the way an advance request for euthanasia is registered and made available to the treating physician[10]
- the Royal Decree of 10 November 1967 concerning the practice of health care professionals[11]

---

[1] Wet van 28 mei 2002 betreffende de euthanasie. *Belgisch Staatsblad* [Belgian State Gazette] (22 June 2002) effective 22 September 2002. For an English translation see: <http://www.kuleuven. ac.be/cbmer/viewpic.php?LAN=E&TABLE=DOCS&ID=23> accessed 10 September 2007. Also in 10 *European Journal of Health Law* 2003, p 329.

[2] Wet van 10 november 2005 tot aanvulling van de wet van 28 mei 2002 betreffende de euthanasie met bepalingen over de rol van de apotheker en het gebruik en de beschikbaarheid van euthanatica. *Belgisch Staatsblad* (13 December 2005).

[3] Wet van 14 juni 2002 betreffende de palliatieve zorg. *Belgisch Staatsblad* (22 October 2002) (effective 22 September 2002).

[4] Wet van 22 augustus 2002 betreffende de rechten van de patiënt. *Belgisch Staatsblad* (26 September 2003).

[5] *Parliamentary Proceedings, Senate,* 2000–01, no 2–244/22. *Parliamentary Proceedings, Chamber of Representatives,* 2001–02, no 50–1488/009. These documents, which are in both Dutch and French, can be found respectively at <http://www.senate.be> and <http://www.dekamer.be>, both accessed 30 September 2007.

[6] *Parliamentary Proceedings, Senate,* 2000–01, no 2–244/21. This document can be found at <http:www.senate.be> accessed 30 September 2007.

[7] Raadgevende Comité voor Bio-ethiek 1997. For an English translation see Nys 1997.

[8] The Code can be found at: <http://195.234.184.64/web-Ned/deonton.htm> accessed 7 September 2007, Dutch, French and German versions.

[9] Koninklijk Besluit van 2 april 2003 houdende vaststelling van de wijze waarop de wilsverklaring inzake euthanasie wordt opgesteld, herbevestigd, herzien of ingetrokken. *Belgisch Staatsblad* (13 May 2003), available at <http://www.ejustice.just.fgov.be/cgi/welcome.pl> accessed 30 September 2007.

[10] Koninklijk Besluit 27 april 2007 tot regeling van de wijze waarop de wilsverklaring inzake euthanasie wordt geregistreerd en via de diensten van het Rijksregister aan de betrokken artsen wordt meegedeeld. *Belgisch Staatsblad* (27 June 2007), available at <http://www.ejustice.just.fgov.be/cgi/ welcome.pl> accessed 30 September 2007.

[11] Koninklijk Besluit no 78 van 10 november 1967 betreffende de uitoefening van de geneeskunst, de verpleegkunde, de paramedische beroepen en de geneeskundige commissies. *Belgisch Staatsblad*

even though, if done by any other person, they would constitute a criminal offence. It is generally accepted that a doctor is not obliged to continue medical treatment that no longer has any curative or palliative[12] effect on a (mortal) disease, and that a possible shortening of life through administration of appropriate pain relief is an acceptable side effect.[13] In the case of a doctor such behaviour is considered to be (implicitly) excluded from the coverage of the criminal law.[14] The Belgian Council of State, in its advice on the then Euthanasia Bill, confirmed this position. The council wrote that the bill would not be applicable to medical behaviour that was considered to be normal medical practice, ie: (a) not starting or ending medical treatment that is useless or disproportionate, and (b) medically indicated pain relief that may result in shortening the life of the patient.[15] In Belgium the basis for this exclusion is considered to lie in the Royal Decree of 1967 Concerning the Practice of the Health Care Professionals. The decree gives—assuming the valid informed consent of the patient—legal permission to doctors to infringe the physical integrity of the patient by surgery and other medical interventions.

The Belgian legislator has delegated authority for laying down professional ('deontological') rules of conduct to professional organisations. In the case of the practice of medicine, this is the Order of Physicians and the Order of Pharmacists.[16] Non-compliance with these rules can result in temporary or permanent professional suspension. The Order of Physicians is responsible for formulating and enforcing a Deontological Code for the medical profession.[17]

(14 November 1967) available at <http://www.ejustice.just.fgov.be/cgi/welcome.pl> accessed 30 September 2007. This law has been changed many times since then.

[12] Art 1 of the Royal Decree of 1967 Concerning the Practice of the Health Care Professions defines medicine as having a 'preventive, experimental, curative, continuous and palliative' character.

[13] See section 9.2.3 for a more comprehensive account of death due to withdrawing or withholding treatment or to pain relief.

[14] But note that the expression 'medical exception', as it is used in the Netherlands to cover these situations (see ch 4.2.1), is as such not used in Belgian medical law.

[15] Advice of the Council of State, *Parliamentary Proceedings, Senate*, 2000–01, no 2–244/21: 10. Not all Belgian legal scholars are convinced by this line of reasoning (see eg Dijon 1982: 537–9). Some argue that if a doctor knows or should have known that the patient would probably die as a result of such treatment, he is in principle guilty of homicide. These authors argue that there is no 'medical exception' but that the behaviour of the doctor can be justified with the help of the idea of a state of necessity. See Nys 2005: 360–61 for the various positions in this debate.

[16] See ch 7.2.3 for the task and role of the Order of Physicians.

[17] Curiously, the Belgian Supreme Court (the *Cour de Cassation*), in a consistent line of decisions, has held that the rules of the Deontological Code of the Order of Physicians are not to be treated as legally-binding rules, either by the disciplinary tribunals of the Order of Physicians or by the courts. This because the code has never been declared binding. But the *Cour de Cassation* does accept that the rules of the code may be considered to describe proper medical behaviour. The effect of this is that while the rules are not legally binding, the disciplinary tribunals can refer to them and impose sanctions on doctors who depart from them. There are no disciplinary judgments known dealing directly with euthanasia or other MBPSL-decisions. This may be at least partly due to the fact that disciplinary judgments are not published or made public. See on all this Nys 2005: 80–81 (with further references).

9.2.1 Refusal of Treatment and Advance Refusal of Treatment

Belgian law recognises unambiguously the right of a patient to refuse medical treatment. Medical treatment against the will of a competent patient may first of all be considered a violation of article 8 (1) of the European Convention for the Protection of Human Rights (ECHR), to which Belgium is a party. This article protects the right to privacy, which includes the right not to be treated medically without consent. In the *Pretty* case (2002) the court held as follows:

> In the sphere of medical treatment, the refusal to accept a particular treatment might, inevitably, lead to a fatal outcome, yet the imposition of medical treatment, without the consent of a mentally competent adult patient, would interfere with a person's physical integrity in a manner capable of engaging the rights protected under article 8(1) of the Convention.[18]

According to article 8 (4) of the Belgian Law on Patients' Rights, patients have the right to refuse or withdraw their consent for any so-called 'medical intervention'. Neither refusal nor withdrawal of consent ends the right to high-quality care referred to in article 5 of the law. In other words, refusal by itself does not terminate the legal relationship between the patient and his doctor.

If at a time when he was still capable of asserting the rights covered in the Law on Patients' Rights, a patient has made a written statement refusing a given medical intervention, this refusal must be respected as long as the patient has not revoked it while he was still competent to exercise his rights himself (art 8 (4), final sentence). This provision, which establishes the binding character of a so-called 'advance refusal', is perhaps the most controversial part of the Belgian Law on Patients' Rights.[19] According to the explanatory report, an advance refusal has in principle the same legal effect as a currently expressed refusal: the health professional is not authorised to act, and must respect the refusal.[20] In order for an advance refusal to be binding, two conditions must be met. First, it must apply to a 'well defined medical intervention' (art 8 (4)) although there are no limits on the treatments that can be refused or on the circumstances (eg terminal illness) in which a refusal is effective. But a refusal that uses vague terms is not binding. Second, there must be no doubt that the refusal was made by the person concerned. In an emergency situation a doctor will often not have enough time to verify this and his duty to provide assistance to a person in great danger (art 422bis Penal Code) will take precedence. The Law does not provide for a system of registration.

The principle of informed consent is also recognised in the Deontological Code of the Order of Physicians, which has recently (2006) been changed under the

---

[18] *Pretty v The United Kingdom*, no 2346/02, 29 April 2002, § 63.

[19] Some members of Parliament who earlier in the year 2002 had approved the Law on Euthanasia refused to approve the binding character of an advance refusal because they considered this a way to circumvent the extensive requirements of the Law on Euthanasia. The Order of Physicians vigorously opposed the binding force of advance refusals but seems more recently to have accepted the idea.

[20] *Parliamentary Proceedings, Chamber of Representatives*, 2001–02, no 1641/001: 28.

influence of the Law on Euthanasia and the Law on Patients Rights. Articles 95 and 97 provide that a doctor should in a timely manner inform the patient about the fact that his life is ending, and also inform him of all the help that can be given in this context (medical, social, psychic, moral, palliative, etc). Article 95 expressly states that the doctor should tell the patient that he always has a right to palliative care. The doctor must make clear in a timely manner what medical care he is prepared to give at the end of life (the implicit reference is to euthanasia),[21] so that the patient has enough time to approach another doctor. Article 96 further states that for all medical behaviour at the end of life the consent of the patient is required.

The Law on Patients' Rights further contains rules to protect the rights of patients who are legally (art 13) or factually (art 14) not capable of exercising their rights as a patient. The rights of adult patients who have the legal status of 'extended minority' or have been declared incompetent are exercised by their parents or guardians. Such patients have to be involved as much as possible, depending on their capacities, in the exercise of their rights (art 13 (1–2)).

The rights of an adult patient who does not belong to one of the categories mentioned in article 13 and who is not capable of exercising his rights as a patient are exercised by a person he previously appointed to act on his behalf when and for as long as he is unable to exercise these rights himself. This so-called 'patient-designated representative' must be appointed in a specific written mandate, dated and signed by the patient and by the appointed person, clearly showing the latter's consent. The patient or his appointed representative may revoke the mandate (art 14 (1)).

If there is no patient-designated representative or if he fails to act, the rights of an incapable adult patient can be exercised by the cohabiting spouse, the legally cohabiting partner or the actual cohabiting partner. If this person refuses or if there is no such person, the rights can be asserted, in descending order, by an adult child, a parent, or an adult brother or sister of the patient. If these persons refuse or if there are no such persons, the physician concerned must act in the patient's interest, possibly after multidisciplinary consultation. This is also the case when there is a conflict between two or more representatives of equal rank, for instance, a conflict between two children of the patient (art 14 (2)). An adult, incapacitated patient must be involved as much as possible in the exercise of his rights (art 14 (3)).

Whereas a patient may make an 'irrational' decision, the legal representative of an incapacitated patient must always act in the interest of the patient. The Law on Patients' Rights provides that a doctor must deviate from the decision taken by the representative, in the interest of the patient, if necessary to avert a threat to the patient's life or serious damage to his health. However, when the decision is taken by a 'patient-designated representative', the physician may deviate from this

---

[21] Art 95 does not mean that a doctor can decide not to provide the patient with medical care, since on the basis of art 8 (4) of the Law on Patients' Rights neither refusal nor withdrawal of consent ends the right to high-quality care. Art 97 of the Deontological Code expressly states that the doctor must help the patient medically and morally at the end of life.

decision only if the representative is unable to refer to the patient's express will, such as an express refusal of a life-saving treatment (art 15 (2)).

In the case of minor patients (under eighteen) the patient's rights are exercised by the parents with authority over the minor or by his guardians (art 12 (1)). The minor patient should be involved in the exercise of his rights, bearing in mind his age and level of maturity.[22] Minor patients who are deemed capable of reasonably grasping their situation may exercise their rights on their own behalf (art 12 (2)). The law nowhere explicitly states who is to judge whether a minor patient can be deemed capable of reasonably grasping the situation, but the most obvious course of action would be to leave this up to the doctor since he may only act if he has obtained valid consent. It is up to him to decide whether the conditions for a valid consent are present.

Article 15 (2) of the Law on Patients' Rights requires a doctor to deviate from the decision taken by the parents in the interest of a minor, when their decision involves a threat to his life or of serious damage to his health. When a minor patient refuses a treatment deemed necessary by the doctor, the doctor must give the treatment nevertheless.

9.2.2 Withholding or Withdrawing Treatment Based on 'Medical Futility'

Up to now, the discussion in Belgium regarding withholding or withdrawing medical treatment based on 'medical futility' has mainly concerned the criminal law consequences of such a decision. Withholding or withdrawing life-prolonging treatment would at first sight seem to violate several articles of the Penal Code. Article 425 prohibits intentionally withholding food or care from a child under 16 years, or from a person who is unable to look after himself due to his physical or mental condition, to the point of endangering his health. Article 426 prohibits negligently withholding care from such a child or person to the point of endangering his health. Article 422bis prohibits failing to give assistance to a person who is in serious danger. Nevertheless, it is commonly accepted that none of these provisions imposes a duty on a physician to start or to continue a treatment when such treatment is or has become futile. There is no case law on this, but according to article 97 of the Deontological Code, so-called 'therapeutic obstinacy'—continuing with treatment that has become futile—must be avoided.

The private law aspects of the participation of the patient or his representative in a non-treatment decision have received little attention. 'Informed consent' by the patient is generally not related to 'medical decisions' but to the narrower concept of 'intervention' or even 'treatment'. An example of this is article 5 of the European Convention on Human Rights and Biomedicine which reads as follows:

> An intervention in the health field may only be carried out after the person concerned has given free and informed consent to it.

---

[22] Art 96 of the Deontological Code expressly provides that the treating physician must involve a minor patient in all MBPSL, having regard to his age, his maturity and the type of decision.

The limitation to 'intervention' seems to imply that other medical decisions regarding the patient, such as non-treatment decisions, are within the authority of the health professional. It might be considered only a matter of good practice to ask for the opinion of the patient, and not a legal duty.[23]

Such a limited approach to patient participation in medical decisions to withhold or withdraw futile treatment reflects the fact that informed consent has traditionally been considered as a justification for a violation of the bodily integrity of the patient. Moreover, medical interventions have been considered only justifiable when a doctor acts with a therapeutic intention.[24] If, according to the doctor, the situation of the patient is such that a given intervention cannot serve any therapeutic purpose, he is obliged to withhold or withdraw the treatment concerned. This reasoning seems to leave no room for a patient or his representative to participate in a non-treatment decision.

Having said all this, the conviction is growing in Belgium that the right to privacy (art 8 ECHR) brings with it that in the case of a non-treatment decision, self-determination and shared decision-making should be taken seriously. Some have argued that article 2 ECHR, which protects the right to life, is relevant in this context. In 1993, the European Commission of Human Rights (whose role was taken over by the European Court of Human Rights a few years ago) was confronted with the question whether this article obliges a Member State to protect its citizens against non-treatment decisions. In the *Widmer* case a Swiss citizen lodged a complaint before the European Commission because of what he considered to be a case of 'passive euthanasia' on his father who suffered from Parkinson's disease.[25] His complaint had been dismissed by the Swiss Courts. Before the European Commission, the applicant complained that Swiss law violates the right to life because it does not prohibit 'passive euthanasia' applied without the express and written consent of the patient. The applicant also considered this situation a violation of 8 ECHR because not respecting the will of the patient constitutes a violation of his right to privacy. According to the European Commission, article 2 obliges a state not only to abstain from intentionally killing a person, but also to take adequate measures to protect life. However, the commission declared the complaint inadmissible because Swiss law prohibits the negligent taking of life. By offering this protection Swiss law complies with the obligation imposed by article 2 ECHR. Unfortunately, the commission did not give an answer with respect to the violation of article 8. In the *Glass* case (2004)[26] the court did not consider it necessary to examine separately the complaint of the applicant (a young boy) regarding the inclusion of a so-called Do Not Resuscitate (DNR) order in his medical file without the knowledge and consent of the second applicant (his mother). But the Court apparently did not exclude the possibility that the informed consent

---

[23] *Cf* Nys 1999: 213.

[24] No reference is made in the literature to a possible palliative intention.

[25] *Widmer v Switzerland*, Application no 20527/92, 10 February 1993. The facts of the application do not reveal what the medical treatment was nor the circumstances under which it was withdrawn.

[26] *Glass v The United Kingdom*, no 61827/00, 9 March 2004.

of the patient or his representative should be sought before making a DNR order.

It is common for Belgian hospitals and nursing homes to have an institutional policy concerning DNR orders, usually consisting of a protocol for DNR decision-making and a special order form to be kept in the files of an individual patient. However, Belgian researchers have concluded that the structure of the order forms needs improvement in order to 'improve decision-making' and 'invite physicians to communicate better with patients, their next of kin, primary care physicians, and other health care providers'.[27] Although there is still a great deal of discussion and confusion in Belgian medical law regarding the position of the patient or his representative in connection with withdrawing or withholding futile treatment,[28] there is a growing consensus that a physician must at least inform the patient of the fact that he proposes to abstain from treatment he considers futile, if only so that the patient can seek a second professional opinion. The greater the role that proportionality or 'quality-of-life' considerations play, the greater the role of the patient in the decision-making should be. Where such considerations are important, the patient has a direct interest in being enabled to express his own views on his situation and the decision should at least be discussed with the patient.[29]

9.2.3 Pain Relief with Life-Shortening Effects and the Idea of 'Double Effect'

The use of drugs by a physician to alleviate pain or symptoms of a dying patient (even though the dose will more or less certainly hasten the moment of death) is accepted medical practice in Belgium. According to a previous version of article 96 of the Deontological Code, it is a doctor's duty to alleviate the mental and physical suffering of his patient and to let him die in dignity. Although the present version of article 96 no longer mentions this duty there is no doubt that pain relief with life-shortening effect is normal medical practice. However, the legal basis for this general acceptance is far from clear. There is only one case on the subject. A home for the elderly filed a complaint against a palliative nurse who had administered morphine to an 82-year-old suffering from terminal lung-cancer. According to the home this was a case of 'active euthanasia'. The expert appointed by the court concluded that only 40 mg were found in the body of the patient, which was certainly not a lethal dose for a terminal cancer patient. According to the court it

---

[27] De Gendt *et al* 2005: 2225. Development of these policies took place in Flanders in the late 1990s.

[28] A recent amendment to the Deontological Code of the Order of Physicians has contributed to the confusion in this regard. Art 96 provides that for any 'intervention' at the end of a patient's life a physician has to obtain the free and informed consent of the patient. Whether 'intervention' includes a non-treatment decision is, however, not certain. The advice of the Advisory Council on Bioethics of 16 April 2007 (not yet published) is divided on the point. For some members the requirement of informed consent provided for in article 8 of the Law on Patients' Rights applies also when a doctor includes a DNR order in the file of a patient, while for other members such a conclusion cannot be derived from this article.

[29] Compare ch 4.2.2.1 and 4.2.2.2 on the legislation in the Netherlands. See also Gevers 1997: 152 (discussing the situation in the Netherlands).

is an accepted medical practice to alleviate intense pain of patients who cannot be cured even if this has an unintended but accepted life-shortening effect. The nurse was acquitted.[30]

Nevertheless, the legal status of pain relief with life-shortening effect remains the subject of discussion. Some criminal lawyers recommend that a doctor who gives such pain relief adhere to all the conditions of the Law on Euthanasia in order to be legally safe.[31] This would imply that pain relief can only be given after an explicit request from the patient and that the doctor must report the case to the Federal Control and Evaluation Commission. During the parliamentary discussion of the Law on Euthanasia, however, the legislator clearly expressed the opinion that pain relief and euthanasia should not be dealt with in the same way.[32]

One widely held view is that shortening the dying process in a way that leads to a death without suffering can be a legitimate subsidiary objective of the administration of pain relief. This reasoning is based on the doctrine of 'double effect'. Shortening life as a result of alleviating pain is in this view morally (and by analogy, legally) permissible because, although it can be foreseen, death in such a case is not intended either for itself or as a means of achieving the goal of alleviating suffering. What is intended is the alleviation of the patient's suffering. Administering the same drug with the intention of causing the patient's death in order to put an end to this suffering would not be permissible.

Critics argue that it is questionable whether the distinction between 'intention' and 'foresight' can be made in the clear-cut way that adherents to the doctrine of double effect suppose.[33] However that may be, Belgian criminal law does not make such a distinction. Article 393 of the Belgian Penal Code provides that 'homicide with the intention of causing death is treated as murder'. According to legal writers there is no difference between 'direct' intention and so-called 'indirect' intention. One speaks of indirect intention if an author does not want the particular consequences of his action, but he does foresee the possibility of these consequences and this does not keep him from acting.[34] If the undesired consequences do occur (ie the patient dies) the physician cannot defend himself by arguing that since he did not want them, he did not intend to end the life of the patient. Thus, under Belgian law, the distinction between intentional and foreseen shortening of the life of the patient is untenable.

The fact that the doctrine of 'double effect' is not consistent with Belgian law does not necessary entail that the use of drugs to alleviate pain with the foreseen consequence that the death of the patient will more or less certainly be hastened is a punishable act. There may be circumstances where doing this is justified. One ground of justification is the so-called 'state of necessity' or conflict of duties. In

---

[30] Cited by Vansweevelt 2006: 383–4.

[31] Dierickx 2003: 8.

[32] *Parliamentary Proceedings, Chamber of Representatives*, 2001–02, 1488/9: 122 and 190.

[33] Dierickx 2003: 7.

[34] Dupont & Verstraeten 1990: 255–6. Compare ch 4.2.2.3 and 4.2.3 on the legal situation in the Netherlands.

the case of pain relief such a conflict may arise between the general duty to respect life and the professional duty to alleviate the pain and suffering of a dying patient. Although such a justification may offer a solution in a particular case, we must come to the conclusion that Belgian law is unsatisfactory in this respect. A doctor is obliged to alleviate pain at the request of or in agreement with a dying patient. However, when the administration of the drugs has the foreseeable consequence that the life of the patient will be shortened, it is up to the doctor to decide whether he accepts this consequence. In other words, the patient is in this respect at the mercy of the doctor who himself is at the mercy of the law.

9.2.4 Palliative and Terminal Sedation

The legal uncertainty that surrounds pain relief also affects palliative and terminal sedation, which are usually not distinguished from each other. Since palliative sedation is not generally a cause of death, it is only when artificial nutrition and hydration are withheld that a MBPSL is involved at all. In its opinion on the then Bill on Euthanasia the Belgian Council of State recommended that the legislator clarify whether 'controlled sedation', as it was called by the council, should be regarded as euthanasia or as palliative care, but it is not clear precisely which of the two the council had in mind.[35] Its recommendation has in any case not been followed.

9.3 The Legal Status of Euthanasia and Physician-Assisted Suicide before 2002

Until the introduction of the Law on Euthanasia in 2002, euthanasia was on its face a criminal offence in Belgium. It was not, however, as in the Netherlands, a discrete offence. It would have been prosecuted under one or another general provision of the Penal Code of 1867, in particular article 393 relating to voluntary manslaughter and article 394 to murder.[36] These offences are tried before the so-called Assize Court.[37]

The matter was more complicated when it came to assisted suicide. Suicide was not and is not a criminal offence in Belgian law, and (in the absence of any specific prohibition, as exists in the Netherlands) assisting with suicide was therefore also not an offence. According to some authors, however, the law could have been so interpreted as to make assisted suicide indirectly punishable. They referred to article 422bis of the Penal Code that deals with not giving help to someone in grave danger.[38] The absence of any Belgian case law on the issue, however, meant that it

---

[35] *Parliamentary Proceedings, Senate*, 2000–01, no 2–244/21: 11–12.
[36] Art 397 relating to poisoning might also have been relevant.
[37] The Assize Court is the criminal court for serious offences; it works with a jury.

was unclear whether such an argument would have been accepted by the courts.[39]

Article 95 of the Deontological Code of the Order of Physicians until recently read:

> A doctor may not intentionally cause the death of one of his patients or help him to take his own life.

And article 96 stated that:

> When the death of a patient is approaching and he is still in some state of awareness, the doctor is bound to give moral support and to give what help is necessary to reduce physical and psychological suffering in order to allow the patient to die a dignified death. When the patient has entered a permanent state of deep unconsciousness the doctor must limit his behaviour to giving palliative care.

These provisions of the Deontological Code reflect the ideas of the medical profession concerning the palliative duties of doctors and the relationship between euthanasia and other MBPSL. They have recently been changed under the influence of the Law on Euthanasia of 2002 and the Law on Patients' Rights of 2002.[40]

Despite the provisions of the Penal Code and the Deontological Code, however, before 2002 the law applicable to euthanasia and physician-assisted suicide was unclear and medical practice took place in a situation of great legal uncertainty. It was known that euthanasia was in fact being practised,[41] but when deciding whether or not to perform euthanasia a doctor would have been unable to predict what the legal consequences might be. There was no relevant case law and until the legislative procedure began in December 1999 the public prosecutor's office had for many decades not initiated proceedings against a doctor in the whole field of MBPSL.[42] Because of this, it was not known, for example, whether the concept of the so-called 'situation of necessity', as this had been applied as early as 1984 by the Dutch Supreme Court to the case of euthanasia,[43] would also be accepted in Belgium.

---

[38] Dijon 1982: 861–2 (with further references). The Council of State was in its advisory report on the then Euthanasia Bill of the opinion that if a doctor actively helps a person to commit suicide, article 422bis of the Belgian Penal Code is applicable. *Parliamentary Proceedings, Senate*, 2000–01, no 2–244/21: 14.

[39] Art 418 of the Penal Code dealing with unintended homicide might conceivably have been applicable. However Dijon (1982: no 859), doubts the applicability of this provision.

[40] See section 9.2.1.

[41] See ch 10.1.

[42] Once euthanasia got on the political agenda, the public prosecutor did begin to investigate cases of possible euthanasia. In January 2000, for example, following reports by nursing personnel, two doctors (a cardiologist and an anaesthetist) in the city of Liège were arrested on suspicion of administering lethal barbiturates to a man suffering from a long-term chronic lung condition, at his own request and in consultation with his family. On 6 February 2003 the Criminal Court of Liège decided not to prosecute the doctors, because under the Law on Euthanasia—which by then had come into force—their behaviour could not be considered an offence. The decision is not published.

At the beginning of 1960s, there had been a prosecution of a doctor in the context of a so-called softenon baby. A mother gave her recently born and badly deformed baby a lethal mixture which she received from her doctor after having put much pressure on him. The jury acquitted both the woman and her doctor. This was of course not a case of euthanasia since there was obviously no request from the baby. See Viernet, Riquet & Roumagnon 1963.

[43] See ch 4.2.3.2 on the 'situation of necessity' in Dutch euthanasia law.

9.4 Euthanasia and Physician-Assisted Suicide under the Law on Euthanasia of 2002

9.4.1 Statutory Requirements

As we have seen in chapter 8, the Law on Euthanasia was passed by the Chamber of Representatives on 28 May 2002. On 23 September 2002 it came into force. This brought to an end a relatively brief legislative process that had begun in the summer of 1999. That the Law on Euthanasia was enacted so quickly is all the more noteworthy given that the legislative process was, as we have just seen in the previous section, in no way legally pre-structured, for example in a body of case law.

An important consequence of this situation is that, by contrast with the Netherlands, one cannot appeal to a qualitatively and quantitatively significant body of law and common understanding when interpreting the new Belgian legislation. One must therefore be cautious and this is all the more the case since the parliamentary debates were not at all clear on a number of important points.

It is precisely the lack of prior law and practical experience in Belgium that helps to explain why the Belgian law, unlike its Dutch counterpart, contains so many detailed provisions. Because of its detailed and complex character we think it important to begin our treatment of the law with a comprehensive and systematic overview of its provisions (Box 9.2). The text that follows will by and large follow this overview.

Box 9.2 The requirements of the Law on Euthanasia of 2002

A. If the patient is expected to die in the near future

The patient:
- must have attained the age of majority (or be an emancipated minor), and be legally competent and conscious at the time of making the request
- must be in a medically hopeless situation of persistent and unbearable physical or mental suffering that cannot be alleviated
- this condition must be the result of a serious and incurable disorder caused by illness or accident

The request:
- must be voluntary, well-considered and repeated
- must not be the result of external pressure

The patient's doctor:
- must inform the patient about his health condition and life expectancy
- must discuss with the patient his request for euthanasia
- must discuss with the patient the possible therapeutic and palliative courses of action and their consequences

---

- must come, together with the patient, to the conclusion that there is no reasonable alternative to the patient's situation
- must be certain of the patient's persistent physical or mental suffering
- must be certain of the durable nature of the patients' request
- must have several conversations with the patient spread out over a reasonable period of time, taking into account the progress of the patient's condition
- must consult another doctor about the serious and incurable character of the disorder
- must inform the consulting doctor about the reasons for his consultation
- must, if there is a nursing team that has regular contact with the patient, discuss the request of the patient with the nursing team or its members
- must, if the patient so desires, discuss the request with relatives appointed by the patient
- must be certain that the patient has had the opportunity to discuss his request with the persons that he wants to meet

The consulted doctor:

- must review the medical record
- must examine the patient and be certain of the patient's persistent and unbearable physical or mental suffering that can not be alleviated
- must report in writing on his findings to the patient's doctor
- must be independent of the patient as well as of the patient's doctor
- must be qualified to give an opinion about the disorder in question

The patient's doctor:

- must inform the patient about the results of the consultation

B. If the patient is not expected to die in the near future.

The patient's doctor must in addition to the requirements under (A):

- consult a second doctor, who is a psychiatrist or a specialist in the disorder in question, and inform him of the reasons for the consultation

The second consulted doctor:

- must review the medical records
- must examine the patient
- must ensure himself of the persistent and unbearable physical or mental suffering that cannot be alleviated
- must ensure himself of the voluntary, and well-considered and repeated character of the euthanasia request
- must be independent of the patient as well as of the doctor initially consulted
- must report in writing on his findings to the patient's doctor

The patient's doctor:

- must inform the patient about the results of the consultation
- must allow at least one month between the patient's request and the performance of the euthanasia

C. The request for euthanasia

If the patient is able to write himself, the request:

- must be in writing
- must be drawn up, dated and signed by the patient himself

If the patient is not able to write himself, the request:

- must be drawn up by a person designated by the patient

The designated person:

- must have attained the age of majority
- must not have any material interest in the death of the patient
- must indicate that the patient is incapable of formulating his request in writing, and state the reasons why
- must draft the request in the presence of a doctor
- must indicate the name of the doctor on the request

The patient:

- can revoke his request at any time (in which case the document on which it is written should be removed from the medical record and returned to the patient)

D. The medical record

- must contain all the requests formulated by the patient
- must contain any actions taken by the doctor and their results
- must contain the reports by the consulted doctor(s)

E. In case of an advance euthanasia request

A legally competent adult (or an emancipated minor) can draw up a written request for euthanasia in case he should become no longer able to express his will.

At the time specified by the patient, the doctor:

- must ensure that the patient suffers from a serious and incurable disorder, caused by illness or accident
- must ensure that the patient is no longer conscious
- must ensure that the condition of unconsciousness is irreversible given the current state of medical science
- must consult another doctor about the irreversibility of the patient's medical condition and inform the consulting doctor about the reasons for this consultation
- must, in case the advance request names a person to be taken into confidence, discuss the advance request with that person
- must inform this person about the results of the consultation by the consulting doctor (see below)
- must discuss the content of the advance request with the nursing team or its members that has regular contact with the patient

The consulted doctor:

- must review the medical record and examine the patient
- must report in writing on his findings to the patient's doctor

- must be independent of the patient and of the attending doctor
- must be qualified to give an opinion on the disorder in question

The advance request:

- may be drafted at any time
- must be composed in writing in the presence of two witnesses, at least one of whom has no material interest in the death of the patient
- must be dated and signed by the drafter and the witnesses
- if the person who wishes to draft an advance request is permanently physically incapable of writing and signing an advance request he/she may designate an adult person who has no material interest in the death of the person, to draft the request in writing in the presence of two witnesses

F. Reporting

- a doctor who has performed euthanasia is required to fill in a registration form, drawn up by the Federal Control and Evaluation Commission
- this form should be delivered to the Commission within four working days

As we have seen in section 9.3, there was never a criminal or other case concerning euthanasia in Belgium before the Law on Euthanasia, nor has there been a prosecution since,[44] so there is no case law to be discussed in conjunction with the statutory provisions. The decisions of the Federal Control and Evaluation Committee, which reviews reported cases of euthanasia, have, to date, all been positive and are not made public, so they, too, do not help us to flesh out the bare bones of the law. On only one point, as we will see in the next section, do the Biennial Reports of the Committee give the law an important interpretation: although physician-assisted suicide is not explicitly covered in the law itself, the committee considers it to fall within the statutory definition of 'euthanasia' and disposes of cases accordingly.

9.4.2 The Definition of Euthanasia and Physician-Assisted Suicide

Article 2 of the Law on Euthanasia defines euthanasia as 'intentional life-terminating action by someone other than the person concerned, at the request of the latter'. The Advisory Committee on Bioethics had proposed this definition in its Advice of 12 May 1997.[45] One of the most important features of the Committee's Advice was that it established for the first time in Belgium an authoritative definition of euthanasia. The definition had its origin in the 1985 report of the Dutch

---

[44] As we will see in ch 10.3.4, no case had at the end of 2006 yet been found 'not careful' by the Federal Control and Evaluation Committee and forwarded to the prosecutorial authorities. However, in notes 75 and 81 (investigation, no prosecution brought) we can see that there have been cases known to the prosecutorial authorities in other ways.

[45] More information on this recommendation can be found in ch 8.3. See also *Parliamentary Proceedings, Senate*, 1999–2000, no 2–244/1: 4.

State Commission on Euthanasia, and had already been suggested in 1977 by a leading Dutch health care lawyer, Henk Leenen.[46] Interestingly, the term euthanasia is not mentioned at all in the Dutch Euthanasia Act, which refers to termination of life on request, as the offence is defined in article 293 of the Dutch Penal Code. Nevertheless, it is clear that the scope of application of the Belgian and Dutch statutes is identical in this respect.

The formal Belgian definition of euthanasia comprises five distinct elements: (a) it is an act, (b) it is committed by a third person, (c) the act must be intentional, (d) the person concerned (ie the patient) must die as a consequence of the act, and (e) the person concerned must have requested the act.[47] Euthanasia thus requires a *positive act*; an omission (eg withdrawing treatment on which the patient's life depends) is not 'euthanasia'.[48] According to the Belgian Council of State, the fact that the act must be intentional entails that the Law on Euthanasia is not applicable to medical behaviour that is intended for pain relief but which has a life-shortening effect.[49] As far as an 'indirect' intention to shorten life in case of pain relief is concerned, however, this reasoning is not convincing.[50]

Unlike its Dutch counterpart, the Belgian Law on Euthanasia does not expressly apply to assisted suicide. On the face of it this seems surprising. It is generally accepted that the differences between euthanasia on the one hand and assisted suicide on the other, are ethically and legally minimal. It would seem logical for both forms of termination of life to be tied to the same legal standards. Why regulate the 'greater' but not the 'lesser'?[51] From the point of view of patient autonomy and of societal control, assisted suicide is preferable to euthanasia,[52] and such a preference could easily have been built into the Law.

In our opinion the most likely explanation for the absence of assisted suicide from the Belgian Law on Euthanasia has to do with the ideological and political context within which the legislative process in Belgium played out.[53] As we have seen in chapter 8, from the beginning of the parliamentary process a hostile atmosphere prevailed between the governing and the opposition parties. Proponents and opponents of the bill did not hesitate to portray each other as extremists. In such a polarised context, the term 'assisted suicide' for a great many members of Parliament apparently came to mean simply killing someone at their request, with no additional conditions. Proponents of the bill obviously did not want to be

---

[46] See ch 4.2.3.1.

[47] On this definition, see especially the Advice of the Council of State, in *Parliamentary Proceedings, Senate*, 2000–01, no 2–224/21: 10. See also Nys 2005: 365–6.

[48] This was confirmed by the Council of State, in *Parliamentary Proceedings, Senate*, 2000–01, no 2–244/21, p 10.

[49] *Parliamentary Proceedings, Senate*, 2000–01, no 2–244/21: 10.

[50] See section 9.2.3.

[51] This was also the opinion of the Council of State, in *Parliamentary Proceedings, Senate*, 2000–01, no 2–244/21: 11.

[52] Compare ch 4.2.3.3(H).

[53] Another possible explanation might lie in the fact that (unlike the situation in the Netherlands) assisting with suicide is not an offence under the Belgian Penal Code (see above section 9.3).

accused of supporting something so 'frivolous'.[54] The fact that the distinction between euthanasia and physician-assisted suicide lies only in details of the way the death of the patient is accomplished, was at a certain point no longer relevant for many of those involved in the debates. One politician who intervened on this issue on several occasions in the Senate noticed the misunderstanding and submitted amendments, but they were all rejected.[55] The time for making refined choices had passed, and the bill's approval, according to politicians from the political majority, could no longer be delayed. The Council of State drew the attention of the legislator to the constitutional principles of equality and non-discrimination in an effort to convince him to enlarge the bill to assisted suicide, but without success.[56]

As could have been foreseen, shortly after the Law became effective, discussion on the matter picked up again. This time it was initiated by the Order of Physicians. This was surprising since the Order had been so silent during the parliamentary discussions.[57] In March 2003, the Order decided that assisted suicide is equivalent to euthanasia so long as the provisions of the Law on Euthanasia have been followed.[58] However, the Deontological Code has not yet been changed to reflect this position.

As we noted at the end of section 9.4.1, the question was settled in 2004 by the Federal Control and Evaluation Commission.[59] The commission is charged not only with reviewing reported cases but also with evaluating in general the practice of euthanasia in Belgium. In its first biennial evaluation report, in September 2004, the commission stated that it considered assisted suicide to fall within the definition of euthanasia.[60] The commission would consider a reported case of assistance with suicide to be a legitimate case of euthanasia so long as all the terms and conditions of the law were met. According to the commission aiding suicide can be regarded as falling under the Law on Euthanasia because the law does not define the means to be used nor prescribe exactly how the drugs get into the patient's body. From a formalistic legal point of view one might quibble with this reasoning because the law clearly requires that a person other than the patient himself intentionally shortens the life of the patient. If the patient himself shortens his life, one might argue, this condition is not fulfilled and the Law on Euthanasia is not applicable.

---

[54] It might also be the case that, as in the Netherlands (see ch 5.2.2.2), some parliamentarians associated assisted suicide with suicide and suicide with psychiatric disorder. But this association was as such never explicitly made during the parliamentary proceedings.

[55] See eg *Parliamentary Proceedings, Senate*, 1999–2000, no 2–244/3, amendment no 5.

[56] *Parliamentary Proceedings, Senate*, 1999–2000, 2–244/21: 14–15.

[57] See ch 8.5 on this.

[58] See *Tijdschrift van de Orde van Geneesheren*, 2003, no 100.

[59] See section 9.4.4.2 on the commission.

[60] FCEC 2004–05: 13–14, 21.

9.4.3 Substantive Requirements under the Law on Euthanasia

Article 3.1 of the Law on Euthanasia provides that a doctor who performs euthanasia does not commit a crime if he ensures that

> the patient is in a medically hopeless situation of persistent and unbearable physical or mental suffering that can not be alleviated, resulting from a serious and incurable disorder caused by illness or accident.

A general requirement (art 3.5) is that all requests formulated by the patient, and all actions performed by the attending doctor and their results, including the report(s) of the other doctor(s) consulted, must be noted in the patient's medical record.

The Law on Euthanasia draws a fundamental distinction between a current written request (art 3) and an advance written request (art 4), a distinction which, as we will see, is particularly important in connection with the requirements concerning a valid request.

9.4.3.1 The Patient

Articles 3 and 4 both speak of the *patient's* request. The term 'patient' is not defined but it does seem to assume the existence of a therapeutic relation with a doctor and that the person requesting euthanasia is suffering from a 'disease'. In the absence of a therapeutic relationship, an advance written request can be made, but it can only be legitimately executed when the substantive conditions required by the Law on Euthanasia have been fulfilled.

Article 3 further requires that in order to make a legitimate request for euthanasia an individual must have attained the age of majority (18 or older or 'emancipated'[61]). The subject of euthanasia for minors turned out to be so controversial during the parliamentary proceedings that including it would have threatened approval of the Euthanasia Bill. And although both the Committee for Public Health of the Chamber of Representatives, which wrote an advisory report for the Commission of Justice Committee, and the Order of Physicians were critical of the exclusion of minors from the bill this did not lead to amendment.[62] As the law stands, euthanasia on a (non-emancipated) minor cannot be justified by appeal to the Law on Euthanasia. However, in a particular case successful invocation of the so-called state of necessity should not be excluded.[63]

The patient does not have to be a Belgian citizen nor be domiciled in Belgium.

---

[61] 'Emancipated' is a legal and not a factual notion: a so-called 'mature minor' is not necessarily an 'emancipated' one. Emancipation requires a decision by a judge. Foreign writers not acquainted with Belgian law have misunderstood this. An example of this is Khorrami 2003: 22: 'Nach Euthanasie kann jeder Volljährige und jeder verstandreife Minderjährige verlangen.'

[62] See *Parliamentary Proceedings, Chamber of Representatives,* 2001–02, 50–1488/9: 379; *Tijdschrift van de Orde Geneesheren,* 2001, no 94: 2.

[63] Nys 2005: 372.

9.4.3.2 The Doctor

Only a *doctor* who is legally qualified to practise medicine in Belgium[64] can legitimately perform euthanasia in Belgium. No further requirements are imposed on the doctor's competence: the doctor performing euthanasia does not have to be the patient's attending doctor, nor is any special expertise required, for instance, in palliative care. In the Netherlands it was generally accepted before the Law of 2002 that the doctor who performs euthanasia must be the doctor responsible for the patient's treatment: there is no longer any such requirement, but the Regional Review Committees have held that he must have 'had such a relationship with the patient as to permit him to form a judgment concerning the requirements of due care.'[65] Perhaps a similar requirement can be derived implicitly from article 3 of the Belgian law, which provides that the doctor must have a number of conversations with the patient, over a reasonable period of time, in order to be certain of the durability of the euthanasia request. In addition, the legal requirements taken as a whole contemplate familiarity with the patient and his symptoms. On the other hand, in the parliamentary documents one finds assertions by members of parliament that a patient should be able to exclude his regular doctor completely from the decision-making process.[66] The situation is not altogether clear.

Article 14 of the Law on Euthanasia provides that a doctor may refuse to perform euthanasia on grounds of conscience or for medical reasons.[67] In such a case, however, he must inform the patient (or the 'person of confidence' of an unconscious patient, appointed in accordance with article 4 of the Law on Euthanasia[68]), within a reasonable time and explain the reasons for his refusal. If the doctor's refusal is based on medical grounds, then these must be noted in the patient's medical record. Moreover, at the request of the patient or his 'person of confidence', the doctor who refuses to fulfil a request for euthanasia must give the patient's medical record to a doctor indicated by the patient or his 'person of confidence'. A doctor may, as provided in articles 3 (2) and 4 (2) of the Law on Euthanasia, also make his willingness to accede to a request for euthanasia subject to additional conditions, such as the application of the so-called 'palliative filter'.[69]

In Belgium there is a widespread opinion among doctors and in the media that euthanasia is a medical act like any other medical activity and therefore should be considered 'normal medical behaviour'.[70] Sometimes this opinion is inspired by a

---

[64] Apart from a diploma this requires a permit from the Ministry of Health and inclusion on the roll of the Order of Physicians (see ch 7.2.3).

[65] See ch 4.2.3.2 (A) and 4.2.3.3 (D).

[66] *Parliamentary Proceedings, Chamber of Representatives*, 2001–02, 1488/9: 236.

[67] See ch 4.2.3.3(I) for the similar, but less well regulated, situation under Dutch law.

[68] See section 9.4.3.5. The 'person of confidence' is a different legal figure with a more limited and specific role than the 'patient-designated representative' under the Patients' Rights Law (see section 9.2.1).

[69] See section 9.4.3.3.

[70] In an interview with the Flemish newspaper *De Standaard* on 28 June 2007 a GP announced that he would assist a patient in dying without consulting another physician and without notifying the Federal Control and Evaluation Commission (he apparently refrained from this action at the last moment). His aim was to have the Law on Euthanasia abolished and to have euthanasia and assisted

misunderstanding: because the Law on Euthanasia explicitly requires that euthanasia be performed by a doctor one can understand that for many people it is 'normal medical behaviour'. If euthanasia fell within 'normal medical behaviour' it could be regarded as part of or a special application of palliative care at the end of life. However, there is no doubt that palliative care is a right of the terminally ill patient: article 2 of the Law on Palliative Care of 14 June 2002 expressly recognises a right to palliative care. This right of the patient corresponds to the professional obligation for the treating physician to give palliative treatment. If palliative care included euthanasia this reasoning would thus create a right to euthanasia and a professional obligation of doctors to perform it.

From a legal point of view, the opinion that euthanasia is 'normal medical behaviour' is not correct. As already stated in section 9.2, under Belgian medical law, medical behaviour that for non-doctors would be criminal can be legally justified under the Royal Decree Concerning the Practice of Health Care Professionals, subject to the consent of the patient. This legal justification does not, however, cover behaviour of physicians for which there is no medical indication, such as (in most cases) abortion, removal of an organ for transplantation, non-therapeutic medical research and also euthanasia. To justify these medical activities specific legislation is required. It is the Law on Euthanasia that creates a specific legal justification for euthanasia while the Royal Decree Concerning the Practice of Health Care Professionals offers the legal justification for 'normal medical behaviour' including palliative care. This distinction—that was accepted by the Belgian Council of State in its advice on the then Bill on Euthanasia[71]—makes it clear that from a legal point of view euthanasia cannot be considered 'normal medical behaviour'.

Misunderstanding on this point is not a coincidence but must be seen against the background of demands for a 'right' to euthanasia. The Law on Euthanasia only recognises a right to *ask for euthanasia* and article 14 of the law expressly provides that no doctor is obliged to perform it and that no other person may be compelled to assist in performing it. Precisely because the Law on Euthanasia is so clear on this point, some want to change it. In the recent past legislative proposals to this effect have been introduced in the Belgian federal Parliament. The motivation of one of them explicitly states that euthanasia should be considered 'normal medical behaviour'[72] and that as a consequence the obligation to guarantee the continuity of care to a patient contained in article 8 of the Royal Decree on the Practice of Health Care Professionals should also apply to the case of euthanasia.

The key to understanding this issue lies in the political context, and ultimately revolves around the question of whether catholic hospitals may prohibit doctors working within their walls from performing euthanasia. The answer to this is not

suicide, like the rest of MBPSL, be governed by the Law on Patients' Rights. See also n 75 concerning the same doctor.

[71] *Parliamentary Proceedings, Senate*, 1999–2000, 2–244/21.

[72] Proposal of law, Senate 2003–04 (7 July 2004), no 3–804/1: 8.

merely academic, since about 80 per cent of the hospitals in Flanders are associated with catholic organisations.[73]

9.4.3.3 Current Requests (art 3)

The Law on Euthanasia regulates in detail the formal and material requirements for a current request. Such a request must be 'voluntary,' 'well-considered,' and 'repeated'; moreover, it must not be 'the result of any external pressure'. The reference to 'external pressure' adds nothing, since any request that is the result of external pressure can by definition not be considered voluntary. It is not clear what 'repeated' means exactly, other than that the request should be made more than once. Article 3 further stipulates that the doctor must verify that the request is 'durable', ascertaining this by means of several discussions.

The chairman of the Justice Committee in the Chamber of Representatives—one of the committees in which the Euthanasia Bill was debated—asserted that the euthanasia request of a psychiatric patient can never meet the statutory standard, since in his view suffering from a psychiatric condition is incompatible with a voluntary and well-considered expression of one's will.[74] This opinion seems to run counter to any meaningful interpretation of the words (and the intention) of the Law on Euthanasia, since mental suffering clearly fulfils the criteria of article 3.1.[75]

Article 3 stipulates that the doctor must inform the patient beforehand about his state of health and his life expectancy, discuss with the patient his request for euthanasia, and discuss any remaining treatment options including palliative care, as well as their consequences.

The Law on Palliative Care (which was approved by Parliament together with the Law on Euthanasia) specifically requires that a patient be informed about the possibilities of palliative care. Article 2 states that 'every patient has a right to palliative care at the end of life'. This means that the health care system must provide sufficient palliative care and that the system of social security must guarantee that this type of care is available to everyone at the end of life. Palliative care comprises all care to patients whose life-threatening disease no longer responds to curative treatment. According to the Law on Palliative Care it is multidisciplinary in approach, focusing on the physical, psychic, social and moral condition of the patient. The aim is to provide the patient with the maximum quality of life and autonomy.

In a majority of Flemish Catholic hospitals (82%) euthanasia for *competent terminally ill patients* is permitted, in accordance with the legal criteria but only after

---

[73] See more on this in section 9.4.3.3. For the policies of catholic health care institutions, see ch 10.3.1.

[74] See *Parliamentary Proceedings, Chamber of Representatives*, 2001–02, 50–1488/9: 217.

[75] The same GP referred to in n 70 performed euthanasia on an 87-year-old woman with dementia and did not formally report this. She had not made an advance request but made a current request in a 'lucid' moment (see Burgemeister 2006: 382). The Public Prosecutor opened an enquiry but closed the case at the end of April 2006 because all the legal conditions had been respected.

implementation of the so called 'palliative filter procedure'.[76] The aim of the palliative filter is to assure that all pertinent caregivers (physicians, nurses, palliative care experts) keep one another informed about a euthanasia request and about the palliative care alternatives. The care for a patient requesting euthanasia should include an obligatory consultation with a specialised palliative care team in order to consider the real needs of the patient. The Law on Euthanasia, however, does not include a 'palliative filter' requirement. The idea was debated during the legislative procedure, especially in the Chamber of Representatives. It was endorsed informally by most politicians. The Commission for Public Health for example, in its advice on the then Euthanasia Bill, unanimously endorsed an amendment proposing to introduce a palliative filter in the bill.[77] Nevertheless, this amendment was disregarded by the Justice Committee. This can only be explained by pointing out that acceptance of the amendment would have meant that the Euthanasia Bill would have had to be sent again to the Senate, and this would have created a considerable delay.[78] It should also be pointed out that the association 'Right to Die with Dignity'[79] was and is firmly opposed to such a 'palliative filter', since they fear that it would function as a kind of test for access to euthanasia, and also would create for the patient a psychological euthanasia threshold.[80] But since a doctor may, as provided in articles 3 (2) and 4 (2) of the Law on Euthanasia, make his willingness to accede to a request for euthanasia subject to additional conditions, a 'palliative filter' can be required by individual doctors and health care institutions.

Finally, the request must be in writing. Nevertheless, the Federal Control and Evaluation Commission has at least once approved a case of euthanasia although no written request was available. Although the decisions of the commission are not published we can know this from the decision of an Arbitration Committee that also dealt with the case.[81] This committee had to assess the dismissal of a doctor by a hospital for the alleged illegal practice of euthanasia. One of the allegations was that there had been no written request. From the decision of the Arbitration Committee it can be deduced that no action was taken by the Order of Physicians and that the Federal Control and Evaluation Commission decided not to ask for additional information from the doctor concerned, nor did they transfer the file to the Public Prosecutor.[82]

In principle, a request must be drafted, dated and signed by the patient himself. It is not required that it be written by hand; it can be typed or written on a com-

---

[76] Gastmans *et al* 2006: 169–78. On the 'palliative filter' see Broeckaert and Janssens 2005: 36–69. See Broeckaert 2003 on the role that the Palliative Care Federation of Flanders and the idea of a 'palliative filter' played in the legislative process leading to the Belgian law of 2002.

[77] *Parliamentary Proceedings, Chamber of Representatives*, 2001–02, no 50–1488/9: 322–85.

[78] See ch 7.1 on the Belgian legislative procedure.

[79] See ch 8.2.

[80] See the statement of 12 January 2004: <http://www.rws.be/nieuws/detail.mv?id=32> accessed 10 September 2007.

[81] Decision of the Arbitration Committee of 10 December 2003, *Tijdschrift voor Gezondheidsrecht* 2005–06, 104–15.

[82] *Ibid* at 108.

puter and printed out. If, as result of a physical disability for example, the patient is incapable of writing the request, then it is to be written by an adult person who has been chosen by the patient and who has no material interest in the patient's death. This person must record the fact that the patient is not able to formulate the request in writing, and give the reasons why. In such a case, drafting of the request must take place in the presence of the doctor, and the person drafting it must record the name of the doctor in the document (it is not required that these two sign the document themselves).

The patient's written request must be appended to the medical record. The patient may revoke the request at any time, in which case it must be physically removed from the medical record and returned to the patient. All requests formulated by the patient, as well as any actions by the attending physician and their results, including the report(s) of the consulted physician(s), are nevertheless to be noted in the patient's medical record.

9.4.3.4 The Patient's Medical Situation in the Case of a Current Request

Article 3 of the Law on Euthanasia requires that the doctor ascertain that the patient who makes a current request is in a 'medically hopeless situation' characterised by 'persistent and unbearable physical or mental suffering that cannot be alleviated' and that this is the result of a 'serious and incurable disorder caused by illness or accident.' This formulation of the requirement provoked copious and confused debates in Parliament.

One can distinguish a more objective and a more subjective element in the definition. The more objective element is that a patient must suffer from a 'disorder' that is of a 'serious and incurable' nature and is caused by 'illness or accident'. The law makes no distinction between conditions of a physical or a mental nature or origin.[83] Nor is a 'terminal' illness required by the Law on Euthanasia.[84]

But what is a 'medically hopeless situation'? Does, for instance, a person suffering from cancer, who could be treated temporarily with intensive chemotherapy and thereby live one or two years longer, fall within the law? Maybe not, at least not on the face of it. However, the fact that a medically hopeless situation is partly defined by a largely subjective element—whether or not the suffering is 'persistent

---

[83] The Chamber of Representatives Committee on Public Health, which fulfilled an advisory role for the Committee of Justice in consideration of the Euthanasia Bill, unanimously recommended that mental suffering alone should never suffice to legitimate euthanasia. See *Parliamentary Proceedings, Chamber of Representatives*, 2001–02, 50–1488/9: 379. However, none of the opinions of this committee were followed.

[84] One of the arguments invoked during the Belgian legislative process for not imposing a requirement of terminal illness is that it is impossible to define what 'terminal' means. This seems less than convincing: doctors are surely capable of determining what the average life expectancy will be of someone who is in the situation of a patient who submits a euthanasia request. That there can be no absolute certainty and that some patients would in fact live shorter or longer than expected does nothing to diminish this fact. In reviewing what the doctor did, the question would be whether a reasonable doctor could have come to the same judgment. The real problem is reaching agreement about what 'terminal' is: an estimated three months, three weeks, or three days?

and unbearable' and cannot be 'alleviated'—would seem to render such a subtle question of interpretation fairly unimportant.

It is the patient, and the patient alone, who determines whether he is suffering from persistent and unbearable physical or mental suffering.[85] The doctor's task is simply to be certain that *the patient finds himself* in such a situation. If the patient says that this is the case—and this assertion is, in the circumstances, believable—then the doctor can do little else but accept the patient's word for it. There is nothing in the Law or in the parliamentary proceedings referring to the doctor's interpretation or understanding of the patient's suffering. It may be that Dutch law is slightly more restrictive on this point.[86]

The Law on Euthanasia does not require a patient to undergo alternative treatment before the doctor may agree to a euthanasia request. It stipulates only that the doctor must *discuss* with the patient 'his request for euthanasia and any remaining therapeutic options, including that of palliative care'. One might conclude from this combination of facts that the patient—for instance the cancer patient mentioned earlier—may refuse a treatment with the result that his situation becomes medically hopeless. A doctor could then legitimately agree to such a patient's euthanasia request. The sole objective requirement of the Law on Euthanasia—of a serious and incurable condition caused by accident or illness—could in this way in effect be created by the patient's refusal.

On the other hand, one could argue that the general legal principles of subsidiarity and proportionality apply, despite the suggestion created by the text of the Law. Consenting to a request from a patient for whom there still is a genuine treatment alternative might from such a perspective be considered a non-subsidiary or disproportionate action on the part of the doctor, given the existence of other treatment possibilities.

Unfortunately, the Law on Euthanasia is not entirely clear concerning the consequences of a refusal of treatment. If the less restrictive interpretation is correct, then there may be a significant difference on this point between Belgian law and Dutch law which (as we have seen in chapter 4.2.3.3(C)) requires the patient's refusal of an alternative to euthanasia to be 'understandable' and that, *together with the patient*, the doctor comes to the conclusion that there is no other reasonable solution to the situation in which the patient finds himself.

Finally, as we have seen, the text of the Law on Euthanasia explicitly requires that the patient's condition be due to 'illness or accident'. The Belgian legislator apparently sought to exclude so-called *Brongersma* ('tired of life') situations from the law's coverage.[87]

---

[85] See *Parliamentary Proceedings, Senate*, 2000–01, 2–244/22: 659 and 896.

[86] See ch 4.2.3.3(C).

[87] See *Parliamentary Proceedings, Senate*, 2000–01, 2–244/22: 852 and 761. Such a limitation raises the question whether it is possible to define the concept of 'illness' clearly enough to make it usable in practice. As was probably the case in the *Brongersma* case itself, it will almost always be possible to discover some disorder that is connected with a patient's euthanasia request. It may well be that the limitation contained in the Belgian Law on Euthanasia in practice is barely relevant. See for further discussion of this matter ch 4.2.3.4(C).

9.4.3.5 Requests in Advance (art 4)

Article 4 of the Law on Euthanasia regulates in detail the formal requirements for a valid advance request for euthanasia. It is important to note that the substantive requirements for a valid current request (such as voluntariness) do not explicitly apply in such a case. On the other hand, broadly speaking, the requirements the doctor must meet in the case of an advance request are the same as those that apply in the case of a current request.

An advance request may be drafted at any time by an adult person or an emancipated minor. The request becomes effective should the author no longer be able to express his will.[88] This does not mean that euthanasia may be performed pursuant to an advance request simply because the author is no longer able to express his will.[89] It means that an advance request becomes a valid request for euthanasia in such a case.

In an advance request, one or more 'person(s) of confidence' can be designated, in order of preference, to inform the attending physician about the patient's will. Each 'person of confidence' replaces his predecessor as mentioned in the advance request, in the case of refusal, hindrance, incompetence or death. The patient's treating physician, the physician consulted and the members of the nursing team may not act as 'persons of confidence'.

The advance request must be drafted (which according to article 2 of the Royal Decree of 2 April 2003 means handwritten or typed out in advance) in the presence of two adult witnesses, at least one of whom has no material interest in the patient's death. It must be dated and signed by the author, by the witnesses, and by the patient's 'person of confidence', if any has been appointed in the request. The advance request may be modified or revoked at any time.

If a person who wishes to draft an advance request is permanently physically incapable of doing so, he may appoint an adult who has no material interest in his death to write down his request, in the presence of two adult witnesses, at least one of whom has no material interest in his death. The advance request must in such a case note that the person concerned is incapable of writing and signing the document and give the reasons why. The advance request must be dated and signed by the person who writes it down, by the witnesses and by the 'person(s) of confidence', if any, of the person concerned. A medical certificate is to be appended to the advance request as proof that the author is permanently physically incapable of writing and signing the advance request.

Finally, the Law on Euthanasia in article 4 (1) provides that an advance request is only valid

---

[88] Later in art 4, §2 uses the expression 'unconscious'.

[89] See, for an example of this misunderstanding, article 1 of the Royal Decree of 2 April 2003 establishing the way an advance request is drafted, confirmed, changed or revoked, which stipulates that

the advance request by which a competent adult person or an emancipated minor expresses his will that, in case he is no longer able to express his will, a doctor performs euthanasia on him in the conditions determined by the Law on Euthanasia, is drafted according to the model attached.

if it has been drafted or confirmed fewer than five years before the moment at which the person in question can no longer express his wishes.

The annex to the Royal Decree of 2 April 2003 contains a model advance request for euthanasia. There is no requirement that one use the model. However, the Law on Euthanasia delegates in article 4 (1) to the King (in effect the Ministers of Health Care and Justice respectively) the power to regulate the way advance requests are registered and made available to the doctors concerned. They have done this in the Royal Decree of 27 April 2007.[90] Only advance requests made up using the model can be registered by the local authorities of the place where the person concerned has drafted an advance request. These authorities are obliged to register the request and transmit it to a database kept at the federal Ministry of Health. The doctor of a patient who is no longer able to express his will and who might be eligible for euthanasia according to the conditions laid down in the Law on Euthanasia must consult the register after due identification and authorisation.

9.4.3.6. The Patient's Medical Condition in Case of an Advance Request

The Law on Euthanasia contains special requirements regarding the patient's state of health when an advance request is to be carried out. He must be suffering from a serious, incurable condition caused by accident or illness and he must be 'irreversibly unconscious'[91] according to the current state of medical science. There is no requirement of unbearable suffering, since the legislature assumed that such patients are no longer capable of suffering. This is one important respect in which the Belgian Law differs from the Dutch Law, where the fact that the requirement of suffering continues to apply in the case of an advance request is one (legal) reason why it is generally supposed that such requests will be largely ineffective.[92]

In spite of the fact that the Law on Euthanasia leaves little room for interpretation as far as the situation in which an advance request can be carried out is concerned, most members of Parliament seem to have assumed that only patients in a so-called persistent vegetative state (PVS) would qualify. There was considerable discussion on this point in the Belgian Parliament. One of the Members of Parliament who had submitted the Euthanasia Bill—the leader of the Dutch-speaking Liberal party in the Senate—believed that the new law would only apply to comatose patients, which is not necessarily the same as 'irreversibly unconscious' patients.[93] This gave rise to questions about the situation of older people with dementia, for instance: are they to be considered 'irreversibly unconscious' because they no longer possess any real powers of awareness? While most Members of Parliament believed that this was not the case, no definitive answer was ever given on the point, and it remains unresolved. There is currently some discussion on whether the issue should be clarified in the future.

---

[90] Published in the *Belgisch Staatsblad* (7 June 2007). It will enter into force on 1 September 2008 (art 8).

[91] See also section 9.4.5 on this terminology.

[92] See ch 4.2.3.3(B) under 'euthanasia pursuant to an advance written request'.

[93] See *Parliamentary Proceedings, Senate*, 2000–01, 2–244/22: 952–953.

9.4.3.7 Consultation

Before carrying out a request for euthanasia a doctor must consult another doctor regarding the serious and incurable nature of the patient's condition, and inform him of the reason for such a consultation. A negative recommendation by the doctor who is consulted is not binding, but of course will be very important for the later judgment of the Federal Control and Evaluation Commission. The doctor consulted must be independent both of the patient and of the consulting doctor and he must be competent to assess the patient's condition.[94] He must inspect the medical record, examine the patient, and make sure that the patient's suffering is persistent and unbearable and cannot be alleviated in another way. He must make a written report of his findings. The attending doctor must inform the patient of the results of the consultation.

If nurses are in regular contact with the patient, then the patient's request must be discussed with them as well. Should the patient so desire, the request must also be discussed with family or friends whom the patient indicates. Of course, the opinions of the family and friends consulted are not determinative of the legitimacy of euthanasia. But this does not prevent the doctor from being influenced by the opinions of family and friends in deciding whether to agree to a euthanasia request.

If the doctor believes the patient is apparently not going to die within a foreseeable period, there are two additional requirements that must be fulfilled. First, at least one month must elapse between the patient's written request and the act of euthanasia. And secondly, article 3 provides that in such a case a *second* doctor, who is a psychiatrist or a specialist in the condition in question, must be consulted after having being informed of the reason for such a consultation. This second doctor must inspect the medical record, examine the patient, and ascertain that the patient's suffering is persistent and unbearable and cannot be alleviated, and determine that the request is voluntary, well-considered and repeated. This doctor must also make a written report of his findings, and he must be independent of the patient, the consulting doctor, and the first doctor consulted. Here, too, the patient's doctor must inform the patient of the results of the consultation.

9.4.3.8 Specially-Trained Consultants (LEIF and *Médecins EOL*)

LEIF (Forum for End of Life Information), a programme very similar to SCEN in the Netherlands (see chapter 4.2.4.4. and 5.4.2), was set up in 2003 in the Dutch-speaking part of Belgium (Flanders) to provide consultation and other services to doctors confronted with a request for euthanasia. Since 2006 there is a similar project to give special training to nurses to give information and advice to other nurses and improve communication between nurses and doctors and others involved in cases of euthanasia. By contrast with the Netherlands, not only GPs but

---

[94] In principle, every doctor is *legally* competent, but the term is used here in the sense of *professionally* competent.

also specialists have been included in the project from the beginning.[95] Recently, an equivalent organisation (*Médecins EOL*) was set up in Wallonia.[96] Unfortunately, the Federal Control and Evaluation Commission, which reviews reported cases of euthanasia and is therefore in a unique position to form an opinion on the matter, has not given any indication concerning the contribution of these specialised consultants to careful euthanasia practice.

9.4.3.9 Carrying Out Euthanasia

Unlike the Dutch Law, the Belgian Law on Euthanasia does not include a requirement that the doctor use 'due medical care' when carrying out euthanasia. There was some debate on this point in Parliament, but the governing parties considered such a requirement superfluous since a doctor is always required to exercise due medical care. The result of this is that there is no statutory ground on which the Federal Control and Evaluation Commission can, like the Dutch Review Committees, develop standards on such things as the physical presence of the doctor, the drugs to be used, the division of role between doctor and nurse and so forth (compare chapter 4.2.3.3(F)).

9.4.3.10 The Role of the Pharmacist and the Availability of Euthanatica

Legislation of 10 November 2005[97] inserted a new article 3bis in the Law on Euthanasia. This article provides that a pharmacist does not commit a crime when he delivers a euthanaticum at the request of a doctor, on condition that the physician explicitly state in writing that he has respected all the conditions of the Law on Euthanasia. This is intended to create more legal security for pharmacists who cooperate in the practice of euthanasia. The same article also enables the King (in effect the competent ministers) to guarantee the availability of euthanatica in pharmacies that are open to the public. Until now such a Royal Decree has not been issued.[98]

In an advice of 4 June 2005 the Order of Physicians recommended that the prescribing doctor personally receive the prescribed drugs from the hands of the pharmacist. The doctor must contact the pharmacist in due time since, according to the Order, 'euthanasia can never be considered an urgency in medicine'.[99]

---

[95] Information received from Prof W Distelmans, professor of palliative medicine, Free University of Brussels, and one of the founders of LEIF. See also the LEIF website: <http://www.leif.be> accessed 4 May 2007.

[96] See the website of the Association 'Right to Die with Dignity': <http://www.admd.be/medecins.html> accessed 4 May 2007.

[97] Law supplementing the Law on Euthanasia with provisions on the role of the pharmacist and the availability of euthanatica of 10 November 2005, *Belgisch Staatsblad* (13 December 2005).

[98] See ch 10.2 on some current problems of availability of euthanatica in Belgium.

[99] *Tijdschrift van de Orde van Geneesheren*, 2005, no 109: 7.

9.4.3.11 The Moral Foundation of the Belgian Law on Euthanasia

Between proponents and opponents of the Belgian Law on Euthanasia there is consensus that the moral foundation of euthanasia is the right to self-determination of the patient: the free request of the patient is the ultimate justification of euthanasia. One might argue that since the law requires that the patient be in a 'medically hopeless situation' characterised by 'persistent and unbearable physical or mental suffering that cannot be alleviated' the ultimate justification of the Belgian Law on Euthanasia is not so much self-determination as beneficence. However, we have also seen that in Belgium it is the patient himself who to a very large extent determines whether or not he is in such a situation. While both self-determination and beneficence are involved, the balance in Belgium seems to be slightly more on the side of self-determination than in the Netherlands.[100]

9.4.4. The System of Control

9.4.4.1 The Reporting Procedure in Case of 'Natural' and 'Non-Natural' Death

In Belgium, the Civil Code (arts 78–80) and the Burial Act contain provisions dealing with death certificates and post mortem examinations.[101] A post mortem examination is considered a medico-legal examination which all doctors are qualified to perform. In case of cremation, a second physician must also carry out a post mortem examination. Usually the attending doctor performs the post mortem examination. The doctor who performs the post mortem can issue a death certificate after examining the body.[102]

The death certificate consists of two parts: one part is for the population registry (which issues permits for burial or cremation) and the second is to be sent in a sealed envelope to the National Institute of Statistics. Both the immediate and the underlying cause of death and the manner of death are covered on the second part.

On the first part of the certificate the doctor must indicate whether there is an indication for a forensic investigation. He must choose between two possibilities: medico-legal objection or no medico-legal objection to funeral or cremation. An explanation on the form states that there is such an objection if death was certainly or probably caused by external factors (accident; suicide; murder; manslaughter). The categories of 'natural' and 'unnatural' are no longer used on the death certificate.[103]

---

[100] *Cf* ch 4.2.3.3(C).

[101] Wet van 20 juli 1971 op de begraafplaatsen en de lijkbezorging. *Belgisch Staatsblad* (3 August 1971) later amended many times.

[102] According to the Civil Code the registrar must visit the deceased in person to make sure of his demise (art 77); in practice this is not done.

[103] See Das 2005: 200–01.

If the certificate indicates that there is a medico-legal objection, the civil servant of the population registry cannot permit burial or cremation and he must inform the public prosecutor. The doctor can himself inform the public prosecutor, but he is not obliged to do so. In case of violent or suspicious death a doctor appointed by the police performs an official inquiry. Based on this inquiry and the findings of the police the prosecutor decides if a medico-legal autopsy is necessary. The number of medico-legal autopsies is low in Belgium.

In light of the changes on the death certificate, which took place in 1998, it is remarkable that article 15 of the Law on Euthanasia still uses the notion of 'natural' death: according to this article euthanasia is to be considered a 'natural death' as far as insurance law is concerned. In practice euthanasia is also considered a natural cause of death for other purposes, including death certificates, where doctors who practice euthanasia uniformly fill in 'no medical-legal objection'. Before the Law on Euthanasia this was a dubious practice, to say the least, but after the Law the Order of Physicians supports such a practice.[104] In effect, albeit via a slightly different route, the situation is the same as in the Netherlands: there is little chance that the prosecutorial authorities will ever learn of a case of euthanasia unless the doctor involved reports it as such (in the Netherlands by reporting a 'non-natural' death to the municipal pathologist; in Belgium by reporting the case to the Federal Control and Evaluation Commission).

9.4.4.2. The Review Procedure

As in the Dutch Euthanasia Law,[105] a special procedure has been designed to review reported cases of euthanasia. The Federal Control and Evaluation Commission (FCEC) established by the Law on Euthanasia assumes the role that in the past would have performed by the public prosecutor if a doctor had reported having performed euthanasia.

The FCEC is, according to article 6 §2 of the Belgian Law on Euthanasia, composed of 16 members (eight doctors, four lawyers and four members 'from groups charged with the problem of incurably ill patients'). As a result, what would previously have been an exclusively criminal assessment has been given form as a professionally and socially oriented assessment with the criminal law present only in the background. The aim of this is to encourage doctors—who are understandably wary of the criminal justice system—to report cases in which they have performed euthanasia. This is expected to yield more effective social control of euthanasia as well as better insight into (and, it is hoped, improvements in) the actual practice of euthanasia.

Article 5 of the Law on Euthanasia provides that a doctor who has performed euthanasia must complete a registration form and submit it within four working

---

[104] See the advice of the Order of Physicians of 22 March 2003 on euthanasia, aiding suicide and other MBPSL, <http://195.234.184.64/web-Ned/nl/a100/a100006n.htm> accessed 10 September 2007.

[105] See ch 4.2.4.3.

days to the FCEC.[106] The registration form consists of two parts, both of them confidential. The first part includes the information shown in Box 9.3.

Box 9.3 Part 1 of the registration form

---

1. the patient's full name and address
2. the full name, address and health insurance registration number of the attending physician
3. the full name, address and health insurance registration number of the doctor(s) consulted about the euthanasia request
4. the full name, address and capacity of all persons consulted by the attending physician, and the date of these consultations
5. if there exists an advance request in which one or more 'persons of confidence' are designated, the full name(s) of such person(s)

The first part is sealed by the reporting doctor and can only be examined by the commission following a formal decision to do so.

The second part of the doctor's report includes the information shown on Box 9.4.

Box 9.4 Part 2 of the registration form

---

1. the patient's sex, date of birth and place of birth
2. the date, time and place of death
3. the nature of the serious and incurable condition, caused by accident or illness, from which the patient suffered
4. the nature of the persistent and unbearable suffering
5. the reasons why this suffering could not be alleviated
6. the elements underlying the assurance that the request was voluntary, well considered and repeated, and not the result of external pressure
7. whether the patient could be expected to die in the near future
8. whether an advance request was drafted
9. the procedure followed by the doctor
10. the capacity of the doctor(s) consulted, their recommendations and their information from the consultation(s)
11. the capacity of the other persons consulted, and the date(s) of these consultations
12. the manner in which euthanasia was performed and the drugs used

---

[106] Art 5:

> Any physician who has performed euthanasia is required to fill in a registration form, drawn up by the Federal Control and Evaluation Commission

This requirement is repeated in article 7:

> The commission drafts a registration form that must be filled in by the physician whenever he/she performs euthanasia.

The FCEC studies the second part of the registration form and determines whether the euthanasia was performed in accordance with the conditions and the procedure stipulated in the Law on Euthanasia. In case of doubt, the commission may decide by simple majority to lift anonymity and examine the first part of the registration form. The commission may also request the responsible doctor to provide any information from the medical record having to do with the euthanasia.[107]

The FCEC renders judgment within two months. If, in a decision taken by a two-thirds majority, the commission is of the opinion that the conditions laid down in the law have not been fulfilled, it turns the case over to the public prosecutor of the jurisdiction in which the patient died. In the first five years of the operation of the law, no such adverse judgment has been rendered.[108]

The FCEC is required to submit regular reports. The first report was due within two years after the Law on Euthanasia came into force; subsequent reports are to be made every two years (art 9). The biennial reports include:

(a) a statistical summary of the information from the second part of the completed registration forms submitted by doctors pursuant to article 8;
(b) a description and evaluation of the implementation of the law;
(c) if appropriate, recommendations that could lead to new legislation or other measures concerning the implementation of the law.

Within six months of receiving the first report and the commission's recommendations referred to in article 9, if any, a debate was to be held in the Chambers of Parliament (art 13).

For the purpose of carrying out its task of evaluating the law, the FCEC may seek information from the various public services and institutions. The information thus gathered is confidential. None of these documents may reveal the identities of any persons named in the dossiers submitted to the commission for the purposes of review (art 8). The commission can decide to supply statistical and purely technical data, purged of any personal information, to university research teams that submit a reasoned request for such data.

Any person who is involved, in whatever capacity, in implementing the Law on Euthanasia is required to maintain confidentiality regarding information provided in the exercise of his function and subject to criminal penalties (under art 458 of the Penal Code) for not doing so (art 12). This provision may perhaps help to explain the lack of transparency characteristic of the FCEC.

---

[107] During the parliamentary debates it became apparent that a doctor might refuse to provide additional information on the basis of professional confidentiality. The requirement of providing information also raises the question of the extent of the *nemo tenetur* principle, which has similarly been a latent problem in the Dutch context (see GB&W: 116–18). Although it is not clear how far the right not to incriminate oneself extends—does it apply to a *potential* suspect such as a doctor who performs euthanasia?—the construction undeniably creates some tension with the *nemo tenetur* principle.

[108] If, after anonymity has been lifted, facts or circumstances come to light which compromise the independence or impartiality of one of the commission members, this member will have an opportunity to explain or to be challenged during the discussion of this matter in the commission (art 8).

9.4.4.3 Criminal Liability in the Case of Failure to Fulfil the Legal Requirements

The Belgian Law on Euthanasia, unlike its Dutch counterpart, does not specify what offence, if any, is committed by a doctor who fails to comply with the norms and procedures established by the Law. This omission is all the more striking since Belgian criminal law—unlike Dutch criminal law—has never recognised euthanasia (or assistance with suicide) as a distinct offence.

The question thus arises: what offence does a doctor in Belgium commit if he performs euthanasia without meeting the conditions set in the Law on Euthanasia? Is it manslaughter,[109] murder,[110] poisoning,[111] or something else? This uncertainty is of course largely due to the fact that there is no case law on the matter. Whatever the reasons may have been for the choice to regulate euthanasia entirely outside the Penal Code,[112] the resulting situation seems, as the Council of State observed, to be an infringement of the principle of legality in criminal law.[113]

As in the Netherlands,[114] the Belgian Law on Euthanasia makes no distinction between the seriousness of the offence in cases of serious or of less serious departures from the requirements for legal euthanasia. Not completing the necessary documents in the proper way is on the face of it just as serious a criminal offence as failure to conform to the essential substantive requirements concerning the patient's request, suffering and medical condition. Thus, in addition to the problem of legality in the Belgian Law, the legislator in both countries seems to have lost sight of the requirement of proportionality.[115]

9.4.5. Possible Future Developments

After the enactment of the Law on Euthanasia in 2002, there have been proposals to change the law. But except for the one change concerning pharmacists (discussed in section 9.4.3.10), none of them has been successful. The most important issues on which change has been suggested concern the position of minors and that of so-called 'unconscious' patients. Both of these issues had also been debated during the parliamentary debates before the enactment of the Law on Euthanasia in 2002.

---

[109] Art 292 of the Penal Code.

[110] Art 394 of the Penal Code.

[111] Art 397 of the Penal Code.

[112] As with some other problematic aspects of the Law on Euthanasia, the consequences of the choice to leave the Penal Code unchanged were realised only after the legislative process had been underway for some time. Doing anything about the problem would have entailed delay. This seems to have been politically unacceptable to the majority parties in Parliament.

[113] Advice of the Council of State, in *Parliamentary Proceedings*, Senate, 2000–01, no 2–244/21: 12–13.

[114] See ch 4.2.3.3(A).

[115] *Cf* Advice of the Council of State, in *Parliamentary Proceedings*, Senate, 2000–01, no 2–244/21: 15–16.

As far as 'unconscious patients' are concerned, we already pointed out in section 9.4.3.6 that there was discussion in Parliament on what exactly the meaning is of 'irreversibly unconscious' in article 4 (1) of the law (dealing with the conditions under which an advance request is effective).[116] Do, for example, patients suffering from dementia fall within the ambit of the law? And what about comatose patients or patients who are brain dead? To resolve the uncertainty surrounding this topic, two legislative proposals have been introduced in recent years. The first was proposed on 7 July 2004,[117] and sought to replace the terms 'conscious' and 'being not conscious' in article 4(1) with the phrases: 'being conscious *of his own personality*' and 'being not conscious *of his own personality*' [italics added]. The proposal was to make the Law on Euthanasia applicable to the broad category of comatose and demented patients, and also to patients who are brain dead. The second proposal had exactly the same ambition.[118]

The position of minors in the Law on Euthanasia is, as we have seen, in marked contrast with their position in the Law on Patients' Rights, which in article 12(2) provides that the minor patient will be involved in exercising his patient rights (eg giving consent or refusing consent to medical treatment), bearing in mind his age and level of maturity.[119] The same article also states that minor patients who are deemed capable of reasonably assessing their situation may exercise their rights on their own behalf. The inclusion of minors in the Law on Euthanasia has been attempted in two legislative proposals: the proposal of 7 July 2004 (just mentioned), and a proposal of 12 December 2006.[120] In both cases the possibility of euthanasia for children under 18 years old was conditional on the child being capable of a reasonable appraisal of its condition. As has been pointed out in section 9.4.3.1, the matter had been debated in Parliament in 2001. At the time, it was deemed so controversial that including it would have threatened approval of the Euthanasia Bill.

9.5 Concluding Remarks

It seems to be a reasonable conclusion from the foregoing description of Belgian law on euthanasia and other MBPSL that the differences between Belgian and Dutch law, on the whole, are fairly minor. The most important differences, as far as euthanasia is concerned, seem to be the special treatment of advance requests for euthanasia and of non-terminal patients in the Belgian Law, in both of which

---

[116] See *Parliamentary Proceedings, Senate,* 2000–01, 2–244/22: 952–3, 982–3, 995 and 1059.

[117] Proposal of law, Senate 2003–04, no 3–804/1.

[118] Proposal of law, Senate 2005–06, no 3–1485/1.

[119] Art 96 of the Deontological Code expressly provides that the treating physician must involve a minor patient in all MBPSL decisions, having regard to his age, his maturity and the type of decision involved.

[120] Proposal of law, Senate 2006–07, no 3–1993/1.

cases it seems fair to say that the Belgian legislator realised distinct improvements over the legal situation in the Netherlands.[121]

From a technical legal point of view, the differences between the two euthanasia laws are striking. They can largely be reduced to the much greater level of detail in the Belgian statutory provisions and the corresponding far greater richness of non-statutory sources of law in the Netherlands.

An important difference between the two countries concerns the position of the medical profession.[122] The Belgian legislature did not have a great deal of confidence in the willingness of the Order of Physicians to support the practice of euthanasia in a constructive manner. In the Netherlands, the Royal Dutch Medical Association (KNMG) had from an early period shown itself willing and able to assume responsibility for euthanasia practice, and the judiciary relied heavily on this when it took upon itself the task of playing a formative role in legal development. The Belgian Order of Physicians, by contrast, has shown no willingness to bear any responsibility for either the content or the maintenance of the new norms.[123] As we have seen in chapter 8.4 and 8.5 the Order reacted timidly to earlier discussions of the subject. It considered legal regulation undesirable and was of the opinion that it would be better if the euthanasia question were left entirely up to individual doctors.

In short, whereas the Royal Dutch Medical Association—together with the judiciary—played a key role in the Dutch process of legal change, the same can not be said of the Belgian Order of Physicians.

---

[121] Other significant differences that have been noted concern so-called *Brongersma* situations ('tired of life', see section 9.4.3.4) and the position of minors (see section 9.4.3.1).

[122] One should also mention an important difference in the character of medical disciplinary law. In Belgium this is in practice primarily concerned with maintaining the honour and dignity of the profession. Disciplinary tribunals rarely hear cases—common in the Netherlands—dealing with the professional behaviour of doctors towards their patients, being more active in the area of behaviour among colleagues (see Nys *et al* 2001–02). The Belgian legislator could therefore not expect much contribution from this quarter in the development or enforcement of norms concerning euthanasia.

[123] As Vander Stichele *et al* (2004: 90) note, 'the legal debate on euthanasia was not accompanied by internal preparation of guidelines among the medical profession.'

10

Belgian Euthanasia Law in Context
and in Practice

Leaving aside MBPSL in neonatology (concerning which some Belgian data was covered in chapter 6), there are only two important sources of information concerning euthanasia and other MBPSL and the operation of the control system in Belgium. The first is the three surveys carried out in Flanders (the Dutch-speaking part of the country) in 1996, 1998 and 2001. For Belgium as a whole, no such data are available.[1] The second is the biennial reports of the Federal Control and Evaluation Committee (FCEC), responsible for reviewing cases of euthanasia pursuant to the Law on Euthanasia of 2002 (see chapter 9.4.4.2).

In interpreting the data to follow, it should be remembered that, as we have seen in chapter 7.2.2, most people in Belgium who are over 75 years of age die in hospitals (49%), 30% die in nursing and rest homes, and 19% die at home. Most people aged between 65 and 75 die in hospitals (60%), 30% at home, and 6.4% in nursing and rest homes.

10.1 Survey Data on the Frequencies of MBPSL in Flanders

The three surveys of MBPSL practice in Flanders—the first, in 1996, was a pilot project in the city of Hasselt; those in 1998 and 2001 covered all of Flanders—used the Dutch death-certificate methodology discussed in chapter 5.1.2.[2]

Unfortunately, the surveys involve samples that are too small to permit reliable measurement of highly infrequent sorts of behaviour (in particular, physician-assisted suicide) and the results of the two most recent studies are—as far as euthanasia and termination of life without a request are concerned—radically inconsistent, as we can see on Table 10.1. Since the certificate studies were not accompanied by interview/questionnaire studies of the experiences and views of doctors, the triangulation of data from different sources and the wealth of

---

[1] The results of new research will not be available until 2008; they will cover Flanders and the city of Brussels, but not Wallonia (information received from L Deliens). Further information on Flanders is covered in the EURELD studies (see ch 17).

[2] Mortier *et al* 2000; Deliens *et al* 2000; Van der Heide *et al* 2003 (EURELD study).

information going beyond basic frequencies available for the Netherlands does not exist in Belgium.

Table 10.1 gives the findings from the three surveys. In the case of abstention, the Belgian researchers add the intermediate intent category ('subsidiary purpose') and classify all three intent categories as abstention. In short, although the route followed is slightly different, the bottom line is the same in both countries: administration of potentially lethal drugs with the 'explicit purpose' of causing death is classified as 'termination of life' whereas abstention with such an 'explicit purpose' is regarded as 'normal medical practice' (without regard to whether there is a request from the patient or a judgment that treatment is 'futile').[3]

The overall frequency of MBPSL—more specifically, of abstention and pain relief with life-shortening effect, which account for the lion's share of all MBPSL—is very similar in Flanders to that in the Netherlands (compare chapter 5, Table 5.1). The differences in the rates of euthanasia and termination of life without a request as estimated by the studies of 1996 and 1998 on the one hand, and 2001 on the other, are difficult to explain,[4] and the existence of the earlier, much higher

Table 10.1. Frequencies of MBPSL in Flanders (percentages of all deaths)

	Hasselt 1996 N = 269	Flanders 1998 N = 1,925	Flanders 2001 N = 2,950
termination of life on request	1.5	1.2	0.31
euthanasia	0.8	1.1	0.3
assistance with suicide	0.7	0.1	0.01
termination of life without request	3.3	3.2	1.5
pain relief with life-shortening effect	16.0	18.5	22
accepting risk*	6.7	13.2	
subsidiary purpose*	9.3	5.3	
death due to abstinence	16.5	16.4	15
accepting risk*	8.5	6.7	
subsidiary purpose*#	3.0	3.9	
explicit purpose*	5.2	5.8	15
total MBPSL	37.3	39.3	38.0
total deaths	970	56,354	55,793

* Data not given in 2001 study.
# This intent category was not included in the Dutch research.

Sources (certificate studies): Mortier *et al* 2000 (Hasselt); Deliens *et al* 2000 (Flanders 1998); Van der Heide *et al* 2003 (Flanders 2001, EURELD study).

[3] No explanation has been given for the different ways both the Dutch and the Belgian studies deal with the classification of abstention and of pain relief.
[4] The difference may have to do with the very low number of cases of euthanasia found in the two years (22 in 1998 and about 9 in 2001), the low response rate (under 50% in 1998—Bilsen *et al* 2004—and 59% in 2001—Van der Heide *et al* 2003) and the fact that in most cases of euthanasia found in 1998, death was probably not caused by the drug used (morphine) (see Vander Stichele *et al* 2004).

estimates is not mentioned in the report of the 2001 findings (although the two studies were carried out, in Flanders, by the same researchers). It is hardly believable that within 3 years the rate of termination of life, with or without request, could have declined so dramatically. As we will see in section 10.3.2, given the number of cases of euthanasia reported to the Federal Control and Evaluation Committee only a few years later, the low estimate for 2001 is implausible. There is no obvious way of accounting for the 2001 finding except as the result of methodological problems leading to classification of much of what was reported as termination of life in 1996 and 1998, as pain relief in 2001. For the time being, the 1998 estimates (similar to those of 1996 but with a far larger sample and covering all of Flanders) seem the safest ones to use.

If we take the 1998 estimates, euthanasia (including assisted suicide) seems to have been about half as frequent in Flanders as in the Netherlands (in 1995 and 2001). Termination of life without a request was about four times as frequent in Flanders as in the Netherlands (even the 2001 estimate is more than double the Dutch figure).

As far as assistance with suicide is concerned, the estimated frequencies—especially at a level of one one-hundredth of a per cent in the 2001 study—have to be taken with a grain of salt. There must have been about a third of a case, whatever that might be, in the sample.[5] Such data fail the 'interocular impact test' for significance.

Table 10.2 gives some basic characteristics of patients who die due to euthanasia/PAS and termination of life without a request, pain relief with life-shortening effect, or withholding or withdrawing life-prolonging treatment. However, because of the doubts just mentioned concerning the measurement of euthanasia in the 2001 study, and because as far as characteristics are concerned 'doctor-assisted dying' is not differentiated into cases with or without a request from the patient, we also give between brackets data on reported cases (see Table 10.3), using here only the data for 2002–03 (as we will see, the other two years for which these data are available are very similar).

Where data from the 2001 study and from cases reported to the FCEC seem to confirm each other, the following comparative observations can be made. Euthanasia takes place in a hospital much more frequently in Flanders than in the Netherlands (over 50% as compared with about 10% over the years in the Netherlands—see chapter 5, Table 5.4). The proportion of euthanasia attributable to patients 80 or older is rather lower in Belgium than in the Netherlands (a fifth or less in Belgium, about a quarter in the Netherlands—see chapter 5, Table 5.2). The estimated shortening of life due to euthanasia is almost the same in Flanders as in the Netherlands: less than a week in half of all cases (chapter 5, Table 5.2).

The data on pain relief with life-shortening effect and on abstention present fewer problems of comparison. The ages of patients are roughly the same (rather

---

[5] There were only 3 observed cases of assisted suicide in the 1998 study, which produced an estimated rate 10 times higher than that in 2001 (Deliens *et al* 2000: 1808, Table 1).

Table 10.2. Characteristics of deaths due to MBPSL in Belgium (Flanders), 2001 (percentages of all cases in a given category)

	'doctor-assisted dying' (E&PAS and termination of life without a request)		*pain relief* with life-shortening effect	*absten-*tion
age				
1–17	3	[age <20: <0.5]	0	0
18–64	25	[age 20–79: 83]	18	12
65–79	52		38	28
80 or older	20	[16]	44	60
sex				
male	66	[50]	52	43
female	34	[50]	48	57
cause of death				
cardiovascular disease	12		14	28
malignant disease	58	[82.5]	55	26
respiratory disease	5		8	12
disease of the nervous system	13		12	14
other/ unknown	12		12	20
place of death				
hospital	50	[54]	55	55
other	50		45	45
estimated shortening of life				
less then 1 week	47		57	45
1 week to 1 month	46		27	42
more then 1 month	7		1	6
unknown	0		15	6

Source: Van der Heide *et al* 2003: Table 3 (EURELD study); data from FCEC between brackets.

older than in cases of euthanasia). Place of death is in Flanders for all MBPSL more often than not a hospital (over 50%). In the Netherlands the proportion of MBPSL deaths that take place in a hospital is considerably lower: 24% of euthanasia, 27% of pain relief, and 42% of abstention.[6] Estimated shortening of life of less than a week was in 2001 somewhat more common in the Netherlands than in Flanders: for pain relief 60% versus 57%, for abstention 73% versus 45%.[7]

---

[6] See Van der Heide *et al* 2003, Tables 1 and 3, for these comparative data. It should be remembered that death in hospital is generally less common in the Netherlands than in Flanders (33% as against 53%).

[7] *Ibid.* The estimated shortening of life in the Netherlands in 2005 was much lower: 81% and 73% respectively (see ch 5, Table 5.2).

10.2 Reported Cases of Euthanasia/PAS in Belgium

For reported cases of euthanasia/PAS, the data in the biennial reports of the Federal Control and Evaluation Commission give some important additional information (Table 10.3). To the extent the FCEC is right in thinking that 'clandestine euthanasia which for years was common in our country and whose dangers speak for themselves' is dying out,[8] these data reflect Belgian euthanasia practice in general.

As in the Netherlands (see Tables 5.2 and 5.5), over 80% of those who receive euthanasia are suffering from cancer. The only other disorders that regularly lead to euthanasia are progressive neuromuscular disorders. The few patients who received euthanasia although they were not considered terminal, were most often suffering from the latter disorders.[9]

As in the Netherlands (see chapter 5.1.2.3), about 80% of all euthanasia takes place with patients aged 40–79, less than 20% with patients 80 or over. For patients below 20, it is very rare.

Unlike the Netherlands (see chapter 5.1.2.3), euthanasia is preponderantly an affair of hospitals and (therefore) of specialists and, slightly less frequently, of GPs. As in the Netherlands, it rarely takes place in a nursing home.

From the commission's second Biennial Report it appears that in most cases (89% in 2004–2005) the drugs used were a combination of general anaesthesia (Pentothal or an equivalent) followed (unless the patient died spontaneously) by a muscle relaxant. Morphine, sometimes in combination with other sedatives, was used in less than 1% of the cases. In a small number of cases (1%), only an oral barbiturate was used (these cases are considered 'assisted suicide' by the commission); incidentally, when death did not occur quickly, this was followed by a muscle relaxant.[10]

A point of concern expressed by the commission in both of its reports concerns the availability of appropriate euthanatica. It seems that these are only generally available in hospital pharmacies, and this gives rise to practical problems in the case of euthanasia performed at home. The commission attributes the problem to the fact that many pharmacists are not adequately informed about drugs suitable for euthanasia or have difficulty acquiring them from wholesalers. It expects the problem to diminish as the result of professional and governmental interventions.[11]

---

  [8] FCEC 2002–03: 18.

  [9] FCEC 2002–03: 24, 26; FCEC 2004–05: 16, 17.

  [10] FCEC 2004–05: 24.

  [11] FCEC 2002–03: 20; 2004–05: 23. In August of 2006, according to news reports euthanasia was temporarily impossible in Belgium due to a shortage of the drug used (see <http://www.medisch contact.artsennet.nl/search/euthanasiemiddel> accessed 1 July 2007. See ch 9.4.3.10 for the Government's attention to this problem.

Table 10.3. Characteristics of reported cases of euthanasia/PAS in Belgium, 2002–2005; percentages of all reported cases [absolute numbers in brackets]

	2002–2003[1] (N = 259)	2004 (N = 349)	2005 (N = 393)
sex (% male)	50	52	52
age			
<20	<0.5	1	0
20–39	3	9	4
40–59	32	33	24
70–79	48	43	54
80 or older	16	14	19
cancer	82.5	81	85
terminal[2]	91.5	93	93
current request	>99.5	99	98
place of death			
hospital	54	56	52
home	41	38	41
'rest and nursing home'	5	4	5
other	<0.5	2	2
consultation			
palliative specialist	19.5	15	11
GP	32.5	41	42
specialist	48	42	47
not specified	0	2	<1
second consultant[3]	[22]	[24]	[27]
psychiatrist	(68)	(42)	(65)
specialist	(32)	(58)	(35)
other consultants[4]	[129]	[206]	[185]
palliative consultation[5]	[101]	[144]	[130]
suffering[6]			
physical	[406]	[511]	[366]
psychic	[174]	[243]	[241]

Source: FCEC 2002–03, 2004–05.

[1] Last quarter of 2002 and four quarters of 2003.
[2] Death expected shortly [*binnen afzienbare termijn*].
[3] These second consultants were required because the patient was not in a terminal state. Percentages of all cases in which there was a second consultant.
[4] Non-mandatory consultations.
[5] Mandatory consultations not included.
[6] More than one sort of suffering possible.

Physician-Assisted Suicide

The Federal Control and Evaluation Committee considers a case one of 'assistance with suicide' if the patient dies shortly after oral administration of a barbiturate and is not thereafter injected with a muscle relaxant.[12] Using this definition, the number of reported cases of 'assistance with suicide' is only 3–5 per year, or about 1% of all reported cases of euthanasia and assisted suicide together (Table 10.4). It seems that the Belgian ratio of assisted suicide to euthanasia is even lower than that in the Netherlands (see chapter 5.2.2.2).[13] It may be that the low Belgian ratio reflects the confusion about the status of physician-assisted suicide in the Belgian parliamentary debates on the Law on Euthanasia of 2002 (see chapter 9.4.1), or that (perhaps for the same reason) 'assisted suicide' is less frequently reported than 'euthanasia'. It is conceivable that the classification of PAS by the FCEC is more restrictive than that used in the death-certificate studies and by the Dutch Review Committees,[14] in which case it might to some extent be differences of classification that account for the different ratios obtained.

If, as we did for the Netherlands (see chapter 5.2.2.2) we ask the question, how many of the cases of euthanasia could probably have been carried out in the form of assistance with suicide, the exercise leads for Flanders to an estimated 362 cases (reported and unreported) in 2005, in which assisted suicide may have been an available alternative.[15] From Table 10.4 we can see that among *reported* cases assisted suicide was occurring in the years from 2002 to 2005 at a rate of roughly 5 times per year in all of Belgium. From Table 10.1 we can calculate that there were an estimated 50 cases or more of PAS in Flanders alone in 1998. Although none of these calculations is more than a stab in the air, it does seem that if there were a (legal or other) preferred position for assisted suicide, the ratio of assisted suicide to euthanasia could change dramatically.

Table 10.4. Reported cases of 'assisted suicide' in Belgium, 2002–2005 [percentage of all cases of euthanasia/PAS in brackets]

2002–2003 (5 quarters)	*2004*	*2005*
5 [2%]	5 [1%]	3 [<1%]

Source: FCEC 2002–03, 2004–05.

[12] As we have seen in ch 9.4.1, the FCEC considers 'assisted suicide' to be a form of 'euthanasia', and the requirements of due care are the same, in particular with respect to the continuous presence of the doctor.

[13] The 1998 survey (see Table 10.1) gives a ratio of PAS to euthanasia similar to those in the Dutch surveys (see ch 5.2.2.2) but because the numbers in the sample were so tiny, comparing them with the actual case load of the Federal Control and Evaluation Committee is risky.

[14] However, this would not affect the results of the surveys in Flanders, where the operational definitions of the Dutch death-certificate studies were used (compare ch 5.2.2.2 under 'euthanasia versus assistance with suicide', n 93).

[15] The rough and ready calculation here is based on Table 10.5 (total deaths in Flanders in 2005), Table 10.1 (frequency of euthanasia/PAS according to the 1998 study), and Table 10.2 (frequency of estimated shortening of life more than a week due to euthanasia/PAS, according to the 2001 study): 56890×1.2%×53% = 362.

10.3 The System of Control

10.3.1 Institutional Policies

A recent study of written euthanasia policies in Belgium (Flanders) documents a positive reception of legalisation of euthanasia by Catholic hospitals and nursing homes that proceeded far more rapidly and went much further than in the Netherlands.[16] The day after the Belgian act legalising euthanasia was passed, Caritas Flanders, the umbrella organisation of Catholic health care institutions in Flanders (responsible for 56% and 33%, respectively, of all hospitals and nursing homes in Flanders), issued a position paper on euthanasia and a clinical practice guideline. These were sent to all Catholic hospitals and nursing homes, who were urged to develop institutional policies. By the end of 2003, almost four-fifths of all Catholic hospitals and a third of all nursing homes had adopted a written policy on euthanasia (in most cases, institutions without such a policy were in the process of drafting one, or planned to do so in the future).[17] The directors of most hospitals and nursing homes reported taking steps to communicate the institution's policy to doctors, nurses and other caregivers, but only nursing homes actively communicated the policy to general practitioners (two-thirds, against a third of the hospitals), and whereas a bit more than half of the nursing homes communicate their ethics policies to patients and their relatives, only one hospital did so.

Very few Catholic institutions (1 of 30 surveyed hospitals, 6 of 47 nursing homes) flatly reject euthanasia as inconsistent with their 'Christian values', but many of them impose conditions additional to those contained in the law. Euthanasia pursuant to the advance written request of an incompetent patient is rejected by almost a third of the hospitals and almost two-thirds of the nursing homes. Two-fifths of the hospitals and two-thirds of the nursing homes limit euthanasia to terminally ill patients. And for competent, terminally ill patients, over four-fifths of both hospitals and nursing homes require a so-called 'palliative filter': consultation with a palliative care expert.[18] Almost half of all hospitals and almost a third of all nursing homes impose no restrictions beyond those contained in the law.[19]

---

[16] The following information is taken from Gastmans *et al* 2006 and Gastmans, Lemiengre & Dierkx de Casterlé 2006. In most hospitals and nursing homes, euthanasia policy was part of a broader policy encompassing abstention and/or symptom or pain control.

[17] In most cases, especially in hospitals, an institutional ethics committee was the key actor involved in drafting and/or adopting the policy.

[18] See ch 9.4.3.3 on the idea of a 'palliative filter'.

[19] The authors of the studies on which this section is based observe that 'The statements of the Roman Catholic Magisterium on euthanasia are, in Catholic health care institutions, no longer generally accepted as the legitimate foundation for developing their own ethics policies.' (Gastmans *et al* 2006: 176)

10.3.2 Consultation[20]

The situation as far as consultation is concerned is essentially the same as in the Netherlands (see Table 10.3). Consultation always takes place in reported cases. The first, legally required consultation is usually with a GP or a specialist; the frequency of first consultation with a palliative specialist seems to be declining (from 19.5% in 2002–03 to 11% in 2005). But in quite a large number of cases, additional palliative consultation takes place (although the frequency of this seems also to have declined slightly, from 39% to 33%).

To date, no information is available concerning the functioning of the system of specially-trained consultants (LEIF and Médecins EOL) (see chapter 9.4.3.8).

10.3.3 Reporting

There has been a more than fourfold increase in the annual number of reported cases over a period of 5 years (see Table 10.6, on which Graphs 10.1 and 10.2 are based).[21] Graph 10.1 shows the development per quarter in the first 5 years. The acceleration was rapid in the first period: 8 per month in the first quarter, 14 per month in the second, 21 per month in the next three; 29 per month in 2004, and 33 per month in 2005. The pattern is reminiscent of the early 1990s in the Netherlands, a comparable period in which the reporting procedure was becoming institutionalised (see chapter 5.4.3, Graph 5.1). However, if we look at the development of reporting over longer periods, and include 2006 (see Graph 10.2[22]) it seems that the rapid increase of the first few quarters is slowing down (whether this is because a high rate of reporting has now been reached, as the FCEC believes, is a matter we will turn to in a moment).

The difference between Dutch- and French-speaking Belgians as far as the number of reports is concerned (see Table 10.6) is striking. Taking account of the fact that the ratio of the two populations is roughly 4:3, one would have expected over 900 French-language reports in the period 2002–06, whereas in fact there have been less than a third that number. A number of considerations have been suggested to explain the difference. One is that there is far less euthanasia being practiced in Wallonia,[23] or that what there is is being far less frequently reported.

---

[20] Consultation with nurses was quite common before the Euthanasia Law of 2002 (about half of all cases of death in an institution and about a quarter in the case of deaths at home). Especially in hospitals, nurses were very often involved in the administration of euthanatica. The frequency of this was even higher in the case of termination of life without an explicit request. See Bilsen *et al* 2004. It should be recalled that these data involve a very small number of cases (see n 4).

[21] There was no such thing as a reporting rate before the Euthanasia Law of 2002, since euthanasia was considered a natural cause of death for registration purposes (see Cohen *et al* 2006c).

[22] For 2002, the number of cases for the last quarter has been multiplied by 4.

[23] 'Wallonia' is not entirely accurate here: the data on reports are only known for 'Dutch language' and 'French language' reports, and these language indicators are only imperfect geographic indicators, especially because the bi-lingual (but predominantly French-speaking) Brussels region with a population of about 1 million is not part of either Wallonia or Flanders. As we have seen in section 10.1, what is known about the frequency of euthanasia, as opposed to that of reports, is known only for Flanders.

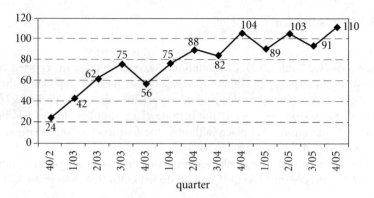

Graph 10.1 Number of Reports per quarter, Belgium, 2005–2005
(FCEC 2002–2003, 2004–2005)

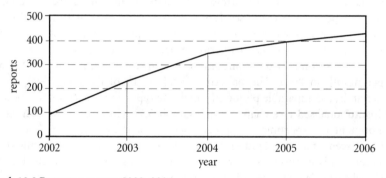

Graph 10.2 Reports per year, 2002–2006

One possible reason for both suppositions is that the population of Flanders may over the past decade or so have been more exposed to and influenced by Dutch practice just across the border and in the same language, and therefore have 'caught up with' Dutch frequencies more quickly. The Federal Control and Evaluation Commission suggests that the existence in Flanders of a corps of specially-trained consultants, something that as we have seen was only set up in Wallonia in 2003 (see ch 9.4.3.8), may account for a higher level of relevant knowledge among Flemish doctors.[24]

The Reporting Rate

Establishing a reporting rate for Wallonia (the French-speaking part of Belgium) is not currently possible, since there has been no nationwide research carried out

---

[24] FCEC 2002–03: 9. The fact that the unfavourable ratio got worse in 2004–05 is hard to explain in terms of unequal exposure to information.

to establish the frequency with which euthanasia is performed.[25] For Flanders, this is possible, but we are confronted with the considerable differences in the frequency of euthanasia according to the three available estimates (see Table 10.1). Table 10.5 gives three reporting rates for Flanders, depending on which estimate one uses. Unfortunately, it is not possible to calculate a reporting rate based on data that all derive from the same year, since the only available estimates of the amount of euthanasia date from 1996, 1998 and 2001, and the first reported cases were in 2002. From Table 10.6 and Graph 10.2 it seems that reporting had only really built up steam by 2004 and 2005, so that even though the survey data for the actual amount of euthanasia date from an earlier period, it would not be sensible to calculate a reporting rate using the earliest data on reporting. For want of a better method, Table 10.5 calculates the amount of euthanasia in 2005 by multiplying the number of deaths in Flanders in that year by the frequencies of euthanasia estimated for Flanders in 1996, 1998 and 2001. Three different reporting rates can then be calculated by dividing the number of reports from Flanders in that year by the calculated amount of euthanasia.

One can conclude two things from this exercise, rough and ready as it has been.[26] In the first place, the 2001 study, whose estimated rate of euthanasia was less than a third of that found in two earlier studies, is almost certainly erroneous.

Table 10.5. Three estimates of the reporting rate in Flanders in 2005

estimated frequency of euthanasia in 3 studies	estimated euthanasia deaths in 2005 (all deaths in Flanders = 56,890)	estimated reporting rate in 2005 (number of Dutch-language reports* = 332)
1996 study –1.5%	853	39%
1998 study –1.2%	683	47%
2001 study –0.31%	176	189%

* See note 23 concerning the identification of Dutch-language reports with the region Flanders.

Source: Tables 10.1 and 10.6; Belgian FOD Economics, Department of Statistics, Population Statistics, available online at <http://aps.vlaanderen.be/statistiek/cijfers/stat_cijfers_demografie.htm> accessed 1 July 2007.

[25] The report of a recent survey (January 2007) on the website of LEIF (the Flemish organisation that supplies specialised consultants—see ch 9.4.3.8) claims that euthanasia is as frequent in Wallonia as in Flanders, so that the differences in the number of reports received from the two regions must be due to a difference in the willingness to report. See <http://www.leif.be/nieuws/euthanasie_Franstalig.html> accessed 30 September 2007.

[26] The weakness of the whole procedure is the latent assumption that the frequency of euthanasia did not radically change over the years. One can do the calculation in a different way that makes the possible effect of this assumption clear. In 2001 the rate of euthanasia is supposed to have been 0.31%. If we were to assume a 100% reporting rate in 2005, so that the number of reported cases is equal to the number of actual cases, then the frequency of euthanasia would be 0.6% in 2005, double what it was only 4 years before. Assuming a lower rate of reporting would make the difference even greater. It seems highly implausible that any such dramatic change in the rate of euthanasia has taken place.

If the rate it found were anywhere near correct, Flemish doctors would be reporting many more cases of euthanasia than they actually perform.

In the second place, if we take the 1998 study as the best estimate available (close to that of 1996 but with a far larger sample covering the whole of Flanders), Flanders has a reporting rate only 4 years after legalisation that is roughly equivalent to that in the Netherlands after more than ten years. Of course, to the extent the actual frequency of euthanasia has gone up since legalisation, we will have calculated too optimistic a rate of reporting. But it is hard to imagine that the picture would change very much.

10.3.4 The Federal Control and Evaluation Commission

As we have seen in chapter 9.4.4.2, the Law on Euthanasia of 2002 provides for reporting to the Federal Control and Evaluation Commission, which is responsible for deciding whether the doctor conformed to the requirements of due care. Only if the doctor is found 'not careful' is the case forwarded to the prosecutorial authorities. The commission began work on 1 September 2002 and issued its first Biennial Report, covering the period through 31 December 2003, in 2004. The second Biennial Report, covering 2004 and 2005, was issued in 2006. Table 10.6 is

Table 10.6. Disposition of cases by the Federal Control and Evaluation Commission, 2002–2006

year	reported cases			commission not competent	additional information requested		'careful'	'not careful'
	Dutch	French	total		remarks[2]	report incomplete[3]		
2002[1]	17	7	24	0	2	4	24	0
2003	199	36	235	1[4]	29	46	235	0
2004	304	45	349	1[5]	15	67	349	0
2005	332	61	393	1[5]	21	59	393	0
2006	380	89	429	?	?	?	429	0
Total	1,232	238	1,430	3	67	176	1,430	0

Source: Biennial Reports, Federal Control and Evaluation Commission (2002–03, 2004–05).
Source 2006: Prof W Distelmans (chairman of the FCEC).

[1] Data for 2002 are for the last quarter of the year since the Commission began work on 22 September 2002.
[2] In the case of a remark, the doctor is not required to reply.
[3] In these cases, the doctor's report is accepted on the condition that missing information be supplied.
[4] This case is not included in the commission's report because it concerned withdrawal of treatment followed by death of the patient several days later. See De Bondt 2005.
[5] These cases are not included in the further statistical data in the report because they concerned withdrawal of treatment followed by sedation.

taken from these two reports and some additional information for 2006 received from the Commission. It offers an overview of the cases dealt with by the Commission in its first five years.

The general conclusion of the FCEC is that 'in the cases that it considers, application of the law does not give rise to significant problems'.[27] As Table 10.6 shows, in the first 5 years of its existence, the FCEC reviewed 1,430 cases and found no doctor 'not careful'. As a result of this, there have been no prosecutions of doctors for euthanasia since the Law on Euthanasia of 2002.

In almost a quarter of all cases the FCEC makes it clear to the reporting doctor that the scrutiny of his behaviour is more than a pure formality. Through 2005 it had sent 'remarks' to the reporting doctor in 67 (7%) of the cases it reviewed and had requested additional information due to an incomplete dossier in 176 (18%). Unfortunately, nothing is known publicly about the contents of these remarks and requests.

Comment on the FCEC Biennial Reports

The statistical reporting by the FCEC is exemplary and affords much more insight into the characteristics of reported cases than do the Annual Reports of the Dutch Regional Review Committees. On the other hand, the FCEC's biennial reports give very little information concerning its own functioning as a control institution. Unlike the Dutch Review Committees, the FCEC is in that respect largely a black box. Except on an incidental point (in particular, the FCEC's decision to regard physician-assisted suicide as a form of euthanasia), its reports provide no information that contributes to legal development, do not provide feedback to the medical profession as a whole, and hardly afford a basis for informed public and political assessments of the functioning of the commission, in particular how it reaches its judgments and why. Nor can one distil from the biennial reports much insight into the range of informal sanctions over which the Commission may dispose. We know that some doctors are asked for additional information, but whether in this context suggestions are made for improvement of practice is unknown. We also do not know whether the FCEC has taken any active steps to influence euthanasia practice in institutions. In short, a commission whose raison d'être is to produce transparency and thereby maintain confidence in euthanasia practice, itself suffers from a regrettable absence of transparency.

10.4 Concluding Comparative Remark

This chapter shows that while there are some differences in the health care context (Belgians die more often than the Dutch in hospitals and Belgian health care

---

[27] FCEC 2002–03: 19; 2004–05: 29.

institutions are still largely organised along religious lines) and striking differences in the processes of legal change the two countries went through (the process in Belgium being characterised by a very low profile of the organised medical profession and the absence of preparatory legal development in the courts and in official and professional reports), nevertheless MBPSL practice in the two countries is quite similar in a number of respects:

- the overall frequency of MBPSL (and especially of pain and symptom relief with possible life shortening effect);
- the high frequency of discussion of MBPSL with patients and relatives and with other caregivers, especially when this is compared with countries in which euthanasia and assisted suicide are prohibited (see chapter 17.2);
- the characteristics of patients who receive euthanasia;
- the strong preference for euthanasia over PAS;
- the rapidly increasing rate of reporting after legalisation.

Termination of life without a request is essentially unregulated in Belgium (formally, it is murder; in fact it is never prosecuted). For reasons we have seen in section 10.1 there is some uncertainty about whether the frequency in Belgium is very different (higher) from that in the Netherlands. But at least as far as termination of life in neonatology is concerned it is clear that differences are marginal (see chapter 6).

Three factors may help to explain the convergence in law and practice between the Belgium and the Netherlands. Their political structure and culture (described in chapters 2 and 7) are in many fundamental respects much more alike than some superficial differences between the two countries might suggest. It is also clear from chapter 17.1 (see also chapter 20) that Dutch and Belgian values relevant to euthanasia and other MBPSL are similar. And finally, it seems (see chapter 9) that geographic and linguistic proximity has been important.

Part III

Other European Countries

Introduction to Part III

This part consists of country reports on eight Western European countries, all written by local experts. We asked the authors to deal with a number of common topics:

- not just euthanasia, but all medical practice that potentially shortens life;
- both law and also whatever is known about actual medical practice;
- both formal law (statutes and judicial decisions) and law in statu nascendi: influential reports of advisory bodies and professional associations, protocols and guidelines, and the like;
- the context of legal development, public debate, public and medical opinion, and so forth.

We have tried to be sure that the terms used at various places in the book are consistent. Our common terminology is that first developed in the Netherlands but now quickly becoming the international standard, used, for example, in comparative empirical research such as the EURELD studies. When, for purposes of an accurate description of a local situation, it is necessary to use a word like 'euthanasia' in a deviant sense (as in 'passive euthanasia'), this has been indicated by the use of single quotation marks. Where our term for a key concept is different from the term used locally, we have given the local term in parentheses at the beginning of a discussion. Thus throughout the book we use the English term 'futility' in connection with withholding or withdrawing life-prolonging treatment, although in southern/Catholic countries variations on the expression '*accanimento terapeutico*' (therapeutic obstinacy) are used to describe treatment that a doctor should not give because it is pointless.

We have made a number of important distinctions that are not yet common currency:

- between 'palliative sedation' (which is not a cause of death) and 'terminal sedation' (which, because artificial nutrition and hydration is not given to the sedated person, is a cause of death);
- between withholding/withdrawing life-prolonging treatment on the authority of the doctor (because it would be 'futile') and doing so because of refusal by the patient;

- between potentially life-shortening pain relief that is medically indicated (and therefore falls within the 'medical exception' or some equivalent legal figure) and pain relief that is not so indicated (and therefore amounts to termination of life, either with or without a request from the patient).

Despite all this striving for uniformity of coverage and terminology, however, we have not tried to force the descriptions of the various countries (including, in the preceding two parts, the Netherlands and Belgium) into a single mould. This would have been impossible (or at least impoverishing) because different countries are at different points in legal development. In the Netherlands and Belgium (and to some extent Switzerland), for example, there is a highly-developed body of 'euthanasia law' to be described and discussed, whereas in most other countries 'euthanasia law' can be pretty well summed up in one sentence ('euthanasia is illegal'), and it is the ongoing processes of political debate and of legal change concerning MBPSL generally, that are interesting. Furthermore, there are major differences between the legal cultures and legal systems involved, which would make it impossible to do justice to local situations by forcing all local variation into a single descriptive scheme.

The result is that variations in the way the various authors describe the situation in their respective countries are often interesting and revealing in themselves. Penney Lewis' account in chapter 11 of the situation in England and Wales could only have been written by a common lawyer about the common law. And Stéphanie Hennette's description in chapter 12 of the French situation is as French as what she describes. But as soon as one has put these words on paper, the subtleties of the differences start giving rise to doubts that are more interesting than stereotypical oppositions between the common and the civil law. Statutes have, of course, for a couple of centuries been central in both legal systems, but one might have expected French judges to treat them more respectfully than English judges. In the case of patients' rights, however, French judges seem in effect to be applying an ancient common law doctrine, used by English judges over the centuries to resist the incursion of statutory law into fields traditionally regulated by judge-made law: 'statutes in derogation of the common law are to be strictly construed'. It is hard to imagine a modern English judge going as far out of his way to emasculate legislative change as his French counterparts seem to have done.

In the final analysis, the basic problems of regulating medical practice at the end of life are everywhere the same. Whether due to spontaneous convergence arising accidentally out of purely endogenous factors, or to mutual influence and imitation, the trend revealed in the following chapters (taken together with those that have gone before) is—with the possible exception of a relatively small part of the whole field of MBPSL, namely euthanasia and physician-assisted suicide—in the direction of a general European law concerning end-of-life medical practice, one that will probably look much like what has most clearly emerged, so far, in the Netherlands. We return to this idea of convergence in chapter 20.

11

England and Wales

PENNEY LEWIS

This contribution describes the law governing medical behaviour that potentially shortens life in England and Wales as well as what is known about medical practice.[1] The situation in Scotland is governed by a separate legal regime which will not be covered here.

11.1 General Principles

The 'Medical Exception'

The medical exception is well established in English law. While consent is generally no defence to assault occasioning actual or grievous bodily harm, 'bodily invasions in the course of proper medical treatment stand completely outside the criminal law'.[2] In *Brown*, Lord Mustill observed that:

> Many of the acts done by surgeons would be very serious crimes if done by anyone else, and yet the surgeons incur no liability. Actual consent, or the substitute for consent deemed by the law to exist where an emergency creates a need for action, is an essential element in this immunity; but it cannot be a direct explanation for it, since much of the bodily invasion involved in surgery lies well above any point at which consent could even arguably be regarded as furnishing a defence. Why is this so? The answer must in my opinion be that proper medical treatment, for which actual or deemed consent is a prerequisite, is in a category of its own.[3]

---

[1] Parts of this chapter are derived from Lewis 2007a and Lewis 2001 with the kind permission of Oxford University Press and Hart Publishing respectively. I am grateful to my colleague Paul Matthews for his advice and guidance relating to coroners and the reporting of deaths.

[2] *Airedale NHS Trust v Bland* [1993] AC 789, 891 (HL, Lord Mustill). See also, *Brown* [1994] 1 AC 212, 258–9 (HL) (holding that it is legitimate to perform 'surgical treatment in accordance with good medical practice and with the consent of the patient'); *AG's Reference (No. 6 of 1980)* [1981] QB 715, 718 (CA, Lord Lane CJ) (listing exceptions to the general rule that consent is no defence to assault causing actual bodily harm, including 'reasonable surgical interference' on the basis of necessity in the public interest).

[3] *Brown* [1994] 1 AC 212, 266 (HL). The other Law Lords agreed: see 231 (Lord Templeman), 245 (Lord Jauncey), 276 (Lord Slynn).

'Double Effect' and the Role of 'Purpose'

The 'doctrine of double effect' has been embraced by English judges in a number of prosecutions of doctors accused of terminating the life of a patient.[4] Thus a doctor who prescribes pain relief that she knows may or will hasten the patient's death, will not be guilty of murder unless her *purpose* was to cause the patient's death.[5] Such purpose can be inferred when the doctor uses a drug whose only medical function is to cause death. In such a case the doctor has gone beyond accepting a risk to her patient's life and intended her death in the sense of purpose or desire: the only possible effect of the drug was to kill her patient.[6]

This is in stark contrast to the law of intention as generally accepted in English criminal law, under which a consequence is intended if the consequence either is the actor's purpose or desire, or is foreseen by the actor as morally certain to occur.[7] The general criminal law concept of intention therefore includes an undesired but known consequence, as in the case where a doctor knows that death will be hastened by the administration of pain-relieving medication. Nevertheless, this is not the approach used when the defendant is a doctor.[8] The approach taken in

---

[4] 'The principle of double effect is a doctrine that distinguishes between the consequences a person intends and those that are unintended but foreseen and may be applicable in various situations where an action has two effects, one good and one bad. In the medical context it is usually relied on when a doctor increases pain-killing medication to a patient; the doctor foresees that the patient may die, although that is not his intention.' Glenys Williams 2001: 41.

[5] See *Re J (A Minor) (Wardship: Medical Treatment)* [1991] Fam 33, 46 (CA) ('the use of drugs to reduce pain will often be fully justified, notwithstanding that this will hasten the moment of death. What can never be justified is the use of drugs or surgical procedures with the primary purpose of doing so.'); *Bland* [1993] AC 789, 867–8 (Lord Goff); *Re A (Children) (Conjoined Twins: Surgical Separation)* [2001] Fam 147, 199 (CA); *Adams (Bodkin)* [1957] Crim LR 365 (Central Crim Ct) ('the doctor is entitled to relieve pain and suffering even if the measures he takes may incidentally shorten life.'). The trial judge in *Adams*, Devlin J (later Lord Devlin), wrote of his experiences in Devlin 1985. See also, Palmer 1957: 375. For a more recent example, see Arlidge 2000; Smith 2000. See also, House of Lords Select Committee on Medical Ethics 1993–94: [242]–[244]; House of Lords Select Committee on the Assisted Dying for the Terminally Ill Bill 2005: [15] (quoting the Attorney-General that it is not murder 'where a doctor acts to do all that is proper and necessary to relieve pain with the incidental effect that this will shorten a patient's life.').

[6] *Cox* (1992) 12 BMLR 38 (Winchester Crown Ct). See also, Kennedy & Grubb 2000: 1963; Price 1997.

[7] *Woollin* [1999] AC 92 (HL).

[8] Although not a case dealing with pain relief, the recent conjoined twins case (described below) confirmed that this narrow view of intention in medical cases survives the enactment of the Human Rights Act 1998 which incorporated the European Convention on Human Rights (ECHR) into English law. Lord Justice Robert Walker commented on the meaning of 'intentionally' in art 2 (1) of the ECHR, which reads in part: 'No one shall be deprived of his life intentionally save in the execution of a sentence of a court following his conviction of a crime for which this penalty is provided by law.' Robert Walker LJ held:

> The Convention is to be construed as an autonomous text, without regard to any special rules of English law, and the word 'intentionally' in article 2(1) must be given its natural and ordinary meaning. In my judgment the word, construed in that way, applies only to cases where the purpose of the prohibited action is to cause death.

Re A (Children) (Conjoined Twins: Surgical Separation) [2001] Fam 147, 256 (Brooke LJ agreed at 238). The passage was also cited with approval in *NHS Trust A v M; NHS Trust B v H* [2001] 2 WLR 942, [22] (HC).

the medical cases is therefore 'less stringent' than the position in the criminal law more generally: a narrow definition of intention is used which results in the exclusion of many pain relief cases from the ambit of the criminal law.[9] This must reflect 'a judgment that some acts (although intended) ought as a matter of moral judgment and public policy to be regarded as attracting no blame because of their social worth.'[10]

It is worth noting, however, that this stretching of the criminal law to accommodate the doctrine of double effect may, although well-intentioned, have unintended side effects. In a review of the medical literature worldwide, Sykes and Thorns conclude that:

> there is no evidence that the use of opioids or sedatives in palliative care requires the doctrine of double effect as a defence . . . Thus, although the doctrine is a valid ethical device, it is, for the most part, irrelevant to symptom control at the end of life. To exaggerate its involvement perpetuates a myth that satisfactory symptom control at the end of life is inevitably associated with hastening death. The result can be a reluctance to use medication to secure comfort and a failure to provide adequate relief to a very vulnerable group of patients.[11]

11.2 Medical Decision-Making in the Case of Incompetent Adults

From 2007, treatment decisions can be made on behalf of an incompetent individual by a proxy or surrogate, whether the proxy was appointed by the individual when still competent or judicially appointed.[12] Prior to this change in the law, the decision-maker for an incompetent person who had not made an anticipatory refusal was the patient's physician.[13] If no proxy has been appointed, or the proxy does not have the authority to make the particular decision,[14] the patient's doctor will be the decision-maker unless the jurisdiction of the Court of Protection is invoked.[15] Incompetent adults are represented in legal proceedings by the Official Solicitor, an office administered by the Ministry of Justice, forming part

---

[9] Ashworth 1996.

[10] Kennedy & Grubb 2000: 2113–14.

[11] Sykes & Thorns 2003: 317.

[12] See Mental Capacity Act 2005, ss 9–14, 22–3 (allowing a competent person to appoint a donee of a lasting power of attorney to make medical decisions on her behalf after the onset of incompetence), 16–20 (allowing a court to appoint a deputy to make medical decisions on behalf of an incompetent person who has not made a lasting power of attorney).

[13] Unless the court's intervention was sought. *Re F* [1990] 2 AC 1 (HL).

[14] For example, a court-appointed proxy may not refuse consent to the carrying out or continuation of life-sustaining treatment. Mental Capacity Act 2005, s 20 (5).

[15] Mental Capacity Act 2005, ss 5, 15. The Court of Protection is a new superior court to deal with matters relating to adults lacking capacity. See Mental Capacity Act 2005, Part II.

of the judicial system. The Official Solicitor provides legal services for vulnerable persons where those services need to be provided by the public sector.[16]

Regardless of the identity of the decision-maker, decisions on medical treatment for incompetent individuals are made using the 'best interests' test, which involves weighing the benefit and detriment that will flow from the proposed procedure.[17] The courts have rejected[18] the alternative 'substituted judgment' test[19] as 'simply a fiction'.[20] The test was also rejected by the Law Commission,[21] although it did recommend that the incompetent's views, wishes and feelings should be considered as a part of the best interests test.[22] Section 4(6) of the Mental Capacity Act 2005 now provides that the person making the determination of what is in the incompetent person's best interests

> must consider, so far as is reasonably ascertainable—
>
> (a) the person's past and present wishes and feelings,
> (b) the beliefs and values that would be likely to influence his decision if he had capacity, and
> (c) the other factors that he would be likely to consider if he were able to do so.

The decision-maker must take into account the views as to the patient's best interests of anyone named by the patient as a consultee, anyone engaged in caring for the patient or interested in his welfare, and any proxy decision-maker.[23]

Withdrawal or Withholding of Life-Prolonging Treatment

The General Medical Council, responsible for regulating the medical behaviour of doctors, published 'guidance'[24] in 2001 entitled *Withholding and Withdrawing*

---

[16] See <http://www.officialsolicitor.gov.uk/about/about.htm> accessed 26 March 2007.

[17] *Re F* [1990] 2 AC 1; Mental Capacity Act 2005, s 4.

[18] *Bland* [1993] AC 789, 895 (Lord Mustill), 872 (Lord Goff). Although see contra, *Re J* [1991] Fam 33, 55, in which Taylor LJ adopts a test which appears to be a form of substituted judgment.

[19] This test requires decisions to conform with those which the incompetent individual would have made were she competent, and is based on respect for the individual's autonomy interests. See Buchanan & Brock 1990: 112–14.

[20] This rejection was based on an apparent failure to distinguish between the substituted judgment test and the concept of proxy decision-making (Kennedy & Grubb 2000: 838). Nevertheless, the rejection of substituted judgment has recently been confirmed. *W Healthcare NHS Trust v H and others* [2005] 1 WLR 834, [12], [23] (CA).

[21] See Law Commission 1991: [4.22]–[4.23].

[22] Law Commission 1995: [3.25]–[3.31].

[23] Mental Capacity Act 2005, s 4(7).

[24] Guidance describes what is expected of all doctors registered with the General Medical Council (GMC). Serious or persistent failure to comply with the guidance issued by the GMC may result in a doctor being found unfit to practise medicine and being struck off the medical register. For a detailed discussion of the regulation of the medical profession, see Pattinson 2006: [2.3.1]. Guidance issued by the GMC and other bodies including the British Medical Association and the Royal Colleges is not binding on the courts, although it is treated with considerable respect. See eg Royal College of Paediatrics and Child Health 1998 and 2004, applied in *Re C (Medical Treatment)* [1998] 1 FLR 384 (HC); *An NHS Trust v MB* [2006] EWHC 507, [21]–[22]; *Re K (A Child)* [2006] EWHC 1007, [37]–[40]. See also *W v Egdell* [1990] Ch 359 (CA) (applying the GMC guidance on confidentiality).

Life-Prolonging Treatment: Good Practice in Decision-Making.[25] The Guidance expands on the application of the best interests test in this context:

> Prolonging life will usually be in the best interests of a patient, provided that the treatment is not considered to be excessively burdensome or disproportionate in relation to the expected benefits. Not continuing or not starting a potentially life-prolonging treatment is in the best interests of a patient when it would provide no net benefit to the patient. In cases of acute critical illness where the outcome of treatment is unclear, as for some patients who require intensive care, survival from the acute crisis would be regarded as being in the patient's best interests.[26]

The decision of the House of Lords in *Bland* remains the leading authority on withdrawal of treatment. Anthony Bland was in a persistent vegetative state (PVS) and his family and medical team agreed that it was in his best interests to withdraw artificial nutrition and hydration (ANH). A declaration that such withdrawal would be lawful was sought from the courts. The House of Lords decided that although the intention of the doctor would be to bring about Bland's death, the proposed withdrawal would be lawful as it constituted an omission rather than an act.[27] The doctor's duty did not require the provision of treatment that was not in the patient's best interests.[28]

Judicial Involvement in PVS Cases

In *Bland*, Lord Goff held that as a matter of practice,[29] judicial approval should be sought in all PVS cases in which the patient's medical team believe it is in her best interests for ANH to be withdrawn.[30] This practice is reflected in a series of subsequent cases[31] and was included in the Code of Practice issued under the Mental

---

[25] The Guidance withstood a recent challenge to its legality. See *R (on the application of Burke) v General Medical Council* [2005] EWCA Civ 1003, [64]–[66], [83]. See also British Medical Association 2007.

[26] General Medical Council 2002: [11].

[27] *Bland* [1993] AC 789, 876 (Lord Lowry), 881 (Lord Browne-Wilkinson), 887 (Lord Mustill).

[28] *Bland* [1993] AC 789, 867–9 (Lord Goff), 883–4 (Lord Browne-Wilkinson), 897 (Lord Mustill, holding that 'the proposed conduct is not in the best interests of Anthony Bland, for he has no best interests of any kind'). It appears unlikely that the withdrawal of ANH will be found to be in the patient's best interests if the patient is not in a PVS or in the dying phase. See *W Healthcare NHS Trust v H and others* [2005] 1 WLR 834, [20], [27]–[32] (CA). See also Dyer 1999 (describing a case in which a doctor was found guilty of serious professional misconduct and suspended from practice for 6 months for authorising the withdrawal of artificial nutrition from an incompetent stroke patient who subsequently died).

[29] That is, judicial approval is desirable but not essential. Failure to obtain judicial approval will not, in and of itself, render the subsequent decision or action unlawful. Judicial approval is in fact always sought in such cases.

[30] *Bland* [1993] AC 789, 873–4.

[31] See eg *NHS Trust A v M; NHS Trust B v H* [2001] 2 WLR 942; *Swindon & Marlborough NHS Trust v S* (1995) 3 Med L Rev 84 (HC); *Frenchay Healthcare NHS Trust v S* [1994] 1 WLR 601 (HC); *Re D (Medical Treatment)* [1998] FLR 411 (HC); *NHS Trust A v H* [2001] 2 FLR 501 (HC); *An NHS Trust v J* [2006] EWHC 3152 (Fam). See also, Practice Note (Official Solicitor: Declaratory Proceedings: Medical & Welfare Proceedings for Adults Who Lack Capacity), 28 July 2006, <http://www.officialsolicitor.gov.uk/docs/PracNoteMedicalandWelfareDecisions.doc> and <http://www.officialsolicitor.gov.uk/docs/PVScases. doc> accessed 26 March 2007.

Capacity Act 2005. It will therefore continue to be the case that even when a patient-appointed donee of a lasting power of attorney or a court-appointed deputy consents to the withdrawal of ANH from a PVS patient, the approval of the Court of Protection will be sought prior to the implementation of the decision.[32] This practice of seeking judicial approval in PVS cases has not been extended to other cases in which a decision is made to withdraw life-sustaining treatment, including ANH and ventilation. Although some such cases have come to court,[33] it is clear that most do not. Decision-making in such cases is governed by the general rules discussed above.

11.3 Medical Decision-Making in the Case of Incompetent Children

If there are legal proceedings, the child[34] will be represented by either the Children and Family Court Advisory and Support Service or the Official Solicitor, depending on the circumstances.[35]

If a child does not meet the test of competence,[36] then she can be treated in her best interests with the consent of a person with parental responsibility or the court.[37] If those with parental responsibility refuse the recommended treatment, then the medical team must take steps to bring the issue before a court if the consequences of the refusal are thought serious enough to warrant such a step.[38] In a series of such cases, courts have considered the appropriate ambit of the autonomous decision-making of those with parental responsibility.

---

[32] Department for Constitutional Affairs 2007: [6.18], [8.18], [8.19]. For a critical view, see Lewis 2007b.

[33] See eg *Re R (Adult: Medical Treatment)* (1996) 31 BMLR 127 (HC); *W Healthcare NHS Trust v H and others* [2005] 1 WLR 834 (CA).

[34] Those below the age of 18.

[35] See Official Solicitor, *Practice Note: Appointment in Family Proceedings*, 2 April 2001, <http://www.officialsolicitor.gov.uk/docs/appointment_in_family_proceedings.doc> accessed 26 March 2007).

[36] See below, n 57.

[37] Children Act 1989; *Gillick* [1986] AC 112 (HL). For a more detailed discussion, see Lewis 2001: 159–63. The consent of one person with parental responsibility is sufficient even if another person with parental responsibility disagrees, unless the decision falls into a 'small group of important decisions' which should only be made if there is agreement between all those having parental responsibility for the child. *Re J (A Minor) (Prohibited Steps Order: Circumcision)* [2000] 1 FLR 571 (HC); *Re C (A Child) (Immunisation: Parental Rights)* [2003] EWCA Civ 1148.

[38] Unless it is an emergency, to proceed without the consent of either those with parental responsibility or the court would be a battery. If in an emergency situation it is impossible or impracticable to seek parental consent, then treatment reasonably necessary to avoid serious harm or death may be given. However, if an emergency is foreseeable, there is an onus on the Hospital Trust to seek a judicial declaration before the situation becomes urgent. *Glass v UK* [2004] 1 FLR 1019, [70]–[83] (Eur Ct HR). There may also be disciplinary consequences for a doctor who proceeds without parental consent. See Dyer 1998 (describing a case of a consultant who was suspended for serious professional misconduct by the General Medical Council for failing to obtain parental consent to a balloon catheterisation on a six-year-old girl).

In the earlier cases, the test adopted was that treatment should be provided unless the child's life post-treatment would be 'intolerable'.[39] The courts accepted that this meant that continued life would not always be in the child's best interests: 'There is without doubt a very strong presumption in favour of a course of action which will prolong life, but . . . it is not irrebuttable'.[40]

The test of intolerability has since been abandoned.[41] Instead, a balancing approach is used, looking at the child's quality of life:[42]

> account has to be taken of the pain and suffering and quality of life which the child will experience if life is prolonged. Account has also to be taken of the pain and suffering involved in the proposed treatment itself.[43]

Courts have also been faced with refusals by those with parental responsibility based on religious convictions. In a series of cases, the courts have consistently overruled the refusals of parents who are Jehovah's Witnesses who refuse life-saving blood transfusions for their children based on their religious convictions.[44] Unconventional medical beliefs have also been treated unsympathetically.[45]

The cases involving quality-of-life determinations and the religious objection cases reflect the fact that judges in England and Wales see themselves as the ultimate arbiters of a child's best interests. The views of the parents are considered, but they do not have determinative weight. This judicial attitude was called into question in *Re T (a minor) (wardship: medical treatment)* which involved an eighteen-month-old boy who, after an earlier unsuccessful operation, needed a liver transplant in order to survive beyond the age of two-and-a-half.[46] The boy's parents refused to consent to the operation, despite the unanimous clinical opinion that the transplant would be in the child's best interests. The Court of Appeal, however, reaffirmed the best interests test, Butler-Sloss LJ observing that 'the welfare of the child is the paramount consideration'.[47] The Court of Appeal held that the trial judge had mistakenly focused on the reasonableness of the parents' decision, rather than on the welfare of the child. While a parent's decision would constitute an important consideration, and the extent to which it is considered would depend on its reasonableness, nevertheless the court retains the power to

---

[39] *Re B (A Minor) (Wardship: Medical Treatment)* [1981] 1 WLR 1421, 1424 (Dunn LJ, CA); *Re J* [1991] Fam 33, 55 (Taylor LJ).

[40] *Re J* [1991] Fam 33, 46.

[41] *Bland* [1993] AC 789, 819–20 (Butler-Sloss LJ, CA); *Burke* [2005] EWCA Civ 1003, [62]–[63]; *Portsmouth Hospitals NHS Trust v Wyatt and another* [2005] EWCA Civ 1181, [76].

[42] *Re J* [1991] Fam 33, 46–7 (Lord Donaldson), 52 (Balcombe LJ), 55 (Taylor LJ); *Re T (A Minor) (Wardship: Medical Treatment)* [1997] 1 WLR 242 (CA). See Lewis 1997–98; Fox & McHale 1997.

[43] *Re J* [1991] Fam 33, 46.

[44] See eg *Re E (A Minor)* (1990) 9 BMLR 1 (HC); *Re S (A Minor) (Medical Treatment)* [1993] 1 FLR 376 (HC); *Re O (A Minor) (Medical Treatment)* (1993) 19 BMLR 148 (HC); *Re R (A Minor)* (1993) 15 BMLR 72 (HC).

[45] *Re C (HIV Test)* [1999] 2 FLR 1004 (HC) (order that a baby be tested for HIV despite her HIV-positive mother's refusal on the basis of her doubts about the validity of the generally accepted theories on HIV and AIDS).

[46] *Re T* [1997] 1 WLR 242. See Lewis 1997–98; Fox & McHale 1997.

[47] *Re T* [1997] 1 WLR 242, 250.

overrule the decision of even a reasonable parent in the best interests of the child. Nevertheless, on the facts of the case each of the three judges concluded that to order the transplant over the parents' refusal would not be in the child's best interests. This case did not, however, mark a move away from the otherwise steadfast position that the court is the ultimate and omniscient guardian of a child's best interests. Subsequent cases have confirmed that the court is the ultimate arbiter of the child's best interests.[48]

Although those with parental responsibility can consent to treatment on behalf of the child patient, they cannot *demand* treatment which the medical team considers not to be in the child's best interests. In the case of *Re C (Medical Treatment)*, the parents were seeking an order *requiring* the medical staff to provide treatment. Judicial opposition to such orders is clear.[49] The child's Orthodox Jewish parents' religious views prevented them from consenting to any course which might have the effect of shortening life. They therefore refused to consent to the withdrawal of their seriously ill sixteen-month-old baby from a ventilator, unless the medical staff would agree in advance to re-ventilation in the event of a further respiratory collapse. The child suffered from spinal muscular atrophy, which is a terminal illness. The parents' objections were overruled on the grounds that it was in the child's best interests to withdraw ventilation in order to prevent her from suffering.[50] This case has been followed by a succession of similar decisions, almost all of which have applied the best interests test and have found that continued treatment would not be in the seriously ill child's best interests.[51]

11.4 Medical Decision-Making in the Case of Competent Patients

Even in relation to competent patients, treatment will not be proposed or continued if it is not in the patient's best interests. The patient cannot insist on treatment against the doctor's clinical judgement. In its recent decision in *Burke*, the Court of Appeal endorsed the position of the appellant General Medical Council to this effect.[52]

---

[48] See eg *Wyatt v Portsmouth NHS Trust* [2005] EWHC 693; *Portsmouth NHS Trust v Wyatt* [2004] EWHC 2247; *Re L (A Child) (Medical Treatment: Benefit)* [2004] EWHC 2713; *Portsmouth Hospitals NHS Trust v Wyatt and another* [2005] EWCA Civ 1181; *An NHS Trust v MB* [2006] EWHC 507.

[49] See *Re J (A Minor) (Child in Care: Medical Treatment)* [1993] Fam 15, 27, 29 (CA); *Re J* [1991] Fam 33, 41 (CA); *Re R (A Minor) (Wardship: Medical Treatment)* [1992] Fam 11, 22, 26 (CA).

[50] *Re C (Medical Treatment)* [1998] 1 FLR 384, 390–91 (HC). See Fortin 1998.

[51] See eg *Portsmouth NHS Trust v Wyatt* [2004] EWHC 2247; *Re L (A Child) (Medical Treatment: Benefit)* [2004] EWHC 2713. For an exception, see *An NHS Trust v MB* [2006] EWHC 507.

[52] *R (on the application of Burke) v General Medical Council* [2005] EWCA Civ 1003, [50].

Consent to Treatment

A mentally competent adult[53] patient has an absolute right to refuse to consent to medical treatment, even where that refusal may lead to death.[54] This right extends to pregnant women, even if the refusal may cause the death of the woman or her foetus.[55] To act without the competent patient's consent will constitute a criminal and tortious assault.[56]

Although competent children[57] may consent to medical treatment regardless of a parental refusal,[58] a competent child's refusal of medical treatment can be over-ridden by a consent given by a person with parental responsibility who acts within the limits of her power, that is, in the best interests of the child.[59] The child's refusal is a very important factor to be weighed but is not conclusive.[60] A court can also overrule a competent child's refusal to consent to treatment, for example if the person with parental responsibility is unwilling or unable to do so.[61]

Some limits have been imposed on this judicial and parental power to overrule a competent child. In *Re W*, Nolan LJ stated that the power should only be exercised if 'the child's welfare is threatened by a serious and imminent risk that the

---

[53] Aged 18 or over.

[54] *Re T (An Adult) (Consent to Medical Treatment)* [1992] 3 WLR 782 (CA); *Re MB (Medical Treatment)* [1997] 8 Med LR 217 (CA); *Re B (Adult: Refusal of Medical Treatment)* [2002] EWHC 429. See generally, Wicks 2001.

[55] *Re MB* [1997] 8 Med LR 217; *St George's Healthcare NHS Trust v S; R (S) v Collins and Others* [1999] Fam 26 (CA).

[56] *St George's Healthcare NHS Trust v S; R (S) v Collins and Others* [1999] Fam 26 (CA).

[57] There is a rebuttable presumption of lack of capacity to consent to medical treatment for children under 16. Family Law Reform Act 1969, s 8. The standard by which one can establish that a child under 16 has the capacity to consent is governed by the House of Lords decision in *Gillick* [1986] AC 112, 186. The child must have 'sufficient understanding and intelligence to be capable of making up his own mind on the matter requiring decision'. Courts are likely to flesh out this test using the capacity test in the Mental Capacity Act 2005, ss 2, 3 (once it comes into force in 2007) although strictly speaking the latter test only applies to adults. This test states that

> a person is unable to make a decision for himself if he is unable (a) to understand the information relevant to the decision, (b) to retain that information, [or] (c) to use or weigh that information as part of the process of making the decision.

There is some evidence that a higher standard of competence is applied to children refusing life-saving or life-sustaining treatment than to adults. See Lewis 2001: 152–4.

[58] See Lord Scarman in *Gillick* [1986] AC 112, 186

> as a matter of law the parental right to determine whether or not their minor child below the age of 16 will have medical treatment terminates if and when the child achieves a sufficient understanding and intelligence to enable him or her to understand fully what is proposed.

[59] *Re R* [1992] Fam 11, 26; *Re W (A Minor) (Medical Treatment: Court's Jurisdiction)* [1993] Fam 64, 84 (Lord Donaldson), 86 (Balcombe LJ), 94 (Nolan LJ, *dubitante*) (CA).

[60] *Re W* [1993] Fam 64, 84. See eg *Re M (Medical Treatment: Consent)* [1999] 2 FLR 1097 (HC) (refusal of heart transplant by 15½-year-old girl overruled).

[61] *Re R* [1992] Fam 11; *Re W* [1993] Fam 64, 81 (Lord Donaldson), 88 (Balcombe LJ), 91 (Nolan LJ); *Re K, W and H (Minors) (Medical Treatment)* [1993] 1 FLR 854 (HC); *Re C (Detention: Medical Treatment)* [1997] 2 FLR 180 (HC); *Re L (Medical Treatment: Gillick Competency)* [1998] 2 FLR 810 (HC) (in *obiter*). These decisions are discussed critically in Lewis 2001: 154–9. Fortin (2006) discusses the slim prospects of success for competent minors seeking to challenge this case law under the European Convention on Human Rights.

child will suffer grave and irreversible mental or physical harm'.[62] Balcombe LJ restricted the power to cases where the child's refusal 'will in all probability lead to the death of the child or to severe permanent injury'.[63]

Advance Refusals

Anticipatory refusals of treatment including life-sustaining treatment are legally valid under the Mental Capacity Act 2005, ss. 24–26.[64] Prior to the enactment of this statute, the common law allowed for persons to refuse unwanted treatment in advance of incapacity.[65] Only adults are covered by the statutory provisions,[66] and while in theory the pre-existing common law position could be applied to a competent child, the case law discussed in the previous section makes this unlikely: if competent children contemporaneously refusing life-saving treatment are in practice always overruled, advance refusals are similarly likely to be overruled.

The Mental Capacity Act 2005 provides that when still competent, a person may decide that if

(a) at a later time and in such circumstances as he may specify, a specified treatment is proposed to be carried out or continued by a person providing health care for him, and
(b) at that time he lacks capacity to consent to the carrying out or continuation of the treatment,
(c) the specified treatment is not to be carried out or continued.[67]

The advance decision may be withdrawn or altered at any time while the individual remains competent.[68] The advance decision will not be applicable if

> there are reasonable grounds for believing that circumstances exist which [the individual] did not anticipate at the time of the advance decision and which would have affected his decision had he anticipated them.[69]

If the advance decision refuses life-sustaining treatment, it must be in writing and signed by the patient or by another person in the presence of the patient and at the patient's direction.[70] The patient must sign or acknowledge the document in the presence of a witness who must sign it (or acknowledge his signature) in the patient's presence.[71]

---

[62] *Re W* [1993] Fam 64, 94.

[63] *Re W* [1993] Fam 64, 88.

[64] If the advance refusal is to apply to life-sustaining treatment, this must be specifically mentioned in the document. Mental Capacity Act 2005, s 25 (5).

[65] *Re T* [1992] 3 WLR 782; *Bland* [1993] AC 789; *Re C (Adult Refusal of Treatment)* [1994] 1 WLR 290 (HC); *Re AK (Medical Treatment: Consent)* [2001] 1 FLR 129 (HC); *HE v A Hospital NHS Trust* [2003] EWHC 1017. For a discussion of the common law requirements, see Morgan 1994; Stern 1994; Michalowski 2005.

[66] Mental Capacity Act 2005, s 24 (1).

[67] Mental Capacity Act 2005, ss 24 (1) (a), (b).

[68] Mental Capacity Act 2005, s 24 (3).

[69] Mental Capacity Act 2005, s 25 (4) (c).

[70] Mental Capacity Act 2005, s 25 (5), (6).

[71] Mental Capacity Act 2005, s 25 (6).

11.5 Palliative and Terminal Sedation

As is the case with pain relief, palliative sedation (in the sense of deep and continuous sedation until death) will be lawful provided that the doctor's purpose was not to cause the patient's death.[72] As the sedation is aimed at relieving suffering, it is unlikely that a doctor providing palliative sedation will be criminally prosecuted, even if it were possible to prove that death was hastened.[73] Indeed, there have been no such criminal prosecutions thus far, nor have any objections been raised to the use of palliative sedation where clinically appropriate.

When continuous, deep sedation is coupled with the withdrawal of artificial nutrition and hydration ('terminal sedation'), the principle of double effect is inapplicable to the latter decision.[74] The withdrawal will only be lawful if it meets the test set out in *Bland*: it must be in the patient's best interests.[75]

11.6 Euthanasia and Assisted Suicide

Euthanasia constitutes murder under English law.[76] An individual convicted of murder faces a mandatory life sentence, although it is for the trial judge to set the minimum period which the defendant must serve before becoming eligible for parole.[77] Neither the consent of the victim[78] nor the offender's motives[79] are relevant in relation to her guilt or innocence, although a 'belief by [the] offender that the murder was an act of mercy' is a relevant factor counting towards reduction of the minimum period.[80] Proposals have been made to adopt a separate offence of mercy-killing, but they have not been successful.[81]

[72] See above, section 11.1.

[73] There is no evidence that death is hastened by palliative sedation. For a review, see Sykes & Thorns 2003: 314, 317.

[74] Williams 2001: 51–2.

[75] This test is likely to be met if, for example, the patient is dying of cancer. See Dunlop *et al* 1995.

[76] *The Queen on the Application of Mrs Dianne Pretty v Director of Public Prosecutions* [2002] 1 AC 800, [5] (HL); *Bland* [1993] AC 789, 865–6 (Lord Goff), 882, 885 (Lord Browne-Wilkinson), 892–3 (Lord Mustill); *Cox* (1992) 12 BMLR 38 (instructing the jury that if the 'primary purpose' of the administration of potassium chloride was to hasten death then it was murder).

[77] The recommendation by the House of Lords Select Committee on Medical Ethics 1993–94: [261] to abolish the mandatory life sentence was rejected by the Government (see UK Government 1994: 5).

[78] *Bland* [1993] AC 789, 890 (Lord Mustill).

[79] *Bland* [1993] AC 789, 867 (Lord Goff), 890 (Lord Mustill).

[80] Criminal Justice Act 2003, s 269, Sch 21, [11 (f)].

[81] See Criminal Law Revision Committee 1976: [82]. The lesser offence of mercy-killing would have applied in cases where the victim was

(1) permanently subject to great bodily pain or suffering, or (2) permanently helpless from bodily or mental incapacity, or (3) subject to rapid and incurable bodily or mental degeneration.

No request requirement was proposed in order to allow the offence to encompass cases where the victim was incompetent. The proposal was dropped due to lack of support from consultees. See Criminal Law Revision Committee 1980: [115]. See also UK Government 1994: 1, 5.

Over the years, there has been recurrent debate on whether euthanasia and physician-assisted suicide should be legalised.[82] Numerous private member's bills have failed to gain parliamentary support.[83] The most recent of these was the Assisted Dying for the Terminally Ill Bill, which was recently defeated in the House of Lords.[84]

One important consequence of the ultimately unsuccessful Assisted Dying for the Terminally Ill Bill was the enquiry by the Select Committee set up to examine the provisions of the bill. This was the first such Parliamentary enquiry since the publication of the influential report by the House of Lords Select Committee on Medical Ethics in 1994. That report had recommended that voluntary euthanasia should not be legalised, raising the familiar concerns of the risk of abuses and the slippery slope.[85] The report of the House of Lords Select Committee on the Assisted Dying for the Terminally Ill Bill took no clear stand either for or against legalisation. Instead, the report recommended a number of considerations which should be taken into account by the drafters of any future bill to legalise assisted dying. These include: drawing a clear distinction between assisted suicide and voluntary euthanasia; providing clear guidance on the actions which a doctor may take in providing assistance in dying; providing a definition of terminal illness which reflects the realities of clinical practice; requiring a psychiatric assessment so that those suffering from psychological or psychiatric disorder can be screened out; using 'unrelievable' or 'intractable' suffering or distress as a criterion rather than 'unbearable' suffering; ensuring real access to palliative care; providing a waiting period which ensures time for reflection without causing increased suffering; not imposing any duty on a doctor with conscientious objections to euthanasia to refer a patient to another doctor; and providing adequate protection for all health care professionals.[86]

Diminished Responsibility

If a person who performs euthanasia is suffering from diminished responsibility at the time, she will be convicted of manslaughter instead of murder. Manslaughter

---

[82] For a flavour of the legalisation debate, see Grubb 2001, Keown 2002a, and the debate between Harris and Finnis in Keown 1995.

[83] See Biggs 2001: 13; Kemp 2002; Otlowski 1997: 334–6.

[84] Assisted Dying for the Terminally Ill Bill, House of Lords, HL Bill 36, 9 November 2005 <http://www.publications.parliament.uk/pa/ld200506/ldbills/036/2006036.pdf> accessed 27 July 2006; Hansard, House of Lords, 12 May 2006, cols 1184–295. See also House of Lords Select Committee on the Assisted Dying for the Terminally Ill Bill 2005; Biggs 2005. 'The Royal Colleges of Physicians and of General Practitioners adopted a neutral stance on the principles underlying the Bill' (House of Lords Select Committee on the Assisted Dying for the Terminally Ill Bill 2005: [108]). The General Medical Council has issued no guidance on assisted dying given its legal status, but in evidence to the House of Lords Select Committee it expressed concerns about the prospect of legalisation (House of Lords Select Committee on the Assisted Dying for the Terminally Ill Bill 2005a: 112). Although the British Medical Association in 2005 briefly adopted a neutral stance, in 2006 it reaffirmed its opposition to 'all forms of assisted dying' (British Medical Association 2006: 3–4).

[85] House of Lords Select Committee on Medical Ethics 1993–94. The committee's enquiry and report are discussed extensively in Otlowski 1997: 336–9.

[86] House of Lords Select Committee on the Assisted Dying for the Terminally Ill Bill 2005a: [269].

does not carry a mandatory life sentence; indeed, a non-custodial sentence may be imposed.[87] This defence has been frequently used successfully in cases of euthanasia involving family members,[88] but it is unlikely to be available to doctors.[89]

The Defence of Necessity: Cannibals and Conjoined Twins

Another possible defence to a charge of murder in a case of euthanasia has received significant academic and judicial attention: the defence of necessity which was used to that end in the development of Dutch euthanasia law.[90] The defence has developed at common law with no statutory intervention. The Law Commission has been reluctant to intervene.[91]

In *Dudley and Stephens* (1884), two sailors who had been shipwrecked were convicted of the murder of a cabin boy whom they had killed and eaten. It was held that necessity was unavailable as a defence to murder.[92] Over a century later,[93] the House of Lords held in *Howe* that neither duress nor necessity are available as defences to a murder charge.[94] The House of Lords refused to accept the choice apparently made by the defendants to prefer their own lives over those of their victims, whom they had killed in response to threats by another that if they did not do so, they would themselves be killed.

> The primary reason for the . . . decision [in Howe] was that the law should not recognize that any individual has the liberty to choose that one innocent citizen should die rather than another.[95]

However, Lord Hailsham observed in *Howe* that 'mercy killing' is an 'almost venial, if objectively immoral' kind of murder,[96] and it seems from this that the

---

[87] Homicide Act 1957, s 2. The defendant must have suffered from an 'abnormality of mind' which has 'substantially impaired his mental responsibility'. See Dell 1984: 35–6.

[88] See House of Lords Select Committee on Medical Ethics 1993–94: [128]. The Law Commission has recently recommended that the defence of diminished responsibility be reformed so as to include the scenario where 'a depressed man who has been caring for many years for a terminally ill spouse, kills her, at her request.' Law Commission 2006: [5.121(2)(c)].

[89] Grubb 2001: 89–90. The Law Commission's recent proposed reformulation of the defence (see n 88) would not appear to be available to doctors, as the defendant would be required to prove that his capacity to form a rational judgment was substantially impaired by an abnormality of mental functioning. Law Commission 2006: [5.112].

[90] See ch 4.2.3.2.

[91] Law Commission 1977: 25–32, rejecting the recommendations contained in Law Commission 1974: 20–42. For criticism, see Williams 1978; Huxley 1978. See also, Law Commission 2005: [1.1(3)], [1.3(1)], [8.3] (exempting issues surrounding necessity and euthanasia from the most recent proposals on homicide), confirmed in Law Commission 2006: [7.26]–[7.33].

[92] (1884) 14 QBD 273. See Simpson 1984.

[93] In the interim, necessity had been allowed as a defence to the crime of procuring a miscarriage in *Bourne* [1939] 1 KB 687, [1938] 3 All ER 615 (KB) (the two reports are different in substantial respects). See Lewis 2007a: 85–6; Williams 1958: 152: 'The only legal principle on which the exception could be based . . . [and] the only principle indicating the extent of legality is the defence of necessity.'

[94] *Howe* [1987] AC 417 (HL). See also, *Pommell* [1995] Cr App R 607 (CA); *Rodger* [1998] 1 Cr App R 143 (CA).

[95] Ashworth 2003: 229.

[96] *Howe* [1987] AC 417, 433.

House of Lords did not distinguish the different choices involved in cannibalism, duress and euthanasia. The choice in cannibalism and duress cases is between the life of the defendant and the life of the victim, while in euthanasia cases the choice is between the duty to preserve life and the duty to relieve suffering.[97] Nevertheless, it is clear from the court's absolute refusal to allow duress and necessity in murder cases that despite the different choices involved, no difference in the availability of necessity exists.

Despite the precedent of *Dudley and Stephens*, in *Re A (Children) (Conjoined Twins: Surgical Separation)*, the Court of Appeal allowed the use of the defence of necessity in a case involving a choice between the lives of two conjoined twins. The case can be distinguished from *Dudley and Stephens* as the choice would not be one made by the person responsible for the killing but rather determined by the poor prognosis of one of the twins,[98] nor would it be one between the life of the actor and that of the victim. Without the operation to separate them, both infant twins would die within a few months. If the operation were performed, the weaker twin would die immediately, but it was hoped that the stronger twin would survive to lead a 'relatively normal life'.[99] In allowing the operation, Brooke LJ adopted Sir James Stephen's formulation of the doctrine of necessity:

> there are three necessary requirements for the application of the doctrine of necessity: (i) the act is needed to avoid inevitable and irreparable evil; (ii) no more should be done than is reasonably necessary for the purpose to be achieved; (iii) the evil inflicted must not be disproportionate to the evil avoided.[100]

The Court of Appeal sought to limit its holding, and Lord Justice Ward specifically excluded the possibility that the defence of necessity could be used to justify or excuse euthanasia.[101] Lord Justice Brooke described the availability of the defence of necessity as 'unique' to the circumstances of the present case. He also observed that '[s]uccessive governments, and Parliaments, have set their face against euthanasia'.[102] Nevertheless, if the 'inevitable and irreparable evil' is the unbear-

---

[97] The suffering would have to be severe as necessity is only available where there is a danger of death or serious injury. *Conway* [1989] 3 All ER 1025 (CA).

[98] [2001] Fam 147, 239 (Brooke LJ) (describing the weaker twin as 'self-designated for a very early death'). See also, Smith 2001: 404. For further discussion of this case, see Wicks 2003: 115; Rogers 2001; Michalowski 2002; Huxtable 2001. One could argue that the victim in *Dudley and Stephens* was also 'self-designated for death' as he had drunk salt-water and was, according to the defendants, extremely unwell at the time that they decided to kill him. *Dudley and Stephens* (1884) 14 QBD 273, 274. See Chan & Simester 2005: 130. Chan and Simester also identify another distinction between *Dudley and Stephens* and *Re A*: 'In *Dudley and Stephens*, the cabin boy's death was directly intended: the defendants aimed to kill him, in order then to eat him. In *Re A*, [the weaker twin's] death was no part of the doctors' aim or purpose, although it was an inevitable consequence of what they sought to achieve.' This distinction was not one relied upon by the court in *Re A*. As death is directly intended in cases of euthanasia, such a limitation on the defence of necessity would prevent the application of the defence to euthanasia cases.

[99] *Re A* [2001] Fam 147, 197. See Laville, 'Surviving Siamese Twin Gracie Goes Home to Gozo' *Daily Telegraph* (16 June 2001).

[100] *Re A* [2001] Fam 147, 240, derived from Stephen 1887: 24.

[101] *Re A* [2001] Fam 147, 204–5.

[102] *Re A* [2001] Fam 147, 239, 211.

able suffering of the patient which cannot be assuaged by other means than euthanasia, then Stephen's formulation could in theory allow for euthanasia provided it is seen as proportionate to the avoidance of unbearable suffering.

Some commentators on the decision in *Re A* have been concerned about such an implication.[103] Their fears are unconvincing as they fail to acknowledge the reality of the choice facing the judges in *Re A*: either both twins would die in a few months, or the stronger twin might be saved if the weaker twin were sacrificed by the operation to separate them. In other words, the choice was between saving one twin and saving neither. This is not the choice faced by the doctor in a euthanasia case. That choice is between the duty to preserve life and the duty to relieve suffering.

In practice, while rejecting the defence of necessity to a charge of murder, judges have tended to use covert tools to reach much the same result, holding or suggesting that a doctor performing euthanasia did not *intend* the death of her patient, or did not *cause* the death.[104] Such escape routes are only available when the medication used can be used to relieve pain as well as to cause death. When a euthanaticum, such as potassium chloride, is used these covert tools are usually unavailable[105] and convictions have ensued.[106]

Another covert tool which may play a role in this context is jury nullification, that is, 'the jury's power to acquit on compassionate grounds, even if instructed that the accused has no defence in law'.[107] Perhaps because of the risk of jury nullification, prosecutors have been willing to accept guilty pleas to lesser offences, thus avoiding the prospect of a jury trial.[108] Selective charging decisions may also make convictions unlikely.[109] In some cases prosecutors may decide not to go forward with a prosecution,[110] or the prosecution may be willing to accept 'a

---

[103] See eg Wicks 2003: 22; Huxtable 2002: 468; McEwan 2001: 248. See further on the scope of the Court of Appeal's decision Lewis 2007a: 87–8.

[104] See para 5.2.1 and Otlowski 1997: 170–84.

[105] Although Robert Walker LJ did make some attempt to bend the concept of intention in *Re A*, a case when the outcome was certain death for the weaker twin. *Re A* [2001] Fam 147, 251, 259.

[106] See eg *Cox* (1992) 12 BMLR 38. This is not invariably the case. Eg, in 1990, the prosecution discontinued its case against Dr Lodwig, an English doctor who had reportedly injected his patient, who was suffering from terminal cancer, with potassium chloride. See Brahams 1990: 586–7 (both causation and intention were apparently doubted).

[107] Sneiderman, Irvine & Osborne 2003: 637. See eg *Arthur* (1981) 12 BMLR 1 (defendant who had administered dihydrocodeine to infant with Down's Syndrome following decision not to feed the child acquitted of attempted murder); *Carr, Sunday Times*, 30 November 1986 (defendant who had administered massive dose of phenobarbitone to cancer patient acquitted of murder).

[108] See House of Lords Select Committee on Medical Ethics 1993–94: [128] (in 22 'mercy-killing' cases between 1982 and 1991, only one defendant was convicted of murder, charges were downgraded to lesser offences in the other cases, resulting in probation or suspended sentences; all of the defendants were family members or acquaintances).

[109] See House of Lords Select Committee on Medical Ethics 1993–94: [128]. Eg, charging the defendant with an offence which will be difficult for the prosecution to prove beyond a reasonable doubt (eg murder) rather than one which would be easier to prove (eg attempted murder).

[110] Interestingly, the presence of prosecutorial and judicial 'flexibility' in assisted suicide and euthanasia cases was considered favourably by the European Court of Human Rights in support of the proportionality of a blanket ban on assisted suicide under Art 8(2) of the European Convention. *Pretty v UK* (2002) 35 EHRR 1, [76] (ECHR).

sympathetic report from a pliant psychiatrist' which 'dress[es] up [a] rational 'mercy' killing . . . as . . . diminished responsibility'.[111]

Assistance with Suicide

Assistance with suicide, whether or not by a doctor, is specifically prohibited by section 2 (1) of the Suicide Act 1961: 'a person who aids, abets, counsels or procures the suicide of another, or an attempt by another to commit suicide, shall be liable on conviction on indictment to imprisonment for a term not exceeding fourteen years'. Under section 2 (4) of the Suicide Act, any prosecution requires the consent of the Director of Public Prosecutions. Very few prosecutions have been brought under this section.[112] However, in *Attorney-General v Able*, the Attorney-General sought a declaration that making available a booklet entitled *A Guide to Self-Deliverance*, which contained guidance on suicide techniques, to members of the Voluntary Euthanasia Society constituted an offence under the Suicide Act. Woolf J held that an offence would only be committed if (a) the defendant intended that the booklet would be used by someone contemplating suicide who would be assisted by its contents; and (b) he distributed the booklet to such a person who used it; and (c) that person was assisted or encouraged by reading the booklet to attempt suicide, whether or not that attempt was successful.[113]

In relation to prosecutorial policy, the House of Lords Select Committee on the Assisted Dying for the Terminally Ill Bill recently observed that there are no published guidelines as to the criteria applied by the Crown Prosecution Service in determining 'whether the evidence presented supports the charge and, if so, whether a prosecution would be in the public interest'[114] because the Director of Public Prosecutions believes it inappropriate to issue a policy the effect of which would be 'to suspend or not to apply part of the law which Parliament has put in place and has not removed'.[115]

It appears that a person who assists another to obtain assistance with suicide in another jurisdiction, such as Switzerland, where it is lawful, will not be prosecuted even if such assistance would amount to assistance in suicide under s.2 of the Suicide Act 1961. In a recent case, the High Court discharged an injunction preventing the husband of a competent woman suffering from cerebellar ataxia from making arrangements to take her to Switzerland where she wished to receive assistance in suicide.[116] The judge pointed out that

---

[111] Law Commission 2006: [7.48].

[112] For some rare examples of such cases see *Attorney-General v Able* [1984] QB 795; *R v UK* (1983) 33 DR 270 (E ComHR) (affirming a conviction of conspiring to aid and abet suicide where the defendant had facilitated contact between individuals desiring assistance in suicide and an individual willing to provide such assistance); *Chard, The Times*, 23 Sept. 1993 (Central Crim Ct) (defendant acquitted on judge's direction of assisting suicide of terminally ill friend whom he had provided with paracetamol).

[113] *Attorney-General v Able* [1984] QB 795, 812.

[114] House of Lords Select Committee on the Assisted Dying for the Terminally Ill Bill 2005a: [16].

[115] House of Lords Select Committee on the Assisted Dying for the Terminally Ill Bill 2005a: [16], quoting the Attorney-General's evidence at Q 2094.

[116] *In re Z (Local Authority: Duty)* [2005] 1 WLR 959 (HC).

[a]lthough not unique, the provision [requiring the consent of the Attorney-General] is rare and is usually found where Parliament recognises that although an act may be criminal, it is not always in the public interest to prosecute in respect of it.[117]

There is no systematic collection of data on such 'suicide tourism'. A newspaper report in May 2007 put the number of British persons who had travelled to Switzerland for assistance in suicide since January 2003 at 76. A two-fold increase in the annual number of such cases was also reported between 2005 and 2006.[118] No one has been prosecuted in any of these cases.

In *Pretty*, the courts were confronted with the question whether the criminal prohibition on assisted suicide complies with the European Convention on Human Rights. Dianne Pretty was suffering from terminal amyotrophic lateral sclerosis or motor neurone disease when she requested an assurance in advance from the Director of Public Prosecutions that her husband would not be prosecuted if he assisted her suicide. Mrs. Pretty relied on her rights to life, freedom from torture and inhuman or degrading treatment, respect for her private and family life, freedom of thought, conscience and religion and freedom from discrimination under the European Convention.[119] She appealed the Director's refusal to provide such assurance through the English courts and then to the European Court of Human Rights but was unsuccessful at every level.[120]

11.7 Termination of Life Without an Explicit Request and 'Help in Dying'

Termination of life without an explicit request by the patient concerned is considered to be murder, which as we have seen carries a mandatory life sentence.

The English courts have not distinguished the practice of intentional intervention to shorten the final process of dying when a patient's vital functions are failing—'help in dying'—from euthanasia or termination of life without request.

---

[117] *In re Z (Local Authority: Duty)* [2005] 1 WLR 959 [14].
[118] Laurance 2007.
[119] European Convention on Human Rights, arts 2, 3, 8, 9, 14.
[120] *The Queen on the Application of Dianne Pretty v Director of Public Prosecutions* [2001] EWHC Admin 788 (QB); *The Queen on the Application of Mrs Dianne Pretty v Director of Public Prosecutions* [2002] 1 AC 800 (HL); *Pretty v UK* (2002) 35 EHRR 1. The constitutionality of the English prohibition on assisting a suicide had been previously considered by the European Commission on Human Rights in *R v UK* (1983) 6 EHRR 140 (see above n 112). The European Commission upheld the prohibition as necessary in a democratic society to prevent abuses and protect health (*R v UK* (1983) 6 EHRR 140, 144).

11.8 The Reporting Procedure in Cases of 'Non-Natural' Death

All deaths must be notified to the local office of the registrar of births and deaths. The person who has this duty to notify the registrar is the 'qualified informant'. If the deceased died in a house, the 'qualified informant' is a relative present at the death or during the deceased's last illness, any other relative living in the district where the death occurred, anyone present at the death, the occupier or inmate of the house if she knew about the death or the person responsible for disposing of the body.[121] If the deceased did not die in a house, the 'qualified informant' is any relative with knowledge of any of the particulars required for registration, any person present at the death, any person finding or taking charge of the body and any person responsible for disposing of the body.[122]

The registrar has a duty to report certain deaths to the coroner, an independent judicial officer charged with inquiring into 'non-natural' death and required in many cases to hold an inquest or public hearing to establish the circumstances of the death. Those deaths which must be reported to the coroner include any death: 'the cause of which appears to be unknown', or 'which appears to the registrar to have occurred during an operation or before recovery from the effect of an anaesthetic.'[123] The registrar must also report to the coroner any death 'which the registrar has reason to believe to have been unnatural . . . or to have been attended by suspicious circumstances'.[124]

If a doctor attended the deceased during her last illness, the doctor must sign a medical certificate of cause of death and forward this to the registrar.[125] If the death occurred in a house, the deceased's general practitioner will usually attend. If she is in a position to certify the cause of death, she will do so. If no doctor is able to certify the cause of death, the general practitioner will report the death to the coroner. 'Although there is no statutory obligation on a medical practitioner to report any death to the coroner, it is normal practice for him to do so in cases of doubt or suspicion.'[126] In theory, this would include any deaths resulting from euthanasia, assisted suicide or termination of life without request as all of these are prohibited by the criminal law. There is no evidence that any of these practices are in fact reported by the attending doctor or general practitioner to the coroner (instead, they are presumably reported to the registrar as 'natural' deaths).

---

[121] Births and Deaths Registration Act 1953, s 16.
[122] Births and Deaths Registration Act 1953, s 17.
[123] Registration of Births and Deaths Regulations 1987, SI 1987/2088, reg 41 (2) (c), (e).
[124] Registration of Births and Deaths Regulations 1987, SI 1987/2088, reg 41 (2) (d).
[125] Under ss 36 and 37 of the Births and Deaths Registration Act 1953 it is a minor criminal offence punishable by a fine for a doctor in such a case to fail to give information or to give false information concerning the cause of death.
[126] Matthews 2006: [951].

The coroner must hold an inquest if 'there is reasonable cause to suspect that the deceased—(a) has died a violent or an unnatural death; [or] (b) has died a sudden death of which the cause is unknown'.[127] The inquest must be adjourned if an individual is charged with the murder or manslaughter of the deceased or with assisting her suicide.[128] The coroner has no criminal jurisdiction and any criminal investigation into the death will be undertaken by the police.

Approximately 45% of all registered deaths were reported to coroners in 2005, the most recent year for which data is available. Inquests were held in just under 13% of all deaths reported to coroners.[129] No data is collected on the percentage of reported deaths which involved medical behaviour which potentially shortened life. Nor is data collected on the number of prosecutions (or decisions not to prosecute) for murder, manslaughter or assisted suicide which involve medical behaviour which potentially shortened life.[130]

11.9 Empirical data concerning MBPSL in the United Kingdom

11.9.1 Prevalence

There is very little reliable information concerning the prevalence of the various sorts of medical behaviour that potentially shortens life in the United Kingdom. In 1994, Ward and Tate conducted an anonymous postal survey of 312 National Health Service doctors in one area of England. The return rate was 73.6%. Of the doctors who had returned a completed questionnaire, 12% reported that they had taken active steps to bring about the death of a patient who had requested this.[131]

---

[127] Coroners' Act 1988, s 8. If an autopsy subsequently establishes a completely natural cause of death, the coroner has the power to dispense with an inquest. Coroners' Act 1988, s 19(3).

[128] Coroners' Act 1988, s 16(1). If the Director of Public Prosecutions notifies the coroner that adjournment is unnecessary then the inquest may proceed or resume. Coroners' Act 1988, s 16(2). The coroner may resume the inquest after the criminal proceedings are over: Coroners' Act 1988, s 16(3).

[129] Department for Constitutional Affairs 2006: 1, Figure 3b.

[130] For examples of such prosecutions, see eg *Adams (Bodkin)* [1957] Crim LR 365 (Central Crim Ct); *Arthur* (1981) 12 BMLR 1; *Carr*, Sunday Times, 30 November 1986; *Cox* (1992) 12 BMLR 38 (Winchester Crown Ct); House of Lords Select Committee on Medical Ethics 1993–94: [128]; *Moor*, discussed in Arlidge 2000 and Smith 2000.

[131] Ward & Tate 1994. See also, McLean & Britton 1996: App III, Table 17, 31–2, discussed in Keown 2002a: 61 and Freeman 2002: 249, fn 31 (4% of responding Scottish health professionals had assisted suicide). In relation to these and similar studies, the House of Lords Select Committee on the Assisted Dying for the Terminally Ill Bill (2005a: [239]) doubted some of the UK survey evidence:

> Bearing in mind . . . the trend towards death taking place in hospital rather than at home, the increasing prevalence of team-working in clinical care, the greater tendency for people to litigate where they suspect malpractice, and the potential for confusion with the legal administration of drugs to prevent restlessness and anxiety in the last hours of life, we would be surprised if covert euthanasia were being practised on anything like the scale which some of these surveys suggest.

Seale recently published the results of a survey in the United Kingdom using the research instrument designed for the Dutch national studies.[132] Where Dutch and other recent European research (the EURELD studies) use a random sample of death certificates to identify the doctors from whom information is obtained, this procedure proved impossible for legal reasons in the UK. A random sample of 1,000 general practitioners and 1,000 hospital specialists were therefore asked to report on the most recent death within the last year for which they acted as the treating or attending doctor. The response rate was 53%.[133] Because doctors asked to comment on the last death in which they were involved often ignore sudden, unexpected deaths in which they played no active role beyond confirming the death, Seale calculates the relative frequencies of various MBPSL as percentages of non-sudden deaths, which means that (unless adjusted, as is done below) they are not directly comparable with the rates for the other countries covered in this book, in particular those included in the pan-European EURELD study presented in chapter 17 (Table 17.2).

Seale reports a rate of alleviation of symptoms with possible life-shortening effect of 32.8% of all deaths. This is higher than any of the rates in the pan-European EURELD survey. Non-treatment decisions occurred in 30.3% of all deaths. This rate, too, is higher than those in any of the countries in the EURELD study.[134]

The rate of euthanasia was 0.16% of all deaths.[135] The UK thus falls in the lower half of the European range. The UK rate for physician-assisted suicide was zero.

Seale reports a rate of termination of life without an explicit request from the patient of 0.33% of all deaths.[136] By European standards, this is in the lower half of the spectrum. There is no UK empirical evidence on the incidence of terminal sedation or help in dying.

11.9.2 Public and Medical Opinion

In 2005, the House of Lords Select Committee on the Assisted Dying for the Terminally Ill Bill commissioned Market Research Services (MRS) to review 'opinion surveys over the course of the last 10–20 years, the state of public opin-

---

[132] Seale 2006a, 2006b.

[133] Seale 2006a: 5. The response rates in the comparative European (EURELD) study (see ch 17, Table 17.2) ranged between 44% in Italy to 75% in the Netherlands.

[134] The wording of the relevant question was subtly different from the wording used in other European surveys and this may have inflated the reporting of this sort of MBPSL. The English questionnaire was based on the translation which had been used in Australia and New Zealand (see Kuhse *et al* 1997 and Mitchell & Owens 2003). In relation to withdrawing or withholding treatment, the relevant phrase used in these surveys was: 'with the explicit intention of not prolonging life or hastening the end of life', while the Dutch, Belgian and EURELD surveys (Van der Heide *et al* 2003: 346) refer to 'the explicit intention of hastening the patient's death'. Personal communication with Clive Seale, 19 March 2006.

[135] The 95% confidence interval for this finding was 0–0.36%. Seale 2006a: Table 2.

[136] The 95% confidence interval for this finding is 0–0.76%. *Ibid.*

ion and any movements in it over that period.'[137] The MRS review concluded that as regards basic public attitudes to assisted suicide and euthanasia,

> it is evident that there is a great deal of sympathy, at least for the concept of euthanasia, and it seems likely that the level of sympathy has grown in recent years.

The review cited survey results of between 72% and 82% in favour of the legalisation of euthanasia.[138] The validity of these surveys was questioned by MRS, which concluded that deficiencies in the surveys meant that 'these polls . . . do not form a very useful guide to public opinion as support for legislative change.'[139]

MRS does, however, recognise that one source of data, the British Social Attitudes Survey, is an

> important source of understanding of public attitudes with regard to a range of social, political and moral issues . . . BSA data is expertly analysed and findings are presented within a broad context of the general understanding of trends in public attitudes which is generated by the survey as a whole.[140]

The most recent BSA data on attitudes to assisted dying dates from 2005 and was therefore not considered by MRS. In 2005, 80% of respondents said that, if a person with an incurable, terminal and painful illness asks for it, a doctor should 'definitely' or 'probably' be allowed by law to end their life.[141] This figure dropped to 74% for a person with an incurable, terminal illness, who says their suffering is unbearable.[142] Public opinion appears to be relatively stable in relation to these issues.[143] Rates from reported surveys of health care professionals are significantly lower, ranging from 22% to 66% in favour of legalisation.[144] MRS concluded that:

> It seems likely that medical professionals view the issue of the legalisation of euthanasia as less straightforward than the lay public as a whole because of their direct experience of working with patients, and there is some evidence to suggest that the closer the experience of end-of-life patients, the less sure the professionals are about the prospect of a change in the law in favour of euthanasia.[145]

However, these surveys were not thought to be a sound guide to medical opinion: 'most research is superficial in coverage and only a few attempts have been made to understand the basis of the opinions of doctors and others, which from the data appear to vary in different directions over time.'[146]

---

[137] House of Lords Select Committee on the Assisted Dying for the Terminally Ill Bill 2005a: [215].
[138] *Ibid* [218].
[139] *Ibid* App 7, s 6.
[140] *Ibid* App 7, s 3.1.
[141] Clery *et al* 2007: 48.
[142] *Ibid* 39.
[143] *Ibid* 48, 50.
[144] House of Lords Select Committee on the Assisted Dying for the Terminally Ill Bill 2005a: [229].
[145] *Ibid* App 7, s 5.1.
[146] *Ibid* App 7, s 6.

11.10 Conclusion

Despite public opinion, neither the judiciary nor the legislature has been willing to legalise assisted dying in England and Wales. Although competent adults may refuse treatment, children and incompetent adults are treated according to their best interests, with the judiciary as the ultimate arbiters of what these are. It remains to be seen what effect the provisions of the Mental Capacity Act 2005 will have on this position. Will a donee of a lasting power of attorney appointed by a patient while still competent routinely be overruled by a judge who disputes the donee's assessment of the patient's best interests?

The empirical evidence suggests that the law prohibiting euthanasia and assisted suicide is generally respected. The rates of assisted dying appear to be low. Other medical behaviour which potentially shortens life is preferred: the rates of non-treatment decisions and alleviation of symptoms with possible life-shortening effect are relatively high, although it is unclear to what extent the latter data reflects mistaken beliefs by doctors about the effects of adequate pain relief.[147]

---

[147] See above, text accompanying n 11.

12

France

STÉPHANIE HENNETTE-VAUCHEZ

12.1 The Public Debate

12.1.1 Historical Background

In 1974, Jacques Monod, recipient of the Nobel Prize for Medicine, was one of the three authors of the 'Plea for a Beneficent Euthanasia' published in the American journal *The Humanist.*[1] In this article the authors propose that there ought to be some control by the individual over the conditions of her death. In November 1979, the main French daily newspaper published a column by Michel Landa, entitled 'A Right'.[2] Suffering from cancer, Landa conceived of his article as a plea for 'the right to die with dignity'. His article, and especially the many reactions it led to, marked the beginning of mobilisation towards what was to become the French *Association pour le Droit de Mourir dans la Dignité* (ADMD).[3] As in most of the countries covered in the present book, end-of-life issues have ever since been continuously present in one way or another on the public agenda in France.[4] As of March 2007, mobilisation of public opinion for change is still ongoing, as for example in the widely publicised call of over 2,000 doctors in a major magazine for the legalisation of euthanasia. This took the form of a proclamation that they themselves had performed it.[5]

To describe the ongoing debate in only one sentence, one could say that since the early 1980s, efforts have continuously been made to keep the question of active termination of life off the public agenda and to present palliative care as an adequate answer to claims for the legalisation of euthanasia—the argument being that requests for active termination of life will vanish of themselves when an appropriate level of palliative care is available to all patients. Over the past 20 years end-of-life issues have mostly been addressed in connection with palliative care. In

---

[1] *Le Figaro* (1 July 1974). The article was signed together with L Parling (Nobel Prize, Chemistry) and G Thompson (Nobel Prize, Physics).

[2] *Le Monde* (17 November 1979).

[3] See <http://www.admd.net> accessed 25 April 2007.

[4] See Castra 2003.

[5] *Le Nouvel Observateur* (16 March 2007).

France physician-assisted suicide has hardly been an issue, probably because, as we will see, suicide itself is not illegal and it follows from this, according to French legal theory, that assistance is necessarily also legal.

The 1980s were a key decade for end-of-life issues in France. In 1978 the first legislative draft proposing legalisation of euthanasia was presented (but not discussed) in Parliament.[6] In 1980, the leading right-to-die association (ADMD) was founded.[7] ADMD regularly convinces Members of Parliament to introduce drafts bills but these are never actually discussed.[8] In 1986, the first major political move was made to improve palliative care: the historic *Circulaire Laroque*[9] laid down the objective of accessible palliative care for terminally ill patients. By 1991, a statute declared palliative care part of the mission of all hospitals,[10] and in 1995 the Code of Medical Deontology[11] included new provisions proclaiming that the relief of suffering[12] is a common objective of all doctors. In 1999 another statute guaranteed access to palliative care to every person as an individual right.[13] This was confirmed in the 2002 Law on Patient's Rights.[14]

---

[6] Draft bill presented by Henri Caillavet, senator and active member (later president) of ADMD, Sénat, Documents, 1977–78, proposition de loi n° 301 relative au droit de vivre sa mort.

[7] It claims today 40,000 members.

[8] See Proposition de loi tendant à rendre licite la déclaration de volonté de mourir dans la dignité et à modifier l'article 63 du Code Pénal, présentée par MM Boeuf et Laucournet, *Journal Officiel*, Sénat, Documents, 1988–89, n 312; Proposition de loi tendant à rendre licite la déclaration de volonté de mourir dans la dignité, présentée par M Bernard Charles, *Journal Officiel*, Assemblée Nationale, Documents, 1989–90, n 999;Proposition de loi relative au droit de mourir dans la dignité, présentée par M Pierre Biarnès, *Journal Officiel*, Sénat, Documents, 1996–97, n 215; Proposition de loi relative au droit de mourir dans la dignité, présentée par M Pierre Biarnès, *Journal Officiel*, Sénat, Documents, 1998–99, n 166. For more recent bills see Proposition de loi relative au droit de mourir dans la dignité, présentée par M Mamère et Mme Billard (AN, 24 February 2004), Proposition de loi relative au droit de finir sa vie dans la liberté, présentée par M Le Déaut (AN, 10 April 2003), Proposition de loi relative à l'autonomie de la personne, le testament de vie et l'euthanasie volontaire (Sénat, 11 May 2004). The more recent of these draft bills can be found at <http://www.assemblee-nationale.fr> accessed 13 September 2007.

[9] DGS/3D, 26 August 1986, relative à l'organisation des soins et à l'accompagnement des maladies en phase terminale, *Bulletin Officiel (BO) du ministère de la solidarité, de la santé et de la protection sociale*, n 86/32bis, 1986. A *circulaire* is a recommendation from a minister to his administration.

[10] Loi n° 91–748 of 3 July 1991.

[11] Since its first version in 1941, the Code of Medical Deontology has been enacted as an Executive Decree after having been developed in collaboration with the National Medical Council (*Conseil National de l'Ordre des Médecins*). Since the 2002 Law on Patients' Rights, the Code has been incorporated in the *Code de la santé publique*, which is composed of both legislative and executive regulations: it is divided into a '*partie legislative*' and a '*partie réglementaire*'. The Code of Medical Deontology belongs to the latter, and can be found under articles R-4127–1 and following.

[12] Art 37 (art R 4127–37) of the *Code de la santé publique*:

A doctor must under all circumstances try to relieve the suffering of the patient by means that are appropriate to his condition and to give him moral support.

[13] Loi n° 99–477 of 9 June 1999, guaranteeing the right of access palliative care. Art 1 provided:

Every ill person whose condition requires this has a right to receive palliative and accompanying care.

[14] Loi n° 2002–303 of 4 March 2002, concerning the rights of patients and the quality of the health care system. See also art L. 1112–4 of the *Code de la santé publique*:

Public and private institutions for health care and medico-social institutions provide appropriate means for dealing with the suffering of their patients and for assuring the palliative care required by their condition.

In the meantime, development was slow and limited as far as active termination of life was concerned. In 1991, the National Consultative Committee on Ethics (*Comité consultatif national d'ethique*) delivered an Opinion that echoed the concurrent legislative endorsement of palliative care as a mission of hospitals.[15] The Opinion had the following to say about euthanasia:

> Legalised euthanasia, even in exceptional cases, would be open to abusive and uncontrollable interpretation: the decision on death would be taken at the request of the patient—a respectable request no doubt—but highly ambivalent. On occasion, economic, hospital, family or ideological considerations unrelated to patient distress would become involved. From its inception the doctor's calling has been one of prevention, care and pain relief. Legal provision for euthanasia would betray the ultimate purpose of this mission and cast suspicion on health care teams thus, in turn, creating anxiety for patients and their families.

The orientation is clear: palliative care is to be encouraged but euthanasia as a way of exercising control over the end of life must be rejected.

The main occasion for public debate about euthanasia was afforded by cases that made the news from time to time. Eventually these probably influenced the National Ethics Committee, which in 2000 took a major step, reversing its 1991 Opinion and adopting a new one favourable to *exceptional* euthanasia.[16] Euthanasia should remain a criminal offence, but under specific conditions (terminally ill patient, no therapeutic options, unbearable and unrelievable pain), a jury should be legally authorised not to convict a doctor. But although the change of position was a major step for the committee, it did not have clear short-term repercussions. The Ministry of Health ordered a report on end-of-life issues that addressed only palliative care and ignored active termination of life.[17]

Public opinion continued to be favourable to euthanasia. And towards the end of the 1990s important information became available concerning the frequency of

---

[15] Comité Consultatif National d'Éthique 1991: 'Concerning a Draft Resolution on the Assistance to the Dying adopted on 25 April 1991 by the Commission for the Environment, Public Health and Consumer Protection of the European Parliament'.

[16] Comité Consultatif National d'Éthique 2000. See in particular the following paragraph:

> The act of euthanasia should continue to be subject to judicial authority. However, it should also be the subject of special consideration if its author presents it as euthanasia. A kind of *plea of defence of euthanasia*, which could be specifically provided for by law, would make it possible to assess both the exceptional circumstances which could lead to a life being ended and the conditions in which the act is committed. [The case] . . . should be the subject of examination by an interdisciplinary commission whose task would be to evaluate well-foundedness of the claims made by those concerned, not so much regarding their guilt in fact and in law, but as regards their motivation, ie concern to end suffering, respect for a request made by the patient, compassion in the face of the inevitable. The judge of course remains in control of the decision [whether there are grounds for bringing the case to trial].

[17] See De Hennezel 2003.

[18] For a presentation to the wider public see *Libération* (12 March 1998) pp 1–4.

death due to withholding or withdrawing treatment.[18] Some 70% of all deaths were taking place in hospitals or similar institutional settings,[19] and studies showed that half of them were occurring as a result of medical decisions.[20]

In the context of all these developments during the 1990s, France seems to have been waiting for a favourable occasion to catalyse legal change.

12.1.2 The *Humbert* Case

At the end of 2003, the death of a youth, Vincent Humbert, after his mother and doctor injected him with sodium pentobarbital, made the headlines.[21] This was not the first major euthanasia affair in France, but it was unusual in many respects. First, it involved a doctor and it took place in a medical setting, while many earlier euthanasia cases reported in the media were 'family' affairs that did not expose the medical profession to public scrutiny.[22] This time the profession was involved and forced to take a position regarding euthanasia. The pressure was all the greater since a couple of years earlier there had been the *Malèvre* case (which was still before the courts when the *Humbert* case became widely known). In that case, a nurse was found guilty of actively terminating the life of a number of her patients.[23] Initially presented in the media as a madonna of 'mercy killing', Christine Malèvre soon appeared to be mentally disturbed and an easy liar. The criminal investigation and trial had nevertheless put the medical profession at large under a cloud of scrutiny in a way it had never experienced before. When Dr Chaussoy—Humbert's doctor—was prosecuted together with Humbert's mother, this was the second time in short succession that members of the medical profession were made to answer questions related to their end-of-life practices in the context of a criminal prosecution. The fact that the courts eventually held that there were no grounds for a trial[24] did not reduce the public impact of the case.

The second respect in which the *Humbert* case is unusual is that, from the beginning, it was linked to the debate on legalisation of euthanasia. The youth had become known to the general public before his death, after he wrote a public letter to the president of the Republic asking for euthanasia. His mother became actively involved in promoting the legalisation of euthanasia. Since her son's death, she has been using his example to promote a change in public policy.[25] And

---

[19] In the middle of the 1960s, over 60% of deaths still took place in private homes (see *Respecter la vie, accepter la mort*, Rapport n° 1708 de la mission d'information parlementaire sur l'accompagnement de la fin de vie, Assemblée Nationale, 2004, vol 1, p 35), available at <http://www.assemblee-nationale.fr/12/rap-info/i1708-t2.asp> accessed 25 April 2007.

[20] See Ferrand *et al* 2001.

[21] See *Le Monde* (26 September 2003) and many subsequent days.

[22] See for a list of more and less famous cases, Py 1997: 51*ff*.

[23] Malèvre was convicted of murder and sentenced to 12 years of imprisonment in 2003: see *Le Monde* (22 October 2003).

[24] Tribunal de Boulogne sur Mer, 27 February 2006: see *Le Monde* (1 March 2006).

[25] She is involved in the *Faut qu'on s'active!* movement, that argues for legalisation of euthanasia. See <http://www.fautquonsactive.com> accessed 25 April 2007.

it would be impossible to deny the link between the *Humbert* case and the 2005 bill on patients' rights at the end of life (see section 12.2.1(C)).

The mid-2000s can thus be seen as presenting the first opportunity for the euthanasia issue to be addressed as such and not bypassed in favour of palliative care. It is probably not coincidental that shortly after the two first euthanasia trials a third case arose. Doctor Tramois and nurse Chanel received extensive media attention after putting a cancerous patient to death (apparently without his request) and being prosecuted despite the fact that the patient's family had not pressed charges. The trial court (*cour d'assises*) finally acquitted the nurse and sentenced the doctor to a symbolic one-year suspended jail sentence.[26]

12.1.3 Medical and Public Opinion

Over the period from 1980 through the mid-2000s, there seems to be a persistent gap between the views of the general public and those of the medical profession concerning euthanasia. Public opinion has been frequently polled on end-of-life issues over the past 20 years. It seems that a 1987 poll was the earliest attempt to measure public opinion on the matter.[27] Although the questions asked are usually imprecise, the general impression they give is that public opinion is rather favourable to euthanasia.[28] The most recent publicised poll took place right after the court delivered a verdict in the *Tramois/Chanel* case, and found that 87% of the respondents wanted to be able to ask for euthanasia should the time come.[29]

On the other hand, the medical profession has always officially opposed any kind of step towards legalisation of active termination of life. The Code of Medical Deontology consistently, through its successive versions, insists that doctors may not intentionally put someone to death.[30] Learned societies such as the Société de reanimation de langue française, and professional associations such as the Société française d'accompagnement et de soins palliatifs have always rejected euthanasia.[31] Similarly, the Académie nationale de médecine recently reemphasised its

---

[26] *Le Monde* (17 March 2007).

[27] Poll conducted by SOFRES on behalf of ADMD. 84% of the respondents would want assistance in dying if they had a 'serious and incurable disease' accompanied by 'unbearable suffering'.

[28] A SOFRES poll of 1990 finds 85% of the population favourable to euthanasia (question: 'Very ill persons must have the possibility of choosing to die if they wish'); the figure is 79% in a 1999 IPSOS poll (question: 'If you suffered an incurable disease and experienced extreme suffering, would you like help in dying?'); and 88% in an IFOP 2002 poll (question: 'Doctors must be authorised to end the suffering of people who are incurably and insupportably ill if they ask for this.'). See for these polls De Hennezel 2003: 18–19.

[29] TNS/SOFRES poll, 17 March 2007 (see *Le Monde* (17 March 2007)).

[30] Art 38 (art R 4127–38 of the *Code de la santé publique*:

> A doctor must accompany the dying person until his last moments, insure the quality of a life that is coming to an end by giving care and taking appropriate measures, safeguard the ill person's dignity and comfort his entourage. He does not have the right to deliberately cause death.

[31] Recently, these positions have been reaffirmed before the French National Assembly's special committee on end-of-life issues (see *Respecter la vie, accepter la mort*, n 19 above, especially volume 2) in which statements by a number of representatives of these organisations are reproduced.

firm rejection of any kind of depenalisation of euthanasia or physician-assisted-suicide.[32] And the National Medical Council (_Conseil national de l'ordre des médecins_), which represents the medical profession and is also responsible for medical disciplinary proceedings, issued a statement the day the _Tramois/Chanel_ trial started, reaffirming the inconsistency of euthanasia with medical ethics.[33]

Nonetheless, one could argue that official bodies of the medical profession are now defending views that differ from those of doctors in the 'field'. A 2002 survey conducted by the regional centre for disease control of south-eastern France and the National Institute of Medical Research (INSERM) showed that 'many French doctors want euthanasia to be legalised'.[34] Further investigation showed that 45% of the generalists, 47% of the neurologists but only 35% of the oncologists stated that they were favourable to a Dutch-like legalisation of active termination of life.[35] Thus even when we look at the views of the grass roots of the medical profession, there still seems to be a big gap between what seems to be the strong support for legalisation among the general public, and the views of doctors and in particular of their official representatives.

Intellectuals, both individually and collectively, have expressed themselves on the subject. Quite prominent figures of the intellectual scene (such as Albert Jacquard, André Comte-Sponville and Pierre-Gilles de Gennes[36]) repeatedly call for legislation. And in 1999, a group of intellectuals published a statement entitled 'Our death belongs to us'.[37]

Most political parties keep their distance from the matter. More accurately, although they all seem to have taken a position,[38] they hardly publicise it, even during the 2007 presidential campaign. The major political leaders of both the right and the left have indicated their support for legislation, albeit in rather vague terms.

---

[32] See Communiqué 'A propos de l'euthanasie', Académie nationale de médecine, 9 December 2003, and its confirmation on 31 January 2006 (texts available at <http://www.academie-medecine.fr/actualites/avis.asp> accessed 25 April 2007).

[33] See _Le Monde_ (14 March 2007).

[34] See Peretti-Watel _et al_ 2003a. This conclusion is based on the answers of 917 respondents (out of a panel of 1,552 doctors).

[35] See Peretti-Watel _et al_ 2003b. This conclusion is based on the answers of 1,000 respondents (out of a panel of 1,852 doctors).

[36] Respectively biologist, philosopher and physicist (and winner of the Nobel Prize).

[37] _Déclaration collective de désobéissance civique._ See _France Soir_ (12 January 1999), and _Libération_ (13 January 1999). Among the signatories were Pierre Bourdieu, Pierre-Gilles de Gennes, Hubert Reeves and Françoise Giroud.

[38] The Socialist Party, for example, writes in its official programme for the 2007 elections that it will present a bill to Parliament to legalise euthanasia. See <http://www.projet.parti-socialiste.fr> accessed 25 April 2007:

> We will submit a _Vincent Humbert_ legislative draft to Parliament on medical assistance with dying with dignity. The draft's aim will be to enable doctors, under strict conditions concerning respect for the patient's will, actively to help persons in a terminal phase of an incurable disease or who are otherwise in a state of dependency that they feel is incompatible with their dignity.

12.1.4 A Concluding Reflection on the French Debate

An interesting shift can be observed in the French debate on end-of-life issues in the period 1980–2007, which we have roughly sketched above. Initially seen as an issue of patients' rights, recent developments seem to have more to do with the legal protection of doctors. The 2005 Law on Patient's Rights at the End of Life, as well as a number of other lesser developments, can be interpreted as aimed primarily at ensuring better legal protection for doctors who make difficult decisions at the end of life. It is with this in mind that in what follows I shall describe the lay of the land, both before and after the 2005 law, from a legal perspective and then present some empirical data about actual end-of-life practice.

12.2 Legal Regulation

When looking at end-of-life issues from a legal perspective, the crucial element has to do with the patient's will and not with the nature of the medical action that is undertaken—active, passive, etc—although the latter dominates in lay contributions to the debate. Positive law regarding end-of-life issues in France deals with three distinct situations: suicide (a potentially solitary will and action that does not necessarily involve anyone other than the author of the action), refusal of medical treatment (a will that must be disclosed to the doctor, but requires no positive action from him, only withdrawal or withholding of the refused treatment), and euthanasia (a will disclosed to another person who performs a lethal act).

12.2.1 Informed Consent and the Right to Refuse Treatment

Refusal of medical treatment is one of the most problematic issues in French medical law. For a long time, informed consent of the patient has been a legal condition of any kind of medical action (diagnosis, treatment, etc).[39] Court decisions over the previous century made this clear. It is considered not only a logical consequence of the often contractual nature of the therapeutic relationship between patient and doctor,[40] but also of 'higher' principles: in 1942, the French highest court (the *Cour de Cassation*) ruled that the consent of the patient must be obtained in the name of 'respect for the human person',[41] and in 2001 the same

---

[39] See L 1111–4 of the Code de la santé publique.

[40] See Cass Civ 1re, 20 May 1936, Mercier. Doctor and patient are in a contractual relationship so long as the doctor is not employed by a public health institution; in the latter case, there is no contract as such, only a legislative and regulatory framework within which the relationship takes place. The legal consequences of the distinction are not great, although they can be important especially with regard to liability. See on that subject Jagueneau 2006.

[41] Cass, Req, 28 January 1942; *Recueil Dalloz*, 1942, p 63.

court held that this requirement is linked to the constitutional principle of human dignity.[42]

12.2.1.1 Medical Paternalism

However clear the law may be in theory, French legal and medical actors have long shown reluctance to accept the logical consequence of the informed consent requirement, at least as far as the right to refuse life-prolonging medical treatment is concerned.

For a long time, medical paternalism was the paradigm of the therapeutic relationship. The various deontology codes from the first one in 1947 onwards denied or ignored the patient's right to refuse medical treatment. The 1947 code said that 'the doctor must try *to impose* the carrying out of his decision'. And the first president of the National Medical Council, Dr Louis Portes, was the author in 1949 of a book on medical ethics in which he wrote that 'every patient should be dealt with [by the doctor] as a child to tame, save or cure,', and 'informed consent is only a myth . . . exceptions aside, consent is never free nor informed'[43]—hence, he asked rhetorically on another occasion, 'what value is to be accorded to the patient's judgment about his own condition?'[44]

When in 1979 a new Code of Medical Deontology was enacted it provided that 'the patient's will must always be respected in all possible cases'. But this left much room for considering it impossible to respect a patient's will to refuse, for example, life-sustaining treatment. It is only since its 1995 version that the code is clear about the fact that a doctor must respect her patient's refusal of treatment: 'When a competent patient refuses the proposed investigations or treatments, the doctor must respect such a refusal, after informing the patient of its consequences.' Nevertheless, the then president of the National Medical Council, Bernard Glorion, continued to interpret such a provision narrowly. He authored ambiguous articles and made ambiguous statements, letting doctors believe that they might be held criminally liable if they respected a patient's decision to refuse medical treatment.[45] In fact, there have been almost no such cases.[46]

The official commentary on the Code of Medical Deontology by the National Medical Board, commenting on the provisions related to the patient's consent and on advance refusal of treatment, includes the following:[47]

---

[42] Civ 1re, 9 October 2001, Pourvoi n° 00–14564.

[43] Portes 1949.

[44] Louis Portes, Speech before the Académie des sciences morales et politiques, 30 January 1964, cited in Louste 1988.

[45] See eg Bernard Glorion, 'Le consentement et ses aspects déontologiques,' *La Gazette du Palais*, 1999, 1, doctrine, p 6:

> If by any chance the patient refuses the care that he is being offered, the doctor must know that if the patient is in a critical condition, he may be criminally liable. If he does not immediately deliver care, this will amount to non-assistance to an endangered person.

[46] See Alt-Maes 2004.

[47] Art 36 available at: <http://www.conseil-national.medecin.fr/?url=rubrique.php&menu=DEOINTEGRAL> accessed 25 April 2007.

If the patient consistently refuses [treatment], the doctor may refuse to continue taking care of the patient, on condition that continuity of care is provided for by another doctor. The doctor may override a patient's refusal to consent when a vital risk is at stake: ultimate stage of hunger strike, suicidal behaviour. . . . When faced with sectarian beliefs, the doctor will have to respect the patients' will, after informing her of the consequences. In case of vital risk, she must act in conformity with her conscience.

Generally speaking, French doctors are given to complaining about the multitude of legal obligations and constraints that weigh on them, especially in terms of their duty to inform their patients fully. After the 2002 Law on Patients' Rights guaranteed a genuine right for patients to obtain medical information prior to any form of treatment, a number of doctors protested that it was too complicated and would be contra-productive to inform patients about all risks, even exceptional ones. A survey by *Espace Éthique* conducted in 2004 showed that almost 20% of the doctors surveyed refused to consider their patients as co-decision-makers concerning medical treatment.[48] An ethnographic study of doctor–patient communication (mostly concerning the way patients are told of their cancer diagnosis and subsequent decisions about treatment) brilliantly demonstrated the structural imbalance of the relationship.[49]

12.2.1.2 Judicial Reluctance to Enforce the Requirement of Informed Consent

Not only the highest organs of the medical profession but also the courts have limited the scope of the right to refuse medical treatment so as to exclude the situation when life is at stake. Quite recent examples of this are the *Garnier* and *Senanayake* cases.[50]

The *Garnier* Case

In 1986, Dr Garnier had a female patient with breast cancer who refused surgery as well as radiotherapy. Together they decided that she would undertake a homoeopathic treatment to ease her pain. Two years later, she was admitted to a hospital. When he realised the seriousness of her condition, the hospital doctor brought the situation to the attention of the regional disciplinary board, arguing that Dr Garnier had not complied with the deontological obligation to deliver careful and appropriate care. The regional and, on appeal, the national disciplinary boards found Dr Garnier guilty and he appealed to the *Conseil d'État* (the supreme administrative court with cassation jurisdiction in cases from medical

---

[48] See the survey on doctors' attitudes toward the 2002 bill on patients' rights conducted by the AP-HP Espace Éthique (Guerrier *et al* 2003), available at: <http://www.espace-éthique.org/fr/enq_4mars.php#preliminaire> accessed 25 April 2007).

[49] See Fainzang 2006.

[50] Older examples could be cited as well. See eg Conseil d'État, 27 January 1982, *Benhamou*:

the [patient's] refusal [of surgery] prohibited the doctor, *except in case of immediate threat to the life or the health of the patient*, ignoring clearly expressed will (italics added).

disciplinary bodies). On 29 July 1994, the *Conseil d'État* ruled that Dr Garnier had indeed made a mistake that justified disciplinary sanction, for he had prescribed illusory treatments that deprived his patient of a chance of cure or survival.[51] The *Conseil d'État* ignored the patient's refusal of other treatments than the ones she chose to undergo.

The *Senanayake* Case

A Jehovah's Witness was admitted to a hospital with a serious condition. He and his wife immediately informed the doctors that he absolutely refused blood transfusions, whatever the consequences for his chance of survival. When his condition worsened, he was given blood transfusions, but he died nonetheless. His wife sued the hospital for failing to respect her husband's refusal. The Administrative Appellate Court of Paris held in June 1998 that: 'the doctor's obligation to respect the will of a patient who is in a condition to express it . . . finds its limit in another obligation, that of protecting his patient's health, that is, in the last instance, his life'.[52] Mrs Senanayake appealed to the *Conseil d'État*. Although it overruled the appellate court's decision, this was only because of the generality of the rule the court had formulated. Reassessing the case itself, the *Conseil d'État* rejected Mrs Senanayake's petition in the following words:

> [G]iven the extreme situation in which M. S. found himself, the doctors have chosen, with as their only objective to save him, to perform a necessary and proportionate act; in such circumstances, and notwithstanding their obligation to respect the patient's will founded on religious beliefs, they have not committed any fault that would give rise to liability on the part of the hospital.

As these two examples show, whether it be on disciplinary or on liability grounds, French courts take a quite restrictive view of the right to refuse medical treatment: a doctor who respects a refusal of treatment apparently risks disciplinary sanction, and the doctor who does not respect a refusal seems to be immune from liability.

The 2002 Law on Patients' Rights

One might have thought that the 2002 Law on Patients' Rights had clarified the situation. Presented and enacted as a way to establish an equilibrium between the roles of doctor and patient within the therapeutic relationship, the law emphasises the importance of the patient's will. The *Code de la Santé publique* now proclaims that:[53]

> [E]very person takes, together with the health professional and given the information and advice provided for, decisions regarding her health. The doctor must respect the person's will, after informing her of the consequences of her choices. If the person's will to refuse or interrupt any treatment puts her life at risk, the doctor must try to have her

---

[51] Conseil d'État, 29 July 1994, *Garnier*, Rec p 407.
[52] Cour administrative d'appel de Paris, 9 June 1998, *Senanayake*.
[53] Art L 1111–4, *Code de la santé publique*.

accept indispensable care. He may ask for another doctor's assistance. In all cases, the patient must reconfirm her decision after a reasonable delay. No medical act or any treatment may be undertaken without the free and informed consent of the patient; and such consent may be withdrawn at any time.

This was the clearest legislative enunciation yet of the patient's right to refuse medical treatment in French law.[54] But even this did not completely clarify the situation, as a number of indications show.

The *Feuillatey* Case

In August 2002—after the 2002 Law on Patients' Rights took effect—*the Conseil* d'État reiterated its limited understanding of the right to refuse medical treatment. In another case involving refusal of blood transfusion by a Jehovah's Witness, it ruled that,[55]

> [T]he right of an adult patient, when he is in the appropriate condition, to give consent to medical treatment certainly is a fundamental liberty; nonetheless, doctors do not gravely and wrongfully injure that liberty when, after trying everything possible to convince a patient to accept indispensable care, they perform, with the objective of saving her life, an act indispensable to her survival and proportionate to her condition.

What we see is, in fact, that although the legislature has enacted a plain and absolute right to refuse medical treatment, the courts make the right conditional by holding that it is no longer absolute when survival is at stake.

Other illustrations of the reluctance of institutional legal actors to enforce the right to refuse medical treatment can be cited. For example, French courts have long accepted that since valid consent to treatment is conditioned on the provision by the doctor of appropriate information, failure to give accurate information concerning the risks of a given medical intervention can be a ground for compensation, since the patient has not been placed in a position to refuse the treatment. Nevertheless, sometimes—in particular when a patient's life is in danger—the courts rule that although the medical information given was insufficient, no compensation is due since given her condition the patient would have accepted the treatment notwithstanding the risks.[56] In effect, despite the right to informed

---

[54] Before this formulation was approved by Parliament, two other tentative formulations of the necessity of consent and of respect for a refusal of treatment had been enacted: in a 1994 law on respect for the human body (law n 94–653 of 29 July 1994 adding art 16–3 to the Civil Code, which provides that

> consent must be obtained prior [to any inteference with physical integrity] except in the case the patient's condition requires a therapeutic intervention he is not in a state to consent to.

And a 1999 law on the right of access to palliative care (n 99–477 of 9 June 1999, published in the *Journal Officiel* of 5 February 1999, but no longer valid as such since the issue was revisited by the 2002 Law on Patients' Rights and the 2005 Law on Patients' Rights at the End of Life provided that

> the patient may refuse any kind of therapeutic intervention.

[55] Conseil d'État, ordonnance de référé, 16 August 2002, *Feuillatey*.
[56] See Cass Civ 1re, 20 June 2000; and also Conseil d'État, 15 January 2001, *Courrech*.

consent, the courts assume the authority to decide for the patient what she would have done in a given situation.

Why is this so? While the paternalistic paradigm is understandable in the case of the reluctance of doctors to accept the right of patients to refuse medical treatment, it is not clear why it has such an effect on judicial reasoning. More confusing still is that this 'reluctant' mode of legal reasoning is more widespread today than it was 20 or 50 years ago. Let us compare the words of a leading figure of French civil law, Professor Jean Carbonnier, who served as a legislative advisor on many topics, with more contemporary literature. In 1947 Carbonnier wrote:[57]

> The inviolability of the person must be seen as an immaterial liberty, not so much physical as personal . . . It is not more acceptable to assault the physical integrity [of the person] when this is benign. Why should it matter that there is no mutilation, that the incision in the flesh is superficial? Flesh itself is not protected here, but a feeling, a liberty—and these are equally assaulted regardless of the nature and importance of the intervention.

In the 2000s, leading lawyers have commented on the Jehovah's Witness cases from a completely different perspective—a generally positive evaluation of decisions described as 'casuistic', 'prudent' and altogether 'satisfying'.[58] Part of the explanation for this shift in the attitude of lawyers to the importance of consent in medicine and their present-day reluctance to accept without important qualifications the patient's right to refuse medical treatment, is to be found in the recent rebirth within the French legal community of the idea that a person does not always have the right to dispose of her own body, because principles weightier than an individual will can be at stake. Different weightier principles appeal to different authors: human dignity,[59] preservation of life,[60] and so forth. What they have in common is that all such principles are said to be limitations on the legal effects of an individual's expression of her will.

12.2.1.3 The Law of 2005 on Patients' Rights at the End of Life

After the *Humbert* case had been prominently in the news, the French Parliament, led by Member of Parliament Jean Leonetti (who also happens to be a doctor), formed a working committee on end-of-life issues. After several months, it released a voluminous report,[61] and eventually a law was passed. Although the title of the Law is 'Patients' Rights at the End of Life,' its real purpose is to give a clear (and thus protective) legislative framework for medical decision-making at the end of life. It does not drastically modify the existing law concerning end-of-life

---

[57] J Carbonnier, commentary on Trib Lille, 18 March 1947, *Recueil Dalloz*, 1947, p 507.
[58] See, for examples of such commentaries, Mathieu 2003: 97*ff*.; De Béchillon 2002: 156*ff*.; Deguergue 2002: 260*ff.*
[59] See eg Mathieu 2003: 99.
[60] See eg Binet 2002: 214.
[61] *Respecter la vie, accepter la mort* (n 19 above).

decision-making. The law was presented by its promoters as a means of addressing end-of-life issues without taking the path of legalisation of euthanasia. It was said to be a useful tool in end-of-life situations. Significantly, the law recognises, for the first time explicitly, the authority of doctors to make decisions to terminate treatment in the case of unconscious patients. Surprisingly, this latter point seems to have escaped the attention of most commentators.

The Right to Refuse Treatment

The Law of 2005 reaffirms the right of a patient to refuse medical treatment, in particular when life is at stake. It states:[62]

> [W]hen a person in an advanced or terminal phase of a grave and incurable condition, for whatever reason decides to limit or forego medical treatment, the doctor respects her will after informing her of the risks entailed by her decision. The patient's decision is recorded in her medical file.

Nothing is known yet about how judges will interpret this new provision. Earlier formulations of the right to refuse were clear enough but as we have seen were interpreted as not implying that a doctor who imposes a refused treatment on a patient is civilly liable, so it is hard to predict what the courts' attitude to the new law will be. One may hope that the legislative reconfirmation will have some effect, especially because the refusal of medical treatment is no longer formulated solely as a patient's right, but also as creating a duty for the doctor.

Advance Treatment Directives

The Law of 2005 is innovative in so far as advance treatment directives are concerned. It is the first legislation in France to recognise such directives, providing that any competent adult may give written instructions as to her wishes in terms of withholding and/or withdrawing treatment, in case she should become incompetent:[63]

> [A]n adult may write advance directives giving instructions for the case she should become incompetent. These directives indicate the person's wishes regarding limitation or withdrawing of treatment at the end of her life. They are revocable at any time.

But while such directives are to be taken into account by the doctor if he considers withdrawing or withholding treatment, they are not binding. Thus the law does not go much beyond acknowledging that when such directives exist they may be used as information concerning the will of an incompetent patient.

---

[62] L 1111–10 of the *Code de la santé publique*.
[63] L 1111–11 of the *Code de la santé publique*. For the details see Décret n° 2006–119 of 6 February 2006.

Representation

The Law of 2005 provides that the patient's 'person of confidence', a figure created by the Law of 2002,[64] is to be consulted if a withholding/withdrawing decision is envisaged. The fact that only 'consultation' is required is not only a further indication that the legal importance of the patient's will concerning treatment (be it directly or indirectly expressed) is rather weak, it is also yet another indication that the primary goal of the law is to give doctors legal protection rather than directly to enhance patients' rights.

In summary, the 2005 law establishes a number of ethical guidelines for medical behaviour at the end of life, and protects the doctor who follows them, but it does not clearly determine the respective rights of patients and obligations of doctors.

Withdrawing or Withholding Life-Prolonging Treatment: 'Futility'

The Law of 2005 recognises for the first time in French law the idea of *acharnement thérapeutique* (the equivalent of 'medically futile treatment'). The law provides that when treatment appears unreasonable given a patient's condition, it must be withheld or withdrawn:[65]

> [Medical treatment] must not be given when persistence is unreasonable. When treatment appears to be useless, disproportionate or only oriented towards artificial prolongation of life, it may be withdrawn or withheld. In such cases, the doctor respects the dying patient's dignity by delivering [palliative] care as defined under L. 1110–10.

Less commented on, although more innovative (subversive?), are the provisions under article 5 of the law:[66]

> When a person is not in a condition to express her own will, the limitation or withdrawal of treatment that might endanger her life cannot be carried out without a collegial procedure provided for in the Code of Medical Deontology[67] and without the *personne de confiance*, the family or a next of kin having been consulted. The [reasons for the] decision to limit or withdraw treatment are recorded in the patient's medical file.

It seems extraordinary that although it is understandable that nothing is said about the patient's consent, for he is supposedly unconscious or otherwise incompetent, nothing is said about *anyone's* will. Indeed, while the family, the next-of-kin and the *personne de confiance* are mentioned, it is only in so far as they ought to be *consulted*. There is no suggestion that their views—or their representation of the patient's views—are entitled to great weight, let alone that they might in certain circumstances be decisive.

---

[64] The Law of 2002 coined the concept of '*personne de confiance*' whom any person can appoint. This representative is to be consulted by the medical staff if the patient herself becomes incompetent. Since only 'consultation' is required, the law does not provide for true proxy decision-making. See L 1111–6 of the *Code de la santé publique*.

[65] L 1110–5 of the *Code de la santé publique*.

[66] L 1111–4 of the *Code de la santé publique*. See also L 1111–13.

[67] See art R 4127–37, inserted by Decree n 2006–120, 6 February 2006.

Concluding Reflection

The legislative treatment of the role of the *personne de confiance*, the family or other close relations of a dying patient is yet one more indication that despite the promise of its title—'patients' rights'—the 2005 law is primarily designed to clarify the legal environment within which doctors take decisions about the treatment of terminally ill patients. What it really does is not so much to establish some fundamental rights of patients as to legalise a number of medical decision-making practices at the end of life that might have been thought threatened by some criminal prosecutions in recent years.

In this connection it is interesting to note how strongly the medical profession was represented in the parliamentary proceedings leading up to the Law of 2005. As noted earlier, the bill was initially proposed by a doctor-member of parliament (Dr Jean Leonetti) after he had led the parliamentary working group for some months. The representation of the medical profession in the working group was very strong (9 of out 31 members). This overrepresentation also characterised the parliamentary debates on the bill.[68]

12.2.2 Pain Relief and Palliative/Terminal Sedation

In France as in other countries there was in the past considerable resistance to giving adequate pain relief at the end of life, for fear it might cause the earlier death of the patient (and that the doctor might therefore be accused of 'euthanasia'). Such concerns now seem archaic. During the 1990s pain relief was the subject of intense public discussion. Following on a number of official reports to the government,[69] policy decisions to improve the situation were taken and since 1999 and the programme of the then Minister Dr Bernard Kouchner, pain management now is a priority of the Ministry of Health.[70] France is both the most important producer of medical morphine and the seventh most frequent prescriber (a proportion that grew dramatically since only ten years ago, when France was number 40).[71] A number of problems still must be solved. In particular, pain management protocols are still not generally present in French hospitals and personnel need better training. A regional study in the south of France in 2002 has shown that 17% of general practitioners still equate high doses of morphine with euthanasia, the percentage dropping to 6% when oncologists are asked the same question.[72]

---

[68] When one searches the professions of the MPs who participated in the debates concerning the 2005 law, it is striking that no less than 22 of them (of a total of 40) are doctors. One might add that another 3 participants are not themselves doctors, but as MPs have specialised in medical or biomedical issues.

[69] See eg Chaillet & Perignon 1995.

[70] See for the first pain management programme: <http://www.sante.gouv.fr/htm/actu/douleur/prog.htm> accessed 17 April 2007 and for the 2006–10 programme: <http://www.sante.gouv.fr/htm/dossiers/prog_douleur/sommaire.htm> accessed 17 April 2007.

[71] See *Respecter la vie, accepter la mort* (n 19 above), vol 1, p 113.

[72] See *Enquête sur les connaissances, attitudes et pratiques médicales face aux soins palliatifs*, by the Observatoire Régional de Santé en Provence-Alpes-Côte d'Azur, available at <http://orspaca.org/depot/pdf/03-SY1.pdf> accessed 17 April 2007.

Nevertheless, the idea that patients should not have to experience avoidable pain is now generally accepted, hospital patients are informed about this in a little booklet that is now to be distributed in hospitals,[73] and the number of individual antalgic pumps in circulation within hospital settings is high and growing.[74]

As to the legal status of pain relief with life shortening effect, it must be noted that the issue was until very recently hardly addressed in France. There seems to have been an implicit consensus around the idea that palliative care as a public policy objective encompasses the acceptance of hastening death as a side effect of the alleviation of pain. But palliative care remained mostly a policy objective with few explicit legal ramifications. However, the 2005 Law on Patient's Rights at the End of Life assumes the legality of pain relief with life-shortening effect when it explicitly provides that,

> if a physician ascertains that he can alleviate the suffering of a person in an advanced or terminal phase of a serious and incurable disease only by administering a treatment that may, as a second effect, shorten her life, he must inform the patient, the *personne de confiance,* the family or a next of kin.[75]

12.2.3 Physician-Assisted Suicide

Suicide has long been legal in France. The 1791 revolutionary Penal Code, drawing mostly on Beccarian principles, put an end to the idea that penal law should prohibit harm to self. The elimination of suicide from the Penal Code was thought logically to imply the legality of complicity in or assistance with suicide. French law has been constant on that issue and not much more can be said on the matter than that assistance to suicide is not a crime in France. The Penal Code does include a general duty to rescue. But it only applies in the case of imminent danger (*peril imminent*) and mostly for that reason has never proved specifically relevant in the case of terminally or incurably ill patients who express a wish to die. The duty to rescue is only rarely a ground for legal action in France and even less frequently in right-to-die cases.[76]

---

[73] See <http://www.sante.gouv.fr/htm/dossiers/prog_douleur/doc_pdf/contr_engag.pdf> accessed 25 April 2007). On the cover one reads: 'Contrat d'engagement: Dans cet établissement, nous nous engageons à prendre en charge votre douleur. Avoir moins mal, ne plus avoir mal, c'est possible.'

[74] There were 11,429 such pumps in circulation in 2004, versus only around 5,000 in a former inventory in 2000; See Ministère de la Santé et des Solidarités, *Plan d'amélioration de la prise en charge de la douleur 2006–2010,* 3 March 2006, pp 25–6 (available at <http://www.sante.gouv.fr/htm/dossiers/prog_douleur/doc_pdf/plan_douleur06_2010.pdf> accessed 17 April 2007.

[75] Art L 1110–5 of the *Code de la santé publique.*

[76] In theory, the prosecution of a doctor present at the time of the suicide is possible, on the ground of the duty to rescue. Nonetheless, prosecution in such a case is unlikely (note that public prosecution in France depends on whether the prosecutor considers it opportune to do so). The legal literature often refers to a 1973 case (Cour de Cassation, chambre criminelle, 3 January 1973, available at: <http://www.legifrance.gouv.fr/WAspad/Visu?cid=86820&indice=1&table=CASS&ligneDeb=1> accessed 28 June 2007, in which a doctor who had not rescued a person who had attempted to commit suicide was not found guilty of failure to rescue, since the patient had refused medical care when the doctor arrived at the scene as well as in a signed document.

The only major legal development concerning suicide since the end of the 18th century is the creation in 1987[77] of a new crime of incitement to suicide.[78] This was intended to make it possible to prosecute publications that are thought to encourage suicidal behaviour. The 1987 law was an immediate response to the re-issue of a book that had been found among the possessions of persons who committed suicide. The book, *Suicide, mode d'emploi* [Suicide: Instructions],[79] gave 'recipes' for the successful performance of suicide and it was believed that the book was responsible for the suicides concerned.[80] The new offence has only very rarely led to prosecution and conviction—and when it has, this has mainly been in the specific context of the media[81] and not that of direct personal assistance with suicide.[82] With this exception, then, assistance with suicide is not a crime in France.

One should add that physician-assisted suicide (PAS) has not yet been a subject of debate in France.[83] If PAS involves only the prescription of legal drugs and not the presence of the doctor at the moment the drugs (or other means) are actually used, the only sanction available in French law would be disciplinary. Disciplinary action under the Code of Medical Deontology would be possible, since the Code provides that a doctor 'must not make [a] patient take an unjustified risk'.[84] Nonetheless, I do not know of any disciplinary action on such grounds.

12.2.4 Euthanasia

Euthanasia—whether by doctors, nurses or lay persons (such as family members of the person asking to be put to death)—is as such unknown in French law (consent of the victim being totally irrelevant in French criminal law) and a prosecution would therefore be brought under a generic offence such as manslaughter or murder (if premeditation can be proved), and the sentence might even be aggravated by considerations linked to the victim's vulnerability.[85] Very few doctors have ever actually been tried for committing euthanasia.[86]

---

[77] Loi nº 87–1133 of 31 December 1987.

[78] See Girault 2002: 360*ff.*

[79] Guillon & Le Bonniec 1982.

[80] Thirty pages of the book, in which the authors gave details on the doses of medicine necessary for committing suicide, how to obtain false medical prescriptions, etc, were presented to Parliament as a justification for legislation. See Jungman 1989.

[81] See eg Cour de Cassation, ch Crim, 13 November 2001 (available at <http://www.legifrance.gouv.fr/WAspad/Visu?cid=101943&indice=1&table=CASS&ligneDeb=1> accessed 28 June 2007, finding *Le Monde* guilty for having in its daily edition of 14 December 1996 included a free supplement in which there was an advertisement for Derek Humphrey's *Final Exit*—presented as a 'suicide guide'—and including the necessary information for obtaining the book (which is forbidden in France). See Isabelle Lucas-Gallay, commentary on TGI Paris, 11 April 1995, *La semaine juridique*, 1996, II, 22729.

[82] See Jacquinot 1995: 954.

[83] See, for the exception that proves the rule, the article of an American law professor describing the Oregon PAS legislation (Charles Baron, *Le Monde* (14 October 2003)).

[84] Art 40 of the *Code de la santé publique*. See also art 38, n 30 above.

[85] See Pin 2002.

[86] This is why, as we noted, the *Humbert* case was extraordinary: it was the first highly publicised case that clearly posed the question of *medical* action at the end of life.

Nevertheless, both journalistic and official sources—including some based on statements by doctors—reveal that active euthanasia is in fact performed by medical staff, although it is impossible to know how often. It is sometimes supposed that the rate of euthanasia is decreasing, in particular because it is thought that the Law on Patients' Rights at the End of Life of 2005, by giving greater protection to doctors, encourages them to withhold or withdraw futile treatment instead of terminating life.

The Leonetti committee of the National Assembly explicitly acknowledged in 2004 the practice of clandestine medical euthanasia.[87] But very few such cases have given rise to prosecution and the sanctions are usually disciplinary rather than penal. One of the best known doctors to have made such information public is Dr Leon Schwartzenberg (1923–2003), who was also a French representative in the European Parliament. Dr Schwartzenberg wrote books in which he actively supported euthanasia and made a number of public declarations in which he acknowledged having practised it. One of those declarations, published in the weekly *Journal du Dimanche*, led to (unsuccesful) disciplinary action against him.[88] At the end of the 1990s, Dr Duffau injected a patient who was suffering unbearably with potassium chloride. He was denounced to the regional medical board by a colleague and found guilty of a disciplinary offence.[89]

The defence of necessity exists in French law, but as far as I am aware it has not been explicitly referred to in criminal cases concerning euthanasia. This probably has to do with the fact that necessity only applies when no other means than the one used was available and when the act was done to safeguard someone's person or property.[90] It is likely that French courts would judge that neither of these conditions has been met in a case of euthanasia, for the preference for palliative care in the French socio-legal debate on medical care at the end of life probably means that such care would be considered available and a judge is unlikely to accept the idea that killing someone is a means to safeguard her person.[91] Nevertheless, criminal courts, more often than not, find ways to acquit people in euthanasia cases, or sentence them to prison for a term corresponding to what they have already spent in pre-trial detention.[92] While, legally speaking, it is not a specific sort of criminal infraction, euthanasia does seem to be treated by the courts as much less serious than the crimes in whose name it is prosecuted. Let us give some further details concerning this practical side of the matter.

Since the French Revolution, serious crimes (*crimes*) are tried before a *cour d'assises*, which consists of nine jury members and three professional judges. The

---

[87] See *Respecter la vie, accepter la mort* (n 19 above) vol 1, pp 145ff.

[88] See Conseil d'État, 11 June 1993, *Léon Schwartzenberg*, concl. Rémy Schwartz, *Revue de droit sanitaire et social*, 1994, p 46 (the disciplinary sanction was cancelled due to procedural irregularity).

[89] The regional medical board forbade him to practice medicine for one year and the national board disciplinary committee and the Conseil d'État affirmed (see Conseil d'État, 29 December 2000, *M Duffau*).

[90] Art L 122–7 of the Code Pénal.

[91] See Lewis 2006.

[92] For examples, see Py 1997.

leniency of the *cours d'assises* in euthanasia cases has become legendary in the end-of-life literature. Although the impression is difficult to verify (since no database of criminal verdicts exists), it seems from press accounts that there have been a number of cases in which people convicted for what amounts to euthanasia have been sentenced very lightly or not at all—when they are not found 'not guilty' altogether. Such leniency is often interpreted by referring to the fact that the general public (supposedly reflected in jury composition) is quite sensitive to the case for euthanasia and mercy killing and wishes to condemn them gently if at all. This supposition is invoked by opponents of any legislative change regarding euthanasia: they argue that the lay element in criminal justice makes it possible to combine the penal rigour of the law with popular morality.[93] But it seems (although, again, it is difficult to verify this) that the cases towards which criminal juries are said to be sympathetic are mostly 'family euthanasia', that is, mercy killing by members of a dying person's family.

12.3 Empirical Data: What Does the End of Life Look Like in France?

As far as we are aware, there are no empirical data on pain relief (in particular, pain relief that is expected to shorten life), palliative care, or palliative/terminal sedation in France.

About 70% of all deaths in France occur in a hospital or other institutional setting.[94] These deaths fall into one of three categories:

- natural deaths (including cases in which death is hastened by pain relieving medication);
- deaths due to a decision to withhold or withdraw life-prolonging treatment;
- deaths due to active termination of life.

The second case is for our purposes the most important, if only because, as shown by the French LATAREA group[95] on the basis of a 1997 study involving 113 Intensive Care Units, 53% of deaths in such services are preceded by a decision to limit life-supporting therapies.[96] The LATAREA study was a crucial step in

---

[93] See eg Perelman 1968.

[94] See *Respecter la vie, accepter la mort* (n 19 above), vol 1, pp 52–3. Official statistics from the National Statistical Institute (INSEE) for 2004, available at <http://www.insee.fr/fr/ppp/ir/accueil.asp?page=SD2004/dd/sd2004_deces.htm> accessed 2 May 2007, indicate that 140,791 deaths occured at home (27% of the total number of deaths that year), versus 350,563 (67%) in hospitals, private clinics or retirement homes and 9,327 (1.7%) in public place (see document T75).

[95] *Limitation et Arrêts de Traitement en Reanimation* (Witholding and Withdrawal of Treatment in ICUs).

[96] The findings of this study were published (Ferrand *et al* 2001) but prior to that they had been presented at the national meeting of the *Société de réanimation de langue française* in 1998. See also Grosbuis *et al* 2000.

assessing French medical practices at the end of life. This is not so much due to the findings as such: similar results had already been found in the Netherlands[97] and were soon to be confirmed at a European level.[98] But it was the first such study in France and at the time no accurate information on medical practice at the end of life in France was available.[99] The LATAREA study was important not only for what it showed about the prevalence of death due to withholding or withdrawing treatment but also because of the ethical questions it raised. It showed that patients' families were involved in the decision-making process leading to the withdrawal or withholding of life-support in only 44% of all cases,[100] and the patients themselves in only 0,5%. Similarly, it established that 11% of the decisions were taken during night shifts, 'which suggests at least some degree of haste,'[101] and only 42% were recorded in the patient's medical file.[102]

The questions raised by the LATEREA study soon gained additional poignancy from research by Ferrand. He showed that doctors working in ICUs often had great doubts about the legality of their behaviour.[103] In May 2002 the francophone intensive care society (*Société de réanimation de langue française*) issued guidelines concerning withholding and withdrawing treatment in intensive care units.[104] The guidelines insist that such decisions be taken collegially—including nursing staff—in order to avoid the shortcomings of individual decision-making (quite frequent according to the LATAREA survey). The family and close relations of the patient (and the patient himself, whenever competent) must be informed. All decisions must be recorded in the patient's file.

About the frequency of active termination of life, as we have seen earlier, nothing of any reliability can be said, since there has been no French research on the subject (with the exception of the situation in neonatology, discussed in section 12.5).

One might want to add to the three possible situations listed above a fourth one: suicide. One hundred and sixty thousand people try to commit suicide in France annually, of whom 11,000 succeed—2% of all deaths, one of the highest rates in Europe.[105] It is rare, however, that suicide occurs in a medical setting; and the

---

[97] See ch 5, Table 5.1.

[98] See ch 17, Table 17.2.

[99] Its findings must thus be read while taking into consideration the fact that the sample of 113 ICUs only amounts to about 1/5 of the total of 568 French ICUs (in 2001), according to Direction de la Recherche, des Études, des Évaluations et des Statistiques (2003: 91), available at <http://www.sante.gouv.fr/drees/donnees/es2001.pdf> accessed 28 June 2007.

[100] See Ferrand *et al* 2001.

[101] See Ferrand *et al* 2001: 12.

[102] As an example of the public impact of the survey, see the daily newspaper *Libération*, whose cover page on 12 March 1998 read: 'Euthanasie passive: la fin d'un tabou?' [Passive Euthanasia: The End of a Taboo?].

[103] Ferrand established that decisions to withhold or withdraw life support in ICUs often led to not informing families (15%), keeping medical behaviour secret (17%) or even lying to other staff (5%). See Ferrand *et al* 2003.

[104] See Ferrand 2002.

[105] See *Respecter la vie, accepter la mort* (n 19 above), vol 1, p 106.

frequency of direct or indirect involvement of a doctor ('physician-assisted suicide') is unknown.

12.4 Neonatology

In France, some 20,000 babies per year are admitted to one of the 50–60 French neonatal intensive care units (NICU). Some 1,800 of them die. At least half of these deaths result from a medical decision, of which most (40%) are decisions to withhold or withdraw treatment.[106] The most important factor leading to decisions to end a baby's life is a poor prognosis for the baby, in particular as a consequence of neurological damage.[107]

No specific legal rules exist concerning end-of-life decisions in the neonatological setting. Medical publications suggest that doctors have been confronting the issue since the 1980s, but it is only during the 2000s that questions surrounding the treatment—more precisely, withholding or withdrawing treatment—of neonates have become more widely known. Illustrative of the development is the opinion issued on the matter by the National Ethics Committee on 14 September 2000.[108] The committee argued that NICU doctors should change certain aspects of their practice. Its report criticised the systematic practice of providing initial resuscitation in all cases, including the extremely premature, and maintained that parents must be involved in the decision-making process.[109] Although strongly critical of daily medical practice in French NICUs, the report did find support among a minority of neonatologists. The 2000 position statement was seen as a major event and a prelude to a reform of decision-making practices. However, this did not happen.[110] A couple of months later, on 23 November 2000, the National Federation of Neonatologist Paediatricians formulated recommendations for perinatal abstention decisions.[111] The recommendations acknowledge that there are situations in which resuscitation is inappropriate. On the issue of parental

---

[106] See Dehan *et al* 2001; Hubert *et al* 2005. The figure 1,800 is a rough calculation based on data given by Dehan (Dehan *et al* 2001: 408).

[107] See Paillet 2007: 7. There are diverging views in the profession concerning infants who have suffered neurological damage, which can only be ascertained after at least three weeks of life. Some teams choose to maintain respiratory dependency, even though this is not strictly speaking necessary, until they can assess the extent of cerebral damage; if it appears to be substantial, they can then decide to withdraw ventilation. Others prefer to let the baby become independent of the ventilator, and to accept responsibility for deciding to end its life later, if the degree of neurological damage justifies this, by the use of strong analgesics. See Paillet 2007: 69–70.

[108] Opinion n 65, 14 September 2000, 'Ethical Considerations Regarding Neonatal Resuscitation,' available at <http://www.ccne-Éthique.fr/english/start.htm> accessed 2 May 2007.

[109] On this last point, the committee was repeating an earlier position: in a statement released on 2 June 1998, the committe had already expressed the view that, for purposes of informed consent, parents should be considered the legal representatives of their children. See Paillet 2007: 273.

[110] See Paillet 2007: 273.

[111] See Dehan *et al* 2001. These recommendations were followed by a similar document, drafted by the Groupe francophone de réanimation et urgences pédiatriques. See Hubert *et al* 2005.

involvement, the document is ambiguous. It suggests that parents should be informed and give their consent to treatment. However, it also suggests that no 'legal constraints' should be imposed on 'medical ethics' and that the responsibility for deciding to let their baby die might be too heavy a responsibility for parents to bear.[112]

On 20 June 2006, the French Academy of Medicine issued a unanimous statement to the effect that resuscitation in prematures of less than 25 weeks (or a birth weight of 700 grams) is not recommended and that fully informing the parents is essential. Resuscitation in premature babies with a gestational age of less than 25 weeks should take place only if the parents insist on it.[113]

An ethnographic study of end-of-life practice in French NICUs, carried out in the late 1990s, was recently published by sociologist Anne Paillet, a pioneer in the field.[114] It describes the situation in French neonatology that lead to the reports discussed above. Paillet shows that withdrawal of life support is conceived of as a technical medical decision. Parents are as a rule entirely excluded. No meetings between parents and the health care team are held. Even information concerning the long-term outcome of their baby is kept hidden from them, for the sake of their 'psychological protection', as senior doctors put it. Parents are never informed of the fact that their child died as a result of a decision by its doctors.

Doctors maintain that end-of-life decision-making in the NICU is 'collective'.[115] However, as a matter of fact only senior doctors participate, with a power of veto of the Head of the NICU over the decisions of others. Junior doctors (specialists in training) and nurses are present at the discussions, but their role is exclusively that of providing senior doctors with information.[116] Only senior doctors are fully informed about the baby's condition and prospects for the future. This factor, together with the fact that end-of-life decisions are not made explicitly, leads to situations in which nurses and junior doctors often do not know what the treatment policy for a baby is.

Withdrawal of ventilation is as a rule accompanied by injection of a medication that stops the heart. Most doctors openly state that this happens and know that it is illegal. It is not reported in the patient's file, and it is done only by senior doctors.[117]

Paillet reports that French NICU doctors 'follow closely' the recent developments of French case law concerning medical responsibility in connection with severely handicapped newborns. However, the only cases there have actually been involve technical-clinical mistakes revealing gross incompetence. A search of the case law shows that through December 2006, no French NICU doctor had ever been prosecuted in connection with MBPSL. Nevertheless, doctors do feel exposed to legal risks. While in theory a doctor might be prosecuted for prolonging the life

---

[112] See Paillet 2007: 276.
[113] See Paillet 2007: 279.
[114] Paillet 2007.
[115] Paillet 2007: 61.
[116] Paillet 2007: 63.
[117] Paillet 2007: 69.

of a severely handicapped child, withdrawing treatment is seen as much more legally problematic than going on with 'futile' treatment. Paillet suggests that legal defensiveness is the reason doctors do not record MBPSL decisions in patient files.[118]

It was only in the 2000s that, thanks to the media, French society became increasingly informed about ethical dilemmas that arise from the availability of IC-technology in neonatology. Public debate on 'futility' in neonatology began. In a major national newspaper, two neonatologist presented opposite views on the issue.[119] One expressed reservations concerning ventilation of the extremely premature; he and his team do not resuscitate babies with a gestational age of less than 25 weeks. He maintains that parental involvement in the decision-making process is indispensible in connection with decisions on whether to resuscitate a very premature baby, and that the parents should have the last word. The other neonatologist stated that setting a limit is arbitrary and stands in the way of medical progress.

12.5 Summary and Conclusions

Anyone interested in French medical law will be struck by the contrast between strong—if recent—legislative affirmations of patients' rights and the equally strong remnants of a paternalist tradition in medicine. Maybe this contrast is an indication that important changes are currently taking place and that the older approach will soon give way and allow the new one to blossom. Nonetheless, until this has taken place, end-of-life issues reflect the tension between the two. Although public opinion as well as the logical application of legal principles should lead to a rather liberal situation where suicide—assisted or not—and refusal of life-sustaining treatments are legally respected options for patients, nevertheless there is an obvious remaining reluctance—both legal and medical—to accept such a conclusion. The result is a tendency to define and apply legal rules in a way that privileges the immunity of doctors over the rights of patients.

Given this state of affairs, it is interesting to note that although euthanasia is not prominent on the political agenda, it is an issue on which all candidates in the 2007 presidential election campaign took positions, some of which seem very advanced when compared to the actual legal situation.[120] But for at least two reasons it

---

[118] Paillet 2007: 224–5.
[119] *Libération* (7 May 2006).
[120] While the 'right-wing' candidate Sarkozy, who was ultimately elected, and also the centrist-catholic candidate, expressed their attachment to the prohibition of euthanasia, and Sarkozy now distinguishes between actively putting to death and letting die, the Socialist candidate promised a '*Vincent Humbert* law' (see above, note 38) and the Green and left-wing parties have argued in favour of legalising euthanasia. For information on these positions see <http://www.genethique.org/doss_theme/dossiers/Presidentielles%202007/acc.presidentielles.htm> accessed 14 September 2007 (the site is of a conservative and pro-life group).

would be surprising if in the near future there were to be major legislative moves on the topic. First, legalising the deliberate taking of life still seems to lack real political support. Second, the general tone of the socio-legal debate on biomedical issues over the past 10 years in France has been marked by a strong reaffirmation of (generally non-liberal) 'principles' and 'values', such as the sacredness of human life, and this does not support but rather undermines the legal recognition of claims formulated as patients' rights.[121]

---

[121] On this development in the debate, see Hennette-Vauchez 2006.

13

Italy

SOFIA MORATTI

13.1 Introduction

There was little public debate on MBPSL in Italy until the 1990s. What there was took place within the Roman Catholic Church, among professionals directly involved in the care of the dying, and among small groups of pro-euthanasia activists. In 1957 Pope Pius XII took (for the time) a progressive position on some ethical issues concerning end-of-life medical care in response to questions posed by medical professional associations.[1] But in 1980, in the papacy of John Paul II, the Church's position became more restrictive when the Sacred Congregation for the Doctrine of the Faith[2] issued the *Declaration on Euthanasia*,[3] a milestone in the process of formulation of the 'sanctity of life' doctrine. And in 1984, a Socialist Member of Parliament, Loris Fortuna,[4] presented a legislative proposal for legalisation of what he called 'passive euthanasia'.[5]

In 1990, a Decree of the Prime Minister established the National Bioethics Committee (*Comitato Nazionale di Bioetica*), an advisory body to the Government composed of experts in the medical, ethical and legal field. In 1995, Pope John Paul II reconfirmed the positions adopted in the *Declaration on Euthanasia* in his encyclical *Evangelium Vitae*.[6] Shortly afterwards, the National Bioethics Committee issued a position paper on end-of-life decisions.[7] The idea of a 'natural' life span, borrowed from the Catholic Church, played a prominent role in this paper, which specifically rejected 'euthanasia'. By the mid-1990s, the unacceptability of 'euthanasia' and the

---

[1] Pope Pius XII 1957a and 1957b.
[2] The Sacred Congregation for the Doctrine of the Faith (*Sacra Congregatio Pro Doctrina Fidei*) is part of the Roman Curia. Its task is to defend those points of Christian tradition which seem in danger from new ideas.
[3] Sacra Congregatio Pro Doctrina Fidei 1980.
[4] Fortuna (1924–85) had earlier drafted the law that introduced divorce in the Italian legal system (Law of 1 December 1970, no 898. *Gazzetta Ufficiale* 1970: 306) and the law that decriminalised abortion (Law of 22 May 1978, no 194. *Gazzetta Ufficiale* 1978:140).
[5] Legislative proposal, 19 December 1984, no 2405.
[6] Pope John Paul II 1995.
[7] Comitato Nazionale di Bioetica 1995.

notion of 'futility' (*accanimento terapeutico*) as a legitimate reason for withdrawing or withholding treatment had become generally accepted ideas in Italian medical ethics discourse. This is reflected in the 1995, 1998 and 2006 reforms of the Medical Ethics Code (*Codice di deontologia medica*).[8] In 1999 public debate got underway, stimulated by press reports of the *Englaro* case. It became particularly lively after the enactment of the Dutch euthanasia law in 2001 led to increased public interest in these matters. We summarise developments here, and return to them in more detail in later sections of the chapter.

In 2002, Giannini and his colleagues administered a questionnaire to intensivists working in all of the 20 ICUs of the city of Milan.[9] Each doctor was asked to report on his end-of-life practice. The study was rather broad and touched all MBPSL. However, the one figure that attracted public attention, causing a scandal, was the 3.6% of the sample that admitted to having administered lethal doses of medications. The media reported that 4% of Italian doctors perform euthanasia.[10] At the same time, a debate on 'Advance Directives' (written refusals of treatment) was taking place. In late 2003, the National Bioethics Committee issued a position paper, stating that there are no ethical objections to the introduction of advance directives in the Italian legal system.[11] This did not, however, lead to legislative change.

In early 2004, the case of 'Maria'—widely covered by the media—showed that, although 'informed consent' is in principle recognised in Italian law, in practice getting a doctor to abide by a refusal of treatment remains problematic. In late 2004, the 'Groningen Protocol' on termination of life in neonatology was reported in the Italian press with outrage and imprecision.[12] The National Bioethics Committee felt the need to issue a new document emphasising the unacceptability of what it called 'euthanasia'.[13]

In late 2006, the *Welby* case was reported by the press. Welby, a terminal MS patient who had been ventilator-dependent for nine years, attracted the attention of the media to his case when he wrote an open letter to the Head of State requesting the right to die by having his ventilator disconnected. The case was one of refusal of treatment, but the terminological confusion characteristic of this stage of Italian legal development was reflected in the fact that many commentators presented it as 'euthanasia' or withdrawal of treatment on grounds of 'futility'. Shortly thereafter, a new case attracted media attention. Giovanni Nuvoli, whose condition was similar to Welby's, refused artificial nutrition and hydration in order to die.

Acceptance of euthanasia among the general public, although among the lowest in Europe, increased considerably between 1981 and 1999.[14] Recent data show

---

[8] See Federazione Nazionale degli Ordini dei Medici 1995, 1998 and 2006.

[9] Giannini *et al* 2003; cf also for earlier studies of rates of requests for euthanasia and assisted suicide, and attitudes towards them, Grassi, Agostini and Magnani 1999 (GPs and hospital doctors in Ferrara) and Grassi, Magnani and Ercolani 1999 (GPs in Ferrara and Mantua).

[10] See eg *Corriere della Sera* (13 November 2002).

[11] Comitato Nazionale di Bioetica 2003.

[12] See eg *Corriere della Sera* (31 August 2004).

[13] Comitato Nazionale di Bioetica 2005a.

[14] See ch 17, Graph 17.1.

that there has been a very significant increase since 2000 in the percentage of Italians who are in favour of MBPSL. In 2006, 68% of Italians considered euthanasia acceptable, 23.5% did not, and 8.5% were uncertain.[15] The highest percentage of supporters of legal euthanasia is to be found among voters on the left of the political spectrum and among residents of central Italy. Three-quarters of the sample was in favour of introduction of binding advance directives. Again, most of the supporters were voters on the left. Doctors and nurses were also interviewed. Among them, 31.8% reported being willing to help a patient to die, but only 'in private'.

13.2 The Position of the Roman Catholic Church

Over the past decennia, the Roman Catholic Church has gradually lost much of its influence on Italian society[16] and politics.[17] However, the Church still enjoys the status of a high moral authority in Italy and has a strong influence on the end-of-life debate. Among Italian ethicists, politicians, lawyers and doctors, the 'sanctity of life' doctrine is certainly not universally subscribed to; however, no expert would write a book or article on end-of-life decisions without making reference to it.

The Church regards suicide and killing as mortal sins. It interprets the Fifth Commandment to mean that no human being is entitled to choose the moment of death for himself or for another. Such a choice is in the hands of God. Nevertheless, medical advances since the late 1950s have greatly increased the technical possibilities of prolonging life and this has made the border between shortening life and prolonging death more uncertain. It became necessary for the Church to define with more specificity which behaviour falls within the prohibition of killing.

The problem of end-of-life decision-making was brought to the attention of the Church in the late 1950s. Associations of professionals directly involved in the care of the dying presented their ethical dilemmas to the highest authority within the Catholic Church. According to Pius XII, the 'doctrine of double effect' implies that administration of pain relief in doses that might hasten death is permissible if based upon 'a clinical indication' such as 'inoperable cancer and incurable illness', 'violent pain' and 'depression and anguish'.[18] Abstention from life-prolonging treatment is justified if the soul has already 'parted from the body'. The example

---

[15] Data from Eurispes Istituto di Studi Politici Economici e Sociali 2007. Euthanasia was defined as 'ending someone's life on request, in order to spare suffering at the last moments of the patient's life'.

[16] Although the vast majority of Italians receive a Catholic baptism and are therefore members of the Roman Catholic Church, the number of observant Catholics is decreasing, especially among young people. Furthermore, the number of immigrants—among them, followers of other religions—is rising rapidly, especially in some areas of the country.

[17] In the early 1990s, the Christian Democratic Party—known as the 'political expression of the Catholic Church'—was dissolved.

[18] Pope Pius XII 1957a.

Pius XII gives is that of an unconscious patient kept alive by artificial ventilation, while the family asks for withdrawal.[19] Under the pontificate of John Paul II, these views—quite advanced for their time—would be replaced by the more conservative 'sanctity of life' principle.

In 1980, the Sacred Congregation for the Doctrine of the Faith issued the *Declaration on Euthanasia*.[20] 'Euthanasia' is defined as 'an action or an omission' which 'causes death' in order to put an end to someone's suffering. There is no reference to the will of the person whose life is at stake. Such a definition in effect encompasses almost all MBPSL. Nevertheless, if the doctor's intention is to relieve pain and not to cause death, administration of pain relief with a potential life-shortening effect is considered acceptable on the basis of the 'double effect' doctrine. Finally, the *Declaration on Euthanasia* states that it is morally acceptable to abstain from 'disproportionate' life-prolonging treatments.[21] This idea seems to be close to that of 'medical futility'. However, the circumstances in which abstention is regarded as admissible are very narrow. A very short life expectancy is the key factor. Death must be 'imminent' and 'inevitable', so that the interference of human intervention with the plans of God for the individual's life is minimal. 'Normal care' cannot be withheld,[22] and artificial nutrition and hydration falls within this category.[23] Refusal of life-prolonging treatment is admissible only in the case of 'futile' treatment. Refusing a life-prolonging treatment that is not 'futile' is regarded as equivalent to suicide and therefore unacceptable. These positions were confirmed in 1992 in the *New Catechism of the Catholic Church*[24] and again in 1995 in the encyclical *Evangelium vitae*.[25] These latter documents do add a new element: financial considerations should play no role in treatment decisions.

---

[19] Pope Pius XII 1957b.
[20] Sacra Congregatio Pro Doctrina Fidei 1980.
[21] Sacra Congregatio Pro Doctrina Fidei 1980: Section IV:

Due proportion [is determined] by studying the type of treatment to be used, its degree of complexity or risk, its cost and the possibilities of using it, and comparing these elements with the result that can be expected, taking into account the state of the sick person and his or her physical and moral resources.

[22] Sacra Congregatio Pro Doctrina Fidei 1980: Section IV:

When inevitable death is imminent in spite of the means used, it is permitted in conscience to take the decision to refuse forms of treatment that would only secure a precarious and burdensome prolongation of life, so long as the normal care due to the sick person in similar cases is not interrupted.

[23] Pope John Paul II 2004.
[24] Sacra Congregratio Pro Doctrina Fidei 1992: paras 2277–9.
[25] Pope John Paul II 1995: ch III, paras 64–7.

13.3 MBPSL: Law and Practice

It is difficult to give a picture of Italian end-of-life medical practice. There is not much empirical information available and some of the most interesting data we have do not refer to the whole country. Such data may not be representative of the national situation, because in Italy there are significant differences between different parts of the country in standards of medical care[26] and in socio-economic respects more generally. The comparative European EURELD study covers only four areas: Emilia-Romagna, the province of Trento, Tuscany and Veneto. Together, these amount to less than one-fifth of Italy's territory and population and are all in the more economically developed northern part of Italy.[27]

13.3.1 Refusal of Treatment

The right not to be subject to medical treatment in the absence of informed consent is guaranteed by article 32, second paragraph, of the Italian Constitution.[28] The Constitution came into force in 1948. However, patient autonomy only started being taken seriously in the early 1990s. In 1992, the National Bioethics Committee issued a document on the right to informed consent.[29] It was not until 1995 that the right to refuse treatment was introduced into the Medical Ethical Code.[30]

In the 1990s, the right to informed consent was supported by several decisions of the Supreme Court involving treatment without the consent of the patient that led to his early and painful death.[31] This is obviously quite a different situation from that of a patient who refuses a life-prolonging treatment, in order to hasten

---

[26] Ministero della Salute 2005.

[27] Other studies also cover only limited areas of the country, eg Giannini *et al* 2003 (city of Milan) and the ITAELD study (14 of the 110 Italian provinces).

[28] Costituzione della Repubblica Italiana. *Gazzetta Ufficiale* 1947: 298:

> No one may be obliged to undergo particular health treatment except under the provisions of the law. The law cannot under any circumstances violate the limits imposed by respect for the human person.

Legal scholars maintain that Articles 2 (protection of human rights) and 13 (inviolability of personal liberty) of the Constitution are also relevant in connection with requirement of informed consent. See Giunta 2001: 379.

[29] Comitato Nazionale di Bioetica 1992.

[30] Art 35, para 4 reads:

> In all cases, in the presence of a documented refusal of a competent patient, the doctor must refrain from all diagnostic or curative interventions, because no treatment against the will of the patient is allowed.

Federazione Nazionale degli Ordini dei Medici 2006.

[31] The best known cases are *Massimo* and *Volterrani* (described respectively in Grande *et al* 1998 and Valmassoi and Mazzon 2005).

a death that could be postponed. Two cases of this latter type took place in the last few years and were widely covered in the press.

The Case of 'Maria'

In January 2004, a 62-year-old woman was admitted to a hospital in Milan where she was found to be suffering from severe diabetes that had long been neglected. The diabetes was so advanced that her right foot was already gangrenous and needed to be amputated in order to avoid septicaemia. The doctors explained her condition to the woman and requested her informed consent for the amputation. They clearly stated that, without the operation, she would die within a few days. But the woman hated the prospect of being 'cut into pieces,' as she later explained to her nephew, and firmly refused. A psychological examination found the woman to be fully competent and clearly aware of her condition and of the consequences of her decision. The internal ethics committee of the hospital discussed the case and confirmed that a refusal of treatment from a competent patient must always be respected: all that could be done in this case was to offer her counselling. The counselling was arranged, but the woman consistently declined the proposed amputation.

At this point, her doctors sought advice from the local prosecutorial authorities. Although, as we have seen, Italian law recognises the patient's right to refuse a life-saving treatment, the doctors felt unsure of their legal position. The prosecutor attached to the Court of Milan declared that intervening in such cases does not fall within the duties of the prosecutorial authorities. Nevertheless, he did take a position on the case, stating that the will of the woman certainly had to be respected. He referred to the judgments of the Supreme Court, referred to above, which had established that a doctor is criminally liable if he treats a patient who is competent, informed and of age despite the patient's explicit and voluntary refusal of the life-saving treatment offered.

The case attracted the attention of the media, which called the woman 'Maria',[32] and generated a rather chaotic debate. The media constantly suggested that 'Maria' could be forced to undergo the proposed treatment against her will, by means of a 'health treatment order' (*trattamento sanitario obbligatorio*).[33] In fact, such an order is an extraordinary measure that can be taken by a mayor on the advice of a patient's doctor only if the patient's pathology is a danger to society, as in the case of a psychiatric patient who could become violent due to his illness.[34] Nevertheless, the idea found a few important supporters, including one of the town councillors of Milan and an advocate of a well-known consumers' association.[35] However, in an open letter, the Mayor of Milan made clear that the law

---

[32] A fictional name, invented in order to protect the woman's privacy.
[33] For example, *Corriere della Sera* (2 and 3 February 2004).
[34] Law of 13 May 1978, no 180. *Gazzetta Ufficiale* 1978: 133.
[35] *Corriere della Sera* (2 February 2004).

did not give him any power of intervention in Maria's case. The Minister of Health, the president of the College of Physicians (*Federazione Nazional degli Ordine dei Medici*)[36]—and the secretary of the Tribunal for the Rights of the Ill (*Tribunale per i diritti del malato*) all intervened in the public discussion, stating that the will of a competent patient must always be respected.[37] 'Maria' did not receive the operation and died at home in February 2004.

The *Welby* Case

Piergiorgio Welby was a muscular dystrophy patient. Despite his illness, he had been living an active life. However, in the late 1990s his condition deteriorated. In 1997 he became ventilator-dependent. He was almost completely paralysed and was fed via a gastric tube. He suffered from chronic, extremely debilitating fatigue. On 12 June 2002, an embittered Welby wrote in his diary: 'Up until a few years ago, muscular dystrophy patients died of severe respiratory insufficiency. Then, portable ventilators, tracheotomy, nasogastric feeding and last generation antibiotics came. Now, most dystrophy patients die of bedsores. Is this scientific progress?'[38] In the same year, Welby joined the 'Luca Coscioni Association for Freedom of Scientific Research' and participated in its campaigns, among them one for legal euthanasia.[39]

Public debate on the *Welby* case began in September 2006, with the publication of an open letter from Welby addressed to the Italian Head of State. In this letter, Welby described the suffering caused by his condition and demanded the 'right to die'. Since the Head of State has no legislative power,[40] Welby's letter was in effect an attempt to get end-of-life issues to the top of the political agenda. The Head of State answered publicly, expressing sympathy and urging a parliamentary debate on the issue.[41] Politicians released statements and gave interviews in major national newspapers.[42] The majority of the Italian political world took a stand against 'euthanasia' but in favour of advance directives.[43] Two minor left-wing parties released statements supporting legalisation of 'euthanasia' and legal

---

[36] See s 13.6.3 on the College of Physicians.

[37] *Corriere della Sera* (3 and 4 February 2004).

[38] Welby 2006: 12.

[39] Founded by Luca Coscioni, an ALS patient, the association also campaigns for liberalisation of the regulation of IVF, abortion, research on embryos and stem cells, improvement in the quality and availability of palliative care, and recognition of the rights of ill and disabled persons.

[40] Roughly speaking, the role of the Italian Head of State is similar to that of the monarch in a Constitutional Monarchy. It should not be confused with the role of Prime Minister.

[41] *Corriere della Sera* (22 and 23 September 2006). In December 2006, the Head of State pardoned a 78-year-old doctor, who was imprisoned for having murdered his severely handicapped son in 2003. The doctor had acted out of fear that he would die before his son, and concern for his son's future. This decision of the Head of State came in the middle of the debate on euthanasia generated by the *Welby* case. See *Corriere della Sera* (6 December 2006).

[42] See eg *Corriere della Sera* (24 September 2006).

[43] *Corriere della Sera* (24 September 2006) and *La Repubblica* (26 September 2006).

recognition of advance directives,[44] whereas a Christian party and a regional right-wing party were opposed to both.[45]

The debate intensified as Welby's condition worsened. He could no longer sleep and breathing became very painful. The media reported similar appeals from other patients. Among them was Giovanni Nuvoli, an ALS patient whose wife declared to the press: 'I am ready to take my husband to Belgium or the Netherlands, where euthanasia is legal, even if this entails running the risk of being arrested when I am back.' She added that legalisation of euthanasia would spare Italian doctors the conflict of duties they face nowadays, between legal rules on one side and professional ethics and common sense on the other.[46] The 'Luca Coscioni Association' and the Radical Party called a hunger strike in support of Welby's demand. More than 700 people joined the strike, which lasted two weeks.[47]

Both doctors taking care of Welby refused to withdraw mechanical ventilation, one *because of* and the other *despite* his ethical-professional principles. In an open letter, the latter doctor stated that the law permits withdrawal of life-prolonging treatment if refused by a competent patient but the law also requires intervention if an incompetent patient's life is in danger. 'Therefore,' the doctor stated, 'I am apparently expected to withdraw the breathing tube now, but to re-insert it as soon as the patient becomes incompetent.' A solution, the doctor stated, had to come from the 'competent authorities.'[48] A few days later, Welby's lawyers brought a case before the Civil Tribunal of Rome. They sought a judicial order requiring his doctors to stop treatment. It was only at this point that a reaction from the 'competent authorities' came. The Minister of Health requested the Health Council (*Consiglio Superiore di Sanità*)[49] to issue an advisory statement. She wanted to know whether, in Welby's case, artificial ventilation was 'futile'.

The negative response of the Health Council was made public a few days later.[50] The council gave three reasons for its negative advice. First, Welby's condition was severe but his death was not 'imminent'. Second, artificial ventilation did serve to improve his quality of life, as it supported his cardiovascular, renal and cognitive functions.[51] Third, the council maintained that artificial ventilation in Welby's case was not 'medical treatment' but 'normal care', and as such could not be withdrawn. While it did not make its reasoning on the point explicit, the council seemed to consider determinative the fact that Welby was still fed orally and taken

---

[44] The Radical Party (Partito Radicale) and Rifondazione Comunista.

[45] The Union of Christian Democrats (UDC) and the Northern League (Lega Nord). However, after Welby's death, a spokesman for the latter party released a statement in favour of withdrawal of treatment and self-determination in such a case.

[46] See *Corriere della Sera* (26 September 2006).

[47] The strike was called on 23 November. At Welby's request, it ended on 8 December.

[48] *Corriere della Sera* (29 November 2006).

[49] The Health Council is a consultative body attached to the Ministry of Health.

[50] *Corriere della Sera* (21 December 2006).

[51] The point of this second remark is not clear. Without ventilation Welby would not have been cognitively impaired or cardiopathic: he would have died. The council seems to suggest that merely being kept alive is in itself an improvement in quality of life.

care of at home. The standpoint of the council was clearly influenced by the official position of the Roman Catholic Church on 'futility'. Surprisingly, the council argued that a competent patient has the right to refuse treatment 'even against medical advice', and considered this general statement compatible with rejecting Welby's request to have ventilation withdrawn. Finally, the council proposed that the content of the notion of 'futility' should be clarified by 'a multidisciplinary body of experts in the medical, legal and ethical field'. The reference here seems to be to the National Bioethics Committee. The decision of the Minister of Health to ask the advice of the Health Council appears, on the contrary, to have been an attempt to turn the issue in the Welby case into a 'technical' one. The Minister of Health said she would visit Welby to check whether he was receiving the best of care and assistance, but she was not willing to do anything more than this.[52]

The prosecutor attached to the Tribunal of Rome stated that an injunction requiring the doctors to withdraw treatment would constitute an invasion of medical-professional autonomy.[53] A few days later, the Tribunal rejected Welby's claim, holding that the regulative gap surrounding refusal of treatment by a competent patient had to be filled by the legislator.[54] Welby could have appealed, but he decided not to wait. The Radical Party and the 'Luca Coscioni Association' were in contact with doctors who were willing to perform the much contested treatment withdrawal. In the night of 20 December, Welby's ventilator was disconnected by an anaesthesiologist who had volunteered to do so. After a long conversation with Welby, the anaesthesiologist was convinced that Welby's request was fully voluntary and well-considered. The withdrawal of ventilation was accompanied by intravenous administration of sedatives and pain-killers. None of this was done in secret. Welby himself chose the day and the hour, and a few friends who knew about his plans came by on that day to pay a last farewell. Welby died in the presence of his wife, his sister, and three members of the Radical Party, among them a minister of the centre-left government coalition then in power.

The next day, the same members of the Radical Party organised a press conference at the Chamber of Deputies. They described how Welby's death had taken place. The anaesthesiologist was also present. He made it clear that his action did not amount to euthanasia, because he had not injected any lethal drug, and that the notion of 'medical futility' was not relevant in Welby's case. All he had done was to stop an unwanted invasion of the body of the patient, at the patient's request. The case had been one of refusal of (further) life-prolonging treatment by a competent patient. The anaesthesiologist defined refusal of treatment as a 'legally recognised and widely practised right' and said it 'takes place daily in Italian ICUs.'[55] A prominent member of the Radical Party said that refusal of treatment

---

[52] The minister told the press that, personally, she was against withdrawal of ventilation in Welby's case. *Corriere della Sera* (6 December 2006).

[53] *Corriere della Sera* (12 December 2006).

[54] Tribunal of Rome, 16 December 2006, *Giurisprudenza di merito* 2007:996.

[55] *Libero* (22 December 2006).

was 'a right that is recognised on paper but denied in practice', and that the *Welby* case marked 'one step ahead in legal certainty'[56]

Political reactions to the *Welby* case were far from unanimous even among members of the same party. The most provocative reaction came from a member of a small right-wing party (the Union of Christian Democrats): 'the people who are responsible for this murder should be arrested,' he reportedly said.[57] Many others criticised this statement, among them some who disapproved of the anaesthesiologist's action, such as a cardinal known for his work in the field of medical ethics.[58] Prominent non-Catholic politicians of the prior centre-right coalition— among them, a former minister—stated that it had been right to put an end to Welby's suffering.[59] There were also significant disagreements among the centre-left parties. The Minister for European Policies had been present at Welby's death and for this reason another centre-left politician asked for her resignation.[60] A large number of politicians and journalists criticised the prominent role played by the Radical Party in the case and considered that the suffering of a severely ill man had been exploited.[61]

The day after Welby's death it became known that, notwithstanding the wishes of his family, he would not be given a religious funeral because high authorities within the Catholic Church were opposed to this.

The anaesthesiologist was required to defend himself before the Council of the College of Physicians of Cremona. On 1 February 2007, the council unanimously decided not to proceed further with the case. The dose of sedatives and pain-killers had been within the limits established by the professional protocols regulating palliation. The injection could therefore not be considered the cause of Welby's death and the action of the doctor did not amount to euthanasia. The case was one of refusal of treatment by a competent patient, a right grounded in articles 20 and 35 of the Medical Ethical Code and Articles 13 and 32 of the Constitution. However, in the Council's view it would have been preferable if the doctor had acted in the context of a long-lasting professional relationship with the patient. Finally, the council criticised the excessive media exposure given the case.[62] Shortly thereafter, the official organ of the Vatican reported that a doctor had resigned his position on the Council of the College of Physicians of Ascoli Piceno, as a protest against what had in his eyes been 'euthanasia' and 'a patent violation of the Hippocratic oath and of the Medical Ethical Code'.[63]

A toxicological examination was performed on Welby's body to ascertain the cause of death.[64] The findings showed that the injection given had not 'directly'

---

[56] *Il Foglio* (22 December 2006).
[57] *Il Foglio* (22 December 2006).
[58] Cardinal Carlo Maria Martini, Archbishop of Milan. See *Il Sole 24 Ore* (21 January 2007).
[59] *Libero* (23 December 2006).
[60] *Il Giornale* (23 December 2006).
[61] *Il Giornale* (22 December 2006) and *Libero* (22 December 2006).
[62] *Corriere della Sera* (1 February 2007).
[63] *L'Osservatore Romano* (4 March 2007).
[64] *Libero* (23 December 2006).

caused Welby's death. Welby died from suffocation in connection with the withdrawal of ventilation. In light of these findings, in early March 2007 the Prosecutor attached to the Court of Rome requested that the case be dismissed. The Prosecutor stated that refusal of treatment is a right grounded in the Constitution and in the Medical Ethical Code.[65] However, about a month later, the investigating magistrate decided to charge the anaesthesiologist with 'homicide of the consenting person' and a preliminary hearing was scheduled.[66]

This decision attracted public attention and there was vigorous protest. Legalisation of abortion had taken place in the 1970s following mass self-reporting to the police by women who said they had had an abortion. A doctor—a well-known proponent of more permissive policies on MBPSL—suggested that should the anaesthesiologist eventually be prosecuted the same should happen in the case of 'euthanasia'. The doctor addressed his colleagues in general and a few well-known personalities in particular, urging them to join him in a collective self-report.[67]

Eventually nothing came of this gesture, because on 23 July 2007, following the preliminary hearing, the magistrate announced her decision to quash the indictment. Welby had the *right* to refuse life-sustaining treatment, the magistrate stated, and the doctor had a correspondent *duty* to comply with Welby's request to cease all vital support.[68] This decision was fully in line with that of the College of Physicians of Cremona and was seen with favour in the medical world. It was commented on very favourably by the President of the College of Physicians and by a spokesman for the Italian Federation of GPs (*Federazione Italiana Medici di Base*). The president of the Italian Association of Hospital Anaesthesiologists (*Associazione Anestesisti Rianimatori Ospedalieri Italiani*) and a spokesman for the Trade Union of Italian Doctors (*Sindacato Medici Italiani*) welcomed the magistrate's decision as a source of legal certainty for the medical profession.[69]

As had been the case after Welby's death a few months earlier, politicians took sides. The Minister of Health reportedly said that the magistrate's decision constituted 'a step in the direction of legal certainty' and stated that she believed that a refusal of treatment by a competent patient must be followed. In light of the rather passive role that the minister had played in the case, her statement is puzzling. The magistrate's decision was commented on favourably by several exponents of centre-left parties and negatively by politicians on the other side of the political spectrum. However, two members of a right-wing party released statements that showed their approval of the decision.[70]

In the Catholic world, reactions were ambivalent. A spokesman for the Vatican chose not to comment on the decision. A former president of the National

---

[65] See *Il Riformista* (7 March 2007).
[66] *Corriere della Sera* (2 April 2007). On the initiative of a senator for the centre-left a fund was opened to cover the legal expenses for the anaesthesiologist (see *L'Unità* (3 April 2007)).
[67] See Viale 2007.
[68] Tribunal of Rome, 22 October 2007. *Bioteca* 2007(3):5.
[69] See <http://www.aduc.it/dyn/eutanasia/noti.php?id=188269> accessed 10 September 2007.
[70] *Ibid.*

Bioethics Committee (and head of an association of Catholic lawyers) reportedly said that the magistrate's decision was 'legally' appropriate; however, 'ethically' a doctor's duty is to preserve life. The director of the Centre for Bioethics of the Catholic University in Rome released a similar statement.[71]

In conclusion, with the *Welby* case it seems to have been established that the informed-consent rule applies to life-sustaining treatment. The case was also a major contribution to conceptual clarification. The distinctions between refusal of treatment, abstention on grounds of 'medical futility', and euthanasia entered the public debate.

The *Nuvoli* Case

On 23 July 2007, the same day in which the indictment against the anaesthesiologist involved in the *Welby* case was dismissed, Giovanni Nuvoli died. Nuvoli, a 53-year-old former soccer referee, had been ill with Lateral Amyotrophic Sclerosis for a few years. In 2003, he received a tracheotomy and had remained on artificial ventilation ever since. He was almost completely paralysed.

Nuvoli's case had many similarities with Welby's. In late 2006, following Welby's example, Nuvoli wrote an open letter to the Head of State. In February 2007, Nuvoli requested the Court of Sassari to issue an order to his doctors to withdraw all life-sustaining treatment. His request was rejected on the same grounds as Welby's had been two months earlier (such an order would constitute an invasion of medical professional autonomy).[72] In early April 2007, Nuvoli was discharged at his request from hospital (where he had been for 14 months) and returned home. He consistently and repeatedly expressed (through a voice synthesiser) his wish to 'die without suffering, to die while asleep'.[73]

In late May 2007, a doctor (a member of the Luca Coscioni Association) volunteered to grant Nuvoli's request.[74] On 7 July, the doctor notified the Prosecutor's office attached to the Court of Sassari that he intended to withdraw Nuvoli's ventilator in order to allow him to die, exactly as had happened in Welby's case. Since the *Welby* case (which clarified the legal status of refusal of treatment) was still pending, there was great uncertainty about whether Welby's anaesthesiologist would eventually be prosecuted. Three days after having received the doctor's notification the Prosecutor replied, warning the doctor that 'in theory' withdrawal of treatment 'might result in an indictment for homicide of the consenting person'. The Prosecutor deemed it necessary to send policemen to patrol Nuvoli's home, in order to prevent the planned withdrawal from taking place.[75] A commentator reported that 'authorities kept an eye upon Nuvoli, in order to avoid a

---

[71] See <http://www.aduc.it/dyn/eutanasia/noti.php?id=188269> accessed 10 September 2007.

[72] Prosecutor's Office of Sassari, 13 February 2007. *Guida al diritto* 2007, no 16:92.

[73] *Corriere della Sera* (25 April 2007).

[74] The doctor was an anaesthesiologist. However, he was not the same anaesthesiologist who had been involved in the *Welby* case.

[75] *Corriere della Sera* (24 July 2007).

new *Welby* case'.[76] In the meantime, there were several initiatives in support of Nuvoli's request, including a collection of signatures in the city of Cagliari (which, like Sassari, is in Sardinia).

The doctor turned to the President of the College of Physicians, expressing concern about what he called 'an arbitrary invasion by the prosecutorial authorities of the doctor–patient relationship'. The president's reply was fully sympathetic. He also urged the media to be more careful than it had been in the past in informing the public about cases like Nuvoli's.

Nuvoli sought a different way to end his life. After 16 July, he refused artificial feeding and hydration. There was some debate in the media as to whether he should be allowed to do so; however, eventually he did not receive forced feeding. He died a week later, a few hours after the magistrate's decision to quash the indictment against Welby's anaesthesiologist. Following Nuvoli's death, the prosecutor attached to the Court of Sassari led a police inspection at Nuvoli's place. After having ascertained that the ventilator had not been withdrawn, the prosecutor issued a certificate of no objection to burial or cremation. The coroner certified that Nuvoli had died from 'natural' causes and did not consider it necessary to perform a post mortem examination of the body.[77] Unlike Welby, Nuvoli received a religious funeral without opposition from the Catholic Church. During his funeral, the priest reportedly said that Nuvoli 'had finally been freed from the cross that he had born for seven years'.[78]

The *Nuvoli* case seems to indicate that if a patient is at home, he can effectively refuse treatment in order to die.

13.3.2 The ITAELD Study[79]

In early 2007, following the *Welby* case, the College of Physicians carried out a survey among its members. A questionnaire was administered to some 15,000 doctors, investigating medical practice and attitudes with regard to MBPSL and palliative care.[80] In mid-2007, an interim report showing the first results of the survey was presented at a conference on end-of-life decisions organised by the College of Physicians. The interim report is based on a very low response rate: only 18.2% (n= 2674) of contacted doctors responded to the questionnaire.

---

[76] *La Repubblica* (16 July 2007).

[77] Source: <http://www.aduc.it/dyn/eutanasia/noti.php?id=188279> accessed 11 September 2007.

[78] *Il Mattino* (26 July 2007).

[79] The source for all information on the ITAELD study is <http://www.fnomceo.it> (the website of the Italian College of Physicians) accessed 10 September 2007.

[80] The sample consisted of 8,950 doctors employed by the National Health Service and 5,710 GPs. All doctors were aged between 30 and 65. The sample covered 14 of the 110 provinces and was geographically stratified with 30.8% of contacted doctors working in northern Italy (provinces of Turin, Bergamo, Trento and Padua) 22.1% in central Italy (provinces of Florence, Forlì-Cesena, Ancona and Pescara), and 47.1% in southern Italy (provinces of Naples, Lecce, Catanzaro, Palermo, Ragusa and Sassari).

The most frequent type of MBPSL appears to be abstention. 19% of the sample reported having withheld or withdrawn life-prolonging treatment. The 19% figure was obtained by averaging the percentages for northern Italy (27%), central Italy (22%) and southern Italy (12%). Eighty per cent of abstention decisions involved incompetent patients. Only 64% of respondents give a positive answer to the question: 'should doctors comply with a patient's request to withhold or withdraw life-sustaining treatment?', with substantial differences between northern Italy (73%), central Italy (66%) and southern Italy (59%). The survey further shows that the informed consent rule is often not applied in medical practice. About half of the respondents reported that in the case of a patient with an 'incurable illness' they 'as a rule' inform the family but not the patient about the diagnosis, the prognosis, and life expectancy. Other results of the survey are given at appropriate places in the following sections.

The President of the College of Physicians argued that the findings of the study cannot be regarded as signs of a cultural change in Italy on MBPSL, because the sample was too small and the response rate too low.[81] However, the very fact that the College of Physicians carried out an official national survey on MBPSL under a Committee of Guarantors which included the Minister of Health is in itself a sign of cultural change. The results of the study were presented at an official conference organised by the College of Physicians. More than 150 representatives of the health care sector participated, including Members of Parliament, university professors and members of the National Bioethics Committee. It is doubtful whether all of this would have been possible a decade earlier.

13.3.3 Advance Refusals of Treatment (Advance Directives)

In 2003, the National Bioethics Committee published an advisory document stating that there are 'no obstacles within the Italian legal system' to the introduction of advance written refusals of treatment, to become operative when the author is no longer competent. In the committee's view, advance directives should not have binding force, as that would violate the professional autonomy of the doctor. However, a doctor who chooses not to comply with the written refusal made by a patient in an advance directive should give reasons for his decision in a written note to be included in the patient's file. It should also be possible for a patient to appoint a health care representative who could participate in the decision-making (the last word, however, would be reserved to the doctor). As always in the Italian debate, artificial nutrition and hydration was given special treatment. There was disagreement within the committee on whether the patient should be allowed to refuse it in an advance directive.[82]

---

[81] *La Repubblica* (6 July 2007).
[82] Comitato Nazionale di Bioetica 2003.

A large number of legislative proposals to give legal force to advance written refusals of treatment have been introduced, but so far to no effect.[83] However, since 1998 the Medical Ethical Code has provided that in a situation of danger for the life of a patient who 'is no longer able to express his will', the doctor must take into consideration the will previously expressed by the patient 'in a clear and documented manner.'[84]

In the ITAELD study discussed above, 55% of respondents (the partial figures for north, centre and south are 60%, 58% and 51% respectively) supported the following statement: 'doctors should always comply with advance directives requesting abstention from life-sustaining treatment, even if this could hasten the end of the incompetent patient's life'.

13.3.4 Health Care Proxies

For lack of a more suitable legal instrument, since 1997 in the *Englaro* case (discussed below) the incapacitation procedure (*procedimento di interdizione*) has been used as a legal basis for substitute health care decision-making.[85] The incapacitation procedure is derived from Roman law and exists in all Civil Law countries to protect individuals who are of unsound mind and therefore unable to see to their financial interests. After a judicial incapacitation decision, the signature of the incapacitated person is deprived of legal validity and the court appoints a guardian (*tutore*) who acts as a proxy financial administrator. The powers of the guardian are in principle limited to financial matters and do not include decision-making concerning the person. Furthermore, legal incapacitation can be declared only after a rather long and cumbersome judicial procedure and the guardianship magistrate (*giudice tutelare*) maintains a substantial power of supervision and veto over the choices made by the guardian. For all of these reasons, the incapacitation procedure is not a suitable legal framework for health care proxy decision-making. This emerged clearly in the *Englaro* case.

A reform of 2004 sought to overcome these problems by creating a new legal figure, the trustee (*amministratore di sostegno*).[86] However, the similarities between the trustee and the guardian are substantial. The trustee is appointed by the guardianship magistrate who has a power of supervision over the choices made by

---

[83] In 2006, five bills aimed at regulating advance directives were introduced in Parliament by members of centre-left parties (numbers 357, 542, 687, 773 and 1463), and two by members of centre-right parties (numbers 3 and 433).

[84] Today art 38 of the Code of Medical Ethics 2006.

[85] The incapacitation procedure is dealt with in Arts 414 and following of the Civil Code.

[86] Law of 9 January 2004, no 6. Gazzetta Ufficiale 2004: 14. The procedure for appointment of a trustee is initiated upon the petition of the person concerned, if still competent, or upon the request of the spouse (or partner) or a close relative, or of the guardian or curator, the health care professionals involved in the care of the person concerned, or the public prosecutor.

the trustee.[87] The guardianship magistrate can even, for 'serious reasons', appoint as a trustee a different person from the one indicated by the petitioner.

In conclusion, it is still not possible in Italy to appoint a health care representative in a manner involving little bureaucracy and minimal interference by the courts with the person chosen and his decisions. When making choices about life-prolonging treatment for an incompetent patient, doctors either consult with the family or proceed to treat (or abstain) without consulting them. A significant portion of life-shortening decisions is apparently made without consulting the family.[88]

The Medical Ethical Code provides in two places—article 32, second paragraph and article 37, third paragraph—that if a parent or guardian opposes treatment that is 'necessary' and cannot be postponed, 'the doctor must inform the prosecutorial authorities'. Temporary removal of parental custody seems therefore to be an option in these cases. This is what happens, for example, in the case of Jehovah's Witnesses who refuse blood transfusions for their children.[89]

Subject to doubts about its representativeness, the ITAELD study has shown that the majority of the medical profession is in favour of legal regulation of health care representation. Sixty-four per cent of respondents (the partial figures being 66% for northern Italy, 67% for the centre and 61% for the south) supported the following statement: 'every patient should be given the possibility to appoint a proxy entitled by law to make end of life decisions in case of incompetence'.

The *Englaro* Case

On 18 January 1992, 21-year-old Eluana Englaro was involved in a car crash. The brain damage immediately appeared to be very serious and forty-eight hours of resuscitative attempts produced a poor result. After two months of coma, the girl started to breathe spontaneously but remained unconscious. She showed no signs of contact with the external world, was paralysed, incontinent and fed through a nasogastric tube. Clinical tests revealed a lack of response to any stimulus, including pain. After two years without any sign of improvement, a very reliable prognosis could be made: because of the severe brain damage she had suffered, she would never recover consciousness. Permanent vegetative state patients have a life expectancy of several years if artificial nutrition and hydration is maintained.[90]

In 1997 Eluana's father was appointed her guardian according to the incapacitation procedure described above. Shortly thereafter, he formally requested the

---

[87] The guardianship magistrate has the power to gather information from (and give instruction to) the trustee, and has the final word on all decisions. The only way for the trustee to contest the decrees of the guardianship magistrate is by appealing to the Court of Appeals (and, in the final instance, to the Supreme Court).

[88] Van der Heide *et al* 2003.

[89] Source: interview with a paediatrician working in the city of Florence.

[90] Together with other relatively simple medical and paramedical care, consisting of daily hygiene, enemas, passive physiotherapy to avoid bedsores, and administration of vitamins and anticonvulsivants. Permanent vegetative state patients are not ventilator-dependent nor in need of intensive care treatment.

director of the hospital to stop Eluana's artificial nutrition and hydration, but the director and doctors refused to do so. Englaro then initiated legal proceedings requesting an end to nasogastric feeding and hydration on the grounds of 'substituted judgment', 'futility', 'presumed will', and (in the final stages of the trial) evidence that the girl, while still competent, had expressed the will not to be kept alive in a condition of unconsciousness.[91] Between 1999 and 2006 there have been seven rulings on the *Englaro* case, all rejecting the father's claim but using a variety of arguments. Most of the rulings end with the remark that it is not within the competence of the judiciary to decide on the permissibility of withdrawal of artificial feeding and hydration in such a situation and call for legislative intervention. However, a Supreme Court ruling in 2007 changed the situation.

In 1999, Englaro addressed a petition for authorisation to him as guardian to direct the doctors to withdraw treatment to the Court of Lecco. The court denied the petition, arguing that the Italian legal system grants unconditional protection to human life.[92] In November 1999 Englaro appealed. The Court of Appeals of Milan held that, in the current state of the scientific debate, artificial nutrition must be regarded as 'basic care' and as such cannot be withdrawn.[93]

In late 2000, the Minister of Health appointed a 'working group on nutrition and hydration in irreversibly unconscious patients', called the 'Oleari Commission' after its president. The commission's report makes explicit reference to the *Englaro* case. According to the report, artificial nutrition and hydration constitutes medical treatment. Decisions to withdraw nutrition and hydration are legitimate, if based on the will of the patient expressed before becoming incompetent. In the absence of such an expression of will, decisions should be made by the patient's guardian. According to the committee, the next of kin should be able to bring legal proceedings for a declaration of incapacitation and the appointment of a guardian.[94] Withdrawal of nutrition and hydration should be possible if requested by the guardian and authorised by the guardianship magistrate.[95]

In 2002, Englaro lodged a new claim with the Tribunal of Lecco, maintaining that the Oleari Report had put an end to the controversy concerning the legal status of artificial nutrition and hydration. But the tribunal pointed to the lack of 'official statements of the College of Physicians (or other medical-scientific institutions)' on the issue and referred to the 'full protection of life' granted by the

---

[91] Eluana had been shocked by the condition of an acquaintance of hers, who was in irreversible coma following a motorbike accident.

[92] Court of Lecco 1 March 1999. *Bioetica* 2000: 1.

[93] Court of Appeals of Milan 31 December 1999. *Bioetica* 2000: 1.

[94] This proposal does not seem very realistic. Incapacitation, as we have seen, involves a cumbersome special judicial proceeding. In the region of Lombardy alone (with a population of about 9 million) there are said to be about 400 new cases of permanent vegetative state per year (statement by a prominent doctor at a conference in Milan in 2003, attended by S Moratti).

[95] There is a major discrepancy between the theoretical assumptions of the document and its regulative conclusions. The document's original idea was that artificial nutrition and hydration constitutes an invasion of physical integrity and that it is therefore its initiation or continuation, not its withdrawal, that needs to be justified.

Italian legal system. Englaro's claim was again rejected. Englaro appealed. On appeal, he presented new evidence of the wish expressed by Eluana, before becoming incompetent, not to be kept alive in a condition of permanent unconsciousness. However, in October 2003 the Court of Appeals of Milan held that advance directives have no legal status in Italy and provide no legal ground for decisions to withdraw treatment. The Court also observed that the Oleari Report is not binding on the courts.[96]

In March 2004, Pope John Paul II gave a speech at a congress on life-sustaining treatments and the permanent vegetative state.[97] His speech confirmed and reinforced the position previously adopted by the Catholic Church rejecting withdrawal of artificial nutrition and hydration.

Englaro appealed the ruling of the Court of Appeals. In March 2005, the Supreme Court declined to review the case.[98] In the court's view, there was a potential conflict of interest between Eluana and her guardian, because the girl's own will concerning withdrawal of nutrition and hydration could not be ascertained.[99] In case of conflict of interest, the Civil Code prescribes the appointment of a special curator (*curatore speciale*) who shares decision-making power with the guardian. No such appointment had been made. The Supreme Court therefore rejected the appeal without considering the case further.

In September 2005, the National Bioethics Committee published an advisory document on artificial nutrition and hydration and the permanent vegetative state.[100] Twenty-two members supported the majority statement, to the effect that artificial nutrition and hydration is 'basic care'. They therefore argued that a request to withdraw artificial nutrition and hydration is the equivalent of a request for euthanasia. Thirteen members issued a dissenting statement to the effect that artificial nutrition and hydration must be regarded as 'medical treatment' that can be withdrawn at the patient's request or at the request of a representative acting as a proxy, or by the doctor on grounds of 'best interests' or 'substituted judgment'. Furthermore, they argued, it should be possible to refuse artificial nutrition and hydration via an advance directive, because a competent patient has the right to refuse any treatment on grounds of article 53 of the Medical Ethical Code.

Eluana's father arranged for the appointment of the 'special curator' requested by the Supreme Court and addressed a new request for withdrawal of artificial nutrition and hydration to the Tribunal of Lecco. In December 2005, the tribunal rejected the claim giving several different reasons. The tribunal maintained that it is not within the power of a guardian or a curator to request withdrawal of artificial nutrition and hydration. Further, the tribunal quoted the majority position of

---

[96] Court of Appeals of Milan, 17 October 2003. *Familia*, 2004: 1167.

[97] John Paul II 2004.

[98] Supreme Court, First Civil Chamber, order of 20 April 2005, no 8291. *Corriere Giuridico* 2005: 88.

[99] The court noted that the applicant had presented no documentation (drafted by the patient while still competent) of her wish not to be subjected to life-prolonging treatment.

[100] Comitato Nazionale di Bioetica 2005b.

the National Bioethics Committee. Finally, reference was made to the unconditional protection of human life in the Italian legal system. Englaro appealed. The Court of Appeals of Milan heard witnesses concerning Eluana's will before she became incompetent. In December 2006 the court affirmed the decision of the tribunal, holding that since the treatment Eluana was receiving was not 'medically futile' it could not be withdrawn.[101] However, on 16 October 2007 the Supreme Court reversed the decision of the lower courts, holding that artificial nutrition and hydration is medical treatment that in principle can be withdrawn from an incompetent patient.[102]

13.3.5 Pain Relief and Palliative Sedation

The quality of palliative care in Italy has improved since the enactment of a law in 2001 that removed some of the legal barriers to administration of opioids in the clinical setting.[103] However, there are still dramatic differences between different areas in Italy concerning the availability and quality of palliative care.[104]

Compared with other European countries, Italy has a higher rate of hospital deaths.[105] Palliativists report that this is connected with the lack of availability of adequate palliative care services at the patient's home. Patients who cannot count on home palliative care are as a rule taken to hospital when their condition takes a turn for the worse and death is expected, and they die there. On 14 March 2007, at a hearing of the Justice and Social Affairs Committees of the Chamber of Deputies, the anaesthesiologist involved in the *Welby* case stated that medical end-of-life behaviour is more likely to take place at home than in the hospital. It is 'almost impossible,' he said, that ending life could take place in the context of critical care (first aid, ICU, coronary unit and surgical department), due to 'the presence of a high number of health care professionals'.[106]

Palliative sedation is common in the case of elderly patients. In northern Italy, it is said to take place regularly in geriatric departments and institutions for the elderly.[107] The EURELD study showed that 'continuous deep sedation until death' takes place more often in Italy than in all other countries involved in the study, although this is least often accompanied by withholding artificial nutrition and hydration.[108] The ITAELD study discussed above showed that (at least among the

---

[101] Tribunal of Lecco, First Civil Chamber, order of 20 December 2005: Court of Appeals of Milan, 18 December 2006. *Il foro italiano* 2007, I, 3025.

[102] Supreme Court, first Civil Chamber, 16 October 2007, no 21748. *Il foro italiano* 2007, I, 3025. The court imposes two conditions: the patient's condition must be medically irreversible and there must be a clear indication that this is what the patient would have wanted.

[103] Law 8 February 2001, no 12. *Gazzetta Ufficiale* 2001: 41. For more information about this reform, see Blengini *et al* 2003.

[104] Source: interview with a palliativist working in Florence.

[105] Van der Heide *et al* 2003.

[106] See <http://www.aduc.it/dyn/eutanasia/noti.php?id=174791> accessed 1 May 2007.

[107] Source: interview with a geriatrist working in the province of Como.

[108] Miccinesi *et al* 2006: 125. Continuous deep sedation until death took place in 8.5% of all deaths, withholding of artificial nutrition and hydration in only a third of these cases. Only Belgium was more

small group of reporting doctors) continuous deep sedation (or induction of chemical coma) until death took place in 18% of deaths (ranging from 23% in northern Italy to 13% in southern Italy). Artificial nutrition and hydration was maintained in 76% of all cases of continuous deep sedation. Remarkably, for this last figure there was no significant difference between various areas of the country.[109] These findings seem to reflect the position of the Catholic Church: on the one hand, the long-standing acceptance of pain relief even when death may be a side-effect, on the other hand the rejection of withholding artificial nutrition and hydration.

13.3.6 'Medical Futility' and Abstention

As we have seen above, according to the Catholic Church 'medical futility' is the only ethically acceptable ground for abstaining from life-prolonging treatment. Two indications suggest that, to some extent, this viewpoint has passed into Italian society: the frequent use of ethical arguments based on 'medical futility' by both specialists and the media, and the uncertainties that until very recently surrounded the right to refuse a life-prolonging treatment.[110]

The many references made to 'medical futility' in the Italian debate, and the unquestioned assumption that 'medical futility' should be (or is already) an acceptable ground for abstention, would lead one to think that 'medical futility' has a strong ethical (if not legal) status in Italy. Article 16 of the Medical Ethical Code prohibits 'futile' treatment, defined as intervention that does not bring about any 'health benefit' or 'improvement of the quality of life'. Article 39 provides that in case of a 'certain fatal prognosis or terminal illness' treatment should be exclusively aimed at preserving 'quality of life and personal dignity'. Paragraph two of the same article provides that if the patient is no longer conscious, life-prolonging treatment should be maintained 'so long as it is considered reasonably useful'.

However, the case law shows that artificial nutrition of a permanent vegetative patient who has been unconscious for 15 years (*Englaro* case) and artificial ventilation of a terminal muscular sclerosis patient (*Welby* case) are not considered 'futile'. If interpreted so restrictively, the notion of 'medically futile treatment' offers doctors, patients and their families no legal certainty. It will always be possible for a court to argue that while 'medical futility' is an acceptable ground for abstention in general, in the specific case the treatment withheld or withdrawn was not 'futile'. And failure to administer a medically indicated treatment—followed by the death of the patient—has very serious criminal law consequences.[111]

or less similar in both respects, the other countries having (much) less palliative sedation, of which a far greater proportion without artificial feeding and hydration.

[109] Source: <http://www.fnomceo.it> (website of the Italian College of Physicians) accessed 16 July 2007.

[110] Although it is widely supposed that Italian law distinguishes between withholding and withdrawing treatment, we have been unable to find legal sources supporting that proposition.

[111] Such consequences range from failure to render assistance (art 593 of the Penal Code) to homicide (art 575 of the Penal Code).

In conclusion, the legal status of abstention on grounds of 'futility' is very uncertain. Furthermore, so far there has been no serious attempt to establish procedures for decision-making when abstention on grounds of 'futility' is being considered.[112] Compared to their European colleagues, Italian doctors are less likely to make an abstention decision and less likely to discuss it with the relatives, the patient (if competent), other doctors and nurses.[113]

13.4 Euthanasia and PAS

Killing on request and assisting suicide are prohibited by articles 579 and 580 of the Penal Code, respectively.[114] Killing on request carries a penalty of a minimum of six and a maximum of fifteen years of imprisonment. The penalty for assisting suicide is imprisonment from five to twelve years if the suicide takes place.

The Medical Ethical Code provides in articles 3 and 5 that protection of life is the first duty of a doctor and article 17—entitled 'euthanasia'—forbids 'treatments aimed at causing death'. The prohibition of 'deliberately provoking the death of a patient' is part of the professional oath that every doctor must swear on being admitted to the College of Physicians. Both article 17 and the professional oath seem to treat the subjective intention of the doctor as determinative.

---

[112] An example of a decision-making procedure for withholding and withdrawal of treatment in the ICU context is to be found in Kleijer 2005.

[113] Seale 2006a.

[114] These read as follows, in the translation of Maitlin & Wise 1978:

Art. 579. *Homicide With Consent.*

Whoever causes the death of a human being, with his own consent, shall be punished by imprisonment for from six to fifteen years.

The provisions relating to homicide shall be applied if the act was committed:

(1) Against a person under the age of eighteen years;
(2) Against a mentally infirm person, or one in a condition of mental deficiency by reason of another infirmity or the abuse of alcoholic or narcotic substances; or
(3) Against a person whose consent was extorted by the offender through violence, threats or undue influence, or obtained by deceit.

Art. 580. *Instigating or Assisting Suicide.*

Whoever brings about another's suicide or reinforces his determination to commit suicide, or in any way facilitates its commission, shall be punished, if the suicide occurs, by imprisonment from five to twelve years. If the suicide does not occur, he shall be punished by imprisonment for from one to five years, provided that the attempted suicide results in serious or very serious personal injury.

These punishments shall be increased if the person instigated or incited or assisted falls within one of the conditions specified in subparagraphs (1) and (2) of the preceding Article. However, if the said person is under the age of fourteen years or is in any way bereft of capacity to understand or to will, the provisions relating to homicide shall be applied.

During the public discussion in Italy following the enactment of the Dutch euthanasia law, there were a few legislative proposals to legalise euthanasia. In late 2002, two bills were introduced to Parliament, both to no effect.[115]

As we have seen in the Introduction to this chapter, a study by Giannini and others in 2002 showed that 3.6% of ICU doctors reported having performed 'euthanasia'. This does not mean that euthanasia, properly speaking, actually takes place at that rate in Italian hospitals. The finding may well be connected with the terminological confusion characteristic of the Italian debate until *Welby*.[116] However that may be, the study triggered public debate. The Minister of Health of the centre-right government then in power stated that the doctors who had admitted to having performed 'euthanasia' should be prosecuted.[117] This would have been impossible, since the study included a strong guarantee of anonymity. A well-known palliativist (and president of a foundation for palliative care) stated that, on the basis of his professional experience, he would be inclined to think that the figure for 'euthanasia' is in fact significantly higher than 3.6%.[118]

In the ITAELD study discussed earlier, fewer than 1% of the respondents gave a positive answer to the following question concerning their most recent case: 'was the death brought about by a drug prescribed, supplied or administered with the specific intention to hasten the end of life?'. Reactions to this finding in the press varied. A far-left newspaper ran a headline: 'Many Italian Doctors Practise Euthanasia'.[119] A newspaper known for its Catholic sympathies maintained instead that, in the light of the results of the ITAELD study, 'there is no such thing as an underground euthanasia practice' in Italy.[120]

Only three trials of for killing on request have come to public attention. None of them involved a doctor. In all three, the courts used 'legal expedients in order to mitigate the rigour of the applicable punishments'.[121] Judges manipulate 'elements of the crime (such as causation or intention), in order to ensure a more lenient penalty for the accused'.[122]

The *Vastalegna* Case

In the early morning of 15 February 1951, a man and his fiancée were found lying unconscious in their house in Rome. They had lost much blood as their wrists had

---

[115] Bill no 2974, 2002 (signed by 17 MPs belonging to very different political tendencies) and bill no 3132, 2002 (signed by a group of MPs belonging to the extreme left). Both bills proposed to amend articles 579 and 580 of the Criminal Code.

[116] The 3.6% of doctors who admitted to having administered drugs in lethal doses also stated that this behaviour accompanied a withdrawal of treatment, and denied having ever used curare. The doctors perceived their behaviour as primarily a withdrawal of treatment. Thus the 3.6% seems in fact to describe the 'grey area' between abstention and euthanasia.

[117] *Corriere della Sera* (13 November 2002).

[118] *Corriere della Sera* (13 November 2002).

[119] *Il Manifesto* (10 July 2007).

[120] *Avvenire* (10 July 2007).

[121] Legal scholar Lanza in his note to the ruling of the Supreme Court in the *Vastalegna* case (Paris 1986: 268).

[122] Viganò 2006: 173.

been cut. They were immediately admitted to hospital. The woman died there, while the man recovered consciousness and explained what had happened. His fiancée had been severely and incurably ill for a few years. At her repeated request, he had helped her to die by means of administration of barbiturates. After having done so, the desperate man had cut both her and his own wrists in an attempt to die together with her. He was tried by the Assizes Court of Rome for premeditated homicide and sentenced to six years, two months and twenty days of imprisonment. He received a reduced sentence on two grounds. The Court held that his action had been inspired by 'motives of particular moral or social value'.[123] But he was also found to have acted with diminished reponsibility. On appeal, the Assizes Court of Appeal of Rome[124] found that the man's action did not amount to premeditated homicide, but rather to 'homicide of the consenting person'. According to the court, the consent of the woman to the man's action was not in question. She had made a fully competent, voluntary and repeated request for help in dying, in order to spare herself further unbearable suffering. The man was sentenced to two years and eight months of imprisonment, to be followed by one year in a mental health institution. The prosecutor did not appeal, but the defendant did, maintaining that his action had only speeded up a dying process that was already taking place and had been aimed at sparing unnecessary suffering. The Supreme Court[125] rejected the appeal, contending that putting an end to the life of a human being is prohibited under the Italian Criminal Law regardless of the amount of life lost or the motives for the action.

The *Papini* Case

On 5 September 1981, a 39-year-old man shot his 18-year-old nephew while the boy was lying asleep in bed. The boy, who had congenital hydrocephalus, had been abandoned by his mother and was entrusted to the care of his uncle. The uncle had obtained extended leave from his job in order to dedicate himself entirely to the care of the boy, who could not walk, was mentally retarded, and had severe difficulties with movement and verbal expression. At the age of 11, the boy had undergone surgical draining of excessive brain fluid. The intervention brought about significant improvement in his clinical condition. However, it worsened his emotional situation, as he became more aware of the impossibility that he would ever lead a normal life. This aggravated further during adolescence. He had increasingly frequent outbursts of violence directed at objects and caretakers, and refused to eat, he said, 'in order to die'. By mid-1980, the situation at home had become intolerable.

The man was tried for homicide by the Assizes Court of Rome. The prosecutor requested a punishment of 10 years imprisonment. However, he called the defendant 'a respectable person' and said that he should receive a reduced sentence

---

[123] Art 62, first paragraph, of the Penal Code.
[124] A summary of the first instance and appeal rulings is reported in Paris 1986: 251.
[125] Supreme Court, first Criminal Chamber, 18 November 1954. *Foro Italiano*, 1955, II, 151.

because his action had been inspired by 'motives of particular moral or social value'. An experts' report by two psychiatrists established that because of his severe mental retardation the boy was incompetent and not capable to consent to his uncle's action. However, in its ruling the court disregarded the experts' report. Based on the testimony of several witnesses, the court came to the conclusion that the boy's wish to die had been conscious and long-lasting. For this reason, in line with what the defence had requested, the court did not consider the case one of murder, but rather of 'homicide of the consenting person' which carries a considerably lighter penalty. The man was sentenced to four years and two months imprisonment. Diminished responsibility was not used to reduce the sentence since a psychiatric examination had found the man to be fully competent. Pending appeal, the court ordered the release of the defendant from detention 'in consideration of his personality and of the nature of his act, which show that he is not a dangerous person'.[126] Neither the prosecutor non the defendant appealed. The case was widely covered in the press[127] and triggered a public debate.[128]

The *Forzatti* Case

In the early morning of 21 June 1998, Ezio Forzatti entered the hospital of Monza. His wife was in the ICU, following brain surgery for sudden and unexpected haemorrhage. She was in a very deep coma and ventilator-dependent. Forzatti told the doctor on shift that he needed to see his wife in order to slip her wedding ring onto her finger. When the doctor answered that he would have to wait a while before being let in, Forzatti pulled out a gun (which, as it later appeared, was unloaded) and the doctor opened the door of the ICU. Forzatti walked to his wife's bed and disconnected her ventilator. After a while, he called one of the nurses and a doctor whom he knew and trusted. They ascertained the woman's death and Forzatti turned himself in to the police. During police interrogations and in court, Forzatti consistently stressed that his had been a conscious and planned action, based on his (and his wife's) personal views about what a 'life worth living' is.

On 20 June 2000, the Assizes Court of Monza sentenced him to six and a half years imprisonment for premeditated homicide, coercion and illegal possession of a firearm.[129] As in the *Vastalegna* case, Forzatti received a reduced sentence on two seemingly inconsistent grounds. On the one hand, the court held that his action had been inspired by 'motives of particular moral or social value'. On the other hand, he was found to have acted with diminished responsibility (Forzatti himself had not raised this defence). The court apparently sought to keep Forzatti's inevitable punishment as low as possible.

Forzatti appealed. The prosecutor attached to the Assizes Court of Appeals of Milan pleaded for a sentence of 9 years and 4 months imprisonment. At the same

---

[126] Court of Assizes of Rome, 10 December 1983. *Foro Italiano* 1985, II, 489.

[127] See *Il Messaggero* (6 September 1981); *Il Messaggero* (30 November and 11 December 1983); *La Repubblica* (13 December 1983).

[128] See *Corriere della Sera* (21 August and 16 September 1985).

[129] A summary of the first instance ruling is reported in *La Repubblica* (20 June 2000).

time, he said that given the peculiarity of the case Forzatti deserved a pardon from the Head of State.[130] However, on 24 April 2002 the Court acquitted Forzatti on the homicide charge. Based on the medical record of the woman and on the post-mortem examination performed on her body the Court found that the woman's condition in the ICU had been one of multi-organ failure, involving multiple bleedings and major brain damage. Her situation had been gradually worsening. She was deeply comatose and was expected to die. The last medical control performed on her took place about one hour before Forzatti's action. Given the woman's desperate condition, the court argued, brain death might have occurred in the period between the last control and the withdrawal of ventilation. Forzatti was given a suspended sentence of one year and five months of imprisonment for coercion and abusive possession of a firearm, and fined 400 euros.[131] Neither Forzatti nor the prosecutor appealed.

13.5 The Neonatology Setting

In the last few years, there have been a few initiatives aimed at limiting life-prolonging treatment in the case of extremely premature babies. That most patients die in hospitals applies also to paediatric practice, as paediatric home palliative care is available only in very few cities.[132] Most deaths of children take place in the ICU, far from the parents, in an extreme and futile attempt to prolong their lives. MBPSL in children is 'almost a taboo topic'.[133] The comparative EURONIC study of MBPSL in neonatology in several European countries showed that compared to other European doctors Italian doctors make abstention decisions considerably less often. The same holds for administration of sedatives and analgesics at the end of life.[134] The same study showed that compared to their European colleagues, Italian doctors appear less inclined to attach importance to 'quality of life' considerations in their treatment decisions.[135]

The University Hospital of Padua Guidelines

In 2002, a multidisciplinary group (including doctors, nurses, midwives, lawyers and ethicists) appointed by the Bioethical Committee of the Paediatrics Department at the University Hospital of Padua drafted guidelines on administration of life-prolonging treatment to premature babies. The guidelines were sub-

[130] The decision to grant a pardon is a discretionary power of the Head of State and neither the prosecutors nor the courts have any power to influence it (see art 87 of the Italian Constitution).
[131] Assizes Court of Appeals of Milan, First Section, 24 April 2002, fn23. *Foro Italiano* 2003, II: 87.
[132] Florence, Padua, Genoa and Naples.
[133] Source: interview with a palliativist working in the city of Florence.
[134] Cuttini *et al* 2000. Data are based on a geographically stratified sample and (in Italy) a 100% response rate.
[135] Rebagliato *et al* 2000. See further ch 6.3.3.
[136] Verlato *et al* 2004.

sequently adopted by all neonatal care centres located in the Veneto region.[136]

The guidelines suggest that premature babies of up to 22 weeks gestational age should not receive any treatment other than comfort care. Prematures with a gestational age of 23 weeks should receive intubation and respiratory support, provided that they display signs of viability. Continuation of life-prolonging treatment for this group of children should be subject to a re-evaluation of their clinical condition. Babies of a gestational age of 24 weeks or more should receive maximum life-prolonging treatment, including not only intubation and respiratory support, but also, if necessary, resuscitation.[137]

The Florence Protocol

The Florence Protocol (*Carta di Firenze* or *Protocollo Degli Innocenti*)[138] was drafted by a Florentine workgroup, composed by representatives of several national medical-professional associations,[139] of the ethical commission of the College of Physicians and of the regional bioethics commission of Tuscany. Most of the members of the workgroup were doctors. However, it also included two ethicists, a lawyer and two judges. Between 2003 and 2006 the protocol received the official approval of a large number of other national medical profession associations.[140] The protocol regulates administration of life-prolonging treatment to prematures and, indirectly, management of high-risk pregnancies.

The protocol stresses the doctor's obligation to provide adequate information to the parents on the dangers (both for the mother and the baby) connected with the choice to carry on a high-risk pregnancy and concerning the prognosis of the child. The protocol emphasises that the views of the parents should be taken into maximum consideration and that the doctor should not impose his own opinions upon the parents.

The Florence Protocol provides that decision-making for the management of high-risk pregnancies of up to 22 weeks should be exclusively based on the health condition of the mother. A caesarian section should be performed only if clinically indicated for protecting the health of the mother. Mothers who want to have a caesarean section performed in the interest of the foetus 'must be informed about the disadvantages and dissuaded'. Once delivered, the baby should receive exclusively comfort care, except for the 'absolutely exceptional' case of the baby who displays significant vital capacities. In the case of a 23 weeks pregnancy caesarean section upon foetal indication is not recommended. The baby's viability should be carefully evaluated at birth and resuscitation undertaken only if the baby shows vital capacities and with parental approval. In case of serious compromise of the baby's clinical condition, the doctor, in consultation with the parents, should consider abstention from (further) life-prolonging treatment, while maintaining comfort

---

[137] Verlato *et al* 2004.
[138] This name derives from the name of a hospital in Florence.
[139] Ranging from the Italian Society of Neonatology to the Italian Society of Legal Medicine.
[140] Ranging from the Italian Society of Neonatal Anaesthesiology to the Italian Society of Obstetrical and Gynaecological Ecography.

care. For a 24 weeks pregnancy, caesarean section upon foetal indication can exceptionally be considered. Life-sustaining treatment for the baby can be administered on the basis of 'favourable objective clinical criteria' such as spontaneous respiratory efforts, heart frequency and facial colour. For a pregnancy of 25 weeks or more, caesarean section upon foetal indication can be considered. Once delivered, the baby should receive resuscitation and intensive care, unless its clinical condition is so poor that survival does not seem possible.

The protocol recommends psychological support and follow-up for the parents, and clinical follow-up for the child, including early treatment of disabilities.[141]

13.6 Modalities of Control

13.6.1. The Criminal Justice System

In the Italian criminal justice system, prosecution is in theory mandatory.[142] However, informal surveys suggest that 90% of reported crimes are in fact not prosecuted.[143] It is therefore possible that cases of 'euthanasia' or other potentially punishable MBPSL come to the attention of the criminal law authorities but are not prosecuted.[144] As the *Forzatti* and other cases suggest, there are a number of doctrinal tools that could be used to justify such a decision.

13.6.2. The Doctor's Duty to Report

The Law on the Disposal of Corpses[145] requires the city clerk's permission for burial (or cremation). Such permission is granted if the doctor responsible for treatment files a death certificate on which he certifies that the death of the patient was not the consequence of a crime.[146] If the doctor is not convinced of this, he must notify the coroner, who inspects the body of the deceased and makes his own judgment about the cause of death. If the coroner is convinced that the death was not the consequence of a crime, he files a death certificate; otherwise, he reports the case to the local prosecutor, who must decide whether to notify the city clerk that he has no objection to burial (or cremation). For a doctor to fail to report a death that might be the consequence of a crime is a distinct if minor criminal offence.[147] However, we have not been able to find any such case.

---

[141] Pignotti, Toraldo di Francia & Donzelli 2007.
[142] Art 112 of the Constitution. This provision has recently been subject to debate.
[143] Lena & Mattei 2002.
[144] Compare the situation in France (see ch 12) and, until recently, in Belgium (see ch 9).
[145] Decree of the President of the Republic of 10 September 1990, no 285. *Gazzetta Ufficiale* 1990: 239.
[146] Royal Decree of 9 July 1939, no 1238. *Gazzetta Ufficiale* 1939: 204.
[147] Art 365 Penal Code.

13.6.3. Medical Disciplinary Law and Tribunals

Each of the 110 Italian provinces has its own College of Physicians. The provincial colleges together form the National Federation of the Colleges of Physicians. Membership of the profession is obtained through enrolment in the provincial Professional Register of Physicians. Only enrolled professionals are entitled to practice medicine. Each college elects a council which among other things hears cases of alleged violation of the Medical Ethical Code. Possible punishments are warning, reprimand, temporary withdrawal of the licence to practise medicine and, in the most serious cases, erasure from the Professional Register of Physicians which permanently deprives the doctor of the right to practise.[148] Appeal is to the Central Commission for Health Professionals (*Commissione Centrale per gli Esercenti le Professioni Sanitarie*). The members of the Central Commission are health professionals appointed by the Head of State. In the final instance, appeal is to the Supreme Court.

The *Conciani* Case

Dr Conciani was a gynaecologist who worked in Florence and had played an important role in the process that lead to legalisation of abortion in 1978. In the mid-1970s, he spent two and a half months in prison as a result of having stated publicly that he had performed abortions on his patients when requested to do so.[149] In the early 1990s, Conciani reported having helped a few severely ill people to die, at their request. As a consequence, he was tried by the Council of the College of Physicians of Florence. The trial ended with the decision to deprive Conciani of the right to practise medicine. In 1995 his name was struck off the Professional Registry. Severely ill, and no longer licensed to prescribe for himself the medications he had used to help his patients to die, Conciani committed suicide by hanging himself.[150]

13.7 Concluding Remarks

Compared with some other European countries, Italy seems rather backward as far as the legal regulation of MBPSL is concerned. The law remains too undevel-

---

[148] Erasure follows automatically in case of conviction for an intentional crime for which the law carries a penalty of imprisonment of a minimum of not less than two years or a maximum of not less than five years. See Legislative Decree 13 September 1946, fn 233, available at <http://portale.fnomceo.it/Jcmsfnomceo/Jarticolo.jsp?lingua=It&idsezione=44&idarticolo=370> accessed 2 May 2007.

[149] See <http://www.radicalparty.org/history/chron/1975_it.htm> accessed 10 September 2007. Conciani also campaigned in favour of introduction of the abortion pill RU486, which replaces more invasive abortion techniques.

[150] See <http://web.radicalparty.org/pressreleases/press_release.php?func=detail&par=2063> accessed 1 May 2007.

oped and too uncertain—too subject to the idiosyncrasies of local courts and prosecutors—to meet the needs either of clinical practice or of effective enforcement. Little is known (even within the medical profession)[151] about actual medical practice, with the partial exception of the recent EURELD and ITAELD studies (which, however, only covered some areas of the country and had low response rates) and of the EURONIC study in the neonatology setting. The Italian debate on MBPSL is influenced by the position of the Roman Catholic Church and dominated by philosophical and legal contributions that mostly limit themselves to doctrinal considerations. However, the *Welby* case changed a situation that had been stagnant for years and showed that the idea of hastening a patient's death by means of a medical intervention no longer belongs in the sphere of taboo. In particular, the medical profession appears to be gradually abandoning its formerly passive attitude with regard to legal regulation (and scientific investigation) of MBPSL practice. The reflections of this change in the public debate, the political world and the attitude of the courts are already visible: charges against the anaesthesiologist involved in the *Welby* case were dropped by the court *after* the man was acquitted by the College of Physicians; the ITAELD survey, whose results were presented in front of several prominent politicians, was commissioned by the Council of the College of Physicians itself.

[151] Source: interview with a palliativist working in the city of Florence.

14

Scandinavia

REIDUN FØRDE, LARS JOHAN MATERSTVEDT, ASLAK SYSE

In a European context, the Scandinavian countries Norway, Denmark and Sweden are relatively conservative when it comes to medical interventions that either end, or have the potential for ending, a patient's life. In this contribution we first describe current legal and ethical regulation and then focus on studies of doctors' attitudes and practices in the three countries.

Because the authors of this chapter are all Norwegians, the situation in Norway will be dealt with most extensively.

14.1 Legal Provisions

Following what has become the international convention we understand by 'euthanasia' the administration of drugs by a doctor with the explicit intention of ending the patient's life at his/her explicit request, and by 'physician-assisted suicide' (PAS) we understand the prescription or supply of drugs at the explicit request of the patient with the explicit intention of enabling the patient to end his/her own life.[1]

Norway

The Norwegian Penal Code dates back to 1902.[2] The taking of human life is prohibited by article 233. A special article 235 makes it a lesser offence to kill a person who consents, which would cover cases of euthanasia. This section also specifically provides that the mercy killing of a hopelessly ill person is unlawful. Assistance with suicide is illegal under article 236. These prohibitions apply to everyone. The sentencing framework is rather indeterminate and the range is wide, ranging from several years of imprisonment to very mild forms of punishment.[3] (For an example of the latter, see the court ruling in the *Sandsdalen* case below.)

---

[1] *Cf* Rurup 2005; Onwuteaka-Philipsen *et al* 2003; Materstvedt *et al* 2003; Van der Heide *et al* 2007.

[2] Norwegian Penal Code 1902 available at <http://www.lovdata.no/all/hl-19020522-010.html> accessed 12 September 2007.

[3] Husabø (1994) notes that the upper limit for both euthanasia and PAS would be 15 years for wilful killing and 21 years for premeditated homicide. Nonetheless, if a person consented to having his life ended by another, the court may go below the lowest possible sentence for killing, which normally is 6 years.

A Penal Code Commission appointed by the Government advised in 2002 that the law should remain unchanged as far as euthanasia and assistance with suicide are concerned.[4] However, two of the five members recommended that the law be changed to allow the defence of necessity for persons assisting another to die. There was no limitation to doctors but the patient would have had to be 'terminally ill'. The Norwegian Parliament's Committee on Justice discussed these proposals in April 2005 and agreed with the commission's majority. In May 2005 the Norwegian Parliament by unanimous vote decided to retain the present definite ban on assistance in dying.[5] It is thus clear that political opposition to changes in the law is strong, and cuts across all parties.

The *Kristina* case has recently drawn the attention of the medical and legal community as well as the general public to the problems surrounding withholding and withdrawing life-sustaining treatment of the seriously ill. This case concerns a little girl who together with her mother was buried under a landslide in September 2005. The mother died, but Kristina was resuscitated and treated in an intensive care unit. Due to severe and comprehensive damage to the brain, the prognosis was that she would never regain consciousness. This view was confirmed by two second opinion examinations outside the hospital. Accordingly, the doctors responsible for the child saw treatment as futile and therefore wanted to terminate life support. Furthermore, it was possible that the child was suffering. Notwithstanding these medical opinions, her father strongly opposed withdrawal and this led to a serious conflict which was widely reported in the media. The father and his lawyers claimed that if life-sustaining treatment were discontinued, Kristina would be deprived of any chance to recover. They brought the case to court seeking an interim measure but the court ruled that the hospital had the right to decide to terminate treatment.[6] An appeal was filed, but then withdrawn after just a few days. After five months in the intensive care unit, the treatment was withdrawn and the child died shortly thereafter.

Subsequent to the *Kristina* case the question of the right of relatives to a voice in end-of-life decisions has been a topic of debate, as has been their right to an independent second opinion in such cases. The appointment of a national—and therefore more independent—clinical ethics committee with the authority to make a final decision has been suggested (no such committee has yet been established). The proposal is based on the position that such decisions reflect not only technical medical considerations but also to a significant degree value judgments. But the legal situation remains unchanged: at the end of the day, the decision in such circumstances is the responsibility of the hospital in charge. Currently, national guidelines to regulate withholding or withdrawing life-prolonging treatment are being worked out by a group consisting of a lawyer, representatives from the Section for Medical Ethics of the University of Oslo, the Norwegian Medical

---

[4] Straffelovkommisjonen 2002; Materstvedt, Syse & Borchgrevink 2005.

[5] See Syse 2005.

[6] In Norwegian law, technically this right resides with the hospital as an institution and not with the individual doctor who makes the final decision.

Association (NMA), the Norwegian Nurses Organisation, and the Norwegian Patients Association. These guidelines will deal with team discussions, patient involvement, second opinions, the decision process and the involvement of the patient's next-of-kin.

The Patients' Rights Act requires 'valid', rather than 'informed', consent.[7] Put briefly, the idea of valid consent calls for more flexible judicial review than the more fixed standard of informed consent. Consent may be given by the representative of a non-competent patient, but a representative cannot insist on treatment against the judgment of the doctor (*cf* the *Kristina* case, above).

Under the Patients' Rights Act, a competent and fully informed patient may, except in emergency situations, refuse life saving treatment. In emergency situations, however, it is the duty of health care personnel to provide the necessary treatment.[8] There are three exceptions to this rule: even in an emergency, a doctor may not override a refusal if it is connected with a hunger strike for some reason of conscience, if it concerns refusal of blood transfusion on the same ground (Jehova's Witnesses would be the usual case), or if the patient is dying. The Patients' Rights Act § 4–9 specifically describes these three situations.[9]

Advance treatment refusals are not binding in Norway.

Denmark

Euthanasia and PAS are forbidden under Articles 239 and 240 of the Danish Penal Code. Article 239 applies to the situation where the killing follows the person's 'definite request' (*bestemte begærning*) and in so doing makes possible a milder sentence than in regular cases of killing or murder.[10] So far no cases of euthanasia or assistance in suicide have been dealt with by the Danish courts.[11]

In 1992 the Physicians Act was amended to include provisions on aid in dying, and these were included in revised form in the Patients' Rights Act of 1999. The new Act makes the right to self-determination of the patient central to Danish health law.[12] This is reflected, among other things, in the right of a patient—if competent and above 15 years of age—to be informed about and to consent to treatment.[13] The Act specifically deals with patients who refuse blood transfusions, and

[7] See Syse 2000.

[8] See the Health Personnel Act of 1999, § 7, which concerns 'immediate help' (*øyeblikkelig hjelp*). Such help is described as being 'acutely necessary' (*påtrengende nødvendig*) and must therefore be given even when a patient 'is opposed to medical help' (*motsetter seg helsehjelpen*). The Health Personnel Act is available at <http://www.lovdata.no/all/hl-19990702-064.html> accessed 1 October 2007.

[9] Norwegian Patients' Rights Act 1999, available at http://www.lovdata.no/all/hl-19990702-063.html> accessed 12 September 2007.

[10] See Husabø 1994: 150.

[11] See Green-Pedersen 2007: 279. However, Vestergaard writes (2000: 423) that a doctor was acquitted 'in a spectacular case years back, and just recently a physician in general practice has been indicted for 5 incidents of manslaughter'. He adds that the latter case would be taken to court in the year 2000 and that charges had been dropped against a nurse who had assisted the doctor, initially accused of 22 homicides.

[12] See Vestergaard 2002: 82.

[13] See Vestergaard 2000: 408.

provides that their wishes should be respected.[14] When the patient is not competent, the doctor has the power to decide.[15] In cases of emergency when 'vital or otherwise urgent treatment' is required 'immediately' and where the patient cannot give consent—due to a permanent or temporary lack of competence—a doctor has a duty to treat even without having sought the consent of a proxy.[16]

Although the right to self-determination is formally at the core of Danish legislation, the reach of the right is limited. Patients have no right to request that treatment be discontinued when death is not imminent, if compliance with the patient's wishes would lead to the patient's immediate death.[17] Advance written treatment refusals are binding on doctors if the patient becomes terminally ill. The assessment of this terminal status is considered in the 1998 Act to be a 'purely medical judgment'. According to Vestergaard a patient is considered terminal 'when it is highly probable that death will occur within days or weeks despite application of available treatment options'.[18] The Penal Code provides sanctions for the offence of 'unlawful coercion, deprivation of liberty or assault'[19] for a doctor who continues treatment despite a terminally ill patient's advance written refusal.[20] Advance treatment directives are not binding in other cases but should be considered as a guide by health care professionals. The Act specifically provides that this applies to cases of severe brain damage, dementia, aphasia, serious lung disease and spinal disorders.[21]

When treatment is deemed futile health care professionals 'have a rather extensive authorisation—and partially an obligation—to perform so-called *"passive aid in dying"*'.[22] Thus an 'irreversibly dying patient' can receive palliative treatment even if that may shorten the dying process.[23] When such a patient is incompetent or cannot express his will 'a health care professional may abstain from initiating or discontinuing life-prolonging treatment'.[24] Such treatment is defined in the Patients' Rights Act in article 17 as

> treatment, where there is no prospect for cure, improvement or palliation, but only for some prolonging of life.[25]

---

[14] See Vestergaard 2002: 83.

[15] *Ibid* at 418.

[16] Arts 250 and 253 of the Penal Code, art 7 of the Physicians Act; art 10 of the Patients' Rights Act. See Vestergaard 2000: 412.

[17] See Vestergaard 2000: 410–11; see also Weyers 2005: 258–9.

[18] See Vestergaard 2000: 413.

[19] *Ibid* at 410.

[20] Advance treatment refusals can be sent to the Living Will Bank. According to Vestergaard more than 70,000 had been sent to the Bank at the end of 1999. He adds that 80% of those who have sent living wills to the bank are above 45 years old. In principle physicians should always consult the Bank when life prolonging treatment is envisaged. However, at the time Vestergaard published his articles such consultation did not seem to be systematically carried out in practice. See Vestergaard 2002: 94.

[21] See Vestergaard 2002: 91.

[22] *Ibid* at 82.

[23] Patients' Rights Act, art 16 s 3. Vestergaard (2000: 417–18) notes that the law does not specify precisely the circumstances in which this should be done. When the patient is competent, his consent is required.

[24] Art 16 s 2 (Vestergaard 2000: 413).

[25] See Vestergaard 2000: 413.

Vestergaard writes that physicians may also abstain from life-prolonging treatment in non-terminal cases under certain circumstances. He adds, however, that the law is somewhat unclear in this respect. It apparently comprehends exceptional circumstances such as those that may cause permanent incapacity 'for every kind of genuine human contact,' for example in the case of comatose patients or patients in a persistent vegetative state.[26]

As to the discussion in the Danish public arena on euthanasia and its possible legalisation, Green-Pedersen writes that although surveys have shown a generally positive attitude of the Danish population towards euthanasia, political parties have not put it on the political agenda and no relevant parliamentary activity has taken place. He refers to an opinion poll published by a newspaper in May 2002 showing that 68% of the population supported euthanasia, to which the Minister of Health reacted by saying that the Government had no intention of legalising it. Green-Pedersen adds that some political figures at that time gave their views on the topic but that no political action resulted from the event, and that so far no political party has included the topic in a campaign manifesto. A pro-euthanasia organisation, *En Værdig Død,* was founded in 2005 but has apparently not been successful at transforming the legalisation of euthanasia into a political or a public issue.[27]

Sweden

The legal situation in Sweden is somewhat different from that in Denmark and Norway. The Swedish Penal Code does not have a special section concerning killing on request, and euthanasia would, in principle, be considered either killing or murder.[28] It is a criminal act intentionally to inject lethal medicine or to prescribe medicines meant for such use. Taking another persons' life is prohibited by chapter 3 article 1 of the Penal Code and carries a jail sentence of 10 years to life in cases of murder. If extenuating circumstances exist, the case may be treated as killing, which would mean 6–10 years imprisonment (see article 2). Chapter 29 article 5 includes a general rule that allows for an even milder sentence. Or the court may dismiss the charge according to article 6.

On the other hand, the exact legal status of PAS is difficult to determine.[29] A lay person, and even a doctor, may contribute to a person's suicide without committing a criminal offence. For a doctor, however, such an act is illegal as a matter of health law. Thus a doctor who assists with suicide might lose his authorisation to practise medicine.

---

[26] *Ibid.*
[27] Green-Pedersen 2007: 278–9. The website of the organisation is <http://www.e-v-d.dk>, accessed 25 February 2008.
[28] See Husabø 1994: 152.
[29] See Westrin & Nilstun 2005; Husabø 1994.

14.2 Medical Ethics Codes

Scandinavian medical ethics codes pretty much reflect the legal situation. In 1988 a meeting in Kolding (Denmark) between all Nordic medical associations—that is, including Iceland and Finland—resulted in a statement opposing the legalisation of euthanasia, while recognising the right of patients to decline life-sustaining treatment.

Norway

The ethical code of the NMA explicitly condemns euthanasia and PAS.[30] The expression used in the code is not 'euthanasia' but '*aktiv dødshjelp*', which literally means 'active help to die'. The term is rather imprecise, it being unclear whether the request of the patient is considered relevant.

Norway does not have a national ethical council. The NMA's Medical Ethics Council is the association's highest competent body in ethical matters. It has laid down general ethical rules that must be adhered to by all members. The NMA distinguishes between acts intended to shorten life and withholding or withdrawing futile medical treatment, which it does not regard as assistance in dying. It also emphasises that the will of a dying patient must be respected.

The acceptability of withholding or withdrawing life-sustaining treatment at the request of a seriously ill patient has been addressed by the council, following a letter from a doctor who raised the following question: if a competent patient with amyotrophic lateral sclerosis requests the stopping of ventilator treatment, should this be honoured? The council's view is that this is morally as well as legally justified, and that preparations for withdrawal should be made before a patient with a chronic and serious disease is put on a ventilator.[31] The council also discussed a case of withdrawing tube-feeding of a young patient with major brain injury who had been in a nursing home for more than 20 years. The parents urged that life-sustaining treatment be stopped. The council concluded that doing so in such circumstances is ethically justified.[32] This case received some attention in the media, but as far as we are aware no one publicly criticised the council's standpoint.

In 1998 a palliative care doctor was accused by a colleague of misusing terminal/palliative sedation as a hidden form of (slow) euthanasia. At the time such treatment was not well known in Norway. The case was examined by the Health Authorities who did not find the treatment illegal. It was also investigated by the police authorities who confirmed the Health Authorities' conclusion. The case received extensive media coverage and is known as the *Bærum* case. In the aftermath of this case, the Medical Ethics Council of the NMA decided to form a

---

[30] Den norske lægeforening 1994.
[31] See Førde 2006.
[32] Den norske lægeforening. Rådet for legeetikk 2003.

task force[33] to formulate guidelines for the regulation of this sort of treatment.[34] In June 2001 the task force came up with comprehensive and detailed guidelines for what it calls 'palliative sedation for the dying (where death is imminent)'.[35] These stipulate:[36]

Box 14.1 Guidelines of the Norwegian Medical Association on Palliative Sedation

1. By palliative sedation for the dying is meant pharmacological depression of the level of consciousness in order to alleviate suffering that cannot be relieved in any other way.
2. Palliative sedation should be an extraordinary measure initiated as a response to intolerable suffering that stems from, and is dominated by, physical symptoms. Mental suffering alone is not an indication for palliative sedation.[37]
3. Palliative sedation for the dying may only be given to patients with a life expectancy of a few days.[38]
4. The causes of the patient's suffering must have been appropriately diagnosed. All other treatments of individual symptoms must have been tried, or at least have been carefully considered and found to be futile. If the ward lacks resources to help the patient, the patient should be referred for specialist palliative care, or the ward should seek the assistance of such expertise. Palliative sedation should not be opted for because it is apparent that lack of resources prevents optimal alternative

---

[33] The task force included members from different medical specialties, law, paramedical health care personnel and a member from the public. The first author of this chapter chaired the task force.

[34] Somewhat later, in July 2000, the Health Authorities formulated their own guidelines for palliative sedation for the dying and these are the ones that have the official status of national guidelines in Norway available at <http://www.helsetilsynet.no/templates/LetterWithLinks____7231.aspx> accessed 22 November 2007. These are very similar to the guidelines authorised by the NMA in 2001. There is however one noteworthy difference: NMA guideline no 6 (latter part) states that, 'If the patient is not competent to give consent, palliative sedation may still be given if, all things considered, it is assumed to be in the patient's best interests.' Such a provision is absent in the Health Authorities' official guidelines.

[35] Den norske lægeforening. Rådet for legeetikk 2001. This document has nine sections; the guidelines themselves are to be found in section 8. Internationally, there is considerable debate about the definition of palliative sedation as well as on the indications for this treatment. A helpful article is De Graeff & Dean 2007. They add clarity to this complex issue by distinguishing three levels of sedation at the end of life: mild (somnolence); intermediate (stupor); and deep (coma—patient is unconscious and unresponsive).

[36] The authors of this chapter wish to thank Professor Jonathan Knowles, Department of Philosophy, Norwegian University of Science and Technology (NTNU), Trondheim, Norway for his invaluable contribution in the translation of the guidelines into English. A professional translator finalised the translation, which has been approved and authorised by the NMA as the official translation of the guidelines.

[37] The Swedish guidelines (see Svenska Läkaresällskapets Delegation för Medicinsk Etik 2003, and the section on Sweden below) state that psychic symptoms include 'anxiety, fear and confusion' and emphasise that the situation is often complex, involving 'a combination of physical and psychic components'. Whether this would exclude psychic suffering as the *only* ground for sedation is thus not entirely clear.

[38] The Swedish guidelines use the formulation that the time left to live 'must be very short—realistically one week' (Svenska Läkaresällskapets Delegation för Medicinsk Etik 2003). Norwegian guideline no 3 seems to give a bit more leeway. Despite the fact that it refers to 'a few days', which could be taken to mean less than a week, the discussion amongst task force members suggests that it could be read to contemplate up to a fortnight at the most.

treatment and care. In such a case, the doctor in charge should notify his or her superiors or the Health Authorities.

5. The ward chief physician is formally responsible for initiating and carrying out palliative sedation of the dying. The decision must be based on an overall medical assessment of the patient's situation, and be made after consultation with the nursing staff and with other doctors familiar with the patient, or others who are qualified to contribute.

6. If the patient is capable of doing so, he or she must give express consent to the treatment. The patient should be informed of his or her state of health and prognosis, what palliative sedation would involve (including information about the level and duration of the sedation), the risks associated with sedation as well as alternatives to sedation. If the patient is not competent to give consent, palliative sedation may still be given if, all things considered, it is assumed to be in the patient's best interests.

7. The patient's next-of-kin should also be informed and involved in the decision-making process, provided the patient is not opposed to this. The next-of-kin have the right to be informed, but cannot be assigned the ultimate responsibility for initialization of the treatment.

8. Patients should only be sedated sufficiently deeply to alleviate suffering.

9. Although sedation of some patients is most likely to be continued until death occurs, raising the level of the patient's consciousness must be considered and attempted. If it becomes clear during the wakening process that the patient's situation is still intolerable, it is justifiable to increase sedation without the patient regaining consciousness.[39]

10. The patient should be adequately monitored with respect to level of consciousness, maintenance of an unrestricted respiratory passage and the efficacy of the treatment. Possible side effects of the treatment must also be monitored, so that these can be dealt with.

11. Patients who have stopped drinking on their own need not be given fluids intravenously. If the patient is still capable of drinking significant amounts, and the sedation renders him or her incapable of this, intravenous fluids should be administered. If the administration of intravenous fluids was started before palliative sedation, it should be continued.[40]

12. The treatment must be documented in the medical records. The following must be emphasized: the grounds for concluding that sedation was necessary; how the decision to sedate was reached; information to the patient and next-of-kin and their views regarding the treatment; how the treatment was carried out and monitored.

---

[39] The formulation 'must be . . . attempted' has sparked some debate. Some have taken this to mean that one should intentionally risk inflicting new, intolerable suffering on the patient. Such criticism seems to miss the point made in the next sentence of the guideline, namely that the procedure should be aborted 'if it becomes clear during the wakening process' that intolerable suffering is likely to result. Any attendant suffering should be very short and probably not intolerable since complete consciousness will not have been achieved. The Swedish guidelines state that 'in principle the level of sedation should be raised intermittently to allow for a new judgment of the indication' (Svenska Läkaresällskapets Delegation för Medicinsk Etik 2003).

[40] The Swedish guidelines are less strict in that they do not demand that fluids be given: 'There is in general no medical reason to start or continue parenteral fluid treatment.' They also underscore that 'cultural differences' should be taken into consideration in this connection (Svenska Läkaresällskapets Delegation för Medicinsk Etik 2003).

One of the crucial messages that comes across in these guidelines is that palliative sedation must be given in such a way that the patient is likely to die of his disease and not of the sedation or complications thereof. This means, for example, that the patient should receive intravenous hydration during sedation unless he or she is so close to death that the natural intake of fluid is negligible (no 11). It also entails that the patient must be watched carefully and regularly so that complications of the sedation, such as respiratory depression, can be treated (no 10). Nonetheless, the NMA acknowledges that one cannot rule out that when given to frail patients palliative sedation may result in the shortening of life. At the same time, the NMA emphasises the distinction between administration of pain relieving drugs that, as an unintended side effect, may shorten life, and actively helping a patient to die.[41]

As far as the ethical justification for palliative sedation is concerned, the following values and principles are discussed and emphasised:[42] respect for patient integrity; respect for patient autonomy; the intrinsic value of human life; the doctrine of double effect.

Denmark

The Danish Medical Association (DMA) has no specific ethical rules dealing with end-of-life decisions.[43] Nevertheless, Green-Pedersen reports that the DMA opposes euthanasia.[44] In 2003 the Danish Council of Ethics,[45] which includes members not employed in health care, also took a stand against legalisation of euthanasia.[46]

Denmark has guidelines concerning pharmacological palliation of terminal patients elaborated by the National Board of Health.[47] The Danish Council of Ethics published a handbook in 2002 on treatment of the dying, dealing with forgoing treatment, but also including palliative sedation—however, the latter topic is not dealt with in as much detail as in Norway and in Sweden.[48] One standpoint is that as far as decisions to forgo treatment of an unconscious and terminally ill patient are concerned, the doctor should have the final say. Another is that a competent patient, irrespective of whether he or she is terminal, ought to have the right to decline life-prolonging treatment even though this may shorten his or her life. The handbook also states that palliative sedation is to be distinguished from euthanasia because the purposes of the two actions are different: relieving suffering versus ending life.

[41] Den norske lægeforening. Rådet for legeetikk 2001.
[42] Den norske lægeforening. Rådet for legeetikk 2001, section 3.
[43] Almindelige Danske Lægeforening 2005.
[44] See Green-Pedersen 2007: 279.
[45] This council is a free-standing body established by the Government and is unrelated to the Danish Medical Association.
[46] Etiske Råd 2003.
[47] Sundhetsstyrelsen 2002.
[48] Etiske Råd 2002.

Sweden

The Swedish Society of Medicine (SSM) includes in its ethical guidelines a section which condemns acts that actively hasten death, but it does not refer specifically to euthanasia and PAS nor does it specify what is meant by 'hasten'.[49]

Like Norway, Sweden has national guidelines concerning palliative sedation.[50] These are not substantially different from their Norwegian counterpart.[51] The Delegation of Medical Ethics of the SSM that worked them out takes at its point of departure the so-called four principles approach to health care ethics: 1. Beneficence (the obligation to provide benefits and balance benefits against risks); 2. Non-maleficence (the obligation to avoid causing harm); 3. Respect for autonomy (the obligation to respect the decision-making capacities of autonomous persons); 4. Justice (obligations of fairness in the distribution of benefits and risks).[52]

In 2006 there was a debate in Sweden over the possible legitimacy of stopping ventilator treatment in the case of a competent patient who asked for this. It is known as the *Jocke* case and involved an individual who was paralysed from the neck down due to a car accident.[53] Surprisingly, such withdrawal was initially regarded by one top government lawyer as a kind of euthanasia and, accordingly, judged to be illegal. Later on, this view was countered by other lawyers, as well as by the SSM. They were of the opinion that rejecting a request for ventilator withdrawal would amount to forced somatic treatment, something which is against Swedish law. Subsequently, in 2006, Swedish national guidelines were worked out to regulate both not initiating and stopping life-sustaining treatment. These guidelines explicitly state the acceptability of withholding or withdrawing such treatment at the request of a competent patient, even when he is not terminally ill and even if the treatment would benefit him.[54]

14.3 Doctors' Attitudes and Medical Practice

Norway, Denmark and Sweden are quite similar with respect to ethnicity, culture, political system and way of life, the languages are close and Scandinavians understand one another fairly well both in writing and orally. A direct comparison

---

[49] Svenska Läkaresällskapets 2006.

[50] Svenska Läkaresällskapets Delegation för Medicinsk Etik 2003.

[51] See the notes to the Norwegian guidelines in Box 14.1 above for some minor differences between the Norwegian and Swedish guidelines.

[52] Svenska Läkaresällskapets Delegation för Medicinsk Etik 2003. This approach was developed in 1979 by Beauchamp & Childress (2001). A helpful discussion of the approach is Gillon 2003. For two papers that use the four principles as a vehicle in the ethical analysis of palliative sedation, see Núñez Olarte & Guillen 2001 and Materstvedt 2006.

[53] The patient in question travelled to Switzerland and received assisted suicide through the right-to-die organisation Dignitas (see ch 16 on Swiss practice in this regard).

[54] Svenska Läkaresällskapets 2006.

between the countries of doctors' attitudes and behaviour regarding end-of-life medical practice is nevertheless not available because no survey has included all three countries. Furthermore, the country-specific surveys differ substantially in design, classification of medical behaviour and wording of the questions asked, which makes comparisons very difficult.[55]

14.3.1 Norway

Attitudes towards Euthanasia and PAS

Unfortunately, the wording of the questions about euthanasia and PAS in Norwegian surveys does not reflect the distinctions that are usually made in the international literature, nor those drawn in the ethical codes of the NMA referred to above.[56] In 1993, a questionnaire exploring attitudes of Norwegian doctors regarding life and death decisions was sent to a representative sample of 1,476 doctors.[57] The questions were designed to permit comparison of doctors' attitudes with those of the population, which had been surveyed earlier.[58] One of the questions was as follows:

> A patient has a painful incurable disease and is close to death. The patient asks the doctor to help him/her to die. In your opinion, should the doctor be permitted to bring the patient's life to an end painlessly?

Sixty-five per cent of the doctors replied 'no', 17% were in favour, while 18% answered 'do not know'. However, the question does not distinguish between euthanasia and PAS. Furthermore, the formulations 'help him or her to die' and 'bring the patient's life to an end painlessly' at the patient's request might be misinterpreted by respondents as referring to acts of abstention from life-prolonging treatment in combination with large doses of pain killers.[59]

Another question dealt with a patient who asks a doctor to end his life and who has a chronic, non-terminal condition causing pain and a severely reduced quality of life. Here 84% of the doctors were negative, 4% positive and 12% did not know what to think.

The survey of the general population which included 1,200 persons, seems to indicate that ordinary Norwegians are far less negative: 32% of those who expressed an opinion were negative in the case of the terminal patient and 59% in case of the chronic patient.[60] 18% of the population was in doubt regarding the first question and 25% regarding the second.

---

[55] See Materstvedt & Kaasa 2002.
[56] See Vigeland 1997; Førde, Aasland & Falkum 1997.
[57] See Førde, Aasland & Falkum 1997 (response rate 66.4%).
[58] See Vigeland 1997.
[59] See Materstvedt & Kaasa 2002.
[60] See Vigeland 1997.

Experience with Euthanasia and PAS

In 2000, the Research Institute of the NMA carried out a survey on a representative sample (1,616 doctors) of all members of the NMA (without regard to specialisation).[61] The questions focused on medical ethics, collegiality and professional autonomy. One question was:

> Have you as a doctor ever committed an act (for example given an injection) with the explicit purpose of shortening the life of a patient? (Do not include termination of life-sustaining treatment to dying patients). [Response alternatives: Never, a few times, several times.]

One per cent of the respondents stated that they had committed such an act and everyone within that group replied 'a few times'. The question, as we can see, is not limited to cases in which there was a request by the patient (euthanasia), so some of the 1% may have involved drug-induced ending of life without an explicit request.

In any event, the answers in the surveys of 1993 and 2000 indicate that Norwegian doctors are conservative in their attitudes and practice when it comes to various types of ending of life by drugs. Based on personal acquaintance with the views of very many doctors across the country—no scientific data exist in this area as far as Norway is concerned—all three authors of this chapter find it safe to conclude that such medical interventions are seen by the majority of doctors as clearly distinct, both clinically and ethically, from death due to 'letting nature take its course'. Additionally, this distinction is found in the vast majority of publications on these topics by Norwegian medical authors.[62]

Two doctors have faced criminal prosecution in connection with euthanasia. In the *Husebø* case (1993), an anaesthesiologist revealed in a television programme that he had administered a lethal drug to a terminal and suffering cancer patient. Not only did the patient consent to the lethal injection, with the support of his next-of-kin he bluntly insisted that it be given.[63] After having investigated the case, the Director General of Public Prosecution gave the doctor a formal reprimand for having performed illegal euthanasia.[64] The doctor has later stated that he is against a change in the law regarding euthanasia.

In the *Sandsdalen* case (1996), a general practitioner associated with a Norwegian right-to-die society turned himself in to the authorities after performing euthanasia on a seriously ill patient suffering from multiple sclerosis. His action was intended to be a test case, with the aim of changing the law. The NMA reacted by expelling the GP for having violated its ethical rules and for publicly

---

[61] See Førde, Aasland & Steen 2002. This is about 10% of all practising doctors in Norway. The response rate was 83%.

[62] See eg Rasmussen 1998.

[63] The case is discussed in Husabø 1994: 265–8.

[64] In such a case, although guilt is deemed to have been proved, prosecution may be waived provided that special circumstances exist such that the prosecuting authority on an overall evaluation finds that there are stronger reasons for not prosecuting the act than for prosecuting. In Norwegian law this is called a 'formal reprimand'.

rejecting them. Ultimately, in 2000, the GP was given a suspended sentence with two-years probation by the Supreme Court.[65] The Health Authorities withdrew his licence to practise.[66]

Experience with Potentially Life-Shortening Pain Relief

The 2000 survey of the Research Institute of the NMA[67] included the question whether the doctors involved had ever experienced unintended patient death following an injection with pain-relieving drugs. Of the 1,616 doctors surveyed, 10.5% said that they had experienced this. The wording 'unintended death' was designed to ensure that pain relief and not medicalised killing was involved. But there are certain grey areas, some think. Palliative sedation is an example of this.

In 2004 a survey exploring doctors' experience with palliative sedation was sent to a representative sample of members of the NMA (1,539 doctors). Of special interest was the doctors' experience with the guidelines that had been produced by the NMA in 2001 (see section 14.2 above).[68] Included in the study were detailed case reports about some of the patients who had received this treatment subsequent to the guidelines. The results indicate that this kind of sedation is used in patients who are suffering very severely. One question concerned whether or not the sedation could have shortened the patient's life. Ninety-one per cent of the 116 respondents who had administered palliative sedation during the preceding 12 months answered that life-shortening had not occurred as a consequence of sedation. Three doctors were of the opinion that the sedation might have shortened their patient's life somewhat, the rest were uncertain because the patients were very frail.

Forgoing Medical Treatment

Decisions to forgo medical treatment resulting in the death of the patient may be clinically, emotionally and ethically difficult for a doctor, and this has not become easier after patients and patients' proxies had their voices in medical decision-making strengthened by the new Patients' Rights Act of 1999.[69] In the 1993 survey conducted among a representative sample of all Norwegian doctors, 76% of the respondents reported having prolonged the life of a patient with a terminal disease at least once when, in their opinion, it would have been more appropriate to discontinue the treatment.[70] One out of three reported having done so every now and then or more frequently. These figures make it clear that over-treatment at the end of life is a significant problem in Norway.

---

[65] Supreme Court, verdict of 14 April 2000, regarding case no 25/2000, snr. 47/1999. Dr Sandsdalen, who died in October 2000, was a board member of the Norwegian right-to-die Society '*Forengingen Ratten til en verdig død*—see <http://www.livstestament.org>, accessed 25 February 2008.

[66] See Syse 2005.

[67] See Førde, Aasland & Steen 2002; see n 61 for information on the sample.

[68] See Førde, Kongsgaard & Aasland 2006.

[69] Norwegian Patients' Rights Act 1999, available at <http://www.lovdata.no/all/hl-19990702-063.html> accessed 12 September 2007.

[70] See Førde, Aasland & Falkum 1997.

Withholding or withdrawing medical treatment is nevertheless becoming more frequent, not least in paediatrics. One Norwegian study scrutinised the medical charts of 178 seriously ill neonates who died in the period 1990–99 at one university hospital.[71] Death after withdrawal of treatment was identified in 65% of the cases; 17% died after treatment was withheld; and 19% died despite maximal treatment efforts. Parents were usually involved in the decision-making, but documentation in patient records of the decision-making process was generally poor.

14.3.2 Sweden and Denmark

Attitudes towards Euthanasia and PAS

In 1995 a questionnaire was sent to 287 Swedish doctors from specialties considered to be among the most likely to be involved in life and death decisions.[72] The questionnaire asked whether the doctors could think of a situation in which it is ethically justifiable to provide what the researchers called 'active help to die' at the patient's request. Thirty-two per cent of the doctors acknowledged that such a situation could exist, and 39% denied this. The same sample was also asked whether the law should be changed so that active help to die at the patient's request would be legal in certain instances. Half were against changing the law and a quarter were in favour. One physician out of five was undecided.

In Denmark a survey was conducted in 1995 of a random sample of 491 doctors who were members of the DMA regarding attitudes and practice towards euthanasia and PAS in the case of terminally ill cancer patients.[73] Thirty-four per cent found euthanasia (as defined above) ethically acceptable; for PAS this was 37%. Thirty-one per cent would be willing to perform euthanasia, and 33% would be willing to give PAS if it were legal.[74]

That Swedish doctors are more conservative regarding euthanasia and PAS than their Danish colleagues is confirmed in a more recent study conducted among doctors in seven European countries including Sweden and Denmark.[75] A questionnaire was sent to doctors who presumably are often involved in end-of-life decisions. Even Italian doctors were less conservative concerning euthanasia than those in Sweden. Thirty-one per cent of Swedish and 42% of Danish doctors agreed with the statement that

> A person should have the right to decide whether or not to hasten the end of his or her life.

Yet it may be remarked that it is not totally clear that this question refers only to euthanasia/PAS. The word 'hasten' in this context could be interpreted by some

---

[71] See Syvertsen & Bratlid 2004.
[72] See Nilstun *et al* 1996 (response rate 85%).
[73] See Folker *et al* 1996 (response rate 64%).
[74] See Folker *et al* 1996.
[75] See Miccinesi *et al* 2005; see for an overview of the results of this survey, ch 17, Table 17.1.

respondents to refer to the hastening of the death of terminal patients that sometimes occurs when a patient requests that life-prolonging treatment be withdrawn
or withheld.

Experience with Euthanasia and PAS

A study carried out in 1998 that drew on a random sample of 1,204 Swedish doctors registered in specialties involved in the care of dying adult patients, revealed
no case of euthanasia and only a few cases of PAS.[76] In a 1995 survey, 5% reported
that they had administered a lethal injection at the patient's request, and 2% had
assisted in a patient's suicide.[77]

The practice of Swedish and Danish doctors can be directly compared in a study
involving doctors in six European countries: the EURELD study.[78] A questionnaire was sent in 2001–02 to doctors responsible for a random sample of death certificates of people older than 1 year. In Sweden 3,248 deaths were studied, of which
36% followed some kind of end-of-life decision. Of 2,939 deaths studied in
Denmark, 41% followed some such decision. According to the respondents, none
of the deaths in Sweden and almost none in Denmark resulted from euthanasia,
and 0.23% of the deaths in Sweden and 0.79% in Denmark were a result of PAS.

Attitudes and Experience with Potentially Life-Shortening Pain Relief

The comparative study of doctors' attitudes mentioned above[79] included questions about attitudes towards pain-relieving treatment that potentially shortens
life. Ninety-two per cent of the Swedish doctors, and 98% of the Danish, found
this morally acceptable. The Danish results are in line with earlier findings by
Folker.[80]

As far as practice is concerned, the comparative EURELD study discussed
above[81] included the following question:

> Did you intensify the alleviation of pain and suffering while taking into account the pos-
> sibility or certainty that this would hasten the patient's death or partly with the intention
> of hastening the patient's death?

Unfortunately as regards the interpretation of the data, this question lumps
together the very different concepts 'possibility', 'certainty' and 'intentionality'.
Having said that, 21% of all Swedish and 26% of all Danish deaths were, according to the doctors, due to such pain relief.

The study by Valverius[82] from 1998 revealed that one-third of all Swedish
doctors had given analgesic or other drugs in such doses that, in the doctor's

---

[76] See Valverius, Nilstun and Nilsson 2000 (response rate 64%).
[77] See Folker *et al* 1996.
[78] See Van der Heide *et al* 2003; see ch17, Table 17.2.
[79] See Miccinesi *et al* 2005.
[80] See Folker *et al* 1996.
[81] See Van der Heide *et al* 2003; see ch 17, Table 17.2.
[82] See Valverius, Nilstun and Nilsson 2000.

judgment, their patients' deaths were hastened. This is more than the 10.6% found in the Norwegian study discussed above,[83] but differences in the wording of the questions make direct comparisons difficult. Folker[84] found that 12% of Danish doctors had doubled morphine dosages at fixed intervals, thus administering doses substantially higher than necessary to control pain, without the informed consent of the patient.

Forgoing Life-Sustaining Treatment

The comparative study of doctors' attitudes mentioned above,[85] included questions concerning forgoing medical treatment. Eighty-eight per cent of Swedish and 97% of Danish doctors agreed that doctors should comply with a patient's request that life-sustaining treatment be withheld or withdrawn.

In the EURELD study,[86] 14% of the Swedish deaths studied and the same proportion of the Danish ones were preceded by a non-treatment decision (not necessarily at the request of the patient).

14.4 Summary and Conclusions

Although there are some noteworthy differences in doctors' attitudes and practices regarding euthanasia and PAS across Norway, Denmark and Sweden, Scandinavian doctors are conservative in both respects.[87]

Public opinion on these issues is a different story altogether. It would appear from various studies that the population in these countries has a much more liberal attitude towards euthanasia and PAS than the medical profession, and that the acceptance of both is increasing.[88] As far as Denmark and Sweden are concerned, the European Values Survey (EVS) shows that public support for legal euthanasia is quite high (only 16% are opposed under all conditions); over the period

---

[83] See Førde, Aasland & Steen 2002.

[84] See Folker *et al* 1996.

[85] See Miccinesi *et al* 2005.

[86] See Van der Heide *et al* 2003; see ch 17, Table 17.2.

[87] As far as attitudes of medical students are concerned, Norwegian students have been surveyed three times (Vigeland 1991; Schioldborg 1999 and 2000). Vigeland 1991 found that 22% of medical students who were at least three years into their study considered euthanasia for a dying and suffering patient acceptable. Schioldborg 1999 is a follow-up to Vigeland, finding that 36% of medical students support euthanasia in cases of terminal disease. He also notes that in cases of terminal illness, younger students are less restrictive than older ones. Schioldborg 2000 finds a significant decrease in support for euthanasia among medical students: a drop to 24%.

A more recent and comprehensive study of the views of Swedish medical students and how the students arrive at and justify them (Karlsson, Strang and Milberg 2007), is methodologically very different from the three Norwegian studies and the results are therefore not directly comparable. Thirty-four per cent of the students expressed a positive opinion regarding legalisation of euthanasia, 52% were negative and 13% undetermined.

[88] See Vigeland 1997; Førde, Aasland & Nilsen 1997.

1981–99 public opinion in Denmark and the Netherlands has been the strongest in the European countries studied; support in Sweden is about the same as that in France and, since 1990, Belgium.[89]

Some complicating factors must however be mentioned in this connection. First, Norway is not included in the EVS so a direct comparison with Denmark and Sweden is not possible. Second, for a number of reasons there is uncertainty as to exactly what the EVS data reflect. These include the fact, in the authors' own words, that 'the description used in the EVS for euthanasia misses an important condition (namely that the act is 'at the explicit request of the patient')'.[90] The Norwegian study presented above has a similar flaw, as we have seen.

We think there is a further problem here, not acknowledged by the authors. The EVS uses the following formulation to explain what is meant by euthanasia: 'terminating the life of the incurably sick'. But this might include withholding or withdrawing life-prolonging treatment that has been deemed futile, since doing so might be considered to cause the patient's death.[91] Emanuel[92] reports that despite careful wording, US physicians frequently confound euthanasia and terminating life-sustaining treatment. There may well also be considerable confusion among ordinary people as to the meaning of 'terminating' in this context.

Politicians in all Scandinavian countries, both left-wing and right-wing as well as those in between, appear quite unwilling to change the law and are thus much more in line with the views of medical associations than with those of the public. At this stage, politicians do not seem to feel pressure from public opinion on these matters; quite the contrary, almost all of them seem to ignore, or not to take seriously or at least not at face value, findings in surveys indicating that the majority of citizens want a change in the law. We predict that because of the absence of political pressure, there will be no euthanasia legislation in any of the Scandinavian countries in the foreseeable future.

The challenges facing the medical profession in Scandinavia concern not so much euthanasia and PAS, but how to deal with withholding and withdrawing life-prolonging treatment in the seriously ill. Some clinicians call for more legal regulation, others for clinical guidelines as a help in the daily decision-making process. The possible involvement of clinical ethics committees, which have now been established within all hospital trusts in Norway and to a much lesser extent in the other Scandinavian countries, is also a bone of contention. Another challenge is to improve the quality of palliative care by securing adequate resources and increased knowledge of pain-relieving treatment among health care personnel.

---

[89] See ch 17, Table 17.1 and Graph 17.1.
[90] See Cohen *et al* 2006b: 667.
[91] See Materstvedt & Kaasa 2002.
[92] Emanuel 2002.

15

Spain

GRACIELA NOWENSTEIN

Spanish law allows doctors to shorten the dying process of a patient if death occurs as a consequence of treatment administered with the aim of easing her pain. It recognises a patient's right to refuse life-prolonging treatment, provides for advance treatment directives, and allows a doctor to withdraw or withhold futile treatment. Assisted suicide and euthanasia are prohibited.

Debate on these issues has been regularly re-opened in Spain since the early 1990s when, in the context of a general discussion that took place in 1995 about the reform of the Penal Code, voices were raised in favour of decriminalising euthanasia and assistance with suicide. What happens in practice is, in the absence of empirical research, difficult to say. One can read in the newspapers that clandestine cases of euthanasia occur. Such suggestions are, however, always undocumented.

Given the absence of reliable empirical information about practice, this contribution focuses on the main lines of change in legislation, on case law and on the political and public debates.

15.1 Law

The Spanish Penal Code punishes the assistance with and cooperation in 'suicide' in article 143. According to legal scholars, although the term 'euthanasia' is not used in the article, it covers euthanasia as well as assistance with suicide. Apart from this article in the Penal Code, the Spanish legal situation concerning MBPSL is structured along two lines: the duties of medical professionals and medical institutions with respect to the treatment of the dying patient on the one hand and the rights of patients on the other. Along the first line we find a duty to help and a duty to obtain consent from the patient for all interventions.[1] Along the second line we find the right of patients to refuse treatment and not to be treated in an undignified way or be submitted to 'inhuman' or 'degrading' treatment.[2]

---

[1] See Arts 195–6 of the Penal Code; health laws regulating patients' rights: Ley Básica 1986, art 10; Ley Básica 41/2002, arts 1–4.

[2] See Constitution, Arts 1 and 5; Ley Básica 41/2002, arts 1–4.

Two articles of the Penal Code impose a duty to help:[3] Article 195 applies to everyone and Article 196 to health professionals. According to article 195 help is due to a person who is in a situation of 'manifest and serious danger'. Article 196 deals with health professionals whose failure to help puts the health of a person in danger at 'serious risk'. This duty is limited, at least formally, by the patients' right to autonomy.[4] If the person to be helped does not want to be helped, Article 172 prohibits it. Nevertheless, article 20 may limit this right to autonomy as it exempts individuals acting in a state of necessity from criminal responsibility. Precisely this argument has been used to defend doctors who gave blood transfusions to patients who are Jehovah's Witnesses despite their refusal or that of their relatives.[5] At the same time, article 20, by rendering certain acts non-punishable when committed in a state of necessity, might make it possible to solve the tension between the culpability of assistance in suicide and the right of a patient not to suffer inhuman and degrading treatment, in favour of the latter.[6]

Suicide as such is not forbidden in Spanish law but, as it has been noted above, assistance with suicide is. According to the legal literature, three developments have in the last three decades affected the way in which the prohibition of assistance with suicide has evolved, both in the text of the Penal Code and in the way it is interpreted: the adoption of the democratic constitution of 1978,[7] the adoption since the mid-1980s of legislation that strengthens the legal rights of patients, and the adoption of a new Penal Code in 1995.

A foundational step in the political and cultural transition from the Franquist regime to democracy was the enactment of a new constitution in 1978. This is said to have given legitimacy to a more liberal interpretation of the prohibition of assistance with suicide. Some legal writers used the explicit value given to individual rights by the new constitution—including rights to freedom, dignity and 'free development of personality'—to effect a shift in the focus of doctrinal analysis from the culpability of those who help or assist a potential suicide toward the right of an individual to dispose over her own life.[8]

These new doctrinal approaches influenced the treatment the new Penal Code of 1995 would give to end of life issues. *The Ley Básica de Sanidad* (Basic Health Law) of 1986 was also important in this regard. This law marked a turning point in the formal recognition of patients' rights, providing in article 10 for the legal right of patients to receive information about available options, as well as the obligation of doctors to seek consent from the patient before any intervention, except in emergency cases. However, as Del Rosal Blasco notes, it remained

---

[3] So long as helping does not put the person who helps or third persons at risk.

[4] We will see below that both in case law and in more recent legislation on advance directives the duty to help may be given priority if it conflicts with the principle of autonomy of the patient.

[5] See Navarro-Michel 2005: 143.

[6] See Tomás-Valiente Lanuza 2000: 18–19.

[7] Franco died in 1975 and in 1978 the current constitution was approved.

[8] See Del Rosal Blasco 1996: 54–5. Del Rosal Blasco also notes that even before the end of the Franquist regime some legal scholars had criticised the fact that the Penal Code did not take into consideration the motives of a person who gives assistance with suicide, treating assistance with suicide in euthanatic cases as common homicide (Del Rosal Blasco 1996: 52–3).

unclear whether a patient had a right to refuse treatment even when such refusal could expose her to the risk of 'irreversible' injuries or death.[9]

This was the legal background against which the discussions that preceded the enactment of the new Penal Code took place. Drafts had been produced in 1990, 1992 and 1994 and along the way questions were raised in Parliament,[10] opinion articles written in newspapers[11] and petitions published. In December 1984 the association *Derecho a Morir Dignamente* (Right to a Dignified Death) was founded.[12] In 1991 and 1993 an association of criminal lawyers and legal scholars, *Grupo de Estudios de Política Criminal*, produced two documents that were signed by a number of politically important legal professionals.[13] The first, *Manifiesto a favor de la disponibilidad de la propia vida* (1991), proposed to reform the Penal Code to make it lawful for a doctor (i) to withhold or withdraw treatment that would 'artificially' prolong the suffering of a dying patient; (ii) to administer analgesic drugs to a patient with a terminal prognosis even if this would hasten her death; (iii) to cause the death of a person at the latter's express and serious request in order to end 'a situation of suffering or of pain, serious and irreversible, no longer bearable for the subject, which could be suppressed in no other way.'

The second document, *Propuesta alternativa al tratamiento jurídico de las conductas de terceros relativas a la disponibilidad de la propia* vida (1993), was a more complete and legally detailed proposal. It contained a draft of a proposed article which proposed (1) that causing the death of a competent person over 18 who has made an 'express, free and serious' request for this should remain a criminal offence but be punished with the minimum applicable penalty; (2) that in such cases 'omissive' behaviour should not be illegal; (3) that a doctor (or 'any person under her supervision') should not be punishable for causing death in response to an 'express, free and serious' request made by a competent person above 18, whose severe and otherwise untreatable suffering derives from an incurable condition that will soon lead to death or permanent and general incapacity.[14] It would also

---

[9] See Del Rosal Blasco 1996: 46–7.

[10] According to information on the website of the Spanish Parliament <http://www.congreso.es> accessed 10 September 2007, MPs raised the issue of euthanasia as part of the reform of the Penal Code in 1988, 1991, 1992 and 1994.

[11] See eg the opinion article published by the vice-president of the association Derecho a Morir Dignamente, who expressed concern that the reform was not going to fulfil what she considered to be the expectations of the majority of the population for the recognition of a right to euthanasia: *El País* (2 March 1994) 'La eutanasia, ¿en lista de espera?'

[12] The first mention one finds of DMD in the archives of the newspaper *El País*—which allow research from 1976 onward—is on 11 December 1984 in a letter to the editor under the title 'Morir dignamente'. Until the mid-1990s there are only rare references (1 in 1986, 2 in 1988, 1 in 1991, 1 in 1993 and 1 in 1994).

[13] Both texts are quoted as annexes in Díez Ripollés & Muñoz Sánchez 1996.

[14] See Díez Ripollés & Muñoz Sánchez 1996: 620. The text reads:

No será punible la producción de la muerte de otro por parte de un médico o de cualquier otra persona bajo su dirección, si media la solicitud expresa, libre y seria de una persona mayor de 18 años que tenga capacidad natural de juicio, siempre que ésta padezca graves sufrimientos no evitables ni notoriamente atenuables de otro modo y que se deriven de una afección incurable que le conducirá próximamente a la muerte o que, siendo permanente, le incapacita de manera generalizada para valerse por sí misma.

not have been necessary to secure the consent of the patient, of her relatives or of her legal representative to withhold or withdraw treatment that only contributes to prolong a life with irreversible lost of consciousness or to 'artificially' prolong life in an 'irreversible process of dying'. This last provision also applied to newborn babies whose life is maintained by the 'massive and permanent use' of intensive care treatment and machines.

In the end, the new Penal Code maintained in article 143 the prohibition of assistance [*cooperación*] in suicide but it did introduce distinctions between different types of assistance. Article 143 begins with incitement to suicide (Art 143.1) which it punishes more severely, with 4 to 8 years of imprisonment, than 'cooperation' with suicide (Art 143.2), punished with 2 to 5 years of imprisonment. If the cooperation goes as far as to cause death (Art 143.3) imprisonment is from 6 to 10 years.[15] Article 143.4 in effect prohibits euthanasia and provides for lesser punishments than those in articles 143.2 and 143.3, if the assistance was given in response to an 'express, serious and unequivocal request' made by a person who 'was suffering from a serious condition that would necessarily lead to her death, or that would cause suffering that was permanent and difficult to bear.'[16] Commenting on article 143.4 in an interview in 2000, Juan Alberto Belloch, Minister of Justice when the new Penal Code was adopted, noted that it marked a turning point in the legislative treatment of end-of-life questions. By subjecting 'active and direct' euthanasia to a fairly limited sanction, he said, the legislator had enabled the courts to punish doctors with short punishments that would not necessarily involve imprisonment.[17] This is because for punishments under 2 years of imprisonment Spanish law allows the court to 'suspend' imprisonment or to substitute weekend arrest or a fine.[18] The turning point Belloch points to was made possible, Tomás-Valiente Lanuza notes, because the new Penal Code introduces distinctions between sorts of homicide that did not exist in the old code (which had not gone further than permitting a reduced punishment for cases of euthanasia based on the idea of a state of necessity). The new code, she writes, distinguishes between 'ordinary', 'consensual' and 'euthanatic' homicide and subjects them to different punishments.[19]

---

[15] This penalty must be compared to that of homicide which in Art 138 imposes penalties between 10 and 15 years.

[16] Here is Art 143 of the new code in full:

1. El que induzca al suicidio de otro será castigado con la pena de prisión de cuatro a ocho años.
2. Se impondrá la pena de prisión de dos a cinco años al que coopere con actos necesarios al suicidio de una persona.
3. Será castigado con la pena de prisión de seis a diez años si la cooperación llegara hasta el punto de ejecutar la muerte.
4. El que causare o cooperare activamente con actos necesarios y directos a la muerte de otro, por la petición expresa, seria e inequívoca de éste, en el caso de que la víctima sufriera una enfermedad grave que conduciría necesariamente a su muerte, o que produjera graves padecimientos permanentes y difíciles de soportar, será castigado con la pena inferior en uno o dos grados a las señaladas en los números 2 y 3 de este artículo.

[17] See Fibla 2000: 110.
[18] See Tomás-Valiente Lanuza 2000: 137.
[19] See Tomás-Valiente Lanuza 2000: 23–4.

The third turning point in this history seems to have been Spain's adherence in 1997 to the Oviedo Convention,[20] which came into force in Spain in 2000. According to Navarro-Michel, this 'triggered an avalanche of laws' in the field of advance treatment directives.[21] Legal development in this area is complicated in Spain because of the federal structure of the Spanish state.[22] Laws on advance treatment directives have been enacted at both the regional and national levels.[23] This is not the place to treat the various laws on such directives in detail.[24] It suffices to note that, according to Navarro-Michel, these laws do not really amount to a very big step toward greater patient autonomy. According to her analysis, with the exception of the Balearic Islands,[25] the refusal contained in an advance directive is not binding on a doctor if,

> it is contrary to 'sound medical practice', or '*lex artis*' . . . or 'professional ethics' . . . or 'better scientific evidence' . . . or gives 'instructions incompatible with . . . [the patient's] pathology' . . . The terms vary in the different statutory regulations. The issue is essentially the same.[26]

Advance directives in Spanish law thus amount on the whole to what Vezzoni calls 'may' directives: doctors are supposed to take them into consideration and are protected from legal liability if they do so, but they are not *legally bound* to follow them.[27]

The courts have gone further, limiting the right of a competent patient to refuse treatment and protecting doctors and medical institutions that impose life-saving treatments against the will of a patient or her relatives. The literature[28] refers to two sorts of cases in which the refusal of treatment by the patient has not been

[20] This is the name under which the European Council's Convention for the Protection of Human Rights and Dignity of the Human Being with regard to the Application of Biology and Medicine is usually referred to.

[21] See Navarro-Michel 2005: 138.

[22] Spain has a central government and 17 autonomous communities that enjoy different levels of autonomy including specific legislative and political competences. See Merino-Blanco 2006.

[23] In chronological order: Catalonia, law 21/2000, 29 December 2000; 3/2001, 28 May 2001; Galicia, law 10/2001, 28 June 2001; 3/2005, 7 March 2005; Extremadura, law 6/2002, 15 April 2002; 3/2005, 8 July 2005; Aragon, decree 100/2003, 6 May 2003; Navarra, law 11/2002, 6 June 2002; 29/2003, 4 April 2003; Ley Básica 41/2002, 14 November 2002; Cantabria, law 7/2002, 10 December 2002; Basque Region, law 7/2002, 12 December 2002; decree 270/2003, 4 November 2003; Valencia, law 1/2003, 28 January 2003; Balearic Islands, law 2/2003, 4 April 2003; Castilla y Leon, law 8/2003, 8 April 2003; Andalusia, law 5/2003, 9 October 2003; Madrid, law 3/2005, 23 May 2005; Castilla la Mancha, law 6/2005, 7 July 2005; decree 15/2006, 21 February 2006; Murcia, decree 80/2005, 8 July 2005; La Rioja, law 9/2005, 30 September 2005; Canary Islands, decree 13/2006, 8 February 2006.

[24] For an exhaustive presentation on the situation of advance directives in Spain see Navarro-Michel 2005.

[25] At the time Navarro-Michel wrote her article, neither the Principado de Asturias, Murcia, La Rioja nor the Canary Islands had enacted legislation on advance treatment directives. According to the association Derecho a Morir Dignamente (DMD), in early 2007 the Principado de Asturias was the only region still in that situation <http://www.eutanasia.ws/dmdTVEspana.html> accessed 22 June 2007.

[26] See Navarro-Michel 2005: 161 (referring to State Act 41/2002, art 11; Community of Madrid, art 28; Navarra Act, art 9; Basque Region Act, art 5).

[27] See Vezzoni 2008: 23.

[28] See eg Del Rosal Blasco 1996: 58–60; Navarro-Michel 2005: 143.

respected. The courts have allowed the forced feeding of inmates on hunger strike whose lives were said to be at risk, based on the special duties of the prison administration to protect the lives of inmates. Had these been normal citizens, it was argued, the same behaviour would not have been legal.[29] The second type of case involves doctors who sought judicial authorisation to proceed with blood transfusions for—or defended ex post the imposition of blood transfusions on—Jehovah's Witnesses who refused transfusions or whose relatives did so on their behalf. Decisions against Jehovah's Witnesses have been justified by invoking the duty to help and a state of necessity in which the doctor was forced to act.[30] The problem with case law in Spain, as Tomás-Valiente Lanuza notes, is that cases in the field of euthanasia, assistance in suicide and refusal of treatment are so few and far between that it is difficult to draw general conclusions. The difficulties are aggravated, she notes, since the cases of inmates on hunger strike are substantially different from the 'normal' case of a free citizen who refuses treatment.[31]

Finally, there is the code of medical ethics of the *Organización Médical Colegial* (OMC).[32] It has a section 'On Death' that condemns 'hopeless, useless and obstinate' treatment; states that when nothing can be done to cure the patient or to improve her state it is the doctor's obligation to 'use adequate measures to secure the patient's wellbeing', even if this has the consequence of shortening her life; and prohibits a doctor from doing anything with the aim of causing the death of a patient, even in the case of an express request by the patient.[33]

In December 2004, the president of the OMC published a letter in the OMC newsletter, in which he defined euthanasia as 'the deliberate act of ending life, at the request of a person or a relative.'[34] He discussed the rights of the terminal patient, giving a key position to the patient's right to autonomy, including the right to refuse 'diagnostic procedures, treatment or feeding' as well as the right to decide whether vital support is to be withdrawn or not initiated.

In April 2005, reacting to a criminal investigation of the doctors of a hospital in the town of Leganés who were accused of having practised illegal terminal sedation (see section 15.4), the OMC issued a joint declaration with other Spanish medical

---

[29] Tribunal Constitucional 120/190. Del Rosal Blasco (1995: 58–60) notes that some local courts decided in favour of inmates' rights not to be fed against their will, but that those decisions were reversed on appeal. All cases have concerned prisoners from political groups engaged in terrorist activities—Grapo and ETA. The last decision on one of these cases was taken in January 2007 (Auto de la Audiencia Nacional, Sala de lo penal, 25 January 2007) against an ETA inmate on a hunger strike. The tribunal decided that it was legal to feed him by force since the judges considered that he had put his life at risk.

[30] Tribunal Constitucional 369/184.

[31] See Tomás-Valiente Lanuza 2000: 31–6.

[32] The OMC is the national society of physicians and the official voice of the medical profession. It represents all of the regional and local medical societies of the country. It enjoys disciplinary and regulatory power (see Real Decreto 757/2006). Real Decreto 1018/1980 gives disciplinary authority for violations of the Code of Deontology to provincial medical associations (art. 34). The maximum sanction is suspension from professional practice (see Real Decreto 1018/1980; see also Pastor Muñoz 2007: 239–40).

[33] Available online at <http://www.cgcom.org/pdf/Codigo.pdf> accessed September 2007.

[34] See Sierra Arredondo 2004.

societies insisting on drawing a conceptual, moral and legal distinction between 'euthanasia' (not acceptable) and 'terminal sedation' (legally and ethically acceptable).[35] The statement stressed 'there is no relation whatsoever between terminal sedation and euthanasia', and that the confusion between the two in the public debate was causing unfair damage to the prestige of medical institutions.

15.2 Medical Practice

Although one sees from time to time suggestions that euthanasia in fact exists in Spain as a clandestine practice,[36] very little of any reliability is actually known about euthanasia or any other MBPSL practice. A national survey on palliative care was conducted in 2000 with 2,500 respondents, including doctors, nurses, relatives of patients who had died of cancer, and members of the general public.[37] Sixty-five per cent of doctors and 85% of nurses declared that they had received requests from patients to hasten the moment of death, either by withdrawing or withholding treatment or by 'active euthanasia' or 'assisted suicide'. Twenty-one per cent of the doctors 'acknowledged' that such hastening 'takes place' and more than 16% of relatives of deceased patients responded that they believed that the moment of the death of their relative had been hastened. Such data, however, do not tell us how much euthanasia is taking place, when and where it takes place, who is involved, and so forth. Research is needed to assess such questions.

In the absence of empirical data the remainder of this chapter focuses on public and professional opinion, on the public debate, and on the actors and institutions that play a prominent role in the debate (politicians, political parties, the national medical organisation, ethics committees, the Spanish Catholic Church and the association *Derecho a Morir Dignamente*).

15.3 Public and Medical Opinion

The methodological and theoretical problems inherent in public opinion surveys are mentioned in chapter 17.1 section 4.2. While it is difficult for a variety of

---

[35] The expression 'terminal sedation' applies in this statement to the last days of a terminal situation in conditions of unbearable and uncontrollable suffering when no therapeutic options are available; it is considered acceptable both ethically and legally. *Declaración conjunta de la Organización Médica Colegial (OMC), y las Sociedades Científicas Españolas de Cuidados Paliativos (SECPAL), Oncología Médica (SEOM), Geriatría y Gerontología (SEGG), Medicina de Urgencias y Emergencias (SEMES).* Available online at <http://www.cgcom.es> accessed 27 September 2007.

[36] See eg 'El 65% de los médicos españoles ha recibido peticiones de eutanasia,' *El Mundo* (30 November 2000).

[37] See Organización de Consumidores y Usuarios 2000.

reasons to say that a particular public opinion on the issues surrounding medical behaviour that potentially shortens life 'exists' and that we know what it is and what significance it may have, the fact is that reference to public opinion is omnipresent in the Spanish public discussion, where participants regularly claim to speak in its name and use surveys to legitimise their positions. 'Public opinion' as constructed in surveys being an important point of reference in public discussions, it is useful to look briefly at the information produced by these surveys.

Using the results of the European Values Survey, Cohen and others write that support for the legalisation of euthanasia in Spain increased significantly between 1981 and 1999.[38] The question asked to a representative sample of the Spanish population in 1981, 1990 and 1999 was: 'Please tell me whether you think euthanasia (terminating the life of the incurably sick) can always be justified, never justified, or something in between.' Respondents were asked to answer on a scale from 1 to 10, from 'never justified' to 'always justified', or to answer 'I don't know'. The answers for the three years indicated a substantial increase in the level of positive opinions, although in 1999 this remained below 5, that is to say, still fairly low relative to other European countries.[39]

Another survey, conducted in 1992 by the *Centro de Investigaciones Sociológicas* and using more precisely formulated questions seems to show stronger support for the legalisation of euthanasia.[40] Two questions were asked to a representative sample of the population (see Table 15.1).

While both surveys purport to be about 'euthanasia', the European Values Survey is vague and general—it does not limit the behaviour concerned to doctors, nor does it specify whether a request for euthanasia would have to be made by patients (and/or their relatives). It seems nonetheless reasonable to conclude that the available surveys reflect an evolution in the views of the respondents since the early 1980s: more people seem to be inclined, as time passes, to respond positively to questions about the legalisation of 'euthanasia'. This noted, however, the level of negative opinions is read by the present Government as consistent enough to suggest the general public is not yet 'ready' for an open and general debate.

Table 15.1. Public support for legalisation of euthanasia in Spain (1992)

When a person suffers from an incurable condition that is causing her grave suffering, do you think that the law should allow her treating doctors to end her life and suffering at her request?

Yes	No	Don't know
66%	22%	22%

And when the person who suffers from an incurable condition and grave suffering cannot request it, but her relatives do, do you think the law should allow it?

Yes	No	Don't know
49%	33%	17%

[38] See Cohen *et al* 2006a. See ch 17.1, Table 17.1 and Graph 17.1, for an overview of the findings.
[39] Response rate 31%; N = 1,200.
[40] See Centro de Investigaciones Sociológicas 1992.

The first time Spanish doctors seem to have been surveyed with regard to their views concerning the legalisation of euthanasia was more than a decade ago, and the results were strongly negative. In 1996, drawing on a national survey from 1994, Stangeland wrote that the medical profession seemed to be massively opposed to the legalisation of euthanasia: only 1 out of 10 doctors had answered positively.[41] A survey conducted in 2002 could be read as a confirmation of Stangeland's conclusion. Although the results were more balanced than in 1994—the frequency of positive answers having increased four-fold—the majority of respondents were not in favour of legalisation of euthanasia (see Table 15.2).[42]

It seems that more than half of the respondents were against the legalisation of euthanasia or assisted suicide. The answers to another question, asked later in the same survey, can however be read as contradicting the idea that doctors were consistently opposed to the legalisation of euthanasia or assisted suicide (Table 15.3).

Table 15.2. Medical opinion concerning legalisation of euthanasia and PAS, 2002 (question 9)

A patient suffering from an incurable and painful illness and who is close to death asks her doctor to hasten the moment of her death. In your opinion, the law should authorise

• the doctor to give a lethal dose of a drug to the patient so that she can end her life herself	21.5
• the doctor to administer a lethal dose of a drug to the patient	21.6
Neither of these	50.7
Don't know	3.7
No answer	2.6
N	1,057

Table 15.3. Medical opinion concerning legalisation of euthanasia and PAS, 2002 (question 19)

Do you think that the law should be changed to allow patients to request and receive from a doctor assisted suicide and/or active euthanasia?

Yes, but only for terminal patients with all their mental faculties intact	41.5
Yes, but only for patients with all their mental faculties intact, whether or not their illness is terminal or chronic (serious or irreversible)	18.4
No	31.4
Don't know	5.4
No answer	3.3
N	1,057

[41] See Stangeland 1996: 32. The results of the survey he refers to were published in *Al Día, Información médica profesional*, vol XL VI, no1073, pp 763–4, March 1994.

[42] See Centro de Investigaciones Sociológicas 2002.

From a methodological perspective this last question deserves criticism, since two questions are being asked at once: about assisted suicide and about euthanasia. Besides both questions assume that assisted suicide or euthanasia would be performed by doctors. It is possible that some respondents would be in favour of legalising active euthanasia or assisted suicide, but not in favour of doctors being involved. The president of the OMC made precisely this point in the article referred to at the end of section 15.1, where he argued that the question of euthanasia is a socio-political, not a medical one, and that, if assistance in suicide were to be legalised, doctors should not be involved in the practice. There is, he concluded, no need to be a doctor to be able to help someone to die peacefully: 'any citizen can do it, we [doctors] have been taught to preserve life.'[43]

We can probably safely conclude from the 2002 survey (in particular from the answers to question 19) that it is no longer the case that a clear majority of doctors opposes the legalisation of euthanasia and assisted suicide and that the profession seems to be equally divided between opponents and supporters of a reform in the direction of legalisation. If legalisation were limited to assisted suicide, and if the principal responsibility were not placed on doctors, it might well be that a majority would now be in favour.

15.4 Criminal Prosecutions and the Public and Political Debate

Analysis of the main national newspapers (*El País, El Mundo, ABC, La Vanguardia*) reveals that public debate on euthanasia and related MBPSL got properly under way in 1993 and has since regularly revived as new cases are reported, either of patients requesting help to end their lives or of patients found dead after having apparently been helped in accomplishing their wish to die. Neither of the two main national parties seems willing to take action on euthanasia, although the socialist party (PSOE) is not opposed to decriminalisation in principle whereas the right-wing Popular Party (PP) is. Further to the left, *Izquierda Unida* is explicitly in favour of legalisation, as are some regional parties, such as the Catalan *Esquerra Republicana de Catalunya*. The strongest opposition to legalisation of euthanasia is that expressed regularly by the Catholic Church through its official voice, the *Conferencia Episcopal Española*. However, as we will see below, in 2005 an ethics committee linked to a Catholic university opened a breach in the unity of the public Catholic voice. Two other major non-Catholic ethics committees have also recently issued statements in support of the decriminalisation of euthanasia. (It is worth noting that all these ethics committees are Catalan.)

---

[43] See Sierra Arredondo 2004.

Let us look first at the cases around which the public discussion has developed and the political and judicial responses these cases received.

The *Sampedro* Case

In July 1993 and in February 1994 the media reported the rejection by two courts in Barcelona of a request to be allowed assistance in dying made by Ramón Sampedro, a man who had been paralysed from the neck down since 1968 when he hit his head while diving in the sea. It was reported that he had legal support from the association *Derecho a Morir Dignamente* (DMD).[44] He asked the courts to guarantee the immunity of his doctor if the latter helped him to end his life.[45] This was apparently the first request of this kind presented to a Spanish court. Both courts rejected the request on grounds of lack of territorial jurisdiction—Sampedro was a resident of the region of Galicia and not of Catalonia where the case was brought.[46] The media reported that in the first decision the court also referred to the above-mentioned decision of 1990 of the *Tribunal Constitucional* which held that inmates engaged in a hunger strike can be fed against their will because of the duty of the state to protect human life.[47] In the second decision, it was reported, the prosecutor argued that although Sampedro's request was for a 'dignified death', since his condition was not terminal what he was asking for was assistance in suicide, prohibited in article 409 of the then Penal Code. The prosecutor added that, on the occasion of the revision of the Penal Code, the legislature might consider adapting the new text to the evolution of 'sensitivities' in Spanish society.[48] Sampedro then brought the case to the *Tribunal Constitucional* which rejected his request in July 1994.[49]

In March 1994, in the context of the ongoing discussion about reform of the Penal Code, the Minister of Justice of the then PSOE government responded in Parliament to a question asked by an MP about the desirability of opening the political debate on euthanasia and of introducing reforms in the new Penal Code. The minister responded that although public surveys had shown increasing public support for the legalisation of euthanasia, the Government would not introduce a proposal to do so; it preferred to reduce the punishment[50]—as indeed happened when article 143 replaced article 409 of the old code.

On 12 January 1998 Sampedro was found dead in his flat.[51] A judicial investigation was begun to find who had given him assistance, namely who procured the

---

[44] See eg *El País* (8 July 1993), 'Un enfermo pide al juez que le deje morir'; *El País* (17 February 1994), 'El fiscal rechaza que se ayude a morir a un inválido, pero pide que se regule la eutanasia'.

[45] See Navarro-Michel 2005: 145.

[46] See Del Rosal Blasco 1996: 60.

[47] *El País* (8 July 1993), 'Un enfermo pide al juez que le deje morir'.

[48] *El País* (17 February 1994), 'El fiscal rechaza que se ayude a morir a un inválido, pero pide que se regule la eutanasia'.

[49] ATC 931/1994.

[50] Diario de Sesiones, Congreso de los Diputados, No 56, 10 March 1994; see also *El País* 10/03/1994, 'El Gobierno considera "insatisfactoria" la actual regulación del derecho a practicar la eutanasia activa'.

[51] *El País* (13 January 1998), 'Muere Ramón Sampedro, el tetrapléjico que reclamó sin éxito su derecho a la eutanasia'.

cyanide that killed him, who put it in a glass of water, and who put this glass with a straw in reach of his lips. Ramona Maneiro, the woman with whom Sampedro was living at the end of his life, was charged. In the weeks that followed, DMD gathered 13,000 signatures of persons who claimed to have participated in Sampedro's death,[52] among them members of the regional parliaments of Catalonia and Galicia.[53] The PSOE—in opposition since 1996—called for the appointment of a special commission to study the problem. The commission began working in the Senate in March 1998,[54] sat until 2000, and conducted a number of hearings without however making any proposals for legislative change. Another consequence of Sampedro's death was that in November 1998 the *Tribunal Constitucional* closed the new request he had brought to this tribunal in July 1996 without judgment.[55]

The PSOE remained in opposition until the general election of March 2004. The programme with which it conducted its electoral campaign had a section on 'Civil Rights' which included a paragraph under the title 'Euthanasia'.[56] It did not argue in favour of new legislation, but instead called for a parliamentary debate. In September 2004 the new PSOE Prime Minister Zapatero and 6 of his ministers attended the première of the movie *Mar adentro*, which tells the story of Sampedro.[57] Nevertheless, the Minister of Justice, the Secretary General of PSOE, the Minister of Health and Prime Minister Zapatero have since their return to power repeatedly stated that euthanasia is not on the Government's parliamentary agenda for the time being. Such statements usually come in response to news accounts of new cases or at moments when tension between the Government and the Catholic Church has increased.

From the beginning of Zapatero's term in March 2004 his Government has had recurring moments of tension with the Catholic Church. Within a few months of taking office, the Government was engaged in three legislative reforms strongly opposed by the Church: legalisation of same sex marriages, simplification of divorce procedure and limitation of the place of religious education in schools. In this context, most newspapers observed that it would seem that the Government and the PSOE had decided to subordinate their support for reform concerning euthanasia to a general strategy of managing relations with the Catholic authorities.

---

[52] *El País* (17 June 1998), '13000 españoles se autoinculpan de la muerte de Sampedro'.

[53] *El País* (14 February 1998), '72 diputados de Cataluña se culpan de la muerte de Ramón Sampedro'.

[54] Comisión Especial de Estudio sobre la Eutanasia, BOCG, Senado, Serie I, 23 February 1998, No 393.

[55] See ATC 242/1998.

[56] The topics raised under the title Civil Rights were (in this order): 'Right to civil marriage' for same sex couples, 'Right to sexual identity' (acknowledgement of the right to formal change of sexual identity and to surgical change of sex), 'Rights of non-married couples', 'Separation and divorce' (acceleration and simplification of divorce procedures), 'Euthanasia', 'Right to intimacy'. Programme available online at <http://www.puedoprometeryprometo.com/descargas/psoe_programa.pdf> accessed 11 September 2007.

[57] *El Mundo* (3 September 2004), 'Zapatero y seis ministros del Gobierno arropan a Amenábar en el estreno de "Mar adentro"'.

In January 2005 Sampedro's case was back in the public arena. Ramona Maneiro, the woman who had been charged with assisting in his suicide and then discharged for lack of evidence, acknowledged in a TV programme that she was the one who had put the lethal dose of cyanide in reach of Sampedro's lips. She recounted having put the quantity of cyanide that Sampedro indicated in a glass of water, having then placed the straw where he asked her to, and finally having turned a video recorder on to film the scene as he wanted. She added that she had then stayed behind the camera and waited.[58] Since the statute of limitations had run out in November 2004, she could no longer be prosecuted. Asked about the Government's position on 'euthanasia' in relation to Maneiro's confession, the Minister of Health confirmed that it was not on the Government's agenda: 'the Government has stated on various occasions that it has no intention to regulate euthanasia.'[59]

The *Leganés* Case

In March 2005 the Minister of Health of the autonomous community of Madrid revealed in a press conference that he had received complaints about a large number of cases of 'abusive sedation' having taken place in a public hospital in the town of Leganés.[60] The whole affair became highly politicised when the central government (PSOE) criticised the way in which the government of the community of Madrid (PP) was handling the situation[61] and several public demonstrations supporting the accused doctors took place.[62] The doctors were accused of having palliatively sedated patients, without having sought appropriate consent, without a medical indication and without having followed the standard procedures.[63] In June 2007 the instructing phase of the investigation ended with the conclusion that there was not enough evidence to charge the doctors criminally. In its decision the tribunal insisted that although there were, according to judicial-medical expertise, consistent signs of improper practice in the 15 cases they assessed (eg incomplete patient files, decisions to sedate taken without having done all the necessary tests to confirm the absence of therapeutic options, available therapeutic

---

[58] *El País* (11 January 2005), 'Una amiga de Sampedro confiesa que fue "la mano" que le ayudó a morir'. In May of 2005 *El País* published an excerpt of the book *Querido Ramón* Maneiro had just published. The article included one paragraph where Sampedro's death was depicted as very painful for both of them: physically for him, psychologically for her. She wrote that she had expected it to happen smoothly but that he had convulsions. At some point she could no longer stand it and left the room to go to the bathroom, from where she could still hear him moan. She added that she lost the sense of time guessing that it lasted for a few minutes which felt like 'eternity' for her. See *El País* (15 May 2005), 'Ramona Maneiro cuenta en "Querido Ramón" cómo ayudó a morir al tetrapléjico Ramón Sampedro'.

[59] *El País* (11 February 2005), 'El delito de auxilio al suicidio prescribió en noviembre'.

[60] *La Vanguardia* (22 March 2005), 'Cesada la dirección de un hospital de Leganés tras hallarse irregularidades administrativas'.

[61] *El País* (6 April 2006), 'Salgado afirma que el Gobierno madrileño "ha fallado" al afrontar la crisis'.

[62] *El País* (4 March 2006),'Miles de personas salen en defensa de los médicos de Leganés'.

[63] *El Mundo* (15 February 2007), 'El juez investigará otras 29 muertes dudosas'.

options not tried before sedation, inconsistencies between doctors' decisions on
the treatment of the same patient), the decision to close the investigation with no
charges against the doctors was due to the lack of sufficient evidence to establish a
criminal offence. It was impossible, it was argued, to ascertain 'with absolute certainty that the direct cause of death had been the medication administered.' Last
but not least, the judge concluded from hearing the doctors under investigation
that, at the time when the events investigated had taken place, they

> believed . . . that they were acting legally and according to standards of medical science.
> They understood that their patients would die in a very short time and that they had to
> relieve their pain. Faced with this situation, they decided to sedate and obtained what
> they had aimed at, which was nothing else than the expected death, yet painless.[64]

The *Léon* Case

In May 2006 a new case with similarities to the *Sampedro* case caught the attention
of the media and brought the issue of assisted suicide back into the public arena.
Jorge León had been paralysed from the neck down since 2000. Unable to breathe
by himself, he was continuously connected to an artificial respirator. On 4 May the
police found him dead in his home. Forensic experts established that he had died
as a consequence of the respirator having been switched off.[65] Once again the
Minister of Health stated publicly that the Government did not consider that the
time had come for a public debate on 'euthanasia' and that it was focusing its
attention on the development of palliative care.[66] In September 2006 the court in
charge of the case closed it due to lack of evidence concerning the person who presumably had disconnected the respirator.[67]

The *Echevarría* Case

Yet another case attracted public attention between October 2006 and March
2007. Inmaculada Echevarría, a woman suffering from muscular dystrophy,
organised a press conference at the hospital in Granada where she was being
treated. She had been confined to bed for the last 20 years and had needed a respi-

---

[64] Auto del Juzgado de primera instancia e instrucción número 7 de Leganés (Madrid), 20 June
2007, DDP t núm 661/2005. See for reports in the media: *El Mundo* (22 June 2007), 'El juez archiva el
caso de las sedaciones en el Severo Ochoa aunque ve 'mala praxis'; *La Vanguardia* (22 June 2007), 'El
juez sobresee el caso de las presuntas sedaciones irregulares en el Severo Ochoa de Leganés'; *El País* (23
June 2007), 'Punto final en Leganés'.

[65] *El País* (7 May 2006), 'El pentapléjico muerto en Valladolid había reclamado que se le facilitara la
eutanasia'.

[66] *El Mundo* (8 May 2006), 'Sanidad considera que el debate político de la eutanasia "no corre-
sponde ahora"'; *El País* (8 May 2006), 'El Gobierno insiste en descartar cualquier regulación de la
eutanasia'. On the development of palliative care policies in Spain since 1990 see the data provided by
the Ministry of Health at <http://www.msc.es/organizacion/sns/planCalidadSNS> accessed 10
September 2007).

[67] *ABC* (23 September 2006), 'La juez archiva las diligencias por la muerte del pentapléjico Jorge
León "por falta de autor conocido"'; *El País* (18 October 2006), 'Los jueces archivan la causa por la
muerte del tetraléjico de Valladolid'.

rator for the last 9. She stated that she wanted to die, to do so with no pain, and to be given the assistance she needed to accomplish this.[68] Supported by her lawyer and later by some legal scholars, she stated that she was not requesting 'euthanasia', but rather insisting on her right to refuse treatment, under the existing law on the autonomy of patients. Once again, the Government made clear that it did not plan for the legislature to deal with the questions of euthanasia or assisted suicide.[69] In February 2007 the ethics committee of the autonomous region of Andalusia rendered an opinion supporting Echevarría's request to have her respirator switched off, arguing that she was entitled, by the law on the autonomy of patients, to reject treatment. The report also indicated that the withdrawal of respiratory assistance should be preceded by profound sedation so as to prevent her from suffering. A member of the committee was reported to have declared to the media that the decision was not only in accord with medical ethics, but also with Catholic moral theology, that condemns the use of futile treatment [*encarnizamiento terapéutico*].[70] She died on 14 March after having been moved to another hospital because the hospital were she was treated at the time of the decision was run by a Catholic order which asked her medical team to move with her to another centre before disconnecting the respirator.[71]

Madeleine Z

The most recent case reported by the media was that of Madeleine Z, a woman suffering from amyotrophic lateral sclerosis who had decided that she wanted to end her life. She is reported to have committed suicide on 12 January 2007, with no material help, although accompanied before and during her suicide by two members of DMD. Journalists from *El País* had had several conversations with her during the weeks that preceded her suicide and published a long article the day after her death.[72] The article gave her reasons for having committed suicide and quoted the volunteers who had accompanied her. Shortly thereafter a judicial investigation was opened, it was reported, 'as always in cases of unnatural death'.[73]

---

[68] *El Mundo* (19 October 2006), 'Inmaculada Echevarría, tetrapléjica: 'Lo único que pido es la eutanasia, no es justo vivir así''; *El País* (18 October 2006), 'Una enferma de 51 años pide una inyección que le pare el corazón'.

[69] *El País* (19 October 2006), 'El Gobierno se inhibe'.

[70] *La Vanguardia* (2 February 2007), 'El Gobierno andaluz avala la retirada del respirador de una enferma que pide morir'. 'Futile treatment' is the expression in English (and Dutch) for what in Latin countries (France, Italy, Spain) is called 'therapeutic obstinacy'.

[71] *El Mundo* (15 March 2007), 'Inmaculada Echevarría, una vida en una cama'.

[72] *El País* (19 January 2007), 'Madeleine Z., una decisión muy meditada'.

[73] *El Mundo* (17 January 2007), 'Un juez investiga el caso de una mujer que murió junto a varios voluntarios proeutanasia'. The normal procedure when a person dies is that if the attending doctor considers the death 'natural' she issues a death certificate giving the apparent causes of death. The doctor does not issue a death certificate but must report the case to the judicial authorities if she suspects death has been 'violent' or caused by a criminal act [*en casos de muerte violenta o sospechosos de criminalidad*]. See Organización Médica Colegial, 'Declaración sobre las cualidades del certificado médico y sobre sus diferencias con los partes y los informes médicos. Peculiaridades del certificado médico de defunción', 26 January 2007, available online at <http://www.cgcom.org/deonto/pdf/07_01_26_certificados.pdf> accessed 10 September 2007.

The cases briefly sketched above—*Sampedro, León, Leganés, Echevarría* and *Madeleine Z*—have afforded the rhythm of the public discussion on euthanasia and assisted suicide in Spain. The responses of political parties and persons in the Government have been—whether for pragmatic or for principled reasons—that the law as it is since the reform of the Penal Code in 1995 should remain unchanged. As we have already seen, the Spanish Medical Organisation (OMC) seems to espouse a similar position, that is, a reluctance to decriminalise medical behaviour that shortens life other than withdrawal or withholding of futile treatment, or pain relief with life-shortening effect.

15.5 The Position of the Spanish Catholic Church[74]

We turn now to the Catholic Church, an institution that plays a prominent role in public discussions of euthanasia and related matters. I have mentioned earlier that the position with regard to euthanasia and assisted suicide of Zapatero's PSOE Government must be at least partly understood as part of a larger strategy of management of the Government's relations with the Church, a strategy that goes beyond the issues treated here. This relationship has regularly been put under strain by disagreements around issues such as same sex marriage, divorce and religion in schools.

The central voice of the Spanish Catholic Church is the *Conferencia Episcopal Española* (CEE). In a nutshell, the CEE is opposed to legalising euthanasia, which it defines broadly as behaviour aimed at causing the death of a human being in order to prevent her from suffering. 'Euthanasia' in this sense can come as a response to a request made by the suffering being, as well as from the judgment, made by others, that her life lacks the minimum quality that makes it worth living.[75] The CEE qualifies as morally acceptable behaviour intended to alleviate the suffering of a dying patient, even if this might hasten a death that is seen as inevitable in the short term.[76]

Four main points underlie the CEE's position on euthanasia and other medical behaviour that potentially shortens life. The first is that life is a holy gift that human beings are not free to dispose of as they wish: 'The right to life is inalienable'. The second is that death should not be resisted or postponed when it is inevitable: 'futile' treatment should not be given. In such a case treatment of pain

---

[74] It is clear from analysis of the written press that the Catholic Church is one of the important voices in the public debate. A voice and an actor, furthermore, to which the present Government recurrently refers in positioning itself in the euthanasia debate.

[75] The non-distinction between euthanasia as a response to a request and euthanasia based on the judgment of others is functional in the context of the slippery slope rhetorical strategy developed in documents issued by the CEE, where it is stressed that the legalisation of euthanasia would put the weak and defenceless at risk (see below).

[76] See Conferencia Episcopal Española 1993.

with the aim of easing the suffering of the patient is a doctor's duty, but it is critical that relief of suffering and not death is the doctor's purpose. The third has to do with the role of the state and legislation in society. The principal end of the state, according to the CEE's public pronouncements concerning euthanasia, is the protection of life; the law should serve this end, and criminal law 'is the last guarantee against homicidal behaviour.'[77] When the state—via the law—does not adequately protect human life, the consequence is the spread of feelings of fear and insecurity, especially among the weakest elements of society—children, the elderly, the ill and so forth.

The CEE's fourth point has to do with the causes of what it sees as the increasing prominence of the euthanasia debate in the public arena, as well as with the consequences that liberalisation may have. The CEE situates the euthanasia debate as a step on the slippery slope from the legalisation—and thereby the banalisation—of abortion to a generalised disdain for life and for the weak. The source of this tendency is to be found, according to the CEE, in the increasing influence of 'hedonism' and 'individualism' in Spanish society. The legalisation of euthanasia 'would open the doors to sinister behaviour, for compassion could be used as an apology for the elimination of the weak, the deficient, the terminally ill.'[78] A document issued in 2001 points to the Netherlands as a forewarning of what could happen in Spain if the 'sirens' of euthanasia were heard. The recently approved Dutch legislation is, notes the CEE, 'the sad and dramatic expression of the dehumanisation that leaves above all the weakest defenceless'.[79]

The official voice of the Spanish Catholic Church sometimes gives guidelines to the faithful for electoral behaviour related to the 'protection of life'. To the question 'What should the attitude of the Christian be towards euthanasia?' the CEE in 1993 gave an answer consisting of eight points, of which one is relevant here:

> To vote, in electoral processes in our country, with responsible attention to the views of each political party on questions such as the family, public health, policies with respect to the disabled and the elderly, euthanasia, etc.[80]

Since the return of the PSOE to Government in 2004, and in spite of representatives of PSOE and Government having repeatedly stated that euthanasia is not on their agenda, the Church has publicly and regularly stressed its increasing concern. In November 2004 it launched a large public campaign with the aim of 'disseminating a Catholic vision on euthanasia' under the slogan 'A whole life to be lived'.[81] Seven million leaflets were produced, to be distributed in churches across the country, as well as posters to be exhibited in schools, churches and religious communities.[82]

---

[77] *Ibid.*
[78] *Ibid.*
[79] See Conferencia Episcopal Española 2001.
[80] See Conferencia Episcopal Española 1993.
[81] See Conferencia Episcopal Española 2004a.
[82] See Conferencia Episcopal Española 2004b; see also *El País* (6 November 2004), 'Los obispos lanzan una campaña de movilizaciones contra la eutanasia'. According to this article from *El País* the Conferencia Episcopal spent more than 81,000 euros in the production of the leaflets.

Nevertheless, as we will see in the next section, a medical ethics committee linked to a Catholic institution was about to break what had until then been a solidly unified Catholic voice against the legalisation of all forms of euthanasia.

15.6 Reports of Institutes for Medical Ethics

Three reports have in the last years been produced by well-established institutes for medical ethics, all of them based in Barcelona. Until October 2006, the report most often referred to by supporters of the decriminalisation of euthanasia was that published in December 2003 by the *Observatori de Bioètica i Dret* of the University of Barcelona.[83] The report supports legalisation of those forms of 'euthanasia' that it regards as protected by the constitutional right to freedom, that is, cases in which a patient is in a position freely to express her will, or when she was in such a position made a written request. When this condition is fulfilled, euthanasia is understood as 'an ethically legitimate decision to end . . . life in a dignified, peaceful manner, taken by a patient suffering from a grave illness which will irrevocably lead to death or entail permanent, unbearable suffering.' The position of the report is limited to these cases and

> does not include cases of non-autonomous patients. Children, the gravely handicapped and all those who have not previously manifested their will—whether through inability or because they did not choose to do so—pose specific problems which must be dealt with separately. None of these cases can be resolved on the basis of respect for the individual's decision-making autonomy. The importance and complexity of these cases—as evidenced in newborn wards and intensive care units—merit separate treatment. This issue will be addressed . . . on another occasion.[84]

This report acknowledges the inspiration its members have found in the 2000 report of the French National Ethics Committee which considers euthanasia legitimate when performed as an act of compassion and solidarity.[85]

In January 2005 the *Institut Borja*, a Catholic institute also based in Barcelona, issued a report in favour of a decriminalisation of euthanasia. Euthanasia was defined as

> the behaviour of a doctor . . . that directly causes the death of a person who suffers from a condition that according to existing medical knowledge is incurable, that causes unbearable suffering, and that will shortly lead to death. Such behaviour responds to a free and repeated request. Its aim is to alleviate suffering . . . Thus, the necessary conditions are an express request of the patient, physical or psychological suffering that is

---

[83] See Grupo de Opinión del Observatori de Bioètica i Dret 2003.
[84] See Grupo de Opinión del Observatori de Bioètica i Dret 2003: 48. To date, no such report has been forthcoming.
[85] See Grupo de Opinión del Observatori de Bioètica i Dret 2003: 9. See ch 12.1.1 on the report of the French National Ethics Committee.

unbearable for the patient, and an irreversible clinical situation that will shortly lead to death.[86]

Publication of this report was presented by some newspapers as a first breach in the hitherto unified Catholic opposition to euthanasia.[87]

In October 2006, again in Barcelona, the first report by an official governmental institution arguing for legalisation of euthanasia and assisted suicide was produced. The *Comitè Consultiu de Bioètica de Catalunya*, of the Health Department of the Catalan Government, published a report entitled *Report on Euthanasia and Assisted Suicide*[88] which lists the conditions under which euthanasia or assisted suicide should be allowed:

• a terminal condition or incurable pathology,
• a capable and informed patient,
• an express, serious, unequivocal and repeated request by the patient,
• acceptance of the request by a doctor,
• death caused in a medically responsible way.

The report states that the doctor concerned must consult another doctor who should not be part of the team that has taken the initial decision. The facts supporting the criteria mentioned must be documented so that an evaluation of the case can be made after the fact. The report recommends that regional committees be created composed of 'at least' two jurists and two doctors 'of which one specialised in psychiatry'. These committees would review cases before or after the fact, depending on the type of case involved. In cases of an incurable but not terminal condition, the review should take place in advance, leading to an authorisation or a rejection of the request. In cases of a terminal condition the control should take place after death. This report refers at length to the Dutch and Belgian situations and seems to find inspiration there, by contrast with the report of the *Observatori di Bioètica i Dret* which seems to have looked primarily to France for inspiration.

15.7 Conclusions

In this chapter a general picture has been given of current law on medical behaviour that potentially shortens life in Spain, in particular euthanasia and assistance with suicide, as well as of the way in which both are presented and discussed in the public and political arena. A distinctive aspect of the Spanish situation is that, due to the federal structure of the Spanish state, political actors and institutions can

---

[86] See Institut Borja de Bioètica 2005: 1–2.
[87] *El Mundo* (14 April 2005), 'Institut Borja y eutanasia'; *El País* (14 April 2005), 'Un instituto católico universitario se muestra a favor de la eutanasia'.
[88] See Comitè Consultiu de Bioètica de Catalunya 2006.

voice opinions different from or opposed to those of the central government. This is clearly the case today when, while the PSOE Government tries for apparently pragmatic reasons to limit the scope of the debate on euthanasia and assisted suicide, Catalan political institutions—which lead the country in giving legal force to advance treatment directives—are once again exhibiting a different legislative and political approach. Another peculiarity of the current Spanish situation is the active role played in the public debate by official Catholic institutions as well as the fact that the present Government and ruling political party, although in open opposition with the Church on important 'civil rights' issues, do not seem to want to push the opposition too far. Although the PSOE Government has passed laws over the vigorous objections of the Church, the sensitivity of church–state relations is definitely not ignored, and it would seem that the treatment the Government gives to euthanasia and assistance to suicide is at least partly to be understood as part of its ongoing management of relations with official Catholic institutions. Last but not least, even among those defending the legalisation of euthanasia and/or assistance in suicide, the debate seems to be limited to patients who are capable of expressing their will, thus excluding the issues associated with minors and other non-competent patients.

16

Switzerland

GEORG BOSSHARD

16.1 Introduction

Medical behaviour that potentially shortens life (MBPSL) in Switzerland is not very different from that in other European countries, whether with regard to legal and professional regulation or with regard to actual practice.

The only point on which Switzerland is substantially different from any other European country is how the Swiss deal with assistance in suicide involving right-to-die societies. The role of these societies is important in this regard, and assistance in suicide in Switzerland is seen as an issue of human rights rather than as a health care issue.[1] Accordingly, it is clearly separated from mainstream health care. And it can be argued that the practice should not be classified as medical behaviour that potentially shortens life (MBPSL) at all.

This contribution deals in its first part with medical end-of-life practice in general, and in its second part with the Swiss model of assisted suicide.

16.2 Medical Behaviour that Potentially Shortens Life

Definitions

The terrible killing performed by the Nazis in the name of destroying those unworthy of living was called *Euthanasie* in the Third Reich. After the war, this led to a sustained taboo on use of this term in the entire German-speaking area of Europe, including the German-speaking part of Switzerland. In order to avoid any associations with the Nazi programme, the term *Sterbehilfe* was introduced in the 1960s. This term covers all medical acts and omissions that foreseeably or intentionally hasten the death of a terminally ill patient, that is to say, it is the functional equivalent of 'medical behaviour that potentially shortens life'.

[1] See Davies 2006.

Sterbehilfe is normally divided into four categories: passive, indirect, active and assisted suicide.[2] Passive *Sterbehilfe* refers to withholding or withdrawing life-prolonging measures. The distinction between withholding and withdrawing is of little importance in the legal and ethical discussion in Switzerland. The term passive *Sterbehilfe* in Switzerland means largely the same thing as the more recent international term *non-treatment decision*.[3]

Indirect *Sterbehilfe* (in Switzerland commonly referred to as *indirekt aktive Sterbehilfe*) refers to the use of agents such as opioids or sedatives to alleviate symptoms of a terminally ill patient, with the unintended side effect of shortening the patient's remaining life. The legitimacy of the practice is commonly supposed to be based on a concept known as the doctrine of double effect in the international literature.

Assisted suicide (*Suizidbeihilfe* or *Beihilfe zum Suizid*) refers to prescribing and/or supplying agents, usually a lethal drug, in order to help someone to end his own life. Whereas in the international discussion such an action is usually referred to as physician-assisted suicide, implying that doing this is normally a physician's task, the analogous German term *ärztliche Beihilfe zum Suizid* is rather unusual in Switzerland since non-physicians play an important role in the Swiss practice of assisted suicide.

Active *Sterbehilfe* (in Switzerland commonly referred to as *direkt aktive Sterbehilfe*) refers to any action to intentionally end the life of a terminally ill patient in order to spare him from further pain and suffering. In Swiss usage, the term active *Sterbehilfe* does not specify whether the decision was made at the explicit request of the patient or with his consent. The same holds for the terms indirect *Sterbehilfe* and passive *Sterbehilfe*.[4]

Box 1 gives an overview of the different sorts of *Sterbehilfe* (MBPSL) and the associated legal regulation, which will be discussed next.

Regulation

As in other European countries, regulation of medical practice is based both on the Penal Code and other statutes on the one hand, and professional guidelines on the other hand. Such guidelines must be in accordance with the law, but since they are usually more specific than formal legal regulations and more abreast of new developments, they have a considerable impact of their own on medical practice and on how statutory regulations are interpreted.

The medical ethics guidelines of the Swiss Academy of Medical Sciences (SAMS) have played an important role in Switzerland. Introduced in the late 1960s, these guidelines were originally a product of medico-ethical discussions among physicians. Non-medical experts have played an increasing role in formulating guidelines released thereafter. SAMS guidelines have long been treated with

---

[2] See Arbeitsgruppe Sterbehilfe 1999: 12–14.
[3] See Van der Maas *et al* 1996; Van der Heide *et al* 2003.
[4] See Bosshard 2005.

Box 16.1 Sterbehilfe *in Switzerland*

MBPSL	death considered to be	legal status	reporting required to
passive *Sterbehilfe* (withdrawing/withholding life-prolonging treatment)	natural	legal	civil authorities
indirect *Sterbehilfe* (pain and symptom relief with life-shortening effect, including terminal sedation)	natural	legal	civil authorities
assisted suicide	non-natural	legal if not self-interested: Art 115 Penal Code	criminal authorities
voluntary active *Sterbehilfe* (euthanasia)	non-natural	illegal: Art 114 Penal Code	criminal authorities
non-voluntary active *Sterbehilfe* (termination of life without request)	non-natural	illegal, eg Art 113 Penal Code	criminal authorities

almost the respect due to legislation. Although in 1996 the Swiss Federal Assembly determined that 'the SAMS guidelines are not legally binding',[5] they still play an important role in a number of cantonal health laws, and are often referred to in the case law on medical-ethical subjects such as end-of-life issues.

16.2.1 Passive *Sterbehilfe* (Withholding and Withdrawing Life-Prolonging Treatment)

Withholding or withdrawing futile life-prolonging treatment is not illegal according to Swiss court decisions,[6] and it is also expressly permitted in the current as well as in earlier SAMS guidelines.[7] This reflects the deeply rooted sentiment in legal and medical practice in Switzerland that in the case of passive *Sterbehilfe* it is the disease rather than the physician's decision or action that is responsible for the patient's death.[8] Deaths due to withholding or withdrawing life-prolonging

---

[5] See Arbeitsgruppe Sterbehilfe 1999: 15.
[6] *Ibid* 13.
[7] See Schweizerische Akademie der Medizinischen Wissenschaften 2005.
[8] See Zimmermann-Acklin 1997: 277.

treatment are considered 'natural' deaths, and reporting to the criminal authorities is not required.

An important and celebrated case more than 25 years ago had a substantial impact on the political, ethical and legal discussion of passive *Sterbehilfe* in Switzerland. In 1975 a member of the Zurich City Council launched a legal investigation against a well-renowned head physician of a municipal hospital. The doctor was arrested and charged with wilful manslaughter for having shortened the lives of severely ill patients by withholding or withdrawing artificial hydration and nutrition.[9] The case ended with the acquittal of the doctor and the political defeat of the member of the council.

Over the following 20 years, a comparatively early and comprehensive acceptance of withholding and withdrawing life-prolonging treatment developed in Swiss law and in professional guidelines, often strikingly different from how these issues were dealt with in neighbouring Germany at the time. In particular, it was early on clear that passive *Sterbehilfe* includes withholding of artificial nutrition and hydration, and turning off life-prolonging devices such as respirators. Broad consensus was also reached that the legitimacy of passive *Sterbehilfe* is not restricted to end-of-life situations, so a competent patient has the right to refuse treatment at any stage of a disease.[10] In the case of incompetent patients with severe brain damage and no hope of recovery, such as patients in a persistent vegetative state, withdrawal of treatment, including artificial feeding and hydration, was already considered acceptable in the 1990s.[11]

Withholding or withdrawing treatment in the case of a non-competent patient is legally justified in terms of the patient's presumed will. In determining this, the patient's next-of-kin are an important source of information. However, the responsibility for the decision remains with the physician.[12] The only exception is when a patient has explicitly appointed a health care proxy, who is thereby empowered to give or withhold consent to treatment on the patient's behalf.[13] However, in today's medical practice such an explicit health care proxy is very rare.[14]

The Swiss Academy of Medical Sciences (SAMS) and many legal experts consider advance directives (ie refusals of treatment) as a tool to determine the presumed will of a patient who has lost decisional capacity, which implies that such directives are not binding on a doctor.[15] Until 1995 SAMS even stated that a refusal of life-preserving treatment in a written directive 'should not be heeded if the patient's condition would, according to general experience, permit a return to

---

[9] See Schär 1998.
[10] See Riklin 1999.
[11] See Fahrländer 1996.
[12] See Seelmann 2003.
[13] See Schweizerische Akademie der Medizinischen Wissenschaften 2005.
[14] See Bosshard, Wettstein & Bär 2003; Bosshard 2005.
[15] See Riklin 1999; Seelmann 2003; Schweizerische Akademie der Medizinischen Wissenschaften 2005.

interpersonal communication and a reinforcement of the will to live.'[16] Today, SAMS views advance treatment directives as binding 'as long as they apply to the actual situation and there is no indication that they no longer reflect the patient's current wish'.[17] The impact of advance treatment directives is nevertheless still limited. A comparative empirical study in six European countries found that such directives were available for fewer than 5% of patients at the end of life in all studied countries including Switzerland—only in the Netherlands was the percentage substantially higher (13%).[18]

16.2.2 Indirect *Sterbehilfe* (Pain Relief) and Palliative Sedation

As with passive *Sterbehilfe*, indirect *Sterbehilfe* is not illegal according to Swiss judicial decisions. Death resulting from pain or symptom relief is considered 'natural', so reporting to the criminal authorities is not required. However, the doctrine of double effect has been rejected by a number of legal experts in Switzerland as elsewhere.[19] One point of criticism is that foreseeing but not intending a certain result amounts at least to *dolus eventualis* (*Eventualvorsatz*) according to normal Swiss as well as German legal doctrine.[20] Another point of criticism is that intentions cannot be objectively established. However, whether or not one considers the concept of double effect useful, to suppose that the concept could enable legislative bodies to regulate life-shortening due to pain and symptom relief without dealing with euthanasia, as recently suggested,[21] seems somewhat illusory.[22]

The Swiss Academy of Medical Sciences states that 'it is the physician's duty to alleviate pain and suffering, even if in individual cases an influence on the duration (shortening or prolongation) of life could be the consequence.' The Academy comments further,

> The life-shortening effect of centrally acting substances has long been overestimated. Generally analgesics and sedatives, if they are correctly used exclusively for the control of symptoms in the last few weeks of life, are not associated with a shortening of the survival time. Analgesics and sedatives can also be misused in order to bring about death. As a general rule, however, a difference between the alleviation of pain and symptoms, in the palliative sense, and the intention to end life, is already clearly evident in the dosage or in the increase of the dosage of the drug.

In this context, palliative sedation should also be mentioned. The practice of keeping a patient in continuous deep sedation or coma until death is increasingly seen as a distinct sort of end-of-life treatment, one that in itself does not shorten life and

[16] See Schweizerische Akademie der Medizinischen Wissenschaften 1995.
[17] See Schweizerische Akademie der Medizinischen Wissenschaften 2005.
[18] See Van der Heide *et al* 2003.
[19] See Schwarzenegger 2003.
[20] See Birnbacher 1995.
[21] See Arbeitsgruppe Sterbehilfe 1999: 46.
[22] See Bosshard, De Stoutz & Bär 2006.

is therefore legally and ethically unproblematic. But the fact that a patient's remaining period of consciousness is shortened is in itself ethically and possibly legally relevant.[23] So far, there are no statutory regulations nor case law on the subject in Switzerland. The SAMS guidelines state (without specifying whether 'palliative sedation' can include withholding of artificial nutrition and hydration):

> With symptoms that are refractory to treatment, palliative sedation may sometimes be necessary. Here it is pointed out that the patient should be sedated only to the extent that this is necessary for alleviation of the symptoms.

16.2.3 Active *Sterbehilfe* (Euthanasia)

Euthanasia—if it occurs at the explicit request of the person concerned—is punishable as death on request under article 114 of the Swiss Penal Code. However, apart from rare cases of serial offences,[24] convictions are extremely rare. One reason may be the simple fact that the criminal authorities are hardly ever aware of such cases since they are reported as natural deaths to the civil authorities. But even in the rare case where the criminal authorities have reason to believe that, for instance, higher dosages of morphine were used than were needed for the relief of pain and symptoms, Ziegler's finding that many US prosecutors feel that 'it is not productive to prosecute doctors unless the doctor's conduct is extremely outrageous' may also hold for most prosecutors in Switzerland.[25] The recent finding of an international study that Swiss doctors carry out euthanasia and termination of life without the explicit request of their patients in almost 1% of all deaths[26] provoked no reaction from Swiss public prosecutors.

Since the mid-1970s a number of political efforts have been made to change or modify article 114 in order to legalise euthanasia. The most important of these efforts was the report of a task force set up by the Swiss Federal Council in 1999, in which the majority of the group argued for decriminalisation of euthanasia, subject to certain restrictions, along the lines of the Dutch model.[27] But in December 2001, the Swiss Parliament rejected the 'Cavalli Initiative'[28] which proposed to put the recommendation of the majority of the working group into practice.[29] In the same session, the Parliament also rejected the 'Vallender Initiative', which would have restricted assistance in suicide performed by right-to-die organisations and prohibited doctors from prescribing lethal drugs. This was the first time the Swiss Parliament had explicitly approved of the existing practice of assisted suicide involving right-do-die societies.[30] Since then, the focus of debate

[23] See Bosshard, De Stoutz & Bär 2006.
[24] See Bachmann 2004.
[25] See Ziegler & Lovrich 2003.
[26] See ch 17, Table 17.2.
[27] See Arbeitsgruppe Sterbehilfe 1999.
[28] See Cavalli 2000.
[29] See Rosenberg 2001.
[30] See Bosshard *et al* 2003.

has largely shifted from euthanasia to assisted suicide and where its legal borders should lie.

16.3 Empirical Findings concerning MBPSL

Attitudes

Swiss doctors strongly support passive and indirect *Sterbehilfe*. An international study of physicians' attitudes towards end-of-life decisions found that 94% of them support withholding and withdrawing life-prolonging treatment at the patient's request, and 96% support pain relief with a life-shortening effect.[31]

Asked whether 'the use of drugs in lethal doses at the explicit request of a terminally ill patient with extreme uncontrollable pain or other distress' is acceptable (a question that covers both assisted suicide and euthanasia) Swiss doctors were more closely divided but still, with the Netherlands and Belgium, at the positive end of the European spectrum (56% affirmative answers).[32] Interestingly, fewer than half (43%) of Swiss doctors agreed that 'assisted suicide should be physician-assisted suicide only'.[33] Support for pain relief with a life-shortening effect as well as for the use of lethal drugs (assisted suicide and euthanasia) was significantly higher among French-speaking than among German- and Italian-speaking doctors. For withholding and withdrawing treatment, on the other hand, support was significantly higher in the German-speaking than in the French- and Italian-speaking regions of Switzerland.

The Swiss population is highly supportive of assistance in dying on request. A representative study among 1,000 Swiss residents produced 82% affirmative answers to the question: 'Do you think that a patient suffering from an incurable disease with intolerable physical and mental suffering has the right to ask to die and to get assistance accordingly?'[34] Seven per cent were undecided and only 11% answered in the negative, a rate that puts Switzerland together with the Netherlands (and to a slightly lesser degree Belgium) at the high end of the European spectrum of public opinion.[35] Interestingly, despite the central role of right-to-die societies in the existing Swiss practice of assisted suicide, most people (68%) put the family doctor at the top of the list of persons to be approached with a request for assistance in dying. Thirty-seven per cent put the family first, and only 22% put a (right-to-die) organisation in first place.[36]

---

[31] See Fischer *et al* 2006.
[32] See ch 17, Table 17.1. In the comparative study presented there, 61% of Swiss doctors supported a less well-formulated statement in favour of legal euthanasia.
[33] See Fischer *et al* 2006.
[34] See *Exit ADMD* 1999.
[35] See ch 17, Table 17.1.
[36] See *Exit ADMD* 1999.

Medical Practice

An international study of medical end-of-life decisions in six European countries found the highest incidence (28% of all deaths) of withholding or withdrawing life-prolonging treatment in Switzerland.[37] The incidence of pain relief with life-shortening effect was roughly the same as in other countries: 22%. The Swiss figure was highest for physician-assisted suicide (0.36%—in 92% of these cases a right-to-die organisation was involved). Euthanasia and termination of life without a request, both as we have seen illegal in Switzerland, accounted for another 0.27% and 0.42% of all deaths. Continuous deep sedation until death was used in 4.8% of all deaths in Switzerland; in more than half of these cases (2.9% of all deaths) deep sedation until death was combined with a decision to forgo artificial hydration and nutrition (Switzerland is about at the middle of the European spectrum in both respects).[38]

Together with the Netherlands and Belgium, and in contrast to Denmark, Sweden and Italy, Switzerland is among those countries where medical end-of-life decisions are comparatively often discussed, with the patient in 78% of cases involving a competent patient, and with the family in 71% of the cases involving an incompetent patient.[39]

16.4 Assisted Suicide in Switzerland

Assisted suicide is, according to article 115 of the Swiss Penal Code, only punishable if it is performed with self-interest.[40] Death due to assisted suicide is considered a 'non-natural', so-called 'extraordinary death' and must therefore be reported to and investigated by the criminal authorities.

16.4.1 Legal Background and Origins

Box 16.2 gives an overview of the Swiss model of assisted suicide.

The legal basis that enabled the Swiss practice of assisted suicide to develop is article 115 of the Swiss Penal Code: 'A person who, for selfish motives, aids or abets another person in suicide will be punished with imprisonment up to five years.'[41] In the Age of Enlightenment the earlier view that suicide is always a sin and a form of murder was rejected and this had a strong impact not only on German, but also

---

[37] See ch 17, Table 17.2 (as the table shows, from a later study in the UK it seems that the rate of death due to abstention is even higher there: 30.3%).
[38] See Miccinesi *et al* 2006; see ch 17, Table 17.2, for comparative data.
[39] See Van der Heide *et al* 2003.
[40] See Hauser & Rehberg 1986.
[41] See Hauser & Rehberg 1986.

Box 16.2 The Swiss model of assisted suicide: legal and professional regulation

source	holds for	substance*
Penal Code	anyone	• assistance in suicide punishable if carried out with selfish motives (art 115) • killing on request punishable (art 114)
narcotics law	doctors	• doctors may use, dispense and prescribe drugs only to the extent that is necessary according to the established rules of medical practice (art 11)
health law (Cantonal)	doctors	• doctors must act according to the established rules of medical practice (article number depends on the Canton)
professional medical guidelines (SAMS)	doctors	• patient terminally ill; alternative possibilities (palliative care) offered; decisional capacity and absence of external pressure
internal guidelines of right-to-die societies	staff of right-to-die societies	• *Exit*: 'poor prognosis, unbearable suffering, or unreasonable disability' • *Dignitas*: 'fatal disease or unacceptable disability' • *Exit ADMD*: 'incurable disease or terminally ill'

* All of these requirements imply or explicitly require that the person wanting assistance be competent.

on Swiss law.[42] At the time, each Swiss canton had its own criminal code. In the last decade of the 19th century, the first steps in the direction of a Swiss Penal Code were taken. From the start it went unchallenged that suicide should not constitute a criminal offence. This entailed that assisting in suicide would not have been an offence either unless the Penal Code were to provide specifically that that should be the case. Unlike Germany, the Swiss experts felt that such a provision should be made.[43] The process leading to the ultimate enactment of Penal Code took decades. Article 115 finally entered into force in January 1942, and has remained unchanged since then.

As a basis for an open practice of assisted suicide, article 115 is interesting for two reasons. First, it makes no mention of doctors—the legality of assisting suicide, in the absence of self-interest, holds good for any person. Second, there is no mention of any medical precondition. The only prerequisite is implicit, namely that the individual wanting help to commit suicide must have decisional capacity,

---

[42] See Guillod & Schmidt 2005.
[43] *Ibid.*

since otherwise he would not be '*handlungsfähig*' (have legal capacity) and his act could not be considered suicide.

Although this legal situation makes it in principle legal for anyone, including relatives or friends, to give assistance in suicide, the development of an open practice of assisted suicide in fact took place in the framework of so-called right-to-die organisations. In 1982, two independent but related organisations were founded, *Exit Deutsche Schweiz* for the German-speaking part of Switzerland (founded and headquartered in Zürich), and *Exit ADMD* ('*Association pour le Droit de Mourir dans la Dignité*') for the French-speaking part of Switzerland (founded and headquartered in Geneva). (In what follows, *Exit Deutsche Schweiz* will generally be referred to simply as *Exit.*)

The basis for what later became the 'Swiss model' was laid in the early decision of *Exit Deutsche Schweiz* not to strive primarily for greater liberalisation of active euthanasia (as so many other right-to-die societies around the world do), but rather to use the liberal legislation concerning assisted suicide to offer such assistance on request to severely ill people wishing to die.[44] During the first ten years of its existence, *Exit* sent a 'suicide manual' to everyone over the age of 18 years who had been a member of the organisation for at least three months. The manual contained precise instructions for committing suicide by placing a plastic bag over one's head or by taking a cocktail of drugs.[45] This cocktail contained a considerable amount of hypnotics. The person wanting to die had to get the pills from different physicians, for instance by pretending to suffer from insomnia. Some members of *Exit* did not find these instructions practicable and, since the early 1990s, *Exit* has offered personal guidance through the process of suicide to members wanting to die. This is carried out by the ingestion of a lethal dose of barbiturates prescribed by a physician with the explicit intention of enabling the patient to end his or her life. This development only became possible once the initial conflict between *Exit* and the medical profession, which characterised *Exit's* early years, had largely abated.[46]

16.4.2 The Role of Doctors in the Swiss Model—Narcotics and Health Law

As assisted suicide is practised in Switzerland today, the doctor's role lies in the prescription of sodium pentobarbital. This is the only drug used for assisted suicide, and the doses used (10, 12 or 15 g) are clearly and exclusively related to the termination of life. Pentobarbital is a prescription drug subject to Swiss narcotics law. This means that a doctor writing a prescription for assistance in suicide has to

---

[44] See Bosshard, Fischer & Bär 2002. The early development of *Exit ADMD* was somewhat different. It focused on securing legal recognition for a certain type of advance treatment directive (see Giroud *et al* 1999).

[45] See Fricker 1999.

[46] See Bosshard, Fischer & Bär 2002.

act according to article 11 of the narcotics law, which requires that the drug be used, dispensed and prescribed according to the established rules of medical practice. A similar reference to the established rules of medical practice can also be found in health law, a subject dealt with at the cantonal level since it regulates the practice of medical doctors licensed by the canton.

It is obviously a matter of interpretation what a reference to the rules of medical practice means in the context of assisted suicide. However, during the last decade judicial decisions have clarified the limits of a doctor's involvement in assisted suicide. The courts have held that assisting in suicide is not in principle incompatible with the rules of medical practice, but that an obligation to ascertain the patient's competence to make such a decision is a prerequisite to the prescription of a lethal drug for the purposes of assistance in suicide.[47] This means that the doctor must examine the patient wanting to die, in person, and assess the medical condition(s) giving rise to the desire to die. An administrative court ruling in 1999 also required the existence of 'a condition indisputably leading to death' if doctors were to assist in this way. However, the court did not specify what medical conditions are covered by this term, and this was not made any clearer by the comment in the ruling that it is 'extremely questionable' whether mental illness would meet the requirement.[48]

In 2006 the Federal Supreme Court recognised that an incurable, permanent, serious mental disorder can be the cause of suffering comparable to that of a physical disorder. The court ruled that a doctor who prescribes a lethal dose of pentobarbital in a case like this does not necessarily violate the rules of medical practice. However, the Federal Supreme Court held, this requires a report by an expert in psychiatry providing evidence that the patient's desire to die is not the expression of a curable, psychiatric disorder but a well-considered and permanent decision based on rational judgment.[49]

The court based its decision not only on the Swiss Penal Code and the Swiss Constitution, but also on the European Convention on Human rights. The fundamental idea underlying Swiss law on suicide is that of the autonomous human individual who has the right to decide on the circumstances and the time of his own death. A 'right to die' in this sense, however, is a negative right ('liberty right'): it protects the individual against legal prohibitions and interventions. Such negative rights can be restricted if other basic rights are at risk.[50] No positive right ('claim right') is involved. The court explicitly rejected the view of Ludwig Minelli, lawyer and founder of the right-to-die society *Dignitas*, that there is an individual right to a pain-free death (using pentobarbital).[51]

---

[47] See Verwaltungsgericht des Kantons Zürich [Zurich Administrative Court], Entscheid der 3. Kammer VB Nr 99.00145, 1999; Verwaltungsgericht des Kantons Aargau [Aargau Administrative Court], Entscheid BE 2003.00354-K3, 2005.

[48] Verwaltungsgericht des Kantons Zürich 1999 (see n 47).

[49] Schweizerisches Bundesgericht [Federal Supreme Court of Switzerland], Entscheid 2A.4812006, 2006.

[50] See Schwarzenegger 2007.

[51] See Minelli 2004.

In November 2004, the Swiss Academy of Medical Sciences released new *Medical Ethics Guidelines for the Care of Patients at the End of Life*. The Academy states that 'a personal decision of a doctor in accordance with his/her conscience to assist a terminally ill patient in suicide has to be respected as such'. The guidelines seem to limit the category of persons who may receive assistance from a doctor more that the Penal Code does, since the latter does not require a patient to be at the end of life in order to qualify for assistance in suicide.[52] The guidelines also insist that 'the final act in the process leading to death must always be undertaken by the patient him/herself' and thereby clearly reject euthanasia in any circumstances.[53]

Apart from the issue whether individual doctors may render assistance in suicide, until the end of the 1990s there was a general understanding that assisted suicide was not allowed in hospitals and probably not in nursing homes, although there were no specific regulations on the subject in most parts of the country. However, in 2000 the Zurich City Council decided to lift an existing ban on assisted suicide in nursing homes.[54] At the same time the council reiterated that assistance in suicide is not allowed in the city hospitals. In January 2006, the Lausanne University Hospital decided to allow right-to-die societies on to their premises to help terminally ill, non-ambulatory patients who seek suicide assistance but are unable to leave the hospital.[55] The Geneva University Hospital followed suit in September 2006.[56] In 2007 the Zurich Cantonal University Hospital reaffirmed the ban on assisted suicide on its premises and adopted a policy of 'studied neutrality'.[57] According to this policy, no health care professional working at the Zurich University Hospital should directly engage in assistance with suicide. But if a competent patient wants assistance from a right-to-die society outside the hospital walls he should not be prevented from seeking it. Such a patient has, as in any other circumstances, the right to a report giving medical information—such as the diagnosis and prognosis—and, if needed, to be transported by ambulance to wherever he chooses, including to a right-to-die society.

16.4.3 The Role of Right-to-Die Organisations—Internal Guidelines

Volunteers of right-to-die societies (often clergymen, social workers or nurses) play an important role in the preliminary assessment of a candidate for assisted suicide. Not infrequently a request for assisted suicide is first made to a volunteer, often by telephone, and not directly to the person's doctor.[58] *Exit's* internal guidelines require a person seeking assistance to be suffering from a disease with 'poor prognosis, unbearable suffering or unreasonable disability'.[59] *Dignitas* and *Exit*

---

[52] See Schweizerische Akademie der Medizinischen Wissenschaften 2005 (see para 16.3.1 above).
[53] See Schweizerische Akademie der Medizinischen Wissenschaften 2005.
[54] See Ernst 2001.
[55] Chapman 2006.
[56] See Schweizerische Depeschenagentur 2006.
[57] See Swissinfo 2007.
[58] See Ziegler & Bosshard 2007.
[59] See homepage *Exit* (see n 88).

ADMD have similar requirements.[60] In practice, there is significant selection even at this early intake stage.

After the volunteer has ascertained that the organisation's criteria are met, the person wanting to die must approach a doctor—if possible his family doctor—and ask him to cooperate by prescribing a lethal dose of pentobarbital. In principle, a doctor who writes such a prescription could be present during the assistance or even give the assistance on his own. The fact is, however, that few doctors are willing to do so, and that most of them prefer to leave on-the-spot participation to the right-to-die societies. In the time between filling the prescription at the pharmacy and the suicide, the drug is usually stored by the right-to-die organisation, which is much safer than if it were to be kept in a medicine chest at home, especially since the prescribed drugs are not always in fact used.

The decision-making process is not complete when the prescription has been issued, since the subsequent course of the illness can also be important. Some of the symptoms that people are desperately afraid of may never materialise, so that there is no need to use the prescribed drug. It is also conceivable that organic disease processes—cerebral metastases, for example—compromise the patient's competence to make decisions, in which case the indication for suicide assistance will no longer be valid.[61]

When the time comes for the suicide, it is a volunteer of the organisation who provides personal guidance. This is a crucial part of the Swiss model, since experience from *Exit's* early days shows that, without on-the-spot assistance, some people have difficulties taking the lethal dose of barbiturate in such a way as to achieve their objective with certainty.[62]

16.4.4 Criminal Prosecutions in the Context of Assisted Suicide

Considering the fact that there are several hundred cases of assistance in suicide in Switzerland every year, convictions are very rare. In the late 1990s, an *Exit* volunteer was convicted for killing (suffocating with a plastic bag) two people who wanted to die. He did so because these individuals were still alive (although in coma) several hours after ingesting the lethal barbiturate.[63]

In 1999 the licence to prescribe controlled substances of a doctor in the Canton of Zurich, and in 2004 the licence to prescribe controlled substances of a doctor in the Canton of Aargau, was withdrawn. In the Zurich case, the doctor had written prescriptions for assistance in suicide without making a personal assessment of the persons wanting to die. In one case he had assisted in the suicide of a 29-year-old woman suffering from a mental illness. Basing his judgment only on her medical files, he had diagnosed the women with a disease different from what her

---

[60] See homepage *Dignitas,* homepage *Exit ADMD* (see n 88).
[61] See Bosshard 2006.
[62] See Ulrich 2002.
[63] See M Meier 2000.

psychiatrist had diagnosed, and he had made wrong assumptions concerning the prognosis.[64] In the Aargau case, the doctor was convicted because he had assisted in the suicide of mentally ill individuals, had assessed their medical diagnosis and prognosis and decisional capacity without due care, and had failed to write a medical report accounting for the findings and conclusions his decision was based on. In several cases he had prescribed a lethal dose of barbiturate based on a single assessment immediately before the suicide took place. In more than one case the doctor's conclusions in terms of psychiatric diagnosis and prognosis were different from what psychiatric specialists had earlier diagnosed.[65]

A recent important court case concerns a psychiatrist who organised his own right-to-die society explicitly for mentally ill people.[66] The psychiatrist was arrested by the Basel authorities in 2003 and spent three months in pre-trial detention. In June 2007 he was sentenced by the Basel criminal court to three years in prison, of which two on probation. The court found the psychiatrist guilty of negligent homicide in one case. He had considered the person he assisted competent; but according to legal experts this was not the case and the psychiatrist would have realised this himself if he had acted with proper care. In a another case the psychiatrist allowed a TV camera team to be present during the assistance with suicide, and the film was subsequently broadcast. The court convicted the psychiatrist of having assisted and abetted a suicide out of selfish motives, namely a desire for publicity. This latter decision is noteworthy since the common legal understanding up to now was that selfish motives in the context of article 115 of the Swiss Penal Code have to do with material benefits. Whether this case will be appealed is not yet known.

16.4.5 Empirical Findings on Assisted Suicide

Suicide assistance carried out by doctors outside the framework of right-to-die societies seems to be rare. Survey research found that a right-to-die society was involved in 92% of all cases in which Swiss doctors assisted a patient in suicide.[67] Cases in which lay people outside the organisations assist relatives or friends to commit suicide with non-medical means seem to be even rarer, or at least the authorities are hardly ever aware of such cases, nor has there been any research on the subject.

At present, four different right-to-die organisations provide assistance in suicide. *Exit Deutsche Schweiz* has about 50,000 members.[68] Its French-speaking counterpart, *Exit ADMD*, accounts for another 10,000 members. The Zurich-based right-to-die organisation *Dignitas*, which was founded in 1998, unlike the two *Exit*

---

[64] Verwaltungsgericht des Kantons Zürich, 1999 (see n 47).
[65] Verwaltungsgericht des Kantons Aargau, 2005 (see n 47).
[66] See Spoendlin 2007.
[67] See Van der Heide *et al* 2003.
[68] See Bundesamt für Justiz 2006: 32.

organisations, offers assistance to people travelling to Switzerland from all over the world.[69] *Dignitas* today has about 5,000 members of whom about 700 are Swiss residents. In addition, a small organisation called *Exit International* can be found near Berne, also offering suicide assistance to people who do not live in Switzerland.[70]

During the 1990s, the number of suicides assisted by *Exit Deutsche Schweiz* tripled to about 100 cases each year.[71] In 2004 it assisted in 153 suicides.[72] *Exit ADMD* accounts for around another 50 cases per year, so that there are currently some 200 cases of assisted suicide among the Swiss population every year.[73] The number of suicides assisted by *Dignitas* has rapidly increased over the last few years. Between 10 October 2002 and 4 April 2004, 22 individuals aged between 40 and 75 ended their lives in Switzerland with the help of *Dignitas*.[74] *Dignitas* today accounts for over 100 cases a year. More than half of these come from Germany, the rest from countries all over the world, but mainly from the UK, France and Austria.[75] The activities of *Exit International* are limited to a few isolated cases of suicide assistance every year; the exact figure is unknown.

Given that Switzerland has a total population of around 7 million, and that there are roughly 62,000 deaths each year,[76] it can be calculated that between 0.3% and 0.4% of all Swiss deaths are assisted suicides, excluding cases of suicide tourism. If one includes suicide tourism the figure is about 0.5% of all deaths.

There are many more requests for assisted suicide than actual assistance. In 2002 an *Exit* representative reported that between 1997 and 2001 the headquarters of *Exit* in Zurich had been contacted each year by about 300 to 400 members who expressed a wish to end their lives with *Exit's* help. Of those, 214 (in 1997) rising to 319 (in 1998) enquiries were followed up each year since they seemed to meet the organisation's criteria and the persons concerned persisted in their wish to die. For 99 (in 1999) to 149 (in 2001) of these persons annually, a doctor wrote a prescription for a lethal dose of barbiturates. And finally, 90 (in 1999) to 124 (in 2001) of these individuals each year ended their lives by assisted suicide with *Exit's* help.[77]

A 2004 *Dignitas* report states that the vast majority of those who inquire from abroad whether *Dignitas* would be willing to help them die and who are given a 'provisional green light' by a doctor working with the organisation, are not heard from again, either for a long time or for good; most of them finally die a natural death.[78]

So far, there has been only one independent study of suicide-related activities in Switzerland.[79] This study is a retrospective analysis of all case files of assisted

[69] See Harding 2004.
[70] See Bosshard, Ulrich & Bär 2003.
[71] See Bosshard, Ulrich & Bär 2003.
[72] See Bundesamt für Justiz 2006: 32.
[73] *Ibid* at 33.
[74] See House of Lords Select Committee on the Assisted Dying for the Terminally Ill Bill (UK) 2005b: 633–7.
[75] See homepage *Dignitas* (see n 88).
[76] See Bundesamt für Statistik 2005.
[77] See Nägeli 2002.
[78] See homepage *Dignitas* (see n 88).
[79] See Bosshard, Ulrich & Bär 2003.

suicide kept by *Exit Deutsche Schweiz* in 1990–2000. *Exit Deutsche Schweiz* assisted 748 suicides in the Swiss population during this period. The deceased were between 18 and 101 years old, with a mean age of 72 years; 54% were women. Residents of German-speaking, more urbanised, predominantly protestant cantons were more common in the *Exit* deaths. In one-third of the cases, the prescription was provided by the family doctor, while a doctor working with the right-to-die organisation prescribed the barbiturate in the remaining cases.

Of the 331 individuals who died with *Exit's* help between 1990 and 2000 in the Canton of Zurich, 79% were suffering from fatal diseases: 47% from cancer, 12% from cardiovascular/respiratory diseases, 7% from HIV/AIDS, and 12% from neurological diseases. The remaining 70 individuals (21%) were suffering from basically non-fatal diagnoses such as musculoskeletal disorders (rheumatoid arthritis, osteoarthritis or osteoporosis), from chronic pain syndromes and diagnoses such as 'blindness' and 'general weakness'. Considering the fact that the mean age among these 70 individuals was very high (80 years for men and 83 years for women), the medical diagnosis may have been something of a pretext, and at least some of these cases were probably in fact close to what is referred to as 'tired of life' or 'suffering from living' in the Dutch euthanasia debate.[80] Also in this group, there were nine cases where mental disorder was the direct reason for the deceased requesting assisted suicide. In eight cases, the individual concerned did not want to carry on living because of a depressive disorder, in one case due to a psychosis.[81]

16.4.6 Safety and Transparency Issues

In 261 *Exit* deaths in Canton Zurich studied in the context of the above-mentioned project, pentobarbital was taken orally. Of these individuals 229 (88%) died within one hour.[82] In 11 cases, death took up to two hours, and in another 20 cases up to twelve hours. In 1 case, almost eighteen hours elapsed between ingestion and death. There were no records of serious complications or cases of re-awakening from coma. These results are in line with findings from the US State of Oregon where serious problems with assisted suicide using oral barbiturates are also extremely rare.[83] An earlier Dutch study had found a higher complication rate for oral assisted suicide than for euthanasia.[84] However, the sample chosen for this particular study included all kinds of assisted suicide, including a number of cases where substances clearly unsuitable for the purpose were used.

As far as the reliability of assisted dying is concerned, the crucial question is whether the staff involved have knowledge, skills and experience sufficient to the task. It may well be safer when assistance is given by a nurse with special training and experience in this field than by a general practitioner who has no particular

---

[80] See Sheldon 2005.
[81] See Bosshard, Ulrich & Bär 2003.
[82] See Bosshard, Ulrich & Bär 2003.
[83] See Oregon Health Division 2006.
[84] See Groenewoud *et al* 2000b.

training and has never engaged in assisted suicide before. For instance, careful prevention of nausea and vomiting in the preparatory phase is crucial. When assisted suicide is based on the oral self-administration of barbiturates, it must be accepted that death may sometimes not occur for hours. Cases of re-awakening from coma in the context of assisted suicide have never been reported in Switzerland.[85] However, unlike in the Netherlands and Belgium, any active intervention to hasten death in these situations would be clearly illegal.

For persons who wish to die but who have difficulties in swallowing, the Swiss practice of assisted suicide allows assistance in dying using iv-drips or stomach tubes. Usually, in particular in people depending on artificial nutrition or tube-feeding, such devices are already in place. However, in some cases a volunteer of the organisation, usually a nurse, puts an intravenous drip in place. Then the volunteer adds the lethal dose of barbiturates to the fluid in the bottle or bag of the drip. All this is viewed as preparatory activity. The legally critical act is the last step of this procedure, opening the tap of the drip or tube.[86] This last step must always be carried out by the individual wanting to die and this must be attested to by a witness.

All 147 suicides in the city of Zurich assisted by *Exit* between 1990 and 2000 were reported to the criminal authorities.[87] The number of assisted suicides reported by the right-to-die societies themselves[88] corresponds with the results of an international study on medical end-of-life decisions based on anonymous reports by a large number of doctors attending dying patients. The study revealed an occurrence of assisted suicide of 0.36% in Switzerland.[89] Since this figure is approximately the same as the number of assisted suicides among Swiss residents reported to the authorities by *Exit* and *Dignitas*, it follows that all cases of assisted suicide are being properly reported, at least when right-to-die societies such as *Exit* or Dignitas are involved. This seems perfectly plausible, since these organisations have a clear policy to report all assisted suicides to the authorities, and the internal social control within these organisations would make it rather difficult for an individual volunteer to make a maverick decision not to report a case.

16.4.7 Current Political Developments

In its 'Opinion on assisted suicide' released in April 2005, the Swiss National Advisory Commission on Biomedical Ethics supports the existing liberal approach towards assisted suicide.[90] The opinion emphasises that assisted suicide should be distinguished from euthanasia. In addition, the commission suggests state

---

[85] See Bosshard, Ulrich & Bär 2003.

[86] See Bosshard *et al* 2003.

[87] See Bosshard, Ulrich & Bär 2003.

[88] Homepage *Exit Deutsche Schweiz* <http://www.exit.ch/wDeutsch> accessed 9 September 2007; homepage *Exit ADMD* <http://www.exit-geneve.ch> accessed 9 September 2007; homepage Dignitas <http://www.dignitas.ch> accessed 9 September 2007.

[89] See Van der Heide *et al* 2003.

[90] See Nationale Ethikkommission im Bereich Humanmedizin 2005.

supervision of right-to-die societies. This suggestion supports a position taken earlier by the Attorney-General of the Canton of Zurich.[91] However, in August 2005 the Parliament of the Canton of Zurich rejected an initiative aimed at making right-to-die societies subject to registration and licensing, and prohibiting suicide tourism in general.[92] And in its proposals for 'Medical End-of-Life Decisions and Palliative Care' released in January 2006, the Swiss Federal Department of Justice and Police denied any need for action at a federal level. According to the department, both assisted suicide and suicide tourism are sufficiently regulated by the existing legal framework, and the department regards state supervision of right-to-die societies, in particular, as neither necessary nor appropriate.[93] Both the Swiss Academy of Medical Sciences and the Swiss National Advisory Commission on Biomedical Ethics have subsequently criticised the Federal Department of Justice for shirking its responsibilities and shifting them to the local prosecutors.[94]

16.5 What can the Swiss Model Contribute to the International Discussion on Assisted Dying?

Most experts agree that assisted dying cannot be properly regulated without doctors being involved. However, it is also true that the basic task of doctors is to heal patients or—when this is not possible—at least to relieve the symptoms caused by their medical condition, and not deliberately to end their patients' lives. It can hardly be denied that there is a basic conflict of roles when doctors assist in the suicide of their patients.

The Swiss model of assisted suicide reduces such role conflict by limiting the doctor's role in assisted suicide and, at the same time, allowing a role for non-physicians.[95] The key question in Switzerland which determines whether someone qualifies for assisted suicide is whether the person is competent to decide or, more specifically, whether there is a persistent and well-considered wish to die.[96] These are basically non-medical preconditions, even if, as mentioned above, the assessment of the medical situation in this respect is also of considerable importance. Although medical expertise must be available at some point in the decision-making process, this does not mean that every person who assists in suicide has to be a doctor or health care professional.

---

[91] See House of Lords Select Committee on the Assisted Dying for the Terminally Ill Bill (UK) 2005b: 624–33; Steudler 2004.

[92] See Hosp 2005.

[93] See Bundesamt für Justiz 2006.

[94] See Leibundgut 2006.

[95] Hurst & Mauron 2003.

[96] See Rippe *et al* 2005.

This position has recently been adopted by the Swiss Academy of Medical Sciences in a revised version of the *Medical-ethical Guidelines for the Care of Patients at the End of Life.*[97] In the very first paragraph of the chapter on assisted suicide, these new guidelines emphasise the fact that Article 115 of the Penal Code applies to everyone. Further on, the guidelines state that 'assisted suicide is not part of a doctor's task'. Rather, 'the doctor's task with patients at the end of life is to alleviate symptoms and to support the patient'. However, the guidelines also recognise, as we have seen, that a doctor who is asked by a patient to help with suicide faces 'a dilemma which calls for a personal decision in accordance with his/her conscience and which has to be respected as such'. To deal with this conflict, the Academy has specified minimum requirements that a doctor should meet if he or she is in principle willing to assist, namely: (1) the patient is approaching the end of life; (2) alternative options have been discussed and, if desired, have been implemented; (3) the patient is capable of making the decision, the wish to end life is well-considered, persistent, and arrived at without external pressure. Whereas (1) and (2) clearly require medical expertise, (3) does not. The Academy emphasises this by stating that the items listed in (3) 'must have been checked by a third person, not necessarily a doctor'. With these guidelines, which were approved by the great majority of the members of the Academy after an extended process of consultation with all parties, the Swiss Academy of Medical Sciences clarified the role of the doctor in assisted suicide while at the same time avoiding putting the responsibility in this field wholly on the shoulders of the medical profession.

[97] See Schweizerische Akademie der Medizinischen Wissenschaften 2005.

17

Some European Comparisons

In this chapter we briefly present the results of some comparative European studies of the frequency of medical behaviour that potentially shortens life and its regulation, and to start off, of public and professional opinion concerning the permissibility of euthanasia.

17.1 Comparative Data on Public and Professional Opinion

Rules concerning personal and professional behaviour obviously do not exist in a socio-cultural vacuum. Part of the relevant context consists of generally held values such as personal autonomy, beneficence, tolerance, liberty ('freedom from'), solidarity and the respect due to (for some, the sacredness of) human life. It seems, for example, a truism that in a society in which autonomy is not considered important but human life is generally regarded as sacred in the sense of beyond intentional human interference, it is unlikely that euthanasia will be allowed or in practice take place.

Nevertheless, how generally held values and the weight attached to them are to be ascertained, and what precisely their relationship is to public action such as the enactment and enforcement of a law, or to the actual use people (in particular, in this case, patients, those close to them and doctors) make of a law, is a notoriously difficult matter.

The problems of ascertaining generally held values—when applied to a concrete topic these are usually referred to as 'opinions'—in a quantitatively responsible way (via surveys) range from banal but crucial methodological problems (unrepresentative samples, a high non-response rate, ambiguous questions) to more fundamental questions: what the meaning is of 'opinions' elicited in the abstract, whether people really know what their operative 'opinions' are, how much weight they attach to them in relation to their other interests and whether a survey is a suitable way of collecting information about 'opinions'.

A further problem is that there is no simple one-to-one relationship between generally held opinions and their translation into political action. Even if in some sense we 'know' what values people (say they) hold in a particular country, there remains the question what this knowledge is worth for understanding or predict-ing political decision-making. How can we explain the fact, which we will see shortly (and which we have seen for a number of countries in chapters 11 through 16), that in most countries where there is well-established strong public support for legal euthanasia, it nevertheless remains illegal and usually does not even get onto the political agenda? Answers to such a question tend to degenerate into a variety of ad hoc observations. Nevertheless, we will attempt to deal with the ques-tion in chapter 20.

None of these problems receives much attention in most 'opinion' research concerning euthanasia.[1] A great deal of energy and expense is devoted to collect-ing numbers, but what question it is that they are supposed to enable one to answer is rarely specified. It is therefore good to approach data on public and pro-fessional 'opinion' about euthanasia in a sceptical frame of mind. But whatever doubts one may have about what this sort of data intrinsically 'means', the fact is that the results of opinion polls are themselves an important part of the local polit-ical debate, with proponents of legal change, for example, invoking the results of favourable opinion polls in support of their position. Opponents can then be por-trayed as in some sense 'undemocratic' for resisting what 'the public wants'.

However all this may be, and for whatever it is worth, Table 17.1 brings together the results of a large number of surveys of public and professional opinion. For most countries, the data come from Cohen's study of public opinion based on questions asked in the context of the European Values Study and from Miccinesi's comparative study of professional opinion. For other countries we have included data from other sources, which means that the table includes data collected in not entirely comparable ways. All of the data are more or less subject to the sorts of reservations one can have about opinion polls (including poorly formulated ques-tions that overlook essential matters such as the role of a doctor and the require-ments of unbearable suffering and of a request). Nevertheless, despite all these reservations, Table 17.1 does strongly suggest that Dutch and Belgian public and professional opinion, while not radically out of line with that in many other Western European countries, is at the favourable end of the spectrum. If this is probably not a sufficient cause of the legal change in those two countries, perhaps it was at least a necessary condition.

Methodological note: We have chosen to present not the degree of 'support' for euthanasia or its legalisation, since it is usually particularly obscure exactly what it is that the people answering a pollster thought they were endorsing and whether

---

[1] Rare exceptions to the general superficiality and ambiguity of opinion research in this area are the data collected in the British Social Attitudes Surveys (see Clery *et al* 2007), the research of Holsteyn and Trappenburg in the Netherlands (see ch 2.3.1), and the use of vignettes by Willems *et al* (2000) in their comparison of the attitudes of Dutch and Oregon doctors toward various end-of-life practice (atti-tudes were quite similar for most situations, including use of morphine in doses likely to shorten life and physician-assisted suicide, but Dutch doctors were much more favourable toward euthanasia whereas a patient's concern about being a burden to his family was much more frequently regarded as relevant by Oregon doctors). See Emanuel 2002 for an interesting critical survey of research concern-ing public and medical opinion in the United States.

Table 17.1. Public and medical opinion on the permissibility of euthanasia (percentages of those polled)

	NL[1]	BE	DK	FR	SW	GB	SP	DE	IT	NO	CH
Public opinion (c2000)											
'euthanasia (terminating the life of the incurably sick)' can never be justified	11	15[2]	16	16[3]	16	27[4]	34	38	47	[n.d.]	[11[5]]
Opinion of doctors (c2002)											
a patient should have the right to decide whether or not to hasten the end of his or her life	68	65[6]	42[7]	[43[8]]	31[7]	[47[9]]	[43[10]]	[25[11]]	37[6]	[17[12]]	61

Sources: except for data in brackets ('n.d.'–no data): Cohen *et al* 2006a (public opinion, based on the European Values Study of 1999–2000; N over 1,000 for all countries included here; response varies from 83% in Italy to 31% in Spain); Miccinesi *et al* 2005 (doctors' opinions; N over 1,000 for all countries; response roughly 60% except for Italy, 39%). All percentages are rounded off. A subsequent study of differences between responders and non-responders in the study of doctors' opinions suggests that the effect of non-response is to produce an overestimation of support for both life-shortening and life-preserving behavior (Fischer *et al* 2006).

[1] Compare the more complete data from other sources given in ch 2.3.1.

[2] A poll by the daily newspaper *La Libre Belgique* in March 2001 (during the Belgian parliamentary proceedings) showed 72% support for the pending bill to legalise euthanasia; in October 1999 an earlier poll had shown 78% support for legislation on the subject: see <http://www.lalibre.be/article_print.phtml?art_id=15963> accessed 13 February 2007.

[3] A more recent poll (SOFRES 8 and 9 March, 2006) gives about 10% opposed to euthanasia under any circumstances, a figure that seems to have been fairly constant for about 2 decades: see <http://www.admd.net/sondage.htm> accessed 22 January 2007.

[4] Data from the British Social Attitudes Surveys (1984, 1989, 1994, 2005) using a constant and better formulated question, show a gradual increase of favorable public attitudes toward legal euthanasia, with those opposed to legalisation declining from 24% in 1984 to 18% in 2005 (see Clery *et al* 2007).

[5] Best available data, from an opinion survey by Exit ADMD Genève (1999): see <http://www.exit-geneve.ch/Sondage1.htm> accessed 8 February 2007.

[6] Belgium: Flanders; Italy: Emilia Romagna, Trento, Tuscany and Veneto.

[7] Compare Folker *et al* 1996 for similar results (37% and 34% in Denmark and Sweden, respectively, consider physician-assisted suicide and euthanasia ethically acceptable).

[8] Peretti-Watel 2003a (per cent who agree or strongly agree that 'euthanasia should be legalized, as in the Netherlands').

[9] This is the result of a study of NHS doctors carried out in 1993 (Ward & Tate 1994). The question was whether the Dutch legal situation should exist in Great Britain. For reasons discussed in a literature survey done for the House of Lords Select Committee (House of Lords 2005a: 136–7,144), it seems despite its limitations to be the best of the studies available. The study also showed that almost half of the doctors had been asked at least once to take active steps to hasten death and of these a third had done so.

[10] CIS poll no 2451 (April–May 2002): 'the law should allow a doctor to hasten the death of a patient suffering from an incurable, painful and terminal condition who requests this'.

[11] Müller-Busch *et al* 2004 (members of German Association for Palliative Medicine 'for' or 'somewhat for' legalising PAS; corresponding figure for euthanasia: 10%).

[12] Førde, Aasland & Falkum 1997a (doctor should be permitted to end life of terminal patient who is suffering and who requests this).

they were all endorsing the same thing. For reasons already set forth in chapter 2.3.1, we take instead the degree of unqualified *opposition* as the least ambiguous measure of changes or differences in public opinion. Unfortunately, it is not possible to do the same for the opinions of doctors because of the way the results of the studies concerned are presented.

Whereas Table 17.1 registers public opinion at one point in time (the beginning of the 21st century), Graph 17.1 deals with changes in public opinion over a period of almost 20 years before that. Respondents were asked to rate their agreement with the statement shown on Table 17.1, on a scale of 1 to 10 (from 'never justified' to 'always justified') and a mean acceptance level was then calculated for each country.[2]

The European Values Survey (EVS) data show an unbroken upward trend in the public acceptance of euthanasia in all but 2 of 9 Western European countries. West Germany is the only country in which public acceptance, roughly in the middle of the nine countries in 1981, has since declined and by 1999 was close to the bottom

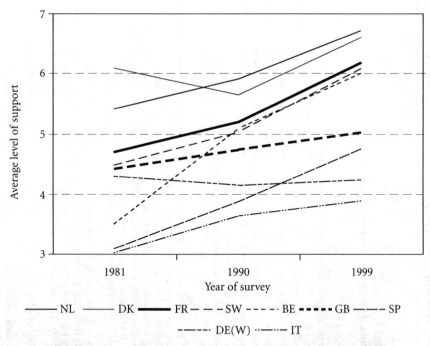

Graph 17.1 Changes in public acceptance of euthanasia in 9 European countries

---

[2] See Cohen *et al* 2006b. As is the case with most of the public opinion data on Table 17.1, the data derive from the European Values Survey, which periodically collects such information from some 33 countries in Western, Central and Eastern Europe. Only those Western European countries that had participated in all three of the surveys held to date are included. Graph 17.1 excludes Iceland, Ireland and Ulster, since we have no further information about them in this book.

(just above Italy, which while very low has distinctly risen over the years). And Denmark, with the highest level of public acceptance in 1981, experienced a slight decline in 1990, but has since risen to almost the same level as the Netherlands. The steepest rise over the years has been in Belgium which, together with the Netherlands, Denmark, France and Sweden, now has the highest level of public acceptance in Europe. Among countries moving in the direction of increased acceptance, the least change has been in Great Britain (although the data from the British Social Attitudes Survey, referred to in note 4 to Table 17.1, strongly suggest that the EVS data do not accurately reflect British public opinion). Except in the Netherlands, Belgium and perhaps Switzerland, the actual legal situation is much more restrictive than the views of (potential) patients would apparently prefer.

The authors of the public opinion studies on which Table 17.1 and Graph 17.1 are based have looked for correlations between the degree of support for euthanasia and other characteristics of their respondents. The results are similar to those that we have seen in chapter 2.3.1 for the Netherlands. Relatively weak religious belief is the most important factor associated with higher acceptance, but also younger people, people from non-manual social classes, and people of higher educational level tend to have a higher level of acceptance. The strength of people's belief in the right of self-determination is also relevant. Taken together, these factors seem to explain the differences between countries, although there are indications that national traditions and history can be important, as in the case of Germany.[3]

Except in the Netherlands, Belgium and Switzerland, only a minority of doctors say they support a patient's 'right' to decide about whether to hasten the end of life, although support in Denmark, Great Britain, France and Spain is close to 50%. Support among doctors seems to be lowest in Norway, followed by Germany and Sweden. In particular in Denmark, France and Sweden, doctors seem to have considerably more reservations about euthanasia than does the general public, but on the whole, as one might expect, in countries where the amount of opposition in the general public is relatively high, the amount of support among doctors is relatively low.[4]

Asking doctors abstract questions concerning their views about euthanasia is probably not nearly as revealing—in any case, it is subject to much more ambiguity—than asking them about their actual experience. We have seen data on this for the Netherlands in chapter 5 (see Table 5.7) and Table 17.2 gives similar data for other countries, to the extent it exists.

---

[3] Cohen *et al* 2006a.

[4] A study in six countries (Czech Republic, Israel, Netherlands, Portugal, Sweden and UK) shows that in connection with end of life decisions intensive care professionals overwhelmingly would consider quality of life more important than the value of life itself (whereas patients and their families are more evenly divided), but only about a third consider quality of life more important for their patients; if diagnosed with a terminal illness, the medical professionals would want admission to ICU, CPR or ventilation much less often than patients and their families would. About a third of the doctors and two-fifths of the nurses would want euthanasia for themselves (slightly more patients and their family would want this). See Sprung *et al* 2007.

17.2 Comparative data on the frequency of MBPSL

Data, mostly collected in the comparative EURELD studies using the Dutch methodology, and therefore comparable with the data for the Netherlands and Belgium presented in chapters 5.1.2.3 and 10.1, are available for a number of other European countries. Table 17.2 gives an overview. Unfortunately, as the notes to the table show, the response rate was disappointing in some countries, especially Italy, and in several countries only some regions were covered. The confidence intervals in the case of (very) small percentages are considerable, which means that results after the decimal point, in particular, should probably be taken with a grain of salt.

The Total Level of MBPSL

As far as the total level of MBPSL is concerned—whether measured as a percentage of all deaths or of non-sudden deaths—the Netherlands are more or less in the middle of the European spectrum. In the Netherlands the rate of death due to withholding or withdrawing treatment was in 2001 about average for European countries (it declined later to 16% in 2005[5]); Switzerland, the UK and especially France had considerably higher rates. The Netherlands stands out, of course, as far as the frequency of euthanasia and assisted suicide is concerned, although Switzerland also has a substantial amount of both and Belgium had a relatively high level of euthanasia even before legalisation in 2002,[6] and seems to have Europe's highest rate of termination of life without a request.

'Permissive' and 'Not Permissive' Countries

For purposes of locating his recent data on the frequency of MBPSL in the United Kingdom among those for other European countries which had already been systematically studied in the EURELD project, Seale[7] divides the other countries into two groups, 'permissive' and 'not permissive', based on the legal status of euthanasia and/or physician-assisted suicide. The Netherlands, Belgium and Switzerland are in the first group; Italy, Denmark and Sweden in the second.

There is a large difference in doctors' estimates of the shortening of life due to MBPSL in the two groups in: 59% in the permissive group and 81% in the non-permissive group estimate that the patient's life in the case studied was shortened by a week or less. The UK is closest to the non-permissive countries in this respect (88%).[8]

---

[5] See ch 5, Table 5.1.
[6] See ch 10.1.
[7] Seale 2006b.
[8] *Ibid*, Table 1.

Table 17.2. **Frequency of euthanasia and other MBPSL in some European countries in 2001–2002 (percentages of deaths)**

	NL	BE[1,2]	CH[1]	DK	SW	IT[1]	UK[3]
euthanasia	2.59	0.30 [1.1]	0.27	0.06	—	0.04	0.16
(% doctors who ever did this)[4]	(57)			(5)	(0)		(12)
physician-assisted suicide	0.21	0.01 [0.1]	0.36[5]	0.06	—	0.00	0.00
(% doctors who ever did this)[4]				(2)	(2)		
abstention (refusal or futility)	20	15 [16.4]	28	14	14	4	30.3
pain relief with life-shortening effect	20	22 [18.5]	22	26	21	19	32.8
termination of life without request	0.60	1.5 [3.2]	0.42	0.67	0.23	0.06	0.33
total MBPSL	44	38 [39.3]	51	41	36	23	64
total MBPSL excluding sudden deaths[6]	65	59	75	61	51	33	70
terminal sedation (without ANH)[7]	3.7	3.2	2.9	1.6	1.8	3.0	?

? = no data;— = no case found.

Source: except for UK and terminal sedation, Van der Heide *et al* 2003 (EURELD study), data collected in 2001–02; this part of the table is set off from the rest with a heavy rule.

Country samples all above 2,500 (for the Netherlands—where data from the 2001 national survey were used—above 5,000). The response rates were: NL 75%, BE 59%, CH 67%, DK 62%, SW 61%, IT 44%. The data do not cover all MBPSL of a given type, but only what the doctor considers to have been the 'most important' MBPSL. Bosshard's data for all abstention decisions (Bosshard *et al* 2005, EURELD study), based on the same data set, are rather higher than those given here: NL 30, BE 27, CH 41, DK 23, SW 22, IT 6.

[1] In Belgium: Flanders; in Italy: Trento, Toscana, Veneto, Emilia Romagna; in Switzerland: German-speaking area.

[2] These figures are probably erroneous, for reasons given in chapter 10.1. Data from the 1998 study (see Table 10.1) seem more reliable and are given between square brackets.

[3] Seale 2006a: Table 2 (data derive from doctors (most recent case) rather than from death certificates and are therefore not entirely comparable with data from death certificate studies). Seale notes (2006b: 658) that the reason for sampling doctors is that privacy legislation makes a death certificate study unfeasible in the UK. Seale's response rate was 53% and his N after non-response 857 (and for MBPSL much smaller than that) so that the confidence intervals are large for euthanasia, assisted suicide and termination of life without a request.

[4] Respectively: Van der Wal *et al* 2003: 45 (Netherlands–euthanasia and PAS); Materstvedt & Kaasa 2002 (Denmark and Sweden); Ward & Tate 1994 (United Kingdom); on Denmark and Sweden, see also respectively Folker *et al* 1996, Valverius Nilstun & Nilsson 2000.

[5] Of 0.36% deaths due to physician-assisted suicide, a right-to-die organization was involved in 92% (see Van der Heide *et al* 2003: 347); the latter are included with the PAS data, because in Swiss practice a doctor always prescribes the lethal drug (see ch 16).

[6] Seale 2006a, Table 3.

[7] Miccinesi *et al* 2006: Table 1 (EURELD study). These data are presented here separately from the other MBPSL data because it is not clear whether or to what extent they are included within the data given for pain relief with life-shortening effect or abstention. See ch 5.2.2.2 for discussion of problems of classification and measurement of terminal sedation.

On a whole range of issues relating to involvement of the patient and his family in the decision-making, and more generally to transparency, the differences between permissive and non-permissive countries are striking and consistent.[9] Doctors in permissive countries consider their MBPSL patients competent far more often than do doctors in non-permissive countries (30% as against 16%) and UK doctors are in between in this respect (24%). Doctors in permissive countries are far more likely to discuss the medical decision-making with their competent patients (81% as against 50%) or with the family of non-competent patients (77% as against 44%). UK doctors were in between, but closer to the permissive countries (69% with competent patients, 63% with family of non-competent patients). Doctors in permissive countries discuss a possible MBPSL decision with other doctors or with nursing staff far more frequently (40% and 47% respectively) than do doctors in non-permissive countries (18% and 28% respectively). UK doctors discuss the decision with other doctors even more often than doctors in permissive countries (52%) and with nurses just as often (47%). In short, despite the fact that the UK is, according to Seale's definition, a non-permissive country, in all respects except their estimates of shortening of life, UK doctors seem more similar to their colleagues in permissive countries than to those in non-permissive countries.[10]

Withdrawing or Withholding Treatment

A study by Bosshard and others focuses specifically on abstention.[11] It shows that the frequency in 2001 of *all* non-treatment decisions (not limited to the 'most important' MBPSL in a given case) as a percentage of all deaths was highest in Switzerland (41%), and lower in the Netherlands (30%), Belgium (27%), Denmark (23%) and Sweden (22%); only Italy seems far out of line (6%). The most common treatments withheld or withdrawn were medication (average of all

---

[9] Miccinesi *et al* 2006, Table 3.

[10] A recent study deals with the access of GPs and general internists to ethical consultation in 4 European countries (Norway, Switzerland, Italy and the UK). Although there are wide differences of access to formal or informal 'ethics support services' (over 50% of doctors in the UK, much less in the other countries), only about 18% of the doctors studied have access in individual cases and even fewer (fewest of all in the UK—10%) actually use the services. Doctors with more training in ethics were more likely to use the resources available to them. About half of all doctors reported some form of training in ethics; in the UK half had had such training in medical school, but only 10% in Italy (Hurst *et al* 2007a). From the same study it appears that in all 4 countries treating patients whose decision-making capacity is impaired, disagreements among caregivers, limiting life-sustaining treatment, and disagreements with the patient are most often mentioned as giving rise to ethical difficulties; in Italy, especially, uncertainty whether to disclose a diagnosis is a common reason for ethical difficulty; in the UK, especially, scarcity of resources is a common reason. Requests for euthanasia or PAS are mentioned by 10% of the doctors in Italy, 20% in Norway, 30% in the UK, and over 40% in Switzerland. In all countries except the UK, requests for euthanasia/PAS give rise to the most difficult ethical issues (over a third of the doctors in Italy and Switzerland, about 15% in Norway); in the UK disagreement among caregivers is more often mentioned, but euthansia/PAS is mentioned by a fifth of the doctors (Hurst *et al* 2007b)

[11] Bosshard *et al* 2005 (EURELD study). The more global data shown on Table 17.2 are slightly different because only the 'most important' MBPSL decision was included.

countries: 44%) and artificial nutrition and hydration (22%), totalling in all countries between 60% and 70% of all treatments forgone. No other treatment amounted to more than 10% for any country. Shortening of life of more than a month when abstention is the 'most important' MBPSL was relatively common in the Netherlands (10%), Belgium (9%) and Switzerland (8%), and rather lower in Sweden (2%), Italy (3%) and Denmark (5%).[12]

An interesting finding, given the common assumption that withdrawing life-prolonging treatment is psychologically, ethically and/or legally more problematic than withholding it in the first place, is that the two forms of abstention were roughly in balance in most countries (about 60:40 in favour of withholding in the six countries as a whole and in Belgium and the Netherlands, a bit more so in Sweden and Switzerland, a bit less so in Italy). Only in Denmark was the balance slightly the other way around.

Discussion of withholding or withdrawing treatment with the patient or his family was normal in all countries (average 82% for all treatments), but systematically higher in the Netherlands (95%) and Belgium (85%) and lower in Italy (68%), Sweden (69%) and Denmark (72%).

As we have seen in chapter 4.2.2.2 and 4.2.3, the legal status of intentional shortening of life by means of withholding or withdrawing treatment can be doubtful, at least from the perspective of traditional criminal law analysis. In six European countries,[13] hastening death is intentional in 45% of all cases of abstention and an accepted but not specifically intended result in 55% (the rate of intentional hastening of death is rather higher in the case of withholding than in that of withdrawing). The specific intention to hasten death is somewhat less frequent in Denmark and Belgium (36% and 38%), more frequent in Sweden and Switzerland (51% and 52%), and about average in Italy and the Netherlands (42% and 45%). Bosshard and others argue that such results are impossible to square with the traditional justification of abstention as a merely non-intentional 'allowing to die':[14]

[T]he conclusion that intentionally allowing a hastened death is always morally wrong would mean disapproval of a considerable number of medical decisions at the end of life. [I]n the context of withholding and withdrawing treatment there is great divergence between the traditional moral rule and today's medical practice.

---

[12] A study by Sprung *et al* (2003) concludes that withholding or withdrawing life-prolonging treatment is 'routine' in European Intensive Care Units (76% of all deaths). Withholding treatment is roughly equally frequent in northern, middle and southern European countries, whereas withdrawing treatment is about half as frequent in the southern countries (Greece, Israel, Italy, Portugal, Spain and Turkey).

[13] See Bosshard *et al* 2006 (EURELD study).

[14] *Ibid* at 325. Bosshard *et al* observe that one might restrict the doctrine of double effect to 'active' measures and use act-omission doctrine for withdrawing and withholding treatment, which they believe is the current legal position in most Western countries.

However, if actively hastening death can be allowed (in indirect euthanasia), and intentionally hastening death can be allowed (in passive euthanasia), the question remains of what is so problematic about their combination. (*Ibid*).

Unfortunately, the number of cases in which abstention was either medically indicated (on grounds of 'futility') or refused by the patient or his representative, is not known. In such cases the problem Bosshard *et al* discuss would not arise (cf ch 4.2.2.1 and 4.2.2.2).

A recent comparative study of the frequency with which a DNR order had been given in cases of non-sudden death in six European countries gives estimates for both Belgium and the Netherlands of 60% (and an additional 5% and 9%, respectively, for 'institutional DNR decisions'—that is, general institutional policy not to resuscitate). The estimates for the other countries were at a comparable level (Denmark, 50%; Sweden, 49%; Switzerland, 73%), except for Italy where the rate was much lower (16%).[15]

Pain Relief with Life-Shortening Effect: Palliative and Terminal Sedation

In most countries covered in the EURELD studies of six European countries between a fifth and a quarter of all deaths were due to pain relief with life-shortening effect (see Table 17.2). Only the United Kingdom was significantly deviant, with almost 33% of all deaths being attributed by the doctor to pain relief (however, as we have seen in chapter 5, Table 5.1, more recent data from the Netherlands show a significant movement in the direction of the UK).[16]

A recent EURELD study gives the following frequencies for deaths following palliative sedation (that is, with ANH) for six European countries in 2001–02: Belgium—5%; Denmark—0.9%; Italy—5.5%; Netherlands—2%; Sweden—1.4%; Switzerland—1.9%.[17] The rate of terminal sedation (without ANH) in the Netherlands, Belgium, Switzerland, and in this case Italy, is roughly similar at ±3% (see Table 17.2) but rather lower in Denmark and Sweden.

Termination of Life Without an Explicit Request from the Patient

From comparative data that have become available over the past few years, it appears that termination of life without an explicit request from the patient occurs in all Western European countries that have been studied. From Table 17.2 we can see that even the lowest rate for Belgium (1.5% of all deaths) is rather higher than that for the other European countries studied, while the Dutch rate is roughly the same as that of Denmark and a bit higher than the rates in Switzerland (0.4%) and the UK (0.3%). Sweden is rather lower (0.2%) and Italy lowest of all (0.06%).

---

[15] Van Delden *et al* 2006 (EURELD study).

[16] A related EURELD study of the drugs used for pain and symptom relief in cases in which the doctor involved believed that life might have been shortened (Bilsen *et al* 2006) concludes that given the generally rather low doses given, the small estimated shortening of life, and the low number of opioid-naïve patients, it can be doubted whether the doctors involved were correct in attributing a life-shortening effect to their behaviour. Pain relief is rarely given with the intention of shortening life, but in these cases, too, the doses given in most cases were unlikely to have had such an effect.

[17] See Miccinesi *et al* 2006: 125. In Belgium and Italy, palliative sedation is about twice as frequent as terminal sedation (with withdrawal of ANH), whereas in the other four countries terminal sedation is more common.

17.3 Conclusions Concerning Medical Practice

MBPSL practice in those European countries covered in the EURELD studies seems on the whole rather similar. Only Italy, where the rates for all MBPSL except pain relief with life-shortening effect and terminal sedation are much lower than in other countries, stands out as a consistent deviant. Leaving Italy aside (and including the UK), the total rate of MBPSL is everywhere over 40% of all deaths and about 60% or more of all non-sudden deaths. The highest rates of death due to 'normal medical practice' (abstention and pain relief) are in the UK.

The Dutch rate of euthanasia/PAS is by far the highest in Europe. The Swiss have the highest rate of assisted suicide, and a surprisingly high rate of euthanasia (given the fact that it is illegal in Switzerland). The Belgian (Flanders) rate—at a time when euthanasia was still illegal—was also high by European standards. In the other countries for which we have data, the rates are much lower but probably not very reliable (among other things because of the large confidence intervals associated with very small percentages).

Although the Netherlands is the only country in which termination of life without a request from the patient is legal in certain circumstances, it is not the country with the highest rate of this most controversial of MBPSLs: the Belgian rate is at least double the Dutch rate, and the Danish rate is slightly higher. Switzerland, the UK and Sweden also have significant rates.

There are, of course, a whole host of questions surrounding these comparative results. Are the results reliable (samples, response)? Are the same things being counted in different countries (in particular when subjective 'intentions' are used to classify behaviour)? Are doctors equally honest in all countries? This is not a reason to reject the results-to-date out of hand: they are, for the time being, the best we have, and a betting man would have to wager that they are not far off the mark. The questions and doubts they give rise to are reasons to do more and better local and comparative research.

In the meantime, the results do seem to justify the conclusion that medical practice at the end of life in the Netherlands and Belgium is not so very deviant from that in other European countries, except that a small part of medical practice that shortens the life of a patient consists of euthanasia or physician-assisted suicide, which are legal, openly practised, and called by their proper names.

17.4 Legal Comparisons

European MBPSL law, at least in the countries we have studied in this book, seems to exhibit convergence. The different sorts of medical behaviour that potentially shorten the life of a patient are now recognised as analytically distinct, and a common vocabulary has emerged for designating them. On most subjects it seems safe to predict that within a few years there will be few and only minor differences (these subjects include the right to refuse treatment and the recognition of advance treatment directives, the legitimacy of withholding or withdrawing life-prolonging treatment and of administering potentially life-shortening pain relief, palliative and terminal sedation). However, based on legal materials alone, it would be rash to venture a prediction whether convergence concerning euthanasia, physician-assisted suicide, and termination of life without a request will follow. We return to that question in chapter 20.

There are rather larger differences concerning the participants in the decision-making. The position of the patient is legally speaking very strong in a number of countries with modern patients' rights legislation (such as Belgium, England, the Netherlands). But in France, Spain and Italy legal acceptance of medical paternalism still seems strong. The legal position of a representative of the patient is even more variable, and only in the Netherlands (and very recently in England) can this be described without qualification as strong. England is idiosyncratic in leaving a key role in some sorts of decision-making (in particular, withdrawal of treatment in PVS cases) to the courts. Considering the direction of change, in countries where it is currently taking place, it seems fair to predict that the modern 'self-determination' model so dominant in the Netherlands will in the not very distant future be characteristic for European countries.

Interpretation and enforcement of legal or professional rules exhibit the greatest differences. In most countries (Belgium being a notable exception) the (criminal) courts have been important vehicles of legal development. In most countries the medical profession produces rules of medical ethics (with or without formal legal status) and especially in the Netherlands, Switzerland and Scandinavia these rules seem to have an important influence on legal development and on MBPSL practice. In countries where there is a legally-organised 'Order of Physicians' or the like, which is responsible for a 'Deontological Code', it seems to play little or no role in legal development. In England and the Netherlands, there are distinct legal bodies responsible for medical disciplinary law, but only in England does the General Medical Council seem to be an important factor in the development and maintenance of professional rules. And finally, in Belgium and the Netherlands a non-criminal procedure for reviewing cases of euthanasia and assisted suicide has taken over the bulk of the control work formerly in the hands of the prosecutorial authorities, and systems of before-the-fact review are gradually becoming more important. It will be interesting to see whether these approaches spread to other countries and also, perhaps, to other forms of MBPSL.

A few more detailed comparative observations can be made:

1. There is general agreement that pain and symptom relief can be given even though it potentially will shorten the patient's life. However, the legal grounds on which this can be done are not clear. Two approaches are available: the 'doctrine of double effect' and the 'medical exception'. The first holds that

potentially life-shortening pain relief is permissible *so long as the doctor's intention is to relieve pain and not to shorten life*. There is a latent doctrinal tension between the subjective conception of 'intent' as used in the doctrine of double effect (purpose or motive) and the objectified intent that is generally used in the criminal law (knowledge and acceptance of consequences). Although it is widely supposed to have legal status, the only country in which the doctrine of double effect has been explicitly accepted for legal purposes is England. The second approach—in effect, the 'medical exception'—holds that doctors are authorised to do things that are otherwise forbidden, *so long as there is a medical indication for what they do*. There seems to be a gradual shift taking place from subjective intention to medical indication as the criterion for distinguishing between pain relief and termination of life. This is most visible in the Netherlands, but there are also indications of a shift in that direction in Switzerland. Nowhere, however, do there seem to be decision-making or review procedures in connection with potentially life-shortening pain relief.

2. All Western European countries give at least lip-service to the principle of informed consent, but although it is anchored in the European Convention on Human Rights[18] the idea that the patient has a right to refuse life-prolonging treatment is only gradually spreading. Belgium, England, the Netherlands, Sweden and Switzerland accept the principle in all situations. In Denmark and France (at least until the new Patients' Rights Law of 2005) treatment cannot be refused if life is at stake; in Norway not in an 'emergency' situation. Until the recent *Welby* case in Italy and the *Echevarría* case in Spain there was doubt about the legitimacy of abstention in such a case, but the law there seems to be developing in the direction of the European norm.

3. There is general agreement that life-prolonging treatment can be withheld or withdrawn if it either would be or has become 'futile'. However, in most countries neither the criteria according to which treatment can be considered 'futile' nor the decision-making procedure required before such a judgment is carried out, are well developed. The key issue is whether doctors (or representatives of the patient) may take 'quality of life' considerations into account. The most limited position on this is that of the Catholic Church, that treatment can be withheld only if death is 'imminent' and 'inevitable'. The Netherlands and England (using the 'best interests' test) explicitly allow judgments based on 'quality of life' considerations. Decision-making procedures that seek to guarantee 'intersubjectivity' in the decision-making when quality of life considerations are involved, are gradually emerging in the Netherlands.

4. Advance treatment directives are known in all countries, but in only some (Belgium, England, the Netherlands, Switzerland) do they have a strong legal status. Nevertheless, the legally binding character of a patient's advance written refusal of treatment seems gradually to be becoming accepted everywhere.[19]

---

[18] See ch 9.2.1 (discussing the *Pretty* case).
[19] However, as Vezzoni (2008) has shown, due among other things to the general absence of supportive policies, their effectiveness in steering medical decision-making is everywhere quite limited.

5. The role of representatives of a non-competent patient (appointed by a court or by the patient, or statutory 'default' representatives) is legally well defined in England, Belgium, the Netherlands and Switzerland. Most other countries accept some form of 'proxy decision-making' (based on the patient's 'best interests' or 'presumed will') if the treatment wishes of a non-competent patient are not known, but the proxy generally only gives information which a doctor can take into account.

6. Palliative sedation, in the sense of deep, continuous sedation until death, seems to be generally accepted as a legitimate form of pain and symptom relief; apparently only in Norway and Sweden, and in the Netherlands (and to a more limited extent in Switzerland), has it been subjected to specific regulatory attention. A clear distinction between 'palliative' and 'terminal' sedation is rarely made (although the empirical data discussed in section 17.2 do distinguish between deep, continuous sedation with and without artificial nutrition and hydration). The legitimacy of withholding artificial nutrition and hydration from a sedated patient at the end of life is everywhere unsettled except in the Netherlands and in England (where the doctrine of double effect is used in connection with pain relief but not terminal sedation, which is regarded as withholding of treatment and therefore falls under the 'best interests' test).

7. Euthanasia is everywhere illegal (either murder or a lesser offence of homicide on request) except in the Netherlands and Belgium. Physician-assisted suicide is legal in the Netherlands and Belgium (where it is assimilated to euthanasia), and in Switzerland (where doctors are involved but the actual help is given by right-to-die societies). It is specifically illegal in Denmark, England, Italy, Norway and Spain. It is in theory legal in France and Sweden, but might be subject to disciplinary action under the codes of medical ethics. Proposals to legalise euthanasia and/or physician-assisted suicide have been introduced in England, France, Italy, Spain and Switzerland, but only in England has serious parliamentary attention been paid to them. Recently, however, there seem to be signs of movement in such a direction in France and Spain.

8. Termination of life without a request from the patient is illegal everywhere. Only in the Netherlands (and in highly unusual circumstances in England, in the 'conjoined-twins' case) have the courts recognised the possibility of a defence of justification in the situation of neonatology. In the Netherlands a national protocol and assessment procedure have recently been established for such cases. There are no signs of any such legal developments in other countries, although termination of life exists as a more or less 'normal' part of neonatal intensive care medicine almost everywhere and for France, Belgium and the Netherlands there are good qualitative descriptions of the practice.

Part IV

Thematic Reflections

Introduction to Part IV

The information density of the preceding three parts has been, on the whole, very high. That is because we have tried to be as comprehensive as possible, and also to stay very close to our sources: to cite chapter and verse for every assertion, so that the reader can challenge it if he likes, or knows where to go if he wants to investigate a given topic further.

In the three chapters of this part, we relax a bit (and we hope the reader will follow us in this). Instead of providing new information, we want to take a step back from all the information in the first three parts and engage in some reflection on what it means for the theoretical themes we mentioned already in the first chapter of the book: changes in the quantity of euthanasia law (chapter 18), the idea of a 'slippery slope' (chapter 19), and the emergence and diffusion of euthanasia law (chapter 20). While we hope it will all be 'evidence based' (to borrow a bit of medical jargon), what we will be doing is engaging in some theoretically and empirically informed speculation.

18

The Nude Beach Phenomenon: Euthanasia and the Juridification of the Doctor–Patient Relationship

A normal person in any other country, upon hearing that euthanasia has been made legal in the Netherlands,[1] could be excused for supposing that what has happened is that existing rules prohibiting euthanasia have been eliminated, that is, that in a general sort of sense, there is 'less law' on the subject now than there was before legalisation. Especially chapters 4 and 9 show how wrong such an idea would be.

On the other hand, the oft-heard fear of 'juridification' of the doctor-patient relationship assumes that more and more law regulates it—that the 'rule pressure' (to use a current Dutch expression) is increasing, and that this is particularly worrisome in an area of life that is too delicate to bear the weight so much law.

Both of these seemingly opposed interpretations of what is going on depend on our being able to measure in some way how much law doctors are exposed to. But how that might be done is not obvious. We are going to approach that problem in a rather rough and ready way, using Black's idea that the 'quantity of law'[2] can be measured in terms of 'the number and scope of prohibitions, obligations and other standards to which people are subject, and by the rate of legislation, litigation, and adjudication'.[3]

Black offers an explanatory theory of difference and change in the 'quantity of law'. Black's theory tells us to expect more law where there is greater inequality of wealth, where social bonds between members of society are looser, where the degree of social integration is lower, and where other forms of social control over the behaviour concerned are weaker. In the case of euthanasia, Black's theory seems to point in precisely the wrong direction. All of his variables would lead us to expect less law on the subject in the Netherlands than elsewhere, whereas, as we will see, quite the opposite is true.

---

[1] Belgium is not included in the argument of this chapter because legal development there is too recent for any kind of settled judgment. On the whole, developments to date seem to support the argument, and where relevant we will note them in the footnotes.

[2] The idea that there is something that might sensibly be called the quantity of law is a classic problem in the sociology of law. The questions it raises include whether the idea is meaningful at all and how to operationalise it for purposes of measurement. For present purposes these problems can be ignored.

[3] Black 1976:3.

Let us turn to what looks like a more hopeful theoretical approach: Elias's civilisation theory'.[4] Elias seeks to explain the growth of social control concerning violence and good manners over the past 1,000 years or so of European history. In his footsteps, Kapteyn has studied the cultural changes of the 1970s in the Netherlands. One chapter in Kapteyn's book *Taboo, Power and Morality in the Netherlands*[5] is devoted to the collapse of the taboo on nudity in public, in particular on beaches. Kapteyn argues that whereas the defenders of traditional Dutch cultural values regarded the whole development as an instance of a more general collapse of civilised order, the fact of the matter was that elimination of an unqualified taboo lead to more rules and more control than there had ever been before. There was, for example, on an old-fashioned beach, not much need for rules about how people look at each other. On nude beaches, however, such rules quickly arose and were effectively—if informally—enforced.

One proposition that can be derived from Elias and Kapteyn is that the decline of an unqualified general prohibition of a given sort of behaviour gives rise to the need for much more and more specific regulation, dealing with when, how, and subject to what restrictions the previously forbidden sort of behaviour is acceptable. Or, in short, taking the idea of 'law' broadly, the end of a taboo brings more law, not less.

The idea of a taboo seems particularly appropriate to the case of euthanasia, which shares with classic examples of taboo, like incest, two important features. The first is that one is not supposed to talk about a subject that is taboo. Early Dutch research revealed, that although some of it did seem to be going on, until the 1980s the idea of 'euthanasia' was not mentioned in Dutch health care institutions.[6] It has been observed that one of the reasons the process of legalisation in the Netherlands got underway lies in the Dutch cultural commitment, from the 1970s onward, to making every imaginable painful sort of subject 'discussable',[7] which is the death knell for a taboo.

A second essential feature of a taboo is that behind the curtain of unmentionability, a lot of the behaviour concerned is in fact going on. Because it was taboo, we cannot know how much euthanasia there actually was in the Netherlands before the legalisation debate began, but it seems pretty clear that under one name or another the practice, although unmentionable, was in fact taking place.[8] Nor, of course, do we know how much is currently going on in other countries where the taboo remains in effect (although comparative research does suggest that euthanasia is by no means unknown[9]).

---

[4] See Elias 1993.
[5] Kapteyn 1980.
[6] See Hilhorst 1983: 35 (discussed in GB&W: 57).
[7] See eg Kennedy 2002.
[8] There are many indications of this, for example the testimony of the Medical Inspector in the *Postma* case (1973—see GB&W: 51–52), Hilhorst's research (see n 6 above), and the *conclusie* [formal written advice] of the Advocate-General in the *Schoonheim* case (1984—see GB&W: 326 n. 11), discussing the trend toward greater acceptance of euthanasia when performed by a doctor.
[9] See ch 17.2. *Cf* also Magnusson 2002.

The way Dutch euthanasia law grew upon the foundation of the traditional criminal law doctrine of necessity (in the sense of conflict of duties) has been described in chapter 3.[10] Although euthanasia is explicitly prohibited by the Dutch Penal Code, doctors were in fact not prosecuted before the 1970s. As late as 1984 a very highly regarded prosecutor and criminal law scholar told the Supreme Court, in arguing that change of euthanasia law should be left to the legislature, that Dutch prosecutors would know better than to prosecute a doctor of good standing for such a thing.[11] A process of legal change became possible when, in the 1970s, prosecutions of doctors began and open public discussion got underway about the legitimacy of various sorts of medical behaviour that shortens the life of patients.[12]

At the beginning of the process of legal change, Dutch law on the subject consisted of two short articles of the Penal Code prohibiting euthanasia and assisted suicide, as well as embryonic versions of some tangentially relevant elements of medical law: informed consent and the right to refuse treatment, advance directives, representation and surrogate decision making, medical futility, the medical exception. All of this was in a very primitive state in the early 1980s, with neither legislation nor authoritative case law to go on, so a few pages would have sufficed to summarise it all, as they would to this day for many other countries.

A little more than 30 years after the taboo was broken and the visible process of legal change began, there is both legislation, delegated and informal rule-making, and extensive case law. Giving a reasonably detailed account of Dutch law concerning euthanasia and related medical behaviour that potentially shortens life has taken over 100 pages in chapter 4.[13] An initial impression, thus, is that there has been a major increase in the amount of law on the subject.

To take the idea of the 'quantity of law' further than such a rough sketch of the growth of euthanasia law permits, we need to return to Black's approach and focus on three forms in which law manifests itself in social life: (1) the official application of legal control to the behaviour of individual doctors; (2) the pressure of legal regulation to which the behaviour of doctors is subject; (3) the amount of rule-following that is taking place.

The *official application of legal control to the behaviour of individual doctors* consists of every instance of official contact between a doctor and a representative of the legal system concerning an individual case of (proposed) euthanasia. The *pressure of regulation* to which euthanasia and other medical behaviour that potentially shortens life is subject consists of the volume of legal rules of various provenance, as described in chapter 4. And the *amount of rule-following* taking place includes

---

[10] See for a fuller account of the early period of legal change, GB&W: ch 2.

[11] See n 8.

[12] See GB&W: ch. 2.1 and 2.2.

[13] As we have seen in chs 8 and 9, the history of legal change in Belgium was very different from that in the Netherlands but the outcome much the same. While there is hardly any relevant case law in Belgium, the Belgian euthanasia statute in effect makes up for this, being far more detailed than that in the Netherlands. Belgian law on the other MBPSL emerged in the same period and is about the same as that in the Netherlands.

both cases in which a doctor applies one or another of the rules to his behaviour as well as rule-following by intermediate institutions such as hospitals and nursing homes, when they incorporate external legal rules into internal policies, procedures and guidelines. In the following sections we examine the amount of each of these manifestations of law, returning in section 18.4 to the question what it all adds up to.

18.1 The Official Application of Legal Control to the Behaviour of Individual Doctors

SCEN Consultation

As we argued in chapters 4 and 5,[14] there is a distinct if low-visibility development taking place in Dutch euthanasia law, from review after the fact to review in advance. In effect, consultation with a specially trained so-called SCEN consultant is gradually becoming the context in which control of a doctor's (proposed) behaviour most frequently takes place.[15] Every such consultation can be considered a particle of law. There were 3,019 SCEN consultations in 2006.[16]

Reporting and Review

Each report by a doctor who carries out euthanasia—and who, by reporting, subjects himself to official scrutiny—is in itself a particle of law, whose 'weight' depends on the amount of official attention it receives. The number of reports has increased dramatically over the past two decades, as Graph 5.1 in chapter 5 shows. In the period 1991–95, before the creation of the Regional Review Committees, Dutch doctors reported 6,324 cases of euthanasia, all of which were reviewed by the prosecutorial authorities. Of these, 120 received full review by the highest authority within the prosecutorial service. In 1996–97 another 3,797 cases were reported. Since 1998 societal control of euthanasia practice has been largely non-criminal, and the burden of control has shifted almost entirely to the Regional Review Committees. 18,042 cases have been reported under this new system from 1998 through 2006. The Dutch system of legal control is currently processing over 1,900 euthanasia cases per year—in 2006 there were 1,923.[17]

Apart from their formal task of deciding whether a doctor was 'careful' (ie followed the rules), the Review Committees also 'sanction' doctors (and consultants)

---

[14] See ch 4.2.4.4 and 4.2.5 (*The System of Legal Control*), and ch 5.4.2.

[15] The development of specialised consultation in the LEIF and Médecins EOL programmes in Belgium may herald a similar shift in the locus of control (see ch 9.4.3.8).

[16] See ch 5, Table 5.16. In 2006 there were also 1,158 requests for information by a doctor considering performing euthanasia.

[17] See ch 5, Tables 5.17 and 5.20; GB&W:243.

in various ways. In a little under 10% of all cases—roughly 200 per year—a reporting doctor, a consultant, or someone else is asked to give further information.[18]

In the course of their first 9 years (1999 through 2006), the Review Committees had found 25 doctors (an average of about 3 per year) 'not careful'—that is to say, one or more of the rules governing euthanasia were not met.[19] All these cases are forwarded to the prosecutorial and medical disciplinary authorities.

The Dutch prosecutorial service decided not to press charges in any of the 25 cases in which the Regional Review Committees came to a 'not careful' judgment. However, in most of these cases the local prosecutor did discuss the case with the doctor concerned. When a decision not to prosecute is taken, the prosecutor sometimes refers the case to the Medical Inspectorate for appropriate action (eg talking to the doctor concerned, calling the attention of the profession to the problem involved, getting the hospital involved to adopt or improve its euthanasia protocol).[20]

Prosecutions, Convictions, Punishments

Since the early 1970s there have been a significant number of prosecutions. From 1973 through 1990 we know of 5 criminal prosecutions of doctors.[21] From 1991 through 1995 there were indictments in 10 cases.[22] For 1996 and 1997 we do not have information on the number of prosecutions, but we do know of two convictions of doctors for multiple violations of the requirements of due care. In the years after 1996, there have been prosecutions in three important cases (one of which antedates the Review Committees, the other two of which were not reported for review because the doctor did not consider what he had done 'euthanasia').[23] Many of these prosecutions ended in acquittal of the doctor concerned, but in a number there have been convictions. In no case has an unconditional sentence of imprisonment been imposed. The sentences have been either 'guilty but without imposition of punishment', fines or a suspended prison sentence.

Apart from prosecutions for the substantive offence of euthanasia, it has always been illegal in the Netherlands for a doctor to report a death due to euthanasia as a 'natural death', and since 1990 there has been a specific procedure that a doctor is required to follow to report a case of euthanasia. There have been a number of prosecutions for not having done so; the usual punishment is a fine.

---

[18] See ch 5.4.4.1.
[19] See ch 5, appendix. In Belgium, a similar reporting and review system was created by the law legalising euthanasia in 2002. In the first 5 years after the new law, 1,430 reported cases have been reviewed. The Belgian Federal Control and Evaluation Committee has so far found all reporting doctors to be in conformity with the rules governing euthanasia and as a consequence there have been no prosecutions. The FCEC did send 'remarks' to the reporting doctor in 67 (7%) of the cases it reviewed and requested additional information due to an incomplete dossier in 176 (18%) (see ch 10, Table 10.6).
[20] See ch 5, appendix.
[21] *Ibid* at 51–72 (the cases *Postma, Schoonheim, Pols, Admiraal,* and one unnamed case (p 72).
[22] See ch 5.4.4.2, Table 5.20.
[23] These are the *Brongersma, Van Oijen* and *Vencken* cases, see ch 3.3 and 3.4.

Medical Disciplinary Cases

In the early days of the development of Dutch euthanasia law the Medical Inspectorate was quite active, bringing disciplinary cases against a number of doctors, sometimes in cases where a criminal conviction or acquittal had already taken place.[24] More recently, the inspectorate has been rather inactive. There have only been incidental medical disciplinary cases since 1998: two against doctors whom the Review Committees found 'not careful'[25] resulting in a warning and a reprimand, and two after criminal prosecutions in cases of doctors who had not reported.[26]

The Total of Legal Control to which Doctors have been Exposed

Putting all the above together, what we get for the year 2006 is shown on Table 18.1.

Table 18.1. The total 'quantity' of legal control of euthanasia in the Netherlands, 2006

Total number of cases of euthanasia (Table 5.1)	2,425
1. involvement of specialised (SCEN) consultant	3,019
2. number of cases reported and reviewed by RRCs	1,923
3. non-routine treatment by RRCs	±200
4. 'not careful' judgments by RRCs	±3
5. informal sanction by prosecutor and/or inspector	±3
6. prosecutions	0
7. convictions	0
8. medical disciplinary cases	0

Source for items 4–8: chapter 5, appendix.

Table 18.1 reflects current Dutch practice. In the past, specialised consultancy did not exist, there were fewer reports, and review by the prosecutorial authorities was far more routine than what the Review Committees do now. On the other hand, prosecutions and medical disciplinary cases, although they have always been rare events, played a relatively more prominent role. How can we weigh almost 3,000 cases of review in advance and almost 2,000 of review after the fact, against the incidental prosecution in the past (13 cases out of 6,324 reported in 1991–95: an average of 3 per year)? Even if we assigned a prosecution 100 times the weight of non-criminal review before and after the fact, there would still be more than 10 times as much law now as there was only a decade ago.

---

[24] See eg GB&W: 338–40 (the *Chabot* case).
[25] See ch 5, appendix.
[26] The *Van Oijen* and *Vencken* cases—see n 23. We know of no medical disciplinary cases in connection with euthanasia in Belgium.

It seems reasonable to conclude that if we look at the official application of legal rules to individual doctors, there has been an enormous increase in the quantity of euthanasia law in the years since euthanasia became legal.

18.2 The Pressure of Regulation

What about the pressure of regulation—the number of rules—to which the behaviour of doctors is exposed? In the Netherlands there is a statute (2002) specifically regulating euthanasia and assisted suicide. It contains explicit exceptions for doctors to the two relevant articles of the Penal Code. It provides for the rules that a doctor must follow in order to fall within these exceptions. It requires a doctor to report such cases. And it provides for a specific legal procedure for reviewing reported cases.[27]

Authoritative reports by the Royal Dutch Medical Association and other professional bodies in effect assume the force of law (being almost automatically followed by prosecutors, courts, and the Review Committees). The most important of these currently provide further detail on matters covered in the statute of 2002, as well as many of the rules that govern assistance in suicide in psychiatric practice, palliative and terminal sedation, appropriate euthanatica and so forth.[28]

For many years the most important determinant of the pressure of regulation in the Netherlands was the considerable body of case law, including half a dozen major decisions of the Supreme Court. This judicial activity first determined that euthanasia can be legally justifiable and later on set out the boundaries of legal and non-legal euthanasia, fixing, refining and interpreting the applicable legal rules. Court decisions remain important in settling major issues that arise from time to time, mostly regarding not euthanasia itself but closely related matters such as, most recently, palliative and terminal sedation.[29]

Since 1998 the Regional Review Committees have largely taken over from the prosecutorial authorities the task of routine evaluation of reported cases of euthanasia. The Annual Reports of the Committees give short presentations of selected cases and discuss the related issues in some detail. From 1998 through 2006 the committees published 93 judgments, in 21 of which the judgment was 'not careful'.

Since 2002 the decisions of the committees are effectively final, and they are now the most productive source of new or clarified rules concerning euthanasia and assisted suicide. In the recent past, for example, they have cleared up confusion

---

[27] See ch 4. In Belgium, as we have seen in ch 9, there is a much more detailed statute (also of 2002), dealing with many of the matters covered in the Netherlands in professional reports and in case law.

[28] Because of the lack of involvement of the Belgian medical profession with the regulation of MBPSL, at least so far, professional reports and guidelines are not a significant source of law.

[29] See the *Vencken* case (ch 4.2.2.4). As we have seen, case law on the subject is non existent in Belgium.

concerning the relationship that must exist between a patient and the doctor who carries out euthanasia at his request, clarified the exact details of the requirement that the consultant be 'independent', explored the possibilities of euthanasia for a patient who falls into coma after all the requirements have been met, examined the implications of a patient's refusal of treatment that might have dealt with his suffering, required the use of appropriate euthanatica, and so forth.[30]

Although in the past the medical disciplinary authorities were occasionally active in euthanasia cases their role as a source of law has always been fairly marginal. As already noted, since the creation of the Regional Assessment Committees there have been only two medical disciplinary proceedings, in both of which the doctor received a minor disciplinary sanction. In effect medical disciplinary proceedings in the case of euthanasia merely ratify substantive decisions already taken by a Review Committee, adding a disciplinary sanction to the committee's judgment of 'not careful' but otherwise not contributing to the development of legal rules.[31]

The publicly-revealed reasons for non-prosecution decisions and other statements of prosecution policy were, in the past, a very important source of Dutch euthanasia law. With the Law of 2002 and the role of the Review Committees as principal decision-makers concerning reported cases of euthanasia, the importance of prosecutorial policy has much diminished. As we have seen, not a single case found 'not careful' by the committees has so far been prosecuted. Most of the recent activity of the prosecutorial authorities has concerned matters that do not fall within the jurisdiction of the Review Committees. It was the head of the prosecutorial service, for example, who first voiced public concern over the phenomenon of 'terminal sedation', resulting in a criminal prosecution, a guideline of the medical association, and a prosecutorial announcement that prosecution decisions would henceforth follow the guideline.

The highest authorities of the prosecutorial service from time to time issue formal prosecutorial guidelines. The recent guideline on prosecutions in cases of euthanasia in effect announces that two (unwise) provisions of the Law of 2002 will not be enforced. The law makes both consultation and reporting formal conditions of legal euthanasia. The prosecution guideline nevertheless provides that when the only reason for the adverse judgment of a Regional Review Committee is that the doctor concerned failed to consult a second doctor, or when a doctor fails to report an otherwise unexceptionable case of euthanasia, this is insufficient ground to justify a prosecution for the offence of euthanasia under article 293 of the Penal Code. Euthanasia law is hereby returned to the condition it was in before

---

[30] In Belgium, apart from the Euthanasia Law itself, the Federal Evaluation and Control Committee (FCEC) is potentially the most important source of legal rules. However, the lack of transparency that so far has characterised the Biennial Reports of the FCEC (see ch 10.3.4) means that—with the notable exception of the committee's decision that assisted suicide falls within the legalisation of euthanasia—the committee has to date made very little contribution to the further development of legal rules.

[31] In Belgium the medical disciplinary authorities seem not to be a relevant source of legal rules concerning euthanasia.

the statute, when the courts considered such procedural failures insufficient reason to deprive a doctor of access to the justification defence.[32]

Table 18.2 summarises the total pressure of regulation concerning euthanasia and assisted suicide. By 'heavy' is meant that the source concerned is productive of a large number of rules and a doctor would be very well advised to take account of them. 'Moderate' pressure means that the source concerned produces a number of rules that a doctor would want to know about, but the rules only concern fairly specific matters. 'Light' means that the source does not produce many rules and on the whole these are derivative of those of other sources.

Table 18. 2. Regulation pressure relating to euthanasia in the Netherlands

legislation	heavy
reports and guidelines of medical associations	heavy
case law	
courts	heavy
Regional Review Committees	heavy
medical disciplinary tribunals	light
prosecutorial policy	moderate

18.3 Rule-Following

According to doctors interviewed in the most recent national research (2005), a patient raises the subject of euthanasia with a Dutch doctor almost 30,000 times a year.[33] A doctor will necessarily have engaged in at least some rule-following—for example, discussing the prognosis and the alternatives with the patient, assessing his competence and the unbearability of his suffering, explaining the requirements that must be met—in all of these cases. This is thus a minimum figure for the amount of rule-following by doctors per year (ignoring for simplicity's sake the fact that in the 8,000+ cases in which there is a concrete request and the almost 2,500 in which it is carried out, much more rule-following will have been involved).

'Secondary' rule-following—that is, the use of legal rules in the internal rule-making processes of intermediate institutions such as nursing homes and hospitals—plays a very important role in the regulation of euthanasia in the Netherlands.[34] We can assume that in many cases, much of what a doctor knows

---

[32] See ch 4.2.4.2. In Belgium, the prosecutorial authorities seem to have played no public role at all in the emergence or development of euthanasia law. The most one can say is that before legalisation in 2002 their disinclination to prosecute a doctor for euthanasia was apparently well known among doctors—a sort of latent legal rule, perhaps (cf ch 8.4, n 40).

[33] See ch 5.2.2.1, Table 5.7.

[34] See ch 5.4.1.

about the legal rules, he will know indirectly through a local protocol that takes account of them. Already in the mid-1990s most Dutch hospitals and nursing homes had an internal policy as far as euthanasia is concerned. In many cases, local prosecutors had been more or less actively involved in the development of written protocols. The prosecutorial authorities, the Medical Inspectorate and the Regional Review Committees actively promote local protocols and intervene when it appears that an institution lacks a protocol or that its protocol is legally inadequate. If we assume that such protocols—or at least initiatives in such a direction—are now practically universal, then there are 130 hospitals and 335 nursing homes where secondary rule-following has taken place.[35] We can estimate the total of cases of secondary rule-following of this sort at about 450 cases over the 15 years from 1990 to 2005.

18.4 Change and Difference in the Quantity of Euthanasia Law

Table 18.3 summarises the foregoing effort to give some rough and tentative content to the idea of the quantity of euthanasia law. In the case of each manifestation of law, those indicators have been used which permit some kind of quantitative judgment.

Table 18.3. Indicators of the quantity of euthanasia law

application of legal rules to individual case (Table 18.1, SCEN plus Review Committees)	±4,000/year
regulation pressure	heavy
rule following	
by doctors	±30,000/year
by institutions	±450 over 15 years

With the foregoing survey of the various elements of the 'quantity of law' in mind, what can we say about geographic and temporal differences? Is there more 'law', item by item or taking it all together, in the Netherlands now than there was in 1985? Is there more in the Netherlands than in places where the taboo has not been broken?

Although our survey has been rather impressionistic, the answer to those two questions seems obvious. Unless one wants to retreat into the position that a taboo is always 'more law' than whatever comes after it has been broken, there is by every measure much more euthanasia law in the Netherlands than there was in 1985,

---

[35] *Cf* ch 10.3.1 for the rapid development of institutional protocols in Belgium.

and much more than there is anywhere else. The only countries in Europe where there is more euthanasia law now than there was in the Netherlands in 1980 are the two where legalisation has taken place: Belgium (see Part II), Switzerland (see chapter 16).

18.5 Explanatory Reflections

So, that is what has happened after the general and absolute prohibition of euthanasia came to an end. It seems reasonable to describe this as an avalanche of 'juridification' and thus a confirmation of the hypothesis with this chapter began: the end of a taboo leads to an increase in the quantity of legal control. The Dutch have not freed doctors from constraints that bind their colleagues in other countries, on the contrary, they have subjected the behaviour of doctors to much more law than used to be the case, and to much more than it attracts elsewhere.

There is a longer-term sociological logic at work here, and the word 'juridification' that we just used to describe the increase in the quantity of law was meant to evoke it. Legalisation of euthanasia and the increase in the quantity of law that accompanies it are not isolated phenomena. They are part of a much more general process of juridification of the doctor–patient relationship. This more general process is manifest in all sorts of developments, of which we mention just a few to give an idea of what we have in mind: the requirement of informed consent, the legal recognition of advance directives, the legal acceptance and regulation of decisions to withhold or withdraw treatment, the burgeoning of medical guidelines, standards and protocols, and so forth and so on.

Why, exactly, such a process of juridification is taking place is not obvious, and it is in any case beyond the scope of this book. But the point we want to emphasise here is that the legalisation of euthanasia must be seen not as part of a process of freeing medical practice from legal restrictions, but on the contrary, as part of a much more general process by which it is increasingly regulated.

With this thought in mind, we can better understand the fact, that even after euthanasia had been declared legal by the Dutch Supreme Court, a substantial number of Dutch doctors in the early years were unwilling to report cases of euthanasia as required because they believed that the state should not be involved in regulating euthanasia at all: it was something that belonged to the authority of the doctor and the privacy of the doctor–patient relationship.[36] The opposition of the Belgian Order of Physicians to the proposal to legalise euthanasia[37] is likewise understandable from such a perspective. Legalisation was not necessary, a spokesman stated to the Belgian Senate, because Belgian doctors practised euthanasia whenever they thought it appropriate and never experienced any interference from the legal

---

[36] See ch 5.4.3.
[37] See chs 8.4, 8.5, 9.5.

authorities. What the law really proposed to do, he argued, was to impose a legal regulatory regime on the decision-making of doctors and patients. We can summarise this reflection on the legal change that has taken place in the Netherlands and in Belgium in one sentence: *He was absolutely right.*

19

Slithering Up the Slippery Slope

The 'slippery slope' argument is by far the most common consideration advanced against proposals to legalise euthanasia. The reason for this is pretty obvious: it is the only significant argument available that does not depend on religious (or equivalent) convictions that are not shared by many or most people in Europe.

The basic idea of a 'slippery slope' is deceptively simple: even if legalising euthanasia is not such a bad idea in itself, it will surely lead to bad things, with the spectre of the Nazi's lurking at the end to scare us off from taking the first step on a downhill slope so fraught with risk. In itself, such an idea is perfectly sensible, and there are many things in life one does not do for just this sort of reason.

19.1 The 'Conceptual' Slippery Slope Argument

There are often thought to be two versions of the slippery slope idea: 'conceptual' and 'empirical'. The difference lies in the nature of the argument made. The conceptual version relies on the meaning of concepts, and the existence of a 'slippery slope' is thought to be a matter of logic. The empirical version relies on generalisations from human experience, and the existence of a 'slippery slope' depends upon empirical evidence.

The 'conceptual' version supposes that by allowing something (A) whose justifying principle necessarily also justifies something else (B), the force of logic will require one to allow B as well. A is supposed to be acceptable, B abhorrent. Applied to legalisation of euthanasia, the notion is that if one accepts autonomy as the justifying principle, then one will be forced to allow not only euthanasia for the terminally ill (A) but also, for example, euthanasia for those who simply want to die (B). The initial restriction to the terminally ill will not be able to resist the force of the underlying justifying principle.[1] Alternatively, if the justifying principle is beneficence, legalising euthanasia for those who ask for it will inevitably lead us to allow doctors to put suffering patients who have not asked for it out of their misery.

The idea of a conceptual slippery slope often seems simply to reflect the 'one law, one principle' fallacy: the common if ill-considered notion that for any law

---

[1] See Burt 2005 for an example of this argument.

there must be one and only one justifying principle.[2] But euthanasia law in the Netherlands, Belgium (and Oregon) is based not only on autonomy but *also* on a second principle: *beneficence*. This second principle is necessary because, unlike the situation of autonomous suicide, not just the person concerned is involved but also another person, the doctor. The behaviour of this second person requires some justification other than the autonomy of the person wanting to die. In the case of a doctor, this additional justification is found in the duty to relieve suffering (the requirement of a terminal illness can be thought—with the help of the idea of proportionality—to reflect the limits of the principle of beneficence). Similarly, the other way around, the fact that euthanasia law is based (in part) on the principle of beneficence—needed to justify the involvement of a doctor—does not entail that the requirement of a voluntary request of the patient will inevitably be swept away by the logic of beneficence (since there are suffering people who cannot or have not asked to die). The requirement of a request will not be swept away precisely because it is based on an entirely different principle.

In short, the conceptual version of the slippery slope argument is intrinsically incoherent. If A is indistinguishable from B, then the one cannot be benign and the other abhorrent. If relevant distinctions can be made, they can be (and in Dutch and Belgian euthanasia law are being) maintained.

19.2 The 'Empirical' Slippery Slope Argument

The empirical slippery slope argument deserves more respect, and in some situations it is almost certainly correct. We should distinguish two variants, depending on what situation B is, which is the supposed reason for not doing A (legalising euthanasia). The two variants correspond to two rather different arguments against legalisation. It is unfortunate for the clarity of debate that those who express concern about a 'slippery slope' tend to mix them up. We can call them the *legal control variant* and the *legal (and moral) change variant* .

Legal Control

In the case of the *legal control variant*, B is a *state of affairs* that as a practical matter we will not be able to prevent if we allow A. Forbidding A is supposed to be the only effective way of making sure that B does not happen: A is the only workable place to draw the line. There are lots of examples of this sort of argument in public discourse, some obviously sound, others little more than expressions of nervousness in the face of change. An example of a probably sound use is the idea that if we allow politicians to accept large contributions *except* if they are being paid for their vote on some issue, we will never be able to enforce the exception;

---

[2] See Keown 2002a: 76–80 for a particularly egregious example of this fallacy.

the only workable line is a complete prohibition of such contributions. An example of a probably unconvincing use is one of the old arguments against mixed secondary schools: the notion that if we allow boys and girls to go to school together this will lead to teenage pregnancies and the like.

The slippery-slope argument against euthanasia, on the legal control variant, is that, in practice, legal control of euthanasia will not be able to prevent the non-voluntary medical killing of the vulnerable (the old and infirm, the poor and deprived, the sick and the handicapped, women and members of other vulnerable minorities). To test the assertion empirically, we would need to be able to compare the frequency of non-voluntary termination of life before and after legalisation of euthanasia, and the situation in places where it is legal with that in places where it is not. The difficulty confronting anyone who seeks to make such a comparison is that there is very little reliable evidence on either point. Keown, one of the most insistent advocates of the 'slippery slope' argument, who apparently believes that the Dutch case proves the predicted evils will in fact take place, in his recent book in effect concedes the lack of evidence (albeit offhandedly and reluctantly).[3]

We simply do not know how much non-voluntary termination of life there was in the Netherlands before the legalisation of euthanasia and the only evidence for the years after legalisation suggests a modest decline.[4] Nor is it the case that there is more non-voluntary termination of life in the Netherlands than in countries where euthanasia remains illegal. The sparse evidence we have suggests that the Dutch are not particularly out of line with medical practice in other European countries where euthanasia is illegal.[5] Most medical behaviour that shortens life is still generally classified as pain relief or abstention (much of which is legally and morally barely distinguishable, if at all, from 'termination of life'). It is known that a great deal of this takes place without consulting the patient or his representatives. As far as respect for patient autonomy in this connection is concerned, countries like the Netherlands that are 'permissive' with regard to euthanasia and physician-assisted suicide score consistently higher than 'not permissive' countries.[6] In the special case of termination of life in neonatology, the case of France makes clear[7] that a flat prohibition is not necessarily associated with a lower level of the behaviour involved, although it definitely is associated with secrecy, lack of control, opaque decision-making and the exclusion of the parents from the whole process. In short, there are many indications that respect for patient autonomy and adequate legal control over the end-of-life behaviour of doctors do not suffer from the legalisation of euthanasia; more probably the reverse is true.

As far as euthanasia proper in the Netherlands is concerned, it is clear that doctors do not like to perform it and that patients who cannot stand up for their

---

[3] See Keown 2002a: 146. See Smith 2005 for an extensive discussion of the empirical evidence relevant in connection with Keown's 'slippery slope' argument against legalisation of euthanasia.

[4] See ch 5.1.2.3, Table 5.1.

[5] See ch 17.2.

[6] *Ibid.*

[7] See chs 6.3.3 and 12.4.

wishes in dealing with their doctor have little chance of persuading him to do so.[8] There is no evidence that members of any of the supposedly vulnerable groups more frequently die from euthanasia than anyone else.[9] If the vulnerable are at risk—and even in the egalitarian Netherlands, with virtually universal and adequate health care coverage, it would be foolish to assume they are not—then the place to look for the danger is among the very large numbers of deaths due to pain relief, palliative/terminal sedation and abstention from life-prolonging treatment, in many of which the patient or his representative are not involved in the decision-making. As we have seen in chapter 17.2, it is precisely these largely unregulated sorts of MBPSL that occur more frequently elsewhere than in the Netherlands.

In short, if they tell us anything about a 'slippery slope', the available data seem to suggest that legalisation of euthanasia leads to less, not more, medical behaviour that potentially shortens life, and to a reduced, not an increased, risk to those particularly vulnerable. One can quarrel with these data, of course, but then one is simply left with empty hands: no quantitative evidence at all one way or the other as far as the legal control variant of the 'slippery slope' argument is concerned.

There is another way to approach the legal control variant: by looking not at the actual results of legal control, about which not very much is known, but at the amount of control activity itself. As we have seen in chapter 18, the legalisation of euthanasia led to an outburst of regulation and other control activity in the Netherlands unequalled in any other country. This concerned not only euthanasia itself. Other sorts of medical behaviour that potentially shorten life but that have traditionally been regarded as 'normal medical practice' not requiring any regulation—such as palliative sedation[10] and withdrawal and withholding treatment[11]—increasingly attract regulatory attention. The result of all this is that the end-of-life practice of Dutch doctors is much more transparent and exposed to far greater regulatory pressure and concrete social control than it ever was before, and in all these respects is subject to more 'juridification' than that of doctors in other countries.

But, it could be argued, the evidence shows that all this control has proven ineffective. Accurate reporting by doctors of what they have done is a precondition of effective control. At the beginning of the process of legal change, in the mid-1980s, the reporting rate was 0. As we have seen in chapter 5.4.3, when first measured in 1990 the reporting rate as calculated by the national researchers was 18%, in 1995 it was 41%, and in 2001 it was still only 54%. And it seemed that it was especially the more problematic cases that in this way escaped the control system. For critics like Keown this was the Achilles Heel of Dutch euthanasia policy. The fact that effective control is impossible—demonstrated in their view by Dutch euthanasia practice—forms a conclusive argument against legalisation.

---

[8] See ch 5.3, Chabot 2001, Van Dam 2007, and GB&W: 247 for indications of this.

[9] See Battin *et al* 2007 for an analysis of the data from the Netherlands and Oregon, concluding that (with the exception of patients with HIV) patients in vulnerable groups are not over-represented among those dying from euthanasia or physician-assisted suicide.

[10] See ch 5.5.2.1.2 and 5.2.2.2.

[11] In particular in neonatology—see ch 6.

Since a few months ago, we know that the rate of reporting as calculated by the national researchers is now 80% (2005). More important, we know that a large part of the apparent short-fall is not due to 'lying', as had always been supposed, but to the fact that doctors and the national researchers interpret the concept 'euthanasia' in different ways. The rate at which doctors report cases that they themselves consider to be 'euthanasia' is just about 100% (the rest they consider to be 'pain relief', 'palliative sedation' or the like—just as do their colleagues in other countries). Looking at these new results in Keown's own terms, they seem to falsify at least an important part of his slippery-slope argument.

Nevertheless, reporting and official review are less than water-tight. What should we make of this? The answer to this question depends on whether you look upon the Dutch regulatory glass as half empty or as half full. Those who seize on the Dutch data as evidence of a failure of control looked at the regulatory glass— at least, before the newest data—as half empty. They emphasised the huge gap between actual control and what we might accept as adequately effective control. But one can also look at the glass as half full. The glass seems to be getting fuller all the time and is now (at 80–99%) probably as full as it realistically can get. This is no small accomplishment for legal regulation in a field as delicate—and as resistant to state regulation—as the doctor–patient relationship. Meanwhile, the regulatory glass is completely empty in most other countries. While we know that euthanasia in fact takes place elsewhere, the reporting rate outside the Netherlands (except for the state of Oregon, Switzerland (see chapter 16.4.6), and very recently Belgium) is everywhere 0.

Looked at in historical and comparative perspective it seems reasonable to regard the steady rise in the rate of reporting as evidence for the *success* of legal control. If a situation of medical anarchy in which euthanasia practice is out of control and the lives of patients are not safe in the hands of their doctors exists anywhere,[12] this is certainly not in the Netherlands or Belgium (or Oregon and Switzerland).

In summary: it is hard to see in the results of the experience with legal euthanasia over a period of more than 20 years any substantial evidence of a slippery slope toward victimisation of the vulnerable. Critics who seek to do this focus on the mote in another's eye and ignore the beam in their own: on imaginary, or real but manageable imperfections in the Dutch and Belgian systems of legal control but not on the gaping defects in the control of 'physician-negotiated death' in other countries. The problems that concern them are assuredly important, but by no means limited to the relatively tiny category of euthanasia. The Dutch experience—if it affords general evidence of anything—shows that legalisation of euthanasia and systematic attention to its control goes hand in hand with more and better control not only of euthanasia itself but also of other medical behaviour that potentially shortens life.

So much for the legal control variant of the empirical slippery-slope argument.

---

[12] For a description of a highly anarchic situation in two countries where euthanasia is firmly illegal, see Magnusson 2002.

Legal (and Moral) Change

In the case of the *legal change variant* of the slippery-slope argument against the legalisation of euthanasia, the prediction is that if once we allow A we will sooner or later find ourselves allowing B: legalisation of A leads to legalisation of B. One can imagine an opponent of privatisation of the steel industry making the following slippery-slope argument. From A (privatisation of steel, not in itself such a bad idea) will come a variety of increasingly objectionable forms of privatisation, each serving as a precedent for the next one: of trains, mail, water, health services and ultimately of the police and the judiciary. Because everyone is against privatising the judiciary, we must therefore oppose privatising steel. Since the relationship between legalising A and legalising B is an empirical one, and not (as in the case of the conceptual slippery slope argument) a logical one, the strength of the argument depends not on the proposition that people in the future will be unable to draw the relevant moral distinctions, but on the prediction that they will in fact not do so.[13]

While the *legal control* variant of the empirical slippery-slope argument is not supported by the evidence and seems if anything to get the empirical relationship between legalisation and effective control upside down, the situation looks quite different as far as the *legal change* variant is concerned. After the legalisation of euthanasia in the Netherlands there have been related legal developments that have not taken place in other countries. Opponents of legalising euthanasia usually point to three areas of later legal change as evidence of a 'slippery slope' in the direction of legalisation of undesirable practices: acceptance of physician-assisted suicide in the case of persons who are not in the 'terminal phase' and whose suffering is not somatically based (in particular, psychiatric patients); acceptance of physician-assisted suicide in the case of persons not suffering from any 'medical' condition; and acceptance of termination of life in the case of non-competent patients (in particular severely defective newborn babies).

Those who think there has been a 'slide' in the direction of accepting physician-assisted suicide in the case of non-somatic suffering and of patients outside the 'terminal phase', are simply unaware of the facts of Dutch legal development. Neither in the case law that over a period of more than 20 years led to the recent Dutch legislation, nor in the Law of 2002 itself, have such restrictions ever been imposed. There has therefore never been a possibility of such a 'slide'.

---

[13] Den Hartogh (2008) argues that legal change may also result from gradual slide in the way indeterminate concepts (such as 'unbearable suffering') are operationalised in practice. However, where there is legitimate concern about such a slide, legal systems have at their disposal a number of devices for preventing it (setting a fixed speed limit instead of a general requirement of 'reasonable speed'; creating decision-making procedures that ensure 'intersubjectivity' in the application of the concept of 'medical futility'; and so forth). If a practice is transparent, then everyone concerned will be witness to any slide that is taking place, and if this is considered undesirable can do something to arrest it. The indeterminacy of concepts seems seldom to be considered a reason for a total prohibition of behaviour. And because of the special importance of transparency of practice for preventing an unwonted slide, a taboo is probably the worst possible way of trying to prevent such a development.

The second supposed form of legal change concerns physician-assisted suicide in the case of persons who are 'tired of life' or whose suffering is otherwise not a matter of any 'medical' condition. While there is considerable and perhaps growing popular demand for such a legal possibility, the Dutch Supreme Court recently held that physician-assisted suicide in such a case does not fall within the scope of the legalisation of euthanasia. The Dutch Parliament is also clearly of this view. In short, this 'slide' turned out not to be inevitable at all: it has not taken place and it is not at all clear that it ever will.[14]

The third example of a slippery slope toward legalisation of the abhorrent is more interesting. As we have seen in chapter 6, the Dutch courts have held that there can be circumstances that justify termination of life in the case of newborn babies. And it is undeniably the case that the form that legal regulation is assuming—for example, the 'requirements of due care' that apply in such cases—has been heavily influenced by the earlier development of euthanasia law.

But what does this prove? So long as one can make moral distinctions between euthanasia and termination of the life of a baby—and the slippery slope argument presupposes that one can—then it is surely possible to permit the first and prohibit the second. If what happens, as in the Dutch case, is that the citizens of a given country decide to legalise B as well as A, this not because they have no real choice in the matter but because they exercise that choice in a particular way.[15]

In short—and this is the essential point that needs to be made—what the *legal change* variant amounts to is distrust of future generations, the idea that they will fail to make morally important distinctions, that we possess a better moral insight than they will. *We* must not choose A, because if we do, *they* may choose B (which we, but not they, find abhorrent).[16] Trying to bind future moral judgments is morally pretentious and mean-spirited, an ethically improper basis for decisions about public policy. In trying in this way to prevent future moral change we think we would disapprove of, we should ask ourselves what sort of society we would live in now, if many of our fundamental moral choices had been made for us in the 19th century.

---

[14] See ch 3.3.

[15] It is not self-evident that there is anything wrong with this choice. Apart from the reiteration of shop-worn formulas, we are not aware of any well-informed, substantial arguments against the direction Dutch law on the matter has taken. It would in any event be an exercise in futility to try to prevent termination of life in neonatology by retaining a prohibition of euthanasia, since the evidence seems to show that the rate of the former is not influenced by the latter. See ch 6.3.1 and 6.3.3.

[16] A curious example of such misguided arrogance is Keown's argument that judicial acceptance of a patient's right to involves life-saving treatment and of the doctor's duty to withdraw treatment when a competent patient insists on this involves a 'slippery slope' from treatment refusal towards (assisted) suicide (see Keown 2002b). The English judges he criticises, however, seem to be taking account of a moral consideration that Keown overlooks: the fact that a doctor has no inherent right to treat and that his authority to do so ceases when the patient withdraws consent. For a doctor to refrain from unlawfully invading a patient's bodily integrity is quite a different matter from the 'intentional termination of life' that according to Keown is involved. In short, it is Keown, and not English judges, who is incapable of making relevant distinctions, in this case between assisted suicide and respecting a patient's right to refuse treatment.

19.3 Conclusion: Slipping into More Control and into More Careful Practice

Legal control over euthanasia and other MBPSL is certainly not perfect in the Netherlands (or Belgium and, mutatis mutandis, Switzerland). However, it is better than in other countries for which information is available, and it has been getting more encompassing, more refined, and in practice more effective in the two decades since euthanasia became legal.

Further legal change has undeniably taken place in the Netherlands as a direct consequence of legalisation. Almost all of it has been in the direction of clarifying and tightening the requirements of due care and improving the system of control. In addition, the practice of 'palliative sedation' has been recognised and subjected to regulation. A modest begin has also been made with the regulation of pain relief and of withdrawing or withholding life-prolonging treatment, the areas of medical end-of-life practice particularly fraught—in the Netherlands and most assuredly elsewhere—with the dangers supposedly inherent in legal euthanasia.

As far as termination of life in neonatology is concerned, there has been important legal change in a direction the opponents of euthanasia regard as confirming their worst fears for a slippery slope. However, there is no reason to suppose that legalisation of euthanasia makes such related legal change inevitable. Nor should one make the mistake of supposing that, just because the practices involved are illegal everywhere else, they are not taking place. As was the case with euthanasia, the Dutch have chosen to bring a practice that is common to neonatology in many countries out into the light of day and subject it to regulation.

Those opposed to the choices the Dutch have made would make a more interesting contribution to the debate in this area if, instead of appealing to an ill-considered metaphor about supposedly inevitable change, they were to address themselves to the question how the absolute prohibition they are in favour of could be made effective.

20

'Prediction is very difficult, especially about the future.'[1]

In the first chapter we set out the aims of this book and explained (in section 1.5.4.) the methodology we were going to use when comparing the law concerning euthanasia and other MBPSL in the various countries covered. We explained why, in our view, a more systematic and broader approach than the one often applied in legal comparison is needed. Euthanasia law emerged in the Netherlands and Belgium in the context of widely held values, of a particular (changing) political and social structure, and of a specific organisation of health care and of the medical profession. Our expectation was that a more systematic and broader approach to legal comparison, which spreads its net wider than traditional legal materials, would help us to understand what the law in these two countries (and elsewhere) means and how it works and to what extent the law taken thus as a whole really differs from one country to the next. We also hoped that an interdisciplinary approach to legal comparison might make it possible to *explain* how and why legal change concerning euthanasia came about in the Netherlands and Belgium and not (yet) in other European countries.

As far as the legal rules, their socio-political context, and medical practice are concerned, we have presented them for the Netherlands and Belgium in detail in parts I and II and in a more summary way for eight other European countries in part III. In chapter 17 we gave a short summary of our findings, arguing that European MBPSL law seems to be converging on all subjects except (perhaps) euthanasia, PAS and termination of life without request. But there remains a question that we have not dealt with explicitly: can we explain and thereby predict changes in MBSPL law, in particular with respect to euthanasia?[2]

Predicting change in law is a precarious undertaking. We nevertheless hope that by focusing on two factors (and keeping several others in mind) we will be able to give at least a plausible account of the reasons why euthanasia was legalised in Belgium and the Netherlands, and to predict developments in some other Western European countries. The two factors that seem to us to be particularly important

---

[1] Attributed to Niels Bohr.

[2] We limit the discussion here to the legalisation of euthanasia. It is interesting to mention, nevertheless, that in most countries the process of legal change gets underway with a dramatic legal case (usually involving withholding or withdrawing treatment) that attracts a great deal of public attention (eg *Quinlan* [US], *Welby* [IT], *Bland* [UK], *Humbert* [FR], *Sampedro* [SP] *Versluis* [NL—see GB&W:48]).

in the Dutch and Belgian cases are changes in generally held values and the accessibility of the political system to demands based on new values.

As far as value change is concerned, we think it is reasonable to assume that more or less democratic states will over the middle-term exhibit congruence between widely held values and legal arrangements.[3] We therefore begin (section 20.1) by examining what is known about changes in relevant values. Next we will look at the accessibility of the political systems in the Netherlands and Belgium and compare these with other Western European countries (section 20.2). Our hypothesis is that political systems which are more open to challengers will be the first to show congruence between value change and legal change.

Apart from endogenous forces that influence legal change in a given country, processes of legal change may be influenced by developments in other countries. In part II we have noted the apparent influence of the Dutch experiment with legal change regarding euthanasia on legal change in Belgium. In section 20.3 we speculate on the possible influence of Dutch, Belgian and Swiss law regarding assisted dying on developments in other European countries.

At the end of the chapter (section 20.4) we will summarise what we have found by way of predicting legal change regarding termination of life in the Western European countries with which we have been concerned.

20.1 Values Relevant to Euthanasia

A first factor that can help to explain changes in the law with respect to euthanasia is changes in widely held values relating to the end of life. This sort of value change is the subject of the European Values Study (EVS). The EVS collects data at regular intervals, asking respondents, for example, to rate their agreement with 'euthanasia'—defined as 'terminating the life of an incurable sick person'—as follows: (a) can always be justified, (b) can never be justified or (c) something in between.[4]

In chapter 2 we went in some detail into the difficulties that are involved in assessing public opinion by polls. In this chapter we try to overcome these shortcomings by combining answers to various questions in the EVS to detect underlying values. Two such clusters seem relevant in connection with euthanasia: Inglehart's idea of a 'post-materialistic value-orientation' and Elchardus's idea that the answers with respect to euthanasia together with those concerning divorce, suicide, abortion and homosexuality reflect an underlying value of 'bodily self-determination'.[5]

---

[3] *Cf* Dicey 1905. Page & Shapiro (1983) have found such congruence between public opinion and public policy for the United States from 1935 to 1979.

[4] See ch 17.1 for an overview of the responses to this question on euthanasia. See ch 14.4 for criticism of the formulation of the question.

[5] Inglehart 1977; Elchardus, Chaumont & Lauwers 1992: 154–5.

Post-Materialism

Inglehart distinguishes between societies with a 'materialistic value-orientation' and those with a 'post-materialistic value-orientation'. A materialistic value orientation emphasises material security and law and order; a post-materialistic value orientation emphasises personal freedom and participation in the political process. People in a society with a post-materialistic value orientation place immaterial life-goals such as personal development and self-esteem above material security. According to Inglehart the populations of advanced industrial societies have moved from a materialistic to a post-materialistic value orientation. A correlation between increasing prosperity and the number of people who consider 'post-materialist values' important has been found in almost all European countries. In the early 1990s in the Netherlands and Denmark, people with a post-materialistic value orientation for the first time outnumbered people with a materialistic value orientation.[6] The most recent results of the EVS show that Austrians and Swedes score highest on post-materialistic values, closely followed by the Danes, the Dutch and the Italians. Countries close behind are England, Belgium, France, Norway and Switzerland.[7]

Bodily Self-Determination

As far as Elchardus's idea of 'bodily self-determination' is concerned the picture is a little more complex.[8] The Dutch are by far the most 'permissive' with respect to homosexuality, suicide and euthanasia, but with respect to divorce and abortion they are less permissive than Scandinavians. Sweden is also a rather permissive country: first with respect to divorce and abortion; second with respect to homosexuality, third with respect to suicide and fourth with respect to euthanasia. Although Denmark is never in the first position, it is second with respect to divorce, abortion and euthanasia and fourth with respect to homosexuality; with respect to suicide the Danes are less permissive: eighth. France is also a permissive country with respect to bodily self-determination: on suicide it is in second place (after the Netherlands); on euthanasia in third place (after the Netherlands and Denmark); on abortion also third (after Sweden and Denmark); on divorce in sixth place (preceded by the Scandinavian countries and the Netherlands); but its

---

[6] Inglehart 1997: 139.

[7] Halman, Luijkx & Van Zundert 2005: 89.

[8] The data of the EVS are reported in different ways in different books (Inglehart, Basañez and Moreno 1998; Halman 2001). Halman gives the means of the scores. To make comparison possible we asked WORC/EVS Tilburg University for the relevant means of the studies of 1980 and 1990 (Weyers 2005). Unfortunately, Switzerland is not included in the EVS.

[9] See Weyers 2005: 261. Halman, Luijkx & Van Zundert 2005 come to a comparable conclusion. They distinguish civic permissiveness from sexual-ethical permissiveness. With respect to the latter (in which to euthanasia, suicide, homosexuality, divorce and abortion are added adultery, sex under the legal age of consent, prostitution and killing in self-defence) they found Sweden, Denmark and the Netherlands to be the most permissive countries in Europe, followed by France (Halman, Luijkx & Van Zundert 2005: 109).

position on homosexuality is rather lower (ninth).[9] Graph 17.1 reflects the steep rise in the Belgian scores on euthanasia in the third survey. The EVS shows that a similar change in public opinion took place in the 1990s with respect to abortion. Permissiveness with respect to divorce, homosexuality and suicide grew more gradually in Belgium.[10] Other European countries (England, Italy and Spain) lie behind the countries mentioned so far with respect to almost all elements of bodily self-determination.[11]

To sum all this up: the value orientations most relevant to legalisation of euthanasia are becoming dominant in all European countries. In both value clusters the Netherlands, Denmark and Sweden have for many years been at the head of the pack.

Public Pressure

Changes in values influence the political process only when interest groups arise that champion an issue as to which the new values are relevant—in our case the legalisation of euthanasia. In almost all European countries dealt with in this book, groups have been founded to promote greater individual choice regarding the end of life. Not all of these groups, however, seek legalisation of euthanasia, some focusing for example on legal recognition of advance treatment directives.[12] The Dutch and Swiss right-to-die societies differ from others in Europe in that they are rather large.[13] In other countries (for example Belgium and England) membership hardly rises above a couple of thousand. As far as political influence is concerned, the Dutch NVVE is not only big enough to be a major political actor, it has also cultivated good relations with political parties and governmental bodies (especially the Minister of Health in the 'Purple'-coalitions of the 1990s). The English right-to-die society differs from others by its long history (it was founded in the 1930s) and its wealth and level of political activity.

Pressure for legalisation of euthanasia can also come from doctors' organisations. To date only the Dutch medical association has played an active role in the process of legal change. In Belgium, as we saw in chapters 8 and 9, the Order of Physicians played essentially no role in the process leading to legalisation of euthanasia. In most other countries medical associations are actively opposed (although it is not clear that this reflects the views of their members). They consider euthanasia to be in violation of the Hippocratic Oath and not compatible with the professional responsibility of doctors. Two medical associations have recently taken steps in the direction of a less vigorous opposition: the Swiss and to a lesser (and so far only temporary) extent the English. Although the process of

---

[10] Austria, the country which has the highest score regarding post-materialism also experienced a steep rise in the latest EVS with respect to 'bodily self-determination'.

[11] In 2000, however, Spain had become rather permissive with respect to homosexuality. As noted on Table 17.1 in ch 17, support for legal euthanasia in England seems as of 2005 to be at about the same level as in the permissive countries.

[12] Most such Scandinavian organisations, for example, do not advocate legalisation of euthanasia.

[13] The Dutch NVVE has 100,000 members, the three Swiss organisations together about 60,000.

legal change with respect to euthanasia in Belgium demonstrates that a positive stance of the medical association is not a necessary condition for legal change, we still assume that where professional organisations are vigorously opposed, legalisation is less likely, even though the values of the general public seem to point in that direction.

Conclusion

If there is a link between, on the one hand, a 'post-materialistic value orientation' and a high value put on 'bodily self-determination' and, on the other hand, legalisation of euthanasia, one would predict that Denmark, Sweden, France and to a lesser extent England will be the next countries to legalise euthanasia. Italy and Spain, on the other hand, will not legalise euthanasia in the near future. If we include the possible importance of doctors' and patients' organisations there is a notable difference between, on the one hand, Switzerland and England and, on the other hand, other Western European countries. If this factor is important then England should be the next country to legalise some form of termination of life on request.

20.2 Political Opportunity Structures and Euthanasia Legislation

The idea of a political opportunity structure is that some political systems are more accessible to post-materialistic issues such as euthanasia than others. Four characteristics are supposed to play a role in relation to accessibility. The first concerns the structure of fundamental political cleavages, the second the political institutional structure, the third political culture, and the fourth temporary changes in parliamentary power relationships. First we examine how each of these four characteristics played a role in the Belgian and Dutch processes of legal change with respect to euthanasia (section 20.2.1). Then (section 20.2.2) we compare the Belgian and Dutch political opportunity structures with those of other Western European countries to see whether correspondences and differences can help to predict the probability of legal change with respect to euthanasia.

20.2.1 The Netherlands and Belgium[14]

National Cleavage Structures

The opportunity for challengers to introduce new conflicts into a polity are shaped

---

[14] See chs 2 and 7 for information on the Dutch and Belgian political structure and culture; and chs 3 and 8 for political developments that were important with respect to the legalisation of euthanasia.

by existing politicised cleavages, such as conflicts over national identities, class conflicts and centre–periphery conflicts. The more such traditional cleavages have been pacified, the more chance that political parties will want to distinguish themselves on post-materialist issues (euthanasia, same sex marriage, etc), and therefore the more chance that these issues will reach the political agenda.

In the Netherlands the traditional cleavages between confessional and non-confessional political parties, and between liberals and socialists, had greatly declined in importance by the 1990s. In Belgium, although the process was not so far advanced, this was also largely the case. Dutch and Belgian political parties were more and more becoming catch-all parties and at the end of the millennium both countries for the first time saw coalition governments in which socialists and liberals worked together.

Green-Pedersen makes an additional observation in this connection:[15]

> If an issue can be linked to an existing conflict in the party system, powerful political actors have an interest in politicizing the issue, and the issue can be framed in a way that makes it a case of an already well-established political conflict.

Non-material issues such as euthanasia can be interpreted as a matter of Christian versus secular morality and thus linked to existing cleavages between religious and secular political parties. So a political history in which the importance of economic cleavages has declined but the non-confessional/confessional cleavage has retained some importance makes it likely that some political parties will seek to distinguish themselves on issues relating to bodily self-determination. In Belgium this had already happened once before, in connection with abortion law reform.

In both the Netherlands and Belgium the non-confessional/confessional cleavage had been very important. In the Netherlands the left-liberals (D66) took the lead in putting euthanasia on the political agenda. D66's profile was that of a party that stresses modern secular values against the doctrinaire moralism of Christian parties. In Belgium the 'Rainbow'-coalition similarly wanted to break with the political past dominated by Christian Democrats by putting the issue of euthanasia on the political agenda.

Political Structure

One of the factors that determines the relative openness of a political system to groups with new demands is its formal institutional structure. Such openness is, in Kriesi's view, a function of three general structural parameters: the degree of the state's (territorial) centralisation; the degree of its (functional) separation of powers; and the institutional make-up of the parliamentary arena. With respect to these features Kriesi notes that

> the greater the degree of decentralisation, the wider the degree of . . . access; the greater the separation of powers between different arenas—that is between the legislature, the executive, and the judiciary—as well within arenas, the greater the degree of . . . access;

---

[15] Green-Pedersen 2007: 273.

and

> the higher the degree of proportionality of the electoral system, the larger will be the number of parties. . . . Where there are large numbers of parties, social movements will be more likely to find allies within the party system.[16]

A decentralised political system offers multiple opportunities for proponents of legal change to get their foot in the legislative door. The way in which advance refusals of treatment got legal recognition in one jurisdiction after another in Spain is a good example of this. The Netherlands is highly centralised and Belgium decentralised. But because criminal law is an exclusively federal responsibility in Belgium, the decentralised character of the Belgian state did not play a role in the process of legal change regarding euthanasia. In short, decentralisation was not important in the Belgian and Dutch cases.

Separation of powers, the second structural parameter, also creates multiple points of access to a political system. The relevant question is whether the judiciary and the executive power have any capacity to effect legal change and therefore are possible places for those seeking rule change to go.

Accessibility resulting from separation of powers played an important role in the Dutch process of legal change with respect to euthanasia. The judiciary took the lead in responding to new demands. This began with the prosecutorial authorities.[17] In the 1980s they sought to clarify the limits of justifiable euthanasia by bringing legal proceedings against doctors who had carried it out.[18] Dutch judges took up the gauntlet, using article 40 of the Penal Code (justification of necessity) to hold that Dutch law did not entirely prohibit euthanasia. It was rulings of the Supreme Court that in effect made euthanasia legal in the Netherlands. The situation was entirely different in Belgium, where the judiciary played no role at all in the legalisation of euthanasia.

The third characteristic of a political system that determines its openness is the proportionality of the electoral system. 'From the point of view of a challenger, proportional representation allows for easier access than plurality or majority methods.'[19] Both the Netherlands and Belgium have a proportional electoral system, and in both countries the minimum number of votes necessary to get a seat in parliament is rather low. Both parliaments therefore include many parties. In both Belgium and the Netherlands there were political parties willing to put the issue of euthanasia on the political agenda.

---

[16] Kriesi *et al* 1995: 28–9.

[17] In the 1980s the prosecutorial authorities were still considered part of the judiciary. This close association has been greatly weakened in recent years.

[18] See GB&W: 60.

[19] Kriesi *et al* 1995: 29. Formal access is also a function of the degree to which direct democratic procedures such as referenda are institutionalised. This feature, however, does not play a role with respect to the legalisation of euthanasia in Europe.

Political Culture

Political culture—informal strategies of dealing with challengers—are, according to Kriesi, either exclusive (repressive, confrontational, polarising) or integrative (facilitative, cooperative, assimilative). Such characteristics are generally very stable.[20] Belgium and the Netherlands, like other small European countries with an open economy, are characterised by integrative political cultures.[21]

The Dutch process of legal change regarding euthanasia is a good example of how an integrative political culture works. Tolerance has for centuries been one of the distinguishing characteristics of Dutch political culture.[22] Proponents of legalisation of euthanasia invoked tolerance by arguing that their opponents did not have the right to impose their (religious) views on others. Because their opponents were sensitive to this argument, the religious argument against euthanasia did not play a role of great importance.

The Belgian process of legal change was rather polarised except at the outset (the role of the Advisory Committee for Bioethics) and the integrative political culture of Belgium was not much in evidence. However, in the way the governing political parties came to a joint legislative proposal, and in the time given to the expression of different views in the parliamentary hearings, we see reflections of the normal Belgian way of doing politics.

Alliance Structure

The idea of an 'alliance structure' refers to the specific balance of power relationships between political actors in Parliament. This fourth element of political opportunity structure sees the accessibility of a political system to new demands such as legalisation of euthanasia as a function not only of the fairly stable characteristics we have considered so far, but also of specific contingencies of power relationships.[23]

The Belgian process of legal change was apparently strongly determined by an unprecedented and unanticipated change in the relationships between political parties that took place in 1999. The elections of 1999 lead to a 'Purple-Green' coalition which for the first time in 40 years did not include the Christian Democrats. Since for more than a decade the Christian Democrats had used their key position in all coalition governments to block any discussion of euthanasia, as soon as they were out of the way, the other parties seized the opportunity to deal with the issue.

Statutory change in the Netherlands can be explained in the same way. In 1994 the Christian Democrats were, for the first time since 1917, not included in the governing coalition. In 1998, under the pressure of new elections, an initiative bill was finally introduced that led ultimately to statutory legalisation. However, the

---

[20] Kriesi *et al* 1995: 33–4.
[21] Kriesi *et al* 1995: 35.
[22] See Zahn 1991.
[23] Kriesi *et al* 1995: 53–60.

Dutch legislative process was less abrupt than that in Belgium. Although a shift in political power relationships was important, the whole issue was politically less charged. First, because euthanasia had been effectively legal for more than a decade, and second because Dutch integrative political culture had been more successful in depoliticising the issue and the Christian-democrats were therefore less resolutely opposed to legal change—in fact, in the decade preceding legalisation, they had as a key member of coalition governments been directly involved in working out essential features of Dutch euthanasia policy.

Conclusion

With respect to political opportunity structure, both Belgium and the Netherlands have political systems that are relatively open to new issues. This openness is a result of their national cleavage structure, their electoral system and their integrative political culture. But ultimately a specific shift in the balance of power between political parties was necessary to make legal change possible. In the Netherlands separation of powers in the sense of the accessibility of the judiciary was also very important, and this helps to account for the more gradual form that legal change took.

20.2.2 Euthanasia and the Political Agenda in Western European Countries

From our discussion of value orientations (section 20.1) it is clear that the Netherlands and Belgium are not the only Western European countries characterised by post-materialistic value orientations and a permissive attitude with respect to bodily self-determination. In several other countries, especially Denmark, Sweden and France, generally held values would lead one to predict that proposals to legalise euthanasia should enjoy broad support. But whether such proposals would find access to the political system is another matter.

With respect to national cleavage structures we have considered two possibilities: (1) the vitality of traditional cleavages can prevent post-materialistic issues from reaching the political agenda, but (2) the existence of an old cleavage to which a post-materialist issue can be linked can give the latter access to the political system. In many countries the old antithesis of liberalism versus socialism is still strong. In such countries post-materialistic issues will not easily reach the national political agenda. Furthermore, many countries do not have an existing cleavage (eg along religious lines) to which euthanasia can be linked.

With respect to institutional structure and political culture we have seen that the political systems in the Netherlands and Belgium are rather open to new issues and that the prevailing political culture is integrative. Although an integrative strategy is not unknown in many European countries, most of them cannot be characterised as easily accessible for groups proposing legal change on non-materialistic issues. Political culture in the Scandinavian countries and England is integrative but structurally these political systems are not very open. Political culture in France and Italy is exclusive. Switzerland is both open and integrative.[24] If the Swiss Criminal Code had had to be changed to make assistance with suicide legal then Switzerland would have been a good bet as the next country where euthanasia would be high on the political agenda.

A second aspect of political structure—access to the political system via the judiciary—was decisive, as we have seen above, in the Netherlands. Although in other countries this path in principle is open, in most countries there have been very few prosecutions of doctors for performing euthanasia. The prosecutorial authorities in most countries apparently consider it wise not to call the taboo on ending life on request into question.[25] In Italy, France, Spain and England there are nevertheless some signs that the taboo is coming to an end.

In short, features of the political opportunity structures in many Western European countries where the relevant value changes have taken place do not support the idea that euthanasia will reach the political agenda soon.

20.3 Diffusion of Law

The Belgian process of legal change regarding euthanasia was undoubtedly influenced by developments in the Netherlands. Vicinity, common history and other similarities will surely have facilitated this.[26] Apart from cultural and geographic vicinity at least two other ways in which European countries influence each other with respect to legislation seem relevant: European unification and 'sin tourism'.

Kurzer investigated the significance of European unification for Dutch drug policy, Nordic alcohol control policy and Irish policy towards sexual morality. National peculiarities in such policies are supposed to reflect a very specific cultural understanding of the relations between state and society, of the responsibility of the state to shield society from human passions and risky behaviour, and of the self or personhood. The policies reflect shared national understandings that function as cultural markers, describing what it means to be Swedish, Dutch or Irish.[27]

In Kurzer's view such national peculiarities are shrinking. Nordic anti-drinking measures are becoming more liberal, Irish attitudes towards abortion less absolute, and the differences between Dutch drug policies and those in other

---

[24] See Kriesi *et al* 1995: 37.

[25] *Cf* Schwitters (2005: 58) on Norway: 'Euthanasia is prohibited but as long as it is carried out in secrecy, prosecutorial authorities spare doctors. In this way both those who want to hold up the prohibition, and those who want to liberalise euthanasia are satisfied.'

[26] The third Benelux-country, Luxemburg, has very recently adopted a law legalising euthanasia along the lines of the Dutch and Belgian laws (see Foreword, p xxv). This event adds credibility to the hypothesis that cultural and geographic proximity facilitate diffusion and are therefore important explanatory factors.

[27] Kurzer 2001: 5–6.

countries are diminishing. Western European societies increasingly share a basic consensus on certain broad values, in particular on allowing individuals to live their lives in accordance with their own personal choices.[28]

Kurzer argues that European intergovernmental agreements to respect national values fail to reckon with the cumulative consequences of the fundamental decision to promote the free circulation of people. In her view, increased exposure to other European cultures has led to changes in national values. And for those who have adopted new values on alcohol, abortion or drugs, the removal of borders has created golden opportunities.[29] Free circulation of people provided Nordic people with the opportunity to buy cheap alcohol, Irish women the opportunity of an abortion abroad and many young people the opportunity to buy and use soft drugs in the Netherlands. European unification thus favours the development of new, European values with respect to bodily self-determination and therefore, it can be predicted, with respect to euthanasia.

Just as Irish women go to England for an abortion, European citizens—especially Germans and Britons—nowadays go to Zurich for assistance with suicide. As with abortion the effect of this 'sin tourism' is twofold: the prohibition in their home country does not stop them—at least a few people—from realising their values regarding bodily self-determination. And by going to Switzerland they challenge the national policy in their home country. The numbers may not be great but the impact on public discussion is profound. Such mechanisms of value diffusion will probably play an important role in getting euthanasia onto local political agendas.

Congruence occurs not only because of physical circulation but also by exchange of information.[30] Dutch and Belgian experiences are becoming better known and less shocking. Thus Dutch euthanasia policy (and more recently, Dutch policy concerning termination of life in neonatology) nowadays elicits at least respectful attention in European media.

20.4 Conclusions

We started this chapter by looking at changes in generally held values. In Europe, the Dutch proved to be the most permissive with respect to bodily self-determination. Other countries (France, Sweden, Denmark and Belgium) are close behind. If public values were one's guide, one would predict legalisation in Denmark, France and Sweden.

---

[28] Kurzer 2001: 11.

[29] Kurzer 2001: 175–6.

[30] Examples of diffusion of this knowledge are the participation by Dutch scholars in a conference organised by the French Minister of Health Kouchner when he was considering a change in policy with respect to euthanasia (see Ministère Délégué à la Santé 2001), and the testimony of Dutch and Belgian scholars during the hearings of the House of Lords Select Committee in England (see House of Lords Select Committee on the Assisted Dying for the Terminally Ill Bill 2005b).

An important difference between the Netherlands and other Western European countries (among them Belgium) is that Dutch public opinion regarding euthanasia found a voice in a large right-to-die society (the NVVE). This voice was complemented by the support for legislation of euthanasia of the Dutch medical association (KNMG). The only country that shares these characteristics is Switzerland, a country where there is little need for a change in the law. If the mobilisation of public values by strong organisations is important, legalisation is not to be expected soon in France, Denmark, or Sweden, nor *a fortiori* in the other countries covered in this book.

Next we looked at political opportunity structure. If the growth in post-materialistic value orientations continues new political cleavages related to this will appear on the scene (or, where already present, they can be expected to grow in political salience). If promotion of legalisation of euthanasia can contribute to a political party's profile then one can predict that in many European countries there will be political parties that pick up the issue.

The next factor we looked at was the openness of political systems to new demands. Belgium and the Netherlands are rather open—because of their pro-portional electoral system—and integrative in their approach to new demands. Except for Switzerland, which is even more open and integrative, no other European political system shows these features. If these conditions are decisive one would predict that euthanasia will not be a political issue in other European countries in the near future.

However, in the Netherlands the change of law did not take place in Parliament but via the courts. This possibility is open in other countries too. An essential condition is that prosecutors be willing to prosecute and judges have an open mind toward novel legal claims. Italy (and perhaps France and Spain) seem promising as far as the first condition is concerned, but judges in these countries seem to be conservative in their approach to legal change.

Both in the Netherlands and in Belgium shifts in power relationships proved to be important. Such shifts are hard to predict but are not very likely in political systems of a more or less two-party or highly polarised character.

The Dutch process of legal change with respect to euthanasia was a rather autonomous project. That the Dutch took the lead could be predicted if we take into account that the country is not only out in front with regard to what Kurzer calls the European common culture but also in giving room for the political expression of new values. If convergence in values takes place, we can predict that other European countries sooner or later will follow the Netherlands and Belgium in realising legal change. Not because of mere imitation but because public pressure will grow and become more effective mobilised. As the Dutch and Belgian experience come to be seen as 'normal', most objections to the legalisation of euthanasia will come to seem far-fetched or old-fashioned.

All in all, we are inclined to predict that legal change in the direction of widely held values will occur first in England, France, Denmark and Sweden.

REFERENCES

Short Titles Used in the Text and Footnotes

AVVV   Algemene Vereniging van Verpleegkundigen en Verzorgenden [General Association of Nurses and Caregivers]

CAL   Commissie Aanvaardbaarheid Levensbeëindigend Handelen [Commission on the Acceptability of Termination of Life of the Royal Dutch Medical Association]

CBS   Centraal Bureau voor de Statistiek [Central Bureau of Statistics]

FCEC   Federale Controle en Evaluatiecommissie Euthanasie/Commission Fédérale de Contrôle et d'Évaluation de l'Euthanasie [Federal Control and Evaluation Commission for Euthanasia] (Belgium)

GB&W   J GRIFFITHS, A BOOD and H WEYERS *Euthanasia and Law in the Netherlands*. Amsterdam, Amsterdam University Press, 1998.

KNMG   Koninklijke Nederlandse Maatschappij ter bevordering van de Geneeskunst [Royal Dutch Medical Association]

KNMP   Koninklijke Nederlandse Maatschappij ter bevordering der Pharmacie [Royal Dutch Association for Pharmacy]

NU'91   Nieuwe Unie '91[New Union '91]

NVK   Nederlandse Vereniging voor Kindergeneeskunde [Dutch Association for Paediatrics]

NVOG   Nederlandse Vereniging voor Obstetrie en Gynaecologie [Dutch Association for Obstetrics and Gynecology]

NVP   Nederlandse Vereniging voor Psychiatrie [Dutch Association for Psychiatry]

NVVE   Nederlandse Vereniging voor Vrijwillige Euthanasie [Dutch Association for Voluntary Euthanasia]

RRC   Regional Review Committees Euthanasia [Regionale Toetsingscommissies Euthanasie]

RRCj   Regional Review Committees Euthanasia judgments [Regionale Toetsingscommissies Euthanasie oordelen]

SCEN   Steun en Consultatie bij Euthanasie in Nederland [Support and Consultation for Euthanasia in the Netherlands]

SCP   Sociaal en Cultureel Planbureau [Social and Cultural Planning Bureau]

SPIEGEL   Overleggroep Toetsing Zorgvuldig Medisch Handelen rond het Levenseinde bij Pasgeborenen [Consultative Committee on Reviewing Due Care in Medical Practice at the End of Life of Newborn Babies]

Bibliographical References

NB Dutch authors are catalogued without regard to prefixes such as 'van' and 'de'; in the
    case of other countries where this is customary (eg Belgium and the United States),
    the prefix is included in the name for purposes of cataloguing.

AARTSEN, J

1989 Letter (signed by 25 persons prominent in the Dutch euthanasia discussion and asso-
    ciated with legal, medical, ethical and health-policy organisations). *Hastings Center
    Report*, special supplement, Jan/Feb: 47–8.

ACHTERBERG, P

2005 *Met de beste vergelijkbaar? Internationale verschillen in sterfte rond de geboorte*
    [Comparable to the Best? International Differences in Perinatal Death]. Bilthoven,
    RIVM.

ADAMS, M

2001 'Euthanasia: The Process of Legal Change in Belgium. Reflections on the
    Parliamentary Debate'. Pp 29–47 in A Klijn, M Otlowski and M Trappenburg (eds).
    Regulating Physician-negotiated Death. The Hague, Elsevier.

ADAMS, M and G GEUDENS

1999–2000 'De regulering van euthanasie in België: principiële beschouwingen naar aanlei-
    ding van een aantal recente wetsvoorstellen [The Regulation of Euthanasia in Belgium:
    Matters of Principle in Connection with Some Recent Legislative Proposals]'.
    Rechtskundig Weekblad 63: 793–816.

ADAMS, M, J GRIFFITHS and G den HARTOGH (eds)

2003 *Euthanasie: nieuwe knelpunten in een voortgezette discussie* [Euthanasia: New
    Problems in a Continuing Discussion]. Kampen, Kok.

ADMIRAAL, P and J GRIFFITHS

2001 'Sterven aan pijnbestrijding [Death from Pain Relief]'. *Medisch Contact* 56: 463–4.

ALBERT SCHWEITZER ZIEKENHUIS (Dordrecht)

2004– *Jaarverslag: Euthanasieconsulent in het Albert Schweitzer ziekenhuis* [Annual Report:
    Euthanasia Consultant in the Albert Schweitzer Hospital]. Dordrecht, Albert
    Schweitzer Ziekenhuis.

ALMINDELIGE DANSKE LÆGEFORENING [DANISH MEDICAL ASSOCIATION]

2005 *Lægeforeningens etiske regler* [Ethical Rules for Doctors 1989, last amended 2005].
    Available at <http://www.laeger.dk/portal/page/portal/LAEGERDK/LAEGER_DK/
    LAEGEFAGLIGT/RET_OG_ETIK/ETIK/LAEGEFORENINGENS_ETISKE_REGLE
    R#3> accessed 1 October 2007.

ALT-MAES, F

2004 'Esquisse et poursuite d'une dépénalisation du droit medical [Outline of a Depenal-
    ization of Medical Law]'. *La Semaine juridique, édition générale*, no 184: 2187–92.

AMERICAN MEDICAL ASSOCIATION

1999 'Medical Futility in End-of-Life Care: Report of the Council on Ethical and Judicial
    Affairs'. *JAMA* 281: 937–41.

ANDEWEG, R and G IRWIN

1993 *Dutch Government and Politics*. London, MacMillan.

ANSPACH, R

1993 *Deciding Who Lives: Fateful Choices in the Intensive-Care Nursery*. Berkeley, University
    of California Press.

ARBEITSGRUPPE STERBEHILFE [TASK FORCE ON ASSISTED DYING]

1999 *Bericht an das Eidgenössisches Justiz- und Polizeidepartement* [Report to the Federal Office of Justice and Police].

ARLIDGE, A

2000 'The Trial of Dr David Moor'. *Criminal Law Review* Jan: 31–40.

ARNEART, A, B VAN DEN HEUVEL and T WINDEY

2005 'Health and Social Care Policy for the Elderly in Belgium'. *Geriatric Nursing* 26: 366–71. Available at <http://statbel.fgov.be/home_nl.asp> accessed 1 October 2007.

ASHWORTH, A

1996 'Criminal Liability in a Medical Context: The Treatment of Good Intentions'. Pp 173–93 in A Simester and A Smith (eds). *Harm and Culpability.* Oxford, Clarendon.

2003 *Principles of Criminal Law.* 4th edn. Oxford, Oxford University Press.

AVVV/NU'91/KNMG [ALGEMENE VERENIGING VERPLEEGKUNDIGEN EN VERZORGENDEN/NIEUWE UNIE '91/KONINKLIJKE NEDERLANDSE MAATSCHAPPIJ TER BEVORDERING VAN DE GENEESKUNST]

2006 *Handreiking voor samenwerking artsen, verpleegkundigen en verzorgenden bij euthanasie* [Guideline for Cooperation between Doctors, Nurses and Caregivers in Cases of Euthanasia]. Utrecht, AVVV *et al.* Available at <http://www.knmg.nl> accessed 1 October 2007.

BACHMANN, U

2004 'Aus Überforderung getötet. Luzerner "Todespfleger" muss wegen 24 Tötungen und 3 Tötungsversuchen vor Gericht [Excessive Demands Led to Killing. Lucerne "Angel of Death" Charged with 24 Killings and 3 Attempts to Kill]'. *Der Bund* (15 January).

BATTIN, M *et al*

2007 'Legal Physician-Assisted Dying in Oregon and the Netherlands: Evidence concerning the Impact on Patients in "Vulnerable" Groups'. *Journal of Medical Ethics* 33 591–7.

BEAUCHAMP, T and J CHILDRESS

2001 *Principles of Biomedical Ethics.* 5th edn. Oxford, Oxford University Press.

BÉCHILLON, D de

2002 Commentary. *Revue française de droit administratif,* no 1: 155–62.

BENJAMINSEN, M

1988 *Bij het einde: een onderzoek naar terminale zorg en euthanasieproblematiek in Utrecht* [At the End: Research Concerning Care of Terminal Patients and Euthanasia in Utrecht]. Utrecht, Gemeente Utrecht.

BIGGS, H

2001 *Euthanasia, Death with Dignity and the Law.* Oxford, Hart Publishing.

2005 'The Assisted Dying for the Terminally Ill Bill 2004: Will English Law Soon Allow Patients the Choice to Die?' *European Journal of Health Law* 12: 43–56.

BILSEN, J *et al*

2004 'Involvement of Nurses in Physician-Assisted Dying'. *Journal of Advanced Nursing* 47: 583–91.

2006 'Drugs Used to Alleviate Symptoms with Life Shortening as a Possible Side Effect: End-of-Life Care in Six European Countries'. *Journal of Pain and Symptom Management* 31: 111–21.

BINDELS, P and A KROL

1996 'Euthanasia and Physician-Assisted Suicide in Homosexual Men with AIDS'. *The Lancet* 347: 499–505.

BINET, J
2002 *Droit et progrès scientifique* [Law and Scientific Progress]. Paris, PUF.

BIRNBACHER, D
1995 *Tun und Unterlassen* [Acting and Omitting]. Stuttgart, Reclam.

BLACK, D
1976 *The Behavior of Law*. New York [etc], Academic Press.

BLAD, J
1990 *Tussen lots-en zelfbeschikking: de stand van het beleid ten aanzien van euthanasie in ziekenhuizen en verpleeghuizen in Nederland* [Between Fate and Self-Determination. Current Policy on Euthanasia in Dutch Hospitals and Nursing Homes]. Arnhem, Gouda Quint.

1996 *Abolitionisme als strafrechtstheorie: theoretische beschouwingen over het abolitionisme van L. Hulsman* [Abolitionism as a Criminal Law Theory: Theoretical Reflections on the Abolitionism of L Hulsman]. Deventer, Gouda Quint.

BLENGINI, C *et al*
2003 'Italy Reforms National Policy for Cancer Pain Relief and Opioids'. *European Journal of Cancer Care* 12: 28–34.

BLOM, A *et al*
2006 'Altijd contact met palliatief consultatieteam: vooraf advies vragen over infusieme-dicatie thuis [There Should Always be Contact in advance with a Palliative Consultation Team Before Giving Intraveneous Medication in the Home Situation]'. *Medisch Contact* 61: 953–5.

BOELE-WOELKI, K and A FUCHS (eds)
2003 *Legal Recognition of Same-Sex Couples in Europe*. Antwerp etc, Intersentia.

BOER, A de
2006 *Rapportage ouderen 2006: veranderingen in de leefsituatie en levensloop* [Report on the Elderly 2006: Changes in Living Arrangements and Course of Life]. The Hague, Sociaal en Cultureel Planbureau.

BOOD, A
1998 'Euthanasie' in de Verenigde Staten [Euthanasia in the United States]'. *RM Themis* no 6: 177–89.

2007 'Levensbeëindiging bij pasgeborenen [Termination of Life of Newborns]'. *Nederlands Juristenblad* 82: 2288–95.

BOOT, J and M KNAPEN
2005 *De Nederlandse gezondheidszorg* [The Health Care System in the Netherlands]. Houten, Bohn Stafleu Van Loghum.

BOSMA, J, G van der WAL and S HOSMAN-BENJAMINSE
1996 'Late zwangerschapsafbreking in Noord-Holland. II. Zorgvuldigheid vooraf en toetsing achteraf [Late-term Abortion in North-Holland. II. Careful Procedure Beforehand and Control Afterwards]'. *Nederlands Tijdschrift voor Geneeskunde* 140: 605–9.

BOSSHARD, G
2005 'Begriffsbestimmungen in der Sterbehilfedebatte [Terminology in the Euthanasia Debate]'. Swiss *Medical Forum* 5: 193–8.

2006 'Die Tätigkeit der Sterbehilfeorganisationen und die Rolle des Arztes [The Practice of Right-to-Die Societies and the Role of the Doctor]'. Pp 21–30 in C Rehmann-Sutter *et al* (eds). *Beihilfe zum Suizid in der Schweiz: Beiträge aus Ethik, Recht und Medizin* [Assisted Suicide in Switzerland: Contributions from Ethics, Law, and Medicine]. Bern, Peter Lang.

BOSSHARD, G, N DE STOUTZ and W BÄR

2006 'Eine gesetzliche Regulierung des Umgangs mit Opiaten und Sedativa bei medizinischen Entscheidungen am Lebensende [Legal Regulation of Opioid and Sedative Use in Medical End-of-Life Decisions]'. *Ethik in der Medizin* 18: 120–32.

BOSSHARD, G, S FISCHER and W BÄR

2002 'Open Regulation and Practice in Assisted Dying: How Switzerland Compares with the Netherlands and Oregon'. *Swiss Medical Weekly* 132: 527–34.

BOSSHARD, G, E ULRICH and W BÄR

2003 '748 Cases of Suicide Assisted by a Swiss Right-to-Die organisation'. *Swiss Medical Weekly* 133: 310–17.

BOSSHARD, G, W WETTSTEIN and W BÄR

2003 'Wie stabil ist die Einstellung Betagter zu lebensverlängernden Massnahmen? Resultate einer 3-Jahres-Katamnese von Pflegeheimbewohnern [How Stable is the Attitude of Aged People towards Life-Extending Measures? Results of a 3-Year Follow-up in Nursing Home Residents]'. *Zeitschrift für Gerontologie und Geriatrie* 36: 124–9.

BOSSHARD, G *et al*

2003 'Assisted Suicide Bordering on Active Euthanasia'. *International Journal of Legal Medicine* 117: 106–8.

2005 'Forgoing Treatment at the End of Life in 6 European Countries'. *Archives of Internal Medicine* 165: 401–7.

2006 'Intentionally Hastening Death by Withholding or Withdrawing Treatment'. *Wiener Klinische Wochenschrift* 118: 322–6.

BOSSUYT, N and H VAN OYEN

2000 *Gezondheidsverwachting volgens socio-economische gradiënt in België* [Health Expectations and Socio-Economic Status in Belgium]. Brussels, Wetenschappelijk Instituut Volksgezondheid/afdeling epidemiologie. Available at <http://www.iph.fgov.be/epidemio/epinl/inegalnl/index.htm> accessed 1 October 2007.

BRAHAMS, D

1990 'The Reluctant Survivor: Part 1'. *New Law Journal* 140 (6453): 586–7.

BRAITHWAITE, J

2002 'Rules and Principles: A Theory of Legal Certainty'. *Australian Journal of Legal Philosophy* 27: 47–82

BRAUW, P de and L KALKMAN-BOGERD

1988 *Rechtspraak medisch tuchtrecht 1976–1987* [Medical Disciplinary Cases 1976–1987]. Deventer, Kluwer.

BRITISH MEDICAL ASSOCIATION

2001 *Withholding and Withdrawing Life-Prolonging Medical Treatment: Guidance for Decision Making*. 2nd edn. London, BMJ Books.

2006 *End-of-Life Decisions: Views of the BMA.*

2007 *Withholding and Withdrawing Life-Prolonging Medical Treatment: Guidance for Decision Making*. 3rd edn. London, BMJ Books.

BROECKAERT, B

2003 'Palliatieve zorg en euthanasie: alternatieven?' [Palliative Care and Euthanasia: Alternatives?]'. Pp 61–84 in Adams, Griffiths & Den Hartogh (eds) 2003.

BROECKAERT, B and R JANSSENS

2005 'Palliative Care and Euthanasia. Belgian and Dutch Perspectives'. Pp 36–69 in T Meulenberghs en P Schotsmans (eds). *Euthanasia and Palliative Care in the Low Countries*. Leuven, Peeters.

BRUCHEM-van de SCHEUR, A van *et al*

2004 *De rol van verpleegkundigen bij medische beslissingen rond het levenseinde: verslag van een landelijk onderzoek naar betrokkenheid en praktijken: Rapport in opdracht van het Ministerie van Volksgezondheid, Welzijn en Sport* [The Role of Nurses in Connection with Medical Decisions at the End of Life: Report of a National Study of Involvement and Practice: Report for the Ministry of Public Health, Welfare and Sport]. Utrecht, Uitgeverij De Tijdstroom.

BUCHANAN, A and D BROCK

1990 *Deciding for Others: The Ethics of Surrogate Decision-Making.* Cambridge, Cambridge University Press.

BUNDESAMT FÜR JUSTIZ [SWISS FEDERAL OFFICE OF JUSTICE AND POLICE]

2006 *Sterbehilfe und Palliativmedizin Bern: Handlungsbedarf für den Bund?* [Assisted Dying: Federal Government Due to Take Action?]. Available at <https://www.news-service. admin.ch/NSBSubscriber/message/de/attachments/5336/9259/2766/20060531_ ber-sterbehilfe-d.pdf> accessed 1 October 2007.

BUNDESAMT FÜR STATISTIK [SWISS FEDERAL OFFICE OF STATISTICS]

2005 *Statistisches Jahrbuch der Schweiz 2005* [Swiss Annuals of Statistics 2005]. Zurich, Verlag Neue Zürcher Zeitung.

BURGEMEISTER, J

2006 'Doctor Reignites Euthanasia Row in Belgium after Mercy Killing'. *British Medical Journal* 332: 382.

BURT, R

1997 'The Supreme Court Speaks: Not Assisted Suicide but a Constitutional Right to Palliative Care'. *New England Journal of Medicine* 337: 1234–6.

2005 'Book review of Dying Justice: A Case for Decriminalizing Euthanasia and Assisted Suicide in Canada by Jocelyn Downie. Toronto, University of Toronto Press, 2004'. *New England Journal of Medicine* 352: 1501–2.

CAL [COMMISSIE AANVAARDBAARHEID LEVENSBEEINDIGEND HANDELEN/ COMMISSION ON THE ACCEPTABILITY OF TERMINATION OF LIFE OF THE ROYAL DUTCH MEDICAL ASSOCIATION]

1990 CAL 1 *Zwaar-defecte pasgeborenen* [Severely Defective Newborn Babies].

1991 CAL 2 *Landurig comateuze patiënten* [Long-Term Comatose Patients].

1993a CAL 3 *Ernstig demente patiënten* [Seriously Demented Patients].

1993b CAL 4 *Hulp bij zelfdoding bij psychiatrische patiënten* [Assistance with Suicide in the Case of Psychiatric Patients].

1997 *Medisch handelen rond het levenseinde bij wilsonbekwamepatiënten* [Medical Behaviour in Connection with the End of Life of Non-Competent Patients]. Houten/Diegem, Bohn Stafleu Van Loghum.

CARLET, J *et al*

2004 'Challenges in End-of-Life Care in the ICU: Statement of the 5th International Consensus Conference in Critical Care: Brussels, Belgium, April 2003'. *Intensive Care Medicine* 30: 770–84.

CASTRA, M

2003 *Bien mourir: sociologie des soins palliatifs* [To Die Well: Sociology of Palliative Care]. Paris, PUF.

CATSBURG, I and C de BOER

1986 'Meningen over euthanasie [Public Opinion about Euthanasia]'. *De Psycholoog* 21: 237–53.

CAVALLI, F

2000 *Strafbarkeit der aktiven Sterbehilfe. Neuregelung* [Punishability of Voluntary Active Euthanasia. Revision]. Parlamentarische Initiative [Parliamentary Initiative] 00.441. Available at <http://www.parlament.ch/afs/data/d/bericht/2000/d_bericht_n_k12_0_20000441_01.htm> accessed 1 October 2007.

CBS [Centraal Bureau voor de Statistiek/Central Bureau of Statistics]

1988 *Overledenen naar doodsoorzaak, leeftijd en geslacht in het jaar 1987* [Deaths by Cause of Death, Age and Sex in the Year 1987]. The Hague, CBS.

1991 *Het levenseinde in de medische praktijk: resultaten van een steekproef uit sterfgevallen, juli-november 1990* [The End of Life in Medical Practice: Results of a Sample of Deaths in the Period July-November 1990]. The Hague, Sdu.

1996 *Het levenseinde in de medische praktijk (1995, 1990): resultaten sterfgevallenonderzoek 1995, deelonderzoek II van het evaluatieonderzoek meldingsprocedure euthanasie* [The End of Life in Medical Practice (1995, 1990): Results of a Study of Deaths in 1995, Part II of the Evaluation Study of the Reporting Procedure for Euthanasia]. Heerlen, CBS.

2003a *Het levenseinde in de medische praktijk: resultaten sterfgevallenonderzoek 2001* [The End of Life in Medical Practice: Results of a Survey of Deaths in 2001]. Voorburg, CBS.

2003b *Vademecum Gezondheidsstatistiek Nederland 2003* [Dutch Health Statistics 2003]. The Hague, Staatsuitgeverij.

2006 *Gezondheidszorg in cijfers* [Health care in Numbers]. The Hague, CBS.

2007 *Statistisch Jaarboek 2007* [Statistical Yearbook]. The Hague, CBS.

CENTRO DE INVESTIGACIONES SOCIOLÓGICAS/CENTRE FOR SOCIOLOGICAL RESEARCH

1992 *Barómetro marzo 1992.* Estudio 1996. Available at <http://www.cis.es/cis/opencms/ES/1_encuestas/estudios/ver.jsp?estudio=988> accessed 1 October 2007.

2002 *Actitudes y opiniones de los médicos ante la eutanasia* [Attitudes and Opinions of Physicians with respect to Euthanasia]. Estudio 2451. Available at <http://www.cis.es/cis/export/sites/default/-Archivos/Marginales/2440_2459/Es2451mar.pdf> accessed 1 October 2007.

1985 'Problèmes de bioéthiques, First Report [Problems of Bioethics, First Report]'. *Cahiers du CEPESS* no 4.

CHABOT, B

1992 'Klaar met leven [Finished with Life]'. *Medisch Contact* 47: 1536–40.

1996 *Sterven op drift: over doodsverlangen en onmacht* [Death Adrift: Powerlessness and the Desire to Die]. Nijmegen, SUN.

2001 *Sterfwerk: de dramaturgie van zelfdoding in eigen kring* [Dying: The Dramaturgics of Suicide without the Help of Doctors]. Nijmegen, SUN.

2003 'Is er toekomst voor de pil van Drion? [Is there a Future for the Drion Pill?]'. Pp 191–213 in J Legemaate and R Dillmann (eds). *Levensbeëindigend handelen door een arts op verzoek van de patiënt* [Termination of Life by a Doctor at the Request of the Patient] Houten, Bohn Stafleu Van Loghum.

2007 *Auto-euthanasie: verborgen stervenswegen in gesprek met naasten* [Self-Euthanasia: Low-Visibility Ways to Die while in Contact with Those to whom One is Close]. Amsterdam, Uitgeverij Bert Bakker.

CHAILLET, S and F PERIGNON

1995 *La prise en charge de la douleur dans les établissements de santé en France* [Pain management in Health Care Institutions in France]. Paris, Ministère des Affaires Sociales, de la Santé et de la Ville. Available at <http://www.ladocumentationfrancaise.fr/rapports-publics/954078100/somm.shtml> accessed 1 October 2007.

CHAN, W and A SIMESTER

2005 'Duress, Necessity: How Many Defences?' *King's College Law Journal* 16: 121–32.

CHAPMAN, C

2006 'Swiss Hospital Lets Terminally Ill Patients Commit Suicide in its Beds'. *British Medical Journal* 332: 7.

CLERY, E *et al*

2007 'Quickening Death: The Euthanasia Debate'. Pp 35–54 in A Park *et al* (eds). *British Social Attitudes: The 23rd Report—Perspectives on a Changing Society*. London, Sage.

COHEN, J *et al*

2006a 'European Public Acceptance of Euthanasia: Socio-Demographic and Cultural Factors Associated with the Acceptance of Euthanasia in 33 European Countries'. *Social Science & Medicine* 63: 743–56.

2006b 'Trends in Acceptance of Euthanasia among the General Public in 12 European Countries (1981–1999)'. *European Journal of Public Health* 16: 663–9.

2006c 'Dying at Home or in an Institution. Using Death Certificates to Explore the Factors Associated with Place of Death'. *Health Policy* 78: 319–29.

COMITATO NAZIONALE DI BIOETICA [NATIONAL BIOETHICS COMMITTEE]

accessed 1 October 2007.

1992 *Informazione e consenso all'atto medico* [Informed Consent].

1995 *Questioni bioetiche relative alla fine della vita umana* [Bioethical Questions concerning the End of Life].

2003 *Dichiarazioni anticipate di trattamento* [Advance Treatment Directives].

2005a *Sull'assistenza a neonati e a bambini afflitti da patologie o da handicap ad altissima gravità e sull'eutanasia pediatrica* [Medical Care and Euthanasia for Newborns and Children with a very Serious Pathology or Handicap].

2005b *L'alimentazione e l'idratazione dei pazienti in Stato Vegetativo Persistente* [Feeding and Hydration of Permanent Vegetative State Patients].

COMITÉ CONSULTATIF NATIONAL D'ÉTHIQUE [NATIONAL CONSULTATIVE COMMITTEE ON ETHICS]

1991 *Avis concernant la proposition de résolution sur l'assistance aux mourants, adopté le 25 avril 1991 au Parlement européen par la Commission de l'environnement, de la santé publique et de la protection des consommateurs* [Opinion concerning a Draft Resolution on Assistance to the Dying adopted on April 25th 1991 by the Commission for Environment, Public Health and Consumer Protection of the European Parliament] no 26. Available at <http://www.ccne-ethique.fr> or <http://www.ccne-ethique.fr/english/start.htm> accessed 1 October 2007.

2000 *Fin de vie, arrêt de vie, euthanasia* [End of Life, Ending Life, Euthanasia]. Opinion no 63, 27 January 2000. Available in English at <http://www.ccne-ethique.fr/english/start.htm> accessed 1 October 2007.

COMITÈ CONSULTIU DE BIOÈTICA DE CATALUNYA [CONSULTIVE COMMITTEE ON BIOETHICS OF CATALUNA]

2006 *Informe sobre la eutanasia y la ayuda al suicidio* [Report on Euthanasia and Assistance with Suicide]. Barcelona.

COMMISSIE PERINATAL AUDIT [COMMITTEE ON PERINATAL AUDIT]

2005 *Landelijk perinatal audit studie* [National Perinatal Audit Study]. Diemen, College voor zorgverzekeringen.

COMMISSIE REMMELINK [COMMISSIE ONDERZOEK MEDISCHE PRAKTIJK INZAKE EUTHANSIE]

1991 *Medische beslissingen rond het levenseinde: rapport van de Commissie onderzoek praktijk inzake euthanasie* [Medical Decisions Concerning the End of Life: Report of the Commission for Research into Medical Practice at the End of Life]. The Hague, Sdu Uitgeverij.

CONFERENCIA EPISCOPAL ESPAÑOLA [SPANISH EPISCOPAL CONFERENCE]

1993 *La Eutanasia. 100 Cuestiones y respuestas sobre la defensa de la vida humana y la actitud de los católicos* [Euthanasia. 100 Questions and Answers about the Defence of Human Life and the Attitudes of Catholics]. Available at <http://www.conferenciaepiscopal.es/ceas/documentos/eutanasia.htm> accessed 1 October 2007.

2001 *Discurso inaugural* [Inaugural Discourse] del Emmo. y Rvdmo. Sr. D Antonio María Rouco Varela Cardenal-Arzobispo de Madrid, Presidente de la Conferencia Episcopal. Madrid, 23–27 Abril 2001. Asamblea plenaria de la conferencia episcopal española LXXVI [Plenary Assembly of the Spanish Episcopal Conference] Available at <http://www.conferenciaepiscopal.es/documentos/plenaria/LXXVI_Plenaria.htm> accessed 1 October 2007.

2004a *Toda una vida para ser vivida* [A Whole Life to be Lived] available at <http://www.conferenciaepiscopal.es/iniciativas/eutanasia.htm> accessed 1 October 2007.

2004b 'Presentación en la Conferencia Episcopal de la iniciativa para difundir la visión católica sobre la eutanasia [Presentation at the Episcopal Conference of the Initiative to Promote the Catholic View on Euthanasia]'. *Boletín Informativo* del 30 de Octubre al 5 de Noviembre 2004. Available at <http://www.conferenciaepiscopal.es/ACTIVIDADES/retablo/2004/octubre-30_nov-5/portada.htm> accessed 1 October 2007.

COOLSAET, A

1995/6 'Een overzicht van de Belgische wetsvoorstellen inzake euthanasie [A Survey of the Belgian Legislative Proposals concerning Euthanasia]'. *Tijdschrift voor Gezondheidsrecht/Revue de Droit de la Santé* 1: 262–71.

CORENS, D

2007 'Belgium. Health System Review'. *Health Systems in Transition* No 9.

CRIMINAL LAW REVISION COMMITTEE

1976 *Working Paper on Offences Against the Person.*

1980 *Offences Against the Person.* Report no 14.

CRUL, B

1999 'Melding en toetsing vooraf, daar had ik wat aan gehad [Reporting and Review in Advance, That Would Have Been Useful]'. *Medisch Contact* 54: 1038–9.

2001a 'Lijdensweg door goed dokterschap [Suffering Due to Good Doctoring]'. *Medisch Contact* 56: 235.

2001b 'Levensmoe dekt de lading volstrekt niet [Tired of Life is a Totally Inadequate Description]'. *Medisch Contact* 56: 772–4.

CUTTINI, M *et al*

2000 'End-of-Life Decisions in Neonatal Intensive Care: Physicians' Self-Reported Practices in Seven European Countries'. *The Lancet* 355: 2112–18.

DAM, H van

2005 *Euthanasie: de praktijk anders bekeken: interviews met nabestaanden* [Euthanasia: Looking at Practice through Other Eyes: Interviews with Next of Kin]. Veghel, Libra & Libris.

2007 *Euthanasie: de praktijk van dichtbij bekeken: interviews met artsen* [Euthanasia: The Practice Close Up: Interviews with Doctors]. Veghel, Libra & Libris.

DAS, C

2005 'Death Certificates in Germany, England, the Netherlands, Belgium and the USA'. *European Journal of Health Law* 12: 193–211.

DAVIES, C

2006 *A Matter of Human Rights. Medically Assisted Dying: The Swiss Experience.* Available at <http://www.geocities.com/friends_at_the_end/swissexperiencechris daviesmep.html> accessed 20 December 2007.

DE BONDT, W

2005 'De eerste evaluatie van de toepassing van de euthanasiewet: capita selecta en kant-tekeningen [The First Evaluation of the Implementation of the Euthanasia Law: Selected Observations]'. *Rechtskundig Weekblad* 69: 81–93.

DE GENDT, C *et al*

2005 'Do-Not-Resuscitate Policy on Acute Geriatric Wards in Flanders, Belgium'. *Journal of the American Geriatric Society* 53: 2221–6.

DE GRAEFF, A and M DEAN

2007 'Palliative Sedation Therapy in the Last Weeks of Life: A Literature Review and Recommendations for Standards'. *Journal of Palliative Medicine* 10: 67–85.

DEGUERGUE, M

2002 Commentary. *Actualité juridique droit administratif*, no 3: 260–63.

DEHAN, M *et al*

2001 'Dilemmes éthiques de la période périnatale: recommandations pour les décisions de fin de vie [Ethical Dilemmas of the Perinatal Period: Recommendations for End-of-Life Decisions]'. *Archives de pédiatrie* 8: 407–19.

DEL ROSAL BLASCO, B

1996 'El tratamiento jurídico-penal y doctrinal de la eutanasia en España [The Penal-Doctrinal Treatment of Euthanasia in Spain]'. Pp 43–74 in J Díez Ripollés and J Muñoz Sánchez (eds) 1996.

DELDEN, J van *et al*

2006 'Do-Not-Rescuscitate Decisions in Six European Countries'. *Critical Care Medicine* 34: 1686–90.

DELFOSSE, M

1995 'Ethische problemen [Ethical Problems]'. Pp 498–518 in W Dewachter and P de Gryse (eds). *Tussen staat en maatschappij: 1945–1995 Christen-democratie in België* [Between State and Society: 1945–1995 Christian-Democracy in Belgium]. Tielt, Lannoo.

DELIENS, L, and J BILSEN

1998 *Handelswijzen van Hasseltse artsen rond het levenseinde van hun patiënten. Een onder-zoek van 269 overlijdens* [The Practice of Doctors in the City of Hasselt Concerning the End of Life. A Study of 269 Deaths]'. Stadsbestuur Hasselt, Vrije Universiteit Brussel and Universiteit Gent.

DELIENS, L *et al*

2000 'End-of-Life Decisions in Medical Practice in Flanders, Belgium: A Nation-wide Survey'. *The Lancet* 356: 1806–11.

2005 'Medical End-of-Life Decisions in Neonates and Infants in Flanders'. *The Lancet* 365: 1315–20.

DELL, S

1984 *Murder into Manslaughter: Diminished Responsibility Defence in Practice.* Oxford, Oxford University Press.

DEMEESTER-DE MEYER, W (ed)

1987 *Bio-ethica in de jaren '90* [Bioethics in the 90s]. Vols I and II. Gent, Omega Editions.

DEN NORSKE LEGEFORENING [NORWEGIAN MEDICAL ASSOCIATION]

1994 *Etiske regler for leger. Vedtatt av landsstyret 1961 med endringer, senest 2002* [Ethical Rules for Doctors 1961, last amended June 2002; section on assisted dying amended October 1994]. Available at <http://www.legeforeningen.no/index.gan?id=485> accessed 1 October 2007.

DEN NORSKE LEGEFORENING. RÅDET FOR LEGEETIKK [NORWEGIAN MEDICAL ASSOCIATION. MEDICAL ETHICS COUNCIL]

2001 *Retningslinjer for lindrende sedering til døende* [Guidelines for Palliative Sedation of the Dying]. Available at <http://www.legeforeningen.no/index.db2?id=3942> accessed 1 October 2007.

2003 *Annual Report.* Available at <http://www.tidsskriftet.no/pls/lts/PA_LT.VisSeksjon?vp_SEKS_ID=906157> accessed 1 October 2007.

DEPARTMENT FOR CONSTITUTIONAL AFFAIRS

2006 *Statistics on Deaths Reported to Coroners England and Wales.* 2005.

2007 *Code of Practice for the Mental Capacity Act 2005.*

DEVLIN, P

1985 *Easing the Passing: The Trial of Dr. John Bodkin Adams.* London, Bodley Head.

DEVROEY, D, V VAN CASTEREN and J DE LEPELEIRE

2002 'Placements in Psychiatric Institutions, Nursing Homes and Homes for the Elderly by Belgian General Practitioners'. *Aging & Mental Health* 6: 286–92.

DICEY, A

1905 *Lectures on the Relation between Law and Public Opinion in England during the Nineteenth Century.* London, Macmillan (2nd edition 1963).

DIERICKX, A

2003 'Als sterven "leven" is…, is helpen sterven dan "doden"? Een commentaar bij de Wet van 28 maart 2002 betreffende de euthanasie. [If dying is "living" . . ., is helping to die then "killing"? A Commentary on the Law on Euthanasia of 28 March 2002]'. *Tijdschrift voor Strafrecht* 3 (Dossier 1): 1–40.

DÍEZ RIPOLLÉS, J and J MUÑOZ SÁNCHEZ (eds)

1996 *El tratamiento jurídico de la eutanasia. Una perspectiva comparada* [The Legal Treatment of Euthanasia. A Comparative Perspective]. Valencia, Tirant lo Blanch.

DIJON, X

1982 *Le sujet de droit en son corps: une mise à l'épreuve du droit subjectif* [The Embodied Legal Subject: A Challenge to the Law of the Person]. Brussels, Ferdinand Larcier.

DILLMANN, R

1996 'Euthanasia in the Netherlands: The Role of the Dutch Medical Profession'. Pp 65–74 in *Euthanasia and Assisted Suicide in the Netherlands and in Europe.* Luxembourg, Office for Official Publications of the European Communities.

DORSCHEIDT, J

2006 *Levensbeëindiging bij gehandicapte pasgeborenen* [Termination of Life of Handicapped Newborns]. The Hague, Sdu Uitgevers.

DORSCHEIDT, J and A VERHAGEN

2004 'Een centrale toetsingscommissie voor beslissingen rond het levenseinde bij pas-geborenen: een brug te ver [A Central Review Committee for Decisions concerning the End of Life in the case of Newborns: A Bridge Too Far]'. *Nederlands Juristenblad* 79: 2141–7.

DREES [DIRECTION DE LA RECHERCHE, DES ÉTUDES, DES ÉVALUATIONS ET DES STATISTIQUES/DIRECTORATE OF RESEARCH, STUDIES, EVALUATIONS AND STATISTICS]

2003 *Les établissements de santé en 2001* [Health Centres in 2001]. Paris, DREES.

DRION, H

1992 *Het zelfgewilde einde van oude mensen* [The Choice for Ending Life by Elderly People]. Amsterdam, Balans.

DUNLOP, R *et al*

1995 'On Withholding Nutrition and Hydration in the Terminally Ill: Has Palliative Medicine Gone Too Far? A Reply'. *Journal of Medical Ethics* 21: 141–3.

DUPONT, L and R VERSTRAETEN

1990 *Handboek Belgisch Strafrecht* [Handbook of Belgian Criminal Law]. Leuven, Acco.

DURKHEIM, E

1897 *La suïcide: Étude de sociologie* [Suicide: A Sociological Study]. Paris, Félix Alcan.

DWORKIN, R

1993 *Life's Dominion. An Argument about Abortion, Euthanasia, and Individual Freedom.* New York, Knopf.

DYER, C

1998 'Consultant Suspended for Not Getting Consent for Cardiac Procedure'. *British Medical Journal* 316: 955.

1999 'Withdrawal of Food Supplement Judged as Misconduct'. *British Medical Journal* 318: 895.

ELCHARDUS, M, J-M. CHAUMONT and S LAUWERS

1992 'Morele onzekerheid en nieuwe degelijkheid [Moral Uncertainties and the New Respectability]'. Pp 153–92 in K Dobbelaere *et al. Verloren zekerheid. De Belgen en hun waarden, overtuigingen en houdingen* [Certainty Lost. The Belgians and their Values, Convictions and Attitutes]. Tielt, Lannoo.

ELIAS, N

1993 *The Civilizing Process: The History of Manners and State Formation and Civlization.* Oxford, Blackwell.

EMANUEL, E

2002 'Euthanasia and Physician-Assisted Suicide. A Review of the Empirical Data from the United States'. *Archives of Internal Medicine* 162: 142–52.

ENGBERTS, D

1997 *Met permissie: morele argumentaties inzake het toestemmingsbeginsel bij de totstand-koming van de Wet Geneeskundige Behandelings-Overeenkomst* [With Permission: Moral Arguments Concerning the Requirement of Informed Consent in Connection with the Enactment of the Law on Contracts for Medical Treatment]. Deventer, Kluwer.

ENSCHEDÉ, C

1985 *De arts en de dood: sterven en recht.* [The Doctor and Death: Dying and the Law]. Deventer, Kluwer.

ERNST, C
2001 'Assistierter Suizid in den Stadtzürcher Alters- und Krankenheimen [Assisted Suicide in Nursing Homes of the City of Zurich]'. *Schweizerische Ärztezeitung* 82: 293–5.

ESER, A and H-G KOCH
2005 *Abortion and the Law. From International Comparison to Legal Policy*. The Hague, TMC Asser Press.

ESMAIL, A
2005 'Physician as Serial Killer: The Shipman Case'. *New England Journal of Medicine* 352: 1843–4.

ETISKE RÅD [DANISH COUNCIL OF ETHICS]
2002 *Behandling af døende. De svære beslutninger* [Treatment of the Dying. The Difficult Decisions]. Available at <http://www.etiskraad.dk/graphics/03_udgivelser/publikationer/doendes_vilkar/svaerebeslut/behandling_af_doeende.pdf> accessed 1 October 2007.

2003 *Det mener rådet om eutanasi* [Opinion on Euthanasia]. Available at <http://www.etiskraad.dk/sw6207.asp#516_6362 > accessed 1 October 2007.

EURISPES ISTITUTO DI STUDI POLITICI ECONOMICI E SOCIALI [INSTITUTE OF POLITICAL ECONOMIC AND SOCIAL STUDIES]
2007 *Rapporto Italia* [Report on Italy]. Rome, Eurispes.

EUROPEAN OBSERVATORY ON HEALTH CARE SYSTEMS
2000 *Health Care Systems in Transition: Belgium*. Copenhagen, European Observatory on Health Care Systems. Available at <http://www.euro.who.int/document/e71203.pdf> accessed 1 October 2007.

EXIT ADMD
1999 *Sondage assistance au décès* [Survey on Assisted Dying]. Available at <http://www.exit-geneve.ch/Sondage1.htm> accessed 1 October 2007.

FAHRLÄNDER, H
1996 'Medizinische, rechtliche und ethische Probleme beim Wachkomapatienten [Medical, Juridical and Ethical Problems in Permanent Vegetative State]'. *Schweizerische Medizinische Wochenschrift* 126: 1191–5.

FAINZANG, S
2006 *La relation médecin malades: information et mensonge* [The Doctor–Patient Relationship: Information and Misinformation]. Paris, PUF.

FCEC [FEDERAL CONTROL AND EVALUATION COMMISSION EUTHANASIA]
2002–03 Premier Rapport aux Chambers Legislative/Eerste Verslag aan de Wetgevende Kamers [First Report for the Legislative Chambers]. (*Parliamentary Proceedings, Senate and Chamber of Representatives*, 2003–2004, 3–860/1 (Senate); DOC 51 1374/001 (Chamber).

2004–05 *Tweede Verslag aan de Wetgevende Kamers* [Second Report for the Legislative Chambers] <https://portal.health.fgov.be/pls/portal/docs/PAGE/INTERNET_PG/HOMEPAGE_MENU/GEZONDHEIDZORG1_MENU/OVERLEGSTRUCTUREN1_MENU/COMMISSIES1_MENU/EUTHANASIA1_MENU/EUTHANASIA1_DOCS/G6635%20RAPPORT%20EUTHANASIE%20NL31–29%20OCT.PDF> accessed 1 October 2007.

FEDERAZIONE NAZIONALE DEGLI ORDINI DEI MEDICI [COLLEGE OF PHYSICIANS]
1995 *Codice di deontologia medica* [Code of Medical Ethics]. Milano: Promopharma, 1996.
1998 *Codice di deontologia medica* [Code of Medical Ethics]. Torino: Mariogros, 1998.

2006 *Codice di deontologia medica* [Code of Medical Ethics]. Torino: Edizioni Medico-Scientifiche, 2007. Available at <http://portale.fnomceo.it/Jcmsfnomceo/cmsfile/attach_3819.pdf> accessed 17 July 2007.

FERRAND, E

2002 'Les limitations et arrêts de thérapeutique(s) active(s) en réanimation adulte: recommandations de la Société de réanimation de langue française [Withholding and Withdrawing Active Therapeutics on Adults in ICUs : Recommendations of the Société de réanimation de langue française]'. *Réanimation* 11: 442–9.

FERRAND, E *et al*

2001 'Withholding and Withdrawal of Life Support in Intensive-Care Units in France: A Prospective Survey'. *The Lancet* 357: 9–15.

2003 'Discrepancies between Perception by Physicians and Nursing Staff of ICU End of Life Decision'. *American Journal of Respiratory and Critical Care Medicine* 167: 1310–15.

FIBLA, C

2000 *Debate sobre la eutanasia* [The Euthanasia Debate]. Barcelona, Planeta.

FINE, R and T MAYO

2003 'Resolution of Futility by Due Process: Early Experience with the Texas Advance Directives Act'. *Annals of Internal Medicine* 138: 743–6.

FISCHER, S *et al*

2006 'Swiss Doctors' Attitudes towards End-of-Life Decisions and their Determinants'. *Swiss Medical Weekly* 135: 370–76.

FOLKER, A *et al*

1996 'Experiences and Attitudes toward End-of-Life Decisions amongst Danish Physicians'. *Bioethics* 10: 233–49.

FØRDE, R

2006 'Respiratorbehandling av pasienter med amyotrofisk lateralsklerose [Artificial Ventilation of Patients with Amyotrofic Lateral Sclerosis]'. *Tidsskrift for Den norske lægeforening* 126: 498.

FØRDE, R, O AASLAND and E FALKUM

1997 'The Ethics of Euthanasia: Attitudes and Practice among Norwegian Physicians'. *Social Science and Medicine* 45: 887–92.

FØRDE, R, O AASLAND and T NILSEN

1997 'Medisinsk avslutning av liv [Ending Life by Medical Means. Do Attitudes of Physicians Differ from those of the Population?]'. *Tidsskrift for Den norske lægeforening* 117: 1135–7.

FØRDE, R, O AASLAND and P STEEN

2002 'Medical End-of-Life Decisions in Norway'. *Resuscitation* 55: 235–40.

FØRDE, R, U KONGSGAARD and O AASLAND

2006 'Lindrende sedering til døende [Palliative Sedation to the Dying]'. *Tidsskrift for Den norske lægeforening* 126: 471–4.

FORTIN, J

1998 'A Baby's Right to Die'. *Child & Family Law Quarterly* 10: 411–16.

2006 'Accommodating Children's Rights in a Post Human Rights Act Era'. *Modern Law Review* 69: 299–326.

FOX, M and J McHALE

1997 'In Whose Best Interests?' *Modern Law Review* 60: 700–09.

FREEMAN, M

2002 'Denying Death its Dominion: Thoughts on the Dianne Pretty Case'. *Medical Law Review* 10: 245–70.

FRICKER, G

1999 *Aus freiem Willen: der Tod als Erlösung: Erfahrungen einer Freitodbegleiterin* [Out of Free Will: Death as Deliverance: Experiences of a Right-to-Die Organisation's Volunteer]. Zürich, Oesch.

FRIELE, R *et al*

1999 *Evaluatie wet klachtrecht cliënten zorgsector* [Evaluation of the Law on Patient Complaints in the Health Care Sector]. The Hague, ZonMw.

GASTMANS, C, L LEMIENGRE and B DIERCKX de CASTERLÉ

2006 'Development and Communication of Written Ethics Policies on Euthanasia in Catholic Hospitals and Nursing Homes in Belgium (Flanders)'. *Patient Education and Counseling* 63: 188–95.

GASTMANS, C *et al*

2006 'Prevalence and Content of Written Ethics Policies on Euthanasia in Catholic Healthcare Institutions in Belgium (Flanders)'. *Health Policy* 76: 169–78.

GB&W [GRIFFITHS, J, A BOOD and H WEYERS]

1985 *Euthanasia and Law in the Netherlands.* Amsterdam, Amsterdam University Press.

GENERAL MEDICAL COUNCIL

2002 *Withholding and Withdrawing Life-Prolonging Treatment: Good Practice in Decision-Making.* London.

GEVERS, J

1997 'Patient Involvement with Non Treatment Decisions'. *European Journal of Health Law* 4: 145–56.

2003 'Zelfbeschikking rond het levenseinde [Self-Determination at the End of Life]'. *Tijdschrift voor Gezondheidsrecht* 27: 314–20.

2007 'Hoe functioneert de euthanasiewet? Bevindingen uit het evaluatie-onderzoek [How is the Euthanasia Law Functioning? Findings of the Evaluation Study]'. *Tijdschrift voor Gezondheidsrecht* 31: 282–7.

GEZONDHEIDSRAAD [HEALTH COUNCIL]

1975 *Advies inzake euthanasie bij pasgeborenen* [Recommendation concerning Euthanasia in the Case of Newborns]. The Hague, Staatsuitgeverij.

1994 *Patiënten in een vegetatieve toestand* [Patients in a Vegetative State]. The Hague, Gezondheidsraad.

2002 *Dementie: advies van een commissie van de Gezondheidsraad aan de Minister van Volksgezondheid, Welzijn en Sport* [Dementia: Advice of a Committee of the Health Council to the Minister of Health, Welfare and Sport]. The Hague, Gezondheidsraad.

2004 *Terminale Sedatie Signalering ethiek en gezondheid 2004* [Terminal Sedation. Current Issues in Ethics and Health 2004]. The Hague, Gezondheidsraad. Available in English at <http://www.gr.nl.pdf/04@12-02E.pdf> accessed 4 March 2008.

2007 *Overwegingen bij het beëindigen van het leven van pasgeborenen* [Considerations in Connection with the Termination of Life of Newborns]. The Hague, Centrum voor ethiek en gezondheid.

GIANNINI, A *et al*

2003 'End of Life Decisions in Intensive Care Units: Attitudes of Physicians in an Italian Urban Setting'. *Intensive Care Medicine* 29: 1902–10.

GILLON R

2003 'Ethics Needs Principles: Four Can Encompass the Rest—and Respect for Autonomy Should Be "First Among Equals" '. *Journal of Medical Ethics* 29: 307–12.

GINKEL, R van

1997 *Notities over Nederlanders* [Notes about the Dutch]. Amsterdam, Boom.

GIRAULT, C

2002 *Le droit à l'épreuve des pratiques euthanasiques* [Law Challenged by the Practice of Euthanasia]. Aix en Provence, Presses Universitaires d'Aix Marseille.

GIROUD, C *et al*

1999 'Exit Association-Mediated Suicide: Toxicologic and Forensic Aspects'. *American Journal of Forensic Medicine and Pathology* 20: 40–44.

GIUNTA, F

2001 'Il consenso informato all'atto medico tra principi costituzionali e implicazioni penalistiche [Informed Consent to Medical Treatment between Constitutional Principles and Criminal Implications]'. *Rivista italiana di diritto e procedura penale* 2001: 377–410.

GLORION, B

1999 'Le consentement et ses aspects déontologiques [Consent and its Deontological Aspects]'. *La Gazette du Palais* 1 doctrine: 6.

GRANDE, A *et al*

1998 'Heart Transplantation without Informed Consent: Discussion of a Case'. *Intensive Care Medicine* 24: 251–4.

GRASSI, L, M AGOSTINI and K MAGNANI

1999 'Attitudes of Italian doctors to euthanasia and assisted suicide for terminally ill patients'. *The Lancet* 354: 1876–7.

GRASSI, L, K MAGNANI and M ERCOLANI

1999 'Attitudes toward euthanasia and physician-assisted suicide among Italian primary care physicians'. *Journal of Pain and Symptom Management* no 3: 188–96.

GREEN-PEDERSEN, C

2007 'The Conflict of Conflicts in Comparative Perspective. Euthanasia as a Political Issue in Denmark, Belgium and the Netherlands'. *Comparative Politics* 39: 273–91.

GRIFFITHS, J

1987 'Een toeschouwersperspectief op de euthanasiediscussie [A Spectators' Perspective on the Euthanasia Discussion]'. *Nederlands Juristenblad* 62: 681–93.

2000 'Self-regulation by the Dutch medical profession of medical behavior that potentially shortens life.' Pp173–90 in H Krabbendam and H ten Napel (eds), *Regulating Mortality: a Comparison of the Role of the State in Mastering the Mores in the Netherlands and the United States.* Antwerp, Maklu.

2003 'The Social Working of Legal Rules'. *Journal of Legal Pluralism* 48: 1–84.

2005 'Geen sprake van euthanasie. Weinig respect voor zelfbeschikkingsrecht in "Million Dollar Baby" [No Question of Euthanasia. Lack of Respect for Self-Determination in "Million Dollar Baby"]'. *Medisch Contact* 60: 608–9.

2007a 'Physician-Assisted Suicide in the Netherlands and Belgium'. In D Birnbacher and E Dahl (eds). *Giving Death a Helping Hand. Physician-assisted Suicide and Public Policy An International Perspective.* Dordrecht, Springer (forthcoming).

2007b 'Criminal Law is the Problem, Not the Solution'. Pp 119–35 in C Erin and S Ost (eds). *The Criminal Justice System and Health Care.* Oxford, Oxford University Press.

2007c Letter to the editor, *Medisch Contact* 62: 964.

GROENEWOUD, J *et al*

1997 'Physician-Assisted Death in Psychiatric Practice in the Netherlands'. *New England Journal of Medicine* 336: 1795–801.

2000a 'A Nationwide Study of Decisions to Forego Life-Prolonging Treatment in Dutch Medical Practice'. *Archives of Internal Medicine* 160: 357–63.

2000b 'Clinical Problems with the Performance of Euthanasia and Physician Assisted Suicide in the Netherlands'. *New England Journal of Medicine* 342: 551–6.

GROSBUIS, S *et al*

2000 'Bases de réflexion pour la limitation et l'arrêt des traitements en réanimation chez l'adulte [Starting Points for Reflection on the Limitation and Stopping of Treatment in Adult Intensive Care]'. *Réanimation Urgences* 9: 11–25.

GRUBB, A

2001 'Euthanasia in England: A Law Lacking Compassion?' *European Journal of Health Law* 8: 89–95.

GRUPO DE ESTUDIOS DE POLÌTICA CRIMINAL ESPAÑA [STUDY GROUP ON CRIMINAL POLICY, SPAIN]

1991 'Manifiesto en favor de la disponibilidad de la propia vida [Manifesto in favour of the Right to Dispose over One's Life]'. Pp 598–605 as annexe in J Díez Ripollés and J Muñoz Sánchez (eds) 1996.

1992 'Propuesta alternativa al tratamiento jurídico de las conductas de terceros relativas a la disponibilidad de la propia vida [Proposal for an Alternative Legal Treatment of the Behaviour of Third Parties related in Connection with the Right to Dispose over One's Life]'. Pp 609–29 as annexe in J Díez Ripollés and J Muñoz Sánchez (eds) 1996.

GRUPO DE OPINIÓN DEL OBSERVATORI DE BIOÈTICA I DRET [OPINION GROUP OF THE OBSERVATORY OF BIOETHICS AND LAW]

2003 *Documento sobre la disposición de la propia vida en determinados supuestos: declaración sobre la eutanasia.* [Document on the Right to Dispose over One's Life under Certain Circumstances: Declaration on Euthanasia]. Available at <http://www.imsersomayores. csic.es/documentos/documentos/obd-eutanasia-01.pdf> accessed 1 October 2007.

GRUPO DE TRABAJO DE LA SOCIEDAD ESPAÑOLA DE NEONATALOGÍA SOBRE LIMITACIÓN DEL ESFUERZO TERAPÉUTICO Y CUIDADOS PALIATIVOS EN RECIÉN NACIDOS

2002 'Decisiones de limitación del esfuerzo terapéutico en recién nacidos críticos: estudio multicéntrico [Decisions to Limit Therapeutic Measures in Critically Ill Newborns: A Multi-Centre Study]. *Anales de Pediatría*, 57: 547–53.

GUERRIER, M *et al*

2003 *Enquête préliminaire sur le loi no. 2002–303 du 4 mars 2002: quelles influences sur l'activité de soin à l'hôpital?* [Preliminary Survey concerning Law no 2002–303 of 4 March 2002: What is its Influence on Care in Hospitals?]. Preliminary Report, 3 March, by the Espace Éthique Assistance Publique: Hôpitaux de Paris. Available at <http://www. espace-ethique.org/fr/enq_4mars.php#preliminaire> accessed 1 October 2007.

GUILLOD, O and A SCHMIDT

2005 'Assisted Suicide under Swiss Law'. *European Journal of Health Law* 12: 25–38.

GUILLON, C and Y LE BONNIEC

1982 *Suicide, mode d'emploi: histoire, technique, actualité.* [Suicide, Instructions: History, Technology, Current State of Affairs] Paris, A Moreau.

GUNNINGHAM, N, R KAGAN and D THORNTON

2003 *Shades of Green: Business, Regulation, and Environment.* Stanford, Stanford University Press.

HALMAN, L

2001 *The European Values Study: A Third Wave. Source book of the 1999/2000 European Values Study Survey.* Tilburg, EVS, WORC, Tilburg University.

HALMAN, L, R LUIJKX and M van ZUNDERT

2005 *Atlas of European Values.* Leiden, Brill; Tilburg, Tilburg University.

HARDING, L

2004 'A Little Sightseeing, a Glass of Schnapps, then a Peaceful Death in a Suburban Flat'. *The Guardian* (4 Dec).

HARTOGH, G den

1996 'Recht op de dood? Zelfbeschikking en barmhartigheid als rechtvaardiging voor euthanasie [Right to Die? Self-Determination and Beneficence as Justification for Euthanasia]. *Recht en Kritiek* 22: 148–68.

2003 'Mysterieuze cijfers: meldingspercentage van euthanasie kan niet meer stijgen [Mysterious Numbers: Further Increase in the Reporting Rate is Not Possible]'. *Medisch Contact* 58: 1063–6.

2006a 'Palliatieve sedatie en euthanasie. Commentaar op een richtlijn [Palliative Sedation and Euthanasia. Comments on a Guideline]'. *Tijdschrift voor Gezondheidsrecht* 30: 109–19.

2006b 'Het recht op inslapen [The Right to a Sedated Death]'. *Medisch Contact* 61: 1463–5.

2008 'The Slippery Slope Argument'. In H Khuse and P Singer (eds). *A Companion to Bioethics.* 2nd edn. Oxford, Blackwell (forthcoming).

HAUSER, R and J REHBERG (eds)

1986 *Schweizerisches Strafgesetzbuch* [Swiss Penal Code]. Zürich, Orell Füssli.

HAVERKATE, M and G van der WAL

1996 'Policies on Medical Decisions concerning the End of Life in Dutch Health Care Institutions'. *Journal of the American Medical Association* 275: 435–9.

HEIDE, A van der *et al*

1997a 'Frequentie van het afzien van (kunstmatige) toediening van voeding en vocht aan het levenseinde [Frequency of Abstinence from (Artificial) Feeding and Hydration at the End of Life]'. *Nederlands Tijdschrift voor Geneeskunde* 141: 1918–24.

1997b 'Medical End of Life Decisions Made for Neonates and Infants in the Netherlands'. *The Lancet* 350: 251–5.

1998 'The Role of Parents in End-of-Life Decisions in Neonatology: Physicians' Views and Practices'. *Pediatrics* 101: 413–18.

2003 'End-of-Life Decision-Making in Six European Countries: Descriptive Study'. *Lancet* 362: 345–50.

2007 'End-of-Life Practices in the Netherlands under the Euthansia Act'. *New England Journal of Medicine* 356: 1957–65.

HENDIN, H

1997 *Seduced by Death: Doctors, Patients and the Dutch Cure.* New York, WW Norton.

HENNETTE-VAUCHEZ, S (ed)

2006 *Bioethique, Biodroit, Biopolitique: réflexions à l'occasion du vote de la loi du 6 août 2004* [Bioethics, Bio-Law, Bio-Politics: Reflections on the Occasion of the Enactment of the Law of 6 August 2004]. Paris, LGDJ.

HENNEZEL, M de

2003 *Fin de vie et accompagnement: rapport au premier ministre* [End-of-Life: the Duty of Accompaniment: Report to the Prime Minister] Available at <http://www.sante. gouv.fr/htm/actu/hennezel/sommaire.htm> accessed 1 October 2007.

HERTOGH, C *et al*

2007 'Would We Rather Lose our Life Than Lose our Self? Lessons from the Dutch Debate on Euthanasia for Patients with Dementia'. *The American Journal of Bioethics* 7: 48–56.

HESSING, D, J BLAD and R PIETERMAN

1996 'Practical Reasons and Reasonable Practice: The Case of Euthanasia in the Netherlands'. *Journal of Social Issues* 52: 149–69.

HILLYARD, D and J DOMBRINK

2001 *Dying Right: the Death with Dignity Movement.* New York/London, Routledge.

HILHORST, H

1983 *Euthanasie in het ziekenhuis: de 'zachte dood' bij ziekenhuispatiënten* [Euthanasia in the Hospital: The 'Gentle Death' of Hospital Patients]. Lochem-Poperinge, De Tijdstroom.

HOLSTEYN, J van and M TRAPPENBURG

1996 *Het laatste oordeel: meningen over nieuwe vormen van euthanasie* [The Last Judgment: Public Opinion concerning New Forms of Euthanasia]. Baarn, Ambo.

1998 'Citizens' Opinions on New Forms of Euthanasia. A Report from the Netherlands'. *Patient Education and Counseling* 35: 63–74.

HORIKX, A and P ADMIRAAL

2000 'Toepassing van euthanatica; ervaringen van artsen bij 227 patiënten, 1998–2000 [Use of Euthanatica; Experience of Doctors with 227 Patients, 1998–2000]'. *Nederlands Tijdschrift voor Geneeskunde* 52: 2497–500.

HOSP, J

2005 'Zürich ist weiterhin offen für Sterbewillige aus dem Ausland [Zurich Still Open for Suicide Tourists]'. *Tages-Anzeiger* (23 Aug).

HOUSE OF LORDS SELECT COMMITTEE ON MEDICAL ETHICS

1993–94 *Report.* HL Paper 21-I.

HOUSE OF LORDS SELECT COMMITTEE ON THE ASSISTED DYING FOR THE TERMINALLY ILL BILL

2005a Volume I: *Report of the Committee.* HL Paper No 86-I. Available at <http://www. parliament.the-stationery-office.co.uk/pa/ld200405/ldselect/ldasdy/86/86i.pdf> accessed 1 October 2007.

2005b Volume II: *Evidence of the Committee.* HL Paper No 86-II. Available at <http://www.publications.parliament.uk/pa/ld200405/ldselect/ldasdy/86/86ii.pdf> accessed 1 October 2007.

HOUT, E

2006 *The Dutch Disciplinary System for Health Care: An Empirical Study.* Amsterdam, EMGO Institute.

HUBERT, P *et al*

2005 'Limitations et arrêts de traitements actifs en réanimation pédiatrique: recommandations du GFRUP [Withholding or Withdrawing Life-Saving Treatment in Pediatric Intensive Care: GFRUP Guidelines]'. *Archives de Pédiatrie* 12: 1501–8. Available at <http://www.gfrup.com/fin_vie/gfrup_fin_vie_recomm_gfrup.pdf> accessed 1 October 2007.

HURST, S and A MAURON

2003 'Assisted Suicide and Euthanasia in Switzerland: Allowing a Role for Non-Physicians'. *British Medical Journal* 326: 271–3.

HURST, S et al

2007a 'Physicians' Access to Ethics Support Services in Four European Countries'. *Health Care Analysis. Journal of Health Philosophy and Policy* 15: 321–5.

2007b 'Ethical Difficulties in Clinical Practice: Experiences of European Doctors'. *Journal of Medical Ethics* 33: 51–7.

HUSABØ, E

1994 *Rett til sjølvvalt livsavslutning?* [Right to Choose to Die?]. Oslo, Ad Notam Gyldendal.

HUXLEY, P

1978 'Proposals and Counter Proposals on the Defence of Necessity'. *Criminal Law Review:* 141–50.

HUXTABLE, R

2001 'Logical separation? Conjoined Twins, Slippery Slopes and Resource Allocation'. *Journal of Social Welfare & Family Law* 23: 459–71.

2002 'Separation of Conjoined Twins: Where Next for English law'. *Criminal Law Review:* 459–70.

INGLEHART, R

1977 *The Silent Revolution.* Princeton, NJ, Princeton University Press.

1997 *Modernization and Postmodernization. Cultural, Economic and Political Changes in 43 Societies.* Princeton, NJ, Princeton University Press.

INGLEHART, R, M BASAÑEZ and A MORENO

1998 *Human Values and Beliefs: A Cross-Cultural Sourcebook. Political, Religious, Sexual and Economic Norms in 43 Societies: Findings from 1990–1993 World Values Survey.* Ann Arbor, University of Michigan Press.

INSTITUT BORJA DE BIOÈTICA [BORJA INSTITUTE OF BIOETHICS]

2005 *Hacia una posible despenalización de la eutanasia: Declaración del Institut Borja de Bioètica* [Towards a Possible Depenalization of Euthanasia: Statement of the Borja Institute of Bioethics]. Barcelona, Universitat Ramon Llull.

ISRAEL, J

1995 *The Dutch Republic: Its Rise, Greatness and Fall 1477–1806.* Oxford, Oxford University Press.

JACQUINOT, C

1995 'Application de la loi sur l'incitation au suicide [Application of the Law on Inciting Suicide]'. *La Gazette du Palais,* 2 October: 954.

JAGUENEAU, N

2006 Essai sur la perte de spécificité du droit de la responsabilité médicale publique [Essay on the Loss of Legal Specificity in the Law Concerning Public Medical Responsibility]. Doctoral dissertation: Pau.

JANS, J

2000 'Euthanasiegesetzgebung in Belgien. Eine Übersicht über die politisch-ethische Debatte 1997–1999 [Euthanasia Law in Belgium. An Overview of the Political-Ethical Debate 1997–1999]'. Pp 175–87 in A Bondolfi and S Grotefeld (eds). *Ethik und Gesetzgebung: Probleme, Lösungsversuche, Konzepte* [Ethics and Law Making: Problems, Attempted Solutions, Concepts]. Stuttgart: Verlag W Kolhammer.

JANSEN-van der WEIDE, M

2005 Handling Requests for Euthanasia and Physician-Assisted Suicide. Dissertation, VU Amsterdam.

JANSEN-van der WEIDE, M *et al*

2005 'Granted, Undecided, Withdrawn, and Refused Requests for Euthanasia and Physician-Assisted Suicide'. *Archives of Internal Medicine* 165: 1698–704.

JUNGMAN, F

1989 D'un livre à une loi: de Suicide, mode d'emploi à la loi no.87–1133 tendant à réprimer la provocation au suicide [From a Book to a Law: From A Guide to Suicide to Law no 87–1133 on Repressing Provocation to Suicide]. Masters Thesis in Sociology of Law, University of Paris.

KAGAN, R

1990 'How Much does Law Matter? Labor Law, Competition, and Waterfront Labor Relations in Rotterdam and US Ports'. *Law & Society Review* 24: 35–69.

KAGAN, R and L AXELRAD (eds)

2000 *Regulatory Encounters: Multinational Corporations and American Adversarial Legalism.* Berkeley, University of California Press.

KAPTEYN, P

1980 *Taboe, ontwikkelingen in macht en moraal in Nederland* [Taboo, Developments in Power and Morality in the Netherlands]. Amsterdam, Arbeiderspers.

KARLSSON, M, P STRANG and A MILBERG

2007 'Attitudes toward Euthanasia among Swedish Medical Students'. *Palliative Medicine* 21: 615–22.

KEMP, N

2002 *'Merciful Release'. The History of the British Euthanasia Movement.* Manchester/New York, Manchester University Press.

KENNEDY, I and A GRUBB

2000 *Medical Law.* 3rd edn. London [etc], Butterworths.

KENNEDY, J

2002 *Een weloverwogen dood: Euthanasie in Nederland* [A Well-Considered Death: Euthanasia in the Netherlands]. Amsterdam, Bert Bakker.

KEOWN, J

2002a *Euthanasia, Ethics, and Public Policy.* Cambridge, Cambridge University Press.

2002b 'The Case of Ms. B: Suicide's Slippery Slope?' *Journal of Medical Ethics* 28: 238–9.

KEOWN, J (ed)

1995 *Euthanasia Examined: Ethical, Clinical and Legal Perspectives.* Cambridge, Cambridge University Press.

KHORRAMI, K

2003 'Die "Euthanasie-Gesetze" im Vergleich. Eine Darstellung der Aktuellen Rechtslage in den Niederlanden und in Belgiën [Euthanasia Laws in Comparative Perspective. An Overview of the Legal Regulation in the Netherlands and Belgium]'. *Medizinrecht* 21: 19–25.

KLEIJER, D

2005 'Het wordt geregeld . . .' Een onderzoek naar (zelf)-regulering bij het staken van de behandeling op Intensive Cares ['It will be taken care of . . .' A Study of the (Self)-Regulation of Withdrawing Treatment in Intensive Cares]. Dissertation, University of Groningen.

KLIJN, A

2003a 'De meldingsfrequentie euthanasie: rekensom of beleidsevaluatie? [The Reporting Frequency in case of Euthanasia: A Problem of Arithmetic or of Policy?]. Pp 171–98 in Adams, Griffiths and Den Hartogh (eds) 2003.

2003b 'The Dutch Experiment in Regulating Euthanasia'. Paper for the 28th International Congress on Law and Mental Health, Sydney, Australia, 28 September–3 October 2003.

KLINKENBERG, M, and R PEREZ

2007 'Verpleegkundige mist arts bij palliative sedatie [Nurse Left on his own to Carry Out Palliative Sedation]'. *Medisch Contact* 62: 1946.

KNMG [KONINKLIJKE NEDERLANDSE MAATSCHAPPIJ TER BEVORDERING VAN DE GENEESKUNST/ROYAL DUTCH MEDICAL ASSOCIATION]

1971 'Richtlijnen ten behoeve van de uitvoering van abortus provocatus [Guidelines for Carrying Out Abortion]'. *Medisch Contact* 26: 1025–8.

1973 'Voorlopig standpunt van het hoofdbestuur inzake het euthanasievraagstuk [Provisional Position of the Governing Board with respect to the Question of Euthanasia]'. *Medisch Contact* 28: 587–8; reprinted in *Medisch Contact* 39 (1984): 997–8.

1975 'Discussienota [Discussion paper of the Working Group on Euthanasia]'. *Medisch Contact* 30: 7–17.

1984 'Standpunt inzake euthanasie [Position on Euthanasia]'. *Medisch Contact* 39: 990–97.

1992 'Richtlijnen KNMG en Nieuwe Unie '91 [Guidelines of the KNMG and Nieuwe Unie '91]'. *Medisch Contact* 47: 29–32.

1995 *Standpunt hoofdbestuur inzake euthanasie* [Position of the Governing Board on Euthanasia]. Utrecht, KNMG [also published as a supplement to] *Medisch Contact* 50, no 33/34: 1037–8 [summary].

1997 *Medisch handelen rond het levenseinde bij wilsonbekwame patienten* [Medical Practice in Connection with the End of Life of Non-competent Patients]. Houten/Diegem, Bohn Stafleu Van Loghum.

2003 *Standpunt Federatiebestuur KNMG inzake euthanasie 2003* [Position of the Federal Board of the KNMG concerning Euthanasia 2003]. Utrecht, KNMG. Available at <http://knmg.artsennet.nl> accessed 1 October 2007.

2004a *Van wet naar praktijk: implementatie van de WGBO. Deel 2: Informatie en toestemming* [From Statute to Practice: Implementation of the WGBO. Vol 2: Information and Consent]. Utrecht, KNMG.

2004b *Op zoek naar normen voor het handelen van artsen bij vragen om hulp bij levensbeëindiging in geval van lijden aan het leven: verslag van de werkzaamheden van een commissie onder voorzitterschap van prof. J Dijkhuis* [Norms for the Behaviour of Doctors in the Case of Requests for Assistance in Suicide due to Suffering from Continued Life: Report of the Dijkhuis Committee]. Utrecht, KNMG.

2005 *KNMG-richtlijn palliatieve sedatie* [KNMG-Guideline on Palliative Sedation]. Utrecht, KNMG.

KNMP [KONINKLIJKE NEDERLANDSE MAATSCHAPPIJ TER BEVORDERING DER PHARMACIE/ROYAL DUTCH ASSOCIATION FOR PHARMACY]

1994 *Toepassing en bereiding van euthanatica* [Application and Preparation of Euthanatica]. The Hague, KNMP.

1998 *Toepassing en bereiding van euthanatica* [Application and Preparation of Euthanatica]. The Hague, KNMP.

2007 *Toepassing en bereiding van euthanatica* [Application and Preparation of Euthanatica]. The Hague, KNMP.

KOLLÉE, L *et al*

1999 'End-of-Life Decisions in Neonates'. *Seminars in Perinatology* 23: 234–41.

KRIESI, H *et al*

1995 *New Social Movements in Western Europe. A Comparative Analysis: Social Movements, Protest, and Contention.* Minneapolis, University of Minnesota Press.

1998 'Verantwoording van een 'nee, tenzij-reanimatiebeleid' in het verpleeghuis [Arguments for a 'no, unless resuscitation policy' in nursing homes].' *Nederlands Tijdschrift voor Verpleeghuiskunde* 1998: 6–10.

KRUIT, A, H WAUTERS and R BREUREN

1998 'Verantwoording van een "nee, tenzij-reanimatiebeleid" in het verpleeghuis [Arguments for a "no, unless resuscitation policy" in nursing homes].' *Nederlands Tijdschrift voor Verpleeghuiskunde* 1998: 6–10.

KUHSE, H *et al*

1997 'End-of-Life Decisions in Australian Medical Practice'. *Medical Journal of Australia* 166: 191–6.

KURZER, P

2001 *Markets and Moral Regulation. Cultural Change in the European Union.* Cambridge, Cambridge University Press.

LAURANCE, J

2007 'The Right to Choose Death'. *The Independent* (8 May).

LAW COMMISSION

1974 *Defences of General Application.* Working Paper No 55.

1977 *Defences of General Application.* Report No 83.

1991 *Mentally Incapacitated Adults and Decision-Making: An Overview.* Consultation Paper No 119.

1995 *Mental Incapacity.* Report No 231.

2005 *A New Homicide Act for England and Wales.* Consultation Paper No 177.

2006 *Murder, Manslaughter and Infanticide.* Report No 304.

LEENEN, H

1977 'Euthanasie in het gezondheidsrecht [Euthanasia in Health Law]' Pp 72–147 in P Muntendam *et al. Euthanasie* [Euthanasia]. Leiden, Stafleu.

1994 *Handboek gezondheidsrecht. Deel 1: Rechten van mensen in de gezondheidszorg* [Handbook of Health Law. Vol 1: Individual Rights in the Context of Medical Care]. 3rd edn. Alphen a/d Rijn, Samsom HD Tjeenk Willink.

2000 *Handboek gezondheidsrecht. Deel 1: Rechten van mensen in de gezondheidszorg* [Handbook of Health Law. Vol 1: Individual Rights in the Context of Medical Care]. 4th edn. Houten/Diegem, Bohn Stafleu Van Loghum.

LEEUW, R de *et al*

1996 'Foregoing Intensive Care Treatment in Newborn Infants with Extremely Poor Prognoses: A Study in Four Neonatal Intensive Care Units in the Netherlands'. *Journal of Pediatrics* 129: 661–6.

LEGEMAATE, J

2005 *De zorgverlening rond het levenseinde: een literatuurstudie naar begripsomschrijvingen en zorgvuldigheidseisen* [Health Care at the End of Life: A Survey of the Literature on the Definition of Concepts and the Requirements of Due Care]. Utrecht, KNMG.

2006 'Symptoombestrijding en palliatie versus levensbeëindiging: een terugblik op de zaak-Vencken [Symptom Relief and Palliation versus Termination of Life: A Review of the Vencken Case]'. *Nederlands Tijdschrift voor Geneeskunde* 150: 1689–92.

LEIBUNDGUT, Y

2006 'Wenn es um Leben und Tod geht [Matters concerning Life and Death]'. *Der Bund* (27 Feb).

LENA, J and U MATTEI

2002 *Introduction to Italian Law.* The Hague, Kluwer Law International.

LEONETTI, J

2004 *Respecter la vie, accepter la mort: rapport no.1708 au nom de la mission d'information sur l'accompagnement de la fin de vie* [Respecting Life, Accepting Death: Report of the National Assembly's Commission on Accompanying End of Life] Tome I Assemblée Nationale]. Available at <http://www.assemblee-nationale.fr/12/rap-info/i1708-t1.asp> accessed 1 October 2007.

LEWIS, P

1997/98 'Proxy Refusals of Medical Treatment'. *King's College Law Journal* 8: 101–3.

2001 'Medical Treatment of Children'. Pp 151–63 in J Fionda (ed). *Legal Concepts of Childhood.* Oxford, Hart Publishing.

2006 'Assisted Dying in France. The Evolution of Assisted Dying in France: A Third Way?' *Medical Law Review* 14: 44–72

2007a *Assisted Dying and Legal Change.* Oxford, Oxford University Press.

2007b 'Withdrawal of Treatment from a Patient in a Permanent Vegetative State: Judicial Involvement and Innovative "Treatment"'. *Medical Law Review* 15: 392–9.

LIJPHART, A

1968 *The Politics of Accomodation. Pluralism and Democracy in the Netherlands.* Berkeley, University of California Press.

1977 *Democracy in Plural Societies: A Comparative Exploration.* New Haven, Yale University Press.

LIJPHART, A (ed)

1981 *Conflict and Coexistence in Belgium: The Dynamics of a Cultural Divided Society.* Berkeley, Berkeley University Press.

LOUSTE, J

1988 Le consentement dans le contrat medical [Consent and Medical Contract]. PhD dissertation, Nice.

LUCAS-GALLAY, I

1996 'Crimes et délits: provocation au suicide [Crime and Offenses : Provocation to Suicide]'. *La Semaine Juridique* no 22729: 447–50.

MAAS, P van der *et al*

1991 *Medische beslissingen rond het levenseinde: het onderzoek voor de Commissie Onderzoek Medische Praktijk inzake Euthanasie* [Medical Decisions Concerning the End of Life: the Research for the Committee to Study Medical Practice concerning Euthanasia]. The Hague, Sdu Uitgeverij.

1992 *Euthanasia and other Medical Decisions concerning the End of Life.* Health Policy Monographs vol 2. Amsterdam [etc], Elsevier.

1995 'Changes in Dutch Opinions on Active Euthanasia, 1966 through 1991'. *Journal of the American Medical Association* 273: 1411–14.

1996 'Euthanasia, Physician-Assisted Suicide, and other Medical Practices involving the End of Life in the Netherlands, 1990–1995'. *New England Journal of Medicine* 335: 1699–705.

MABILLE, X

1990 'Political Decision-Making'. Pp 201–20 in R Bryssinck, M Boudart and M Boudart (eds). *Modern Belgium*. Palo Alto, The Society for the Promotion of Science and Scholarship.

MACHIELSE, A

2004 'Recht in zicht: Onbeschermde seks en opzet bij levensberoving [Unprotected Sex and the Intentionality Requirement for Homicide]'. *Ars Aequi* 53: 155–60.

MACKENBACH, J and P van der MAAS (eds)

2004 *Volksgezondheid en gezondheidszorg* [Health and Health Care]. Maarsen, Elsevier Gezondheidszorg.

MAGNUSSON, R

2002 *Angels of Death. Exploring the Euthanasia Underground.* New Haven, Yale University Press.

MAITLIN, A and E WISE

1978 *The Italian Penal Code.* Littleton, CO, Fred B Rothman & Co.

MARQUET, R *et al*

2003 'Twenty Five Years of Requests for Euthanasia and Physician Assisted Suicide in Dutch General Practice: Trend Analysis'. *British Medical Journal* 327: 201–2.

MATERSTVEDT, L

2006 'Lindrende sedering: problem eller plikt? [Palliative Sedation: Problem or Obligation?]'. *Tidsskrift for den norske lægeforening* 126: 430.

MATERSTVEDT, L and S KAASA

2002 'Euthanasia and Physician-Assisted Suicide in Scandinavia: With a Conceptual Suggestion regarding International Research in relation to the Phenomena'. *Palliative Medicine* 16: 17–32.

MATERSTVEDT, L, A SYSE and P BORCHGREVINK

2005 'Straffelovkommisjonen om aktiv dødshjelp. [The Penal Code Commission on Assisted Dying]'. *Tidsskrift for Den norske lægeforening* 125: 614–16.

MATERSTVEDT, L *et al*

2003 'Euthanasia and Physician-Assisted Suicide: A View from an EAPC Ethics Task Force'. *Palliative Medicine* 17: 97–101.

MATHIEU, B

2003 'De la difficulté de choisir entre la liberté et la vie [On the Difficulty of Choosing between Liberty and Life]'. *Revue générale de droit médical* no 9: 97–104.

MATTHEWS, P

2006 *Halsbury's Laws of England* no 9: 949–52.

MCEWAN, J

2001 'Murder by Design: The Feel-Good Factor and the Criminal Law'. *Medical Law Review* 9: 246–58.

MCLEAN, S and A BRITTON

1996 *Sometimes a Small Victory.* Glasgow, Institute of Law and Ethics in Medicine.

MEER, S van der *et al*

1999 'Hulp bij zelfdoding bij een patiënt met een organisch-psychiatrische stoornis [Assistance with Suicide of a Patient with an Organic-Psychiatric Disorder]'. *Nederlands Tijdschrift voor Geneeskunde* 143: 881–4.

MEIER, M

2000 'Sterbehilfe via Plastiksack verurteilt [Conviction for Assistance in Dying with Plastic Bag]'. *Tages-Anzeiger* (29 Dec).

MEIJER, A, C van KAMPEN and A KERKSTRA

2000 'A Comparative Study of the Financing, Provision and Quality of Care in Nursing Homes. The Approach of Four European Countries: Belgium, Denmark, Germany and the Netherlands'. *Journal of Advanced Nursing* 32: 554–61.

MERINO-BLANCO, E

2006 *Spanish Law and Legal System*. 2nd edn. London, Sweet and Maxwell.

MESMAN, J

2002 *Ervaren pioniers: omgaan met twijfel in de intensive care voor pasgeborenen* [Experienced Pioneers: Dealing with Doubt in the Intensive Care of Newborns]. Amsterdam, Aksant.

MICCINESI, G *et al*

2005 'Physicians' Attitudes towards End-of-Life Decisions: A Comparison between Seven Countries'. *Social Science & Medicine* 60: 1961–74.

2006 'Deep Sedation until Death and Medical End-of-Life Decisions: A Death Certificate Study in Six European Countries'. *Journal of Pain and Symptom Management* 31: 122–9.

MICHALOWSKI, S

2002 'Sanctity of Life: Are Some Lives More Sacred than Others?' *Legal Studies* 22: 377–97.

2005 'Advance Refusals of Life-Sustaining Medical Treatment: The Relativity of an Absolute Right'. *Modern Law Review* 68: 958–82.

MINELLI, L

2004 'Die EMRK schützt die Suizidfreiheit. Wie antwortet darauf das Schweizer Recht? [The European Convention on Human Rights Protects the Right to Commit Suicide. What is Swiss Law's Response?]'. *Aktuelle Juristische Praxis*: 491–540.

MINISTÈRE DÉLÉGUÉ À LA SANTÉ [MINISTRY OF HEALTH]

2001 *Fin de Vie* [End of Life]. Paris, Ministère de l'Emploi et de la Solidarité.

MINISTERO DELLA SALUTE [MINISTRY OF HEALTH]

2005 *Relazione sullo stato sanitario del Paese: 2003–2004* [Report on the Health Condition of the Country: 2003–2004]. Rome, Istituto Poligrafico e Zecca dello Stato.

MISTIAEN, P and A FRANCKE

2007 *Quick scan informatiebehoeften en informatievoorziening bij palliatieve zorg* [Quick Scan of Information Requirements and Facilities in Connection with Palliative Care]. Utrecht, NIVEL.

MITCHELL, K and G OWENS

2003 'National Survey of Medical Decisions at End of Life Made by New Zealand General Practitioners'. *British Medical Journal* 327: 202–3.

MORGAN, D

1994 'Odysseus and the Binding Directive: Only a Cautionary Tale?' *Legal Studies* 14: 411–42.

MORTIER, F *et al*

2000 'End-of-Life Decisions of Physicians in the City of Hasselt (Flanders, Belgium)'. *Bioethics* 14: 254–67.

2003 'Attitudes, Sociodemographic Characteristics, and Actual End-of-Life Decisions of Physicians in Flanders, Belgium'. *Medical Decision Making* 23: 502–10.

MULLER, M

1996 *Death on Request: Aspects of Euthanasia and Physician-Assisted Suicide, with Special Regard to Dutch Nursing Homes*. Amsterdam, Thesis Publishers [based in part on articles which appeared in *Journal of the American Geriatric Society* 42 (1994): 620–23, 624–9].

MÜLLER-BUSCH, H *et al*

2004 'Attitudes on Euthanasia, Physician-Assisted Suicide and Terminal Sedation: A Survey of the Members of the German Association for Palliative Medicine'. *Medicine, Health Care and Philosophy* 7: 333–9.

NÄGELI, H

2002 Beihilfe zum Suizid: doch eine ärztliche Tätigkeit? [Assistance in Suicide: Nevertheless a Doctor's Activity?]. Presentation held at the open vocational education session of the Zurich Cantonal Medical Association, 10 January 2002.

NATIONALE ETHIKKOMMISSION IM BEREICH HUMANMEDIZIN [SWISS NATIONAL ADVISORY COMMISSION ON BIOMEDICAL ETHICS]

2005 *Beihilfe zum Suizid* [Assisted Suicide]. Stellungnahme No 9. Available at <http://www.bag.admin.ch/nek-cne/04229/04232/index.html?lang=de> accessed 4 March 2008.

NATIONALE ORDE VAN GENEESHEREN/ORDRE DES MÉDECINS

2003 *Advies betreffende palliatieve zorg, euthanasie en andere medische beslissingen omtrent het levenseinde* [Advice concerning Palliative Care, Euthanasia and Other Medical Decisions concerning the End of Life]. Available at <http://195.234.184.64/web-Ned/nl/a100/a100006n.htm> accessed 1 October 2007.

NAV/JPV [NEDERLANDS ARTSENVERBOND [DUTCH LEAGUE OF DOCTORS]/JURISTENVERENIGING PRO VITA [LAWYERS' ASSOCIATION PRO VITA]]

2006 'Standpunt inzake de KNMG-richtlijn palliatieve sedatie [Position on the KNMG-Guideline regarding Palliative Sedation]'. *Pro Vita Humana* 13 no 3: 24–9.

NAVARRO-MICHEL, M

2005 'Advance Directives: The Spanish Perspective'. *Medical Law Review* 13: 137–69.

NEDERLANDSE VERENIGING VAN VERPLEEGHUISARTSEN [DUTCH ASSOCIATION OF NURSING-HOME DOCTORS]

1997 *Medische zorg met beleid: handreiking voor de besluitvorming over verpleeghuisgeneeskundig handelen bij dementerende patiënten* [Responsible Medical Care: A Support Document for Decision-Making Concerning Medical Treatment of Demented Patients in Nursing-Homes]. Utrecht, NVVA.

NEDERLANDSE VERENIGING VOOR INTENSIVE CARE [DUTCH ASSOCIATION FOR INTENSIVE CARE]

2001 *Criteria voor opname en ontslag van Intensive Care afdelingen in Nederland: een concept-richtlijn ontwikkeld door de commissie richtlijnen en protocollen van de Nederlandse Vereniging voor Intensive Care* [Criteria for Admission and Release from Intensive Care Units in the Netherlands: A Proposed Guideline of the Committee for Guidelines and Protocols of the NVIC]. Adopted 15 February 2001. NVIC Available at <http://www.nvic.nl> accessed 1 October 2007.

NILSTUN, T *et al*

1996 'Oenighet bland läkare om aktiv dödshjälp. 245 läkarsvar i svensk enkät speglar osäkerhet. [Disagreement among Physicians about Active Euthanasia. 245 Answers from a Swedish Questionnaire Reflects Uncertainty]'. *Läkartidningen* 93: 1350–51.

560   *References*

NISBETT, R and T WILSON
1977 'Telling More Than We Can Know: Verbal Reports on Mental Processes'. *Psychological Review* 84: 230–59.

NIVEL [NEDERLANDS INSTITUUT VOOR ONDERZOEK VAN DE GEZONDHEIDS-ZORG/DUTCH INSTITUTE FOR RESEARCH ON HEALTH CARE]
2004 *Monitor Palliatieve Zorg* [Palliative Care Monitor]. Utrecht, NIVEL Available at <http://www.nivel.nl> accessed 1 October 2007.
2007 *Continue morbiditeits registratie peilstations Nederland 2006* [Dutch Sentinel Practice Network 2006]. Utrecht, Nivel Available at <http://www.nivel.nl> accessed 1 October 2007.

NORWOOD, F
2005 Euthanasia Talk. Euthanasia Discourse, General Practice and End-of-Life Care in the Netherlands. Dissertation, University of California Berkeley and San Francisco.
2006 'A Hero and a Criminal: Dutch *Huisartsen* and the Making of Good Death through Euthanasia Talk in The Netherlands'. *Medische Antropologie* 18: 329–47.
2007 'Nothing More to Do: Euthanasia, General Practice, and End-of-Life Discourse in the Netherlands'. *Medical Anthropology* 26: 139–74.

NÚÑEZ OLARTE, J and D GUILLEN
2001 'Cultural Issues and Ethical Dilemmas in Palliative and End-of-Life Care in Spain'. *Cancer Control* 8: 46–54.

NUY, M and A HOOGERWERF
2000 'De verlegenheid ten aanzien van het menselijk beheer: over de grens tussen normaal en buitengewoon medisch handelen [Embarrassment regarding Management of People: Concerning the Boundaries between Normal and Exceptional Medical Behaviour]'. *Tijdschrift voor Geneeskunde en Ethiek* 10: 121–5.

NVK [NEDERLANDSE VERENIGING VOOR KINDERGENEESKUNDE/DUTCH ASSOCIATION FOR PEDIATRICS]
1992 *Doen of laten? Grenzen van het medisch handelen in de neonatologie* [To Act or to Abstain? The Limits of Medical Practice in Neonatology]. Utrecht, NVK.

NVOG [NEDERLANDSE VERENIGING VOOR OBSTETRIE EN GYNAECOLOGIE/ DUTCH ASSOSIATION FOR OBSTETRICS AND GYNECOLOGY
1994 *Nota late zwangerschapsafbreking* [Memorandum Late Abortion]. Utrecht, NVOG.
2007 *Medisch handelen late zwangerschapsafbreking* [Medical Behaviour in the Case of Late Abortion]. Available at <http://www.nvog-documenten.nl/index.php?pagina=/ richtlijn/item/pagina.php&richtlijn_id=756> accessed 1 October 2007.

NVP [NEDERLANDSE VERENIGING VOOR PSYCHIATRIE/DUTCH ASSOCIATION FOR PSYCHIATRY]
1998 *Hulp bij zelfdoding door patiënten met een psychiatrische stoornis: richtlijnen voor de psychiater* [Assistance with Suicide in the Case of Patients with a Psychiatric Disorder; Guidelines for the Psychiatrist].
2004 *Het verzoek om hulp bij zelfdoding door patiënten met een psychiatrische stoornis: richtlijn hulp bij zelfdoding* [The Request for Assistance with Suicide in the Case of Patients with a Psychiatric Disorder: Guideline for the Psychiatrist]. Revised version of NVP 1998.

NVVE [NEDERLANDSE VERENIGING VOOR VRIJWILLIGE EUTHANASIE/DUTCH ASSOCIATION FOR VOLUNTARY EUTHANASIA]
1989 *Men moet ten slotte het recht hebben om als een heer te sterven* [After All, One Should Have the Right to Die Like a Gentleman]. Amsterdam, NVVE.

1996 *Voorontwerp euthanasiewet* [Draft Euthanasia Bill]. Amsterdam, NVVE.

2003 *Het Schotse boekje over methoden van zelfdoding* [The Scottish Booklet on Ways to Carry out Suicide]. Amsterdam, NVVE.

NYS, H

1997 'Advice of the Federal Advisory Committee on Bioethics concerning legalisation of Euthanasia'. *European Journal of Health Law* 4: 389–93.

1999 'Physician Involvement in a Patient's Death: A Continental European Perspective'. *Medical Law Review* 7: 208–246 [revised version pp 279–96 in T Jost (ed). *Readings in Comparative Health Law and Bioethics*. 2nd edn. Durham, Carolina Academic Press, 2007.

2003 *International Encyclopaedia of Medical Law. Belgium.* Pp 61–5. Mechelen, Kluwer.

2005 *Geneeskunde: recht en medisch handelen* [Medicine: Law and Medical Behaviour]. Mechelen, Story-Scientia.

NYS, H *et al*

2001–02 'Oordelen volgens de eer en waardigheid van het beroep [Judging in Accordance with the Honour and Dignity of the Profession]'. *Rechtskundig Weekblad* 22: 1445–8.

O'DOWD, A

2005 'Joffe will Amend Role for Doctors in New Bill on Assisted Dying'. *British Medical Journal* 331: 863.

O'NEILL, C *et al*

2003 'Physician and Family Assisted Suicide: Results from a Study of Public Attitudes in Britain'. *Social Science and Medicine* 57: 721–31.

OCU [ORGANIZACIÓN DE CONSUMIDORES Y USUARIOS/ORGANISATION OF CONSUMERS AND USERS].

2000 *Enfermos terminales: encuesta sobre los cuidados paliativos* [Terminal Patients: Survey on Palliative Care] Available at <http://www.ocu.org> accessed September 2007.

OECD [ORGANISATION FOR ECONOMIC CO-OPERATION AND DEVELOPMENT]

1999 *Belgium.* OECD Economic Surveys, Belgium Luxembourg 48. Available at <http://doc-store.ingenta.com/cgi-bin/ds_deliver/1/u/d/ISIS/39737972.1/oecd/03766438/1999/00001999/00000004/1099291e/CF339782D37989591191327276CF118C8A61BDE1C9.pdf?link=http://www.ingentaconnect.com/error/delivery&format=pdf> accessed 1 October 2007.

ONWUTEAKA-PHILIPSEN, B and G van de WAL

1998 *Rapport steun en consultatie bij euthanasie in Amsterdam* [Report on SCEA]. Amsterdam, Instituut voor extramuraal geneeskundig onderzoek/Afdeling Sociale Geneeskunde Vrije Universiteit Amsterdam.

2001 'Consultatie bij euthanasie: verslagen van SCEA-artsen en andere consulenten vergeleken [Consultation in connection with Euthanasia: Comparison of the Reports of SCEA-Doctors and Other Consultants]'. *Medisch Contact* 56: 1201–4.

ONWUTEAKA-PHILIPSEN, B *et al*

2003 'Euthanasia and Other End-of-Life Decisions in the Netherlands in 1990, 1995 and 2001'. *The Lancet* 362: 395–9.

2007 *Evaluatie Wet toetsing levensbeëindiging op verzoek en hulp bij zelfdoding* [Evaluation of theTermination of Life on Request and Assisted Suicide (Review Procedure) Act of 2002]. The Hague, ZonMw.

OREGON HEALTH DIVISION

1999– *Annual Reports on Oregon's Death with Dignity Act.* Portland, OR, Department of Human Services. Available at <http://www.oregon.gov/DHS/ph/pas/ar-index.shtml> accessed 22 November 2007.

ORENTLICHER, D

1997 'The Supreme Court and Physician-Assisted Suicide: Rejecting Assisted Suicide but Embracing Euthanasia'. *New England Journal of Medicine* 337: 1236–9.

OTLOWSKI, M

1997 *Voluntary Euthanasia and the Common Law.* Oxford, Oxford University Press.

2000 *Voluntary Euthanasia and the Common Law.* Oxford, Oxford University Press [rev pbk edn].

OVERBEEK, R van

1996 *Tussen wens en werkelijkheid: een onderzoek naar het proces van omgaan met een ver-zoek om euthanasie of hulp bij zelfdoding* [Between Will and Reality: A Study of the Process of Reacting to a Request for Euthanasia or Assistance with Suicide]. Utrecht, Verwey-Jonker Instituut.

OVERLEGGROEP LATE ZWANGERSCHAPSAFBREKING [CONSULTATION GROUP LATE TERM ABORTION]

1998 *Late zwangerschapsafbreking: zorgvuldigheid en toetsing* [Late Term Abortion: Due Care and Review]. Rijswijk, Ministerie van Volksgezondheid, Welzijn en Sport.

PACOLET, J *et al*

2004 *Vergrijzing, gezondheidszorg en ouderenzorg in België. Rapport voor de FOD Sociale Zekerheid Directie-Generaal Sociaal Beleid* [Aging of the Population, Health Care and the Care of the Elderly in Belgium]. DGSOC 32036. Brussels, FOD Sociale Zekerheid. Available at <http://socialsecurity.fgov.be/NL/nieuws_publicaties/publicaties/vergrijzing/rapport_vergrijzing.pdf> accessed 1 October 2007.

PAGE, B and R SHAPIRO

1983 'Effects of Public Opinion on Policy'. *The American Political Science Review* 77: 175–90.

PAILLET, A

2007 *Sauver la vie, donner la mort. Une sociologie de l'éthique en reanimation néonatale.* [Save Life, Give Death. A Sociology of Ethics in Neonatal Intensive Care] Paris, La Dispute.

PALMER, H

1957 'Dr Adams' Trial for Murder'. *Criminal Law Review* 365–96.

PANS, E

2003 'De Hoge Raad en de onzekere arts: kanttekeningen bij het arrest over hulp bij zelf-doding in de zaak Brongersma [The Supreme Court and the Uncertain Doctor: Comments on the Judgment concerning Assistance with Suicide in the *Brongersma* Case]'. *Nederlands Juristenblad* 78: 870–78.

2006 *De normatieve grondslagen van het Nederlandse euthanasierecht* [The Normative Foundations of Dutch Euthanasia Law]. Nijmegen, Wolf Legal Publishers.

PARIS, G (ed)

1986 *Atti del convegno giuridico 'Vivere un diritto o un dovere? Problematiche dell'eutanasia'* [Proceedings of the Legal Conference 'Is Living a Right or a Duty? Questions about Euthanasia']. Rieti, Banca Popolare di Rieti.

PASMAN, H, and B ONWUTEAKA-PHILIPSEN

forthcoming 'When Requests do Not Result in EAS: A Qualitative Interview Study'.

PASMAN, H *et al*

2004a 'Foregoing Artificial Nutrition and Hydration in Nursing Home Patients with Dementia'. *Alzheimers Disease and Associated Disorders* 18: 154–62.

2004b 'Participants in the Decision Making on Artificial Nutrition and Hydration to Demented Nursing Home Patients: A Qualitative Study'. *Journal of Aging Studies* 18: 321–35.

PASTOR MUÑOZ, N

2007 'Euthanasia in the Spanish Legal System'. Pp 237–55 in M Groenhuijsen and F van Laanen (eds). *Euthanasia in International and Comparative Perspective*. Nijmegen, Wolf Legal Publishers.

PATTINSON, S

2006 *Medical Law and Ethics*. London, Sweet & Maxwell.

PERELMAN, C

1968 'Le droit et la morale devant l'euthanasie [Law and Ethics Confronted by Euthanasia]'. Pp 121–6 in C Perelman. *Droit, morale et philosophie* [Law, Ethics and Philosophy]. Paris, Librairie Générale de Droit et de Jurisprudence.

PERETTI-WATEL, P *et al*

2003a 'Doctors' Opinion on Euthanasia, End of Life Care and Doctor–Patient Communication: Telephone Survey in France'. *British Medical Journal* 327: 595–6.

2003b 'Les soins palliatifs en France. Accès aux soins, expérience des médecins, usage de morphiniques et opinions sur l'euthanasie. Premiers résultats de l'enquête "Attitudes et pratiques face aux soins palliatifs, 2002" [Palliative Care in France. Access to Treatment, Doctors' Experience, Use of Morphine and Opinions on Euthanasia. First Results of a Survey]'. *Annales de médicine interne* 154: 441–7. Available at <http://orspaca.org/depot/pdf/03-SY1.pdf> accessed 1 October 2007.

PHILIPSEN, N and M FAURE

2002 'The Regulation of Pharmacists in Belgium and the Netherlands: In the Public or Private Interest?' *Journal of Consumer Policy* 25: 155–201.

PIGNOTTI, M, M TORALDO DI FRANCIA and G DONZELLI

2007 'Intensive Care at Extremely Low Gestational Age: Ethical Issues and Treatment Choices'. *La Pediatria Medica e Chirurgica* 29: 84–93.

PIN, X

2002 *Le consentement en droit pénal* [Consent in Penal Law]. Paris, LGDJ.

PLOEG-JUK, T van der

2003 'Het proces van zelfregulering van levensverkortend handelen bij pasgeborenen [The Process of Self-Regulation of Life-Shortening Behaviour in the case of Newborns]'. Pp 107–32 in H Weyers and J Stamhuis (eds). *Zelfregulering* [Self-Regulation]. The Hague, Reed Business Information.

POPE JOHN PAUL II

1995 'Evangelium vitae'. *Acta Apostolicae Sedis* 87: 401–522.

2004 'I trattamenti di sostegno vitale e lo stato vegetativo. Progressi scientifici e dilemmi etici [Address to the participants in the international congress on life-sustaining treatments and the vegetative state]'. *L'Osservatore Romano* (20 March) 5.

POPE PIUS XII

1957a 'Summus Pontifex, coram praeclaris medicis, chirurgis atque studiosis, quaesitis respondit de catholica doctrina quoad anaesthesiam, a Societate Italica de anaesthesiologia propositis'. [Address on catholic doctrine concerning anaesthesia]. *Acta Apostolicae Sedis* 49: 129–47.

1957b 'Adstantibus multis honorabilibus Viris ac praeclaris Medicis et Studiosis, quorum plerique Nosocomiis praesunt vel in magnis Lyceis docent, qui Romam convenerant invitatu et arcessitu Instituti Genetici 'Gregorio Mendel', Summus Pontifex propositis quaesitis de 'reanimatione' respondit [Address on resuscitation]'. *Acta Apostolicae Sedis* 49: 1027–33.

1954 *A la recherche d'une éthique médicale* [In Search of an Ethics of Medicine]. Paris, Masson.

PRICE, D

1997 'Euthanasia, Pain Relief and Double Effect'. *Legal Studies* 17: 323.

PROVOOST, V

2005 End-of-Life Decisions in Neonates and Infants in Flanders, Belgium. Dissertation, Vrije Universiteit Brussel.

PROVOOST, V *et al*

2006 'The Use of Drugs with a Life-Shortening Effect in End-of-Life Care in Neonates and Infants'. *Intensive Care Medicine* 32: 133–9.

PY, B

1997 *La mort et le droit* [Death and the Law]. Paris, PUF.

RAAD VOOR DE VOLKSGEZONDHEID EN ZORG [COUNCIL FOR HEALTH AND HEALTH CARE]

2003 *De wensen van zorgcliënten in Europa* [What European Health Care Clients Want]. Zoetermeer, Raad voor de Volksgezondheid en Zorg.

RAADGEVEND COMITÉ VOOR BIO-ETHIEK [ADVISORY COMMITTEE FOR BIOETHICS]

1997 *Recommendation* no 1, 12 May 1997, on the Desirability of Legislation on Euthanasia. Available at <https://portal.health.fgov.be/pls/portal/docs/PAGE/INTERNET_PG/HOMEPAGE_MENU/GEZONDHEIDZORG1_MENU/OVERLEGSTRUCTUREN1_MENU/COMITEES1_MENU/BIOETHISCHECOMMISSIE1_MENU/AVIS25_MENU/AVIS25_DOCS/ADVIES1-EUTHANASIE.PDF>accessed 1 October 2007.

1999 *Recommendation* no 9, 22 February 1999. Available at: <https://portal.health.fgov.be/pls/portal/docs/PAGE/INTERNET_PG/HOMEPAGE_MENU/GEZONDHEIDZORG1_MENU/OVERLEGSTRUCTUREN1_MENU/COMITEES1_MENU/BIOETHISCHECOMMISSIE1_MENU/AVIS25_MENU/AVIS25_DOCS/ADVIES9-EUTHANASIE.PDF> accessed 22 November 2007.

RANG, J

1977 *Rechtspraak medisch tuchtrecht, 1930–1976* [Medical Disciplinary Case Reports, 1930–1976]. Deventer, Kluwer.

RASMUSSEN, K

1998 'Er det forskjell mellom å drepe og å la dø? [Is there a Difference between Killing and Letting Die?]'. *Tidsskrift for Den norske lægeforen* 118: 422–4.

REBAGLIATO, M *et al*

2000 'Neonatal End-of-Life Decision Making: Physicians' Attitudes and Relationship with Self-Reported Practices in 10 European Countries'. *JAMA* 284: 2451–9.

RIETJENS, J

2006 Medical Decision-Making at the End of Life: Experiences and Attitudes of Physicians and the General Public. Dissertation, Rotterdam Erasmus MC.

RIETJENS, J *et al*

2005 'Dutch Experience of Monitoring Euthanasia'. *British Medical Journal* 331: 691–3.

2006 'Terminal Sedation and Euthanasia. Comparison of Clinical Practices'. *Archives of Internal Medicine* 166: 749–53.

RIKLIN, F

1999 'Die strafrechtliche Regelung der Sterbehilfe in der Schweiz [Swiss Penal Law on assisted dying]'. Pp 322–44 in A Holderegger (ed). *Das medizinisch assistierte Sterben: zur Sterbehilfe aus medizinischer, ethischer, juristischer und theologischer Sicht* [Medically Assisted Dying]. Freiburg, Universitätsverlag.

RIPPE, K *et al*

2005 'Urteilsfähigkeit von Menschen mit psychischen Störungen und Suizidbeihilfe [Decision-Making Competence of Persons with Mental Disorder and Assisted Suicide]'. *Schweizerische Juristenzeitung* 101: 53–62 and 101: 81–91.

RIZIV [RIJKSINSTITUUT VOOR ZIEKTE EN INVALIDITEITSVERZEKERING/ NATIONAL INSTITUTE FOR HEALTH AND INVALIDITY INSURANCE]

2005 *Jaarverslag* [Annual Report]. Available at <http://www.riziv.fgov.be/presentation/nl/ publications/annual-report/2005/index.htm> accessed 1 October 2007.

ROGERS, J

2001 'Necessity, Private Defence and the Killing of Mary'. *Criminal Law Review*: 515–26.

ROOIJ, E van *et al*

2002 *Health and Health Care in the Netherlands: A Critical Self-Assessment of Dutch Experts in Medical and Health Sciences.* 2nd rev edn. Maarsen, Elsevier Gezondheidszorg.

ROSENBERG, M

2001 'Sterbehilfe soll nicht straffrei werden [Voluntary Active Euthanasia Must not be Decriminalised]'. *Neue Zürcher Zeitung* (12 Dec).

ROYAL COLLEGE OF PAEDIATRICS AND CHILD HEALTH

1998 *Withdrawing and Withholding Treatment in Children.* [London].

2004 *Withholding or Withdrawing Life Sustaining Treatment in Children: A Framework for Practice.* 2nd edn. London.

RRC [REGIONAL REVIEW COMMITTEES EUTHANASIA/REGIONALE TOETSINGS-COMMISSIES EUTHANASIE]

1998– *Annual Reports* [Jaarverslag]. The Hague, Ministry of Health. Available at <http://www.toetsingscommissieseuthanasie.nl/Toetsingscommissie/jaarverslag/> in English, French and German beginning in 2005; accessed 1 October 2007.

2003 'Richtlijnen betreffende de werkwijze van de Regionale Toetsingscommissies Euthanasie [Guidelines for the the Operations of the Regional Review Committees for Euthanasia]'. Published in RRC 2003: 50–54.

RRCj [REGIONAL REVIEW COMMITTEES EUTHANASIA JUDGEMENTS/ REGIONALE TOETSINGSCOMMISSIES EUTHANASIE OORDELEN]

2006– *Judgements* [Oordelen]. Available at <http://www.toetsingscommissieseuthanasie. nl>accessed 1 October 2007.

RURUP, M

2005 Setting the Stage for Death: New Themes in the Euthanasia Debate. Dissertation, Amsterdam VU.

RURUP, M *et al*

2005a 'Attitudes of Physicians, Nurses and Relatives towards End-of-Life Decisions concerning Nursing Home Patients with Dementia'. *Patient Education and Counseling* 61: 372–80.

2005b 'Requests for Euthanasia or Physician-Assisted Suicide from Older Persons who do Not Have a Severe Disease: An Interview Study'. *Psychological Medicine* 35: 665–71.

2006a 'Frequency and Determinants of Advance Directives concerning End-of-Life Care in the Netherlands'. *Social Science and Medicine* 62: 1552–63.

2006b 'Trends in gebruikte geneesmiddelen bij euthanasie en samenhang met het aantal meldingen [Trends in the Use of Drugs for Euthanasia and their Relationship to the Number of Reported Cases]'. *Nederlands Tijdschrift voor Geneeskunde* 150: 618–24.

SACRA CONGREGATIO PRO DOCTRINA FIDEI [SACRED CONGREGATION FOR THE DOCTRINE OF THE FAITH]

1980 'Declaratio de euthanasia [Declaration on Euthanasia]'. *Acta Apostolicae Sedis* 72: 542–52.

1992 *Catechismo della Chiesa Cattolica* [Catechism of the Catholic Church]. Vatican City, Libreria Editrice Vaticana.

SCEN [STEUN EN CONSULTATIE BIJ EUTHANASIE IN NEDERLAND/SUPPORT AND CONSULTATION IN CONNECTION WITH EUTHANASIA IN THE NETHERLANDS]

2004 *Newsletter* no 11. Available at <http://knmg.artsennet.nl/uri/?uri=AMGATE_6059_100_TICH_R1583971184458200> accessed 1 October 2007]

2005– *Spiegelinformatie SCEN*. Available at <http://knmg.artsennet.nl/content/resources/AMGATE_6059_100_TICH_L898614605/AMGATE_6059_100_TICH_R158394118 6246791//> accessed 22 November 2007.

SCHÄR, M

1998 'Der Arzt als Sterbehelfer [The Doctor as Assistant in Dying]'. *Therapiewoche* 4: 174–5.

SCHIOLDBORG, P

1999 'Studenters holdninger til aktiv dødshjelp [Students' Attitudes towards Active Euthanasia]'. *Tidsskrift for Den norske lægeforening* 119: 2515–9. For an abstract in English see <http://www.ncbi.nlm.nih.gov/sites/entrez?Db=pubmed&Cmd=Show DetailView&TermToSearch=10425907&ordinalpos=2&itool=EntrezSystem2.PEntrez .Pubmed.Pubmed_ResultsPanel.Pubmed_RVDocSum> accessed 28 November 2007.

2000 'Studenters holdninger til aktiv dødshjelp, assistert suicid og foreslått lovendring [Students' Attitudes towards Active Euthanasia, Assisted Suicide and Proposed Legal Change]'. *Tidsskrift for Den norske lægeforening* 120: 2283–8. For an abstract in English see <http://www.ncbi.nlm.nih.gov/sites/entrez?Db=pubmed&Cmd=Show DetailView&TermToSearch=10997089&ordinalpos=1&itool=EntrezSystem2. PEntrez.Pubmed.Pubmed_ResultsPanel.Pubmed_RVDocSum> accessed 29 November 2007.

SCHOTSMANS, P

1997 'Wenselijkheid van een wettelijke regeling van euthanasie: het eerste advies van het Belgisch Raadgevend Comité voor Bio-ethiek [Desireability of a Statutory Regulation of Euthanasia: The First Advice of the Belgian Advisory Committee for Bio-Ethics]'. *Ethische Perspectieven* 7: 87–97.

SCHRIJVERS, A (ed)

1997 *Health and Health Care in the Netherlands. A Critical Self-Assessment by Dutch Experts in the Medical and Health Sciences*. Utrecht, De Tijdstroom.

SCHWARZENEGGER, C

2003 'Strafbare Handlungen gegen Leib und Leben [Criminal act against body and life]'. Pp 1–69 in M Niggli. *Strafgesetzbuch II: Art.111–401* [Penal Code Art 111–401] Basel, Helbing und Lichtenhahn.

2007 'Das Mittel zur Suizidbeihilfe und das Recht auf den eigenen Tod [The Means to Assistance in Suicide and the Right to Die]'. *Jusletter* (19 March).

SCHWEIZERISCHE AKADEMIE DER MEDIZINISCHEN WISSENSCHAFTEN [SWISS ACADEMY OF MEDICAL SCIENCES]

1995 'Medizinisch-ethische Richtlinien für die ärztliche Betreuung sterbender und zerebral schwerst geschädigter Patienten [Medical-Ethical Guidelines for the Care of Patients who Suffer from Severe Brain Damage or who are Dying]'. *Schweizerische Ärztezeitung* 76: 1223–5.

2005 'Betreuung von Patienten am Lebensende. Medizinisch-ethische Richtlinien [Care of Patients at the End of Life. Medical-Ethical guidelines]'. *Schweizerische Ärztezeitung* 86: 172–6.

SCHWEIZERISCHE DEPESCHENAGENTUR [SWISS NEWS AGENCY]

2006 'Genfer Unispital lässt Sterbehilfe zu [Geneva University Hospital Allows Assistance in Dying]'. *Neue Zürcher Zeitung* (15 Sept).

SCHWITTERS, R

2005 'Signaalwerking: positieve symbolische effecten in het werk van Vilhelm Aubert [Signals: Positive Symbolic Effects in Vilhelm Aubert's Work]'. *Recht der Werkelijkheid* 26: 47–67.

SCP [SOCIAAL EN CULTUREEL PLANBUREAU/SOCIAL AND CULTURAL PLANNING BUREAU]

1992 *Sociaal en cultureel rapport 1992* [Social and Cultural Report 1992]. The Hague, VUGA.

1996 *Sociaal en cultureel rapport 1996* [Social and Cultural Report 1996]. The Hague, Staatsuitgeverij.

2000 *Sociaal en cultureel rapport 2000. Nederland in Europa* [Social and Cultural Report 2000. The Netherlands in Europe]. The Hague, Sociaal en Cultureel Planbureau.

2002 *Sociaal en cultureel rapport 2002. De kwaliteit van de quartaire sector* [Social and Cultural Report 2002. The Quality of Public Service]. The Hague, Sociaal en Cultureel Planbureau.

2004 *Sociaal en cultureel rapport 2004. In het zicht van de toekomst* [Social and Cultural Report 2002. In Sight of the Future]. The Hague, Sociaal en Cultureel Planbureau.

SEALE, C

2006a 'National Survey of End-of-Life Decisions Made by UK Medical Practitioners'. *Palliative Medicine* 20: 3–10.

2006b 'Characteristics of End-of-Life Decisions: Survey of UK Medical Practitioners'. *Palliative Medicine* 20: 653–9.

SEELMANN, K

2003 'Sterbehilfe: Die Rechtslage in der Schweiz [Assisted dying: The Legal situation in Switzerland]'. Pp 135–46 in G Brudermüller *et al* (eds). *Suizid und Sterbehilfe* [Suicide and Assistance in Dying]. Würzburg, Könighausen und Neumann.

SEYMOUR, J, R JANSSENS and B BROECKAERT

2007 'Relieving Suffering at the End of Life: Practitioners' Perspectives on Palliative Sedation from Three European countries'. *Social Science & Medicine* 64: 1679–91.

SIERRA ARREDONDO, G

2004 'La eutanasia: ¿debate médico o social? [Euthanasia: Medical or Social Debate?]'. *El Periódico de la OMC* [*Journal of the Medical Colegial Organisation*] (Dec). Available at

<http://www.cgcom.org/notas_prensa/2005/05_01_19_eutanasia.htm> accessed 1 October 2007.

SHELDON, T

2005 'Dutch Euthanasia Law Should Apply to Patients "suffering through living", report says'. *British Medical Journal* 330: 61.

SIMPSON, A

1984 *Cannibalism and the Common Law: The Story of the Tragic Last Voyage of the Mignonette and the Strange Legal Proceedings to Which It Gave Rise.* Chicago, University of Chicago Press.

SLUIJTERS, B and M BIESAART

2005 *De geneeskundige behandelingsovereenkomst* [The Contract for Medical Treatment]. 2nd edn. Deventer, Kluwer.

SMITH, J

2000 'A Comment on Moor's Case'. *Criminal Law Review*. 41–4.

2001 'Case Comment'. *Criminal Law Review*. 400–5.

SMITH, S

2005 'Evidence for the Practical Slippery Slope in the Debate on Physician-Assisted Suicide and Euthanasia'. *Medical Law Review* 13: 17–44.

SNEIDERMAN, B, J IRVINE and P OSBORNE

2003 *Canadian Medical Law: An Introduction for Physicians, Nurses and other Health Care Professionals.* 3rd edn. Scarborough, Ont, Carswell.

SORGDRAGER, W and E BORST-EILERS

1995 'Euthanasie. De stand van zaken [Euthanasia. The Current State of Affairs]'. *Medisch Contact* 50: 381–4.

SPIEGEL

1997 *Toetsing als spiegel van de medische praktijk: rapport van de overleggroep toetsing zorgvuldig medisch handelen rond het levenseinde bij pasgeborenen* [Review as a Reflection of Medical Practice]. Rijswijk, Ministerie van VWS.

SPOENDLIN, R

2007 'Suizidhelfer muss hinter Gitter. Neue Gesetzesauslegung in der Schweiz [Suicide assistant to jail. New Interpretation of Swiss Law]'. *Soziale Medizin* (2 July).

SPRUNG, C *et al*

2003 'End-of-Life Practices in European Intensive Care Units'. *Journal of the American Medical Association* 290: 790–97.

2007 'Attitudes of European Physicians, Nurses, Patients, and Families regarding End-of-Life Decisions: The ETHICATT Study'. *Intensive Care Medicine*, 33: 104–10.

STAATSCOMMISSIE EUTHANASIE [STATE COMMISSION ON EUTHANASIA]

1985 *Euthanasie: rapport van de Staatscommissie Euthanasie.* Vol 1: Advies [Report of the State Commission on Euthanasia]. The Hague, Staatsuitgeverij.

STANGELAND, P

1996 'Aspectos sociológicos de la eutanasia en España [Sociological Aspects of Euthanasia in Spain]'. Pp 25–40 in Díez Ripollés and Muñoz Sánchez 1996.

STEPHEN, J

1887 *A Digest of the Criminal Law.* 4th edn. London, Macmillan.

STERN, K

1994 'Advance Directives'. *Medical Law Review* 2: 57–76.

STEUDLER, M

2004 'Kanton Zürich plant Suizidhilfe-Gesetz [Canton of Zurich Planning to Legislate Assisted Suicide]'. *NZZ am Sonntag* (22 Feb).

STICHTING GESCHILLENCOMMISSIES VOOR CONSUMENTENZAKEN [ORGANISATION OF DISPUTE-SETTLEMENT COMMITTEES FOR CONSUMER CASES]

2006 *Annual Report.* Available at <http://www.sgc.nl> accessed 1 October 2007.

STRAFFELOVKOMMISJONEN

2002 *Norges offentlige utredninger. Ny straffelov. Straffelovkommisjonens delutredning VII* [Norway's Official Reviews. New Penal Code. The Penal Code Commission's Review, Part VII]. Oslo: Ministry of Justice and Police. Available at <http://www. regjeringen.no/nb/dep/jd/dok/NOUer/2002/NOU-2002-04.html?id=380296> accessed 4 March 2008.

SUNDHETSSTYRELSEN [NATIONAL BOARD OF HEALTH]

2002 *Vejledning i medikamentel palliation i terminalfasen* [Guidance regarding pharmacological palliation in the terminal phase]. Available at <http://www.sst.dk/publ/ love_regler/Vejledningmedikamentalpellation.pdf> accessed 1 October 2007.

SVENSKA LÄKARESÄLLSKAPETS DELEGATION FÖR MEDICINSK ETIK [SWEDISH SOCIETY OF MEDICINE DELEGATION OF MEDICAL ETHICS]

2003 *Riktlinjer för palliativ sedering av döende patienter—etiska aspekter* [Guidelines for Palliative Sedation of Dying Patients: Ethical Aspects]. Available at <http://www.svls. se/cs-media-old/xyz/000001435.pdf> accessed 1 October 2007.

SVENSKA LÄKARESÄLLSKAPETS [SWEDISH SOCIETY OF MEDICINE]

2006 *Etiska riktlinjer vid ställningstagande till att avstå från och avbryta livsuppehållande behandling* [Ethical Guidelines regarding Withholding and Withdrawing Life-Sustaining Treatment]. Available at <http://www.svls.se/cs-media/xyz/000003352. pdf> accessed 1 October 2007.

SWARTE, N, *et al*

2003 'Effects of Euthanasia on the Bereaved Family and Friends: A Cross Sectional Study'. *British Medical Journal* 327: 189–93.

SWISSINFO

2007 'Zurich University Hospital Rejects Assisted Suicide'. *Neue Zürcher Zeitung* [English version] (9 March).

SYKES, N and A THORNS

2003 'The Use of Opioids and Sedatives at the End of Life'. *The Lancet Oncology* 4: 312–18.

SYSE, A

2000 'Norway : Valid (as Opposed to Informed) Consent'. *The Lancet* 356: 1347–8.

2005 'Uutholdelige liv: et rettslig perspektiv [Intolerable Lives: A Legal Perspective]'. Pp 84–107 in H Herrestad and L Mehlum (eds). *Uutholdelige liv. Om selvmord, eutanasi og behandling av døende* [Intolerable Lives. On Suicide, Euthanasia and Treatment of the Dying]. Oslo, Gyldendal Akademisk.

SYVERTSEN, L and D BRATLID

2004 'Avslutning av behandling ved alvorlig sykdom hos nyfødte [Withdrawal of Treatment in Severely Ill Newborn Infants]'. *Tidsskrift for Den norske laegeforening* 124: 2483–5. Available at <http://www.tidsskriftet.no/pls/lts/PA_LT.VisSeksjon?vp_ SEKS_ID=1077418> accessed 1 October 2007.

THE, A-M

1997 'Vanavond om 8 uur . . .' Verpleegkundige dilemma's bij euthanasie en andere beslissingen rond het levenseinde ['This Evening at 8 o'Clock . . .' Nursing Dilemmas in

Connection with Euthanasia and Other Decisions Concerning the End of Life]. Houten/Diegem, Bohn Stafleu Van Loghum.

1999 *Palliatieve behandeling en communicatie. Een onderzoek naar het optimisme op herstel van kankerpatiënten* [Palliative Treatment and Communication. A Study of Optimism about Recovery among Cancer Patients]. Houten, Bohn Stafleu Van Loghum.

2005 *In de wachtkamer van de dood. Leven en sterven met dementie in een verkleurende samenleving* [In the Waiting Room of Death. Living and Dying with Dementia in a Changing Society]. Amsterdam, Thoeris.

THIEL, G van, A HUIBERS and K de HAAN

1997 *Met zorg besluiten: medische beslissingen rond het levenseinde in de zorg voor mensen met een verstandelijke handicap* [Deciding with Care: Medical Decisions in Connection with the End of Life in Institutions for Persons with a Mental Handicap]. Assen, Van Gorcum.

THOLEN, A

2003 'Levensbeëindiging en psychisch lijden [Termination of Life and Mental Suffering]'. *Medisch Contact* 58: 64–7.

TOL, D van

2005 Grensgeschillen: een rechtssociologisch onderzoek naar het classificeren van euthanasie en ander medisch handelen rond het levenseinde [Boundary Disputes: a Legal-Sociological Study of the Classification of Euthanasia and Other Medical Behaviour at the End of Life]. Dissertation, University of Groningen.

2007 'Making Sense of Suffering: An Empirical Study'. Paper for the Conference on *Making Sense of Dying and Death*. Oxford, Mansfield College, 7–12 July 2007.

TOMÁS-VALIENTE LANUZA, C

2000 *La cooperación al suicidio y la eutanasia en el nuevo CP (art. 143)* [Cooperation in Suicide and Euthanasia in the New Penal Code (Art 143)]. Valencia, Tirant lo Blanch.

TWINING, W

2000 *Globalization and Legal Theory.* London, Butterworths.

nd. *General Jurisprudence: Law from a Global Perspective.* Cambridge, Cambridge University Press (forthcoming).

UK GOVERNMENT

1994 *Response to the House of Lords Select Committee on Medical Ethics.* Cm 2553.

ULRICH, E

2002 'Exit': Beihilfe zum Suizid zwischen 1990 und 2000 ['Exit': Assistance in Suicide between 1990 and 2000]. Dissertation, University of Zurich.

VALMASSOI, G and D MAZZON

2005 'Informed Consent to Proposed Course of Medical Treatment: Recent Case Law Stances'. *Minerva Anestesiologica* 71: 659–69.

VALVERIUS, E, T NILSTUN and B NILSSON

2000 'Palliative Care, Assisted Suicide and Euthanasia: Nationwide Questionnaire to Swedish Physicians'. *Palliative Medicine* 14: 141–8. Available at <http://pmj.sagepub.com/cgi/reprint/14/2/141> accessed 1 October 2007.

VANDE LANOTTE, J, S BRACKE and G GOEDERTIER

2006 *Belgium for Beginners. A Guide through the Belgian Labyrinth.* Brugge, Die Keure/La Chartre.

VANDER STICHELE, R *et al*

2004 'Drugs Used for Euthanasia in Flanders, Belgium'. *Pharmacoepidemiology and Drug Safety* 13: 89–95.

VANSWEEVELT, T

2006 'Comparative Legal Aspects of Pain Management'. Pp 377–84 in *Book of Proceedings of the 16th World Congress on Medical Law.* Vol 1. Toulouse.

VEENHOVEN, R

1998 'Vergelijken van geluk in landen [Comparing Happiness in Countries]'. *Sociale Wetenschappen* 41: 58–85.

VELDINK, J *et al*

2002 'Euthanasia and Physician-Assisted Suicide among Patients with Amyotrophic Lateral Sclerosis in the Netherlands'. *New England Journal of Medicine* 346: 1638–44.

VERHAGEN, A and P SAUER

2005 'The Groningen Protocol: Euthanasia in Severely Ill Newborns'. *New England Journal of Medicine* 352: 959–62.

VERHAGEN, A *et al*

2005 'Actieve levensbeëindiging bij pasgeborenen in Nederland: analyse van alle 22 meldingen uit 1997/'04 [Active Termination of Life of Newborns in the Netherlands: Analysis of all 22 Reported Cases from 1997/'04]'. *Nederlands Tijdschrift voor Geneeskunde* 149: 183–8.

2007a 'Uitzichtloos en ondraaglijk lijden en actieve levensbeëindiging bij pasgeborenen [Hopeless and Unbearable Suffering and the Active Termination of Life of Newborns]'. *Nederlands Tijdschrift voor Geneeskunde* 151: 1474–7.

2007b 'Physician medical Decision-Making at the End of Life in Newborns: Insight into Implementation at 2 Dutch Centers'. *Pediatrics* 120: e20-e28.

VERLATO, G *et al*

2004 'Guidelines for Resuscitation in the Delivery Room of Extremely Preterm Infants'. *Journal of Child Neurology* 19: 31–4.

VERMEERSCH, E

2000 'Euthanasie in België [Euthanasia in Belgium]'. *Filosofie en Praktijk* 21: 48–56.

VERMEULEN, E

2001 Een proeve van leven: praten en beslissen over extreem te vroeg geboren kinderen [A Test of Life: Talking and Deciding about Extreme Premature Children]. Dissertation, University of Amsterdam.

2003 'Uit nood geboren: Levensbeëindigend handelen in de Belgische en Nederlandse neonatologie [Born in a State of Necessity: End-of-Life Treatment in Belgian and Dutch Neonatology]. Pp 277–302 in Adams, Griffiths & Den Hartogh (eds). 2003.

2004 'Dealing with Doubt: Making Decisions in a Neonatal Ward in the Netherlands'. *Social Science and Medicine* 59: 2071–85.

VERPEET, E, T MEULENBERGS and C GASTMANS

2003 'Professional Values and Norms for Nurses in Belgium'. *Nursing Ethics* 10: 654–65.

VESTERGAARD, J

2000 'Medical Aid in Dying under Danish Law: Mainly regarding Living Wills and Other Forms of renouncing Life Prolonging Treatment'. *European Journal of Health Law* 7: 405–25.

2002 'Danish Law concerning Medical Aid in Dying'. Pp 77–103 in R Dameno (ed). *Autodeterminarsi nonostante.* Milano, Edizioni Angelo Guerini e Associati.

VEZZONI, C

2008 *Advance Treatment Directives and Autonomy for Incompetent Patients in Law and Practice.* Lampeter, Ceredigion (Wales), The Edwin Mellen Press (forthcoming).

VIALE, S

2007 'Autodenunciamoci. Un appello a Veronesi, Marino, e a tutti i medici che hanno coscienza [Let Us All Incriminate Ourselves. An Appeal to Veronesi, Marino and All Doctors with a Conscience]'. *Micromega* 76: 7–12.

VIERNET, J, M RIQUET and Y ROUMAGNON

1963 'Réflexion sur le proces de Liège (le point de vue religieux, moral et médical) [Reflections on the Liege Case (the Religious, Moral and Medical Point of View)]'. *Revue de sciences criminelles* 18: 83–100.

VIGANÒ, F

2006 'Euthanasia in Italy'. Pp 167–86 in M Groenhuijsen and F van Laanen (eds). *Euthanasia in International and Comparative Perspective*. Nijmegen, Wolf Legal Publishers.

VIGELAND, K

1991 'Holdning til aktiv voluntær eutanasi [Attitude towards Active Voluntary Euthanasia]'. *Tidsskrift for Den norske lægeforening* 111: 460–3. (For an abstract in English see <http://www.ncbi.nlm.nih.gov/sites/entrez?Db=pubmed&Cmd=ShowDetailView& TermToSearch=2006486&ordinalpos=5&itool=EntrezSystem2.PEntrez.Pubmed. Pubmed_ResultsPanel.Pubmed_RVDocSum> accessed 28 November 2007).

1997 *Assistert død: en etisk utfordring* [Assisted Death: An Ethical Challenge]. Oslo, Tano Aschehoug.

VINCENT, J

1999 'Forgoing Life Support in Western European Intensive Care Units: The Results of an Ethical Questionnaire'. *Critical Care Medicine* 27: 1626–33.

VRAKKING, A *et al*

2005 'Physicians' Willingness to Grant Requests for Assistance in Dying for Children: A Study of Hypothetical Cases'. *Journal of Pediatrics* 146: 611–17.

WAGNER, C and M de BRUIJNE

2007 *Onbedoelde schade in Nederlandse ziekenhuizen* [Unintended Harm in Dutch Hospitals]. Amsterdam/Utrecht, EMGO Institute/NIVEL.

WAL, G van der

1992 *Euthanasie en hulp bij zelfdoding door huisartsen* [Euthanasia and Assistance with Suicide by Family Doctors]. Rotterdam, WYT Uitgeefgroep.

WAL, G van der and P van der MAAS

1996 *Euthanasie en andere medische beslissingen rond het levenseinde: de praktijk en de meldingsprocedure* [Euthanasia and Other Medical Decisions in Connection with the End of Life: Medical Practice and the Reporting Procedure]. The Hague, Sdu Uitgevers.

WAL, G van der, J BOSMA and S HOSMAN-BENJAMINSE

1996 'Late zwangerschapsafbreking in Noord-Holland. I. Incidentie en aandoeningen [Late-Term Abortion in North-Holland. I. Frequency and Diagnosis]'. *Nederlands Tijdschrift voor Geneeskunde* 140: 600–04.

WAL, G van der, G SIEMONS and J VERHOEFF

1994 'Weigeren van euthanasie. Zijn artsen verplicht om te verwijzen? [Refusal to Perform Euthanasia. Is a Doctor Required to Refer the Patient to Another Doctor?]'. *Medisch Contact* 49: 1240–42.

WAL, G van der *et al*

1996 'Evaluation of the Notification Procedure for Physician-Assisted Death in the Netherlands'. *New England Journal of Medicine*. 335: 1706–11.

2003 *Medische besluitvorming aan het einde van het leven: de praktijk en de toetsingsprocedure euthanasie en het Verslag van de begeleidingscommissie van het evaluatieonderzoek naar de medische besluitvorming aan het einde van het leven* [Medical Decision Making at the End of Life: Medical Practice and the Assessment Procedure for Euthanasia]. Utrecht, de Tijdstroom.

WARD, B and P TATE

1994 'Attitudes among NHS Doctors to Requests for Euthanasia'. *British Medical Journal* 308: 1332–4.

WEISZ, F

1994 'Hulp bij zelfdoding: verslag van een huisarts' [Assistance with Suicide: Report from a GP]. *Medisch Contact* 49: 700–03.

WELBY, P

2006 *Lasciatemi morire* [Let Me Die]. Milano, Rizzoli.

WERF, G van der and J ZAAT

2005 'Klaar-met-leven of lijden aan het leven [Finished with Life or Suffering from Life]'. *Huisarts en Wetenschap* 18: 556–9.

WESTRIN, C and T NILSTUN (eds)

2005 *Att få hjälp att dö: synsätt, erfarenheter, kritiska frågor* [Being Helped to Die: Viewpoints, Experiences, Critical Questions]. Lund, Studentlitteratur.

WEYERS, H

2001 'Euthanasia: the process of legal change in the Netherlands. The making of requirements of careful practice.' Pp 11–27 in A Klijn, M Otlowski and M Trappenburg (eds). *Regulating Physician-negotiated Death.* the Hague, Elsevier.

2004 *Euthanasie: het proces van rechtsverandering* [Euthanasia: The Process of Legal Change]. Amsterdam, Amsterdam University Press.

2005 'Legal Recognition of the Right to Die'. Pp 253–67 in A Garwood-Gowers, J Tingle and K Wheat (eds). *Contemporary Issues in Healthcare Law and Ethics.* Edinburgh [etc], Elsevier.

2006 'Explaining the Emergence of Euthanasia Law in the Netherlands: How the Sociology of Law Can Help the Sociology of Bioethics'. *Sociology of Health and Illness* 28: 802–16.

WHITE, P

1988 'Knowing More about What We Can Tell: "Introspective Access" and Causal Report Accuracy 10 Years Later'. *British Journal of Psychology* 79: 13–45.

WICKS, E

2001 'The Right to Refuse Medical Treatment under the European Convention on Human Rights'. *Medical Law Review* 9: 17–40.

2003 'The Greater Good? Issues of Proportionality and Democracy in the Doctrine of Necessity as Applied in *Re A'. Common Law World Review* 32: 115–34.

WIJKERSLOOTH, J de

2003 'Twee lacunes in de euthanasieregeling [Two Gaps in the Regulation of Euthanasia]'. *Oppertuun* 9: no 10.

WIJSBEK, H

2001 Taking Lives Seriously. Philosophical Issues in the Dutch Euthanasia Debate. Dissertation, Free University of Amsterdam.

WILLEMS, D *et al*

2000 'Attitudes and Practices concerning the End of Life. A Comparison between

Physicians from the United States and from the Netherlands'. *Archives of Internal Medicine* 160: 63–8.

WILLIAMS, GLANVILLE

1958 *The Sanctity of Life and the Criminal Law.* London, Faber.

1978 'Necessity'. *Criminal Law Review.* 128–36.

WILLIAMS, GLENYS

2001 'The Principle of Double Effect and Terminal Sedation'. *Medical Law Review* 9: 41–53.

WINDT, W van der, H CALSBEEK, H TALMA and L HINGSTMAN

2003 *Feiten over verpleegkundige en verzorgende beroepen in Nederland 2003* [Facts on Nursing and Caregivers, 2003]. Maarssen, Elsevier/De Tijdstroom en LCVV [Landelijk Centrum Verpleging & Verzorging].

WIT, M de

2005 'De geloofwaardigheid van de inspectie [Can the Medical Inspectorate be Taken Seriously?]'. *Medisch Contact* 60: 683.

WOLF, S

2005 'Assessing Physician Compliance with the Rules for Euthanasia and Assisted Suicide'. *Archives of Internal Medicine* 165: 1677–9.

WOZZ [STICHTING WETENSCHAPPELIJK ONDERZOEK NAAR ZORGVULDIGE ZELFDODING/FOUNDATION FOR SCIENTIFIC RESEARCH INTO CAREFUL SUICIDE]

2006 *Guide to a Humane Self-Chosen Death.* Delft, WOZZ.

ZAHN, E

1991 *Regenten, rebellen en reformatoren. Een visie op Nederland en de Nederlanders* [Regents, Rebels and Reformers. A Perspective on the Netherlands and the Dutch]. Amsterdam, Uitgeverij Contact.

ZELDERS, T

1996 'Patient Risks: An Underdeveloped Area'. *Journal of Clinical Monitoring* 12: 237–41.

ZIEGLER, S and N LOVRICH

2003 'Pain Relief, Prescription Drugs and Prosecution: A Four-State Survey of Chief Prosecutors'. *Journal of Law, Medicine and Ethics* 31: 75–100.

ZIEGLER, S and G BOSSHARD

2007 'Role of Non-Governmental Organisations in Physician Assisted Suicide'. *British Medical Journal* 334: 295–8.

ZIMMERMANN-ACKLIN, M

1997 Euthanasie: eine theologisch-ethische Untersuchung. [Euthanasia: A Theological-Ethical Survey]. Dissertation, University of Freiburg.

ZUSSMAN, R

1992 *Intensive Care: Medical Ethics and the Medical Profession.* Chicago, University of Chicago Press.

ZUURMOND, W *et al*

2006 'Medische beslissingen rond het levenseinde, in het bijzonder de incidentie van euthanasia bij bewoners van een hospice in Nederland [Medical Decisions at the End of Life, in particular the Frequency of Euthanasia among the Inhabitants of One Hospice]'. *Nederlands Tijdschrift voor Palliatieve Zorg,* 7: 10–11.

ZWAVELING, J

1994 'Euthanasie legt te zware last bij de arts [Euthanasia Puts Too Heavy a Burden on the Doctor]'. *NRC Handelsblad* (25 November).

INDEX

University Centre Library
The Hub at Blackburn College

Customer ID: * * * * * *84

Title: Euthanasia and the law in Europe : with special reference to the Netherlands and Belgium (2nd ed.)
ID: BB19546
Due: 20120503

Total items: 1
15/03/2012 10:18

Please retain this receipt for your records
Contact Tel. 01254 292165

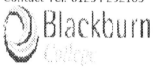